John Benson Presents

FUTURE STARS

The Rookies of 2001 - 2002

EXECUTIVE EDITOR
Tony Blengino

SENIOR EDITOR
John Benson

MANAGING EDITOR
Douglas DelVecchio

ASSOCIATE EDITORS
Lary Bump
Eric Marino
Karl Mordhorst
Kevin Wheeler

LAYOUT AND DESIGN
Wade Lunsford
Joe Palys

Library of Congress Cataloging-in-Publication Data:
Benson, John
Future Stars - The Rookies of 2001-2002
1. Baseball — United States — History
2. Baseball — United States — Records
I. Title

ISBN 1-880876-92-2

For information address: Diamond Library.

Published by Diamond Library, a division of Diamond Analytics Corporation, with offices at:
15 Cannon Road, Wilton, Connecticut, 06897.
Telephone: 203-834-1231.

PRINTED IN THE UNITED STATES OF AMERICA

Cover Photos:
Ryan Anderson courtesy of the New Haven Ravens
Josh Beckett courtesy of Pete Wagner and the Kane County Cougars
Sean Burroughs courtesy of Chip English
Hee Seop Choi courtesy of the West Tenn Diamond Jaxx
Michael Cuddyer courtesy of the New Britain Rock Cats
Alex Escobar courtesy of the Binghamton Mets
Marcus Giles courtesy of the Greenville Braves
Josh Hamilton courtesy of the Charleston, S.C. RiverDogs
Drew Henson courtesy of the Norwich Navigators
Corey Patterson courtesy of the West Tenn Diamond Jaxx
C.C. Sabathia courtesy of Ken Carr
Ben Sheets courtesy of the Indianapolis Indians
Chin-Hui Tsao courtesy of the Asheville Tourists
Barry Zito courtesy of the Sacramento River Cats

Cover design by Digital Grafx

Statistics are provided by STATS, Inc., 8131 Monticello Ave., Skokie, IL 60076
Telephone: 847-676-3322.

TABLE OF CONTENTS

TABLE OF CONTENTS (continued)

Preface

by John Benson

Just a few short years ago, there would have been little interest in a book featuring players like Sean Burroughs and Ben Sheets. But within the world of baseball fandom, the minor leagues have been discovered — big time!

Like all major changes in all fields, the discovery of minor league stars came about through the confluence of diverse forces. The first big force was the emergence of Bill James and his methods. James demonstrated (among his numerous other findings) that minor league performance really can be used as an indicator of future major league performance — if you know what you are doing and consider all the relevant data.

Before the Jamesian era, minor league performances tended to be dismissed wholesale. The world was simpler then. Almost everyone accepted the myth, now disproved, that minor league stats were universally unhelpful and misleading. Using a microscope, it was easy to find evidence supporting this theory. Smallish players with only warning-track power sometimes amassed shocking home run totals; obviously minor league fences had to be too close for home runs to mean anything. Pitchers with 82 MPH fastballs and mediocre control would sometimes lead their league in strikeouts; obviously minor league batters would swing at anything.

The trail of misleading minor league numbers continued (and continues) long after James gave us methods to make sense of confusion. Glenn Braggs hit .390 in the Appalachian League and .360 in the Pacific Coast League and then "flopped" in front of major league crowds before moving on to Japan. James, who knew how to read minor league numbers and transform them into useful information, never predicted more than a mid-.260's average from Braggs in the majors.

After the 1990 season, the winner of the Pacific Coast League batting title (Luis Lopez, with a .353 average) was dismissed by the Dodgers organization at the age of 26. He barely hung on to a professional baseball career, with another club. To many observers, such events remain mysterious and inexplicable. But with increasing understanding (Lopez' team, the Albuquerque Dukes, hit a collective .307 that year, and most of them were younger than Lopez) the average fan is becoming more discerning. Tony Blengino and the Diamond Library staff are miles ahead of the average fan. The point is: the world has changed. We have new methods.

Another major force in the discovery of the minor league player population has been the emergence of *Baseball America*. It took a long time, but the baseball industry finally developed its own professional journal. I have a strong belief that you can tell who reads any publication by looking at the advertising in it. (Who knows more about readers, than the people paying to reach them?) Look in *Baseball America*, and you will find ads for radar guns, baseball job openings and professional services, bats, glove repair services and Beam Clay, Obviously, baseball people read *Baseball America*, and no other publication has a such a following. And these readers get far more information on minor leaguers than can be found in any other source. The general public gets a huge benefit from this critical mass of information.

Minor league interest has been further elevated by the emergence of the personal computer as a home appliance. Especially through the use of a modem to access news and statistics from sources such as STATS Inc. and Howe Sportsdata International, following minor league baseball has become much easier. The existence of carefully coded data blends nicely with the Jamesian and related methods for making sense of this data, so you can begin to see the notions of critical mass and confluence at work in this field.

Major league expansion has been another force pushing minor league players into our collective consciousness. I'm not sure how many people actually taped the expansion drafts on ESPN in 1992 and 1997, and replayed it for entertainment and educational value as I have done more times than I'd want to admit, but I do know that fans everywhere were stimulated by thinking about the 15-man freeze lists going into the draft, and that fans in every city followed with passionate interest as the expansion teams dipped into each of the previously-existing farm systems.

Most rookie starting pitchers do badly, of course. I spend a great deal of time reminding rookie-lovers, if they begin brimming with enthusiasm for an unproven starting pitcher, that Bob Gibson (3-6, 5.61 ERA), Sandy Koufax (2-4, 4.91), and Greg Maddux (6-14, 5.61) all struggled when young. When anyone expects a rookie starter to do well, I ask earnestly: is he really much better than Greg Maddux? If not, be prepared to wait a couple years or longer.

Hitting is a different story. I find it instructive to go back and look at "top ten" lists from *Baseball America* from a few years ago. Whether it's the top ten from a minor league or the top ten from one organization, there is notable trend: if the list includes five hitters and five pitchers, you will find that four of the five hitters won regular major league jobs, and three of them became stars; while of five top pitching prospects it is likely that only one became a major league success.

Baseball's owners have finally ceased the pretense that they are fun-loving sportsmen [sportspersons?] and have come to grips with the reality that baseball is show business. Given a stage of sorts, and a live audience, the show business model for profitable operation will necessarily be more like a Broadway play than a Hollywood film. What does that have to do with minor leaguers? Simple: the Hollywood model means all-star casts and huge budgets; it won't work. The Broadway model features one or two (or maybe three) high-priced stars and a supporting cast making the industry minimum wage.

All these factors portend more minor leaguers reaching the majors faster and taking more prominent roles earlier in their careers than ever before. Certainly for the next five years that will be the trend. So if you weren't much interested in minor leaguers before, now is the time to start getting educated.

For getting educated about minor leaguers, you couldn't find better tutors than Tony Blengino and the Diamond Library staff. That's why I chose them, and that's why I know you will enjoy this book and benefit from it, immensely. Tell us what you think.

Tony Blengino brings a wonderfully diverse bundle of talent to this book. Tony first came to my attention as one of the more savvy, energetic and insightful research presenters at the annual conventions of the Society for American Baseball Research (SABR, the source of the term sabermetrics to describe baseball analysis). Tony's quantitative work in this book speaks for itself; he is on the frontiers of knowledge in baseball analysis. Tony is much more than a baseball researcher, however. He is an accredited journalist who covers minor league games for national publications, and at the same time he has done scouting on behalf of major league executives. And beyond the skills of observation and analysis, Tony is a true friend in the best definition of that word.

Please do write and tell us what you think. This book is still taking shape, now in its fifth edition. Suggestions from readers are the main source of improvement for all our publications, and we are all reachable by mail at Diamond Library, 15 Cannon Road, Wilton, CT 06897.

John Benson, October, 2000

TONY'S ACKNOWLEDGMENTS

As usual, it feels exceptionally rewarding to bring a major project to its successful conclusion. It feels even more so as the writing of the sixth edition of *"Future Stars"* comes to a close. It's been a wild and woolly year on the ballfield, and also in the personal and professional life of yours truly. At the end of the day, however, things are looking up, and the euphoric adrenaline rush of spotting the finish line brings with it satisfaction and hope for the future.

For *"Future Stars"* to become a reality, the contributions of many diverse and uniquely talented individuals are required. I believe that we have steadily developed a superb product over the years. There are plenty of competing titles out there — many of them are solid in their own right, and some are in my collection next to my own. I do believe, however, that the combination of statistical analysis and traditional scouting crafted in *"Future Stars"* can't be matched in the marketplace, and the comments of many of you, the readers, have served to reaffirm that belief.

First and foremost, John Benson made this project possible in the first place. He listened intently as I first pitched this project many years ago, when I first explained my methods of rating minor league prospects to him. He believed in me, gave me enough rope to shape the book according to my vision, and stood behind me every step of the way. He's much more than a publisher and colleague — he's a true friend. There have been many points in both our lives when one of us needed to speak about something totally unrelated to baseball, and we have been there for each other. You're the man, John.

Doug DelVecchio spends an astronomical amount of time crafting every facet of the operation that enables this book to exist. He manages, writes, edits copy, typesets, acts as the clearinghouse for every bit of info that finds its way into the book, obtains the cover photos — you name it. What has been most notable about Doug's contribution this year, however, is the tremendous extent of his ongoing professional growth. Doug has made countless suggestions regarding potential current and future improvements to *"Future Stars"*, all of which have been inspired and rooted in a true belief in the concept. He's got a whole lot more than *"Future Stars"* to worry about in his work day, but he always has time for me and this book. Keep up the super work, Doug — you've got an extremely bright future ahead of you.

Kudos to Eric Marino and Karl Mordhorst, office interns whose contributions to the layout of the book were invaluable. Doug speaks quite highly of your work, and your enthusiasm in bringing this project to a successful conclusion is truly appreciated.

Steve Lunsford is the Tony Phillips (remember him?) of our contingent. Over the years, his *"Future Stars"* role has morphed many times, and he has always stepped to the plate and delivered the key base hit. His cover design efforts were instrumental, as usual. The Olympic success of Ben Sheets just prior to our cover deadline pressed Steve into closer duty, but he delivered. Thanks, Steve.

Kevin Wheeler is the 162-game horse in our lineup. He writes all of the "Other Prospects" essays, and requires very little oversight, editing, etc. His excellence frees me up during the minor league season to sharpen the other aspects of the book, of which I write virtually all of the content. He knows his stuff, is wholly committed to this project, and has fun doing his work. I especially enjoyed communicating with him via e-mail regarding obscure "other" prospects while he was covering the Olympic Games this past September. G'day, mate.

I'd like to pay respects to the other stalwarts in this industry, who have been successful in bringing the numbers behind the game of baseball to the masses in recent decades. Bill James, Pete Palmer and others got the ball rolling, and organizations such as SABR, STATS, Inc., *Baseball America* and *USA Today Baseball Weekly* have made huge contributions in developing the heightened consciousness of the contemporary baseball fan. The Internet has made voluminous statistical information instantly available to baseball fans around the world.

Many players are finding success in this market, though I am obviously partial to SportsWritersDirect (sportswritersdirect.com), to whom I contribute during the season. Steve Moyer and John Sickels, among many others, are doing excellent work there, and I thank them for their ongoing contributions.

I have made many new friends among the people I've met since beginning to contribute to various Diamond Library publications back in 1993. Right there at the top of the list are Bill Gilbert and Lawr Michaels, two super guys who are about as different as any two people I know. You can oversimplify things and sum them up in one word, the states they respectively live in — Bill is Texas and Lawr is California. Bill's a little bit country, Lawr's a little bit rock and roll. Despite any such superficial differences, they share a passion for the game of baseball, and are real people that I value as friends. Along with Matt Olkin of *USA Today Baseball Weekly*, we compose a truly dangerous SABR Trivia Contest team that has advanced to the national finals and semifinals at the last two SABR conferences.

Thanks to the McManus Family of Cooperstown, the proprietors of the Adalaide Country Inn, where I go every summer, along with my family, to recharge my batteries and reassess life's priorities. It was fate that we found them back in 1994 — and now I can't imagine life without our midsummer trip. If you want to do Cooperstown right, give them a call.

However, even more so than all of the considerable contributors listed above, there is one individual who must be singled out for performance well above and beyond the call of duty. That's my wife, Kathy. 2000 has been a fairly interesting year on a lot of levels in the Blengino household. Our core beliefs, respective work ethics and priorities have been tested in new and exciting ways this year. They've been tested, but have been proven to be wise and inspired. I'm sure that there are others out there who found and married the one person on earth that they were truly destined to spend the rest of their lives with — but there probably aren't many. She has helped me learn to view every potential problem as a potential opportunity, and to see what I might have once considered barriers to actually be pathways to a new and exciting future. We have our differences, as all couples do, but I wake up each and every morning secure in the belief that I have someone special with whom to experience all of life's ups and downs. Jessica, Anthony and I all thank you and love you from the bottom of our hearts.

Tony Blengino October 2000

INTRODUCTION

Minor league performance analysis inevitably travels down one of two paths — one based on objective statistical performance, the other on subjective assessment of physical tools. Both roads have their merits — most successful major leaguers don't make it without skills and credentials. When we undertook this project, we decided to try to incorporate the best of both worlds, combining relevant, statistical analysis with first-person scouting.

Why the emphasis on the word "relevant"? Well, when many people evaluate prospects, they tend to rely on traditional-media-friendly statistics such as batting average, home runs and runs batted in. Even worse, players at various classifications, at various ages and in various ballparks are often compared to one another statistically without any adjustment for context. The statistical analysis in this book is based on more pertinent categories — on-base percentage and slugging percentage for hitters, and strikeout/walk and strikeout/innings pitched ratios for pitchers. These statistics are good barometers of current performance, and even better barometers of future performance. All of the statistical analysis in this book is compiled RELATIVE TO THE LEAGUE. A player who hits for average and power in the hitting-rich Triple-A Pacific Coast League may be nothing special, but one who does so in the pitching-rich High-A Carolina League may be truly special. The last, and possibly most important, factor is the prospect's age in relation to his level of competition. At first glance four years ago, Dodgers-system second baseman Adam Riggs looked like a megaprospect with a massive California League campaign — further analysis shows that he is only four months younger than established major league star Manny Ramirez.

A combination of reviewing pertinent statistical performance, adjusted for league and age context, gives a clear perspective of a prospect's capabilities. As Bill James clearly proved in his landmark *Baseball Abstracts*, minor league performance can provide a clear picture of future major league output, if you look at the right stats in the right way.

Stats only tell part of the story, however. First-person scouting is essential when evaluating a prospect. Seeing a player in action uncovers the facets of a player's game — positive or negative — that are not visible in numbers. Both Tony Blengino and the Diamond Library staff, have seen plenty of minor league prospects.

It's not always a matter just of seeing players playing the game. It's helpful to see and talk to players off the field, and Tony and the Diamond Library staff do that. During one locker room visit, one of us shocked to see a flabby, but highly regarded, pitching prospect in the Red Sox organization, despite a good statistical record, just didn't look like an athlete — and his subsequent major league career was predictably brief.

The most important questions for young players have to do with their self-evaluation. The best is "What do you have to do to improve enough to get to the majors?" Some players answer that they don't have to make any improvement; they seldom succeed. Others don't seem to know, or give an answer that makes it clear they are either unaware of their weaknesses or slinging BS. The best answer was from Mo Vaughn, then playing at Triple-A Pawtucket. Vaughn not only knew what improvements he had to make, but he was able to expound on his entire theory of hitting and how it fit in with what he had to do. Right then, Mo Vaughn went from our list of "promising" prospects to a list of those "sure" to make it.

Both the statistical and scouting approaches toward prospect evaluation have their virtues. All of us have a healthy respect for both methods — each other's methods. We will not try to steer you one way or the other — we will simply lay all of our cards on the table, and allow you to choose the combination however you prefer.

Best of all, none of what you'll read in this book is based on hype. It isn't the team's public relations office giving you information about its players. Nor is it coming from the scout who has a vested interest because the kid he recommended as a first round draft pick may be taking the scout's job down with him if he fails. Instead, we have written from the perspective of knowledgeable baseball fans, students of the game, with no axe to grind and no hidden agenda. If Alan Benes didn't make it — well, then we'd simply be wrong, no more, no less. (But we don't think we'll be wrong too often.)

This book will also place players in their current organizational context. Opportunity is at least as important as talent when projecting future major league stars. Sure, the Blue Jays' Carlos Delgado has proven many times over that he is a devastating major league power hitter, but he waited the better part of three seasons for a position to open. Conversely, the Royals' Johnny Damon was air-expressed to a waiting starting position in the majors the instant he was ready. Delgado did finally arrive in 1996, but the much younger Damon had already arrived because he got a full, no-strings opportunity.

Organizational drafting and promotion strategies also vary, and are explored in detail in this book. Some organizations tend to have winning minor league affiliates, giving the illusion of a solid organization, when in fact they are winning with players older than the league average, with little major league potential. This attention to organizational perspective allows for evaluation of entire systems — such long-dormant organizations as Texas finally appear to be on the rise, and the Los Angeles system, long a standard-bearer of excellence, is beginning to show wear. Recent changes in front office personnel, and the resulting changes in draft and promotion strategy, are often at the core of such shifts. The Rangers have focused upon Latin American talent. As for the Dodgers, Tommy Lasorda undid several years of hard work with three months of recklessness in the GM role.

Detailed draft analysis is also a focus of this book. Our goal is not simply to predict which rookies will have a significant impact in 2001, though that's part of it. More important is to look down the road and identify which players will have the most impact over the long haul, even if they don't make the majors until 2002 or even 2003. There are surely some future major league studs who toiled in Low-A or Rookie ball in 2000 who you will read about for the first time in this book.

The authors will not always agree on a prospect's virtues — we will simply state the reasons for our positions and let you make the call. If you're looking for a minor league reference book, there are others out there who will give you more categories of information — hit by pitch totals and sacrifice flies are not the types of things upon which we're going to spend precious space. This book, however, is a perfect addition to the baseball library of the discerning fan who is willing to consider fresh approaches to the science/art of prospect evaluation. A few years down the road, you will open this book and see a list of most of the game's newest All-Stars.

HOW TO USE THIS BOOK

(Customer Safety Information)

We have organized the bulk of the information in this book on a team-by-team basis. Below is a guide on how to interpret data presented in each organization's section:

Organizational Grids — For each team, a grid is presented, showing all of the starting players and other important contributors for all of its full-season minor league teams. Included is each player's position, age, and whether they bat or throw left or righthanded (or are switch hitters). This is a snapshot of an organization at a moment in time — it can help you determine how much competition a prospect will face for a future major league job. A glance at the ages of players at various levels within an organization gives clues as to an organization's attitude regarding promotion. It is not a coincidence that the aggressive promoters such as the Braves and Indians also tend to have the best minor league systems.

You should refer to these grids often. We're not going to tell you how old each player is every time we refer to him, or that he bats righthanded. The grid will give you that info at a glance. Instead, we'll use space to describe what kind of player he is and what his chances are.

Draft Analysis Grids — Another grid for each team highlights the best and worst draft picks for each organization between the last five years. Tony has rated notable selections as major league stars, major league starters, major leaguers (at any time to date), solid prospects, potential prospects and Round 1-5 flops. Each organization is assigned an overall grade for each year. The evaluations are subjective, but based on the methods applied in this book.

Organization Overview — Each gives a brief description of where the organization stands — if it is changing key personnel or philosophies, how deep its talent is, which positions are strong or weak, who its top prospects are. After that, a paragraph each is devoted to commentary on the leading players at each position group — infield, outfield, catchers, starting pitchers, relief pitchers. If a position group paragraph is missing, so are prospects for that team at that position.

Top Ten Lists — These are based on the players' long-term major league potential — not their 2000 potential. Any player who spent a material portion of the 2000 season (generally at least 100 at bats or 50 innings pitched) in a full-season minor league was eligible for this list. Players promoted to the majors from June 2000 forward might still be included on their organization's prospect list. Each player's abilities, strengths and weaknesses are presented in some level of detail. An estimated major league arrival date is generally forecasted, along with some indication of their major league upside.

Other Prospects — Because there are more than 10 players worthy of mention from every organization we have capsule profiles for players not included in the top 10, with comments from the author in most cases. The level of detail in this section is generally not as deep as on the Top Ten lists.

In addition to the team-by-team sections, we have prepared statistical analyses and other features. The following helpful hints should prepare you on how to use the information presented:

"Relative Production Potential" essay and lists — The RPP method projects the major league potential of full-season minor league hitters based on their on-base and slugging percentages relative to the league, and adjusted for their age relative to their peers. This analysis results in an ordered list of the top minor league hitting prospects. Another list ranking organizations' relative batting strength is presented.

"Relative Control/Power Potential" essay and lists — The RC/PP method projects the major league potential of full-season minor league pitchers based on their strikeout/walk and strikeouts/nine innings ratios relative to the league, and adjusted for their age relative to their peers. This analysis also results in an ordered list of the top minor league pitching prospects, and a list ranking organizations' relative pitching strength.

Major League Equivalencies — The major league equivalencies for the 2000 minor league batting performances by Double and Triple-A hitters who ranked high on the RPP list, using a method based on landmark studies by the Patron Saint of Sabermetrics, Bill James.

"Class-A Batting Prospects and Their Major League Comparables" — It is silly to project major league equivalencies for players so far removed from the major leagues. Instead, we compared the Class-A players who fared the best in the RPP analysis to players with comparable major league RPPs. It's a pretty solid bet that some of these comparisons will prove to be prophetic a few years down the road.

"Heirs to the Throne" — Projecting future major league performance of top minor league pitchers is dicy because of a higher frequency of injuries, sudden attacks of wildness and other factors. Therefore, instead of projecting the stats of future major league hurlers, we have used the RC/PP figures to compare top minor leaguers with their major league counterparts. We have divided major league superstar pitchers into seven different groups, based on their RC/PP levels. We have then taken some of the top minor league hurlers and assigned them to one of those groups based on their RC/PP levels. Again, we expect these comparisons to look pretty darn good down the road.

A Look Back — A historical look back at Tony's Top 10 organizational lists starting from the books inception in 1995.

The List — A *NEW* addition to the *Future Stars* book in 2001-2002. This chapter looks deeper into the minors; at players who are in Rookie ball and who are much harder to predict future success.

2001-2003 All Rookie Teams — Tony's list projecting the All-Rookie teams for the next three seasons, based upon both the players' ability and their likelihood of getting a major league opportunity.

Will Lingo's 2000 Draft Recap — The Pride of *Baseball America* has graciously allowed us to present his annual review of the top players chosen in the 2000 draft.

THE 2000 AMATEUR DRAFT REPORT

by Will Lingo & James Bailey

In the weeks before the 2000 draft, Major League Baseball convened a meeting with the scouting directors for all 30 teams, encouraging everyone to do their part to keep signing bonuses in line.

MLB described it as a negotiating seminar, in which information was provided to help teams when the time came to start dickering dollars after the draft. The word some others used to describe it was collusion. Regardless, the meeting was credited months later with helping some teams hold the line on spiraling bonuses, though the cost in many cases was summer-long holdouts that delayed the pro debuts of numerous early-round picks until 2001.

The tactic many teams used come draft day to ensure signability was to seek out players who were willing to agree to terms ahead of time. Though this type of negotiating is technically against the rules, it was obvious it had occurred when several teams announced the signing of their first-round picks almost immediately after the draft. The Florida Marlins, who held the No. 1 overall pick, were rumored to be seriously considering about a half-dozen players in the week before the draft. They finally settled on first baseman Adrian Gonzalez, who signed on draft day for $3 million.

Texas prep phenom Jason Stokes was one of the players the Marlins were said to be strongly looking at before the draft. Unlike Gonzalez, he refused to negotiate before the draft, and he slipped accordingly. But when the Marlins' second turn came at pick No. 41, he was still on the board and they took a stab at him. He did not prove to be an easy sign, holding out for two months before choosing to sign instead of going to college.

Thirteen first-round picks signed within two weeks of the draft, by which point the average signing bonus had decreased nearly 10 percent from 1999. The commissioner's office was pleased. The top agents, including Scott Boras who represented nine early-round picks, were not. Many teams seemed content to just wait out negotiations on their top picks, figuring this would be the year the other side blinked.

Then along came the Joe Borchard deal. Borchard, an outfielder who doubled as the starting quarterback of the football team at Stanford, signed a record $5.3 million deal with the White Sox in mid-July. His bonus was the largest ever given to a player who signed with the team that drafted him. (Several loophole free agents in 1996 received more.)

Though no one came close to Borchard's bonus the rest of the summer, negotiations got creative in many cases, as several players signed deals that included major league contracts, requiring them to be placed on the 40-man roster (though not on the 25-man active roster) in 2001.

By the end of the summer, most of the teams had come to terms with their top picks, though not before at least a dozen players skipped the first days of classes at colleges around the country. Once a player attends classes, he's no longer eligible to sign. The Twins lost two of their top three picks when righthander Aaron Heilman and first baseman Taggert Bozeid chose to return to school after a summer of grueling negotiations.

They were consoled somewhat, however, by the sensational debut of their first selection, righthander Adam Johnson, whom they selected with the second overall pick in the draft out of Cal State Fullerton. Johnson jumped right into the high Class A Florida State League and immediately showed he was up to the competition.

Here's a look at some 2000 draftees, who, like Johnson, seem to have bright futures ahead of them. Players who signed late and did not play were not considered.

AMERICAN LEAGUE

CATCHER

Scott Heard, Rangers: Heard was strongly considered by the Marlins as the No. 1 pick in the draft but his signability and a poor offensive showing in the spring caused him to slip all the way to the Rangers at No. 25. He refound his stroke in the Rookie-level Gulf Coast League, hitting .351 with 16 doubles. But what makes Heard an outstanding prospect is his defense which some scouts say is already near major league average. If he can continue to hit even a little as he climbs, he will reach the big leagues, though it will probably take several years as most high school catchers move a level at a time.

FIRST BASE

Sean Swedlow, Indians: This would be Bozeid had the Twins signed him, but instead Swedlow takes it by default. All of the first basemen who were drafted early went to NL teams. Swedlow, who was a catcher in high school, made the transition to first at Rookie-level Burlington and has a lot of work to do defensively. The Indians' third-round pick has a nice lefthanded stroke, though he hit just .226 without a home run in his debut. Like Heard, he could take awhile to reach the big leagues, but he's also capable of showing dramatic improvement as early as next year.

SECOND BASE

Chris Amador, White Sox: An eighth-round pick out of Puerto Rico, Amador played shortstop in high school. He came to the White Sox with a reputation as a slap hitter who could run and that's what he showed in the Rookie-level Arizona League. Amador hit .302 without much power and tied the league record with 40 stolen bases. He's already willing to take a walk and could develop into a fine top-of-the-order hitter. When he fills out he'll add a little pop, but that's really not his game.

THIRD BASE

Corey Smith, Indians: A teammate of Swedlow's at Burlington, Smith showed dramatic improvement as the summer progressed. Though he was error-prone defensively, he has all the tools to become a fine third baseman when he learns how to play the position. A shortstop in high school, he owns a strong arm and he's athletic enough to make just about any play. He's got tremendous power

potential and will knock his share of home runs, though he managed only four in his debut while hitting .256. Smith's name was tossed around early as the top high school prospect in his draft class, but others passed him during the spring. The early reports might have been right, however, and he could prove a steal with the No. 26 overall pick.

SHORSTOP

Freddie Bynum, Athletics: The A's didn't have a first-round pick thanks to their signing of free agent lefthander Mike Magnante. That was acknowledged later as a front-office snafu. When Oakland called Bynum's name in the second round it was viewed by many as a reach — a big reach. The Pitt County (N.C.) CC product might have been an unknown in June, but by September everyone in the Northwest League knew who he was. He batted just .256 for Vancouver, but stole 22 bases and displayed all-round athleticism that made him the No. 1 prospect in the league. He's raw and could take awhile to get to Oakland, but he definitely has an interesting tool box.

OUTFIELD

Rocco Baldelli, Devil Rays; Joe Borchard, White Sox; Jamal Strong, Mariners: Baldelli was a four-sport star in high school and had scholarship offers in basketball and volley ball as well as baseball. His athleticism was so attractive that the Devil Rays took him with the No. 6 overall pick even though they have another center fielder named Josh Hamilton who is one of the top prospects in the game. Baldelli can do everything but throw, but he won't move as quickly as Hamilton or some of the other top high school prospects because he comes from Rhode Island where the weather — not to mention his other sporting pursuits — cut into his development in high school. He batted just .216 at Rookie-level Princeton. Borchard, on the other hand, climbed all the way to Double-A Birmingham in his debut. Several teams regarded him as the top talent in the draft, and his fall to No. 12 can be chalked up almost entirely to money, though no one expected him to walk away with the $5.3 million deal. He batted .311 with two homers in 103 at-bats at three different stops and is likely to begin the 2001 season back at Birmingham. He's a strong candidate to be the first player from the 2000 draft to reach the big leagues. The Mariners lost their first three draft choices due to free agent signings, so sixth-rounder Strong was their third pick. The speedster from the University of Nebraska was the co-MVP of the Northwest League after hitting .314 and stealing an eye-popping 60 bases.

RIGHTHANDED PITCHING

Adam Johnson, Twins: As mentioned earlier, Johnson enjoyed one of the best debuts of any 2000 draftee, and he did it at a higher level than most of his classmates. Ironically, he was viewed as a signability pick when the Twins chose him second overall. He quickly came to terms on a $2.5 million deal and began wowing the Florida State League almost immediately. In 13 appearances for Fort Myers Johnson went 5-4 with a 2.47 ERA and struck out a staggering 92 hitters in 69 innings. That came with just 45 hits and 20 walks. He had a reputation as a cocky competitor at Fullerton, often showing up opponents after a strikeout. But he's proven he can back it all up. His fastball reaches 94 MPH and he certainly knows what to do with it.

LEFTHANDED PITCHING

Joe Torres, Angels: Torres struck out a mind-boggling 128 hitters in 55 innings in the spring, so it's easy to see why the Angels were interested in him with the 10th pick in the draft. They had enough confidence to start him at Boise in the Northwest League, which can be a tough assignment for a high school draftee. He was definitely up to the task, going 4-1 with a 2.54 ERA and striking out 52 in 46 innings. The Angels have shown a willingness lately to move pitchers rapidly through the system, jumping 1999 draftee John Lackey twice during his first full season. Torres could be on the express soon himself.

NATIONAL LEAGUE

CATCHER

Brad Cresse, Diamondbacks: Cresse may have had the best debut of any 2000 draftee, starting at high Class A High Desert, where he hit .324 with 17 homers in 173 at-bats, and finishing at Double-A El Paso. High Desert is a notorious home run haven, but Cresse's ratio of a homer every 10 at-bats was sensational nonetheless and proved he was not an aluminum-bat hero. He had an outstanding senior season at Louisiana State, hitting .388 with 30 homers and 106 RBI to lead the Tigers to the national championship. Baseball America named him to its All-America Team as the DH. The Diamondbacks selected him in the fifth round of the draft, though he'd likely have gone higher if he weren't a senior.

FIRST BASE

Garrett Atkins, Rockies: Atkins, another fifth-round find, was a third-team All-American last spring after hitting .352 with 17 homers and 72 RBI for UCLA. He had been projected as a higher pick, but questions about his power pushed his stock down. He didn't conclusively answer them over the summer, hitting seven homers in 251 at-bats for Portland in the short-season Northwest League. But he showed enough to share co-MVP honors in the league with Strong by batting .303 with 47 RBI and drawing 45 walks. Atkins will have to hit for power, as he doesn't have the athleticism to play anywhere but first.

SECOND BASE

Chase Utley, Phillies: A teammate of Atkins' at UCLA, Utley went to the Phillies with the 15th overall pick in the draft. He was one of the top prospects to appear in the New York-Penn League in 2000, hitting .307 with 13 doubles for Batavia. He managed just two home runs after hitting 22 and earning All-America honors in the spring, but the belief is that he will still have above-average power for a second baseman as he develops. He's adequate defensively, though his bat will be what carries him. If Marlon Anderson can't claim the Phillies job once and for all in 2001, it could be Utley's before long, because there's no one else in the organization to stand in his way.

THIRD BASE

Lance Niekro, Giants: His father Joe and uncle Phil made their livings baffling big league hitters with knuckleballs, but Lance is aiming to make his mark with a bat in his hands. He broke onto the scene with a tremendous season in the Cape Cod League in the summer of '99, then followed up with a poor spring at Florida Southern. The Giants put enough stock in their old scouting reports to spend their second-round pick on him and he made them look smart in his debut. Niekro won the Northwest League batting title with a .362 mark for Salem-Keizer. He showed enough power and defensive ability to project as a solid third baseman down the road.

SHORTSTOP

Luis Montanez, Cubs: The third overall pick in the draft, Montanez has the tools to someday join the upper echelon of run-producing shortstops. He could bring the full package to the position and give the Cubs their best shortstop in a generation. Montanez certainly got off to a good start, earning MVP honors in the Rookie-level Arizona League, where he was also the best prospect. He hit .344 with 16 doubles and seven triples. Much has been made of the rejuvenated Cubs' farm system, led by center fielder Corey Patterson, but the organization lacked a bona fide middle infield prospect until Montanez came along.

OUTFIELD

Josh Kroeger, Diamondbacks; Dave Krynzel, Brewers; Grady Sizemore, Expos: Krynzel is the class of the outfield as far as NL teams go. He's got all the tools to become an outstanding leadoff man and was turning the Pioneer League on its ear when he went down with a thumb injury midway through the season. The 11th overall pick in the draft, he hit .359 in his brief debut. Kroeger was the only high school player the Diamondbacks took with their first 10 picks. He started his career by hitting .297 and leading the Arizona League Diamondbacks with four homers and 28 RBI. The Expos stunned everyone by granting a $2 million bonus to Sizemore, the fifth pick in the third round of the draft. They had to buy him away from a football scholarship to the University of Washington, but the negotiations were short and sweet and he was under contract within days of the draft. He showed good speed and though he didn't hit for much power, he has the size to do so in the future. He's a center fielder now, and could eventually move to a corner, following the career path of former Expos phenom Cliff Floyd.

RIGHTHANDED PITCHING

Adam Wainwright, Braves: Atlanta is typically conservative with its young pitchers and they tried to be with Wainwright, the first of four Braves first-round picks in 2000. The Braves began him in the Rookie-level Gulf Coast League, but it just wasn't a fair match, as he tore through the competition, posting a 4-0 record and 1.13 ERA in seven appearances. In 32 GCL innings he allowed just 15 hits and 10 walks while striking out 42. He was on

such a roll when he moved to the Appalachian League that it took four starts for him to issue his first walk. As it was, he finished with just two walks and 39 strikeouts in 29 innings for Danville, while going 2-2 with a 3.68 ERA. He ranked among the top prospects in both leagues and secured himself a spot on the pitching pipeline to Atlanta.

LEFTHANDED PITCHING

Mark Phillips, Padres: Cardinals prospect Chris Narveson had a better debut, going 2-4 with a 3.27 ERA at Rookie-level Johnson City, but Phillips has a higher ceiling. He was one of the multitude of young players the Marlins were said to have had their eye on in the weeks before the draft, but he slid to the Padres at No. 9. He's a power pitcher with a mid-90s fastball and lefthanders with that kind of heat are truly coveted. He was on a tight pitch count at Rookie-level Idaho Falls and managed just 37 innings in 10 starts, posting a 1-1 record and 5.35 ERA. He did, however, strike out a batter per inning.

DOWN ON THE FARM

by John Benson

Some fans still don't pay much attention to the minor leagues. They don't bother scouting beyond the STATS Red Book. They feel that a minor league draft pick is less important than a 35-year-old utility infielder who had a home run in a major league box score yesterday. They scoff at their peers who read *Baseball America* and chatter with enthusiasm about this year's baby-faced phenoms. And of course: they lose their Rotisserie leagues every year, because they are chumps.

Major leaguers come in all shapes and sizes. They come not only from Texas, New York and California; they also come from Australia, Japan, Taiwan, Korea, The Netherlands, Mexico, Panama, and every Caribbean island large enough to have an airport. And they all (well, almost all) have one thing in common: they play minor league baseball before reaching the majors. Even Hideki Irabu, the Nolan Ryan of Japanese baseball, played in the minors before reaching the majors and had his share of problems.

Scrutinizing two minor league box scores and worrying over a player's post-game comments in Double-A competition would have been unthinkable in Rotisserie circles during the 1980's, but such activities are typical of a winning competitor's approach during the new millennium. The general method of paying attention to Double-A performances has become the norm. For the average player, we may wait until the season is over before forming opinions, but Double-A stats have become a major source for armchair scouts.

Mets third baseman Edgardo Alfonzo first caught my eye with his Double-A performance in 1994. Playing second base for Binghamton, Alfonzo hit .293 with 15 home runs and 75 RBI. The most impressive stat was his age: 20 (he turned 21 on November 8). Even more importantly, I knew that the Mets front office had plans for him.

Ryne Sandberg played Double-A ball in the same Eastern League. His numbers were .310-11-79, and Sandberg did this at the same age as Alfonzo, two months older, in fact. So we had the same league, same age, similar results (yes,

I know, we should be looking at on-base percentage and slugging, and comparing to the league as a whole from the same year, and I did that, but this essay is about the numbers used in stat leagues) and these results were confirmed by scouting reports. A very good bat-handler, Alfonzo on defense was arguably superior to Sandberg at the same age, though statistical measures (like errors) favor Sandberg's steadiness to Alfonzo's better range and stronger throwing arm.

So before the 1995 season, I was writing that Alfonzo could be compared to Sandberg, which in the Rotisserie world, where Sandberg was king, sounded like blasphemy. When Alfonzo got off to a slow start in the majors, at least a couple of people forgot that I was talking about Alfonzo over the course of his career, not Alfonzo in 1995 or even 1996. And they forgot that Sandberg had taken a while to become the player we later knew as Sandberg (in his first two years in the majors, he hit .271 with seven home runs and then .261 with eight homers). And people also forgot that Wrigley field is a much easier place to be a hitter than Shea Stadium, but I will save that nitpicky argument for later in Alfonzo's career.

Two people sent me letters (yes, I do read almost everything that comes my way, as a learning exercise, although it can be July or August before I finally have time to look) and one letter called attention to the "misleading" comment about Alfonzo (my numbers forecasts were actually pretty good; this reader just didn't like the mention of Sandberg in the same sentence) and another put Alfonzo on a list of players I had "overrated."

Then 1997 arrived, and Alfonzo hit .315 with double digits in homers and steals, which is exactly what the Rotisserie people love: power and speed. And for the sabermetric readers of this book, Alfonzo's .391 on-base percentage in 1997 was higher than Sandberg ever achieved, and Alfonzo's .432 slugging percentage was within .020 of Sandberg's career mark.

Alfonzo is still just age 27. Though his development temporarily plateaued in 1998, I expected him to improve further in 2001 and beyond — and he's doing just that. But we are getting away from the subject of minor league performances and their meaning. The point of this essay is that minor league stats really do matter, if you know how to use them. And there was a time when nobody knew how to use them. Bill James changed all that, and Tony Blengino continues pioneering on the frontier that James first explored.

Which brings us to Ken Phelps, a player who was much studied by James. In 1982, Phelps hit .333, smashed 46 homers, and drove in 141 runs. These huge stats were largely ignored. At that time, nobody paid much attention to minor league numbers. Conventional wisdom was that minor league stats are all misleading; the parks are too small, the pitchers can't throw strikes, and nobody has a good curveball in the minors.

Phelps put up his Ruthian numbers in the Triple-A American Association, a league known for good pitching. Phelps had to face pitchers like Bud Black, later a highly successful major leaguer, who had a 2.48 ERA that year in Phelps' league. Bryn Smith, another major league success, was one of Phelps' teammates, and a 1.90 ERA in exactly the same ballparks where Phelps played. Ken Phelps really did have a tremendous season in 1982.

Phelps finally got promoted to the major leagues, but never got a chance to play full time. The most at-bats he ever had in a season was 344, in 1986. Remarkably, he still produced 24 to 27 homers every year from 1983 through 1988, except for 1985 when he got a paltry 116 at bats. Phelps finished his career with more than one home run for every 15 at bats, equal to Mickey Mantle and Jimmy Foxx in home run ratio, and ahead of Lou Gehrig, Henry Aaron and Willie Mays.

Today, thanks to James and Blengino, among others, a player doesn't have to put up huge statistics to raise high expectations. What would the scouts and media today think of a player who hit, say 45 to 50 homers, and about 140 RBI, with a .330 batting average in Triple-A? Such numbers would create unimaginable excitement!

The point of this essay is not that Ken Phelps was a great player. I am not even going to argue the point that minor league stats are useful indicators, as James proved. The point is: today, everybody studies minor league numbers extensively. To compete in a Rotisserie league, you must study them, too.

The increased scrutiny of minor league numbers has pushed their perceived importance all the way to the other end of the spectrum. Finding each season's top rookies is vital. Almost every armchair league now includes some kind of minor league draft. Rotisserie Ultra and the 40-man roster have made farm systems (and even college programs) the new battlefield of fantasy roster management.

There are numerous tools for fans who spend their winters on the peach-fuzz watch. Bill James produces annual projections for rookies based on minor league numbers, as do my *Rotisserie Baseball Annual* and Draft Software.

My advice is to spend less time crunching numbers and poring over statistical tables, and spend more time studying managerial style and thinking about which teams actually have job openings. Too often, people focused just on the numbers come up with names like Phil Hiatt and Tyrone Horne, who had terrific seasons in the high minors in 1999, but didn't even play in the majors in 1999.

The record books are full of players who simply couldn't fit into a major league lineup. Rob Nelson had the misfortune to compete with Mark McGwire, Jack Clark, and Frank Thomas for time at first base. Mike Laga gave up waiting in line behind Pedro Guerrero and Will Clark, and went to Japan long ago, as did Cecil Fielder when he was stuck behind Fred McGriff (but then Laga didn't come back young enough to have a career here). Same with Roberto Petagine, their '90's equivalent.

Fine players get stuck in log jams. Only a few become unstuck. Geronimo Berroa spent the first half of his career on the Braves' farm, passed by rising stars like David Justice and Ron Gant. In 1991, I wrote: "Berroa's minor league stats say he could hit 25 homers with 90 RBI in the majors, but that potential doesn't do him a lot of good in Richmond." Two years after I wrote that, Berroa produced 22 homers and 98 RBI for Oakland, and then he became even better. Here's another lament from 1991: "Slugger Tino Martinez of Seattle must wait for Alvin Davis or Pete O'Brien to move aside."

Dodger super-talents Tom Goodwin and Henry Rodriguez had to get out of Los Angeles to find success. When evaluating any rookie's chances, consider the team's status (pennant contender or rebuilding) before you draw conclusions based on a minor league track record. Travis Lee, Brad Fullmer and Todd Helton put up great numbers in their 1997 minor league seasons. In 1998 they were able to play in the majors because their parent clubs were not contenders and could afford to have them learn in the majors.

When you start using prediction methods based on minor league stats, you find all the exceptions that prove your rules. Eventually, the old myths about minor league numbers regain some of the credibility that technicians have stripped from them. Minor league numbers, under the microscope, look just as mysterious and confusing as they did 15 years ago when viewed collectively from a long and safe distance.

The outfield fences really are too close. Minor league pitchers really can't throw their curves for strikes. In The Show, they really do throw wicked breaking stuff, as Crash Davis told us. Real baseball people know these things, and fantasy managers are only just beginning to get the feel for them.

RELATIVE PRODUCTION POTENTIAL 2000

by Tony Blengino

It is time for my annual foray into the field of statistical evaluation of minor league hitting prospects using the Relative Production Potential method. Most other prospect lists that you will see tend to rely either upon raw athletic tools, or upon traditional, politically correct statistics, such as batting average, home runs and RBI, and either underestimate or fail to consider at all the role of a prospect's age when determining his long-term potential.

Yes, Relative Production Potential is all about statistics — but it's about the "right" statistics. It's about the ones that truly measure offensive performance: on-base percentage and slugging percentage. The method adjusts for league context, measuring all players' performance relative to their league. Therefore, a massive offensive season as measured in traditional numbers in the pitcher-dominated High-A Carolina League carries more weight than a similar campaign in the hitting-crazy Triple-A Pacific Coast League.

The method also adjusts for a prospect's age in relation to his level, weeding out all of the Chris Hatchers and Luis Ravens who create the illusion that they are long-term major league prospects with their pounding of minor league hurlers. The end result is an ordered list of 305 minor leaguers who established some level of expected major league production based upon their 2000 minor league performance.

The method has eight years under its belt now, and its track record is now well documented. Virtually all of the Top Ten alumni have made major league appearances or remain solid prospects. It must be emphasized that this method does not purport to project which players will have the most major league impact in 2001: it measures long-term potential.

The 2000 Top Ten is a fairly inexperienced group - the top five finishers all toiled at the High or Low-A levels in 2000. None of the Top Ten have had a single big league at bat, though #6 Brad Wilkerson likely would have if he didn't make the Olympic team.

This method has proven to be quite effective at unearthing minor league prospects very early in their careers; 17-year-old (or was it 16?) Edgar Renteria batted all of .203 in 1993, but made the list. The Jose Vidros and Mike Sweeneys of this world made the upper reaches of this list long before they caught the attention of other minor league talent evaluators. This method heralded Alex Rodriguez as a god five years ago, and has predicted stardom for Nomar Garciaparra, Andruw Jones, Vladimir Guerrero, Pat Burrell, Troy Glaus, Eric Chavez, Adrian Beltre, Ben Grieve, Paul Konerko, Scott Rolen, Mike Sweeney, Darin Erstad, Johnny Damon, Shawn Green, Bob Abreu, Carlos Delgado, Cliff Floyd, Jim Thome, Manny Ramirez and Chipper Jones, all former Top Tenners, along the way. Other players who ranked highly in last year's analysis who largely escaped mainstream baseball media attention were Luis Rivas, Jimmy Rollins, and Brent Abernathy, who are now widely heralded as top prospects.

Also, one can get a feel for the overall offensive depth of the respective minor league organizations by calculating cumulative RPP scores. Those results are always good for a few surprises.

METHODS

For those of you who are familiar with the method, this might seem a bit tedious. Bear with me. The first step in the evaluation process is the calculation of on-base and slugging percentages for all regulars on all full-season minor league teams. To capture them all, all players with 250 or more at bats were included, as well as any other players who had the most at bats on their club at a given position. In some cases, players who met neither qualification because they split their season at multiple classifications were qualified at both classifications. If more than one RPP score qualified them for the list of top prospects, their low score was dropped.

Each player's OBP and SLG are then compared to the average of all the qualifiers in his league. Each player is awarded points equal to the number of standard deviations above or below the average of all of his league's qualifiers. For instance, Jack Cust of Double-A El Paso had an on-base percentage 2.19 standard deviations above the average of his league's qualifiers, and a slugging percentage 1.04 standard deviations above the average of his league's qualifiers. Adding 2.19 and 1.04 gives Cust an unadjusted RPP score of 3.23, which is excellent.

For each minor league, the sum of all OBP and SLG factors is zero. This enables hitters' leagues to be fairly compared to pitchers' leagues. Red Sox' Triple-A first baseman Dernell Stenson (.346 OBP, .487 SLG) had very similar statistics to A's Triple-A outfielder Mario Encarnacion (.347 OBP, .472 SLG). However, Stenson posted his numbers in the International League, much less conducive to hitting than Encarnacion's Pacific Coast League. Therefore, Stenson's unadjusted RPP was higher, by 0.97 to 0.19.

After calculating unadjusted RPP for all minor league qualifiers, the population of top minor league prospects is assembled. At this point, a prospect's age is compared to the "optimal" age for his minor league level. For Triple-A, the optimal age is 22, for Double-A 21, for High-A 20, and for Low-A 19. First, all starters who were at or below their level's optimal age (July 4 cutoff date) are placed in the prospect pool. Next, all players who were one year above optimal age and had positive unadjusted RPP scores are added. Then, all players who were two years above optimal age, and had unadjusted RPP of at least 1.00 are added. Finally, all players who were three years above optimal age and had unadjusted RPP of at least 2.00 are added. The pool is now full, 305 players qualified in 2000, slightly above the 1999 total of 294. The pool includes players who performed at very high offensive levels, but also many who did not, but were among the youngest prospects in their leagues.

Each of the 305 qualifying prospects' RPP scores is then adjusted for age. For each year younger than his level's optimal age, a player's RPP is increased by 1.00; for each year older than his league's optimal age, a player's RPP is decreased by 1.00. #1 finisher Antonio Perez, for example, received a positive 2.00 age adjustment for his High-A performance at Lancaster at age 18. This process can bring together two seemingly starkly different seasons. Rangers' High-A outfielder Kevin Mench, 22, had an unadjusted RPP of 6.00, adjusted downward by (2.00)

to 4.00, ranking him 3rd overall. Meanwhile, Mariners' Low-A outfielder Chris Snelling, 18, posted an unadjusted RPP of 2.92. However, his positive 1.00 age adjustment boosted his adjusted RPP to 3.92, ranking him just behind Mench, and 4th overall. Both should be standout major league outfielders down the road.

THE 2000 RESULTS

Let's check out this year's Top Ten. All of the players in the Top Ten are covered in detail in their respective organizational Top Ten lists.

The #1 finisher is the Mariners' Antonio Perez, 18, also known as "The Other Guy They Got for Griffey". Yes, Mr. Perez came over from the Reds in the Griffey deal, and should someday soon join Junior in a major league All-Star Game. Perez stands only 5'11", 175, but packs serious extra-base punch for a middle infielder. He batted .276 with 36 doubles, 17 homers, 63 RBI and 28 steals in the California League. The Mariners will obviously be pretty well fortified at shortstop should Alex Rodriguez remain in town, but Perez would be a snug fit at second base by 2002 in that event. It must be noted that, though Perez finished first on this year's list, his adjusted 4.22 RPP figure would have ranked him only fifth in 1999 and seventh in 1998; 2000 wasn't a stellar year for minor league hitters.

This year's second place finisher is Pirates' Low-A catcher/designated hitter J.R. House, 20, their 1999 fifth round draft pick. The 6'2", 215, righthanded hitter got off to an explosive start at Low-A Hickory and never looked back, batting .348 with 29 doubles, 23 homers and 90 RBI in only 420 at bats. He might lack the defensive chops to remain at catcher, but still has enough offensive juice to eventually be a starting major league first baseman, and a potential All-Star.

Rangers' High-A outfielder Kevin Mench, 22, is this year's #3 finisher. The Rangers' 1999 fourth round pick is a former NCAA home run champion who has made an easy adjustment to the wooden bat. The 6'0", 215, right-handed hitter absolutely tore apart the High-A Florida State League, batting .334 with 39 doubles, nine triples, 27 homers, 121 RBI, 76 walks and 19 steals. He was a bit old for his level last season, and should be able to handle a two-level jump to Triple-A in 2001.

This year's #4 finisher is Mariners' Low-A outfielder

Chris Snelling. A mere lad of 18, the 5'10", 165, lefthanded hitter was extremely productive on a per at bat basis in an injury-shortened season at Low-A Wisconsin, batting .305 with nine doubles, five triples, nine homers, 56 RBI, 34 walks and seven steals in only 259 at bats. The young Australian lacks a single eyecatching tool, but is above average across the board and knows how to play the game. He could be an eventual fit in four or five different spots in a big league order.

The #5 finisher is Reds' Low-A outfielder Austin Kearns, 20, a 1998 first round pick who tore apart the Midwest League last season. The 6'4", 210, righthanded hitter is a complete offensive player who batted .306 with 110 runs scored, 37 doubles, 27 homers, 104 RBI, 90 walks and 18 steals at Low-A Dayton. He should be able to handle a two-level jump to Double-A in 2001.

We get our first look at an upper-level prospect at #6 in the person of Expos' outfielder Brad Wilkerson. The 6'0", 190, Wilkerson, 23, began the 2000 season by torching the Double-A Eastern League, batting .336 with an amazing 36 doubles in only 229 at bats, adding six homers, 44 RBI and 42 walks for good measure. Wilkerson is a bit more complete as a prospect as compared to the Class A guys ranking above him, but likely lacks their upside. He projects as a solid on-base guy with 20-homer pop in the majors, and could arrive in 2001.

Marlins' outfield prospect Abraham Nunez, 20, checks in at #7 on this year's list. Nunez was part of the haul in the Matt Mantei deal that also brought Brad Penny to the Marlins. The 6'2", 165, switch-hitter has battled shoulder problems over the past two seasons, but still projects as an elite power/speed prospect who will likely play right field in the majors. Nunez only scratched the surface of his potential at Double-A Portland last season, batting .276 with 17 doubles, six homers, 44 RBI and eight steals in only 221 at bats. He is an injury risk, but has a 30/30 power/speed upside.

Padres' Double-A third base prospect Sean Burroughs, 19, checks in at #8, slightly down from his 1999 #3 ranking. The 6'1", 195, lefthanded hitter was the youngest upper minor league regular last season, and more than held his own at Mobile, batting .291 with 29 doubles and an excellent 45/58 strikeout/walk ratio in 450 plate appearances, but managed only two homers and 42 RBI. Don't worry, the power will come as he begins to face pitchers closer to his own age, beginning in 2001 at the Triple-A level. He'll eventually be a 25-homer guy.

#9 finisher Brad Cresse, 21, is by far the highest ranking 2000 draftee on this year's list. Cresse, a righthanded-hitting catching prospect, was the Diamondbacks' fifth round draft pick. He immediately asserted himself with the wooden bat, batting .324 with seven doubles and an amazing 17 homers and 56 RBI in only 173 at bats in the High-A California League. He played his home games at hitter-friendly High Desert, and did post a poor 50/17 strikeout/walk ratio there. Still, durable defensive receivers with serious longball pop don't exactly grow on trees, so keep an eye on Cresse.

Rounding out this year's Top Ten is last year's #2 finisher, Diamondbacks' Double-A outfielder Jack Cust. The 6'1", 205, lefthanded-hitting Jim Thome bash-alike combines extreme power and patience, and projects as a big league number three or four hitter. Cust hit .293 with 32 doubles, 20 homers, 75 RBI, 117 walks and 150 strikeouts at El Paso, and could be ready for the majors sometime next year. His defense is quite forgettable, but his bat will carry the day.

How did last year's Top Ten fare? Quite well. #4 Pat Burrell established himself as a long-term power force, and #6 Aramis Ramirez showed signs of becoming a legitimate big league starting third baseman. #2 Cust and #3 Burroughs returned to this year's Top Ten. #5 Vernon Wells, 21, dropped to #101 after a poor Triple-A season, but appears to be in line to earn a starting outfield job in Toronto in 2001.

Cubs' first base prospect Hee Choi, 21, dropped from #7 in 1999 to #19 in 2000, but remains one of the most highly regarded power prospects in the game. He could move into the major league lineup in 2001 if Mark Grace isn't re-signed. Last year's #8 finisher, Royals' Triple-A outfielder Dee Brown, 22, dropped to 147th in 2000. A poor start resulted in a midseason trip to the Florida Instructional League for Brown, but he reasserted himself as a top power prospect in the second half of the season. He still should make a material big league impact.

1999 #9 finisher Rico Washington, 22, a Pirates' prospect who can play catcher, second base and third base, narrowly missed this year's list. He projects as a likely future all-purpose backup at the major league level. Last year's #10 prospect, Reds' Double-A shortstop Travis Dawkins, 22, dropped way down to 238th on this year's list. Though he batted only .231 this season, he remains an impact player with the glove and still should be at least major league average with the bat. He finished the 2000 season on the US Olympic team, and could reach the majors sometime in 2001.

By the way, last year's #11 finisher was some guy named Rafael Furcal. You might have heard of him. The biggest mystery of the 1999 group was #1 Nick Johnson. The Yankees' blue-chip first base prospect missed the entire season with a mysterious wrist ailment, casting his future into doubt. If he proves himself healthy, however, Johnson should quickly reassert himself as a likely future major league #3 hitter.

Of the 1998 Top Ten, #3 Eric Chavez and #7 Troy Glaus look like entrenched stars. #1 Russell Branyan, #6 Jeremy Giambi and #8 Carlos Beltran have shown extended flashes of brilliance, and should stand out in 2001. 1998 #2 Marcus Giles (#43 in 2000), #4 Alex Escobar (#21 in 2000), #9 Nick Johnson (injured in 2000) and #10 Jackie Rexrode (#58 in 2000) remain highly rated prospects. Only 1998 #5 Calvin Pickering, who has likely eaten his way out of a bright major league future, has dropped off of the major league fast track.

Of the 1997 Top Ten, #1 Adrian Beltre, #2 Ben Grieve, #4 Paul Konerko, #5 Travis Lee, #6 Branyan, #7 Aramis Ramirez, #8 Lance Berkman, and #9 Ruben Mateo are all established major leaguers, and some are stars. #3 Mark Bellhorn and #10 Cole Liniak remain at the Triple-A level, watching their respective windows of big league opportunity beginning to close.

1996 Top Tenners include such luminaries as #1 Andruw Jones, #2 Vladimir Guerrero, #3 Beltre, #4 Scott Rolen, #5 Nomar Garciaparra and #7 Konerko. Of the 1995 Top Ten, #1 Alex Rodriguez exceeded even the loftiest expectations, while #6 Jones, #7 Mike Sweeney, #8 Darin Erstad, #9 Guerrero and #10 Johnny Damon are entrenched big league studs. #3 Ruben Rivera continues to show flashes of brilliance, and could still break out.

Of the 1994 Top Ten, #1 Rodriguez, #4 Shawn Green, #5 Bob Abreu and #6 Carlos Delgado are established stars. The 1993 Top Ten is well represented in the major leagues - #1 Cliff Floyd, #2 Jim Thome, #3 Manny Ramirez, #4 Delgado, #6 Chipper Jones, #9 Roger Cedeno and #10 Dmitri Young are all entrenched stars.

THE BLUE CHIPPERS

In addition to Top Tenners Antonio Perez, Abraham Nunez, Sean Burroughs and Jack Cust, who each cracked the Top 50 in both 1999 and 2000, seven other top prospects similarly asserted themselves by posting high RPP ranks in both seasons. Reds Low-A outfielder Adam Dunn, 20, ranked 32nd in 1999 and 15th in 2000, and is nearly as good a power/speed prospect as Kearns, his Low-A Dayton teammate last season. He could be a 30/30 man in the majors someday.

Cubs' outfield gem Corey Patterson, 20, ranked 21st in 1999 and 18th in 2000. He moved into center field in Chicago in September, and should stay awhile. With added plate discipline, he could be truly special. Cubs' first base prospect Hee Choi, 21, ranked seventh in 1999 and 19th in 2000, and could join Patterson in the Cubs' major league lineup in 2001. He should hit for power and average and play solid defense in the majors.

Mets' center field prospect Brian Cole, 21, ranked 42nd in 1999 and 23rd in 2000. Though he exhibited poor plate discipline after a promotion to Double-A Binghamton last season, Cole remains an exciting power/speed prospect who will duel Escobar for the Mets' center field job by 2002.

Reds' third base prospect Drew Henson, 20, came over from the Yankees last summer in the Denny Neagle deal. Henson is a blue-chip power stud, but needs to put his football career, he's the University of Michigan's quarterback, behind him before realizing his baseball potential. Braves' second base prospect Marcus Giles, 22, ranked 30th in 1999 and 43rd in 2000 after ranking 2nd in 1998. He packs an extra-base wallop for a middle infielder and has excellent bloodlines; the Pirates' stud outfielder Brian is his older brother. He could team up with Rafael Furcal in Atlanta for the next 15 years or so.

Cubs' third base prospect Eric Hinske, 22, ranked 45th in 1999 and 48th in 2000. Hinske is a sleeper in this company, a high average hitter with 20-homer pop that can play solid defense at either infield corner. He could be a valuable bench guy in the majors.

Several other prospects ranked in the Top 100 in both 1999 and 2000. Those whose rankings improved in 2000 were Pirates' first baseman Dan Meier (83rd to 12th), Rangers' first baseman Travis Hafner (98th to 13th), Marlins' first baseman Nate Rolison (84th to 16th), Devil Rays' third baseman Aubrey Huff (59th to 20th), Diamondbacks' outfielder Carlos Urquiola (60th to 30th), Blue Jays' first baseman Jay Gibbons (91st to 42nd),

Orioles' second baseman Richard Paz (99th to 50th), and Rockies' outfielder Jody Gerut (78th to 51st).

Those whose ranks declined in 2000 were Expos' outfielder Milton Bradley (24th to 54th), Rockies' catcher Ben Petrick (18th to 56th), Red Sox' first baseman Dernell Stenson (58th to 68th), Rangers' outfielder Corey Wright (73rd to 76th), A's outfielder Rusty Keith (72nd to 91st), Rockies' third baseman Matt Holliday (74th to 94th) and Red Sox' second baseman Angel Santos (53rd to 95th).

Besides Top Tenners J.R. House, Kevin Mench, Chris Snelling and Brad Cresse, other upper echelon prospects playing in full-season leagues for the first time in 2000 included Cardinals third baseman Albert Pujols (11th), Indians' outfielder Jorge Moreno (14th), Pirates' first baseman Jeremy Cotten (17th), Mariners' second baseman Willie Bloomquist (22nd), Astros' catcher John Buck (24th), Rangers' third baseman Hank Blalock (28th), Expos' outfielder Valentino Pascucci (31st), Devil Rays' outfielder Josh Hamilton (32nd), Devil Rays' shortstop Jorge Cantu (34th), Devil Rays' outfielder Carl Crawford (35th), Pirates' shortstop Jose Castillo (37th), Indians' shortstop Jhonny Peralta (40th), Mets' outfielder Timoniel Perez (45th) and Tigers' shortstop Omar Infante (46th).

Last year's corresponding group included Furcal, Antonio Perez, Patterson, Henson, Dunn and others. It's the list that tends to produce the following year's breakout stars: review it carefully.

Also, many players arrive on this list based on their relative youth, then advance because of drastically improved production as their bodies and skills mature. Such players include Reds' outfielder Kearns (106th in 1999 to 5th in 2000), Expos' third baseman Scott Hodges (242nd to 29th), Red Sox' second baseman Carlos Leon (277th to 38th), Rangers' first baseman Carlos Pena (115th to 41st), Phillies' shortstop Jimmy Rollins (105th to 44th), Giants' third baseman Tony Torcato (131st to 49th), and Blue Jays' first baseman Matt Logan (263rd to 57th).

DROPOUTS AND OTHER ASSORTED OVERRATED PROSPECTS

Some who earned high RPP ranks in 1999 fell on hard times in 2000. The aforementioned Vernon Wells is a case in point. Other major dropoffs include A's outfielder Mario Encarnacion (34th in 1999, 107th in 2000), Twins'

outfielder Michael Restovich (43rd to 122nd), Twins' third baseman Mike Cuddyer (23rd to 133rd), Pirates' outfielder J.J. Davis (46th to 141st), Reds' outfielder Jackson Melian (51st to 145th), Royals' outfielder Dee Brown (8th to 147th), Orioles' catcher Jayson Werth (48th to 150th), Mariners' outfielder Alex Fernandez (50th to 163rd), Rangers' second baseman Jason Romano (26th to 203rd), White Sox' first baseman Jeff Liefer (38th to 208th), Angels' outfielder Nathan Haynes (33rd to 217th), A's catcher Miguel Olivo (54th to 221st), A's outfielder Gary Thomas (35th to 226th), Cubs' outfielder Roosevelt Brown (14th to 234th), Reds' shortstop Travis Dawkins (10th to 238th), Dodgers' outfielder Tony Mota (28th to 275th), Blue Jays' shortstop Cesar Izturis (64th to 285th) and Cubs' catcher Jeff Goldbach (49th to 297th).

Of that group, many should still bounce back and have solid major league careers. Raul Mondesi and Todd Walker are two examples of players who experienced large drops in their final minor league seasons.

Some players who appear to be somewhat overrated include Tigers' first baseman Eric Munson (140th), Twins' catcher Matt LeCroy (164th), Phils' outfielder Eric Valent (185th), Padres' catcher Ben Davis (191st), Devil Rays' outfielder Kenny Kelly (199th), Orioles' second baseman Jerry Hairston (201st), White Sox' outfielder Aaron Rowand (231st), Devil Rays' outfielder Jason Tyner (248th), and Red Sox' third baseman Wilton Veras (303rd). In past years, media darlings such as J.R. Phillips, Todd Greene, Antone Williamson, Juan Melo and the aforementioned Veras were similarly covered in this space, though I must admit that Mondesi, Tony Clark and Ben Grieve were as well.

RELATIVE ORGANIZATIONAL POTENTIAL

This system makes it simple to compare the relative offensive strength of minor league systems' position players. A cumulative organizational RPP is calculated by assigning the number one prospect 305 points, and lowering each successive prospect's value by one.

The Top Five offensive organizations in 2000 were Pittsburgh (3,158 points), followed by Oakland (2,849), Seattle (2,463), Colorado (2,222) and Chicago Cubs (2,172). Three of last year's Top Five are repeaters, with the Mariners (24th in 1999) and Rockies (8th in 1999) the only newcomers.

The Mariners are quite a success story. Spirits were low during the 1999 offseason in Seattle, as Ken Griffey Jr. left town, and Alex Rodriguez seemed to be on his way out. Instead, they fared much better than Mr. Griffey's new team, the Reds, and may actually turn out to get their money's worth out of that trade once Mr. Perez reaches the majors.

The Pirates Low-A Hickory squad was quite possibly the most prospect-loaded individual team since the Chipper Jones-led Richmond Braves. J.R. House, Jose Castillo, Tony Alvarez, Aron Weston and Jovanny Sosa joined pitcher Bobby Bradley and a strong starting rotation, and offer the Bucs a solid future big league foundation.

The A's have developed into a prospect machine; Jose Ortiz should be their second baseman next season, and could be joined by a number of strong bench bats. The Tigers' system also took a strong step forward, moving from 26th in 1999 to 12th in 2000, led by top teenage shortstop prospects Ramon Santiago and Alex Infante.

The Bottom Five organizations were Milwaukee (304), Anaheim (535), St. Louis (634), New York Yankees (816) and Los Angeles (820). The Yanks, who dropped from 11th in 1999, were hurt by parting with multiple top prospects in the Denny Neagle deal, and by the Nick Johnson wrist injury, among other factors. Other big droppers included the Dodgers (14th in 1999), Braves (13th to 24th), Expos (7th to 17th), Blue Jays (2nd to 15th) and Rangers (6th to 14th). The Blue Jays' decline is particularly notable, as they have been a regular in the top five over most of the past decade.

SUMMARY

Relative Production Potential is a method of evaluating minor league position players. Measuring players' on-base and slugging percentages relative to their peers and adjusting for their relative age gives an unbiased view of their long-term major league potential. Performance can be viewed within league context, and can be compared across minor league levels. In its eight years of existence, this method has consistently unearthed prospects: Edgar Renteria, Vladimir Guerrero, Jose Vidro, Mike Sweeney and Nick Johnson, to name a few; ahead of most of the baseball media establishment. Next year's "discoveries" are likely to be somewhere on this year's RPP list.

RELATIVE PRODUCTION POTENTIAL
2000

2000 Rank	1999 Rank	1998 Rank		LEVEL	TEAM	ORG	POS	AGE	REL. OBP	REL. SLG	REL. TOT.	AGE ADJ.	RPP	PTS
1	27		Antonio Perez	HI-A	LNC	SEA	SS	18	0.49	1.73	2.22	2.00	4.22	305
2			J.R. House	LO-A	HCK	PIT	C	20	2.15	2.97	5.12	-1.00	4.12	304
3			Kevin Mench	HI-A	CHR	TEX	OF	22	2.55	3.45	6.00	-2.00	4.00	303
4			Chris Snelling	LO-A	WSC	SEA	OF	18	1.30	1.62	2.92	1.00	3.92	302
5	106		Austin Kearns	LO-A	DAY	CIN	OF	20	1.98	2.71	4.68	-1.00	3.68	301
6			Brad Wilkerson	AA	HRB	MON	OF	23	2.84	2.80	5.64	-2.00	3.64	300
7	22	26	Abraham Nunez	AA	PRT	FLA	OF	20	1.65	0.87	2.51	1.00	3.51	299
8	3		Sean Burroughs	AA	MOB	SD	3B	19	1.22	0.21	1.43	2.00	3.43	298
9			Brad Cresse	HI-A	HD	AZ	C	21	0.82	3.53	4.36	-1.00	3.36	297
10	2		Jack Cust	AA	ELP	AZ	OF	21	2.19	1.04	3.23	0.00	3.23	296
11			Albert Pujols	LO-A	PEO	STL	3B	20	1.25	2.80	4.05	-1.00	3.05	295
12	83		Dan Meier	HI-A	LYN	PIT	1B	22	1.59	3.27	4.86	-2.00	2.86	294
13	98		Travis Hafner	HI-A	CHR	TEX	1B	23	2.76	2.94	5.70	-3.00	2.70	293
14			Jorge Moreno	LO-A	CLM	CLE	OF	19	0.89	1.63	2.52	0.00	2.52	292
15	32		Adam Dunn	LO-A	DAY	CIN	OF	20	2.08	1.42	3.51	-1.00	2.51	291
16	84	62	Nate Rolison	AAA	CLG	FLA	1B	23	1.75	1.71	3.46	-1.00	2.46	290
17			Jeremy Cotten	LO-A	HCK	PIT	1B	19	0.57	1.87	2.44	0.00	2.44	289
18	21		Corey Patterson	AA	WTN	CUB	OF	20	-0.05	1.49	1.44	1.00	2.44	288
19	7		Hee Choi	HI-A	DAY	CUB	1B	21	0.98	2.26	3.24	-1.00	2.24	287
20	59	53	Aubrey Huff	AAA	DUR	TB	3B	23	1.39	1.81	3.20	-1.00	2.20	286
21	4		Alex Escobar	AA	BNG	NYM	OF	21	0.93	1.26	2.19	0.00	2.19	285
22			Willie Bloomquist	HI-A	LNC	SEA	2B	22	2.41	1.69	4.10	-2.00	2.10	284
23	42		Brian Cole	HI-A	STLC	NYM	OF	21	0.91	2.18	3.10	-1.00	2.10	283
24			John Buck	LO-A	MCH	HOU	C	19	0.95	1.06	2.01	0.00	2.01	282
25	222	131	Jose Ortiz	AAA	SAC	OAK	2B	23	1.35	1.62	2.97	-1.00	1.97	281
26	180		Nate Espy	LO-A	PDT	PHL	1B	22	2.78	2.18	4.96	-3.00	1.96	280
27			Ntema Ndungidi	HI-A	FRD	BAL	OF	21	1.72	1.22	2.95	-1.00	1.95	279
28			Hank Blalock	LO-A	SAV	TEX	3B	19	1.23	0.70	1.92	0.00	1.92	278
29	242		Scott Hodges	HI-A	JUP	MON	3B	21	1.34	1.57	2.91	-1.00	1.91	277
30	60		Carlos Urquiola	HI-A	HD	AZ	OF	20	1.53	0.34	1.87	0.00	1.87	276
31			Valentino Pascucci	HI-A	JUP	MON	OF	21	1.50	1.37	2.87	-1.00	1.87	275
32			Josh Hamilton	LO-A	CHSC	TB	OF	19	0.48	1.37	1.85	0.00	1.85	274
33	102		Jason Hart	AA	MID	OAK	1B	22	1.20	1.64	2.84	-1.00	1.84	273
34			Jorge Cantu	LO-A	CHSC	TB	SS	18	0.25	0.58	0.83	1.00	1.83	272
35			Carl Crawford	LO-A	CHSC	TB	OF	18	0.35	0.43	0.78	1.00	1.78	271
36	25		Drew Henson	AA	NRW	CIN	3B	20	0.24	0.53	0.78	1.00	1.78	270
37			Jose Castillo	LO-A	HCK	PIT	SS	19	0.25	1.45	1.70	0.00	1.70	269
38	277	123	Carlos Leon	HI-A	SAR	BOS	2B	20	1.48	0.20	1.68	0.00	1.68	268
39	227		John Barnes	AAA	SLK	MIN	OF	24	2.18	1.49	3.67	-2.00	1.67	267
40			Jhonny Peralta	LO-A	CLM	CLE	SS	17	0.63	-1.01	-0.37	2.00	1.63	266
41	115		Carlos Pena	AA	TUL	TEX	1B	22	1.49	1.11	2.60	-1.00	1.60	265
42	91		Jay Gibbons	AA	TEN	TOR	1B	23	1.61	1.98	3.59	-2.00	1.59	264
43	30	2	Marcus Giles	AA	GRV	ATL	2B	22	1.33	1.22	2.55	-1.00	1.55	263
44	105	170	Jimmy Rollins	AAA	SWB	PHL	SS	21	0.09	0.43	0.52	1.00	1.52	262
45			Timoniel Perez	AAA	NRF	NYM	OF	23	1.36	1.12	2.48	-1.00	1.48	261
46			Omar Infante	HI-A	LAK	DET	SS	18	0.01	-0.54	-0.53	2.00	1.47	260
47	282	13	Joe Crede	AA	BRM	CWS	3B	22	0.97	1.47	2.45	-1.00	1.45	259
48	45		Eric Hinske	AA	WTN	CUB	3B	22	0.97	1.42	2.39	-1.00	1.39	258
49	131		Tony Torcato	HI-A	SJ	SF	3B	20	0.66	0.71	1.37	0.00	1.37	257

2000 Rank	1999 Rank	1998 Rank		LEVEL	TEAM	ORG	POS	AGE	REL. OBP	REL. SLG	REL. TOT.	AGE ADJ.	RPP	PTS
50	99	20	Richard Paz	HI-A	FRD	BAL	2B	22	2.96	0.36	3.32	-2.00	1.32	256
51	78		Jody Gerut	AA	CAR	COL	OF	22	1.86	0.41	2.27	-1.00	1.27	255
52			Brian Specht	HI-A	LE	ANA	SS	19	0.47	-0.21	0.26	1.00	1.26	254
53			Ryan Gripp	LO-A	LNS	CUB	3B	22	1.95	2.25	4.20	-3.00	1.20	253
54	24	87	Milton Bradley	AAA	OTT	MON	OF	22	1.21	-0.03	1.18	0.00	1.18	252
55	193	12	Pablo Ozuna	AA	PRT	FLA	2B	21	0.73	0.44	1.17	0.00	1.17	251
56	18	76	Ben Petrick	AAA	CSPR	COL	C	23	1.03	1.14	2.16	-1.00	1.16	250
57	263		Matt Logan	HI-A	DUN	TOR	1B	20	0.42	0.71	1.13	0.00	1.13	249
58	159	10	Jackie Rexrode	AA	BRM	CWS	2B	21	1.83	-0.71	1.12	0.00	1.12	248
59			Sheldon Fulse	LO-A	WSC	SEA	OF	18	0.84	-0.73	0.11	1.00	1.11	247
60			Ron Paulino	LO-A	HCK	PIT	C	19	0.56	0.52	1.08	0.00	1.08	246
61			Mike Lockwood	HI-A	MOD	OAK	OF	23	2.65	1.42	4.07	-3.00	1.07	245
62			Todd Sears	AA	CAR	MIN	1B	24	2.54	1.50	4.04	-3.00	1.04	244
63			Ed Rogers	LO-A	DEL	BAL	SS	18	-0.14	0.18	0.04	1.00	1.04	243
64	147	65	Craig Wilson	AAA	NSH	PIT	C	23	0.05	1.98	2.02	-1.00	1.02	242
65			Jorge Padilla	LO-A	PDT	PHL	OF	20	0.53	1.48	2.00	-1.00	1.00	241
66			Ramon Castro	AAA	CLG	FLA	C	24	0.71	2.29	2.99	-2.00	0.99	240
67			Juan Diaz	AA	TRN	BOS	1B	24	0.25	3.73	3.99	-3.00	0.99	239
68	58	32	Dernell Stenson	AAA	PAW	BOS	1B	22	0.17	0.80	0.97	0.00	0.97	238
69	127	54	Mario Valdez	AAA	SAC	OAK	1B	25	2.27	1.67	3.94	-3.00	0.94	237
70	212		Dave Kelton	HI-A	DAY	CUB	3B	20	-0.22	1.13	0.91	0.00	0.91	236
71	188		Kevin Burford	HI-A	SLM	COL	OF	22	1.05	1.85	2.89	-2.00	0.89	235
72	163		Brian Gordon	HI-A	HD	AZ	OF	21	0.58	1.32	1.89	-1.00	0.89	234
73	124	28	Joe Lawrence	HI-A	DUN	TOR	C	23	2.16	1.72	3.88	-3.00	0.88	233
74			Cody Ross	LO-A	WM	DET	OF	19	0.46	0.37	0.83	0.00	0.83	232
75			Ben Broussard	AA	CHT	CIN	OF	23	1.77	1.03	2.80	-2.00	0.80	231
76	73		Corey Wright	HI-A	CHR	TEX	OF	20	1.53	-0.73	0.80	0.00	0.80	230
77			Lyle Overbay	AA	ELP	AZ	1B	23	1.68	1.11	2.80	-2.00	0.80	229
78	208		Josh Pressley	LO-A	CHSC	TB	1B	20	1.04	0.73	1.77	-1.00	0.77	228
79			Eric Sandberg	LO-A	QC	MIN	1B	20	1.47	0.27	1.74	-1.00	0.74	227
80			Terrmel Sledge	HI-A	LNC	SEA	OF	23	2.10	1.62	3.72	-3.00	0.72	226
81	104		Eric Byrnes	AAA	SAC	OAK	OF	24	1.43	1.27	2.71	-2.00	0.71	225
82			Tim Hummel	LO-A	BUR	CWS	SS	21	1.92	0.77	2.69	-2.00	0.69	224
83			Rich Lane	LO-A	CF	MON	1B	20	1.05	0.62	1.67	-1.00	0.67	223
84			Keith Ginter	AA	RR	HOU	2B	24	2.05	1.61	3.66	-3.00	0.66	222
85			Cesar Saba	LO-A	AUG	SD	SS	18	-0.40	0.01	-0.38	1.00	0.62	221
86			Joe Thurston	HI-A	SBR	LA	SS	20	0.46	0.15	0.61	0.00	0.61	220
87	211		Shawn McCorkle	LO-A	WSC	SEA	1B	22	1.83	1.77	3.60	-3.00	0.60	219
88			Ryan Ludwick	HI-A	MOD	OAK	OF	21	0.14	1.44	1.59	-1.00	0.59	218
89	75		Bucky Jacobsen	AA	HNT	MIL	1B	24	1.46	2.04	3.50	-3.00	0.50	217
90			Ben Johnson	LO-A	FTW	SD	OF	19	-0.17	0.67	0.50	0.00	0.50	216
91	72		Rusty Keith	HI-A	MOD	OAK	OF	22	1.93	0.55	2.48	-2.00	0.48	215
92			Anderson Machado	HI-A	CLW	PHL	SS	19	0.14	-0.67	-0.53	1.00	0.47	214
93			Donovan Ross	LO-A	CHWV	KC	OF	22	1.77	1.66	3.43	-3.00	0.43	213
94	74		Matt Holliday	HI-A	SLM	COL	3B	20	0.21	0.21	0.42	0.00	0.42	212
95	53		Angel Santos	AA	TRN	BOS	2B	20	-0.04	-0.55	-0.60	1.00	0.40	211
96	233	263	Juan Silvestre	HI-A	LNC	SEA	OF	22	0.69	1.70	2.39	-2.00	0.39	210
97	269		Alex Hernandez	AA	ALT	PIT	OF	23	1.12	1.26	2.38	-2.00	0.38	209
98			Ramon Santiago	LO-A	WM	DET	SS	18	0.04	-0.66	-0.62	1.00	0.38	208
99	179	132	Mike Darr	AAA	LVG	SD	OF	24	1.58	0.79	2.37	-2.00	0.37	207
100	111	79	Luis Rivas	AA	NB	MIN	2B	20	-0.36	-0.30	-0.66	1.00	0.34	206
101	5	77	Vernon Wells	AAA	SYR	TOR	OF	21	-0.77	0.11	-0.66	1.00	0.34	205
102	61		Robert Stratton	HI-A	STLC	NYM	OF	22	0.19	2.14	2.33	-2.00	0.33	204
103			Nate Frese	HI-A	DAY	CUB	SS	22	1.61	0.71	2.31	-2.00	0.31	203
104	93	124	Cesar Crespo	AA	PRT	FLA	OF	21	0.63	-0.34	0.29	0.00	0.29	202

2000 Rank	1999 Rank	1998 Rank		LEVEL	TEAM	ORG	POS	AGE	REL. OBP	REL. SLG	REL. TOT.	AGE ADJ.	RPP	PTS
105			Neil Jenkins	LO-A	WM	DET	3B	19	-0.32	0.59	0.27	0.00	0.27	201
106			Ryan Christianson	LO-A	WSC	SEA	C	19	-0.02	0.28	0.26	0.00	0.26	200
107	34	31	Mario Encarnacion	AAA	SAC	OAK	OF	22	-0.14	0.33	0.19	0.00	0.19	199
108	282		Pedro Feliz	AAA	FRS	SF	3B	23	-0.38	1.56	1.18	-1.00	0.18	198
109	55		Alfonso Soriano	AAA	CLM	NYY	SS	22	-0.35	0.52	0.17	0.00	0.17	197
110	69		Felipe Lopez	AA	TEN	TOR	SS	20	-0.67	-0.20	-0.87	1.00	0.13	196
111	181		Juan Uribe	HI-A	SLM	COL	SS	20	-0.41	0.53	0.12	0.00	0.12	195
112	87	281	Nick Leach	AA	NRW	NYY	1B	22	1.07	0.04	1.12	-1.00	0.12	194
113			Marlon Byrd	LO-A	PDT	PHL	OF	22	1.14	1.95	3.08	-3.00	0.08	193
114			Jorge Piedra	HI-A	DAY	CUB	OF	21	0.53	0.55	1.07	-1.00	0.07	192
115			Andres Torres	HI-A	LAK	DET	OF	22	1.71	0.36	2.07	-2.00	0.07	191
116			Keith Reed	LO-A	DEL	BAL	OF	21	0.63	1.44	2.07	-2.00	0.07	190
117	231		Alejandro Giron	HI-A	CLW	PHL	OF	21	0.39	0.66	1.05	-1.00	0.05	189
118	161		Bobby Kielty	AA	NB	MIN	OF	23	1.57	0.46	2.03	-2.00	0.03	188
119			Julio Cordido	HI-A	BAK	SF	3B	19	-0.57	-0.43	-0.99	1.00	0.01	187
120			Brian Wiese	HI-A	SAR	BOS	OF	22	0.79	1.21	2.00	-2.00	0.00	186
121			Angel Berroa	HI-A	VIS	OAK	SS	20	-0.47	0.47	0.00	0.00	0.00	185
122	43		Michael Restovich	HI-A	FTM	MIN	OF	21	0.54	0.45	1.00	-1.00	-0.00	184
123	117		Jeff Winchester	LO-A	ASH	COL	C	20	-0.23	1.21	0.98	-1.00	-0.02	183
124			Karim Garcia	AAA	ROC	BAL	OF	24	0.36	1.61	1.97	-2.00	-0.03	182
125	176		Joe Dillon	AA	WCH	KC	3B	24	1.73	1.25	2.97	-3.00	-0.03	181
126			Hiram Bocachica	AAA	ABQ	LA	2B	24	0.53	1.43	1.97	-2.00	-0.03	180
127			Jon Helquist	LO-A	MCH	HOU	3B	19	0.16	-0.20	-0.04	0.00	-0.04	179
128	267	72	Brent Butler	AAA	CSPR	COL	2B	22	0.11	-0.17	-0.06	0.00	-0.06	178
129	101		Choo Freeman	HI-A	SLM	COL	OF	20	-0.07	0.00	-0.07	0.00	-0.07	177
130	250		Juan Pierre	AA	CAR	COL	OF	22	1.00	-0.07	0.92	-1.00	-0.08	176
131			Josh Bonifay	LO-A	HCK	PIT	2B	21	0.92	0.99	1.92	-2.00	-0.08	175
132	239	49	Jermaine Clark	AA	NH	SEA	2B	23	1.98	-0.09	1.89	-2.00	-0.11	174
133	23	38	Mike Cuddyer	AA	NB	MIN	3B	21	0.02	-0.15	-0.14	0.00	-0.14	173
134			Aron Weston	LO-A	HCK	PIT	OF	19	0.42	-0.57	-0.15	0.00	-0.15	172
135	63		Ty Wigginton	AA	BNG	NYM	3B	22	-0.45	1.30	0.85	-1.00	-0.15	171
136			Francisco Ferrand	LO-A	KNC	FLA	OF	20	-0.41	1.25	0.84	-1.00	-0.16	170
137	122	55	Ryan Lehr	LO-A	MAC	ATL	1B	21	0.81	1.03	1.84	-2.00	-0.16	169
138	279		Paul Weichard	HI-A	LYN	PIT	OF	20	0.01	-0.21	-0.19	0.00	-0.19	168
139			Alexis Gomez	HI-A	WLM	KC	OF	19	-0.16	-1.03	-1.20	1.00	-0.20	167
140	174		Eric Munson	AA	JCK	DET	1B	22	-0.18	0.98	0.80	-1.00	-0.20	166
141	46		J.J. Davis	HI-A	LYN	PIT	OF	21	-0.25	1.05	0.80	-1.00	-0.20	165
142	260		Alfredo Castro	HI-A	MYR	ATL	SS	20	0.04	-0.25	-0.21	0.00	-0.21	164
143			Jim Deschaine	LO-A	LNS	CUB	SS	22	1.22	1.57	2.78	-3.00	-0.22	163
144			Carlos Mendoza	AAA	CSPR	COL	OF	25	2.40	0.39	2.78	-3.00	-0.22	162
145	51	144	Jackson Melian	AA	NRW	CIN	OF	20	-1.16	-0.06	-1.22	1.00	-0.22	161
146	187	204	Eddy Martinez	HI-A	FRD	BAL	SS	22	1.68	0.10	1.78	-2.00	-0.22	160
147	8	88	Dee Brown	AAA	OMA	KC	OF	22	-0.79	0.57	-0.23	0.00	-0.23	159
148	253		Toby Hall	AA	ORL	TB	C	24	1.22	1.54	2.76	-3.00	-0.24	158
149			Chris Duncan	LO-A	PEO	STL	1B	19	-0.45	0.20	-0.25	0.00	-0.25	157
150	48	116	Jayson Werth	AA	BOW	BAL	C	21	0.49	-0.74	-0.25	0.00	-0.25	156
151			Morgan Ensberg	AA	RR	HOU	3B	24	1.51	1.24	2.75	-3.00	-0.25	155
152	270		Dave Callahan	LO-A	KNC	FLA	1B	20	0.57	0.17	0.75	-1.00	-0.25	154
153			Royce Huffman	HI-A	KIS	HOU	3B	23	2.11	0.62	2.73	-3.00	-0.27	153
154			Brian Roberts	HI-A	FRD	BAL	SS	22	1.74	-0.01	1.73	-2.00	-0.27	152
155	128	61	Brent Abernathy	AAA	DUR	TB	2B	22	0.11	-0.40	-0.29	0.00	-0.29	151
156			Simon Pond	HI-A	KIN	CLE	3B	23	1.22	1.46	2.68	-3.00	-0.32	150
157			Lamont Matthews	HI-A	SBR	LA	OF	22	0.38	1.30	1.68	-2.00	-0.32	149
158			Alvin Morrow	LO-A	BLT	TOR	OF	22	1.01	1.66	2.67	-3.00	-0.33	148
159			Andy Brown	LO-A	GRB	NYY	OF	20	-0.38	1.04	0.65	-1.00	-0.35	147

2000 Rank	1999 Rank	1998 Rank		LEVEL	TEAM	ORG	POS	AGE	REL. OBP	REL. SLG	REL. TOT.	AGE ADJ.	RPP	PTS
160			Elpidio Guzman	HI-A	LE	ANA	OF	21	0.21	0.43	0.64	-1.00	-0.36	146
161			Tony Alvarez	LO-A	HCK	PIT	OF	21	0.45	1.18	1.63	-2.00	-0.37	145
162			Jake Messner	HI-A	BAK	SF	OF	23	0.71	1.92	2.63	-3.00	-0.37	144
163	50		Alex Fernandez	AA	NH	SEA	OF	19	-1.67	-0.71	-2.38	2.00	-0.38	143
164	157	104	Matt LeCroy	AA	NB	MIN	C	24	1.06	1.56	2.62	-3.00	-0.38	142
165			Mike Rivera	HI-A	LAK	DET	C	23	0.26	2.35	2.60	-3.00	-0.40	141
166	1		Russell Branyan	AAA	BUF	CLE	3B	24	-0.34	1.94	1.60	-2.00	-0.40	140
167			Carlos Valderrama	HI-A	BAK	SF	OF	22	0.54	1.05	1.59	-2.00	-0.41	139
168	71	171	Mike Edwards	AA	AKR	CLE	3B	23	1.27	0.30	1.57	-2.00	-0.43	138
169	175		Nick Sosa	HI-A	MOD	OAK	1B	22	0.85	0.72	1.57	-2.00	-0.43	137
170			Pete LaForest	HI-A	STP	TB	C	22	0.55	1.02	1.56	-2.00	-0.44	136
171			Nilson Teilon	LO-A	BUR	CWS	2B	19	-0.70	0.26	-0.44	0.00	-0.44	135
172			Pat Burns	HI-A	STLC	NYM	OF	22	1.31	0.24	1.55	-2.00	-0.45	134
173			Ruben Salazar	HI-A	FTM	MIN	2B	22	0.83	0.72	1.55	-2.00	-0.45	133
174			Victor Rodriguez	HI-A	KIN	CLE	SS	23	1.42	1.12	2.54	-3.00	-0.46	132
175			Josue Perez	HI-A	CLW	PHL	OF	22	0.92	0.61	1.53	-2.00	-0.47	131
176	92	58	Luke Allen	AA	SANT	LA	3B	21	-0.20	-0.28	-0.48	0.00	-0.48	130
177	136		Jack Wilson	AA	ARK	PIT	SS	22	0.26	0.25	0.51	-1.00	-0.49	129
178	139		Oscar Salazar	AA	MID	OAK	SS	22	0.18	0.33	0.51	-1.00	-0.49	128
179			Rafael Pujols	HI-A	VIS	OAK	1B	22	1.04	0.47	1.51	-2.00	-0.49	127
180			Justo Rivas	LO-A	MAC	ATL	OF	20	0.16	0.34	0.50	-1.00	-0.50	126
181			Alex Requena	LO-A	CLM	CLE	OF	19	0.58	-1.10	-0.52	0.00	-0.52	125
182	90	108	Aaron McNeal	AA	RR	HOU	1B	22	0.06	0.43	0.48	-1.00	-0.52	124
183	52	183	John Rodriguez	HI-A	TAM	NYY	OF	22	0.38	1.06	1.44	-2.00	-0.56	123
184	172	62	John Roskos	AAA	LVG	SD	OF	25	1.27	1.16	2.43	-3.00	-0.57	122
185	144	141	Eric Valent	AA	REA	PHL	OF	23	0.48	0.95	1.43	-2.00	-0.57	121
186	66		Terrell Merriman	HI-A	WS	CWS	OF	22	0.97	0.45	1.42	-2.00	-0.58	120
187			Marvin Seale	LO-A	CAP	NYM	OF	21	1.00	0.42	1.42	-2.00	-0.58	119
188	191	285	Mike Peeples	AA	TEN	TOR	OF	23	0.29	1.13	1.42	-2.00	-0.58	118
189	227		Alex Cintron	AA	ELP	AZ	SS	21	-0.33	-0.25	-0.58	0.00	-0.58	117
190	145		Jared Sandberg	AA	ORL	TB	3B	22	0.36	0.05	0.42	-1.00	-0.58	116
191	103		Ben Davis	AAA	LVG	SD	C	23	0.46	-0.08	0.38	-1.00	-0.62	115
192	125		Alejandro Diaz	AA	CHT	CIN	OF	21	-1.07	0.45	-0.62	0.00	-0.62	114
193	66		Kevin Eberwein	AA	MOB	SD	1B	23	0.28	1.09	1.36	-2.00	-0.64	113
194			Cory Aldridge	HI-A	MYR	ATL	OF	21	-0.49	0.84	0.35	-1.00	-0.65	112
195	142	166	Brett Roneberg	HI-A	BRV	FLA	OF	21	1.13	-0.78	0.35	-1.00	-0.65	111
196	192		Ryan Freel	AAA	SYR	TOR	2B	24	0.67	0.68	1.35	-2.00	-0.65	110
197			Gary Johnson	HI-A	DAY	CUB	OF	23	1.10	1.25	2.35	-3.00	-0.65	109
198			Ron Wright	AA	CHT	CIN	1B	24	0.81	1.53	2.34	-3.00	-0.66	108
199	133	118	Kenny Kelly	AA	ORL	TB	OF	21	0.01	-0.68	-0.67	0.00	-0.67	107
200	218		Maikell Diaz	HI-A	FRD	BAL	2B	20	0.38	-1.06	-0.67	0.00	-0.67	106
201	85		Jerry Hairston	AAA	ROC	BAL	2B	24	1.14	0.18	1.32	-2.00	-0.68	105
202			A.J. Zapp	HI-A	MYR	ATL	1B	22	0.83	0.49	1.32	-2.00	-0.68	104
203	26	190	Jason Romano	AA	TUL	TEX	2B	21	-0.27	-0.41	-0.68	0.00	-0.68	103
204	121	51	Mike Rose	AA	ELP	AZ	C	23	1.21	0.10	1.31	-2.00	-0.69	102
205	171	177	Elvis Pena	AA	CAR	COL	SS	23	1.37	-0.06	1.31	-2.00	-0.69	101
206			Brandon Phillips	LO-A	CF	MON	SS	19	-0.69	-0.02	-0.71	0.00	-0.71	100
207	210		Craig Monroe	AA	TUL	TEX	OF	23	0.45	0.83	1.29	-2.00	-0.71	99
208	38	152	Jeff Liefer	AAA	CHA	CWS	1B	25	0.47	1.81	2.28	-3.00	-0.72	98
209	274		Juan Melo	AAA	FRS	SF	SS	23	-0.08	0.34	0.26	-1.00	-0.74	97
210			Mark Ellis	HI-A	WLM	KC	SS	23	1.70	0.54	2.24	-3.00	-0.76	96
211	243	290	Carlos Mendoza	HI-A	SJ	SF	SS	20	-0.17	-0.59	-0.76	0.00	-0.76	95
212			Carlos Rosario	HI-A	MOD	OAK	2B	20	0.25	-1.02	-0.76	0.00	-0.76	94
213	266	100	Yorvit Torrealba	AA	SHR	SF	C	21	-0.21	-0.57	-0.77	0.00	-0.77	93
214			Ismael Gallo	HI-A	VB	LA	2B	23	1.49	0.74	2.23	-3.00	-0.77	92

2000 Rank	1999 Rank	1998 Rank		LEVEL	TEAM	ORG	POS	AGE	REL. OBP	REL. SLG	REL. TOT.	AGE ADJ.	RPP	PTS
215			Luis Garcia	LO-A	AUG	BOS	1B	21	0.10	1.11	1.21	-2.00	-0.79	91
216			Maxim St. Pierre	LO-A	WM	DET	C	20	0.82	-0.62	0.21	-1.00	-0.79	90
217	33	112	Nathan Haynes	AA	ERIE	ANA	OF	20	-0.92	-0.88	-1.80	1.00	-0.80	89
218	234		Jovanny Sosa	LO-A	HCK	PIT	OF	20	-0.31	0.52	0.20	-1.00	-0.80	88
219	213		Ramon Vazquez	AA	NH	SEA	SS	23	0.85	0.35	1.20	-2.00	-0.80	87
220			Mark Ernster	AA	HNT	MIL	SS	22	0.55	-0.35	0.20	-1.00	-0.80	86
221	54		Miguel Olivo	HI-A	MOD	OAK	C	21	-0.37	0.57	0.20	-1.00	-0.80	85
222			Eric Johnson	LO-A	CLM	CLE	OF	22	1.72	0.47	2.19	-3.00	-0.81	84
223			Lee Evans	HI-A	LYN	PIT	C	22	0.56	0.62	1.18	-2.00	-0.82	83
224	292		Jon Prieto	HI-A	LYN	PIT	2B	20	0.20	-1.03	-0.82	0.00	-0.82	82
225	109		Tim Raines	HI-A	FRD	BAL	OF	20	0.16	-0.99	-0.83	0.00	-0.83	81
226	35		Gary Thomas	AA	MID	OAK	OF	20	-0.47	-1.35	-1.83	1.00	-0.83	80
227	198		Richard Gomez	HI-A	LAK	DET	OF	22	0.58	0.59	1.17	-2.00	-0.83	79
228			Corey Erickson	HI-A	KIN	CLE	3B	23	0.47	1.69	2.16	-3.00	-0.84	78
229	213		Brian Benefield	HI-A	KIN	CLE	2B	23	1.18	0.98	2.16	-3.00	-0.84	77
230	286		Marco Pernalete	HI-A	BAK	SF	2B	21	0.61	-0.45	0.15	-1.00	-0.85	76
231	110	56	Aaron Rowand	AA	BRM	CWS	OF	22	-0.59	0.74	0.15	-1.00	-0.85	75
232			Ranier Olmedo	LO-A	DAY	CIN	SS	19	-0.47	-0.39	-0.86	0.00	-0.86	74
233			J.D. Closser	LO-A	SBD	AZ	C	20	0.30	-0.16	0.14	-1.00	-0.86	73
234	14	63	Roosevelt Brown	AAA	IOW	CUB	OF	24	0.51	0.63	1.14	-2.00	-0.86	72
235			Chone Figgins	HI-A	SLM	COL	2B	22	0.78	0.35	1.13	-2.00	-0.87	71
236			Chip Ambres	LO-A	KNC	FLA	OF	20	0.20	-0.07	0.13	-1.00	-0.87	70
237			Juan Rivera	HI-A	TAM	NYY	OF	22	0.12	1.02	1.13	-2.00	-0.87	69
238	10	224	Travis Dawkins	AA	CHT	CIN	SS	21	-0.61	-0.27	-0.87	0.00	-0.87	68
239	80		Gary Schneidmiller	HI-A	MOD	OAK	3B	20	0.72	-1.60	-0.88	0.00	-0.88	67
240	274		Franklin German	LO-A	LNS	CUB	OF	20	-0.11	0.23	0.12	-1.00	-0.88	66
241			Brian Schmitt	LO-A	MCH	HOU	1B	21	0.52	0.60	1.12	-2.00	-0.88	65
242			Wily Mo Pena	LO-A	GRB	NYY	OF	18	-1.64	-0.26	-1.90	1.00	-0.90	64
243	141		Jeff Bailey	HI-A	BRV	FLA	1B	21	-0.13	0.23	0.10	-1.00	-0.90	63
244			Steve Neal	HI-A	HD	AZ	1B	23	0.81	1.29	2.10	-3.00	-0.90	62
245			Doug Devore	LO-A	SBD	AZ	OF	22	0.67	1.42	2.09	-3.00	-0.91	61
246	273		Matt Boone	HI-A	LAK	DET	3B	20	-0.54	-0.37	-0.92	0.00	-0.92	60
247			Craig Kuzmic	HI-A	LNC	SEA	1B	23	0.76	1.32	2.08	-3.00	-0.92	59
248	205		Jason Tyner	AAA	NRF	TB	OF	23	1.02	-0.95	0.08	-1.00	-0.92	58
249	236	78	Chris Haas	AA	ARK	STL	3B	23	0.21	0.86	1.07	-2.00	-0.93	57
250			Andy Bevins	AA	ARK	STL	OF	24	0.49	1.58	2.06	-3.00	-0.94	56
251			Chad Santos	LO-A	CHWV	KC	1B	19	-0.41	-0.53	-0.94	0.00	-0.94	55
252			Angel Mendoza	HI-A	SAR	BOS	OF	21	-0.38	0.43	0.06	-1.00	-0.94	54
253	198		Mark Bellhorn	AAA	SAC	OAK	3B	25	1.11	0.94	2.05	-3.00	-0.95	53
254			Rolando Segura	HI-A	LYN	PIT	3B	21	-0.28	0.33	0.04	-1.00	-0.96	52
255			Willie Harris	LO-A	DEL	BAL	2B	22	1.58	0.46	2.04	-3.00	-0.96	51
256	111		Matt Erickson	AA	PRT	FLA	SS	24	1.92	0.12	2.04	-3.00	-0.96	50
257	135	194	Papo Bolivar	AA	NB	MIN	OF	21	-0.51	-0.45	-0.96	0.00	-0.96	49
258			Josh McKinley	LO-A	CF	MON	3B	20	0.16	-0.12	0.04	-1.00	-0.96	48
259			Jay Sitzman	LO-A	PDT	PHL	OF	22	1.18	0.84	2.02	-3.00	-0.98	47
260			Gary Johnson	AA	ERIE	ANA	OF	24	0.97	1.04	2.01	-3.00	-0.99	46
261			Joe Jester	HI-A	SJ	SF	2B	21	0.42	-0.42	0.00	-1.00	-1.00	45
262			Sean McGowan	HI-A	SJ	SF	1B	23	0.84	1.16	2.00	-3.00	-1.00	44
263			Ramon Carvajal	LO-A	PEO	STL	SS	19	-0.80	-0.27	-1.07	0.00	-1.07	43
264	288		Wilmy Caceres	AA	CHT	CIN	2B	21	-0.39	-0.69	-1.08	0.00	-1.08	42
265			Casey Rogowski	LO-A	BUR	CWS	1B	19	-0.48	-0.65	-1.14	0.00	-1.14	41
266			B.J. Garbe	LO-A	QC	MIN	OF	19	-0.17	-0.98	-1.15	0.00	-1.15	40
267	192	275	Carlos Maldonado	AA	RR	HOU	C	21	-0.63	-0.60	-1.23	0.00	-1.23	39
268			Danny Solano	AA	TUL	TEX	SS	21	-0.66	-0.72	-1.38	0.00	-1.38	38
269	177		Leo Daigle	HI-A	LAK	DET	1B	20	-1.05	-0.40	-1.46	0.00	-1.46	37

2000 Rank	1999 Rank	1998 Rank		LEVEL	TEAM	ORG	POS	AGE	REL. OBP	REL. SLG	REL. TOT.	AGE ADJ.	RPP	PTS
270	257	115	Jaisen Randolph	AA	WTN	CUB	OF	21	-0.27	-1.21	-1.48	0.00	-1.48	36
271			Gary Cates	LO-A	DEL	BAL	SS	19	-0.81	-0.69	-1.51	0.00	-1.51	35
272	268		Arturo McDowell	HI-A	BAK	SF	OF	20	-0.39	-1.25	-1.64	0.00	-1.64	34
273			Fred Torres	HI-A	CHR	TEX	C	20	-1.03	-0.62	-1.65	0.00	-1.65	33
274	160		Humberto Cota	AA	ALT	PIT	C	21	-1.15	-0.54	-1.69	0.00	-1.69	32
275	28	37	Tony Mota	AAA	ABQ	LA	OF	22	-0.84	-0.96	-1.80	0.00	-1.80	31
276			Jeff Brooks	HI-A	HD	AZ	3B	20	-1.43	-0.37	-1.80	0.00	-1.80	30
277	254	119	Julio Ramirez	AAA	CLG	FLA	OF	22	-1.16	-0.64	-1.80	0.00	-1.80	29
278	262		Tyler Minges	HI-A	KIN	CLE	OF	20	-1.12	-0.68	-1.81	0.00	-1.81	28
279	75		Thomas Pittman	HI-A	JUP	MON	1B	20	-0.83	-0.98	-1.81	0.00	-1.81	27
280			Tim Lemon	LO-A	PEO	STL	OF	19	-1.81	-0.08	-1.89	0.00	-1.89	26
281			Juan Salas	LO-A	CHSC	TB	3B	18	-1.82	-1.08	-2.89	1.00	-1.89	25
282			Vince Faison	LO-A	FTW	SD	OF	19	-1.62	-0.29	-1.91	0.00	-1.91	24
283	97		Ryan Langerhans	HI-A	MYR	ATL	OF	20	-1.33	-0.68	-2.01	0.00	-2.01	23
284			Victor Castillo	LO-A	GRB	NYY	SS	19	-0.17	-1.89	-2.06	0.00	-2.06	22
285	64	273	Cesar Izturis	AAA	SYR	TOR	SS	20	-2.31	-1.84	-4.14	2.00	-2.14	21
286	226	233	Eddy Garabito	AA	BOW	BAL	2B	21	-1.29	-0.90	-2.19	0.00	-2.19	20
287			Robert Cosby	LO-A	HAG	TOR	3B	19	-1.18	-1.01	-2.19	0.00	-2.19	19
288			John Hernandez	HI-A	SBR	LA	C	20	-1.31	-0.89	-2.21	0.00	-2.21	18
289	86		Belvani Martinez	AA	CAR	COL	2B	21	-1.52	-0.72	-2.24	0.00	-2.24	17
290			Brant Ust	AA	JCK	DET	3B	21	-1.27	-1.10	-2.37	0.00	-2.37	16
291	271	299	Eddy De los Santos	AAA	DUR	TB	SS	22	-0.92	-1.48	-2.41	0.00	-2.41	15
292	95	21	Chad Hermansen	AAA	NSH	PIT	OF	22	-1.73	-0.76	-2.48	0.00	-2.48	14
293	149	267	Darnell McDonald	AA	BOW	BAL	OF	21	-1.39	-1.10	-2.49	0.00	-2.49	13
294	261	264	Aaron Capista	AA	TRN	BOS	SS	21	-1.11	-1.40	-2.51	0.00	-2.51	12
295			Julio Collazo	LO-A	PDT	PHL	SS	19	-0.79	-1.92	-2.72	0.00	-2.72	11
296	170		Javier Colina	AA	CAR	COL	3B	21	-1.01	-1.73	-2.74	0.00	-2.74	10
297	49		Jeff Goldbach	HI-A	DAY	CUB	C	20	-1.82	-0.95	-2.76	0.00	-2.76	9
298			Francisco Belliard	HI-A	HD	AZ	2B	20	-1.59	-1.21	-2.80	0.00	-2.80	8
299			Ruben Castillo	LO-A	WSC	SEA	SS	19	-1.52	-1.29	-2.80	0.00	-2.80	7
300			Gil Velazquez	HI-A	STLC	NYM	SS	20	-1.41	-1.45	-2.85	0.00	-2.85	6
301			Bret Boyer	LO-A	CF	MON	2B	19	-1.54	-1.54	-3.08	0.00	-3.08	5
302			Pedro Guerrero	HI-A	CHR	TEX	2B	20	-1.10	-1.99	-3.09	0.00	-3.09	4
303	252	69	Wilton Veras	AAA	PAW	BOS	3B	22	-2.32	-1.64	-3.96	0.00	-3.96	3
304	265	275	Tomas De la Rosa	AAA	OTT	MON	SS	22	-1.86	-2.23	-4.09	0.00	-4.09	2
305	216		Derry Hammond	HI-A	MUD	MIL	OF	20	-2.69	-1.80	-4.49	0.00	-4.49	1

RELATIVE PRODUCTION POTENTIAL
By Organization

2000 Rank	1999 Rank	1998 Rank		LEVEL	TEAM	ORG	POS	AGE	REL. OBP	REL. SLG	REL. TOT.	AGE ADJ.	RPP	PTS
52			Brian Specht	HI-A	LE	ANA	SS	19	0.47	-0.21	0.26	1.00	1.26	254
160			Elpidio Guzman	HI-A	LE	ANA	OF	21	0.21	0.43	0.64	-1.00	-0.36	146
217	33	112	Nathan Haynes	AA	ERIE	ANA	OF	20	-0.92	-0.88	-1.80	1.00	-0.80	89
260			Gary Johnson	AA	ERIE	ANA	OF	24	0.97	1.04	2.01	-3.00	-0.99	46
43	30	2	Marcus Giles	AA	GRV	ATL	2B	22	1.33	1.22	2.55	-1.00	1.55	263
137	122	55	Ryan Lehr	LO-A	MAC	ATL	1B	21	0.81	1.03	1.84	-2.00	-0.16	169
142	260		Alfredo Castro	HI-A	MYR	ATL	SS	20	0.04	-0.25	-0.21	0.00	-0.21	164
180			Justo Rivas	LO-A	MAC	ATL	OF	20	0.16	0.34	0.50	-1.00	-0.50	126
194			Cory Aldridge	HI-A	MYR	ATL	OF	21	-0.49	0.84	0.35	-1.00	-0.65	112
202			A.J. Zapp	HI-A	MYR	ATL	1B	22	0.83	0.49	1.32	-2.00	-0.68	104
283	97		Ryan Langerhans	HI-A	MYR	ATL	OF	20	-1.33	-0.68	-2.01	0.00	-2.01	23
9			Brad Cresse	HI-A	HD	AZ	C	21	0.82	3.53	4.36	-1.00	3.36	297
10	2		Jack Cust	AA	ELP	AZ	OF	21	2.19	1.04	3.23	0.00	3.23	296
30	60		Carlos Urquiola	HI-A	HD	AZ	OF	20	1.53	0.34	1.87	0.00	1.87	276
72	163		Brian Gordon	HI-A	HD	AZ	OF	21	0.58	1.32	1.89	-1.00	0.89	234
77			Lyle Overbay	AA	ELP	AZ	1B	23	1.68	1.11	2.80	-2.00	0.80	229
189	227		Alex Cintron	AA	ELP	AZ	SS	21	-0.33	-0.25	-0.58	0.00	-0.58	117
204	121	51	Mike Rose	AA	ELP	AZ	C	23	1.21	0.10	1.31	-2.00	-0.69	102
233			J.D. Closser	LO-A	SBD	AZ	C	20	0.30	-0.16	0.14	-1.00	-0.86	73
244			Steve Neal	HI-A	HD	AZ	1B	23	0.81	1.29	2.10	-3.00	-0.90	62
245			Doug Devore	LO-A	SBD	AZ	OF	22	0.67	1.42	2.09	-3.00	-0.91	61
276			Jeff Brooks	HI-A	HD	AZ	3B	20	-1.43	-0.37	-1.80	0.00	-1.80	30
298			Francisco Belliard	HI-A	HD	AZ	2B	20	-1.59	-1.21	-2.80	0.00	-2.80	8
27			Ntema Ndungidi	HI-A	FRD	BAL	OF	21	1.72	1.22	2.95	-1.00	1.95	279
50	99	20	Richard Paz	HI-A	FRD	BAL	2B	22	2.96	0.36	3.32	-2.00	1.32	256
63			Ed Rogers	LO-A	DEL	BAL	SS	18	-0.14	0.18	0.04	1.00	1.04	243
116			Keith Reed	LO-A	DEL	BAL	OF	21	0.63	1.44	2.07	-2.00	0.07	190
124			Karim Garcia	AAA	ROC	BAL	OF	24	0.36	1.61	1.97	-2.00	-0.03	182
146	187	204	Eddy Martinez	HI-A	FRD	BAL	SS	22	1.68	0.10	1.78	-2.00	-0.22	160
150	48	116	Jayson Werth	AA	BOW	BAL	C	21	0.49	-0.74	-0.25	0.00	-0.25	156
154			Brian Roberts	HI-A	FRD	BAL	SS	22	1.74	-0.01	1.73	-2.00	-0.27	152
200	218		Maikell Diaz	HI-A	FRD	BAL	2B	20	0.38	-1.06	-0.67	0.00	-0.67	106
201	85		Jerry Hairston	AAA	ROC	BAL	2B	24	1.14	0.18	1.32	-2.00	-0.68	105
225	109		Tim Raines	HI-A	FRD	BAL	OF	20	0.16	-0.99	-0.83	0.00	-0.83	81
255			Willie Harris	LO-A	DEL	BAL	2B	22	1.58	0.46	2.04	-3.00	-0.96	51
271			Gary Cates	LO-A	DEL	BAL	SS	19	-0.81	-0.69	-1.51	0.00	-1.51	35
286	226	233	Eddy Garabito	AA	BOW	BAL	2B	21	-1.29	-0.90	-2.19	0.00	-2.19	20
293	149	267	Darnell McDonald	AA	BOW	BAL	OF	21	-1.39	-1.10	-2.49	0.00	-2.49	13
38	277	123	Carlos Leon	HI-A	SAR	BOS	2B	20	1.48	0.20	1.68	0.00	1.68	268
67			Juan Diaz	AA	TRN	BOS	1B	24	0.25	3.73	3.99	-3.00	0.99	239
68	58	32	Dernell Stenson	AAA	PAW	BOS	1B	22	0.17	0.80	0.97	0.00	0.97	238
95	53		Angel Santos	AA	TRN	BOS	2B	20	-0.04	-0.55	-0.60	1.00	0.40	211
120			Brian Wiese	HI-A	SAR	BOS	OF	22	0.79	1.21	2.00	-2.00	0.00	186
215			Luis Garcia	LO-A	AUG	BOS	1B	21	0.10	1.11	1.21	-2.00	-0.79	91
252			Angel Mendoza	HI-A	SAR	BOS	OF	21	-0.38	0.43	0.06	-1.00	-0.94	54
294	261	264	Aaron Capista	AA	TRN	BOS	SS	21	-1.11	-1.40	-2.51	0.00	-2.51	12
303	252	69	Wilton Veras	AAA	PAW	BOS	3B	22	-2.32	-1.64	-3.96	0.00	-3.96	3
5	106		Austin Kearns	LO-A	DAY	CIN	OF	20	1.98	2.71	4.68	-1.00	3.68	301
15	32		Adam Dunn	LO-A	DAY	CIN	OF	20	2.08	1.42	3.51	-1.00	2.51	291
36	25		Drew Henson	AA	NRW	CIN	3B	20	0.24	0.53	0.78	1.00	1.78	270
75			Ben Broussard	AA	CHT	CIN	OF	23	1.77	1.03	2.80	-2.00	0.80	231

2000 Rank	1999 Rank	1998 Rank		LEVEL	TEAM	ORG	POS	AGE	REL. OBP	REL. SLG	REL. TOT.	AGE ADJ.	RPP	PTS
145	51	144	Jackson Melian	AA	NRW	CIN	OF	20	-1.16	-0.06	-1.22	1.00	-0.22	161
192	125		Alejandro Diaz	AA	CHT	CIN	OF	21	-1.07	0.45	-0.62	0.00	-0.62	114
198			Ron Wright	AA	CHT	CIN	1B	24	0.81	1.53	2.34	-3.00	-0.66	108
232			Ranier Olmedo	LO-A	DAY	CIN	SS	19	-0.47	-0.39	-0.86	0.00	-0.86	74
238	10	224	Travis Dawkins	AA	CHT	CIN	SS	21	-0.61	-0.27	-0.87	0.00	-0.87	68
264	288		Wilmy Caceres	AA	CHT	CIN	2B	21	-0.39	-0.69	-1.08	0.00	-1.08	42
14			Jorge Moreno	LO-A	CLM	CLE	OF	19	0.89	1.63	2.52	0.00	2.52	292
40			Jhonny Peralta	LO-A	CLM	CLE	SS	17	0.63	-1.01	-0.37	2.00	1.63	266
156			Simon Pond	HI-A	KIN	CLE	3B	23	1.22	1.46	2.68	-3.00	-0.32	150
166	1		Russell Branyan	AAA	BUF	CLE	3B	24	-0.34	1.94	1.60	-2.00	-0.40	140
168	71	171	Mike Edwards	AA	AKR	CLE	3B	23	1.27	0.30	1.57	-2.00	-0.43	138
174			Victor Rodriguez	HI-A	KIN	CLE	SS	23	1.42	1.12	2.54	-3.00	-0.46	132
181			Alex Requena	LO-A	CLM	CLE	OF	19	0.58	-1.10	-0.52	0.00	-0.52	125
222			Eric Johnson	LO-A	CLM	CLE	OF	22	1.72	0.47	2.19	-3.00	-0.81	84
228			Corey Erickson	HI-A	KIN	CLE	3B	23	0.47	1.69	2.16	-3.00	-0.84	78
229	213		Brian Benefield	HI-A	KIN	CLE	2B	23	1.18	0.98	2.16	-3.00	-0.84	77
278	262		Tyler Minges	HI-A	KIN	CLE	OF	20	-1.12	-0.68	-1.81	0.00	-1.81	28
51	78		Jody Gerut	AA	CAR	COL	OF	22	1.86	0.41	2.27	-1.00	1.27	255
56	18	76	Ben Petrick	AAA	CSPR	COL	C	23	1.03	1.14	2.16	-1.00	1.16	250
71	188		Kevin Burford	HI-A	SLM	COL	OF	22	1.05	1.85	2.89	-2.00	0.89	235
94	74		Matt Holliday	HI-A	SLM	COL	3B	20	0.21	0.21	0.42	0.00	0.42	212
111	181		Juan Uribe	HI-A	SLM	COL	SS	20	-0.41	0.53	0.12	0.00	0.12	195
123	117		Jeff Winchester	LO-A	ASH	COL	C	20	-0.23	1.21	0.98	-1.00	-0.02	183
128	267	72	Brent Butler	AAA	CSPR	COL	2B	22	0.11	-0.17	-0.06	0.00	-0.06	178
129	101		Choo Freeman	HI-A	SLM	COL	OF	20	-0.07	0.00	-0.07	0.00	-0.07	177
130	250		Juan Pierre	AA	CAR	COL	OF	22	1.00	-0.07	0.92	-1.00	-0.08	176
144			Carlos Mendoza	AAA	CSPR	COL	OF	25	2.40	0.39	2.78	-3.00	-0.22	162
205	171	177	Elvis Pena	AA	CAR	COL	SS	23	1.37	-0.06	1.31	-2.00	-0.69	101
235			Chone Figgins	HI-A	SLM	COL	2B	22	0.78	0.35	1.13	-2.00	-0.87	71
289	86		Belvani Martinez	AA	CAR	COL	2B	21	-1.52	-0.72	-2.24	0.00	-2.24	17
296	170		Javier Colina	AA	CAR	COL	3B	21	-1.01	-1.73	-2.74	0.00	-2.74	10
18	21		Corey Patterson	AA	WTN	CUB	OF	20	-0.05	1.49	1.44	1.00	2.44	288
19	7		Hee Choi	HI-A	DAY	CUB	1B	21	0.98	2.26	3.24	-1.00	2.24	287
48	45		Eric Hinske	AA	WTN	CUB	3B	22	0.97	1.42	2.39	-1.00	1.39	258
53			Ryan Gripp	LO-A	LNS	CUB	3B	22	1.95	2.25	4.20	-3.00	1.20	253
70	212		Dave Kelton	HI-A	DAY	CUB	3B	20	-0.22	1.13	0.91	0.00	0.91	236
103			Nate Frese	HI-A	DAY	CUB	SS	22	1.61	0.71	2.31	-2.00	0.31	203
114			Jorge Piedra	HI-A	DAY	CUB	OF	21	0.53	0.55	1.07	-1.00	0.07	192
143			Jim Deschaine	LO-A	LNS	CUB	SS	22	1.22	1.57	2.78	-3.00	-0.22	163
197			Gary Johnson	HI-A	DAY	CUB	OF	23	1.10	1.25	2.35	-3.00	-0.65	109
234	14	63	Roosevelt Brown	AAA	IOW	CUB	OF	24	0.51	0.63	1.14	-2.00	-0.86	72
240	274		Franklin German	LO-A	LNS	CUB	OF	20	-0.11	0.23	0.12	-1.00	-0.88	66
270	257	115	Jaisen Randolph	AA	WTN	CUB	OF	21	-0.27	-1.21	-1.48	0.00	-1.48	36
297	49		Jeff Goldbach	HI-A	DAY	CUB	C	20	-1.82	-0.95	-2.76	0.00	-2.76	9
47	282	13	Joe Crede	AA	BRM	CWS	3B	22	0.97	1.47	2.45	-1.00	1.45	259
58	159	10	Jackie Rexrode	AA	BRM	CWS	2B	21	1.83	-0.71	1.12	0.00	1.12	248
82			Tim Hummel	LO-A	BUR	CWS	SS	21	1.92	0.77	2.69	-2.00	0.69	224
171			Nilson Teilon	LO-A	BUR	CWS	2B	19	-0.70	0.26	-0.44	0.00	-0.44	135
186	66		Terrell Merriman	HI-A	WS	CWS	OF	22	0.97	0.45	1.42	-2.00	-0.58	120
208	38	152	Jeff Liefer	AAA	CHA	CWS	1B	25	0.47	1.81	2.28	-3.00	-0.72	98
231	110	56	Aaron Rowand	AA	BRM	CWS	OF	22	-0.59	0.74	0.15	-1.00	-0.85	75
265			Casey Rogowski	LO-A	BUR	CWS	1B	19	-0.48	-0.65	-1.14	0.00	-1.14	41
46			Omar Infante	HI-A	LAK	DET	SS	18	0.01	-0.54	-0.53	2.00	1.47	260
74			Cody Ross	LO-A	WM	DET	OF	19	0.46	0.37	0.83	0.00	0.83	232
98			Ramon Santiago	LO-A	WM	DET	SS	18	0.04	-0.66	-0.62	1.00	0.38	208

2000 Rank	1999 Rank	1998 Rank		LEVEL	TEAM	ORG	POS	AGE	REL. OBP	REL. SLG	REL. TOT.	AGE ADJ.	RPP	PTS
105			Neil Jenkins	LO-A	WM	DET	3B	19	-0.32	0.59	0.27	0.00	0.27	201
115			Andres Torres	HI-A	LAK	DET	OF	22	1.71	0.36	2.07	-2.00	0.07	191
140	174		Eric Munson	AA	JCK	DET	1B	22	-0.18	0.98	0.80	-1.00	-0.20	166
165			Mike Rivera	HI-A	LAK	DET	C	23	0.26	2.35	2.60	-3.00	-0.40	141
216			Maxim St. Pierre	LO-A	WM	DET	C	20	0.82	-0.62	0.21	-1.00	-0.79	90
227	198		Richard Gomez	HI-A	LAK	DET	OF	22	0.58	0.59	1.17	-2.00	-0.83	79
246	273		Matt Boone	HI-A	LAK	DET	3B	20	-0.54	-0.37	-0.92	0.00	-0.92	60
269	177		Leo Daigle	HI-A	LAK	DET	1B	20	-1.05	-0.40	-1.46	0.00	-1.46	37
290			Brant Ust	AA	JCK	DET	3B	21	-1.27	-1.10	-2.37	0.00	-2.37	16
7	22	26	Abraham Nunez	AA	PRT	FLA	OF	20	1.65	0.87	2.51	1.00	3.51	299
16	84	62	Nate Rolison	AAA	CLG	FLA	1B	23	1.75	1.71	3.46	-1.00	2.46	290
55	193	12	Pablo Ozuna	AA	PRT	FLA	2B	21	0.73	0.44	1.17	0.00	1.17	251
66			Ramon Castro	AAA	CLG	FLA	C	24	0.71	2.29	2.99	-2.00	0.99	240
104	93	124	Cesar Crespo	AA	PRT	FLA	OF	21	0.63	-0.34	0.29	0.00	0.29	202
136			Francisco Ferrand	LO-A	KNC	FLA	OF	20	-0.41	1.25	0.84	-1.00	-0.16	170
152	270		Dave Callahan	LO-A	KNC	FLA	1B	20	0.57	0.17	0.75	-1.00	-0.25	154
195	142	166	Brett Roneberg	HI-A	BRV	FLA	OF	21	1.13	-0.78	0.35	-1.00	-0.65	111
236			Chip Ambres	LO-A	KNC	FLA	OF	20	0.20	-0.07	0.13	-1.00	-0.87	70
243	141		Jeff Bailey	HI-A	BRV	FLA	1B	21	-0.13	0.23	0.10	-1.00	-0.90	63
256	111		Matt Erickson	AA	PRT	FLA	SS	24	1.92	0.12	2.04	-3.00	-0.96	50
277	254	119	Julio Ramirez	AAA	CLG	FLA	OF	22	-1.16	-0.64	-1.80	0.00	-1.80	29
24			John Buck	LO-A	MCH	HOU	C	19	0.95	1.06	2.01	0.00	2.01	282
84			Keith Ginter	AA	RR	HOU	2B	24	2.05	1.61	3.66	-3.00	0.66	222
127			Jon Helquist	LO-A	MCH	HOU	3B	19	0.16	-0.20	-0.04	0.00	-0.04	179
151			Morgan Ensberg	AA	RR	HOU	3B	24	1.51	1.24	2.75	-3.00	-0.25	155
153			Royce Huffman	HI-A	KIS	HOU	3B	23	2.11	0.62	2.73	-3.00	-0.27	153
182	90	108	Aaron McNeal	AA	RR	HOU	1B	22	0.06	0.43	0.48	-1.00	-0.52	124
241			Brian Schmitt	LO-A	MCH	HOU	1B	21	0.52	0.60	1.12	-2.00	-0.88	65
267	192	275	Carlos Maldonado	AA	RR	HOU	C	21	-0.63	-0.60	-1.23	0.00	-1.23	39
93			Donovan Ross	LO-A	CHWV	KC	OF	22	1.77	1.66	3.43	-3.00	0.43	213
125	176		Joe Dillon	AA	WCH	KC	3B	24	1.73	1.25	2.97	-3.00	-0.03	181
139			Alexis Gomez	HI-A	WLM	KC	OF	19	-0.16	-1.03	-1.20	1.00	-0.20	167
147	8	88	Dee Brown	AAA	OMA	KC	OF	22	-0.79	0.57	-0.23	0.00	-0.23	159
210			Mark Ellis	HI-A	WLM	KC	SS	23	1.70	0.54	2.24	-3.00	-0.76	96
251			Chad Santos	LO-A	CHWV	KC	1B	19	-0.41	-0.53	-0.94	0.00	-0.94	55
86			Joe Thurston	HI-A	SBR	LA	SS	20	0.46	0.15	0.61	0.00	0.61	220
126			Hiram Bocachica	AAA	ABQ	LA	2B	24	0.53	1.43	1.97	-2.00	-0.03	180
157			Lamont Matthews	HI-A	SBR	LA	OF	22	0.38	1.30	1.68	-2.00	-0.32	149
176	92	58	Luke Allen	AA	SANT	LA	3B	21	-0.20	-0.28	-0.48	0.00	-0.48	130
214			Ismael Gallo	HI-A	VB	LA	2B	23	1.49	0.74	2.23	-3.00	-0.77	92
275	28	37	Tony Mota	AAA	ABQ	LA	OF	22	-0.84	-0.96	-1.80	0.00	-1.80	31
288			John Hernandez	HI-A	SBR	LA	C	20	-1.31	-0.89	-2.21	0.00	-2.21	18
89	75		Bucky Jacobsen	AA	HNT	MIL	1B	24	1.46	2.04	3.50	-3.00	0.50	217
220			Mark Ernster	AA	HNT	MIL	SS	22	0.55	-0.35	0.20	-1.00	-0.80	86
305	216		Derry Hammond	HI-A	MUD	MIL	OF	20	-2.69	-1.80	-4.49	0.00	-4.49	1
39	227		John Barnes	AAA	SLK	MIN	OF	24	2.18	1.49	3.67	-2.00	1.67	267
62			Todd Sears	AA	CAR	MIN	1B	24	2.54	1.50	4.04	-3.00	1.04	244
79			Eric Sandberg	LO-A	QC	MIN	1B	20	1.47	0.27	1.74	-1.00	0.74	227
100	111	79	Luis Rivas	AA	NB	MIN	2B	20	-0.36	-0.30	-0.66	1.00	0.34	206
118	161		Bobby Kielty	AA	NB	MIN	OF	23	1.57	0.46	2.03	-2.00	0.03	188
122	43		Michael Restovich	HI-A	FTM	MIN	OF	21	0.54	0.45	1.00	-1.00	-0.00	184
133	23	38	Mike Cuddyer	AA	NB	MIN	3B	21	0.02	-0.15	-0.14	0.00	-0.14	173
164	157	104	Matt LeCroy	AA	NB	MIN	C	24	1.06	1.56	2.62	-3.00	-0.38	142
173			Ruben Salazar	HI-A	FTM	MIN	2B	22	0.83	0.72	1.55	-2.00	-0.45	133
257	135	194	Papo Bolivar	AA	NB	MIN	OF	21	-0.51	-0.45	-0.96	0.00	-0.96	49

2000 Rank	1999 Rank	1998 Rank		LEVEL	TEAM	ORG	POS	AGE	REL. OBP	REL. SLG	REL. TOT.	AGE ADJ.	RPP	PTS
266			B.J. Garbe	LO-A	QC	MIN	OF	19	-0.17	-0.98	-1.15	0.00	-1.15	40
6			Brad Wilkerson	AA	HRB	MON	OF	23	2.84	2.80	5.64	-2.00	3.64	300
29	242		Scott Hodges	HI-A	JUP	MON	3B	21	1.34	1.57	2.91	-1.00	1.91	277
31			Valentino Pascucci	HI-A	JUP	MON	OF	21	1.50	1.37	2.87	-1.00	1.87	275
54	24	87	Milton Bradley	AAA	OTT	MON	OF	22	1.21	-0.03	1.18	0.00	1.18	252
83			Rich Lane	LO-A	CF	MON	1B	20	1.05	0.62	1.67	-1.00	0.67	223
206			Brandon Phillips	LO-A	CF	MON	SS	19	-0.69	-0.02	-0.71	0.00	-0.71	100
258			Josh McKinley	LO-A	CF	MON	3B	20	0.16	-0.12	0.04	-1.00	-0.96	48
279	75		Thomas Pittman	HI-A	JUP	MON	1B	20	-0.83	-0.98	-1.81	0.00	-1.81	27
301			Bret Boyer	LO-A	CF	MON	2B	19	-1.54	-1.54	-3.08	0.00	-3.08	5
304	265	275	Tomas De la Rosa	AAA	OTT	MON	SS	22	-1.86	-2.23	-4.09	0.00	-4.09	2
21	4		Alex Escobar	AA	BNG	NYM	OF	21	0.93	1.26	2.19	0.00	2.19	285
23	42		Brian Cole	HI-A	STLC	NYM	OF	21	0.91	2.18	3.10	-1.00	2.10	283
45			Timoniel Perez	AAA	NRF	NYM	OF	23	1.36	1.12	2.48	-1.00	1.48	261
102	61		Robert Stratton	HI-A	STLC	NYM	OF	22	0.19	2.14	2.33	-2.00	0.33	204
135	63		Ty Wigginton	AA	BNG	NYM	3B	22	-0.45	1.30	0.85	-1.00	-0.15	171
172			Pat Burns	HI-A	STLC	NYM	OF	22	1.31	0.24	1.55	-2.00	-0.45	134
187			Marvin Seale	LO-A	CAP	NYM	OF	21	1.00	0.42	1.42	-2.00	-0.58	119
300			Gil Velazquez	HI-A	STLC	NYM	SS	20	-1.41	-1.45	-2.85	0.00	-2.85	6
109	55		Alfonso Soriano	AAA	CLM	NYY	SS	22	-0.35	0.52	0.17	0.00	0.17	197
112	87	281	Nick Leach	AA	NRW	NYY	1B	22	1.07	0.04	1.12	-1.00	0.12	194
159			Andy Brown	LO-A	GRB	NYY	OF	20	-0.38	1.04	0.65	-1.00	-0.35	147
183	52	183	John Rodriguez	HI-A	TAM	NYY	OF	22	0.38	1.06	1.44	-2.00	-0.56	123
237			Juan Rivera	HI-A	TAM	NYY	OF	22	0.12	1.02	1.13	-2.00	-0.87	69
242			Wily Mo Pena	LO-A	GRB	NYY	OF	18	-1.64	-0.26	-1.90	1.00	-0.90	64
284			Victor Castillo	LO-A	GRB	NYY	SS	19	-0.17	-1.89	-2.06	0.00	-2.06	22
25	222	131	Jose Ortiz	AAA	SAC	OAK	2B	23	1.35	1.62	2.97	-1.00	1.97	281
33	102		Jason Hart	AA	MID	OAK	1B	22	1.20	1.64	2.84	-1.00	1.84	273
61			Mike Lockwood	HI-A	MOD	OAK	OF	23	2.65	1.42	4.07	-3.00	1.07	245
69	127	54	Mario Valdez	AAA	SAC	OAK	1B	25	2.27	1.67	3.94	-3.00	0.94	237
81	104		Eric Byrnes	AAA	SAC	OAK	OF	24	1.43	1.27	2.71	-2.00	0.71	225
88			Ryan Ludwick	HI-A	MOD	OAK	OF	21	0.14	1.44	1.59	-1.00	0.59	218
91	72		Rusty Keith	HI-A	MOD	OAK	OF	22	1.93	0.55	2.48	-2.00	0.48	215
107	34	31	Mario Encarnacion	AAA	SAC	OAK	OF	22	-0.14	0.33	0.19	0.00	0.19	199
121			Angel Berroa	HI-A	VIS	OAK	SS	20	-0.47	0.47	0.00	0.00	0.00	185
169	175		Nick Sosa	HI-A	MOD	OAK	1B	22	0.85	0.72	1.57	-2.00	-0.43	137
178	139		Oscar Salazar	AA	MID	OAK	SS	22	0.18	0.33	0.51	-1.00	-0.49	128
179			Rafael Pujols	HI-A	VIS	OAK	1B	22	1.04	0.47	1.51	-2.00	-0.49	127
212			Carlos Rosario	HI-A	MOD	OAK	2B	20	0.25	-1.02	-0.76	0.00	-0.76	94
221	54		Miguel Olivo	HI-A	MOD	OAK	C	21	-0.37	0.57	0.20	-1.00	-0.80	85
226	35		Gary Thomas	AA	MID	OAK	OF	20	-0.47	-1.35	-1.83	1.00	-0.83	80
239	80		Gary Schneidmiller	HI-A	MOD	OAK	3B	20	0.72	-1.60	-0.88	0.00	-0.88	67
253	198		Mark Bellhorn	AAA	SAC	OAK	3B	25	1.11	0.94	2.05	-3.00	-0.95	53
26	180		Nate Espy	LO-A	PDT	PHL	1B	22	2.78	2.18	4.96	-3.00	1.96	280
44	105	170	Jimmy Rollins	AAA	SWB	PHL	SS	21	0.09	0.43	0.52	1.00	1.52	262
65			Jorge Padilla	LO-A	PDT	PHL	OF	20	0.53	1.48	2.00	-1.00	1.00	241
92			Anderson Machado	HI-A	CLW	PHL	SS	19	0.14	-0.67	-0.53	1.00	0.47	214
113			Marlon Byrd	LO-A	PDT	PHL	OF	22	1.14	1.95	3.08	-3.00	0.08	193
117	231		Alejandro Giron	HI-A	CLW	PHL	OF	21	0.39	0.66	1.05	-1.00	0.05	189
175			Josue Perez	HI-A	CLW	PHL	OF	22	0.92	0.61	1.53	-2.00	-0.47	131
185	144	141	Eric Valent	AA	REA	PHL	OF	23	0.48	0.95	1.43	-2.00	-0.57	121
259			Jay Sitzman	LO-A	PDT	PHL	OF	22	1.18	0.84	2.02	-3.00	-0.98	47
295			Julio Collazo	LO-A	PDT	PHL	SS	19	-0.79	-1.92	-2.72	0.00	-2.72	11
2			J.R. House	LO-A	HCK	PIT	C	20	2.15	2.97	5.12	-1.00	4.12	304
12	83		Dan Meier	HI-A	LYN	PIT	1B	22	1.59	3.27	4.86	-2.00	2.86	294

2000 Rank	1999 Rank	1998 Rank		LEVEL	TEAM	ORG	POS	AGE	REL. OBP	REL. SLG	REL. TOT.	AGE ADJ.	RPP	PTS
17			Jeremy Cotten	LO-A	HCK	PIT	1B	19	0.57	1.87	2.44	0.00	2.44	289
37			Jose Castillo	LO-A	HCK	PIT	SS	19	0.25	1.45	1.70	0.00	1.70	269
60			Ron Paulino	LO-A	HCK	PIT	C	19	0.56	0.52	1.08	0.00	1.08	246
64	147	65	Craig Wilson	AAA	NSH	PIT	C	23	0.05	1.98	2.02	-1.00	1.02	242
97	269		Alex Hernandez	AA	ALT	PIT	OF	23	1.12	1.26	2.38	-2.00	0.38	209
131			Josh Bonifay	LO-A	HCK	PIT	2B	21	0.92	0.99	1.92	-2.00	-0.08	175
134			Aron Weston	LO-A	HCK	PIT	OF	19	0.42	-0.57	-0.15	0.00	-0.15	172
138	279		Paul Weichard	HI-A	LYN	PIT	OF	20	0.01	-0.21	-0.19	0.00	-0.19	168
141	46		J.J. Davis	HI-A	LYN	PIT	OF	21	-0.25	1.05	0.80	-1.00	-0.20	165
161			Tony Alvarez	LO-A	HCK	PIT	OF	21	0.45	1.18	1.63	-2.00	-0.37	145
177	136		Jack Wilson	AA	ARK	PIT	SS	22	0.26	0.25	0.51	-1.00	-0.49	129
218	234		Jovanny Sosa	LO-A	HCK	PIT	OF	20	-0.31	0.52	0.20	-1.00	-0.80	88
223			Lee Evans	HI-A	LYN	PIT	C	22	0.56	0.62	1.18	-2.00	-0.82	83
224	292		Jon Prieto	HI-A	LYN	PIT	2B	20	0.20	-1.03	-0.82	0.00	-0.82	82
254			Rolando Segura	HI-A	LYN	PIT	3B	21	-0.28	0.33	0.04	-1.00	-0.96	52
274	160		Humberto Cota	AA	ALT	PIT	C	21	-1.15	-0.54	-1.69	0.00	-1.69	32
292	95	21	Chad Hermansen	AAA	NSH	PIT	OF	22	-1.73	-0.76	-2.48	0.00	-2.48	14
8	3		Sean Burroughs	AA	MOB	SD	3B	19	1.22	0.21	1.43	2.00	3.43	298
85			Cesar Saba	LO-A	AUG	SD	SS	18	-0.40	0.01	-0.38	1.00	0.62	221
90			Ben Johnson	LO-A	FTW	SD	OF	19	-0.17	0.67	0.50	0.00	0.50	216
99	179	132	Mike Darr	AAA	LVG	SD	OF	24	1.58	0.79	2.37	-2.00	0.37	207
184	172	62	John Roskos	AAA	LVG	SD	OF	25	1.27	1.16	2.43	-3.00	-0.57	122
191	103		Ben Davis	AAA	LVG	SD	C	23	0.46	-0.08	0.38	-1.00	-0.62	115
193	66		Kevin Eberwein	AA	MOB	SD	1B	23	0.28	1.09	1.36	-2.00	-0.64	113
282			Vince Faison	LO-A	FTW	SD	OF	19	-1.62	-0.29	-1.91	0.00	-1.91	24
1	27		Antonio Perez	HI-A	LNC	SEA	SS	18	0.49	1.73	2.22	2.00	4.22	305
4			Chris Snelling	LO-A	WSC	SEA	OF	18	1.30	1.62	2.92	1.00	3.92	302
22			Willie Bloomquist	HI-A	LNC	SEA	2B	22	2.41	1.69	4.10	-2.00	2.10	284
59			Sheldon Fulse	LO-A	WSC	SEA	OF	18	0.84	-0.73	0.11	1.00	1.11	247
80			Terrmel Sledge	HI-A	LNC	SEA	OF	23	2.10	1.62	3.72	-3.00	0.72	226
87	211		Shawn McCorkle	LO-A	WSC	SEA	1B	22	1.83	1.77	3.60	-3.00	0.60	219
96	233	263	Juan Silvestre	HI-A	LNC	SEA	OF	22	0.69	1.70	2.39	-2.00	0.39	210
106			Ryan Christianson	LO-A	WSC	SEA	C	19	-0.02	0.28	0.26	0.00	0.26	200
132	239	49	Jermaine Clark	AA	NH	SEA	2B	23	1.98	-0.09	1.89	-2.00	-0.11	174
163	50		Alex Fernandez	AA	NH	SEA	OF	19	-1.67	-0.71	-2.38	2.00	-0.38	143
219	213		Ramon Vazquez	AA	NH	SEA	SS	23	0.85	0.35	1.20	-2.00	-0.80	87
247			Craig Kuzmic	HI-A	LNC	SEA	1B	23	0.76	1.32	2.08	-3.00	-0.92	59
299			Ruben Castillo	LO-A	WSC	SEA	SS	19	-1.52	-1.29	-2.80	0.00	-2.80	7
49	131		Tony Torcato	HI-A	SJ	SF	3B	20	0.66	0.71	1.37	0.00	1.37	257
108	282		Pedro Feliz	AAA	FRS	SF	3B	23	-0.38	1.56	1.18	-1.00	0.18	198
119			Julio Cordido	HI-A	BAK	SF	3B	19	-0.57	-0.43	-0.99	1.00	0.01	187
162			Jake Messner	HI-A	BAK	SF	OF	23	0.71	1.92	2.63	-3.00	-0.37	144
167			Carlos Valderrama	HI-A	BAK	SF	OF	22	0.54	1.05	1.59	-2.00	-0.41	139
209	274		Juan Melo	AAA	FRS	SF	SS	23	-0.08	0.34	0.26	-1.00	-0.74	97
211	243	290	Carlos Mendoza	HI-A	SJ	SF	SS	20	-0.17	-0.59	-0.76	0.00	-0.76	95
213	266	100	Yorvit Torrealba	AA	SHR	SF	C	21	-0.21	-0.57	-0.77	0.00	-0.77	93
230	286		Marco Pernalete	HI-A	BAK	SF	2B	21	0.61	-0.45	0.15	-1.00	-0.85	76
261			Joe Jester	HI-A	SJ	SF	2B	21	0.42	-0.42	0.00	-1.00	-1.00	45
262			Sean McGowan	HI-A	SJ	SF	1B	23	0.84	1.16	2.00	-3.00	-1.00	44
272	268		Arturo McDowell	HI-A	BAK	SF	OF	20	-0.39	-1.25	-1.64	0.00	-1.64	34
11			Albert Pujols	LO-A	PEO	STL	3B	20	1.25	2.80	4.05	-1.00	3.05	295
149			Chris Duncan	LO-A	PEO	STL	1B	19	-0.45	0.20	-0.25	0.00	-0.25	157
249	236	78	Chris Haas	AA	ARK	STL	3B	23	0.21	0.86	1.07	-2.00	-0.93	57
250			Andy Bevins	AA	ARK	STL	OF	24	0.49	1.58	2.06	-3.00	-0.94	56
263			Ramon Carvajal	LO-A	PEO	STL	SS	19	-0.80	-0.27	-1.07	0.00	-1.07	43

2000 Rank	1999 Rank	1998 Rank		LEVEL	TEAM	ORG	POS	AGE	REL. OBP	REL. SLG	REL. TOT.	AGE ADJ.	RPP	PTS
280			Tim Lemon	LO-A	PEO	STL	OF	19	-1.81	-0.08	-1.89	0.00	-1.89	26
20	59	53	Aubrey Huff	AAA	DUR	TB	3B	23	1.39	1.81	3.20	-1.00	2.20	286
32			Josh Hamilton	LO-A	CHSC	TB	OF	19	0.48	1.37	1.85	0.00	1.85	274
34			Jorge Cantu	LO-A	CHSC	TB	SS	18	0.25	0.58	0.83	1.00	1.83	272
35			Carl Crawford	LO-A	CHSC	TB	OF	18	0.35	0.43	0.78	1.00	1.78	271
78	208		Josh Pressley	LO-A	CHSC	TB	1B	20	1.04	0.73	1.77	-1.00	0.77	228
148	253		Toby Hall	AA	ORL	TB	C	24	1.22	1.54	2.76	-3.00	-0.24	158
155	128	61	Brent Abernathy	AAA	DUR	TB	2B	22	0.11	-0.40	-0.29	0.00	-0.29	151
170			Pete LaForest	HI-A	STP	TB	C	22	0.55	1.02	1.56	-2.00	-0.44	136
190	145		Jared Sandberg	AA	ORL	TB	3B	22	0.36	0.05	0.42	-1.00	-0.58	116
199	133	118	Kenny Kelly	AA	ORL	TB	OF	21	0.01	-0.68	-0.67	0.00	-0.67	107
248	205		Jason Tyner	AAA	NRF	TB	OF	23	1.02	-0.95	0.08	-1.00	-0.92	58
281			Juan Salas	LO-A	CHSC	TB	3B	18	-1.82	-1.08	-2.89	1.00	-1.89	25
291	271	299	Eddy De los Santos	AAA	DUR	TB	SS	22	-0.92	-1.48	-2.41	0.00	-2.41	15
3			Kevin Mench	HI-A	CHR	TEX	OF	22	2.55	3.45	6.00	-2.00	4.00	303
13	98		Travis Hafner	HI-A	CHR	TEX	1B	23	2.76	2.94	5.70	-3.00	2.70	293
28			Hank Blalock	LO-A	SAV	TEX	3B	19	1.23	0.70	1.92	0.00	1.92	278
41		115	Carlos Pena	AA	TUL	TEX	1B	22	1.49	1.11	2.60	-1.00	1.60	265
76	73		Corey Wright	HI-A	CHR	TEX	OF	20	1.53	-0.73	0.80	0.00	0.80	230
203	26	190	Jason Romano	AA	TUL	TEX	2B	21	-0.27	-0.41	-0.68	0.00	-0.68	103
207	210		Craig Monroe	AA	TUL	TEX	OF	23	0.45	0.83	1.29	-2.00	-0.71	99
268			Danny Solano	AA	TUL	TEX	SS	21	-0.66	-0.72	-1.38	0.00	-1.38	38
273			Fred Torres	HI-A	CHR	TEX	C	20	-1.03	-0.62	-1.65	0.00	-1.65	33
302			Pedro Guerrero	HI-A	CHR	TEX	2B	20	-1.10	-1.99	-3.09	0.00	-3.09	4
42	91		Jay Gibbons	AA	TEN	TOR	1B	23	1.61	1.98	3.59	-2.00	1.59	264
57	263		Matt Logan	HI-A	DUN	TOR	1B	20	0.42	0.71	1.13	0.00	1.13	249
73	124	28	Joe Lawrence	HI-A	DUN	TOR	C	23	2.16	1.72	3.88	-3.00	0.88	233
101	5	77	Vernon Wells	AAA	SYR	TOR	OF	21	-0.77	0.11	-0.66	1.00	0.34	205
110	69		Felipe Lopez	AA	TEN	TOR	SS	20	-0.67	-0.20	-0.87	1.00	0.13	196
158			Alvin Morrow	LO-A	BLT	TOR	OF	22	1.01	1.66	2.67	-3.00	-0.33	148
188	191	285	Mike Peeples	AA	TEN	TOR	OF	23	0.29	1.13	1.42	-2.00	-0.58	118
196	192		Ryan Freel	AAA	SYR	TOR	2B	24	0.67	0.68	1.35	-2.00	-0.65	110
285	64	273	Cesar Izturis	AAA	SYR	TOR	SS	20	-2.31	-1.84	-4.14	2.00	-2.14	21
287			Robert Cosby	LO-A	HAG	TOR	3B	19	-1.18	-1.01	-2.19	0.00	-2.19	19

RELATIVE MINOR LEAGUE STRENGTH
OFFENSE

2000 Rank	1999 Rank	1998 Rank	TEAM	2000 CUM. RPP	2000 # OF PLAYERS	1999 CUM. RPP	1999 # OF PLAYERS	1998 CUM. RPP	1998 # OF PLAYERS
1	3	5	Pittsburgh	3158	19	2214	15	2110	14
2	1	4	Oakland	2849	17	3267	19	2130	12
3	24	23	Seattle	2463	13	833	6	1113	8
4	8	29	Colorado	2222	14	1865	11	512	4
5	4	16	Chi. Cubs	2172	13	2106	12	1570	12
6	16	28	Tampa Bay	2097	13	1406	9	691	6
7	9	14	Baltimore	2029	15	1807	11	1591	10
8	12	3	Florida	1929	12	1602	13	2216	14
9	5	1	Minnesota	1853	11	1971	14	2600	20
10	10	17	Arizona	1785	12	1799	9	1535	11
11	18	26	Philadelphia	1689	10	1327	8	1016	7
12	26	22	Detroit	1681	12	675	8	1211	9
13	15	21	Cincinnati	1660	10	1484	9	1231	8
14	6	10	Texas	1646	10	1894	14	1770	12
15	2	2	Toronto	1563	10	2475	15	2345	15
16	20	8	Cleveland	1510	11	1182	7	1964	11
17	7	12	Montreal	1509	10	1893	13	1652	8
18	17	27	New York Mets	1463	8	1358	7	1014	5
19	27	30	San Francisco	1409	12	617	9	487	6
20	28	25	San Diego	1316	8	574	3	1045	7
21	21	7	Boston	1302	9	1181	10	1989	13
22	22	15	Houston	1219	8	1111	7	1573	10
23	19	6	Chi. White Sox	1200	8	1244	10	2066	13
24	13	13	Atlanta	961	7	1590	12	1609	11
25	29	11	Kansas City	871	6	466	5	1662	8
26	14	19	Los Angeles	820	7	1486	13	1381	12
27	11	18	NY Yankees	816	7	1765	9	1532	10
28	30	9	St. Louis	634	6	383	4	1793	11
29	25	24	Anaheim	535	4	812	4	1051	7
30	23	20	Milwaukee	304	3	978	8	1294	8

TOP CLASS A BATTING PROSPECTS
AND THEIR MAJOR LEAGUE COMPARABLES
by Tony Blengino

How does one project the eventual major league performance of Class A prospects, who are so far away from the big time? Their distance from the majors makes it impossible to calculate a statistically viable "major league equivalent" based on their raw minor league numbers.

As it is in home buying, another highly inexact science, the term "comparables" is a key factor in determining the "value" of the greenest of prospects. Determining the most comparable major league player to a low minor league prospect is not a guarantee of similar eventual major league success, but it is a key indicator of the potential for such success.

By using relative statistics, especially in the key categories of on-base and slugging percentages, comparable major league performers can readily be matched to their Class A counterparts. From the list of the Top 305 minor league batting prospects ranked by Relative Production Potential, the Class A players in the Top 125 were isolated for this analysis.

Their relative on-base and slugging percentages (quantified in terms of the number of standard deviations above or below the league average) are used as the original basis for comparison. These numbers are adjusted downward by the amount of any negative age adjustments resulting from the RPP study (split 50-50 between on-base and slugging percentage factors).

However, relative on-base and slugging percentage are not adjusted upward for any positive age adjustments, such an increase would inappropriately anticipate increases in power that might not materialize, we would then be comparing minor league spray hitters with major league power hitters.

After the minor leaguers' relative on-base and slugging percentage factors have been adjusted, we simply identify the 2000 major league regular with the closest match; not just to the sum of the two factors, but to each factor individually. Thus, the minor leaguer is not only matched with a major leaguer who was similarly effective in 2000, but also to a player with a similar combination of on-base and power skills.

You are going to see raw minor leaguers compared to some proven studs. So be it, four years ago we compared Andruw Jones, Richie Sexson and Jose Vidro to Larry Walker, Mike Sweeney to Mike Piazza, Darin Erstad to Albert Belle, Vladimir Guerrero to Belle, Scott Rolen to Ryan Klesko, Steve Cox to Reggie Sanders, Derrek Lee to Ray Lankford, Russell Branyan to Dante Bichette, Luis Castillo to Dave Magadan (check out Magadan's career OBP before you laugh), Bobby Estalella to Eric Karros, Fernando Tatis to Tino Martinez, Juan Encarnacion to Vinny Castilla, Ricky Ledee to Benito Santiago, and Ben Grieve to John Olerud.

Four years ago we compared Adrian Beltre to Ellis Burks, Branyan to Juan Gonzalez, Geoff Jenkins to Roberto Alomar, David Ortiz to Klesko, Sean Casey to Bernie Williams, Tatis to Castilla, Daryle Ward to Scott Brosius, Mitch Meluskey to Kevin Seitzer (again, check out the OBP's), Carlos Febles to Julio Franco, Brad Fullmer to Lankford, Terrence Long to Glenallen Hill, Carlos Lee to Brian Jordan, and Miguel Tejada to Carlos Delgado.

Three years ago we compared Beltre to Piazza, Branyan to Ken Griffey, Jr., Lance Berkman to Jeff Bagwell, Gabe Kapler to Raul Mondesi, Jimmy Rollins to Jeff Cirillo, Peter Bergeron to Knoblauch, Warren Morris to Jay Bell, Carlos Lee to a 21-year-old version of Alex Rodriguez, and Mark Quinn to Neifi Perez.

Two years ago, we compared Pat Burrell to Will Clark, Aubrey Huff to Jeff Kent, Brent Abernathy to Tony Fernandez, Luis Rivas to Mike Bordick, and Adam Piatt to Jay Buhner.

Last year, we compared Rafael Furcal to Rickey Henderson: enough said. For good measure, we added Jack Cust to Larry Walker, Sean Burroughs to Bob Abreu, Corey Patterson to Sammy Sosa, Antonio Perez to Tony

Gwynn, Adam Dunn to Sean Casey and Austin Kearns to Preston Wilson. That's a pretty decent record, if I may say so myself.

We can't draw too many conclusions from this method. These are Single-A players; many will never approach the stature of their major league counterparts. The method does not take speed into account beyond the effect it has on on-base and slugging percentages. The phase in the current major leaguer's career must also be taken into consideration. A comparison of 18-year-old Orioles' shortstop prospect Ed Rogers to a breaking-down 33-year-old Albert Belle must be taken with a grain of salt. The two never would have been matched up during a typical Belle season.

Also, Rangers' High-A outfielder Kevin Mench is matched up with 24-year-old baseball god Vladimir Guerrero, though Mench is only two years, and three levels of competition, his junior. Though Mench can flat out hit, it would be asking a lot of him to even scratch the surface of Guerrero's accomplishments by age 24.

Many intriguing comparisons were unearthed by this analysis, however. The Austin Kearns/Sammy Sosa tandem matches up one of the last decade's top power threats with one of the next decade's. The Reds' Adam Dunn matches up with Edgardo Alfonzo; both are powerful on-base guys who would easily function anywhere in the top third of a batting order.

The Devil Rays' Carl Crawford and Rondell White couldn't possibly be more similar outfield prospects. Ditto Giants' third baseman Tony Torcato and Sean Casey. The Indians' Omar Vizquel is matched up with his likely eventual successor, Jhonny Peralta, who also projects as a decent on-base guy with no power.

Not one, but two Tigers' Low-A shortstop prospects, Omar Infante and Ramon Santiago, are matched up with A's second baseman Randy Velarde. All are crafty top-of-the-order types. Mark Quinn was just a rookie in 2000, but has already been matched up with Orioles' Low-A outfielder Keith Reed. Both have decent power upsides and hit for average, but have subpar plate discipline.

Matched pairs of players who share the same position include Mench and Guerrero, Kearns and Sosa, Diamondbacks' catcher Brad Cresse and Ivan Rodriguez, Mets' outfielder Brian Cole and Carl Everett, Phils' first baseman Nate Espy and Mike Sweeney, Expos' outfielder Valentino Pascucci and Jeffrey Hammonds, Crawford and White,

Peralta and Vizquel, Orioles' second baseman Richard Paz and Quilvio Veras, A's outfielder Mike Lockwood and Matt Lawton, Phillies' outfielder Jorge Padilla and Steve Finley, Rockies' outfielder Kevin Burford and Jay Buhner, Diamondbacks' outfielder Brian Gordon and Buhner, Tigers' outfielder Cody Ross and Rondell White, Twins' first baseman Eric Sandberg and John Olerud, Expos' outfielder Terrmel Sledge and Rusty Greer, Royals' outfielder Donovan Ross and Gabe Kapler, Mets' outfielder Robert Stratton and Garret Anderson, Reed and Quinn, and Red Sox' outfielder Brian Wiese and Albert Belle.

Some matched pairs simply couple players with eerily matched offensive skills; check out the correlations between Orioles' outfielder Ntema Ndungidi and Mike Sweeney, Devil Rays' outfielder Josh Hamilton and Todd Hundley, Devil Rays' shortstop Jorge Cantu and Derrek Lee, Crawford and White, Torcato and Casey, Cubs' third baseman Ryan Gripp and Cliff Floyd, Phillies' Padilla and Finley, Gordon and Buhner, Cody Ross and White, Devil Rays' first baseman Josh Pressley and Roberto Alomar, Sledge and Greer, Padres' shortstop Cesar Saba and Terrence Long, Dodgers' shortstop Joe Thurston and Trot Nixon, Mariners' first baseman Shawn McCorkle and Gabe Kapler, A's outfielder Rusty Keith and Mark Grace, Donovan Ross and Kapler, Rockies' third baseman Matt Holliday and Kapler, Mariners' outfielder Juan Silvestre and Brook Fordyce, Tigers' shortstop Ramon Santiago and Randy Velarde, Tigers' third baseman Neil Jenkins and Juan Gonzalez, Cubs' outfielder Jorge Piedra and Todd Zeile, this year's closest match, and Wiese and Belle. That's an unusually large number of very close matches.

Obviously, many of the listed minor league prospects will not reach the levels attained by their major league counterparts. Opportunity is the x-factor, not to mention the ever-rising requirement for offensive achievement as prospects advance through their respective minor league systems.

The key point is to not take this approach too seriously. This is more of a fun exercise, matching up the legends of today's game with the youngest of prospects; the ultimate in crystal ball-gazing. Some of these combos, like Furcal/Henderson, could prove prophetic, but many will be worth a chuckle in the not-too-distant future. Being a dominant Savannah Sand Gnat is a lot different from being a dominant major leaguer.

2000 RELATIVE PRODUCTION COMPARABLES

	POS	ORG	AGE	REL. OBP	REL. SLG	REL. PROD.
Antonio Perez	SS	SEA	18	0.49	1.73	2.22
Carl Everett	OF	BOS	29	0.38	1.58	1.96
J.R. House	C	PIT	20	1.65	2.47	4.12
Vladimir Guerrero	OF	MON	24	1.24	2.38	3.62
Kevin Mench	OF	TEX	22	1.55	2.45	4.00
Vladimir Guerrero	OF	MON	24	1.24	2.38	3.62
Chris Snelling	OF	SEA	18	1.30	1.62	2.92
Troy Glaus	3B	ANA	23	1.24	1.78	3.02
Austin Kearns	OF	CIN	20	1.48	2.21	3.69
Sammy Sosa	OF	CUB	31	1.32	2.03	3.35
Brad Cresse	C	AZ	21	0.32	3.03	3.35
Ivan Rodriguez	C	TEX	28	0.69	2.53	3.22
Albert Pujols	3B	STL	20	0.75	2.30	3.05
Ivan Rodriguez	C	TEX	28	0.69	2.53	3.22
Dan Meier	1B	PIT	22	0.59	2.27	2.86
Richard Hidalgo	OF	HOU	25	0.54	2.05	2.59
Travis Hafner	1B	TEX	23	1.26	1.44	2.70
Jim Edmonds	OF	SEA	30	1.37	1.42	2.79
Jorge Moreno	OF	CLE	19	0.89	1.63	2.52
Mike Piazza	C	NYM	31	1.02	1.79	2.81
Adam Dunn	OF	CIN	20	1.58	0.92	2.50
Edgardo Alfonzo	2B	NYM	26	1.69	0.94	2.63
Jeremy Cotten	1B	PIT	19	0.57	1.87	2.44
Richard Hidalgo	OF	HOU	25	0.54	2.05	2.59
Hee Choi	1B	CUB	21	0.48	1.76	2.24
Carl Everett	OF	BOS	29	0.38	1.58	1.96

	POS	ORG	AGE	REL. OBP	REL. SLG	REL. PROD.
Willie Bloomquist	2B	SEA	22	1.41	0.69	2.10
Jorge Posada	C	NYY	28	1.45	0.87	2.32
Brian Cole	OF	NYM	21	0.41	1.68	2.09
Carl Everett	OF	BOS	29	0.38	1.58	1.96
John Buck	C	HOU	19	0.95	1.06	2.01
Lance Berkman	OF	HOU	24	0.96	1.16	2.12
Nate Espy	1B	PHL	22	1.28	0.68	1.96
Mike Sweeney	1B	KC	26	1.22	0.82	2.04
Ntema Ndungidi	OF	BAL	21	1.22	0.72	1.94
Mike Sweeney	1B	KC	26	1.22	0.82	2.04
Hank Blalock	3B	TEX	19	1.23	0.70	1.93
Mike Sweeney	1B	KC	26	1.22	0.82	2.04
Scott Hodges	3B	MON	21	0.84	1.07	1.91
Luis Gonzalez	OF	AZ	32	0.82	0.96	1.78
Carlos Urquiola	OF	AZ	20	1.53	0.34	1.87
Derek Jeter	SS	NYY	26	1.48	0.42	1.90
Valentino Pascucci	OF	MON	21	1.00	0.87	1.87
Jeffrey Hammon	OF	COL	29	0.96	0.78	1.74
Josh Hamilton	OF	TB	19	0.48	1.37	1.85
Todd Hundley	C	LA	31	0.58	1.37	1.95
Jorge Cantu	SS	TB	18	0.25	0.58	0.83
Derrek Lee	1B	FLA	24	0.27	0.53	0.80
Carl Crawford	OF	TB	18	0.35	0.43	0.78
Rondell White	OF	CUB	28	0.37	0.36	0.73
Jose Castillo	SS	PIT	19	0.25	1.45	1.70
Carl Everett	OF	BOS	29	0.38	1.58	1.96
Carlos Leon	2B	BOS	20	1.48	0.20	1.68
Will Clark	1B	BAL	36	1.39	0.23	1.62

	POS	ORG	AGE	REL. OBP	REL. SLG	REL. PROD.
Jhonny Peralta	SS	CLE	17	0.63	-1.01	-0.38
Omar Vizquel	SS	CLE	33	0.59	-0.93	-0.34
Omar Infante	SS	DET	18	0.01	-0.54	-0.53
Randy Velarde	2B	OAK	37	0.00	-0.64	-0.64
Tony Torcato	3B	SF	20	0.66	0.71	1.37
Sean Casey	1B	CIN	26	0.67	0.64	1.31
Richard Paz	2B	BAL	22	1.96	-0.64	1.32
Quilvio Veras	2B	ATL	29	1.35	-0.63	0.72
Brian Specht	SS	ANA	19	0.47	-0.21	0.26
Delino DeShield	2B	BAL	31	0.53	-0.12	0.41
Ryan Gripp	3B	CUB	22	0.45	0.75	1.20
Cliff Floyd	OF	FLA	27	0.50	0.78	1.28
Matt Logan	1B	TOR	20	0.42	0.71	1.13
Cliff Floyd	OF	FLA	27	0.50	0.78	1.28
Sheldon Fulse	OF	SEA	18	0.84	-0.73	0.11
Bill Spiers	3B	HOU	34	0.78	-0.84	-0.06
Ron Paulino	C	PIT	19	0.56	0.52	1.08
Sean Casey	1B	CIN	26	0.67	0.64	1.31
Mike Lockwood	OF	OAK	23	1.15	-0.08	1.07
Matt Lawton	OF	MIN	28	1.21	0.07	1.28
Ed Rogers	SS	BAL	18	-0.14	0.18	0.04
Albert Belle	OF	BAL	33	-0.20	0.24	0.04
Jorge Padilla	OF	PHL	20	0.03	0.98	1.01
Steve Finley	OF	AZ	35	0.09	0.96	1.05
Dave Kelton	3B	CUB	20	-0.22	1.13	0.91
Brad Fullmer	DH	TOR	25	-0.35	1.24	0.89
Kevin Burford	OF	COL	22	0.05	0.85	0.90
Jay Buhner	OF	SEA	35	0.15	0.81	1.20

	POS	ORG	AGE	REL. OBP	REL. SLG	REL. PROD.
Brian Gordon	OF	AZ	21	0.08	0.82	0.90
Jay Buhner	OF	SEA	35	0.15	0.81	0.96
Joe Lawrence	C	TOR	23	0.66	0.22	0.88
Benny Agbayani	OF	NYM	28	0.72	0.17	0.89
Cody Ross	OF	DET	19	0.46	0.37	0.83
Rondell White	OF	CUB	28	0.37	0.36	0.73
Corey Wright	OF	TEX	20	1.53	-0.73	0.80
Luis Castillo	2B	FLA	24	1.55	-0.88	0.67
Josh Pressley	1B	TB	20	0.54	0.23	0.77
Roberto Alomar	2B	CLE	32	0.59	0.26	0.85
Eric Sandberg	1B	MIN	20	0.97	-0.23	0.74
John Olerud	1B	SEA	31	1.03	-0.17	0.86
Terrmel Sledge	OF	MON	23	0.60	0.12	0.72
Rusty Greer	OF	TEX	31	0.64	0.07	0.71
Tim Hummel	SS	CWS	21	0.92	-0.23	0.69
John Olerud	1B	SEA	31	1.03	-0.17	0.86
Rich Lane	1B	MON	20	0.55	0.12	0.67
Rusty Greer	OF	TEX	31	0.64	0.07	0.71
Cesar Saba	SS	SD	18	-0.40	0.01	-0.39
Terrence Long	OF	OAK	24	-0.33	-0.02	-0.35
Joe Thurston	SS	LA	20	0.46	0.15	0.61
Trot Nixon	OF	BOS	26	0.44	0.09	0.53
Shawn McCorkle	1B	SEA	22	0.33	0.27	0.60
Gabe Kapler	OF	TEX	24	0.27	0.23	0.50
Ryan Ludwick	OF	OAK	21	-0.36	0.94	0.58
Brad Fullmer	DH	TOR	25	-0.35	1.24	0.89
Ben Johnson	OF	SD	19	-0.17	0.67	0.50
Andres Galarraga	1B	ATL	39	-0.11	0.75	0.64

	POS	ORG	AGE	REL. OBP	REL. SLG	REL. PROD.
Rusty Keith	OF	OAK	22	0.93	-0.45	0.48
Mark Grace	1B	CUB	36	0.95	-0.39	0.56
Anderson Machado	SS	PHL	19	0.14	-0.67	-0.53
Chuck Knoblauch	2B	NYY	31	0.14	-0.81	-0.67
Donovan Ross	OF	KC	22	0.27	0.16	0.43
Gabe Kapler	OF	TEX	24	0.27	0.23	0.50
Matt Holliday	3B	COL	20	0.21	0.21	0.42
Gabe Kapler	OF	TEX	24	0.27	0.23	0.50
Juan Silvestre	OF	SEA	22	-0.31	0.70	0.39
Brook Fordyce	C	BAL	30	-0.29	0.63	0.34
Ramon Santiago	SS	DET	18	0.04	-0.66	-0.62
Randy Velarde	2B	OAK	37	0.00	-0.64	-0.64
Robert Stratton	OF	NYM	22	-0.81	1.14	0.33
Garret Anderson	OF	ANA	28	-0.93	0.78	-0.15
Nate Frese	SS	CUB	22	0.61	-0.29	0.32
Denny Hocking	OF	MIN	30	0.64	-0.45	0.19
Neil Jenkins	3B	DET	19	-0.32	0.59	0.27
Juan Gonzalez	OF	DET	30	-0.38	0.61	0.23
Ryan Christianson	C	SEA	19	-0.02	0.28	0.26
Mike Bordick	SS	BAL	34	0.05	0.32	0.37
Juan Uribe	SS	COL	20	-0.41	0.53	0.12
Juan Gonzalez	OF	DET	30	-0.38	0.61	0.23
Marlon Byrd	OF	PHL	22	-0.36	0.45	0.09
Jose Valentin	SS	CWS	30	-0.22	0.45	0.23
Jorge Piedra	OF	CUB	21	0.03	0.05	0.08
Todd Zeile	1B	NYM	34	0.05	0.05	0.10
Andres Torres	OF	DET	22	0.71	-0.64	0.07
Brent Mayne	C	COL	32	0.81	-0.53	0.28

	POS	ORG	AGE	REL. OBP	REL. SLG	REL. PROD.
Keith Reed	OF	BAL	21	-0.37	0.44	0.07
Mark Quinn	OF	KC	26	-0.25	0.41	0.16
Alejandro Giron	OF	PHL	21	-0.11	0.16	0.05
Herbert Perry	3B	CWS	30	-0.25	0.16	-0.09
Julio Cordido	3B	SF	19	-0.57	-0.43	-1.00
Tino Martinez	1B	NYY	32	-0.72	-0.38	-1.10
Brian Wiese	OF	BOS	22	-0.21	0.21	0.00
Albert Belle	OF	BAL	33	-0.20	0.24	0.04
Angel Berroa	SS	OAK	20	-0.47	0.47	0.00
Wil Cordero	OF	PIT	28	-0.58	0.51	-0.07
Michael Restovich	OF	MIN	21	0.04	-0.05	-0.01
Todd Zeile	1B	NYM	34	0.05	0.05	0.10
Jeff Winchester	C	COL	20	-0.73	0.71	-0.02
Garret Anderson	OF	ANA	28	-0.93	0.78	-0.15

2000 MAJOR LEAGUE EQUIVALENCIES
by Tony Blengino

Once again, we are presenting major league equivalencies for all Triple-A and Double-A batters included on the Relative Production Potential list. These projected statistics are based on actual 2000 minor league performance, translated to an approximate major league equivalent based upon the concepts first set forth in Bill James' landmark essay in the 1985 *Baseball Abstract*. The minor league stats are "deflated" by estimating a percentage dropoff from the high minors to the majors for all players, and then adjusting upward or downward based upon the offensive context of their 2000 minor league club's league in relation to the offensive context of their parent club's major league. Only 11 of the players on last year's list became major league regulars for the bulk of 2000, way down from 17 in 1999.

Here are their 2000 major league stats along with their 1999 major league equivalents. On the whole, these players underperformed their major league equivalents in 2000, though most players did perform similarly to their MLE in one or more key areas. Some, however, performed eerily in line with the projected numbers. Julio Lugo is a case in point, and Lance Berkman, Terrence Long, Adam Kennedy, Mark Quinn and Derrek Lee are examples of others who performed quite similarly to the level suggested by their earlier minor league statistics. Certain players, like David Ortiz and Steve Cox, hit for about the expected batting average, but fell well short in the power categories. Pat Burrell didn't dominate to the level expected, largely because his strikeout/walk ratio fell short of the projected ratio, causing a shortfall in his batting average. Peter Bergeron and Mike Lamb fell short pretty much across the board. Unfortunately, Rafael Furcal wasn't on last year's MLE list, as we only prepare projections for Double and Triple-A players, not taking into consideration 19-year-old shortstops who dare to jump straight to the major league leadoff slot for a championship-caliber team. How dare he!

A couple of other points. Why didn't Lance Berkman, A: Get more playing time after Roger Cedeno came off of the disabled list, and B: Get even a smidgeon of Rookie of the Year support? Berkman had one awesome year, easily outperforming his MLE on a per at-bat basis. Also, the Steve Cox case bears some examination. He's been posting major league caliber numbers in the minors for years now, but had been written off as a career minor leaguer. Folks, he can play, and there are scores of others like him wasting away in the minors. Maybe the success of the US Olympic Team will open some eyes to the plight of the Mike Neills and Ernie Youngs; guys who are certainly more deserving of major league jobs than the Rob Duceys, Kevin Sefciks and John Mabrys who appear to be grandfathered in.

	AB	R	H	2B	3B	HR	RBI	AVG	BB	K	SB
Pat Burrell											
Actual	408	57	106	27	1	18	79	.260	63	139	0
'99 MLE	471	84	147	30	5	28	90	.312	79	126	3
Peter Bergeron											
Actual	518	80	127	25	7	5	31	.245	58	100	11
'99 MLE	486	77	149	40	5	11	48	.306	64	94	24
David Ortiz											
Actual	415	59	117	36	1	10	63	.282	57	81	1
'99 MLE	484	71	139	33	2	25	92	.286	66	117	2
Steve Cox											
Actual	318	44	90	19	1	11	35	.283	46	47	1
'99 MLE	497	84	156	43	3	20	100	.314	53	75	2

	AB	R	H	2B	3B	HR	RBI	AVG	BB	K	SB
Lance Berkman											
Actual	353	76	105	28	1	21	67	.297	56	73	6
'99 MLE	483	72	140	39	0	14	84	.291	67	111	12
Terrence Long											
Actual	584	104	168	34	4	18	80	.288	43	77	5
'99 MLE	517	59	155	32	5	10	68	.299	33	76	20
Mike Lamb											
Actual	493	65	137	25	2	6	47	.278	34	60	0
'99 MLE	507	80	153	45	3	17	82	.302	43	66	3
Adam Kennedy											
Actual	598	82	159	33	11	9	72	.266	28	73	22
'99 MLE	517	78	152	28	4	11	71	.294	33	56	23
Mark Quinn											
Actual	500	76	147	33	2	20	78	.294	35	91	5
'99 MLE	522	68	172	31	0	25	85	.329	28	93	7
Derrek Lee											
Actual	477	70	134	18	3	28	70	.281	63	123	0
'99 MLE	514	73	130	28	1	23	88	.253	36	149	4
Julio Lugo											
Actual	420	78	119	22	5	10	40	.283	37	93	22
'99 MLE	507	75	149	26	4	10	41	.295	43	66	24

On balance, this was a fairly lean group of rookie position players. The 2001 group might be similarly thin compared to say, the 1997 Andruw Jones/Vladimir Guerrero/Nomar Garciaparra/Scott Rolen class. Look for the Class of 2001 to include players from a group including Brad Wilkerson, Jack Cust, Corey Patterson, Aubrey Huff, Alex Escobar, Jose Ortiz, John Barnes, Marcus Giles, Jimmy Rollins, Timoniel Perez, Joe Crede, Milton Bradley, Ben Petrick, Ramon Castro, Dernell Stenson, Mike Darr, Luis Rivas, Vernon Wells, Pedro Feliz, Alfonso Soriano, Hiram Bocachica, Brent Butler, Juan Pierre, Dee Brown, Toby Hall, Brent Abernathy, Russell Branyan, Matt LeCroy, Ben Davis, and Jerry Hairston.

2000 MAJOR LEAGUE EQUIVALENCIES
DOUBLE-A & TRIPLE-A PLAYERS ON RELATIVE PRODUCTION POTENTIAL LIST

	AGE	POS	TEAM	AB	R	H	2B	3B	HR	RBI	AVG.	BB	K	OBP	SLG	SB
Brad Wilkerson	23	OF	MON	472	98	150	71	3	11	82	0.317	78	85	0.414	0.552	15
Abraham Nunez	20	OF	FLA	467	74	121	34	5	11	79	0.259	83	145	0.371	0.426	15
Sean Burroughs	19	3B	SD	481	55	136	35	4	2	50	0.282	69	59	0.372	0.387	7
Jack Cust	21	OF	AZ	452	84	120	30	4	17	63	0.267	98	165	0.398	0.464	10
Nate Rolison	23	1B	FLA	488	78	145	37	2	20	78	0.296	62	142	0.375	0.507	3
Corey Patterson	20	OF	CUB	501	80	127	29	5	24	89	0.253	49	138	0.320	0.473	29
Aubrey Huff	23	3B	TB	493	82	149	42	3	22	85	0.302	57	93	0.375	0.536	2
Alex Escobar	21	OF	NYM	492	80	133	27	6	16	68	0.271	58	138	0.347	0.448	24
Jose Ortiz	23	2B	OAK	511	89	165	31	4	20	90	0.323	39	69	0.371	0.515	18
Jason Hart	22	1B	OAK	497	78	151	38	2	24	96	0.304	53	111	0.371	0.533	3
Drew Henson	20	3B	CIN	509	80	137	20	3	14	80	0.269	41	184	0.324	0.406	0
John Barnes	24	OF	MIN	496	101	167	39	5	12	82	0.336	54	59	0.401	0.509	7
Carlos Pena	22	1B	TEX	472	91	131	30	1	22	82	0.277	78	104	0.381	0.486	9
Jay Gibbons	23	1B	TOR	487	88	154	39	1	20	78	0.317	63	73	0.396	0.524	3
Marcus Giles	22	2B	ATL	477	74	134	29	2	17	63	0.282	73	79	0.376	0.457	25
Jimmy Rollins	21	SS	PHL	504	63	129	29	9	11	65	0.256	46	63	0.319	0.416	23
Timoniel Perez	23	OF	NYM	524	72	176	29	7	10	59	0.336	26	49	0.367	0.473	21
Joe Crede	22	3B	CWS	497	79	150	33	0	20	89	0.303	53	109	0.370	0.489	3
Eric Hinske	22	3B	CUB	469	79	118	22	8	21	76	0.251	81	152	0.361	0.465	15
Jody Gerut	22	OF	COL	457	59	126	40	3	4	70	0.276	93	72	0.398	0.401	22
Milton Bradley	22	OF	MON	493	74	140	27	1	8	37	0.285	57	87	0.359	0.391	13
Pablo Ozuna	21	2B	FLA	511	73	148	26	5	7	58	0.290	39	65	0.341	0.402	35
Ben Petrick	23	C	COL	499	61	141	40	4	14	76	0.282	51	88	0.349	0.467	11
Jackie Rexrode	21	2B	CWS	457	82	130	14	4	0	19	0.285	93	56	0.406	0.330	26
Todd Sears	24	1B	MIN	442	81	132	31	0	18	108	0.298	108	119	0.436	0.491	18
Craig Wilson	23	C	PIT	505	84	128	28	2	33	87	0.252	45	169	0.313	0.513	1
Ramon Castro	24	C	FLA	519	84	156	48	0	27	86	0.301	31	100	0.340	0.548	0
Juan Diaz	24	1B	BOS	525	90	158	36	2	42	132	0.300	25	159	0.332	0.620	0
Dernell Stenson	22	1B	BOS	496	71	127	18	0	28	86	0.255	54	138	0.329	0.460	0
Mario Valdez	25	1B	OAK	480	93	151	32	1	21	102	0.316	70	82	0.403	0.520	1
Ben Broussard	23	OF	CIN	442	96	109	12	5	21	76	0.247	108	128	0.394	0.440	22
Lyle Overbay	23	1B	AZ	502	74	162	31	3	14	84	0.323	48	88	0.383	0.479	5
Eric Byrnes	24	OF	OAK	497	94	152	44	1	15	81	0.305	53	67	0.373	0.493	21
Keith Ginter	24	2B	HOU	479	94	146	29	2	23	80	0.305	71	144	0.395	0.516	21
Bucky Jacobsen	24	1B	MIL	465	74	124	24	0	30	84	0.268	85	127	0.381	0.514	7
Angel Santos	20	2B	BOS	496	54	122	30	3	5	54	0.247	54	115	0.321	0.349	30
Alex Hernandez	23	OF	PIT	519	66	165	40	2	9	80	0.317	31	118	0.355	0.457	2
Mike Darr	24	OF	SD	502	87	156	29	5	10	72	0.310	48	83	0.371	0.446	14
Luis Rivas	20	2B	MIN	499	80	119	34	7	4	57	0.239	51	66	0.310	0.362	16
Vernon Wells	21	OF	TOR	505	72	117	31	6	15	62	0.231	45	96	0.295	0.405	22
Cesar Crespo	21	OF	FLA	481	86	116	20	5	8	54	0.241	69	126	0.336	0.352	37
Mario Encarnacion	22	OF	OAK	500	71	122	25	4	18	84	0.245	50	171	0.313	0.416	21
Pedro Feliz	23	3B	SF	525	71	140	32	1	27	87	0.267	25	108	0.300	0.491	1
Alfonso Soriano	22	SS	NYY	524	95	145	35	5	13	70	0.276	26	104	0.311	0.437	15
Felipe Lopez	20	SS	TOR	515	59	131	20	4	10	46	0.254	35	129	0.301	0.367	14
Nick Leach	22	1B	NYY	479	56	127	30	1	9	62	0.265	71	114	0.360	0.389	6
Bobby Kielty	23	OF	MIN	457	75	114	30	2	13	62	0.250	93	118	0.377	0.413	6
Karim Garcia	24	OF	BAL	501	75	136	26	3	31	101	0.271	49	129	0.336	0.518	5
Joe Dillon	24	3B	KC	476	66	141	33	3	19	81	0.296	74	89	0.391	0.498	0
Hiram Bocachica	24	2B	LA	516	85	149	37	3	20	72	0.289	34	118	0.333	0.487	9

	AGE	POS	TEAM	AB	R	H	2B	3B	HR	RBI	AVG.	BB	K	OBP	SLG	SB
Brent Butler	22	2B	COL	509	68	133	37	1	7	50	0.261	41	59	0.316	0.381	1
Juan Pierre	22	OF	COL	513	71	162	19	4	0	36	0.316	37	32	0.363	0.368	52
Jermaine Clark	23	2B	SEA	465	78	131	23	7	2	43	0.281	85	77	0.392	0.376	37
Mike Cuddyer	21	3B	MIN	496	71	130	31	7	6	60	0.263	54	105	0.336	0.388	5
Ty Wigginton	22	3B	NYM	525	66	140	30	3	21	80	0.267	25	133	0.301	0.453	5
Eric Munson	22	1B	DET	496	72	124	29	5	21	94	0.249	54	138	0.322	0.451	7
Carlos Mendoza	25	OF	COL	485	86	155	20	13	0	46	0.319	65	75	0.400	0.413	28
Jackson Melian	20	OF	CIN	521	55	123	14	5	14	61	0.236	29	133	0.276	0.366	27
Dee Brown	22	OF	KC	517	68	127	25	5	21	63	0.245	33	131	0.290	0.431	18
Toby Hall	24	C	TB	517	72	176	27	0	17	97	0.340	33	48	0.379	0.493	6
Jayson Werth	21	C	BAL	465	74	101	26	3	8	41	0.218	85	90	0.339	0.337	14
Morgan Ensberg	24	3B	HOU	475	78	130	31	0	23	74	0.273	75	115	0.373	0.484	7
Brent Abernathy	22	2B	TB	511	64	141	30	2	5	53	0.276	39	52	0.327	0.372	24
Alex Fernandez	19	OF	SEA	534	46	130	33	1	6	57	0.243	16	83	0.265	0.341	14
Matt LeCroy	24	C	MIN	483	77	130	29	2	23	88	0.270	67	90	0.359	0.483	0
Russell Branyan	24	3B	CLE	494	92	115	19	3	42	120	0.232	56	214	0.310	0.539	2
Mike Edwards	23	3B	CLE	486	68	137	25	2	10	60	0.283	64	93	0.367	0.405	7
Luke Allen	21	3B	LA	501	67	121	21	5	9	73	0.241	49	114	0.308	0.354	17
Jack Wilson	22	SS	PIT	506	80	136	27	8	7	42	0.268	44	95	0.327	0.399	2
Oscar Salazar	22	SS	OAK	509	73	142	31	1	14	59	0.278	41	92	0.332	0.422	4
Aaron McNeal	22	1B	HOU	521	48	147	27	2	13	83	0.283	29	143	0.321	0.419	0
John Roskos	25	OF	SD	494	79	141	35	0	19	78	0.286	56	97	0.358	0.470	2
Eric Valent	23	OF	PHL	485	75	117	22	4	20	83	0.242	65	99	0.331	0.428	2
Mike Peeples	23	OF	TOR	501	75	139	28	4	19	78	0.277	49	79	0.341	0.462	12
Alex Cintron	21	SS	AZ	526	70	144	28	4	3	49	0.274	24	61	0.306	0.363	8
Jared Sandberg	22	3B	TB	484	60	123	30	2	10	70	0.255	66	115	0.345	0.387	10
Ben Davis	23	C	SD	484	66	113	32	1	12	69	0.233	66	103	0.325	0.381	9
Alejandro Diaz	21	OF	CIN	535	73	138	20	7	14	70	0.258	15	89	0.278	0.400	19
Kevin Eberwein	23	1B	SD	492	73	126	21	2	23	91	0.255	58	108	0.333	0.447	3
Ryan Freel	24	2B	TOR	493	100	135	24	7	16	49	0.273	57	82	0.348	0.447	49
Ron Wright	24	1B	CIN	478	70	123	36	0	23	97	0.258	72	150	0.355	0.479	4
Kenny Kelly	21	OF	TB	490	74	122	17	7	3	29	0.249	60	126	0.330	0.330	31
Jerry Hairston	24	2B	BAL	485	96	136	35	2	9	47	0.280	65	83	0.365	0.416	13
Jason Romano	21	2B	TEX	504	71	127	31	1	7	57	0.251	46	85	0.314	0.357	20
Mike Rose	23	C	AZ	474	65	122	27	1	11	69	0.258	76	103	0.361	0.391	9
Elvis Pena	23	SS	COL	482	90	140	16	6	3	36	0.291	68	82	0.378	0.366	47
Craig Monroe	23	OF	TEX	491	82	129	34	4	18	82	0.262	59	104	0.341	0.460	11
Jeff Liefer	25	1B	CWS	495	77	133	31	1	33	94	0.268	55	127	0.340	0.535	2
Juan Melo	23	SS	SF	516	57	136	29	5	12	49	0.264	34	121	0.310	0.409	13
Yorvit Torrealba	21	C	SF	514	54	134	25	1	4	34	0.260	36	77	0.309	0.338	2
Nathan Haynes	20	OF	ANA	515	59	125	18	4	6	45	0.243	35	129	0.291	0.328	39
Ramon Vazquez	23	SS	SEA	491	66	135	30	4	9	67	0.274	59	98	0.352	0.406	1
Mark Ernster	22	SS	MIL	472	60	111	20	0	11	58	0.236	78	112	0.344	0.350	22
Gary Thomas	20	OF	OAK	496	63	113	17	0	2	59	0.229	54	84	0.305	0.277	11
Aaron Rowand	22	OF	CWS	513	78	131	25	4	20	96	0.255	37	119	0.305	0.434	21
Roosevelt Brown	24	OF	CUB	509	75	141	41	0	13	62	0.276	41	92	0.331	0.436	11
Travis Dawkins	21	SS	CIN	498	70	111	27	7	8	40	0.223	52	102	0.297	0.351	29
Jason Tyner	23	OF	TB	507	78	155	8	2	0	40	0.307	43	53	0.361	0.331	48
Chris Haas	23	3B	STL	494	73	122	22	2	24	83	0.246	56	155	0.323	0.446	0
Andy Bevins	24	OF	STL	516	84	151	30	3	25	88	0.293	34	114	0.337	0.510	0
Mark Bellhorn	25	3B	OAK	466	99	113	17	8	21	65	0.242	84	140	0.357	0.451	18
Matt Erickson	24	SS	FLA	482	64	130	30	4	2	47	0.270	68	98	0.360	0.363	9
Papo Bolivar	21	OF	MIN	521	55	139	24	7	2	51	0.266	29	95	0.305	0.354	17
Gary Johnson	24	OF	ANA	488	78	134	18	6	18	99	0.275	62	127	0.357	0.447	7
Wilmy Caceres	21	2B	CIN	515	64	134	22	3	2	31	0.259	35	73	0.306	0.325	34

	AGE	POS	TEAM	AB	R	H	2B	3B	HR	RBI	AVG.	BB	K	OBP	SLG	SB
Carlos Maldonado	21	C	HOU	515	46	126	27	2	5	52	0.245	35	94	0.293	0.333	5
Danny Solano	21	SS	TEX	501	44	115	17	3	9	40	0.230	49	99	0.298	0.327	12
Jaisen Randolph	21	OF	CUB	495	74	116	15	4	1	30	0.235	55	103	0.311	0.288	45
Humberto Cota	21	C	PIT	527	54	129	23	1	9	48	0.245	23	105	0.276	0.343	7
Tony Mota	22	OF	LA	519	63	124	14	4	7	52	0.239	31	93	0.282	0.319	9
Julio Ramirez	22	OF	FLA	525	54	124	25	3	8	62	0.236	25	141	0.271	0.342	24
Cesar Izturis	20	SS	TOR	528	60	109	19	5	0	30	0.207	22	57	0.239	0.261	24
Eddy Garabito	21	2B	BAL	523	73	125	22	3	6	53	0.240	27	64	0.278	0.327	22
Belvani Martinez	21	2B	COL	536	64	129	23	4	4	46	0.241	14	88	0.260	0.322	32
Brant Ust	21	3B	DET	506	49	108	20	5	5	37	0.214	44	132	0.277	0.303	3
Eddy De los Santos	22	SS	TB	513	47	122	7	1	5	56	0.239	37	101	0.290	0.289	5
Chad Hermansen	22	OF	PIT	515	65	102	19	1	15	53	0.199	35	169	0.249	0.328	22
Darnell McDonald	21	OF	BAL	519	63	120	14	5	6	46	0.231	31	105	0.274	0.313	12
Aaron Capista	21	SS	BOS	509	57	115	23	3	2	40	0.227	41	85	0.284	0.295	10
Javier Colina	21	3B	COL	500	38	105	14	1	2	39	0.210	50	100	0.281	0.254	6
Wilton Veras	22	3B	BOS	523	40	105	21	0	7	55	0.200	27	46	0.239	0.278	0
Tomas De la Rosa	22	SS	MON	509	36	96	14	1	1	47	0.188	41	69	0.248	0.228	13

RELATIVE CONTROL/POWER POTENTIAL 2000
A Method of Evaluating Minor League Starting Pitchers
by Tony Blengino

INTRODUCTION

Evaluating the major league potential of minor league starting pitchers is a very inexact science; it is much more difficult than it is to evaluate minor league hitters. Many attempt to do so by focusing solely on tools (physical size, velocity of fastball, repertoire of pitches, etc.), while others focus on mainstream, user-friendly statistics such as won-lost record or ERA. The former approach tends to overrate pitchers who don't have the savvy and maturity to cut it in the majors, while the latter tends to overrate pitchers who received obscene run support, had exceptional clubs behind them or hurled in pitcher-friendly parks or leagues.

The following statistical approach combines the finer points of both methods. It inherently favors pitchers with excellent tools, and focuses on statistics that truly matter. Further, it gives priority to pitchers who are younger than most of the hurlers at their level. The most important qualities for a pitching prospect are precision and dominance, the ability to place the ball where desired, and to blow it past hitters when necessary. These abilities are quite accurately measured by strikeout/walk and strikeout/nine innings ratios. Pitchers who can combine relative precision, dominance and youth relative to their minor league level are the best prospects of all.

Relative Control/Power Potential measures these traits quite well. The Relative Control/Power Factor is actually the sum of two components. The first, the control factor, is obtained by measuring a pitcher's strikeout/walk ratio to the average of other qualifiers in his league. The c factor is equal to the number of standard deviations above or below the league average. The second, the power factor, is obtained by measuring a pitcher's strikeout/nine innings ratio to the average of the other qualifiers in his league. The p factor is equal to the number of standard deviations above or below the league average. The two factors are then simply added together, resulting in the unadjusted relative c/p factor. This figure is then adjusted for age as the final step in compiling the Relative Control/Power Potential list.

This list of prospects is not intended to be a projection of the best major league prospects for 2001. It instead measures long-term potential.

FILLING THE PROSPECT POOL

The first step in the evaluation process is the calculation of the K/W and K/9 IP ratios for all qualifying starters in full-season minor leagues. The five pitchers with the most starts for each minor league club were considered qualifiers. Pitchers who split their season between more than one minor league club qualified at each level in which they had nine or more starts and 50 or more innings pitched. If such pitchers qualified for the RCPP list more than once, all but the highest ranking were disregarded. The basic rule of thumb: it is preferable to include deserving pitchers with limited stats rather than omit them entirely.

Next, the relative control/power factors of all qualifiers in each full-season minor league are calculated. Since the sum of the relative c/p factors in each league is zero, an inherent adjustment allows the precision and dominance of hurlers in both hitting and pitching-oriented leagues to be readily compared to one another. The last key component in compiling the RCPP list is the age of qualifiers. The optimal age for a Triple-A hurler for the purposes of this analysis is 22, for Double-A, 21, for High-A, 20, and for Low-A, 19. Consideration of a prospect's age prevents the inclusion of career minor leaguers like Rick Krivda and Pat Ahearne on this list on an annual basis.

All qualifiers at or below a league's optimal age were first placed on the RCPP list. Next, all qualifiers one year older than their league's optimal age possessing a positive relative c/p factor were placed on the list. Then, all qualifiers two years older than their league's optimal age possessing a relative c/p factor of at least 1.00 were placed on the list. Finally, all qualifiers three years older than their league's optimal age possessing a relative c/p factor of at least 2.00 were placed on the list. The prospect pool is now complete, 211 players qualified in 2000, down slightly from 226 in 1999. The list includes pitchers who exhibited well above average levels of precision and dominance in 2000, as well as some who did not, but who were among the youngest prospects in their leagues.

Next, the relative c/p factors of the 211 starting pitchers on the list were adjusted for age. For each year younger than his league's optimal age, a prospect's factor was increased by 1.00; for each year older than his league's optimal age, a prospect's relative c/p factor was decreased by 1.00. This process can bring together two starkly different seasons. For instance, #44 prospect Jon Garland, 20, of the White Sox, posted a mere (0.56) unadjusted relative c/p factor in the Triple-A International League, which was adjusted upward by 2.00 to 1.44 for his age. Meanwhile, Randey Dorame, 21, who was later traded from the Dodgers to the Rockies, posted a comparatively excellent 2.41 unadjusted RPP for Vero Beach in the High-A Florida State League, which was adjusted downward by (1.00) to 1.41 based upon his age, dropping his final ranking to 45th, just behind Garland.

It is difficult to project Class A ball performance, with the bat or on the mound, into equivalent major league performance. It is particularly tough for pitchers, as many that excel against undisciplined A-ball hitters predictably wilt against better hitters. Pitchers are also much more susceptible to major injuries. In particular, many Class A control pitchers have ranked high on these annual lists, and then have been unable to repeat their successes at higher minor league levels. However, the top of this year's list appears to be short on such pitchers, a welcome change from previous seasons. Though the list of 211 pitching prospects will undoubtedly shrink over time for these and other reasons, many prospects on this list are either unfairly ignored or underrated by the mainstream baseball media.

2000 RESULTS

The 2000 Top Ten includes prospects from all four minor league levels. Only one made his major league debut in 2000, though another sat on a major league bench for part of September and two others were key starting pitchers for the US Olympic team. All of this year's Top Ten can confidently be projected as future top members of their respective major league teams' rotations, barring injury, of course. Below are thumbnail sketches of the 2000 Top Ten; more detailed descriptions of these prospects can be found in their respective organizations' Top Ten lists.

The Mariners' Ryan Anderson, 20, moved from 11th on the 1998 list to 7th on the 1999 list, to the top of this year's list. The 6'10", 215, southpaw features a high-90's fastball and a curveball and slider that will likely both be deadly secondary pitches once he establishes a consistent release point. His control is eerily advanced for such a young power pitcher. Comparisons of him to Randy Johnson at a similar developmental stage are inevitable, and favorable for Anderson. Anderson finished with a brilliant 146/55 strikeout/walk ratio in only 104 Triple-A innings as his league's youngest hurler, resulting in an adjusted RCPP of 6.95, even higher than 1999 leader Rick Ankiel's 6.84 mark. Anderson is a near future major league ace, and will arrive to stay in 2001.

Red Sox' righthander Paxton Crawford, 22, ranks second on this year's list on the strength of nine dominant Double-A Eastern League starts in which he unfurled a gaudy 54/6 strikeout/walk ratio in 52 innings. While he isn't nearly as overpowering as those stats would suggest, he does have a diverse four-pitch repertoire and exceptional command of all of his pitches. His fastball only reaches the high-80's, so his margin of error in the majors won't be great. Look for him to be a productive long-term member of the Red Sox' rotation.

Twins' righthander Adam Johnson, 20, was by far the best pitching performer among 2000 draftees. The third overall pick in this year's first round, Johnson waxed High-A Florida State League hitters, recording a scary 92/20 strikeout/walk ratio with only 45 hits allowed in 69 innings. The 6'2", 200, righty relies on a 90 MPH fastball and a tight, hard slider, and should soon join Brad Radke and Eric Milton at the top of the Twins' big league rotation.

Astros' Double-A righthander Roy Oswalt, 22, is the first of this year's Olympic team studs among the Top Ten. The 6'0", 170, Oswalt dominated the Texas League after making a daunting two-level jump from Low-A ball in 1999. He posted a lethal 141/22 strikeout/walk ratio in 130 innings in a hitters' league, despite his lack of an overpowering fastball. He places his low-90's heater and darting curve on the edges of the strike zone at will, and pitched exceedingly well under Olympic pressure. He should reach the majors sometime in 2001.

Pirates' 1999 first round pick Bobby Bradley, 19, ranked #5 on this year's list. Limited to 83 innings by minor injuries at Low-A Hickory, Bradley posted a scary 118/21 strikeout/walk ratio with only 62 hits allowed. The 6'1", 170, righty is often compared to Greg Maddux. He can place his 90 MPH fastball anywhere he desires, and his curveball is his answer to Maddux' changeup. It's a true A-level major league out pitch. Bradley should race through the minors quickly and arrive in Pittsburgh sometime in 2002.

Along with Bradley, #6 finisher Chin-Hui Tsao, 18, dominated the Low-A South Atlantic League in 2000. The 6'1", 180, Taiwanese righthander throws a heavy mid-90's fastball, a sharp slider and a decent changeup, and posted an imposing 187/40 strikeout/walk ratio in 145 innings as his level's youngest starting pitcher. He could finally be the one to test the theory that a pure power pitcher should be able to succeed in the mile-high altitude of Coors Field, around Opening Day 2003.

Angels' righthander Francisco Rodriguez, 18, the #7 finisher, was quite overpowering as the youngest starter in the hitter-friendly High-A California League last season. The 6'0", 165, has a free, easy motion, a mid-90's heater and a sharp slider, and recorded an excellent 79/32 strikeout/walk ratio with only 43 hits allowed in 64 innings. If he can toss 180-plus innings of solid upper minor league ball in 2001, he could be ready for the majors in 2002. He's a likely future big league ace.

This year's #8 finisher is Olympic ace starter Jon Rauch, 21, *Baseball America's* Minor League Player of the Year. At 6'11", 230, Rauch relegates Anderson to second-tallest status among this year's Top Ten. Though his size is obviously an asset, Rauch is more than a raw, hard-throwing power-pitching prospect. He complements his low-90's fastball with a well above average curve and slider, and has finely tuned mechanics and command for his size. He posted a 63/16 strikeout/walk ratio with only 36 hits allowed in 56 Double-A innings after a midseason promotion, and then dominated to an even greater extent in the Olympics. He could crack the White Sox' rotation as early as the beginning of 2001, and should be a long-term top-of-the-rotation force.

The #9 finisher is Cards' lefthander Bud Smith. Smith, 20, is a 1998 fourth round draftee who has sliced through the minors, posting a 17-2 combined Double/Triple-A mark in 2001 and a 102/27 Double-A strikeout/walk ratio in 109 innings. He's by no means overpowering, but spots his upper-80's fastball, curve and changeup expertly, and consistently lasts deep into ballgames. The Cards are well-fortified in their starting rotation for now, but Smith will be ready the second a spot opens. He'll be a solid long-term complement to the mighty Rick Ankiel.

Rounding out this year's Top Ten is Indians' lefty C.C. Sabathia, 19, who was called back from the Olympic team after not being used as a starter as promised. He then sat a spell on the Indians' big league bench. The strapping 6'7", 235, southpaw was the Indians' 1998 first round pick, and dominated the High-A Carolina League in 2000, posting a 69/24 strikeout/walk ratio in 56 innings before a midseason promotion. Though he went just 3-7 after his promotion to Double-A, his strikeout/walk ratio held up well, speaking very well for his future. Sabathia's fastball reaches the mid-90's, excellent peak velocity for a lefty, and he also possesses a top-shelf curveball. He'll have a crack at the Indians' rotation in 2001, and should be a long-term major league ace alongside Bartolo Colon.

How did the 1999 group fare? Pretty well on balance, with standout successes and failures. #1 Rick Ankiel established himself as a long-term star with the Cardinals, and #10 Brad Penny appears to be a keeper for the Marlins. #4 Juan Pena of the Red Sox missed the entire 2000 season due to elbow surgery, and #5 Matt Riley will miss all of 2001 with the same, after being limited by physical and disciplinary problems throughout 2000. 1999 #7 Ryan Anderson (#1 in 2000) and #9 Nick Neugebauer of the Brewers (#17 in 2000) remain star prospects likely to be major league aces for their respective clubs. 1999 #6 Andy Pratt of the Rangers (#16 in 2000) and #8 Jason Jennings of the Rockies (#129 in 2000) have somewhat more limited upsides, but should both eventually be long-term fixtures in the middle of their respective clubs' rotations. #2 Dan Wheeler of the Devil Rays and #3 Scott Comer of the Marlins hit the Minor League Finesse Pitcher Wall in 2000. Wheeler posting a 5-11, 5.63, mark at Triple-A Durham with 183 hits allowed in 150 innings, while Comer did him one worse at Double-A Portland, going 4-10, 6.42, allowing an amazing 180 hits in 130 innings. Wheeler still has a shot to someday be a productive member of the Rays' rotation, but Comer's utter inability to retire upper minor league hitters in his first crack at them speaks poorly about his eventual upside.

Of the 1998 Top Ten, #1 Ankiel, #2 Penny, and #5 Bruce Chen appear on the verge of varying levels of major league stardom. #4 Luke Prokopec of the Dodgers (#12 in 2000) and #9 Dicky Gonzalez of the Mets (#23 in 2000) remain highly regarded prospects likely to make long-term big league impacts. #6 Josh Towers of the Orioles (#20 in 2000) remains highly rated, but likely lacks the power to be a top major league performer. He could get his chance to prove me wrong in Baltimore in 2001, however. #3 Riley's all-around travails have already been explained. If he can get his act together in 2002 after rehabbing from elbow surgery, he could still be heard from. #7 Pena of the Red Sox and #8 Odalis Perez of the Braves have both been injured for the better part of a season and a half , but they could still be major league factors. #10 Comer's future, chronicled a paragraph ago, is questionable at best.

The 1997 Top Ten is turning out to be a pretty special group. #1 Eric Milton, #2 Kerry Wood, #3 Carl Pavano, #5 Tony Armas, #6 Scott Elarton, #7 Brett Tomko and #9 Esteban Yan have all shone brightly at various times in their careers to date. A few of them are on their way to being among the best of their generation. #4 Ted Lilly of the Yankees (74th in 2000), and #10 Lorenzo Barcelo of the White Sox (#36 in 2000) remain highly rated, but need to make moves soon. #8 Jason Brester of the Phillies dropped off the 2000 list due to poor control at Double-A Reading, but might still evolve into at least a useful major league southpaw swingman.

The 1996 Top Ten is turning out pretty good after all. Though #1 Elvin Hernandez has been a washout, #2 Jeff D'Amico of the Brewers was a major 2000 success story, and #3 Jeff Suppan, #4 Sidney Ponson and #7 Wood are fixtures in the Royals', Orioles' and Cubs' rotations, respectively. #8 John Snyder has struggled recently with the Brewers, and #10 Mark Brownson of the Phillies is now a fringe Triple-A prospect.

The 1995 Top Ten is quite solid. Again, the #1 finisher, the Phils' Rich Hunter, is long gone, but #3 Bartolo Colon and rehabbing #8 Billy Wagner are established big league stars, and #5 Suppan is a steady major league producer. #2 Paul Wilson (Devil Rays), #4 Rocky Coppinger (Brewers), #6 Damian Moss (Braves), #7 Bryan Rekar (Devil Rays), #9 Alan Benes (Cardinals) and #10 Amaury Telemaco (Phillies) have all shown flashes of excellence, but have been hampered by a combination of injuries, ineffectiveness and lack of opportunity at the major league level. Expect at least one or two from that group to rise up and experience big league success within the next season or two; all but Coppinger are currently healthy.

Of the 1994 Top Ten, the first such list, #1 Ismael Valdes, #4 Jimmy Haynes and #5 Suppan are entrenched major leaguers, and #10 Tony Saunders' career was tragically shortened by frightening arm injuries. #6 Ramon Morel, #7 Brian Barber, #8 Jim Pittsley, and #9 Mike Bovee all pitched in the majors. #2 Johnny Pantoja was found to be lying about his age, by 10 years, and #3 Hugo Pivaral of the Dodgers was stonewalled by injuries.

Several pitchers made the Top 50 in both 1999 and 2000, led by 2000 #1 finisher Ryan Anderson and #9 finisher Bud Smith (#18 in 1999).

Orioles' High-A righthander John Stephens, 20, ranked 12th in 1999 and 13th in 2000. Though his fastball only reaches the mid-to-upper-80's, he has excellent control and an above average curve and changeup. Watch his 2001 Double-A numbers carefully. His allowance of a hit per inning in the Carolina League last season raises a small red flag about his future.

Cubs' High-A righty Ruben Quevedo, 21, ranked 14th in both 1999 and 2000 after ranking 41st in 1998. He received an extended major league trial last season, and annoyed Cubs' brass with his ordinary conditioning and a lack of aggressiveness on the mound. He's still a kid, however, and possesses the stuff and command to get over the hump and then some if given the chance. Striking out more than a batter per inning (77 in 75 innings) as a 21-year-old Triple-A starter usually isn't a mirage.

Rangers' High-A finesse lefty Andy Pratt, 20, ranked 6th in 1999 and 16th in 2000. The 1998 ninth round draftee stands only 5'11", 160, and doesn't throw very hard, but he makes his fastball appear harder by setting it up with quality breaking stuff. After dominating both Class A levels in 1999 and 2000, he failed miserably in his first Double-A audition late last season, going 1-6, 7.22, with 99 baserunners allowed, including 33 walks, in only 52 innings. Look for Pratt to bounce back at that level in 2001, but he'll need to be consistently precise to become a solid mid-rotation big league starter.

Brewers' Double-A righty Nick Neugebauer, 19, ranked 9th in 1999 and 17th in 2000. This big-time power pitching prospect posted an almost unbelievable 174/134 strikeout/walk ratio in 128 minor league innings at two levels last season, allowing only 78 hits. The 6'3", 225, righty throws a high-90's heater and a killer slider, and could be a dominant major leaguer with improved command and mechanics. He's no more than a year away.

Mets' righthander Dicky Gonzalez, 21, ranked 35th in 1999 and 23rd in 2000. You could call the 5'11", 170, Gonzalez the anti-Neugebauer; a true finesse hurler who overcomes middling raw stuff with impeccable command and mechanics. He passed the key Double-A test for finesse pitchers, posting a 138/36 strikeout/walk ratio in 148 innings, allowing only 130 hits despite possessing only slightly above average peak velocity on his fastball.

Red Sox' righthander Sun-Woo Kim, 22, ranked 39th in 1999 and 27th in 2000. OK, so he only went 11-7, 6.03, with 170 hits allowed in 134 Triple-A innings last season, posting a fine 116/42 strikeout/walk ratio. The 6'2", 180, righty simply hasn't developed the requisite breaking ball arsenal to go with his mid-90's heater. He's a feisty type whose stuff and demeanor might be best suited for a short relief role. Look for him to step forward in 2001, possibly at the major league level.

Padres' righthander Buddy Carlyle, 22, ranked 23rd in 1999 and 35th in 2000. The 6'3", 175, finesse hurler has long been overlooked in favor of power pitchers like Matt Clement and Adam Eaton in the Padres' system, and is now held in lower regard by most observers compared to the likes of Mike Bynum, Wascar Serrano and Junior Herndon. Though Carlyle possesses only an average major league fastball, he has a diverse array of breaking stuff, exceptional command, and varies speed and location well. A 127/44 strikeout/walk ratio and a 4.29 ERA in 151 innings as one of the youngest starters in the hitter-friendly Triple-A Pacific Coast League is nothing to be sneezed at. Carlyle is a sleeper looking to make a splash in San Diego in 2001.

Orioles' lefty Matt Riley, 20, ranked 5th in 1999 and 43rd in 2000, and as mentioned earlier, will miss all of 2001 due to elbow ligament transplant surgery. Like Kerry Wood, who underwent that same surgery, Riley featured a mid-90's heater and a killer curve before surgery. Like Wood, expect Riley to return with only the heater totally intact. Even before the injury, Riley's stock was dropping due to immature behavior in major league camp during 2000 spring training. Let's hope Riley returns with a better head, even if it's with less of an arm. A player with his immense talent can never be totally discounted.

Rockies' lefthander Randey Dorame, 21, acquired from the Dodgers in the Tom Goodwin deal, ranked 25th in 1999 and 45th in 2000. The 6'2", 205, southpaw posted a solid 49/13 strikeout/walk ratio over 57 innings in nine early-season High-A starts before posting much less

imposing strikeout numbers after a promotion to Double-A. His fastball only reaches the mid-to-upper-80's, and he requires precise command of his curve and changeup early in the count to be effective. Watch his Double-A strikeout rate early in 2000. It will need to improve greatly for him to have a chance for high-altitude success at the Triple-A and major league levels.

Many other pitchers ranked in the Top 100 in both 1999 and 2000. Those whose ranks improved in 2000 include the Dodgers' Luke Prokopec (57th in 1999, 12th in 2000), Astros' Mike Nannini (77th, 19th), Dodgers' Eric Gagne (65th, 29th), Rangers' Joaquin Benoit (64th, 29th), Mets' Pat Strange (72nd, 32nd), Mariners' Joel Pineiro (71st, 34th), Cubs' Joey Nation (96th, 35th), Padres' Adam Eaton (59th, 38th), Red Sox' Justin Duchscherer (70th, 58th), Rockies' Mark DiFelice (67th, 64th), Astros' Tim Redding (90th, 65th), Orioles' Jacobo Sequea (73rd, 72nd), Royals' Chad Durbin (88th, 78th), and Cardinals' Chad Hutchinson (95th, 91st). Gagne, Benoit and Sequea have all moved higher within the Top 100 in three consecutive seasons, and Prokopec, Nation and Durbin also each logged their third consecutive Top 100 season. Others whose ranks declined within the Top 100 in 2000 include the A's Barry Zito (21st in 1999, 61st in 2000), Royals' Chris George (31st, 69th), Angels' Seth Etherton (40th, 73rd), Yankees' Ted Lilly (69th, 74th), White Sox' Mark Buehrle (15th, 83rd), Devil Rays' Jesus Colome (47th, 85th), Padres' Brian Lawrence (52nd, 96th), Twins' Joe Foote (94th, 97th) and Giants' Ryan Vogelsong (44th, 98th). Lilly and Lawrence have ranked in the Top 100 in each of the last three seasons.

Several pitchers made positive first impressions in their first full pro season in 2000. Obviously, Top Tenners Johnson, Bradley, Tsao, Rodriguez, Rauch and Sabathia are prime examples. Beyond the Top Ten, pitchers such as the Padres' Jacob Peavy (11th), Braves' Matt Belisle (15th), Giants' Jerome Williams (18th), Padres' Dennis Tankersley (21st), Yankees' Ricardo Aramboles (22nd), Marlins' Josh Beckett (24th), Rangers' Colby Lewis (26th), Angels' John Lackey (28th), Brewers' Jose Mieses (39th), Cubs' Ben Christensen (40th), Braves' John Ennis (47th), Mariners' Craig Anderson (49th) and Royals' Jimmy Gobble (50th) led a group of strong hurlers making full-season league debuts. This list has always been a fertile source of future Top Ten hurlers, and appears to be stronger than ever in 2000.

Pitchers whose stock dropped in 2000 but could still be heard from include the Astros' Wilfredo Rodriguez (46th in 1999, 104th in 2000), Orioles' Lesli Brea (33rd, 114th), Rockies' Jason Jennings (8th, 129th), Devil Rays' Dan Wheeler (2nd, 136th), Cubs' Mike Meyers (38th, 148th), Devil Rays' Cedrick Bowers (36th, 161st), Red Sox' Tomokazu Ohka (16th, 175th), Royals' Junior Guerrero (11th, 185th), Expos' T.J. Tucker (61st, 201st) and Rangers' Alan Webb (89th, 211th). Players listed in this group last season included the Marlins' A.J. Burnett, Expos' Tony Armas, Braves' Jason Marquis, and the Red Sox' Paxton Crawford, who either emerged as promising big leaguers or re-established themselves as top prospects in 2000.

RELATIVE ORGANIZATIONAL STRENGTH

Relative Control/Power Potential can also be used to compare the relative strength of starting pitching within minor league organizations. A cumulative organizational RCPP factor is calculated by assigning the number one prospect with a point value of 211, and reducing each successive prospect's value by one.

The Padres, led by eight Top 100 pitching prospects: Jacob Peavy, Dennis Tankersley, Buddy Carlyle, Adam Eaton, Wascar Serrano, Ben Howard, Gerik Baxter and Brian Lawrence; led the way with 1,718 points after finishing a lowly 17th in 1999.

The Orioles crept up from 3rd in 1999 to 2nd in 2000, with 1,438 points. They had three of the top 43 pitching prospects in John Stephens, Josh Towers and Matt Riley.

The Rockies jumped from 18th in 1999 to 3rd in 2000 with 1,132 points, led by #6 Chin-Hui Tsao and #45 Randey Dorame.

The Cubs fell from 2nd in 1999 to 4th in 2000 with 1,066 points. They had five of the top 54 prospects in #14 Ruben Quevedo, #35 Joey Nation, #40 Ben Christensen, #52 Carlos Zambrano and #54 Juan Cruz.

The Red Sox, who finished first in 1999 and second in 1998, rounded out the 2000 top five with 1,051 points, a point ahead of the #6 Twins and two points ahead of the #7 Mariners. The Sox were led by #2 Paxton Crawford and #27 Sun-Woo Kim.

The Twins (24th in 1999, 6th in 2000), Devil Rays (20th, 9th), Brewers (21st, 11th), Yankees (22nd, 12th) and Indians (27th, 15th) also made strong upward moves.

The Bottom Five were the Diamondbacks (191 points: a three-year major league low), Expos (205), Reds (260), Blue Jays (273) and Cardinals (344). Major downward movers besides the Diamondbacks (14th in 1999) and Expos (19th) include the Giants (15th in 1999, 25th in 2000), Dodgers (5th, 24th), Marlins (9th, 20th), Mets (8th, 19th) and Royals (4th, 17th).

SUMMARY

Relative Control/Power Potential is a performance evaluation system for minor league starting pitchers. The statistic measures pitchers' precision and dominance relative to their peers by measuring their comparative strikeout/walk and strikeout/9 innings ratios, then adjusting for relative age. This method gives an unbiased view of pitchers' long-term major league potential. The concept of relativity allows pitchers to be evaluated not only within the context of their respective leagues, but also to pitchers of all ages at all levels. Injury and other factors can easily detour top minor league pitching prospects on the road to the majors. This method, however, does a solid job of defining the population from which the next generation of star major league pitchers will come.

RELATIVE CONTROL/POWER POTENTIAL
2000

2000 Rank	1999 Rank	1998 Rank		AGE	TEAM	ORG	LEVEL	C FACT	P FACT	CP FACT	AGE ADJ.	ADJ. RCPP	PTS
1	7	11	Ryan Anderson	20	TAC	SEA	AAA	0.88	4.07	4.95	2.00	6.95	211
2	166	74	Paxton Crawford	22	TRN	BOS	AA	5.28	2.09	7.37	-1.00	6.37	210
3			Adam Johnson	20	FTM	MIN	HI-A	2.70	3.62	6.32	0.00	6.32	209
4	176		Roy Oswalt	22	RR	HOU	AA	4.19	2.23	6.41	-1.00	5.41	208
5			Bobby Bradley	19	HCK	PIT	LO-A	2.56	2.84	5.40	0.00	5.40	207
6			Chin-Hui Tsao	18	ASH	COL	LO-A	1.76	2.18	3.94	1.00	4.94	206
7			Franc Rodriguez	18	LE	ANA	HI-A	0.58	1.77	2.36	2.00	4.36	205
8			Jon Rauch	21	BRM	CWS	AA	1.93	2.32	4.25	0.00	4.25	204
9	18		Bud Smith	20	ARK	STL	AA	1.62	1.21	2.82	1.00	3.82	203
10			C.C. Sabathia	19	KIN	CLE	HI-A	0.28	2.43	2.71	1.00	3.71	202
11			Jacob Peavy	19	FTW	SD	LO-A	1.00	2.66	3.67	0.00	3.67	201
12	57	4	Luke Prokopec	22	SANT	LA	AA	3.19	1.38	4.57	-1.00	3.57	200
13	12		John Stephens	20	FRD	BAL	HI-A	2.35	1.17	3.52	0.00	3.52	199
14	14	41	Ruben Quevedo	21	IOW	CUB	AAA	0.65	1.86	2.51	1.00	3.51	198
15			Matt Belisle	20	MYR	ATL	HI-A	3.11	0.39	3.50	0.00	3.50	197
16	6		Andy Pratt	20	CHR	TEX	HI-A	1.61	1.68	3.29	0.00	3.29	196
17	9		Nick Neugebauer	19	HNT	MIL	AA	-1.20	2.27	1.07	2.00	3.07	195
18			Jerome Williams	18	SJ	SF	HI-A	0.48	0.33	0.81	2.00	2.81	194
19	77		Mike Nannini	19	KIS	HOU	HI-A	2.01	-0.22	1.79	1.00	2.79	193
20	101	6	Josh Towers	23	ROC	BAL	AAA	3.62	0.12	3.74	-1.00	2.74	192
21			Dennis Tankersley	21	FTW	SD	LO-A	1.48	3.26	4.74	-2.00	2.74	191
22			Ricardo Aramboles	18	GRN	NYY	LO-A	0.50	1.17	1.67	1.00	2.67	190
23	35	9	Dicky Gonzalez	21	BNG	NYM	AA	1.25	1.41	2.66	0.00	2.66	189
24			Josh Beckett	20	KNC	FLA	LO-A	2.20	1.46	3.66	-1.00	2.66	188
25	65	79	Eric Gagne	24	ABQ	LA	AAA	2.63	2.02	4.65	-2.00	2.65	187
26			Colby Lewis	20	CHR	TEX	HI-A	1.32	1.12	2.44	0.00	2.44	186
27	39	33	Sun-Woo Kim	22	PAW	BOS	AAA	0.96	1.46	2.42	0.00	2.42	185
28			John Lackey	21	ERIE	ANA	AA	1.99	0.27	2.26	0.00	2.26	184
29	64	75	Joaquin Benoit	20	TUL	TEX	AA	0.27	0.81	1.08	1.00	2.08	183
30	23	84	Buddy Carlyle	22	LV	SD	AAA	1.20	0.77	1.98	0.00	1.98	182
31	179		Chris Cervantes	21	SBN	AZ	LO-A	3.24	0.71	3.95	-2.00	1.95	181
32	72		Pat Strange	19	STLC	NYM	HI-A	0.18	0.76	0.94	1.00	1.94	180
33	108		Josue Matos	22	LNC	SEA	HI-A	2.93	0.92	3.85	-2.00	1.85	179
34	71	30	Joel Pineiro	21	NH	SEA	AA	1.06	0.73	1.79	0.00	1.79	178
35	96	53	Joey Nation	21	WTN	CUB	AA	0.33	1.43	1.76	0.00	1.76	177
36			Lorenzo Barcelo	22	CHR	CWS	AAA	2.08	-0.35	1.73	0.00	1.73	176
37	216	120	Mike Bacsik	22	KIN	CLE	HI-A	3.54	0.16	3.70	-2.00	1.70	175
38	59	174	Adam Eaton	22	MOB	SD	AA	1.11	1.59	2.70	-1.00	1.70	174
39			Joses Mieses	20	BLT	MIL	LO-A	1.59	1.10	2.69	-1.00	1.69	173
40			Ben Christensen	22	DAY	CUB	HI-A	2.24	1.44	3.68	-2.00	1.68	172
41	172		Claudio Vargas	21	BRV	FLA	HI-A	1.15	1.46	2.60	-1.00	1.60	171
42			Matt Kinney	23	SLK	MIN	AAA	0.36	2.13	2.49	-1.00	1.49	170
43	5	3	Matt Riley	20	BOW	BAL	AA	-0.68	1.15	0.47	1.00	1.47	169
44	119	160	Jon Garland	20	CHR	CWS	AAA	-0.05	-0.51	-0.56	2.00	1.44	168
45	25		Randey Dorame	21	VB	COL	HI-A	1.74	0.67	2.41	-1.00	1.41	167
46	169		Dave Williams	21	HCK	PIT	LO-A	1.99	1.41	3.41	-2.00	1.41	166
47			John Ennis	20	MAC	ATL	LO-A	1.36	1.04	2.40	-1.00	1.40	165
48	170	185	Shane Loux	20	JCK	DET	AA	0.12	0.27	0.39	1.00	1.39	164

2000 Rank	1999 Rank	1998 Rank		AGE	TEAM	ORG	LEVEL	C FACT	P FACT	CP FACT	AGE ADJ.	ADJ. RCPP	PTS
49			Craig Anderson	19	WSC	SEA	LO-A	1.23	0.16	1.39	0.00	1.39	163
50			Jimmy Gobble	18	CHWV	KC	LO-A	0.66	-0.29	0.37	1.00	1.37	162
51	159		James Johnson	23	HNT	MIL	AA	1.27	2.07	3.34	-2.00	1.34	161
52	175		Carlos Zambrano	19	WTN	CUB	AA	-0.24	-0.45	-0.69	2.00	1.31	160
53			Neal Frendling	20	CHSC	TB	LO-A	1.00	1.28	2.28	-1.00	1.28	159
54			Juan Cruz	19	LNS	CUB	LO-A	-0.63	1.90	1.27	0.00	1.27	158
55			Casey Fossum	22	SAR	BOS	HI-A	1.98	1.29	3.27	-2.00	1.27	157
56			Geoff Geary	23	REA	PHL	AA	2.23	1.00	3.23	-2.00	1.23	156
57			Ben Sheets	21	IND	MIL	AAA	-0.13	0.35	0.22	1.00	1.22	155
58	70		Justin Duchscherer	22	TRN	BOS	AA	1.07	1.08	2.15	-1.00	1.15	154
59	194		Donnie Bridges	21	JUP	MON	HI-A	1.20	0.94	2.15	-1.00	1.15	153
60			Julio DePaula	20	ASH	COL	LO-A	0.35	1.77	2.12	-1.00	1.12	152
61	21		Barry Zito	22	SAC	OAK	AAA	0.02	1.07	1.09	0.00	1.09	151
62			Dave Walling	21	NRW	NYY	AA	0.36	0.71	1.08	0.00	1.08	150
63	131	78	Corey Thurman	21	WCH	KC	AA	-0.16	1.24	1.08	0.00	1.08	149
64	67		Mark DiFelice	23	CAR	COL	AA	3.33	-0.31	3.02	-2.00	1.02	148
65	90		Tim Redding	22	KIS	HOU	HI-A	0.84	2.14	2.98	-2.00	0.98	147
66	126		Juan Rincon	21	NB	MIN	AA	-0.16	1.12	0.97	0.00	0.97	146
67	106	138	Wascar Serrano	22	MOB	SD	AA	0.47	1.47	1.94	-1.00	0.94	145
68			Joe Kennedy	21	CHSC	TB	LO-A	1.95	0.96	2.91	-2.00	0.91	144
69	31		Chris George	20	WCH	KC	AA	-0.54	0.45	-0.09	1.00	0.91	143
70			Jovanny Cedeno	20	SAV	TEX	LO-A	0.24	1.62	1.86	-1.00	0.86	142
71	180		Juan Pena	21	MOD	OAK	HI-A	0.44	1.39	1.83	-1.00	0.83	141
72	73	88	Jacobo Sequea	18	FRD	BAL	HI-A	-0.71	-0.47	-1.18	2.00	0.82	140
73	40		Seth Etherton	23	EDM	ANA	AAA	0.85	0.90	1.75	-1.00	0.75	139
74	69	64	Ted Lilly	24	CLM	NYY	AAA	0.81	1.93	2.74	-2.00	0.74	138
75			David Moraga	24	CAR	COL	AA	2.94	0.78	3.72	-3.00	0.72	137
76			Matt Ford	19	HAG	TOR	LO-A	-0.18	0.86	0.68	0.00	0.68	136
77	213	72	John Parrish	22	ROC	BAL	AAA	-0.58	1.24	0.66	0.00	0.66	135
78	88	51	Chad Durbin	22	OMA	KC	AAA	0.55	0.10	0.65	0.00	0.65	134
79			Ben Howard	21	RC	SD	HI-A	-0.91	2.53	1.62	-1.00	0.62	133
80			Erik Bedard	21	DLM	BAL	LO-A	0.97	1.64	2.61	-2.00	0.61	132
81			Wilfredo Ledezma	19	AUG	BOS	LO-A	-0.80	1.40	0.60	0.00	0.60	131
82	152		Jason Stumm	19	BUR	CWS	LO-A	-0.26	0.86	0.60	0.00	0.60	130
83	15		Mark Buehrle	21	BRM	CWS	AA	2.00	-1.43	0.57	0.00	0.57	129
84	114		Adam Pettyjohn	23	JCK	DET	AA	1.71	0.79	2.51	-2.00	0.51	128
85	47		Jesus Colome	21	MID	TB	AA	-0.22	0.71	0.50	0.00	0.50	127
86			Gerik Baxter	20	FTW	SD	LO-A	0.08	1.37	1.45	-1.00	0.45	126
87			Eric Thompson	22	MID	OAK	AA	1.28	0.16	1.44	-1.00	0.44	125
88	225	131	Horacio Ramirez	20	MYR	ATL	HI-A	0.36	0.06	0.42	0.00	0.42	124
89			Enger Veras	19	CHSC	TB	LO-A	-0.10	0.51	0.41	0.00	0.41	123
90	177	118	Travis Phelps	22	ORL	TB	AA	0.06	1.35	1.40	-1.00	0.40	122
91	95		Chad Hutchinson	23	ARK	STL	AA	-0.12	2.50	2.38	-2.00	0.38	121
92			Kurt Ainsworth	21	SHR	SF	AA	-0.06	0.43	0.38	0.00	0.38	120
93			Ryan Madson	19	PDT	PHL	LO-A	0.11	0.26	0.37	0.00	0.37	119
94			Brad Salmon	20	CLN	CIN	LO-A	0.38	0.99	1.37	-1.00	0.37	118
95			Andy Van Hekken	20	WM	DET	LO-A	1.39	-0.04	1.35	-1.00	0.35	117
96	52	34	Brian Lawrence	24	MOB	SD	AA	2.29	1.04	3.33	-3.00	0.33	116
97	94		Joe Foote	20	QC	MIN	LO-A	0.86	0.46	1.32	-1.00	0.32	115
98	44		Ryan Vogelsong	22	SHR	SF	AA	0.01	1.29	1.30	-1.00	0.30	114
99	148		Justin Miller	22	SAC	OAK	AAA	0.83	-0.53	0.30	0.00	0.30	113
100	144		Zach Day	22	AKR	CLE	AA	-0.14	1.43	1.29	-1.00	0.29	112
101			Blair DeHart	22	FTW	SD	LO-A	2.82	0.46	3.29	-3.00	0.29	111
102			Brand. Duckworth	24	REA	PHL	AA	0.93	2.35	3.28	-3.00	0.28	110

2000 Rank	1999 Rank	1998 Rank		AGE	TEAM	ORG	LEVEL	C FACT	P FACT	CP FACT	AGE ADJ.	ADJ. RCPP	PTS
103	166		Brad Thomas	22	FTM	MIN	HI-A	1.50	0.77	2.28	-2.00	0.28	109
104	46	46	Wilfredo Rodriguez	21	RR	HOU	AA	-1.04	1.29	0.25	0.00	0.25	108
105	141	62	Grant Roberts	22	NRF	NYM	AAA	-0.23	0.45	0.22	0.00	0.22	107
106	85	142	Kyle Lohse	21	NB	MIN	AA	0.02	0.19	0.22	0.00	0.22	106
107			Enmanuel Ulloa	21	LNC	SEA	HI-A	0.81	0.40	1.21	-1.00	0.21	105
108			Ryan Baerlocher	22	CHWV	KC	LO-A	1.37	1.83	3.20	-3.00	0.20	104
109			Jeff Heaverlo	22	LNC	SEA	HI-A	1.37	0.81	2.17	-2.00	0.17	103
110	108		Shawn Chacon	22	CAR	COL	AA	-0.27	1.39	1.13	-1.00	0.13	102
111			Roger Luque	20	FTW	SD	LO-A	0.64	0.45	1.10	-1.00	0.10	101
112	81		Greg Miller	20	KIS	HOU	HI-A	0.13	-0.04	0.09	0.00	0.09	100
113			Brian Wolfe	19	QC	MIN	LO-A	0.49	-0.40	0.09	0.00	0.09	99
114	33		Lesli Brea	21	BOW	BAL	AA	-0.74	0.82	0.07	0.00	0.07	98
115	82		Sean Douglass	21	BOW	BAL	AA	-0.06	0.13	0.07	0.00	0.07	97
116	139		Grant Balfour	22	FTM	MIN	HI-A	0.45	1.61	2.06	-2.00	0.06	96
117			Brad Baker	19	AUG	BOS	LO-A	-0.27	0.31	0.04	0.00	0.04	95
118	107	93	Aaron Myette	22	CHR	CWS	AAA	-0.62	0.65	0.03	0.00	0.03	94
119			Aaron Cook	21	ASH	COL	LO-A	2.15	-0.13	2.01	-2.00	0.01	93
120			Gary Majewski	20	BUR	CWS	LO-A	-0.32	1.34	1.01	-1.00	0.01	92
121			Jeremy Blevins	22	TAM	NYY	HI-A	-0.15	2.13	1.98	-2.00	-0.02	91
122	66	21	Allen Levrault	22	IND	MIL	AAA	-0.40	0.37	-0.02	0.00	-0.02	90
123	127		Steve Bechler	20	FRD	BAL	HI-A	-0.09	0.07	-0.03	0.00	-0.03	89
124			Brandon Claussen	21	TAM	NYY	HI-A	0.38	0.58	0.97	-1.00	-0.03	88
125			Danys Baez	22	KIN	CLE	HI-A	0.22	1.75	1.97	-2.00	-0.03	87
126			Carlos Hernandez	20	MCH	HOU	LO-A	-0.56	1.47	0.92	-1.00	-0.08	86
127	203		Brett Jodie	23	TAM	NYY	HI-A	2.25	0.59	2.83	-3.00	-0.17	85
128	51	137	John Grabow	21	ALT	PIT	AA	-0.43	0.25	-0.17	0.00	-0.17	84
129	8		Jason Jennings	21	SLM	COL	HI-A	0.51	0.32	0.83	-1.00	-0.17	83
130	92		Anastacio Martinez	19	AUG	BOS	LO-A	-0.39	0.20	-0.19	0.00	-0.19	82
131	198		Nate Cornejo	20	LAK	DET	HI-A	-0.37	0.16	-0.20	0.00	-0.20	81
132	212	111	Paul Stewart	21	MUD	MIL	HI-A	-0.09	0.87	0.79	-1.00	-0.21	80
133			Steve Watkins	21	RC	SD	HI-A	-0.29	1.08	0.78	-1.00	-0.22	79
134	202	107	Tim Drew	21	BUF	CLE	AAA	-0.38	-0.87	-1.25	1.00	-0.25	78
135	163		Vladimir Nunez	25	CLG	FLA	AAA	0.67	2.03	2.70	-3.00	-0.30	77
136	2	127	Dan Wheeler	22	DUR	TB	AAA	0.20	-0.50	-0.30	0.00	-0.30	76
137			Randy Perez	20	DLM	BAL	LO-A	0.95	-0.26	0.69	-1.00	-0.31	75
138	224	197	Jake Westbrook	22	CLM	NYY	AAA	-0.51	0.09	-0.42	0.00	-0.42	74
139	80	129	Matt White	21	ORL	TB	AA	-0.65	0.23	-0.42	0.00	-0.42	73
140			Richard Stahl	19	DLM	BAL	LO-A	-0.83	0.40	-0.43	0.00	-0.43	72
141			Steve Green	22	ERIE	ANA	AA	-0.22	0.79	0.57	-1.00	-0.43	71
142	110	104	Wade Miller	23	NO	HOU	AAA	0.17	0.37	0.54	-1.00	-0.46	70
143			Rodrigo Lopez	24	LV	SD	AAA	0.29	1.22	1.51	-2.00	-0.49	69
144			Christian Parra	22	MYR	ATL	HI-A	0.31	1.20	1.51	-2.00	-0.49	68
145			Delvis Pacheco	22	GRN	ATL	AA	-0.04	0.55	0.51	-1.00	-0.49	67
146			Mike Bynum	22	RC	SD	HI-A	0.66	0.83	1.49	-2.00	-0.51	66
147	186	59	Willie Martinez	22	BUF	CLE	AAA	-0.75	0.23	-0.52	0.00	-0.52	65
148	38	96	Mike Meyers	22	IOW	CUB	AAA	-0.74	0.22	-0.52	0.00	-0.52	64
149			Ken Chenard	21	CAP	NYM	LO-A	-0.23	1.70	1.47	-2.00	-0.53	63
150			Scott Martin	22	SBR	LA	HI-A	1.58	-0.13	1.44	-2.00	-0.56	62
151	140		Mike Wuertz	21	DAY	CUB	HI-A	-0.04	0.48	0.44	-1.00	-0.56	61
152	154	17	Jason Marquis	21	GRN	ATL	AA	-0.14	-0.42	-0.57	0.00	-0.57	60
153			Jim Magrane	21	CHSC	TB	LO-A	0.99	0.42	1.41	-2.00	-0.59	59
154			Javier Calzada	21	VIS	OAK	HI-A	0.37	0.03	0.40	-1.00	-0.60	58
155	181	92	Brian Reith	22	TAM	CIN	HI-A	0.89	0.50	1.39	-2.00	-0.61	57
156			Cha Baek	20	WSC	SEA	LO-A	0.58	-0.19	0.39	-1.00	-0.61	56
157			Martire Franco	18	PDT	PHL	LO-A	-0.89	-0.72	-1.61	1.00	-0.61	55

2000 Rank	1999 Rank	1998 Rank		AGE	TEAM	ORG	LEVEL	C FACT	P FACT	CP FACT	AGE ADJ.	ADJ. RCPP	PTS
158	162	51	Brian Fuentes	24	NH	SEA	AA	-0.04	2.39	2.35	-3.00	-0.65	54
159			Scott Chiasson	22	VIS	OAK	HI-A	0.80	0.55	1.35	-2.00	-0.65	53
160			Ben Kozlowski	19	MAC	ATL	LO-A	-0.75	0.09	-0.66	0.00	-0.66	52
161	36	44	Cedrick Bowers	22	ORL	TB	AA	-0.19	0.52	0.33	-1.00	-0.67	51
162			Wilson Guzman	22	LYN	PIT	HI-A	0.42	0.91	1.33	-2.00	-0.67	50
163	54		Scot Shields	24	EDM	ANA	AAA	-0.14	1.45	1.31	-2.00	-0.69	49
164	199	68	Matt Wise	24	EDM	ANA	AAA	1.57	-0.28	1.29	-2.00	-0.71	48
165			Brett Myers	19	PDT	PHL	LO-A	-0.49	-0.26	-0.75	0.00	-0.75	47
166			Aaron Harang	22	CHR	TEX	HI-A	0.54	0.71	1.24	-2.00	-0.76	46
167			Carlos Ortega	21	VB	LA	HI-A	-0.49	0.72	0.23	-1.00	-0.77	45
168			Pasqual Coco	22	TEN	TOR	AA	-0.19	0.42	0.23	-1.00	-0.77	44
169	91		Jung Bong	19	MAC	ATL	LO-A	-0.51	-0.27	-0.79	0.00	-0.79	43
170			Lindsay Gulin	23	WTN	CUB	AA	-0.52	1.73	1.21	-2.00	-0.79	42
171	128		Jorge Julio	21	JUP	MON	HI-A	-0.39	0.59	0.20	-1.00	-0.80	41
172	28		Juan Figueroa	21	BRM	BAL	AA	-0.58	-0.22	-0.80	0.00	-0.80	40
173	49		Wes Anderson	20	BRV	FLA	HI-A	-1.01	0.20	-0.81	0.00	-0.81	39
174	75	143	Gary Glover	23	SYR	TOR	AAA	-0.11	0.30	0.19	-1.00	-0.81	38
175	16		Tomokazu Ohka	24	PAW	BOS	AAA	1.76	-0.59	1.17	-2.00	-0.83	37
176			Nick Maness	21	STLC	NYM	HI-A	-0.49	0.64	0.14	-1.00	-0.86	36
177			Ty Howington	19	DAY	CIN	LO-A	-1.10	0.22	-0.88	0.00	-0.88	35
178	218	152	Rick Palma	20	DAY	CUB	HI-A	-0.71	-0.20	-0.91	0.00	-0.91	34
179			Ryan Moskau	22	BRV	FLA	HI-A	0.70	0.36	1.07	-2.00	-0.93	33
180			Justin Lehr	22	MOD	OAK	HI-A	1.29	-0.23	1.06	-2.00	-0.94	32
181			Jorge Cordova	22	CLN	CIN	LO-A	0.81	1.24	2.06	-3.00	-0.94	31
182			Mario Ramos	22	MOD	OAK	HI-A	0.86	0.19	1.05	-2.00	-0.95	30
183			Ryan Cameron	22	SLM	COL	HI-A	-0.29	1.32	1.03	-2.00	-0.97	29
184	206		Kevin Olsen	23	PRT	FLA	AA	0.01	1.01	1.02	-2.00	-0.98	28
185	11		Junior Guerrero	20	WCH	KC	AA	-0.95	-1.07	-2.02	1.00	-1.02	27
186			Andy Cavazos	19	SAV	TEX	LO-A	-1.12	0.07	-1.04	0.00	-1.04	26
187	214		Brad Baisley	20	CLW	PHL	HI-A	-0.56	-0.49	-1.05	0.00	-1.05	25
188	171	97	Junior Herndon	21	LV	SD	AAA	-1.17	-0.90	-2.07	1.00	-1.07	24
189			Dennis Ulacia	19	BUR	CWS	LO-A	-0.76	-0.34	-1.10	0.00	-1.10	23
190			Gustavo Chacin	19	DUN	TOR	HI-A	-1.21	-0.94	-2.15	1.00	-1.15	22
191			Dan Curtis	20	MYR	ATL	HI-A	-0.20	-0.95	-1.15	0.00	-1.15	21
192			Cristobal Correa	20	PTM	STL	HI-A	-0.77	-0.46	-1.23	0.00	-1.23	20
193	29		John Curtice	20	SAR	CIN	HI-A	-1.19	-0.07	-1.26	0.00	-1.26	19
194			Franklyn German	20	MOD	OAK	HI-A	-0.84	-0.53	-1.37	0.00	-1.37	18
195			Edwin Moreno	19	SAV	TEX	LO-A	-0.57	-0.91	-1.48	0.00	-1.48	17
196	204	38	Clayton Andrews	22	SYR	TOR	AAA	-0.77	-0.76	-1.52	0.00	-1.52	16
197			Ryan Kibler	19	ASH	COL	LO-A	-0.82	-0.71	-1.52	0.00	-1.52	15
198			Fernando Rodney	19	WM	DET	LO-A	-0.83	-0.81	-1.65	0.00	-1.65	14
199			Marcos Sandoval	19	HAG	TOR	LO-A	-0.48	-1.21	-1.68	0.00	-1.68	13
200	222		Eric Fischer	20	WS	CWS	HI-A	-0.92	-0.83	-1.75	0.00	-1.75	12
201	61		T.J. Tucker	21	HAR	MON	AA	-0.63	-1.14	-1.78	0.00	-1.78	11
202			Phil Wilson	19	CR	ANA	LO-A	-0.74	-1.06	-1.81	0.00	-1.81	10
203			Franklin Perez	19	PDT	PHL	LO-A	-0.82	-0.99	-1.81	0.00	-1.81	9
204	226		Hatuey Mendoza	20	HD	AZ	HI-A	-1.25	-0.59	-1.85	0.00	-1.85	8
205			Adam Barr	19	CLM	CLE	LO-A	-1.49	-0.78	-2.27	0.00	-2.27	7
206			Randy Galvez	21	SANT	LA	AA	-0.93	-1.39	-2.33	0.00	-2.33	6
207			Brian West	19	BUR	CWS	LO-A	-1.29	-1.24	-2.52	0.00	-2.52	5
208			Charlie Kegley	20	DUN	TOR	HI-A	-1.57	-0.99	-2.55	0.00	-2.55	4
209			Jason Standridge	21	ORL	TB	AA	-1.12	-1.46	-2.58	0.00	-2.58	3
210	173	218	Ben Norris	22	TUC	AZ	AAA	-1.43	-1.17	-2.60	0.00	-2.60	2
211	89	12	Alan Webb	20	CHR	TEX	HI-A	-1.41	-1.69	-3.10	0.00	-3.10	1

RELATIVE CONTROL/POWER POTENTIAL
By Organization

2000 Rank	1999 Rank	1998 Rank		AGE	TEAM	ORG	LEVEL	C FACT	P FACT	CP FACT	AGE ADJ.	ADJ. RCPP	PTS
7			Franc. Rodriguez	18	LE	ANA	HI-A	0.58	1.77	2.36	2.00	4.36	205
28			John Lackey	21	ERIE	ANA	AA	1.99	0.27	2.26	0.00	2.26	184
73	40		Seth Etherton	23	EDM	ANA	AAA	0.85	0.90	1.75	-1.00	0.75	139
141			Steve Green	22	ERIE	ANA	AA	-0.22	0.79	0.57	-1.00	-0.43	71
163	54		Scot Shields	24	EDM	ANA	AAA	-0.14	1.45	1.31	-2.00	-0.69	49
164	199	68	Matt Wise	24	EDM	ANA	AAA	1.57	-0.28	1.29	-2.00	-0.71	48
202			Phil Wilson	19	CR	ANA	LO-A	-0.74	-1.06	-1.81	0.00	-1.81	10
15			Matt Belisle	20	MYR	ATL	HI-A	3.11	0.39	3.50	0.00	3.50	197
47			John Ennis	20	MAC	ATL	LO-A	1.36	1.04	2.40	-1.00	1.40	165
88	225	131	Horacio Ramirez	20	MYR	ATL	HI-A	0.36	0.06	0.42	0.00	0.42	124
144			Christian Parra	22	MYR	ATL	HI-A	0.31	1.20	1.51	-2.00	-0.49	68
145			Delvis Pacheco	22	GRN	ATL	AA	-0.04	0.55	0.51	-1.00	-0.49	67
152	154	17	Jason Marquis	21	GRN	ATL	AA	-0.14	-0.42	-0.57	0.00	-0.57	60
160			Ben Kozlowski	19	MAC	ATL	LO-A	-0.75	0.09	-0.66	0.00	-0.66	52
169	91		Jung Bong	19	MAC	ATL	LO-A	-0.51	-0.27	-0.79	0.00	-0.79	43
191			Dan Curtis	20	MYR	ATL	HI-A	-0.20	-0.95	-1.15	0.00	-1.15	21
31	179		Chris Cervantes	21	SBN	AZ	LO-A	3.24	0.71	3.95	-2.00	1.95	181
204	226		Hatuey Mendoza	20	HD	AZ	HI-A	-1.25	-0.59	-1.85	0.00	-1.85	8
210	173	218	Ben Norris	22	TUC	AZ	AAA	-1.43	-1.17	-2.60	0.00	-2.60	2
13	12		John Stephens	20	FRD	BAL	HI-A	2.35	1.17	3.52	0.00	3.52	199
20	101	6	Josh Towers	23	ROC	BAL	AAA	3.62	0.12	3.74	-1.00	2.74	192
43	5	3	Matt Riley	20	BOW	BAL	AA	-0.68	1.15	0.47	1.00	1.47	169
72	73	88	Jacobo Sequea	18	FRD	BAL	HI-A	-0.71	-0.47	-1.18	2.00	0.82	140
77	213	72	John Parrish	22	ROC	BAL	AAA	-0.58	1.24	0.66	0.00	0.66	135
80			Erik Bedard	21	DLM	BAL	LO-A	0.97	1.64	2.61	-2.00	0.61	132
114	33		Lesli Brea	21	BOW	BAL	AA	-0.74	0.82	0.07	0.00	0.07	98
115	82		Sean Douglass	21	BOW	BAL	AA	-0.06	0.13	0.07	0.00	0.07	97
123	127		Steve Bechler	20	FRD	BAL	HI-A	-0.09	0.07	-0.03	0.00	-0.03	89
137			Randy Perez	20	DLM	BAL	LO-A	0.95	-0.26	0.69	-1.00	-0.31	75
140			Richard Stahl	19	DLM	BAL	LO-A	-0.83	0.40	-0.43	0.00	-0.43	72
172	28		Juan Figueroa	21	BRM	BAL	AA	-0.58	-0.22	-0.80	0.00	-0.80	40
2	166	74	Paxton Crawford	22	TRN	BOS	AA	5.28	2.09	7.37	-1.00	6.37	210
27	39	33	Sun-Woo Kim	22	PAW	BOS	AAA	0.96	1.46	2.42	0.00	2.42	185
55			Casey Fossum	22	SAR	BOS	HI-A	1.98	1.29	3.27	-2.00	1.27	157
58	70		Justin Duchscherer	22	TRN	BOS	AA	1.07	1.08	2.15	-1.00	1.15	154
81			Wilfredo Ledezma	19	AUG	BOS	LO-A	-0.80	1.40	0.60	0.00	0.60	131
117			Brad Baker	19	AUG	BOS	LO-A	-0.27	0.31	0.04	0.00	0.04	95
130	92		Anastacio Martinez	19	AUG	BOS	LO-A	-0.39	0.20	-0.19	0.00	-0.19	82
175	16		Tomokazu Ohka	24	PAW	BOS	AAA	1.76	-0.59	1.17	-2.00	-0.83	37
94			Brad Salmon	20	CLN	CIN	LO-A	0.38	0.99	1.37	-1.00	0.37	118
155	181	92	Brian Reith	22	TAM	CIN	HI-A	0.89	0.50	1.39	-2.00	-0.61	57
177			Ty Howington	19	DAY	CIN	LO-A	-1.10	0.22	-0.88	0.00	-0.88	35
181			Jorge Cordova	22	CLN	CIN	LO-A	0.81	1.24	2.06	-3.00	-0.94	31
193	29		John Curtice	20	SAR	CIN	HI-A	-1.19	-0.07	-1.26	0.00	-1.26	19
10			C.C. Sabathia	19	KIN	CLE	HI-A	0.28	2.43	2.71	1.00	3.71	202
37	216	120	Mike Bacsik	22	KIN	CLE	HI-A	3.54	0.16	3.70	-2.00	1.70	175
100	144		Zach Day	22	AKR	CLE	AA	-0.14	1.43	1.29	-1.00	0.29	112
125			Danys Baez	22	KIN	CLE	HI-A	0.22	1.75	1.97	-2.00	-0.03	87
134	202	107	Tim Drew	21	BUF	CLE	AAA	-0.38	-0.87	-1.25	1.00	-0.25	78
147	186	59	Willie Martinez	22	BUF	CLE	AAA	-0.75	0.23	-0.52	0.00	-0.52	65
205			Adam Barr	19	CLM	CLE	LO-A	-1.49	-0.78	-2.27	0.00	-2.27	7

2000 Rank	1999 Rank	1998 Rank		AGE	TEAM	ORG	LEVEL	C FACT	P FACT	CP FACT	AGE ADJ.	ADJ. RCPP	PTS
6			Chin-Hui Tsao	18	ASH	COL	LO-A	1.76	2.18	3.94	1.00	4.94	206
45	25		Randey Dorame	21	VB	COL	HI-A	1.74	0.67	2.41	-1.00	1.41	167
60			Julio DePaula	20	ASH	COL	LO-A	0.35	1.77	2.12	-1.00	1.12	152
64	67		Mark DiFelice	23	CAR	COL	AA	3.33	-0.31	3.02	-2.00	1.02	148
75			David Moraga	24	CAR	COL	AA	2.94	0.78	3.72	-3.00	0.72	137
110	108		Shawn Chacon	22	CAR	COL	AA	-0.27	1.39	1.13	-1.00	0.13	102
119			Aaron Cook	21	ASH	COL	LO-A	2.15	-0.13	2.01	-2.00	0.01	93
129	8		Jason Jennings	21	SLM	COL	HI-A	0.51	0.32	0.83	-1.00	-0.17	83
183			Ryan Cameron	22	SLM	COL	HI-A	-0.29	1.32	1.03	-2.00	-0.97	29
197			Ryan Kibler	19	ASH	COL	LO-A	-0.82	-0.71	-1.52	0.00	-1.52	15
14	14	41	Ruben Quevedo	21	IOW	CUB	AAA	0.65	1.86	2.51	1.00	3.51	198
35	96	53	Joey Nation	21	WTN	CUB	AA	0.33	1.43	1.76	0.00	1.76	177
40			Ben Christensen	22	DAY	CUB	HI-A	2.24	1.44	3.68	-2.00	1.68	172
52	175		Carlos Zambrano	19	WTN	CUB	AA	-0.24	-0.45	-0.69	2.00	1.31	160
54			Juan Cruz	19	LNS	CUB	LO-A	-0.63	1.90	1.27	0.00	1.27	158
148	38	96	Mike Meyers	22	IOW	CUB	AAA	-0.74	0.22	-0.52	0.00	-0.52	64
151	140		Mike Wuertz	21	DAY	CUB	HI-A	-0.04	0.48	0.44	-1.00	-0.56	61
170			Lindsay Gulin	23	WTN	CUB	AA	-0.52	1.73	1.21	-2.00	-0.79	42
178	218	152	Rick Palma	20	DAY	CUB	HI-A	-0.71	-0.20	-0.91	0.00	-0.91	34
8			Jon Rauch	21	BRM	CWS	AA	1.93	2.32	4.25	0.00	4.25	204
36			Lorenzo Barcelo	22	CHR	CWS	AAA	2.08	-0.35	1.73	0.00	1.73	176
44	119	160	Jon Garland	20	CHR	CWS	AAA	-0.05	-0.51	-0.56	2.00	1.44	168
82	152		Jason Stumm	19	BUR	CWS	LO-A	-0.26	0.86	0.60	0.00	0.60	130
83	15		Mark Buehrle	21	BRM	CWS	AA	2.00	-1.43	0.57	0.00	0.57	129
118	107	93	Aaron Myette	22	CHR	CWS	AAA	-0.62	0.65	0.03	0.00	0.03	94
120			Gary Majewski	20	BUR	CWS	LO-A	-0.32	1.34	1.01	-1.00	0.01	92
189			Dennis Ulacia	19	BUR	CWS	LO-A	-0.76	-0.34	-1.10	0.00	-1.10	23
200	222		Eric Fischer	20	WS	CWS	HI-A	-0.92	-0.83	-1.75	0.00	-1.75	12
207			Brian West	19	BUR	CWS	LO-A	-1.29	-1.24	-2.52	0.00	-2.52	5
48	170	185	Shane Loux	20	JCK	DET	AA	0.12	0.27	0.39	1.00	1.39	164
84	114		Adam Pettyjohn	23	JCK	DET	AA	1.71	0.79	2.51	-2.00	0.51	128
95			Andy Van Hekken	20	WM	DET	LO-A	1.39	-0.04	1.35	-1.00	0.35	117
131	198		Nate Cornejo	20	LAK	DET	HI-A	-0.37	0.16	-0.20	0.00	-0.20	81
198			Fernando Rodney	19	WM	DET	LO-A	-0.83	-0.81	-1.65	0.00	-1.65	14
24			Josh Beckett	20	KNC	FLA	LO-A	2.20	1.46	3.66	-1.00	2.66	188
41	172		Claudio Vargas	21	BRV	FLA	HI-A	1.15	1.46	2.60	-1.00	1.60	171
135	163		Vladimir Nunez	25	CLG	FLA	AAA	0.67	2.03	2.70	-3.00	-0.30	77
173	49		Wes Anderson	20	BRV	FLA	HI-A	-1.01	0.20	-0.81	0.00	-0.81	39
179			Ryan Moskau	22	BRV	FLA	HI-A	0.70	0.36	1.07	-2.00	-0.93	33
184	206		Kevin Olsen	23	PRT	FLA	AA	0.01	1.01	1.02	-2.00	-0.98	28
4	176		Roy Oswalt	22	RR	HOU	AA	4.19	2.23	6.41	-1.00	5.41	208
19	77		Mike Nannini	19	KIS	HOU	HI-A	2.01	-0.22	1.79	1.00	2.79	193
65	90		Tim Redding	22	KIS	HOU	HI-A	0.84	2.14	2.98	-2.00	0.98	147
104	46	46	Wilfredo Rodriguez	21	RR	HOU	AA	-1.04	1.29	0.25	0.00	0.25	108
112	81		Greg Miller	20	KIS	HOU	HI-A	0.13	-0.04	0.09	0.00	0.09	100
126			Carlos Hernandez	20	MCH	HOU	LO-A	-0.56	1.47	0.92	-1.00	-0.08	86
142	110	104	Wade Miller	23	NO	HOU	AAA	0.17	0.37	0.54	-1.00	-0.46	70
50			Jimmy Gobble	18	CHWV	KC	LO-A	0.66	-0.29	0.37	1.00	1.37	162
63	131	78	Corey Thurman	21	WCH	KC	AA	-0.16	1.24	1.08	0.00	1.08	149
69	31		Chris George	20	WCH	KC	AA	-0.54	0.45	-0.09	1.00	0.91	143
78	88	51	Chad Durbin	22	OMA	KC	AAA	0.55	0.10	0.65	0.00	0.65	134
108			Ryan Baerlocher	22	CHWV	KC	LO-A	1.37	1.83	3.20	-3.00	0.20	104
185	11		Junior Guerrero	20	WCH	KC	AA	-0.95	-1.07	-2.02	1.00	-1.02	27
12	57	4	Luke Prokopec	22	SANT	LA	AA	3.19	1.38	4.57	-1.00	3.57	200
25	65	79	Eric Gagne	24	ABQ	LA	AAA	2.63	2.02	4.65	-2.00	2.65	187

2000 Rank	1999 Rank	1998 Rank		AGE	TEAM	ORG	LEVEL	C FACT	P FACT	CP FACT	AGE ADJ.	ADJ. RCPP	PTS
150			Scott Martin	22	SBR	LA	HI-A	1.58	-0.13	1.44	-2.00	-0.56	62
167			Carlos Ortega	21	VB	LA	HI-A	-0.49	0.72	0.23	-1.00	-0.77	45
206			Randy Galvez	21	SANT	LA	AA	-0.93	-1.39	-2.33	0.00	-2.33	6
17	9		Nick Neugebauer	19	HNT	MIL	AA	-1.20	2.27	1.07	2.00	3.07	195
39			Joses Mieses	20	BLT	MIL	LO-A	1.59	1.10	2.69	-1.00	1.69	173
51	159		James Johnson	23	HNT	MIL	AA	1.27	2.07	3.34	-2.00	1.34	161
57			Ben Sheets	21	IND	MIL	AAA	-0.13	0.35	0.22	1.00	1.22	155
122	66	21	Allen Levrault	22	IND	MIL	AAA	-0.40	0.37	-0.02	0.00	-0.02	90
132	212	111	Paul Stewart	21	MUD	MIL	HI-A	-0.09	0.87	0.79	-1.00	-0.21	80
3			Adam Johnson	20	FTM	MIN	HI-A	2.70	3.62	6.32	0.00	6.32	209
42			Matt Kinney	23	SLK	MIN	AAA	0.36	2.13	2.49	-1.00	1.49	170
66	126		Juan Rincon	21	NB	MIN	AA	-0.16	1.12	0.97	0.00	0.97	146
97	94		Joe Foote	20	QC	MIN	LO-A	0.86	0.46	1.32	-1.00	0.32	115
103	166		Brad Thomas	22	FTM	MIN	HI-A	1.50	0.77	2.28	-2.00	0.28	109
106	85	142	Kyle Lohse	21	NB	MIN	AA	0.02	0.19	0.22	0.00	0.22	106
113			Brian Wolfe	19	QC	MIN	LO-A	0.49	-0.40	0.09	0.00	0.09	99
116	139		Grant Balfour	22	FTM	MIN	HI-A	0.45	1.61	2.06	-2.00	0.06	96
59	194		Donnie Bridges	21	JUP	MON	HI-A	1.20	0.94	2.15	-1.00	1.15	153
171	128		Jorge Julio	21	JUP	MON	HI-A	-0.39	0.59	0.20	-1.00	-0.80	41
201	61		T.J. Tucker	21	HAR	MON	AA	-0.63	-1.14	-1.78	0.00	-1.78	11
23	35	9	Dicky Gonzalez	21	BNG	NYM	AA	1.25	1.41	2.66	0.00	2.66	189
32	72		Pat Strange	19	STLC	NYM	HI-A	0.18	0.76	0.94	1.00	1.94	180
105	141	62	Grant Roberts	22	NRF	NYM	AAA	-0.23	0.45	0.22	0.00	0.22	107
149			Ken Chenard	21	CAP	NYM	LO-A	-0.23	1.70	1.47	-2.00	-0.53	63
176			Nick Maness	21	STLC	NYM	HI-A	-0.49	0.64	0.14	-1.00	-0.86	36
22			Ricardo Aramboles	18	GRN	NYY	LO-A	0.50	1.17	1.67	1.00	2.67	190
62			Dave Walling	21	NRW	NYY	AA	0.36	0.71	1.08	0.00	1.08	150
74	69	64	Ted Lilly	24	CLM	NYY	AAA	0.81	1.93	2.74	-2.00	0.74	138
121			Jeremy Blevins	22	TAM	NYY	HI-A	-0.15	2.13	1.98	-2.00	-0.02	91
124			Brandon Claussen	21	TAM	NYY	HI-A	0.38	0.58	0.97	-1.00	-0.03	88
127	203		Brett Jodie	23	TAM	NYY	HI-A	2.25	0.59	2.83	-3.00	-0.17	85
138	224	197	Jake Westbrook	22	CLM	NYY	AAA	-0.51	0.09	-0.42	0.00	-0.42	74
61	21		Barry Zito	22	SAC	OAK	AAA	0.02	1.07	1.09	0.00	1.09	151
71	180		Juan Pena	21	MOD	OAK	HI-A	0.44	1.39	1.83	-1.00	0.83	141
87			Eric Thompson	22	MID	OAK	AA	1.28	0.16	1.44	-1.00	0.44	125
99	148		Justin Miller	22	SAC	OAK	AAA	0.83	-0.53	0.30	0.00	0.30	113
154			Javier Calzada	21	VIS	OAK	HI-A	0.37	0.03	0.40	-1.00	-0.60	58
159			Scott Chiasson	22	VIS	OAK	HI-A	0.80	0.55	1.35	-2.00	-0.65	53
180			Justin Lehr	22	MOD	OAK	HI-A	1.29	-0.23	1.06	-2.00	-0.94	32
182			Mario Ramos	22	MOD	OAK	HI-A	0.86	0.19	1.05	-2.00	-0.95	30
194			Franklyn German	20	MOD	OAK	HI-A	-0.84	-0.53	-1.37	0.00	-1.37	18
56			Geoff Geary	23	REA	PHL	AA	2.23	1.00	3.23	-2.00	1.23	156
93			Ryan Madson	19	PDT	PHL	LO-A	0.11	0.26	0.37	0.00	0.37	119
102			Bran. Duckworth	24	REA	PHL	AA	0.93	2.35	3.28	-3.00	0.28	110
157			Martire Franco	18	PDT	PHL	LO-A	-0.89	-0.72	-1.61	1.00	-0.61	55
165			Brett Myers	19	PDT	PHL	LO-A	-0.49	-0.26	-0.75	0.00	-0.75	47
187	214		Brad Baisley	20	CLW	PHL	HI-A	-0.56	-0.49	-1.05	0.00	-1.05	25
203			Franklin Perez	19	PDT	PHL	LO-A	-0.82	-0.99	-1.81	0.00	-1.81	9
5			Bobby Bradley	19	HCK	PIT	LO-A	2.56	2.84	5.40	0.00	5.40	207
46	169		Dave Williams	21	HCK	PIT	LO-A	1.99	1.41	3.41	-2.00	1.41	166
128	51	137	John Grabow	21	ALT	PIT	AA	-0.43	0.25	-0.17	0.00	-0.17	84
162			Wilson Guzman	22	LYN	PIT	HI-A	0.42	0.91	1.33	-2.00	-0.67	50
11			Jacob Peavy	19	FTW	SD	LO-A	1.00	2.66	3.67	0.00	3.67	201
21			Dennis Tankersley	21	FTW	SD	LO-A	1.48	3.26	4.74	-2.00	2.74	191
30	23	84	Buddy Carlyle	22	LV	SD	AAA	1.20	0.77	1.98	0.00	1.98	182

FUTURE STARS - The Rookies of 2001-2002

2000 Rank	1999 Rank	1998 Rank		AGE	TEAM	ORG	LEVEL	C FACT	P FACT	CP FACT	AGE ADJ.	ADJ. RCPP	PTS
38	59	174	Adam Eaton	22	MOB	SD	AA	1.11	1.59	2.70	-1.00	1.70	174
67	106	138	Wascar Serrano	22	MOB	SD	AA	0.47	1.47	1.94	-1.00	0.94	145
79			Ben Howard	21	RC	SD	HI-A	-0.91	2.53	1.62	-1.00	0.62	133
86			Gerik Baxter	20	FTW	SD	LO-A	0.08	1.37	1.45	-1.00	0.45	126
96	52	34	Brian Lawrence	24	MOB	SD	AA	2.29	1.04	3.33	-3.00	0.33	116
101			Blair DeHart	22	FTW	SD	LO-A	2.82	0.46	3.29	-3.00	0.29	111
111			Roger Luque	20	FTW	SD	LO-A	0.64	0.45	1.10	-1.00	0.10	101
133			Steve Watkins	21	RC	SD	HI-A	-0.29	1.08	0.78	-1.00	-0.22	79
143			Rodrigo Lopez	24	LV	SD	AAA	0.29	1.22	1.51	-2.00	-0.49	69
146			Mike Bynum	22	RC	SD	HI-A	0.66	0.83	1.49	-2.00	-0.51	66
188	171	97	Junior Herndon	21	LV	SD	AAA	-1.17	-0.90	-2.07	1.00	-1.07	24
1	7	11	Ryan Anderson	20	TAC	SEA	AAA	0.88	4.07	4.95	2.00	6.95	211
33	108		Josue Matos	22	LNC	SEA	HI-A	2.93	0.92	3.85	-2.00	1.85	179
34	71	30	Joel Pineiro	21	NH	SEA	AA	1.06	0.73	1.79	0.00	1.79	178
49			Craig Anderson	19	WSC	SEA	LO-A	1.23	0.16	1.39	0.00	1.39	163
107			Enmanuel Ulloa	21	LNC	SEA	HI-A	0.81	0.40	1.21	-1.00	0.21	105
109			Jeff Heaverlo	22	LNC	SEA	HI-A	1.37	0.81	2.17	-2.00	0.17	103
156			Cha Baek	20	WSC	SEA	LO-A	0.58	-0.19	0.39	-1.00	-0.61	56
158	162	51	Brian Fuentes	24	NH	SEA	AA	-0.04	2.39	2.35	-3.00	-0.65	54
18			Jerome Williams	18	SJ	SF	HI-A	0.48	0.33	0.81	2.00	2.81	194
92			Kurt Ainsworth	21	SHR	SF	AA	-0.06	0.43	0.38	0.00	0.38	120
98	44		Ryan Vogelsong	22	SHR	SF	AA	0.01	1.29	1.30	-1.00	0.30	114
9	18		Bud Smith	20	ARK	STL	AA	1.62	1.21	2.82	1.00	3.82	203
91	95		Chad Hutchinson	23	ARK	STL	AA	-0.12	2.50	2.38	-2.00	0.38	121
192			Cristobal Correa	20	PTM	STL	HI-A	-0.77	-0.46	-1.23	0.00	-1.23	20
53			Neal Frendling	20	CHSC	TB	LO-A	1.00	1.28	2.28	-1.00	1.28	159
68			Joe Kennedy	21	CHSC	TB	LO-A	1.95	0.96	2.91	-2.00	0.91	144
85	47		Jesus Colome	21	MID	TB	AA	-0.22	0.71	0.50	0.00	0.50	127
89			Enger Veras	19	CHSC	TB	LO-A	-0.10	0.51	0.41	0.00	0.41	123
90	177	118	Travis Phelps	22	ORL	TB	AA	0.06	1.35	1.40	-1.00	0.40	122
136	2	127	Dan Wheeler	22	DUR	TB	AAA	0.20	-0.50	-0.30	0.00	-0.30	76
139	80	129	Matt White	21	ORL	TB	AA	-0.65	0.23	-0.42	0.00	-0.42	73
153			Jim Magrane	21	CHSC	TB	LO-A	0.99	0.42	1.41	-2.00	-0.59	59
161	36	44	Cedrick Bowers	22	ORL	TB	AA	-0.19	0.52	0.33	-1.00	-0.67	51
209			Jason Standridge	21	ORL	TB	AA	-1.12	-1.46	-2.58	0.00	-2.58	3
16	6		Andy Pratt	20	CHR	TEX	HI-A	1.61	1.68	3.29	0.00	3.29	196
26			Colby Lewis	20	CHR	TEX	HI-A	1.32	1.12	2.44	0.00	2.44	186
29	64	75	Joaquin Benoit	20	TUL	TEX	AA	0.27	0.81	1.08	1.00	2.08	183
70			Jovanny Cedeno	20	SAV	TEX	LO-A	0.24	1.62	1.86	-1.00	0.86	142
166			Aaron Harang	22	CHR	TEX	HI-A	0.54	0.71	1.24	-2.00	-0.76	46
186			Andy Cavazos	19	SAV	TEX	LO-A	-1.12	0.07	-1.04	0.00	-1.04	26
195			Edwin Moreno	19	SAV	TEX	LO-A	-0.57	-0.91	-1.48	0.00	-1.48	17
211	89	12	Alan Webb	20	CHR	TEX	HI-A	-1.41	-1.69	-3.10	0.00	-3.10	1
76			Matt Ford	19	HAG	TOR	LO-A	-0.18	0.86	0.68	0.00	0.68	136
168			Pasqual Coco	22	TEN	TOR	AA	-0.19	0.42	0.23	-1.00	-0.77	44
174	75	143	Gary Glover	23	SYR	TOR	AAA	-0.11	0.30	0.19	-1.00	-0.81	38
190			Gustavo Chacin	19	DUN	TOR	HI-A	-1.21	-0.94	-2.15	1.00	-1.15	22
196	204	38	Clayton Andrews	22	SYR	TOR	AAA	-0.77	-0.76	-1.52	0.00	-1.52	16
199			Marcos Sandoval	19	HAG	TOR	LO-A	-0.48	-1.21	-1.68	0.00	-1.68	13
208			Charlie Kegley	20	DUN	TOR	HI-A	-1.57	-0.99	-2.55	0.00	-2.55	4

RELATIVE MINOR LEAGUE STRENGTH
STARTING PITCHING - 2000

2000 Rank	1999 Rank	1998 Rank	TEAM	2000 # OF P'S	2000 CUM. RCPP	1999 # OF P'S	1999 CUM. RCPP	1998 # OF P'S	1998 CUM. RCPP
1	17	8	San Diego	14	1718	7	821	8	756
2	3	4	Baltimore	12	1438	11	1301	7	950
3	18	16	Colorado	10	1132	7	816	7	585
4	2	6	Chicago Cubs	9	1066	12	1311	10	872
5	1	2	Boston	8	1051	11	1328	11	1221
6	24	29	Minnesota	8	1050	6	682	4	306
7	12	9	Seattle	8	1049	7	959	5	726
8	6	28	Chicago White Sox	10	1033	10	1079	5	408
9	20	23	Tampa Bay	10	937	6	757	6	509
10	7	12	Houston	7	912	10	1048	6	650
11	21	11	Milwaukee	6	854	9	743	7	661
12	22	19	New York Yankees	7	816	7	721	5	569
13	13	1	Atlanta	9	797	8	917	13	1678
14	16	20	Texas	8	797	6	831	5	530
15	27	26	Cleveland	7	726	6	514	6	438
16	10	17	Oakland	9	721	9	996	7	579
17	4	25	Kansas City	6	719	8	1160	5	484
18	11	30	Anaheim	7	706	7	996	4	267
19	8	15	New York Mets	5	575	7	1023	5	635
20	9	3	Florida	6	536	8	1019	9	1023
21	26	7	Philadelphia	7	521	4	519	8	853
22	30	13	Pittsburgh	4	507	4	369	9	649
23	25	27	Detroit	5	504	6	565	7	416
24	5	18	Los Angeles	5	500	9	1087	5	575
25	15	10	San Francisco	3	428	8	886	6	679
26	23	14	St. Louis	3	344	5	684	4	640
27	28	5	Toronto	7	273	5	428	10	885
28	29	24	Cincinnati	5	260	3	414	6	506
29	19	21	Montreal	3	205	12	774	5	525
30	14	22	Arizona	3	191	8	903	5	525

HEIRS TO THE THRONE

by Tony Blengino

It is much more difficult to translate minor league pitching statistics into their major league equivalencies than it is to similarly translate hitting statistics. A hitter who bats extremely well at lower minor league levels can usually be expected to hit at higher levels, but pitchers tend to go through a rigorous weeding-out process at the Double-A level. Pitchers are also much more vulnerable to career-threatening injuries, causing any forecast to be at risk.

However, by examining the relative control/power factors of current major league pitching stars and looking for close matches among the pitchers listed near the top of the Relative Control/Power Potential list, we can make educated guesses as to the identity of their eventual successors from within the current minor league population.

The relative control/power factor is used as the basis for comparison. The minor league c/p factors are adjusted downward for negative age adjustments (splitting the difference 50/50 between power and control) but are conservatively not adjusted upward for positive age adjustments.

The adjusted c/p factor is then matched with that of the most comparable major leaguer. By breaking down the control and power sub-factors and evaluating them separately, we can also group current and future pitching stars by pitching style. It must be noted that the major leagues were again dominated by two hurlers: Pedro Martinez, and to a lesser extent, Randy Johnson. Since their relative c/p factors were so high, and all factors in a league must add to zero, it stands to reason that there were fewer high factors among other pitchers than in other recent seasons.

It also must be noted that 2000 was a particularly strong year for minor league pitchers; much more so than for hitters. A new pitching elite is currently being developed that will soon the supplant the aging warriors named Johnson, Wells, Clemens, Maddux, Glavine, Leiter, etc. Pedro, again, was in a class by himself in 2000. Johnson was next best at combining control and power. Four minor league hurlers that combined control and power as well as

anyone were the Twins' Adam Johnson, Pirates' Bobby Bradley, Rockies' Chin-Hui Tsao and the White Sox' Jon Rauch.

Johnson, 20, is the most advanced 2000 draftee, he was the second overall pick in the first round, on this year's list. Though he lacks a dominating fastball, he has an awesome slider and very advanced command.

Bradley, 19, lost part of 2000 with a strained elbow ligament, but regained his health by season's end. He too has just a low-90's fastball, but gets supplemental power from an excellent curveball.

Tsao, 18, is a prototypical power pitcher, possessing a mid-to-upper-90's heater. Within a couple of years, Tsao is likely to test the hypothesis that a true power pitcher should be relatively unaffected by the mile-high Coors Field altitude.

Lastly, the 6'11", 230, Rauch, 21, combines awesome size and a deceptive but smooth delivery with a lively low-90's fastball. He is incredibly polished for his age and size, and was unhittable in the Olympic Games.

Last year's selections in this category were the Marlins' Brad Penny and the Orioles' John Stephens. Penny established himself as a solid big league starter in 2000, while Stephens is compared to Kevin Brown (below) this year.

Greg Maddux and David Wells shared the distinction of being the game's best finesse pitcher in 2000. The Braves' Matt Belisle and the Astros' Mike Nannini are his closest matches. Belisle, 20, has four quality big league pitches, impeccable command, and a live low-90's fastball that should keep big league hitters honest. Nannini, 19, stands only 5'11", 175, but throws a sneaky-fast, but fairly straight, low-90's fastball plus a solid changeup and an improving slider. He needs to develop a true strikeout pitch to reach his potential, but is quite solid for his tender age.

Last year's selections in this category were the Red Sox' Tomokazu Ohka and the Marlins' Scott Comer. Ohka finished the season in the Red Sox' rotation and settled in nicely by the end of the year. He should be a mid-rotation guy for the foreseeable future. Comer blew up in Double-A, not an uncommon occurrence for Class A finesse pitchers who never develop a true out pitch. His future is uncertain at best. This section correctly predicted "growing pains" for Comer in 2000.

Youngsters Rick Ankiel, 20, and Bartolo Colon, 25, stepped up as the majors' premier high-power/average-control pitchers in 2000. The Mariners' Ryan Anderson, Indians' C.C. Sabathia and Brewers' Nick Neugebauer best fit this profile in 2000. Anderson, 20, might actually be too good a pitcher for this list. In fact, he might have performed near Ankiel's level had he spent 2000 in the majors. His combination of 6'10" size, an upper-90's fastball, an improving breaking ball repertoire and exceptional control make him a treasured prospect.

Sabathia, 19, at 6'7", 235, is as scary a prospect physically as Anderson. His heater reaches 100 MPH on occasion and he has a solid curve. Conditioning and mechanical consistency are both concerns, but Sabathia's upside is rivaled by few.

Neugebauer, 19, has put up some wild strikeout/walk numbers in his brief pro career. His upper-90's fastball and nasty slider are unhittable when he's throwing them for strikes, which isn't all that often. He's a classic high-risk/high-reward prospect.

Last year's selections in this category were repeaters Anderson and Neugebauer, along with the A's Barry Zito. Zito was superb in his rookie year in the majors, and his control has caught up with the strikeout potential of his fastball/curve combination. Kevin Brown's control still ranks among the game's best, and his power is well above average, though not spectacular.

The closest minor league fits with Brown are the Astros' Roy Oswalt and the Orioles' John Stephens. Oswalt, 22, dominated after a daunting two-level jump to the Double-A Texas League on the strength of pinpoint control and a low-90's fastball/sharp curveball combination. Like Rauch, the 6'0", 170, Oswalt overmatched the competition in the Olympics. His power upside doesn't match Rauch's, but Oswalt isn't far from being ready to achieve in the show. Stephens, 20, rarely reaches 90 MPH with his fastball, but consistently throws his heater, curve and changeup to precise spots.

Double-A could be a challenge for Stephens; watch his 2001 performance closely. Last year's picks in this category were the Devil Rays' Dan Wheeler and the Rockies' Jason Jennings. Wheeler got a taste of the majors, but struggled mightily there and in Triple-A because of a dropoff in command and a continuing inability to develop an out pitch. He'll get more chances, but likely projects as no better than a major league mid-rotation guy.

Jennings, 21, was good but not great in the High-A Carolina League, but still rates as a solid prospect. He'll need to make hitters miss more often to get it done in Colorado. Mike Mussina doesn't reach the Maddux/Wells control level or the Johnson/Ankiel/Colon power threshold, but isn't that far off of either mark. His 2000 minor league counterparts were the Cards' Bud Smith and the Marlins' Josh Beckett.

Smith, 20, fit this profile in 1999 as well. He pitched no-hitters at two levels last season, and has a feel for pitching that transcends his stuff. His stuff isn't bad, however, he has a high-80's fastball plus a solid curve and changeup, and throws quality strikes consistently. Kind of like Mussina.

Beckett, 20, is considered a prototypical power pitcher prospect, but has fallen a tad short in that area thus far in his pro career, though his command has been solid. He was limited by minor injuries in 2000, and his mid-to-upper-90's fastball has proven to be fairly straight to date. He could really take off in 2001 with continued enhancement of his mechanics and fine-tuning of his breaking stuff.

Last year's selections in this category were the Orioles' Matt Riley, Angels' Ramon Ortiz, Dodgers' Randey Dorame and the Cards' Smith. Riley underwent an elbow ligament transplant late in 2000, and will miss all of 2001. He also proved to be quite immature prior to the injury, setting back his development.

Ortiz was dominant at times in a star-crossed 2000 campaign split between the majors and Triple-A. He out-dueled Pedro Martinez 1-0 one memorable late-summer night in Anaheim.

Dorame was dealt to the Rockies in the Tom Goodwin deal, and his strikeout rate dropped precipitously after his promotion to Double-A. That act might not play at high altitude.

Al Leiter's control is a bit better than that of young guns Ankiel and Colon, while his power rates around the Mussina/Brown level. He is most closely aligned with 18-year-old minor leaguers Francisco Rodriguez of the Angels and Ricardo Aramboles of the Yankees.

Rodriguez was nearly unhittable as the youngest High-A California League hurler last season, combining a high-90's fastball and a sharp curveball with solid command for his age. Once he builds arm strength and becomes an eight or nine-inning guy, watch out.

Aramboles was one of the Yanks' recent high-profile 16-year-old signees, but quickly needed elbow surgery after turning pro and fell out of the spotlight. He reentered it at Low-A Greensboro last season, relying heavily on his live low-90's fastball that he consistently threw for quality strikes. He needs to improve his breaking stuff to reach his potential, but hey, he's eighteen.

Last year's selections in this category were Ankiel, you all know what became of him, and the Diamondbacks' John Patterson, whose future is in doubt because of 2000 elbow surgery. It is dangerous to predict future major league pitching stars solely on the basis of minor league stats: the legacies of Steve Ontiveros, Dave Eiland and Rick Krivda attest to that.

However, by examining minor leaguers' relative control/power factors and their component sub-factors and comparing them to those of current major leaguers in their prime, we can isolate the pitchers most likely to follow in the major leaguers' footsteps. Some of the young hurlers mentioned in this section will be contending for Cy Young Awards in the not too distant future.

THE NEXT GENERATION 2001-2003
Projected All Rookie Teams
by Tony Blengino

Time to break out the crystal ball. In this space last year, I incorrectly predicted that Ben Petrick and Ruben Mateo would be the Rookies of the Year; ditto J.D. Drew and Eric Chavez in 1999. On the other hand, I did correctly predict Ben Grieve and Todd Helton would be 1998 Rookies of the Year, and that Nomar Garciaparra and Scott Rolen would do the same in 1997. Here goes:

POSITION	2001	2002	2003
First Base:	Hee Choi (Cub)	Carlos Pena (Tex)	Jeremy Cotton (Pit)
	Dernell Stenson (Bos)	Nick Johnson (NYY)	Travis Hafner (Tex)
	Mario Valdez (Oak)	Jason Hart (Oak)	Josh Pressley (TB)
Second Base:	Brent Abernathy (TB)	Jason Romano (Tex)	Willie Bloomquist (Sea)
	Luis Rivas (Min)	Marcus Giles (Atl)	Carlos Leon (Bos)
	Jose Ortiz (Oak)	Jackie Rexrode (CWS)	Richard Paz (Bal)
Shortstop:	Jimmy Rollins (Phl)	Antonio Perez (Sea)	Jose Castillo (Pit)
	Alfonso Soriano (NYY)	Felipe Lopez (Tor)	Joe Thurston (LA)
	D'Angelo Jimenez (NYY)	Jorge Cantu (TB)	Ramon Santiago (Det)
Third Base:	Aubrey Huff (TB)	Sean Burroughs (SD)	Hank Blalock (Tex)
	Joe Crede (CWS)	Tony Torcato (SF)	Albert Pujols (StL)
	Pedro Feliz (SF)	Scott Hodges (Mon)	Neil Jenkins (Det)
Utility:	Pablo Ozuna (Fla)	Drew Henson (Cin)	Omar Infante (Det)
Outfield:	Corey Patterson (Cub)	Jack Cust (Az)	Chris Snelling (Sea)
	Vernon Wells (Tor)	Alex Escobar (NYM)	Adam Dunn (Cin)
	Brad Wilkerson (Mon)	Austin Kearns (Cin)	Josh Hamilton (TB)
	Milton Bradley (Mon)	Kevin Mench (Tex)	Carl Crawford (TB)
	Mike Darr (SD)	Abraham Nunez (Fla)	Ben Johnson (SD)
	Timoniel Perez (NYM)	Jody Gerut (Col)	Jorge Padilla (Cin)
Catcher:	Toby Hall (TB)	Brad Cresse (Az)	J.R. House (Pit)
	Matt LeCroy (Min)	Jayson Werth (Bal)	John Buck (Hou)
	Craig Wilson (Pit)	Joe Lawrence (Tor)	Ryan Christianson (Sea)
Pitchers:	Ryan Anderson (Sea)	Adam Johnson (Min)	Bobby Bradley (Pit)
	Paxton Crawford (Bos)	Roy Oswalt (Hou)	Chin-Hui Tsao (Col)
	Jon Rauch (CWS)	Bud Smith (StL)	Francisco Rodriguez (Ana)
	C.C. Sabathia (Cle)	Nick Neugebauer (Mil)	Jacob Peavy (SD)
	Luke Prokopec (LA)	Dicky Gonzalez (NYM)	John Stephens (Bal)
	Joel Pineiro (Sea)	John Lackey (Ana)	Matt Belisle (Atl)
	Joey Nation (Cub)	Pat Strange (NYM)	Jerome Williams (SF)
	Ben Sheets (Mil)	Ben Christensen (Cub)	Mike Nannini (Hou)
	Kurt Ainsworth (SF)	Carlos Zambrano (Cub)	Josh Beckett (Fla)

Obviously, the competition levels vary from position to position, and from year to year. As predicted in this space a few years back, we have entered the Era of the Shortstop. Though the major leagues are already loaded at that position, it also remains the deepest spot in the minors. Undoubtedly, some of the above shortstops will slide over to second base, currently the thinnest position in the minors. There are top-shelf shortstop prospects that I couldn't find room for above (like Anderson Machado of the Phillies), even with the inclusion of a "utility" slot. Believe it or not, we are in a slight "down" cycle with regard to position player talent in the minors. Nowhere above do I see an Alex Rodriguez, Andruw Jones or Vladimir Guerrero, a potential future first-team all-timer. Pitching, now that's where it's at currently in the minor leagues. There are some true studs listed above; just ask the Cuban, Japanese and Korean Olympic teams, who had to face the likes of Rauch, Sheets, Oswalt and Ainsworth in Sydney. Toss in Ryan Anderson, C.C. Sabathia, Jerome Williams, Bobby Bradley, and Chin-Hui Tsao. Rick Ankiel is going to have some company real soon in building the list of successors to the mantle of the Madduxes, Glavines, Clemenses, Cones, and Johnsons who are just beginning to move on.

Time to break my two-year Rookie of the Year drought. I absolutely loved Rafael Furcal and Ankiel, as any of my readers surely know. I just couldn't imagine that they would get full major league shots so soon. In 2001, some of these pitchers are going to get full shots. I'm going to go with Ben Sheets in the NL and Ryan Anderson in the AL. Sheets will be fronting a fairly weak team, but appears to have the guts to perform immediately. Anderson could be scary right away with a solid outfit behind him. Other contenders in the NL could include Jimmy Rollins and Corey Patterson, while other AL contenders could include Brent Abernathy, Luis Rivas, Vernon Wells and Jon Rauch. As a frame of reference, here are last year's selections:

POSITION	**1999**	**2000**	**2001**
First Base:	Erubiel Durazo (Az)	Nick Johnson (NYY)	Hee Choi (Cub)
	Kevin Barker (Mil)	Dernell Stenson (Bos)	Thomas Pittman (Mon)
	Calvin Pickering (Bal)	Eric Munson (Det)	
Second Base:	Adam Kennedy (StL)	Brent Abernathy (Tor)	Antonio Perez (Cin)
	Jerry Hairston (Bal)	Marcus Giles (Atl)	Esteban German (Oak)
	Chad Meyers (Cub)	Jason Romano (Tex)	Jorge Nunez (Tor)
Shortstop:	D'Angelo Jimenez (NYY)	Pablo Ozuna (Fla)	Rafael Furcal (Atl)
	Alfonso Soriano (NYY)	Luis Rivas (Min)	Felipe Lopez (Tor)
	Travis Dawkins (Cin)	Jimmy Rollins (Phl)	Ramon Soler (TB)
Third Base:	Aramis Ramirez (Pit)	Adam Piatt (Oak)	Drew Henson (NYY)
	Russell Branyan (Cle)	Michael Cuddyer (Min)	Sean Burroughs (SD)
	Wilton Veras (Bos)	Luke Allen (LA)	Tony Torcato (SF)
Utility:	Cole Liniak (Cub)	Adam Everett (Bos)	Cesar Izturis (Tor)
Outfield:	Vernon Wells (Tor)	Dee Brown (Royals)	Jack Cust (Az)
	Pat Burrell (Phl)	Alex Escobar (NYM)	Corey Patterson (Cub)
	Chad Hermansen (Pit)	Chin-Feng Chen (LA)	Abraham Nunez (Az)
	Ruben Mateo (Tex)	Julio Ramirez (Fla)	Mike Restovich (Min)
	Edgard Clemente (Col)	Milton Bradley (Mon)	Alex Fernandez (Sea)
	Peter Bergeron (Mon)	Jason Tyner (NYM)	Josh Hamilton (TB)
Catcher:	Ben Petrick (Col)	Matt LeCroy (Bos)	Steve Lomasney (Bos)
	Ramon Hernandez (Oak)	Jayson Werth (Bal)	Jeff Goldbach (Cub)
	Ramon Castro (Fla)	Javier Cardona (Det)	Humberto Cota (Pit)
Pitchers:	Rick Ankiel (StL)	Barry Zito (Oak)	Randey Dorame (LA)
	Matt Riley (Bal)	Ruben Quevedo (Cub)	Wilfredo Rodriguez (Hou)
	Ed Yarnall (NYY)	Brad Penny (Fla)	Nick Neugebauer (Mil)
	Ramon Ortiz (Angels)	Ryan Anderson (Sea)	Jason Jennings (Col)
	Ted Lilly (Mon)	John Patterson (Az)	Wes Anderson (Fla)
	A.J. Burnett (Fla)	Jon Garland (CWS)	Junior Guerrero (KC)
	Tony Armas (Mon)	Chad Hutchinson (StL)	Brad Baisley (Phl)
	Juan Pena (Bos)	Jason Marquis (Atl)	Pat Strange (NYM)
	Francisco Cordero (Det)	Adam Eaton (Phl)	John Stephens (Bal)

THE LIST

by Tony Blengino

Faithful readers of "*Future Stars*" know that I am hesitant to focus on rookie ball accomplishments when evaluating prospects. The woods are full of players, Gary Redus, Bobby Cripps and Greg Morrison immediately come to mind, who absolutely detonated rookie-level pitching, only to never deliver on their supposed "promise". Though I'm still not going to put a whole lot of faith in rookie-ball statistics, I am, however, going to attempt to isolate the potential top achievers in the four most advanced rookie-ball leagues: the Appalachian, New York-Penn, Northwest and Pioneer Leagues, by identifying players who were on-field achievers while still teenagers. No Gulf Coast or Arizona League players need apply. The caliber of play in such circuits is simply too far from the major league level to place any stock at all in such numbers. The combination of performance and youth is key, many other lists of top prospects in these leagues will include older players who performed well and similarly young players who didn't. I'd be willing to bet that a significant number of 2001 full-season league breakout prospects are on this very short list. Enjoy.

ROOKIE BALL STUDS ON THE HORIZON

PITCHERS	AGE	ORG	TEAM	LG	W	L	ERA	IP	H	BB	K	THE SKINNY
Adam Wainwrigh	19	ATL	DAN	APPY	2	2	3.68	29	28	2	39	How do they do it?
Rafael Lopez	19	NYM	KNG	APPY	3	3	3.04	56	50	9	43	Needs more power
Josh Girdley	19	MON	VER	NYP	5	0	2.95	79	60	28	70	More than "signable"
Wilton Chavez	19	CUB	EUG	NW	7	1	1.69	90	69	25	103	Three nice pitches

HITTERS	AGE	ORG	TEAM	LG	POS	AVG	H	AB	2B	3B	HR	RBI	BB	K	SB	THE SKINNY
Alejandro Macha	18	ATL	DAN	APPY	2B	.341	74	217	6	2	0	16	53	29	30	Top of the order guy
Wilson Betemit	19	ATL	JAM	NYP	SS	.331	89	269	15	2	5	37	30	37	3	Developing power
Enrique Cruz	18	NYM	KNG	APPY	3B	.251	56	223	14	0	9	39	26	56	19	Power/speed sleeper
Noel Devarez	18	NYM	KNG	APPY	OF	.305	60	197	14	2	9	35	14	46	8	Take some pitches
Mike Jacobs	19	NYM	KNG	APPY	C	.270	55	204	15	4	7	40	33	62	6	1999 38th round steal
Josh Wilson	19	FLA	UTI	NYP	SS	.344	89	259	13	6	3	43	29	47	9	No weaknesses
Adam Morrissey	19	CUB	EUG	NW	2B	.275	74	269	16	2	7	36	42	50	12	MI with power
Dave Krynzel	18	MIL	OGD	PION	OF	.359	47	131	8	3	1	29	16	23	8	Born to lead off
Cristian Guerrero	19	MIL	OGD	PION	OF	.341	87	255	14	4	12	54	37	42	24	Vladi bloodlines
Jason Belcher	18	MIL	HEL	PION	C	.333	54	162	18	2	4	36	20	25	3	Here comes the......
Garett Gentry	19	HOU	AUB	NYP	C	.286	66	231	15	3	4	34	26	27	5	...next generation of......
Ryan Doumit	19	PIT	WMS	NYP	C	.313	77	246	15	5	2	40	23	33	2	..... catching studs
Manuel Ravelo	18	PIT	WMS	NYP	OF	.303	59	195	4	7	0	17	26	30	28	No power at all
Victor Hall	19	AZ	MIS	PION	OF	.307	74	241	7	9	3	26	77	38	47	Check out those walks
Shawn Lagana	19	AZ	MIS	PION	2B	.288	65	226	12	2	2	20	33	33	10	Performance over tools
Nick Trzesniak	19	SD	IDA	PION	C	.341	45	132	6	2	7	30	23	30	4	Best of the catcher lot
Ron Davenport	18	TOR	MED	PION	1B	.345	79	229	16	2	4	46	21	28	5	Natural born hitter
Guillermo Reyes	18	CWS	BRS	APPY	2B	.296	76	257	10	2	3	31	22	24	21	Little-ball expert
Corey Smith	18	CLE	BUR	APPY	3B	.256	53	207	8	2	4	39	27	50	8	Upside lower each year
Chad Santos	19	KC	SPK	KC	1B	.251	67	267	18	0	14	47	36	103	1	Too many whiffs
Jared Abruzzo	18	ANA	BUT	PION	C	.255	53	208	11	0	8	45	61	58	1	Another nice catcher
Josh Gray	18	ANA	BUT	PION	DH	.327	48	147	11	3	8	36	19	41	1	Find a position, sir

A LOOK BACK ...
Historical Organizational Top Tens

ARIZONA DIAMONBACKS

1995	1996	1997	1998	1999
(NONE)	(NONE)	1 - 1B Travis Lee	P John Patterson	P John Patterson
		2 - P Nick Bierbrodt	P Brad Penny	OF Abraham Nunez
		3 - P John Patterson	2B Jackie Rexrode	1B Erubiel Durazo
		4 - 2B Jackie Rexrode	OF Jhensy Sandoval	OF Jack Cust
		5 - P Vladimir Nunez	SS Danny Klassen	OF Dante Powell
		6 -	P Nick Bierbrodt	P Nick Bierbrodt
		7 -	P Vladimir Nunez	SS Danny Klassen
		8 -	C Mark Osborne	2B Carlos Urquiola
		9 -	OF Jack Cust	OF Jhensy Sandoval
		10 -	OF Garry Maddox	P Ben Norris

ATLANTA BRAVES

1 - OF Andruw Jones	OF Andruw Jones	P Jason Marquis	P Bruce Chen	SS Rafael Furcal
2 - P Jason Schmidt	P Damian Moss	P Damian Moss	OF George Lombard	P Jason Marquis
3 - P Damian Moss	3B Wes Helms	3B Wes Helms	2B Marcus Giles	2B Marcus Giles
4 - OF Jermaine Dye	OF Jermaine Dye	OF George Lombard	P Jason Marquis	OF George Lombard
5 - P Terrell Wade	P Winston Abreu	P Bruce Chen	P Rob Bell	P Luis Rivera
6 - 1B Ron Wright	OF George Lombard	P Rob Bell	P Odalis Perez	P Jung Bong
7 - OF Gator McBride	SS Danny Magee	3B Mike Hessman	P Kevin McGlinchy	OF Ryan Langerhans
8 - OF Damon Hollins	3B Bobby Smith	P Kevin McGlinchy	3B Wes Helms	1B Wes Helms
9 - 3B Bobby Smith	P Ismael Villegas	P Jimmy Osting	1B A.J. Zapp	C Jean Boscan
10 - OF Anton French	OF Juan Williams	SS Bobby Smith	SS Troy Cameron	3B Troy Cameron

CHICAGO CUBS

1 - P Amaury Telemaco	P Kerry Wood	P Kerry Wood	C Pat Cline	OF Corey Patterson
2 - OF Brooks Kieschnick	C Pat Cline	C Pat Cline	2B Chad Meyers	1B Hee Choi
3 - C Pat Cline	3B Kevin Orie	SS Dennis Abreu	OF Jaisen Randolph	P Ruben Quevedo
4 - 2B Bobby Morris	OF Pedro Valdez	P Jeremi Gonzalez	P Chris Gissell	C Jeff Goldbach
5 - OF Robin Jennings	OF Robin Jennings	P Amaury Telemaco	P Phillip Norton	3B Cole Liniak
6 - P Terry Adams	1B Brooks Kieschnick	P Courtney Duncan	C Brad Ramsey	2B Chad Meyers
7 - OF Pedro Valdes	P Steve Rain	2B Elinton Jasco	SS Dennis Abreu	3B Dave Kelton
8 - P Jason Ryan	2B Elinton Jasco	OF Pedro Valdes	P Courtney Duncan	1B Eric Hinske
9 - 1B Brant Brown	1B Brant Brown	OF Quincy Carter	P Brian McNichol	OF Jaisen Randolph
10 - P Javier Martinez	1B Bobby Morris	P Steve Rain	2B Franklin Font	OF Roosevelt Brown

CINCINNATI REDS

1995	1996	1997	1998	1999
1 - OF Steve Gibralter	P Curt Lyons	SS Damian Jackson	SS Travis Dawkins	SS Travis Dawkins
2 - SS Pokey Reese	SS Pokey Reese	OF Darron Ingram	OF Mike Frank	OF Austin Kearns
3 - 3B Willie Greene	OF Steve Gibralter	3B Aaron Boone	SS Damian Jackson	P Rob Bell
4 - IF Eric Owens	P Brett Tomko	C Justin Towle	P Scott Williamson	2B Antonio Perez
5 - OF Pat Watkins	3B Aaron Boone	P Buddy Carlyle	C Jason LaRue	OF Alejandro Diaz
6 - OF Chad Mottola	C Justin Towle	UT Chris Stynes	OF DeWayne Wise	OF Adam Dunn
7 - P Kevin Jarvis	P Gabe White	OF Pat Watkins	P Jacobo Sequea	OF DeWayne Wise
8 - P Johnny Ruffin	OF Curtis Goodwin	P Danny Graves	3B Brandon Larson	OF Mike Frank
9 - P Jim Nix	OF Decomba Conner	C Paul Bako	1B Roberto Petagine	OF Andy Burress
10 - 3B Aaron Boone	OF Pat Watkins	UT Eric Owens	OF Darron Ingram	OF Samone Peters

COLORADO ROCKIES

1 - P Bryan Rekar	P Jamey Wright	1B Todd Helton	C Ben Petrick	C Ben Petrick
2 - OF Edgard Clemente	OF Edgard Clemente	SS Neifi Perez	P Mike Kusiewicz	P Jason Jennings
3 - OF Derrick Gibson	1B Todd Helton	C Ben Petrick	OF Derrick Gibson	OF Choo Freeman
4 - SS Neifi Perez	C Ben Petrick	OF Edgard Clemente	OF Edgard Clemente	SS Juan Uribe
5 - P Mike Kusiewicz	SS Neifi Perez	OF Derrick Gibson	P Lariel Gonzalez	P Jermaine Van Buren
6 - P Doug Million	OF Derrick Gibson	P Jake Westbrook	P Shawn Chacon	3B Matt Holliday
7 - OF Q. McCracken	P Doug Million	P Mark Brownson	P Jason Brester	OF Edgard Clemente
8 - P Jamey Wright	P Bryan Rekar	2B Elvis Pena	P Josh Kalinowski	OF Jody Gerut
9 - OF Angel Echevarria	P Mike Kusiewicz	P Mike Saipe	2B Elvis Pena	2B Belvani Martinez
10 - 2B Roberto Mejia	P John Thomson	P Mike Kusiewicz	P Mark Brownson	P Josh Kalinowski

FLORIDA MARLINS

1 - SS Edgar Renteria	2B Luis Castillo	OF Mark Kotsay	SS Alex Gonzalez	SS Pablo Ozuna
2 - 2B Luis Castillo	P Livan Hernandez	SS Alex Gonzalez	OF Julio Ramirez	P A.J. Burnett
3 - 2B Ralph Milliard	OF Todd Dunwoody	P Livan Hernandez	P A.J. Burnett	OF Julio Ramirez
4 - OF Todd Dunwoody	OF Jaime Jones	C John Roskos	P Ed Yarnall	P Brad Penny
5 - C John Roskos	OF Billy McMillon	OF Julio Ramirez	2B Luis Castillo	P Jason Grilli
6 - OF Billy McMillon	P Ryan Dempster	OF Jaime Jones	P Todd Noel	P Wes Anderson
7 - P Andy Larkin	P Tony Saunders	OF Todd Dunwoody	1B Nate Rolison	P Nate Bump
8 - P Jay Powell	2B Ralph Milliard	2B Victor Rodriguez	3B Jose Santos	C Ramon Castro
9 - P Matt Mantei	1B Nate Rolison	2B Ralph Milliard	OF Preston Wilson	2B Cesar Crespo
10 - P Chris Seelbach	SS Victor Rodriguez	1B Nate Rolison	OF Jaime Jones	2B Amaury Garcia

HOUSTON ASTROS

1 - P Billy Wagner	P Billy Wagner	OF Richard Hidalgo	OF Lance Berkman	OF Lance Berkman
2 - OF Bobby Abreu	OF Bobby Abreu	P Scott Elarton	P Scott Elarton	1B Daryle Ward
3 - OF Richard Hidalgo	OF Richard Hidalgo	1B Daryle Ward	OF Daryle Ward	P Wilfredo Rodriguez
4 - SS Jhonny Perez	SS Carlos Guillen	1B Lance Berkman	P Wade Miller	P Wade Miller
5 - SS Bry Nelson	P Scott Elarton	SS Carlos Guillen	C Mitch Meluskey	P Mike Nannini
6 - P Tony Mounce	P Edgar Ramos	2B Carlos Hernandez	P Wilfredo Rodriguez	SS Julio Lugo
7 - P Donne Wall	SS Jhonny Perez	C Ramon Castro	P Brian Sikorski	P Tony McKnight
8 - P Scott Elarton	2B Nelson Samboy	P Oscar Henriquez	SS Julio Lugo	P Jeriome Robertson
9 - P Alberto Blanco	SS Russ Johnson	3B Russ Johnson	IF Jhonny Perez	P Eric Ireland
10 - P Chris Holt	P Alberto Blanco	P Wade Miller	3B Russ Johnson	C Mike Rose

LOS ANGELES DODGERS

1995	1996	1997	1998	1999
1 - OF Karim Garcia	3B Adrian Beltre	3B Adrian Beltre	3B Adrian Beltre	OF Chin-Feng Chen
2 - SS Wilton Guerrero	OF Karim Garcia	3B Paul Konerko	OF Hiram Bocachica	P Randey Dorame
3 - P Antonio Osuna	1B Paul Konerko	OF Karim Garcia	OF Luke Allen	3B Luke Allen
4 - OF Roger Cedeno	2B Wilton Guerrero	P Dennis Reyes	1B Glenn Davis	P Luke Prokopec
5 - P Chan Ho Park	P Dennis Reyes	OF Roger Cedeno	P Onan Masaoka	OF Tony Mota
6 - 1B Paul Konerko	3B Brian Richardson	P Onan Masaoka	P Luke Prokopec	P Marcos Castillo
7 - P Hugo Pivaral	P Onan Masaoka	P Ted Lilly	1B Nick Leach	1B Nick Leach
8 - 2B Adam Riggs	2B Adam Riggs	SS Alex Cora	3B Damian Rolls	P Mike Judd
9 - P Rick Gorecki	P Eric Gagne	3B Brian Richardson	SS Alex Cora	OF Glenn Davis
10 - P Kym Ashworth	P Luke Prokopec	1B Jon Tucker	OF Tony Mota	3B Damian Rolls

MILWAUKEE BREWERS

1 - P Jeff D'Amico	P Jeff D'Amico	2B Ron Belliard	2B Ron Belliard	P Nick Neugebauer
2 - OF Geoff Jenkins	2B Ron Belliard	SS Danny Klassen	1B Kevin Barker	P J.M. Gold
3 - SS Mark Loretta	OF Geoff Jenkins	1B Kevin Barker	OF Geoff Jenkins	1B Kevin Barker
4 - 3B Antone Williamson	P Valerio De los Santos	OF Geoff Jenkins	P Val. De los Santos	P Kyle Peterson
5 - SS Danny Klassen	1B Antone Williamson	OF Chad Green	SS Santiago Perez	OF Derry Hammond
6 - OF Duane Singleton	OF Mike Rennhack	P Val. De los Santos	P Kyle Peterson	P Allen Levrault
7 - P Tyrone Narcisse	OF Brian Banks	P Steve Woodard	P Jose Garcia	P Jose Garcia
8 - OF Brian Banks	SS Danny Klassen	1B Antone Williamson	OF Chad Green	3B Jeff Deardorff
9 - 1B Tim Unroe	3B Tim Unroe	OF Mike Rennhack	P Allen Levrault	SS Santiago Perez
10 - P Doug Webb	C Kelly Stinnett	P Allen Levrault	P Doug Johnston	SS Jose Guillen

MONTREAL EXPOS

1 - OF Vladimir Guerrero	OF Vladimir Guerrero	SS Hiram Bocachica	OF Peter Bergeron	P Tony Armas
2 - SS Hiram Bocachica	SS Hiram Bocachica	1B Brad Fullmer	C Michael Barrett	OF Peter Bergeron
3 - P Ugueth Urbina	P Jose Paniagua	C Michael Barrett	P Ted Lilly	P T.J. Tucker
4 - 1B Brad Fullmer	2B Jose Vidro	P Jose Paniagua	1B Jon Tucker	P Ted Lilly
5 - P Everett Stull	OF Yamil Benitez	P Javier Vazquez	P Tony Armas	OF Milton Bradley
6 - 2B Jose Vidro	C Michael Barrett	P Keith Evans	OF Milton Bradley	1B Thomas Pittman
7 - OF Yamil Benitez	P Javier Vazquez	3B Jose Vidro	P John Nicholson	1B Fern. Seguignol
8 - P Derek Aucoin	OF Jon Saffer	OF Jon Saffer	SS Tomas De la Rosa	P Shane Arthurs
9 - OF Jon Saffer	OF Brad Fullmer	P Mike Thurman	P Jake Westbrook	SS Albenis Machado
10 - OF Ray McDavid	P Everett Stull	SS Jason Camilli	P Mike Johnson	1B Jon Tucker

NEW YORK METS

1 - P Paul Wilson	OF Alex Ochoa	P Grant Roberts	OF Alex Escobar	OF Alex Escobar
2 - P Jason Isringhausen	P Arnold Gooch	P Jesus Sanchez	2B Cesar Crespo	OF Jason Tyner
3 - P Bill Pulsipher	OF Jay Payton	OF Jay Payton	P Grant Roberts	P Octavio Dotel
4 - OF Jay Payton	3B Jose Lopez	3B Jose Lopez	P Arnold Gooch	P Pat Strange
5 - OF Alex Ochoa	OF Scott Hunter	OF Scott Hunter	OF Jason Tyner	1B Jorge Toca
6 - 3B Butch Huskey	1B Roberto Petagine	OF Preston Wilson	P Octavio Dotel	P Lesli Brea
7 - SS Rey Ordonez	P Ethan McEntire	OF Carlos Mendoza	OF Scott Hunter	P Grant Roberts
8 - OF Dwight Maness	P Lindsay Gulin	P Ed Yarnall	OF Terrence Long	2B Ty Wigginton
9 - OF Scott Hunter	OF Terrence Long	P Arnold Gooch	3B Jose Lopez	OF Brian Cole
10 - P Arnold Gooch	P Jesus Sanchez	C Pee Wee Lopez	P Dicky Gonzalez	P Dicky Gonzalez

PHILADELPHIA PHILLIES

1995	1996	1997	1998	1999
1 - 3B Scott Rolen	3B Scott Rolen	SS Jimmy Rollins	1B Pat Burrell	1B Pat Burrell
2 - P Rich Hunter	C Bobby Estalella	SS Desi Relaford	SS Jimmy Rollins	P Brad Baisley
3 - C Bobby Estalella	P Calvin Maduro	P Ryan Brannan	OF Eric Valent	P Adam Eaton
4 - P Wayne Gomes	SS Desi Relaford	C Bobby Estalella	C Bobby Estalella	SS Jimmy Rollins
5 - P Larry Wimberly	OF Reggie Taylor	OF Reggie Taylor	P Carlton Loewer	OF Reggie Taylor
6 - 2B Manny Amador	P Rich Hunter	P Adam Eaton	P Randy Wolf	C Bobby Estalella
7 - P Mike Grace	P Randy Knoll	P Kris Stevens	OF Reggie Taylor	OF Josue Perez
8 - OF Wendell Magee	P David Coggin	OF Billy McMillon	P David Coggin	OF Eric Valent
9 - P Carlton Loewer	2B Marlon Anderson	P David Coggin	P Adam Eaton	P Franklin Nunez
10 - C Mike Lieberthal	P Rob Burger	2B Marlon Anderson	P Ryan Brannan	P Jason Brester

PITTSBURGH PIRATES

1 - C Jason Kendall	SS Chad Hermansen	OF Chad Hermansen	OF Chad Hermansen	3B Aramis Ramirez
2 - P Ramon Morel	P Elvin Hernandez	P Kris Benson	SS Abraham Nunez	OF Chad Hermansen
3 - OF Trey Beamon	1B Ron Wright	SS Abraham Nunez	2B Warren Morris	C Humberto Vota
4 - SS Lou Collier	P Jimmy Anderson	3B Aramis Ramirez	P Kris Benson	OF J.J. Davis
5 - P Jimmy Anderson	OF Jose Guillen	1B Ron Wright	3B Kevin Haverbusch	OF Jovanny Sosa
6 - OF Charles Peterson	OF T.J. Staton	P Elvin Hernandez	P Bronson Arroyo	OF Alex Hernandez
7 - 1B Rich Aude	OF Jerm. Allensworth	P Jimmy Anderson	OF Emil Brown	OF Kory DeHaan
8 - OF T.J. Staton	OF Trey Beamon	P Bronson Arroyo	OF Alex Hernandez	OF Tike Redman
9 - SS Tony Robinson	SS Lou Collier	C Craig Wilson	SS Victor Gutierrez	3B K. Haverbusch
10 - P Kevin Pickford	OF Charles Peterson	OF Alex Hernandez	1B Ron Wright	P Jimmy Anderson

ST. LOUIS CARDINALS

1 - P Alan Benes	1B Dmitri Young	SS Brent Butler	P Rick Ankiel	P Rick Ankiel
2 - 2B David Bell	C Eli Marrero	C Eli Marrero	OF J.D. Drew	2B Adam Kennedy
3 - P Brian Barber	P Matt Morris	SS Jason Woolf	SS Pablo Ozuna	P Chad Hutchinson
4 - P Matt Morris	P Kris Detmers	P Braden Looper	P Chad Hutchinson	SS Brent Butler
5 - P T.J. Mathews	P Manny Aybar	P Manny Aybar	SS Brent Butler	P Bud Smith
6 - OF Miguel Mejia	P Corey Avrard	3B Chris Haas	P Braden Looper	SS Jason Woolf
7 - C Eli Marrero	1B Chris Richard	3B Jose Leon	SS Adam Kennedy	3B Chris Haas
8 - OF Dmitri Young	P Blake Stein	OF Scarb. Green	3B Chris Haas	SS Jack Wilson
9 - P Corey Avrard	P Eric Ludwick	2B Placido Polanco	SS Jason Woolf	P Matt DeWitt
10 - P Kris Detmers	P Britt Reames	OF Kerry Robinson	2B Placido Polanco	OF Jason Lariviere

SAN DIEGO PADRES

1 - 1B Derrek Lee	1B Derrek Lee	OF Ruben Rivera	P Matt Clement	3B Sean Burroughs
2 - P Ron Villone	SS Juan Melo	1B Derrek Lee	C Ben Davis	P Junior Herndon
3 - P Dustin Hermanson	P Dustin Hermanson	SS Juan Melo	OF Mike Darr	P Buddy Carlyle
4 - OF Marc Newfield	3B Gabe Alvarez	C Ben Davis	SS Juan Melo	OF Mike Darr
5 - P Marc Kroon	P Heath Murray	3B George Arias	P Buddy Carlyle	SS Kevin Nicholson
6 - P Glenn Dishman	C Ben Davis	P Rafael Medina	3B George Arias	P Wascar Serrano
7 - C Raul Casanova	P Marc Kroon	P Matt Clement	P Junior Herndon	P Isabel Giron
8 - SS Juan Melo	P Matt Clement	P Marc Kroon	OF Gary Matthews	SS Cristian Berroa
9 - P Heath Murray	SS Jorge Velandia	OF Mike Darr	SS Kevin Nicholson	OF Gary Matthews
10 - SS Jorge Velandia	2B Homer Bush	P Heath Murray	OF Kevin Burford	C Wilbert Nieves

SAN FRANCISCO GIANTS

1995	1996	1997	1998	1999
1 - 2B Jay Canizaro	OF Dante Powell	OF Dante Powell	P Jason Grilli	3B Tony Torcato
2 - OF Jacob Cruz	P Shawn Estes	P Joe Fontenot	P Nate Bump	P Scott Linebrink
3 - SS Rich Aurilia	P Russell Ortiz	OF Jacob Cruz	SS Wilson Delgado	OF Arturo McDowell
4 - SS Wilson Delgado	2B Jay Canizaro	SS Wilson Delgado	P Scott Linebrink	P Joe Nathan
5 - C Marcus Jensen	OF Jacob Cruz	P Russell Ortiz	SS Carlos Mendoza	P Jeff Urban
6 - OF Dante Powell	P Lorenzo Barcelo	P Jason Brester	OF Dante Powell	P Chris Jones
7 - P Shawn Estes	P Mike Villano	C Yorvit Torrealba	P Jeff Andra	SS Carlos Mendoza
8 - P Ricky Pickett	C Marcus Jensen	OF Mike Glendenning	OF Mike Byas	C Sammy Serrano
9 - 1B Jesse Ibarra	P Joe Fontenot	P Darin Blood	3B Pedro Feliz	SS Wilson Delgado
10 - P Fausto Macey	P Darin Blood	3B Pedro Feliz	3B Edwards Guzman	OF Mike Byas

ANAHEIM ANGELS

1 - OF Darin Erstad	OF Darin Erstad	C Todd Greene	3B Troy Glaus	P Ramon Ortiz
2 - C Todd Greene	3B George Arias	P Jarrod Washburn	P Jarrod Washburn	OF Nathan Haynes
3 - 3B George Arias	C Todd Greene	OF Norm Hutchins	P Scott Schoeneweis	P Seth Etherton
4 - P Shad Williams	P Jarrod Washburn	P Matt Perisho	P Ramon Ortiz	OF Elpidio Guzman
5 - SS Tim Harkrider	P Scott Schoeneweis	P Scott Schoeneweis	C Jason Dewey	P Jarrod Washburn
6 - SS Paul Failla	P Jose Cintron	P Ramon Ortiz	OF Norm Hutchins	OF Mike Colangelo
7 - P Matt Beaumont	IF Keith Luuloa	OF Rich Stuart	P Matt Wise	P Steve Green
8 - OF Marquis Riley	2B Aaron Guiel	2B Trent Durrington	OF Marcus Knight	2B Trent Durrington
9 - P Jose Cintron	P Jason Dickson	OF Jason Herrick	OF Mike Colangelo	OF Norm Hutchins
10 - P David Holdridge	P Brian Cooper	P Fausto Macey	P Renney Duarte	OF Darren Blakely

BALTIMORE ORIOLES

1 - P Rocky Coppinger	P Rocky Coppinger	P Sidney Ponson	1B Calvin Pickering	P Matt Riley
2 - P Jimmy Haynes	P Chris Fussell	P Brian Falkenborg	P Matt Riley	C Jayson Werth
3 - P Calvin Maduro	P Sidney Ponson	1B Calvin Pickering	OF Darnell McDonald	1B Calvin Pickering
4 - 1B Kevin Curtis	SS Eddy Martinez	SS Eddy Martinez	C Jayson Werth	OF Darn. McDonald
5 - OF Kimera Bartee	OF Eugene Kingsale	P Julio Moreno	2B Jerry Hairston	P John Stephens
6 - SS David Lamb	3B Scott McClain	SS Augie Ojeda	SS Eddy Martinez	2B Jerry Hairston
7 - P Billy Percibal	P Billy Percibal	OF Eugene Kingsale	OF Eugene Kingsale	OF Luis Matos
8 - P Garrett Stephenson	OF Carlos Akins	P Chris Fussell	P Brian Falkenborg	P Jacobo Sequea
9 - C B.J. Waszgis	1B Tommy Davis	OF David Dellucci	P John Stephens	P B.J. Ryan
10 - OF Danny Clyburn	P Julio Moreno	OF Danny Clyburn	P Chris Fussell	P Brian Falkenborg

BOSTON RED SOX

1 - SS Nomar Garciaparra	SS Nomar Garciaparra	P Carl Pavano	OF Dernell Stenson	1B Dernell Stenson
2 - P Jeff Suppan	P Jeff Suppan	OF Michael Coleman	3B Cole Liniak	C Steve Lomasney
3 - SS Donnie Sadler	P Carl Pavano	P Jeff Suppan	P John Curtice	3B Wilton Veras
4 - P Rafael Orellano	SS Donnie Sadler	P Tony Armas	P Jin Ho Cho	SS Adam Everett
5 - OF Trot Nixon	P Juan Pena	3B Cole Liniak	P Juan Pena	P Tomokazu Ohka
6 - OF Michael Coleman	P Brian Rose	P Brian Rose	OF Trot Nixon	P Jin Ho Cho
7 - P Shayne Bennett	C Damian Sapp	2B Donnie Sadler	OF Michael Coleman	P Juan Pena
8 - 1B Ryan McGuire	3B Cole Liniak	P Juan Pena	3B Wilton Veras	OF Michael Coleman
9 - OF Jose Malave	OF Trot Nixon	P Chris Reitsma	P Sun Kim	P Sun Woo Kim
10 - P Carl Pavano	OF Michael Coleman	OF Dernell Stenson	P Paxton Crawford	SS Aaron Capista

CHICAGO WHITE SOX

1995	1996	1997	1998	1999
1 - OF Jeff Abbott	OF Jeff Abbott	1B Mario Valdez	3B Carlos Lee	P Jon Garland
2 - SS Chris Snopek	3B Jeff Liefer	SS Mike Caruso	P Aaron Myette	P Kip Wells
3 - P Tom Fordham	OF Mike Cameron	3B Carlos Lee	1B Mario Valdez	P Aaron Myette
4 - OF Lyle Mouton	1B Mario Valdez	OF Jeff Abbott	3B Joe Crede	3B Joe Crede
5 - 3B Greg Norton	C Josh Paul	P Lorenzo Barcelo	P Jon Garland	SS Jason Dellaero
6 - P Luis Andujar	P Tom Fordham	P Jim Parque	C Mark Johnson	OF Mc. Christensen
7 - P Scott Ruffcorn	P Scott Ruffcorn	OF Jeff Liefer	1B Jeff Liefer	P Josh Fogg
8 - P Bill Simas	SS Greg Norton	OF Brian Simmons	OF Brett Caradonna	OF Aaron Rowand
9 - P Andrew Lorraine	3B Olmedo Saenz	C Josh Paul	P Lorenzo Barcelo	1B Mario Valdez
10 - P James Baldwin	3B Carlos Lee	OF Magglio Ordonez	P Jason Lakman	OF Jeff Abbott

CLEVELAND INDIANS

1 - P Bartolo Colon	P Bartolo Colon	P Jaret Wright	1B Richie Sexson	3B Russell Branyan
2 - 1B Richie Sexson	P Jaret Wright	P Bartolo Colon	3B Russell Branyan	P C.C. Sabathia
3 - P Alan Embree	SS Enrique Wilson	3B Russell Branyan	2B Enrique Wilson	P Willie Martinez
4 - SS Enrique Wilson	OF Brian Giles	2B Enrique Wilson	P Willie Martinez	P Tim Drew
5 - OF Brian Giles	1B Richie Sexson	1B Sean Casey	C Edgar Cruz	C Edgar Cruz
6 - P Jaret Wright	P Danny Graves	P Willie Martinez	P Tim Drew	OF Alex Ramirez
7 - P Paul Shuey	3B Russell Branyan	1B Richie Sexson	OF Alex Ramirez	P Rob Pugmire
8 - SS Damian Jackson	P Frankie Sanders	OF Danny Peoples	P Alberto Garza	P Jamie Brown
9 - P Casey Whitten	1B Sean Casey	2B Marcos Scutaro	P Frankie Sanders	2B Marcos Scutaro
10 - P Daron Kirkreit	OF Alex Ramirez	OF Chad Whitaker	P Jamie Brown	P David Riske

DETROIT TIGERS

1 - P Mike Drumright	P Mike Drumright	OF Juan Encarnacion	P Matt Anderson	P Francisco Cordero
2 - P C.J. Nitkowski	P Justin Thompson	P Mike Drumright	OF Juan Encarnacion	1B Eric Munson
3 - OF Juan Encarnacion	P Matt Drews	2B Richard Almanzar	P Alan Webb	P Alan Webb
4 - 2B Richard Almanzar	2B Richard Almanzar	2B Rene Capellan	OF Gabe Kapler	P Nate Cornejo
5 - P Cade Gaspar	OF Juan Encarnacion	OF Gabe Kapler	3B Gabe Alvarez	P Shane Loux
6 - 1B Daryle Ward	OF Anton French	P Matt Drews	P Seth Greisinger	P Dave Borkowski
7 - 1B Tony Clark	1B Daryle Ward	2B Frank Catalanotto	P Shane Loux	C Javier Cardona
8 - OF Mike Darr	OF Gabe Kapler	P Seth Greisinger	P Francisco Cordero	P Adam Pettyjohn
9 - OF Micah Franklin	OF Bubba Trammell	P Clayton Bruner	P Dave Borkowski	2B Pedro Santana
10 - P Cam Smith	2B Frank Catalanotto	P Francisco Cordero	C Javier Cardona	3B Matt Boone

KANSAS CITY ROYALS

1 - OF Johnny Damon	C Mike Sweeney	OF Dee Brown	OF Jeremy Giambi	OF Dee Brown
2 - C Mike Sweeney	P Jim Pittsley	OF Carlos Beltran	OF Carlos Beltran	P Dan Reichert
3 - P Jim Pittsley	P Glendon Rusch	OF Jeremy Giambi	OF Dee Brown	P Junior Guerrero
4 - P Glendon Rusch	P Jose Rosado	SS Felix Martinez	P Dan Reichert	P Orber Moreno
5 - OF Michael Tucker	3B Mendy Lopez	2B Sergio Nunez	2B Carlos Febles	P Jeff Austin
6 - 2B Sergio Nunez	2B Sergio Nunez	2B Carlos Febles	P Chad Durbin	P Chris George
7 - SS Anthony Medrano	2B Jed Hansen	2B Jed Hansen	P Orber Moreno	P Chris Fussell
8 - C Sal Fasano	OF Jon Nunnally	IF Mendy Lopez	OF Juan LeBron	P Chad Durbin
9 - 3B Mendy Lopez	P Jaime Bluma	OF Yamil Benitez	P Enrique Calero	OF Jeremy Dodson
10 - P Ken Ray	SS Anthony Medrano	OF Juan LeBron	OF Goefrey Tomlinson	OF Goef. Tomlinson

MINNESOTA TWINS

1995	1996	1997	1998	1999
1 - C Javier Valentin	3B Todd Walker	SS Luis Rivas	SS Luis Rivas	SS Luis Rivas
2 - 2B Todd Walker	C Javier Valentin	3B Todd Walker	SS Michael Cuddyer	3B Michael Cuddyer
3 - OF Matt Lawton	P Dan Serafini	1B David Ortiz	SS Cristian Guzman	OF Mike Restovich
4 - P Dan Serafini	OF Torii Hunter	OF Jacque Jones	C Matt LeCroy	C Matt LeCroy
5 - OF Torii Hunter	P Jason Bell	C Javier Valentin	OF Torii Hunter	1B David Ortiz
6 - OF Chris Latham	OF Rafael Alvarez	P Dan Serafini	C A.J. Pierzynski	P Kyle Lohse
7 - OF Rafael Alvarez	P Mark Redman	SS Dan Cey	OF Jacque Jones	P Jason Ryan
8 - OF J.J. Johnson	OF J.J. Johnson	P Mark Redman	OF John Barnes	C A.J. Pierzynski
9 - P Hector Trinidad	2B Ryan Lane	C A.J. Pierzynski	OF Chad Allen	P Juan Rincon
10 - P LaTroy Hawkins	P LaTroy Hawkins	P Jason Bell	P Jason Bell	OF Papo Bolivar

NEW YORK YANKEES

1 - SS Derek Jeter	OF Ruben Rivera	P Eric Milton	1B Nick Johnson	1B Nick Johnson
2 - OF Ruben Rivera	SS D'Angelo Jimenez	OF Ricky Ledee	P Ryan Bradley	SS Alfonso Soriano
3 - P Matt Drews	OF Ricky Ledee	SS D'Angelo Jimenez	3B Mike Lowell	SS D'Angelo Jimenez
4 - P Ray Ricken	P Rafael Medina	P Luis De los Santos	OF Ricky Ledee	OF Jackson Melian
5 - 3B Andy Fox	P Ray Ricken	1B Nick Johnson	SS D'Angelo Jimenez	P Ed Yarnall
6 - C Jorge Posada	P Dan Rios	OF Donzell McDonald	OF Jackson Melian	3B Drew Henson
7 - OF Shane Spencer	C Jorge Posada	SS Cristian Guzman	P Luis De los Santos	P Ryan Bradley
8 - C Chris Ashby	OF Brian Buchanan	3B Mike Lowell	P Jay Tessmer	P Todd Noel
9 - P Brett Schlomann	P Jay Tessmer	OF Brian Buchanan	P Brian Reith	P Luis De los Santos
10 - C Mike Figga	C Chris Ashby	IF Gabby Martinez	P Zach Day	C Victor Valencia

OAKLAND ATHLETICS

1 - 1B Steve Cox	SS Miguel Tejada	OF Ben Grieve	3B Eric Chavez	P Barry Zito
2 - OF Ben Grieve	OF Ben Grieve	SS Miguel Tejada	P Chad Harville	P Chad Harville
3 - 1B Jason Giambi	SS Mark Bellhorn	3B Eric Chavez	OF Nathan Haynes	P Mark Mulder
4 - OF Ernie Young	1B Steve Cox	2B Mark Bellhorn	C Ramon Hernandez	P Jesus Colome
5 - P John Wasdin	SS Tony Batista	C A.J. Hinch	3B Mark Bellhorn	C Ramon Hernandez
6 - P Jay Witasick	OF Mario Encarnacion	SS Jose Ortiz	OF Mario Encarnacion	OF Mario Encarnacion
7 - OF Jose Herrera	P Willie Adams	C Ramon Hernandez	P Eric DuBose	3B Adam Piatt
8 - P Bret Wagner	P Jay Witasick	OF Mario Encarnacion	P Chris Enochs	OF Gary Thomas
9 - P Willie Adams	C Ramon Hernandez	P Chris Enochs	2B Jose Ortiz	2B Esteban German
10 - SS Tony Batista	3B Scott Spiezio	1B Steve Cox	P Kevin Gregg	SS Jose Ortiz

SEATTLE MARINERS

1 - SS Alex Rodriguez	OF Jose Cruz, Jr.	P Ken Cloude	P Ryan Anderson	P Ryan Anderson
2 - SS Desi Relaford	1B David Ortiz	OF Shane Monahan	P Freddy Garcia	OF Alex Fernandez
3 - P Bob Wolcott	C Chris Widger	P Denny Stark	P Gil Meche	P Joel Pineiro
4 - OF Jose Cruz, Jr.	P Ken Cloude	3B Jason Regan	2B Carlos Guillen	SS Vaughn Schill
5 - 3B Arquimedez Pozo	OF Shane Monahan	P Brian Fuentes	2B Adonis Harrison	2B Adonis Harrison
6 - 1B Greg Pirkl	1B Jim Bonnici	P Joe Mays	OF Shane Monahan	P Chris Mears
7 - OF Darren Bragg	C Jason Varitek	3B Luis Figueroa	2B Jermaine Clark	2B Jermaine Clark
8 - C Jason Varitek	OF Raul Ibanez	2B Adonis Harrison	3B Jason Regan	1B Peanut Williams
9 - P Matt Wagner	P Makoto Suzuki	OF Mike Burrows	P Brian Fuentes	C Carlos Maldonado
10 - C Raul Ibanez	OF Marcus Sturdivant	SS Ramon Vazquez	P Joel Pineiro	P Brian Fuentes

TAMPA BAY DEVIL RAYS

1995	1996	1997	1998	1999
(NONE)	(NONE)	1 - P Matt White	P Matt White	SS Ramon Soler
		2 - OF Alex Sanchez	OF Alex Sanchez	OF Josh Hamilton
		3 - P Rolando Arrojo	OF Kenny Kelly	P Matt White
		4 - P Bobby Seay	P Cedrick Bowers	P Bobby Seay
		5 - P Cedrick Bowers	P Bobby Seay	P Jason Standridge
		6 -	OF Carlos Mendoza	OF Kenny Kelly
		7 -	SS E. De los Santos	3B Jared Sandberg
		8 -	P Pablo Ortega	3B Aubrey Huff
		9 -	1B Steve Cox	OF Alex Sanchez
		10 -	OF Paul Wilder	P Dan Wheeler

TEXAS RANGERS

1 - 2B Edwin Diaz	2B Edwin Diaz	OF Ruben Mateo	OF Ruben Mateo	OF Ruben Mateo
2 - 3B Fernando Tatis	3B Mike Bell	3B Fernando Tatis	1B Carlos Pena	2B Jason Romano
3 - 3B Mike Bell	3B Fernando Tatis	P Corey Lee	C Cesar King	1B Carlos Pena
4 - C Kevin Brown	OF Ruben Mateo	2B Warren Morris	1B Shawn Gallagher	P Corey Lee
5 - P Mark Mimbs	C Kevin Brown	C Cesar King	2B Jason Romano	3B Tom Evans
6 - OF Andrew Vessel	P Jonathan Johnson	2B Mike Bell	P Corey Lee	C Cesar King
7 - P Rick Helling	P Danny Kolb	2B Edwin Diaz	P Brandon Knight	3B Mike Lamb
8 - P Julio Santana	P Ted Silva	C Kevin Brown	P Jonathan Johnson	SS Kelly Dransfeldt
9 - P Jose Alberro	OF Mark Little	P Brandon Knight	OF Juan Piniella	1B Shawn Gallagher
10 - P Rod Seip	OF Andrew Vessel	SS Hanley Frias	OF Mike Zywica	P Andy Pratt

TORONTO BLUE JAYS

1 - 1B Carlos Delgado	OF Shannon Stewart	OF Shannon Stewart	OF Vernon Wells	OF Vernon Wells
2 - OF Shannon Stewart	3B Tom Evans	P Kelvim Escobar	P Roy Halladay	SS Cesar Izturis
3 - P Marty Janzen	P Jose Pett	P Roy Halladay	3B Tom Evans	SS Felipe Lopez
4 - P Jose Pett	P Kelvim Escobar	P Chris Carpenter	P Isabel Giron	2B Brent Abernathy
5 - 2B Felipe Crespo	1B Ryan Jones	3B Tom Evans	2B Brent Abernathy	2B Jorge Nunez
6 - 3B Tom Evans	P Roy Halladay	P Bill Koch	SS Joe Lawrence	P Clayton Andrews
7 - SS Kevin Witt	P Chris Carpenter	1B Kevin Witt	P Clayton Andrews	3B Joe Lawrence
8 - P Jose Silva	SS Kevin Witt	2B Jeff Patzke	3B Andy Thompson	1B Kevin Witt
9 - P Chris Carpenter	2B Felipe Crespo	3B Andy Thompson	1B Kevin Witt	2B Mike Young
10 - 2B Miguel Cairo	1B Mike Whitlock	P Clint Lawrence	OF Peter Tucci	P Gary Glover

ARIZONA DIAMONDBACKS
ORGANIZATIONAL GRID

	AAA	AA	HI-A	LO-A
1B	Luis Ortiz - R - 30	Lyle Overbay - L - 23 Victor Sanchez - R - 28	Steve Neal - L - 23	Billy Martin - R - 24
2B	Vick Brown - R - 27	Walt White - R - 28 Jamie Saylor - L - 25 Junior Spivey - R - 25	Francisco Belliard - B - 20 Jeff Powers - L - 24	Jack Santora - B - 23
SS	Esteban Beltre - R - 32 Jhonny Carvajal - R - 25	Alex Cintron - B - 21	Yuri Sanchez - L - 26 Luis Santos - R - 21 Jason Williams - R - 21	Matt Kata - B - 22
3B	Bry Nelson - B - 26	Doug Newstrom - L - 28 Brian Dallimore - R - 26	Jeff Brooks - R - 20	Javier Fuentes - R - 25 Ryan Owens - R - 22
OF	Chip Sell - L - 29 David Dellucci - L - 26 Jamie Gann - R - 25 Damon Mashore - R - 30	Jack Cust - L - 21 Fletcher Bates - B - 26 Carlos Urquiola - L - 20 Ramon Gomez - R - 24	Brian Gordon - L - 21 Jamie Sykes - R - 25 Cedrick Harris - R - 21 Steve Woodward - B - 21	Kevan Burns - L - 23 Doug DeVore - L - 22 Jhensy Sandoval - R - 21 Julius Foreman - R - 21 Tim Olson - R - 21
C	Rod Barajas - R - 24 Ken Huckaby - R - 29	Mike Rose - R - 23 Brad Cresse - R - 21 Robby Hammock - R - 23	Josh Glassey - L - 23 Travis Oglesby - R - 22	J.D. Closser - B - 20 Joe Kalczynski - R - 22 John Massey - R - 21
SP	Erik Sabel - R - 25 John Patterson - R - 22 Steve Randolph - L - 26 Kennie Steenstra - R - 29 Shawn Boskie - R - 33 Dan Carlson - R - 30 Bill Pulsipher - L - 26 Dave Tuttle - R - 30 Jeff Andrews - R - 25	Brian Scott - R - 24 Martin Sanchez - R - 23 Nick Bierbrodt - L - 22 Ben Norris - L - 22 Chris Cervantes - L - 21 Blake Mayo - R - 27 Rafael Pina - R - 28 Todd Thorn - L - 23	Jason Jensen - L - 24 Javier Lopez - L - 22 Hatuey Mendoza - R - 20 Scott Barber - R - 21 Mike Rooney - R - 24 Mike Schultz - R - 21 Oscar Villarreal - R - 18	Duaner Sanchez - R - 20 Greg Valera - R - 21 Chris Capuano - L - 22 Juan Ovalles - R - 18 Francisco Trejo - L - 20 Bill White - L - 21
CLOSER	Clint Davis - R - 30 Dave Evans - R - 32	Bret Prinz - R - 23 Mike Koplove - R - 23	Greg Belson - R - 21	Brandon Webb - R - 21 Brian Matzenbacher -R- 23

ARIZONA DIAMONDBACKS

The Diamondbacks' overall development strategy has been called into question due to some questionable early round draft selections, most notably 1999 first rounder Corey Myers, and a willingness to part with many early round picks as compensation for the signing of such iffy Type-A free agents as Greg Swindell and Russ Springer. They have filled some of the cracks with the free agent signings of some superior, if somewhat advanced in age, prospects such as Erubiel Durazo, Alex Cabrera and Geraldo Guzman.

At first base, the Diamondbacks rolled the dice and hit the jackpot in consecutive years with the signings of Durazo and Cabrera. Both are legitimate prospects, and should be big contributors at the major league level in the intermediate term. The club believes it has another sleeper in Lyle Overbay, but he's not in the league of the other two.

There are no significant second base prospects in the system, so Jay Bell had better remain productive for a while longer.

6'2", 180, switch-hitter Alex Cintron has made substantial progress in each successive season, and now appears to have a shot to challenge for the starting major league shortstop job sometime in the next two seasons. Teenager Maximo Vizcaino has promising raw skills, but was unable to produce in a full-season league in his first attempt last season.

Only Jeff Brooks has a significant upside among the club's third base prospects. However, the 6'5", 235, righthanded hitter has yet to meet a pitch that he didn't like, and appears to lack a single defining tool.

The Diamondbacks possess a handful of top quality outfield prospects, as well as a few scrappy overachievers who could contribute in supplementary big league roles down the road. Jason Conti clearly fits into the latter category. He squeezes the most out of humble raw tools, and is an instinctive winner. The once-promising career of David Dellucci appears to have been stalled by injuries. He

was unproductive in a limited Triple-A role last season. Jack Cust is the premier prospect in the system. Think Jim Thome. The only downside, he could evoke memories of Greg Luzinski in left field. Carlos Urquiola was shifted from second base to the outfield last season. He has no power, and despite his multiple complementary skills, not many starting major league outfielders are utterly powerless these days. Lefthanded hitter Brian Gordon was the best on-field performer among Diamondbacks' Class A outfielders last season, but others such as Jhensy Sandoval, Luis Terrero and Victor Hall have much better tools and power/speed upsides, though each has one or more glaring flaws at this stage in their development.

At catcher, Rod Barajas has the best chance of eventually earning a major league role. He'll never hit enough to contend for more than a share of a major league job, however. Among others, only Low-A receiver J.D. Closser, a switch-hitter with some power potential, merits attention.

The pitching depth of the system was relatively lean before top prospect John Patterson went down with a serious elbow injury that required reconstructive surgery. Nelson Figueroa is the epitome of the "Quadruple-A" pitcher. He's a bit too good for Triple-A hitters, but doesn't likely have good enough stuff or command to consistently retire major leaguers. Geraldo Guzman might be different. The club found him in Taiwan in 1999, and saw him rocket through the system last season. He can pitch in any role, and has a rubber arm. The club has always had high hopes for lefties Nick Bierbrodt and Ben Norris, but both were cuffed around by Triple-A hitters last season due to control and consistency issues. Neither should be counted upon at the major league level in 2001. Lean righthander Hatuey Mendoza has the makings of a promising arsenal, but had abysmal control last season. A couple of members of the 2000 Low-A South Bend staff bear watching. Dominican Duaner Sanchez and Mexican Oscar Villarreal both have an advanced feel for pitching for their age, but could be sternly tested in the pitchers' nightmare that is High-A High Desert in 2001.

The Diamondbacks' system advanced first baseman Cabrera and pitchers Guzman and Vicente Padilla into second-half 2000 major league roles, and closer Byung-Hyun Kim was brilliant in his first full major league season. Durazo suffered through an injury-plagued season, but remains a top hitting prospect. Outfielder Conti, infielder Danny Klassen and pitcher Figueroa also showed promise in cameo appearances in the majors.

TOP TEN PROSPECTS

1 - OF Jack Cust - Cust, 21, is a natural power prospect who is likely to assume a long-term position in the middle of the Diamondbacks' major league lineup. The 6'2", 200, 1997 first round pick evokes memories of a youthful Jim Thome. The lefthanded hitter has exceptional plate discipline, but will quite often swing through high fastballs, and therefore accumulate high strikeout and walk totals. The ball simply explodes off his bat, and he has light-tower power from gap to gap. He has worked hard to make himself a passable left fielder, but it's pretty clear that power is his only tool that projects to be above major league average. He is a smart baserunner who will occasionally steal a base via the element of surprise. A shift to first base also could be in his future, though the Diamondbacks are quite deep at that position. Cust is likely to step into the major league lineup sometime in 2001, and should be a long-term 30-plus homer, 100-plus RBI guy in the majors.

2 - C Brad Cresse - Cresse, 21, made an immediate offensive impact after being selected on the fifth round of the 2000 draft, tearing apart the High-A California League and earning a promotion to Double-A El Paso by season's end. The 6'3", 225, righthander is a natural power hitter who made a seamless transition to the wooden bat, drilling 17 homers in 173 High-A bats, albeit in a cozy hitters' environment at High Desert. He is a fairly wild swinger who often expands his strike zone to an unacceptable size, and has a tendency to be too pull-conscious. Still, you simply can't teach this kind of power. Defensively, he's got some work ahead of him. His mechanics are decent for a big man, but his arm strength and release quickness are both below average at this stage in his development. He'll advance quickly, and will reach the majors as soon as his glove allows him. He could get a September 2001 audition, and will battle with the Twins' Adam Johnson to be the first 2000 draftee to get to the show.

3 - OF Carlos Urquiola - Urquiola, 20, is a small 5'8", 150, speed merchant who rose to the Double-A level in 2000, where he ranked as one of the youngest regulars in the Texas League. Urquiola is a switch-hitter who knows and is comfortable with his strengths and weaknesses. He is adept at keeping the ball on the ground, a good thing since he is unlikely to ever develop significant home run power, even with increased physical development. He is one of the fastest players in the minors, and should emerge as a 30-plus stolen base threat once he develops better technique. He is almost impossible to strike out, and should emerge as a top-of-the-order major league prospect by 2003. His ability to also play a fair second base enhances his eventual major league value. Think of Tony Womack with a little better plate discipline, and you've got Urquiola.

4 - 1B Alex Cabrera - Cabrera, 27, much like Erubiel Durazo in 1999, was an out-of-nowhere success story last season, and could end up playing a significant, long-term role with the club. A Brewers' prospect in an earlier life, Cabrera nomadically wandered among leagues in Mexico, Taiwan and Venezuela before resurfacing at Double-A El Paso at the beginning of the 2000 season. All he did was hit 35 homers in 54 games there, even at his advanced age for a prospect, you don't put up numbers like that by accident. Cabrera was recognized as the Texas League's most exciting player by its managers, and continued his power exploits at Triple-A, and, in early opportunities, the major leagues. Then, an inability to fight off quality breaking stuff at this stage in his development limited him. The strapping righthanded hitter has the raw power to be a major league contributor, but starting opportunities at that level don't open up often. Look for Cabrera, who can also play a respectable left field, to help out in Arizona in a complementary role in Arizona for the foreseeable future.

5 - SS Alex Cintron - Cintron, 21, is a switch-hitting, 6'3", 180, shortstop who is likely to be the next Diamondbacks' starter at that position. All that remains to be seen is whether he emerges as a defensively oriented number eight hitter, or as a polished, all-around prospect. Cintron can hit; he has batted around .300 everywhere he's been, most recently at Double-A El Paso. However, his plate discipline remains poor, and despite playing his home games in a hitters' paradise last season, he only slightly tapped into the extra-base power that his frame suggests should exist. His basestealing upside is quite limited as well. Defensively, Cintron is quite solid, combining fine range with a strong throwing arm. Unlike many gifted young shortstops, Cintron is quite reliable on the routine play. At this point, the best guess is that Cintron will be the starting major league shortstop in 2003, and that he will emerge as a .270ish hitter with low power and speed upsides who will fit snugly near the bottom of the major league order.

6 - OF Luis Terrero - I don't make it a habit to include prospects without significant full-season league experience on organizational Top Ten lists, but the combination of the Diamondbacks' dearth of prospects at upper levels and Terrero's exceptional all-around skills qualifies him for an exception. This 6'2", 183, righthanded hitter has eyecatching raw tools, including excellent speed and raw power potential, plus well above average defensive range in center field and a howitzer throwing arm. His glaring weakness, extremely poor plate discipline, is a potential career-breaker, however. Even in rookie ball, Terrero, 20, made it a habit to get himself out regularly last season. I had the good fortune to watch him dominate the annual Hall of Fame Game, against major league competition, last summer. He had two key hits and made two astonishing defensive plays in center field that saved the game and earned him MVP honors. Watch that strikeout/walk ratio; with improvement, he could make a major move upward in 2001.

7 - OF Victor Hall - Hall, 19, was an unheralded 1998 12th round pick who is on the verge of emerging as a potential top of the order major league threat. The 6'0", 170, lefthanded hitter's main asset is pure speed. He ranks as the Diamondbacks' fastest minor leaguer, and one of the fastest prospects anywhere. Though he has earned little full season experience to this point, he has already made significant strides in various areas of his game in rookie ball. He's a consistent line drive hitter who hit the ball with much more authority to the gaps last season, and has developed uncanny plate discipline for a youngster. He's a year younger than Terrero, and much more polished offensively, but has nowhere near the defensive potential. Hall is most likely to wind up in left field as he advances. Look for a full-season league breakout next year, and a major league debut as either a leadoff man or fourth outfielder by late 2003 or early 2004.

8 - RHP John Patterson - Patterson, 22, arguably the Diamondbacks' best prospect ever since his arrival to the system in 1996, slid backward in 2000, undergoing Tommy John reconstructive elbow surgery at midseason. He won't be ready to pitch again until mid-2001 at the earliest. At his best, Patterson appeared to be a solid contender for a long-term upper rotation role in the major leagues. The 6'6", 197, righty relied on a mid-to-upper 90s fastball and a deadly curveball that was his out pitch, and possibly the pitch that hastened his elbow woes. Kerry Wood's 2000 major league comeback could offer some insight into Patterson's future. Getting the fastball back wasn't Wood's problem, and likely won't be Patterson's. It's their exceptional, almost unnatural, breaking pitches that once defined them, and that will be hard to recapture. If Patterson proves healthy in 2001, he will likely retain a big league future. He won't likely be the dominant hurler he was previously, and a shift to the bullpen might be necessary for him to become an impact big leaguer.

9 - RHP Jeremy Ward - The Diamondbacks plucked Ward, 22, on the second round of the 1999 draft. He had become a closer during his final season at Long Beach State, and he initially thrived in the role, as narrowing his repertoire to his mid 90s heater and hard slider worked wonders for him psychologically. His mechanics, quite inconsistent in his days as a college starter, suddenly were much improved. A combination of injury and recurrence of his mechanical woes led to a wasted 2000 season The 6'3", 220, righthander has prototypical closer's stuff and mindset. He's a dogged competitor who wants the ball with the game on the line. For all of his promise, however, Ward has only a few innings of professional ball under his belt. The Diamondbacks need to see him excel over a full season somewhere before penciling him into their major league plans. He'll likely be the Triple-A closer in 2001, and if all goes well, could do some time as a big league situational righty.

10 - LHP Nick Bierbrodt - The Diamondbacks are getting a bit tired of waiting for their 1996 first round pick to develop. Bierbrodt, 22, is a 6'5", 190, lefthander who has been plagued by elbow injuries throughout his professional career. Even when healthy, however, Bierbrodt has been unable to throw quality strikes consistently. His fastball is only a bit above major league average, and when it is working, he keeps it low in the strike zone. He needs to keep hitters off balance with his curve and changeup to succeed. The trickiest pitch for Bierbrodt to throw, however, has been strike one. He has consistently run up high pitch counts and has averaged no better than five innings per start for his career to date. Bierbrodt has reached a crossroads; if he does not remain healthy and show substantial progress in 2001, his window of opportunity to reach his considerable potential will likely close. As a lefty, he'll always have situational bullpen possibilities ahead if he enhances his command.

OTHER PROSPECTS

3B Jeff Brooks - The righthanded batter spent his first three pro seasons in Rookie ball until he got it right. Last year at High-A High Desert, he showed power to the gaps, but who doesn't? He struck out at an alarming rate (117 Ks, 25 walks), which gave him just a .288 on-base average. At 21, he still has time to develop, though it may be difficult to evaluate him in the offense-oriented parks in the Arizona organization.

OF Jason Conti - At 26, Conti is a bit old for a prospect, but he did make it to the majors last season. In the lower minors, he was an on-base machine; Conti scored 125 runs at Double-A Tulsa in 1998. The lefthanded batter is a good, strong-armed center fielder and can steal a base, but in Triple-A and the majors he hasn't walked enough to be a top-echelon leadoff batter. He was born to play ball; his first name is Stanley, after Stan Musial. A 36th-round draft choice in 1996, Conti has succeeded because of the kind of intense desire that enabled him to be in the opening-day lineup at Tucson in 2000 after a quick recovery from a broken hamate bone.

OF Brian Gordon - After taking three years to get past Low-A ball, Gordon showed major progress in High-A last season. And the lefty batter's .311-12-66 finish wasn't entirely related to the ideal hitting environment at High Desert. Gordon showed significantly increased patience at the plate. He also had enough speed to run out 13 triples and steal 19 bases.

LHP Ben Norris - At the very least, 2000 was an interesting season for Norris, a 6'3", 185, lefthander. The 1996 13th round pick started out by getting tattooed in his first shot at Triple-A hitters, then regained his footing at Double-A El Paso, earning him a major league audition. He then promptly became one of the few hurlers in big league history to yield four homers in a single inning. That inning is evidence of what can happen to pitchers without top-shelf stuff when they're missing their spots. Norris, 22, throws a fairly straight 90 MPH heater which he absolutely must keep low and on the edges of the strike zone, and supplements it with an above average changeup and an ordinary curve. It does not appear that Norris will be able to develop a true strikeout pitch for use against upper level hitters. Thus, his main chance for a major league future lies in situational relief, or as a swingman or spot starter. Norris will likely begin 2001 in the Triple-A rotation, where anything resembling his 2000 disaster could end his Diamondbacks' career.

OF Jhensy Sandoval - A year ago, we rated Sandoval as the Diamondbacks' ninth-best prospect, following a Double-A season greatly reduced by a hamstring injury. Then the 22-year-old righthanded batter began 2000 as the right fielder at High-A High Desert, and finished it on the disabled list at Low-A South Bend. In five minor league seasons, he has struck out more than six times as often as he has walked, and he didn't show much sign of improving that ratio last year. His strikeout rate is unacceptable for a player who hasn't hit more than 11 homers in any season. The 5'11", 200-pound Sandoval is fast enough to play center, though he hasn't translated his speed into base-stealing ability.

RHP Oscar Villareal - The 19-year-old has plenty of time, and room, for improvement. In his two pro seasons, he has pitched well, but that hasn't translated into success in terms of wins. He performed at four levels from Rookie ball to Triple-A in 2000. He isn't overpowering, and is likely to find himself used increasingly in relief roles.

RHP Duaner Sanchez - The 21-year-old has pretty good control. He hasn't been easy to hit, but he also hasn't been an overpowering Class A pitcher. As a pro rookie in 1999, he finished the season in High-A ball. Last year he went back down to Low-A. Starting like clockwork every fifth day at South Bend, Sanchez was 8-8 with a 3.65 ERA.

ATLANTA BRAVES
ORGANIZATIONAL GRID

	AAA	AA	HI-A	LO-A
1B	Toby Rumfield - R - 27 Andy Barkett - L - 25	Mike Glavine - L - 27	A.J. Zapp - L - 22	Jaeme Leal - R - 21 Curt Fiore - R - 22 Ryan Lehr - R - 21
2B	Steve Sisco - R - 30 Louis Martinez - R - 23 Chris Petersen - R - 29	Marcus Giles - R - 22	Travis Wilson - R - 22	Pat Manning - R - 20
SS	Mark DeRosa - R - 25	Steve Lackey - R - 25	Alfredo Castro - B - 20 David Dalton - R - 24 Nick Green - R - 21	Keoni DeRenne - R - 21 Erick Contreras - B - 21
3B	Wes Helms - R - 24	Mike Hessman - R - 22	Troy Cameron - B - 21	Astrubal Oropeza - R - 20
OF	George Lombard - L - 24 Tyrone Pendergrass -B- 23 Pedro Swann - L - 29 Tim Unroe - R - 29	Demond Smith - B - 27 Stewart Smothers - R - 24 Mike Terhune - B - 24 Marty Gazarek - R - 27 Mike Moore - R - 29 David Miller - L - 26 Jason Ross - R - 26	Junior Brignac - R - 22 Cory Aldridge - L - 21 Ryan Langerhans - L - 20 Nataniel Reinoso - L - 25	Damien Jones - L - 20 Justo Rivas - R - 20 Jerry Simmons - R - 24 Nick Crocker - L - 22
C	Jeff Horn - R - 29 Mike Hubbard - R - 29	Dax Norris - R - 26 Pasqual Matos - R - 25	Steve Torrealba - R - 22 Josh Pugh - R - 22 Mark Mortimer - R - 24	Jean Boscan - R - 20 Scott Bronowicz - L - 24 Jeff Rodriguez - R - 23
SP	Derrin Ebert - L - 23 Damian Moss - L - 23 Chris Seelbach - R - 27 Don Wengert - R - 30 Steve Avery - L - 30 Jason Marquis - R - 21 Tim Pugh - R - 33	L.J. Yankosky - R - 25 Winston Abreu - R - 23 Derrick Lewis - R - 24 Scott Sobkowiak - R - 22 Matt McClendon - R - 22 Jason Flach - R - 26 Delvis Pacheco - R - 22	Horacio Ramirez - L - 20 Christian Parra - R - 22 Dan Curtis - R - 20 Tony Pierce - R - 24 Matt Belisle - R - 20 Jung Bong - L - 19 Tim Spooneybarger - R - 20 Nathan Kent - R - 21	Matt Butler - R - 20 Ben Kozlowski - L - 19 John Ennis - R - 20 Mike Smalley - L - 21 Justin Willoughby - L - 22
CLOSER	Gabe Molina - R - 25 Dave Stevens - R - 30	Jacob Shumate - R - 24 Brian Barnes - L - 33	Brad Voyles - R - 23 Billy Sylvester - R - 23	Shanin Veronie - R - 23

ATLANTA BRAVES

Just as the long-standing members of the Braves' major league pitching rotation near the end of their respective primes, their minor league system appears ready to spit out a high-ceiling group of potential replacements. However, position player talent appears to be relatively lean, with only second baseman Marcus Giles a surefire future major league starter.

A.J. Zapp, 22, a 1996 first round pick, has the highest ceiling of any first base prospect in the organization, but had been a poor performer before a solid High-A campaign in 2000. Jaeme Leal, 21, doesn't have Zapp's overall upside, but has taken more quickly to the pro game than the late-blooming Zapp. Neither is likely to play more than a part-time role at the major league level, however.

With the quick advancement of Rafael Furcal to the major leagues, Giles, 22, is now the Braves' marquee prospect. He's a future major league starter with a chance to be a star, combining solid tools with brother Brian's work ethic. He's not too far away. New Zealander Travis Wilson, 22, snuck onto the World team's Futures Game roster in 2000, but isn't an elite prospect. Like Giles, he packs power for a middle infielder, but Wilson's complementary skills aren't nearly as good. Pat Manning, 20, is a 1999 third round draftee who struggled at bat for much of the 2000 season. He too has a solid power upside and should bypass Wilson once he irons out some of his rough edges.

With Furcal in place at the major league level, only future utility spots are available to the Braves' minor league shortstops. Switch-hitter Alfredo Castro, 20, has solid defensive skills and decent speed, but a very limited overall offensive game. If he develops a bit more power, he could have a chance to make a big league dent. Nick Green, 21, lacks in-your-face raw skills, but has a sneaky power/speed upside. He can play both middle infield positions at a respectable level, and is a sleeper to break out to the upside in the near term.

If Chipper Jones is ever moved to a less demanding defensive position, the Braves have a number of decent prospects to groom as potential replacements. Wes Helms, 24, is a longtime prospect whose star has fallen a bit. He retains significant power potential, but his lack of plate discipline and defensive progress pegs him as a major league supporting player. Troy Cameron's inability to make consistent contact has held him back, more than offsetting his considerable power potential. He'll have to show major improvement in 2001 to remain in the Braves' plans. Astrubal Oropeza, 20, also has a sizeable power upside, and could explode as his 6'2", 170, frame naturally fills out. He remains quite raw, however.

George Lombard, 24, has long been considered a prime prospect, but has been very slow to polish his immense raw tools. He'll play in the majors, but at this point, he's very unlikely to become a star. The Braves' other outfield prospects are a fair distance from the majors. Junior Brignac, 22, a 1996 third round draftee, took major steps backward last season, and now appears to be a longshot to thrive in the upper minors, let alone the majors. Cory Aldridge, 21, is a lefthanded hitter with average tools who has a chance to be a major league role player. Like Brignac, Ryan Langerhans, 20, is a potential power/speed prospect with a plate discipline problem. Langerhans' relative youth works in his favor, however, don't give up on his upside just yet. Damien Jones, 20, is a speed demon who could mature into a top-of-the-order prospect if he begins to hit more grounders. Justo Rivas, 20, is a line drive machine who could emerge as a sleeper prospect if physical development turns some of his doubles to the gaps into homers.

There isn't a lot of help on the horizon at catcher. Jean Boscan, 20, is a fairly accomplished defensive receiver who could become a durable horse as his 6'2", 160, frame develops. Though he's a low average hitter, he does have power potential, and could compete for a share of a major league job down the road.

Pitching options are plentiful. Derrin Ebert, 23, is a crafty lefty who projects as little more than a second bullpen lefty at the big league level. Damian Moss, 23, is an oft-injured southpaw who managed to stay healthy last season, though his control remained a problem. He's got the raw stuff to take a turn in the majors, but there might never be room in Atlanta. Scott Sobkowiak, 22, was shut down for elbow surgery last season, but the 6'5", 235, has arguably the highest upside among Braves' pitching prospects. He'll have to prove his health and get back in line, however. The Braves stole righty Matt McClendon, 22, on the fifth round in 1999, as other clubs shied away from his bonus demands. He's a polished hurler who could evolve into a nine-inning bull.

The lower levels of the Braves' system are loaded with high-ceiling hurlers. Horacio Ramirez, Dan Curtis and Tim Spooneybarger, all 20, experienced significant success at High-A Myrtle Beach last season. Southpaw Ramirez is the most complete of the three, and the first to develop a strikeout pitch. Matt Belisle and Matt Butler (both age 20) and Jung Bong and Ben Kozlowski (19) anchored a youthful Macon rotation. Belisle was brilliant in 2000, combining power and control as few minor league hurlers can. He's a future Braves' major league stand out. 1999 second rounder Butler doesn't have Belisle's stuff but could evolve into a top-shelfer in his own right if he develops a consistent strikeout pitch. Bong's upside is considerable, but he actually took baby step backwards in his second Low-A season. Kozlowski is a 6'6", 220, lefthander who is likely best suited for the bullpen, his role when he torched rookie ball the previous season.

TOP TEN PROSPECTS

1 - 2B Marcus Giles - Giles, 22, the brother of Pirates' star outfielder Brian, is on the verge on making some of his own noise at the major league level. The 5'8", 180, 1996 53rd round draftee has always been a exceptional power producer for his size and for a middle infielder, but he has worked hard to flesh out the remainder of a solid all-around package. His walk total has increased while his strikeout total has decreased over recent seasons, and his defensive game, while it will never be pretty, is consistent and reliable. He is built like a brick wall, and is an expert basestealer though his raw speed is only a bit above average. Giles is a bulldog who will extract the utmost from his unspectacular raw tools and become a major league stand out. He is no more than a year away from

seizing the Braves' second base job, and could make a Rafael Furcal-like sneak attack in 2001 spring training. He will be a 25/25 power/speed guy, and a likely All-Star in the majors.

2 - RHP Matt Belisle - Belisle, 20, a 1998 first round draftee, enjoyed a breakout 2000 season who saw him overmatching High-A Carolina League hitters at times by season's end. The 6'3", 195, righthander combines a hard low 90s fastball and an excellent changeup, both of which he consistently places on the low edges of the strike zone. His early 2000 destruction of the Low-A South Atlantic League resulted in Belisle being recognized for having the best control, and for being the circuit's best pitching prospect by its managers. Belisle also made significant strides in the psychological aspects of pitching. He was much more adept at setting up hitters and taking charge of ballgames last season, compared to a mediocre 1999 rookie ball campaign during which he often reacted poorly to adversity. Belisle now looks like a future major league #1 or 2 starter, a worthy successor to the Madduxes, Glavines, and Smoltzes of this world.

3 - LHP Horacio Ramirez - Ramirez, 20, is a lean 6'1", 170, southpaw who made major strides as one of the many aces on a brilliant High-A Myrtle Beach pitching staff. Ramirez was always considered to have a live, rubber arm that could eventually be utilized in a variety of roles, but the 1997 fifth round pick added both velocity and movement to all of his pitches in 2000, and became a strikeout pitcher for the first time in his career. Ramirez still doesn't overpower hitters, but his fastball appears much quicker when compared to the offspeed pitches he often uses to get ahead in the count. The key jump for any pitcher, but especially for those without overpowering heaters, is the advance to Double-A. Ramirez will get his chance at a fairly young age in 2001, and maintenance of a solid strikeout rate would indicate that he is squarely on the fast track to the majors. Ramirez could play Glavine to Belisle's Maddux at the major league level by late 2002.

4 - RHP Matt McClendon - The strategy of signing high-ceiling, high-bonus prospects after the first round has been an effective one in recent years. Just ask the Cards, who signed Rick Ankiel on the second round in 1997, or the Braves, who inked fifth rounder McClendon after offering him a $950,000 bonus in 1999. The Braves quickly honed the 6'6", 220, righthander's mechanics and watched him knife through High-A hitters and then average nearly seven innings per start after being advanced to

Double-A Greenville. McClendon combines a lively low to mid 90s heater with an improving curveball and changeup, and has a chance to be a pitcher who can either overpower or finesse hitters. He has the look of a future nine-inning horse at the major league level, and though he might not have Belisle's upside, he's a fairly safe bet to make a favorable major league impression before long. The best guess is that McClendon will get a look in the majors in 2001, and make the rotation for good in 2002. He'll be the next Smoltz, at best.

5 - LHP Jung Bong - Bong, 19, is a 6'3", 175, southpaw with comparable raw skills to the aforementioned hurlers. However, though Bong is still a baby, it has been mildly disappointing that he has virtually stood still developmentally over two years spent in the Low-A Macon rotation. Bong mixes a low to mid 90s fastball with and a curve and changeup, either of which could develop into a plus pitch. Despite his solid stuff and above average control for a youngster, Bong has allowed just over a hit per inning in both of the last two seasons due to poor location within the strike zone. The Braves are likely to challenge Bong by moving him ahead to High-A Myrtle Beach next season; success there could well put him on the same fast track as the aforementioned hurlers. In most other organizations, Bong would be seen as a gem, in this one, where pitchers take quantum leaps with regard to performance consistently, Bong is just another multi-talented prospect from whom much is expected. Look for a major step forward in 2001.

6 - OF George Lombard - Lombard, 24, has long been heralded as one of the minors' most talented prospects, and as the Braves' left fielder in waiting. Unfortunately for the 6'0", 212, lefthanded hitter, his inability to both develop passable plate discipline and make consistent contact against quality breaking stuff has prevented the true breakout season necessary to vault him into the Atlanta lineup. With Reggie Sanders playing poorly at the major league level in early 2000, Lombard was a hot streak away from the Atlanta job, and it never materialized. With B.J. Surhoff now in place, Lombard's window of opportunity may be closed in Atlanta. He has torched the Arizona Fall league more than once, showcasing a 30/30 power/speed upside, but his penchant for whiffing in over a third of his at bats simply hasn't subsided. Lombard could well be used as trade bait, and still get a chance to be a starting left fielder in the majors for someone. Expect him to continue to tease, and ultimately frustrate big league talent evaluators.

7 - LHP Damian Moss - Moss, 23, was once one of the premier pitching prospects in the game, but 1998 reconstructive elbow surgery set him back significantly. The 6'0", 187, southpaw was healthy enough to take a regular turn at Triple-A Richmond last season, and his stuff appeared to be intact. Moss combines a low 90s fastball plus a curve and a solid changeup, and has remained a strikeout pitcher despite the serious injury setback. Now he needs to get back to combating what has always been his major shortcoming, inconsistent command, which has led to consistently high walk and pitch totals. Moss has been a six-inning starter at best during his pro career, though the six innings have generally been effective. Moss is in a tight spot; there is a horde of higher-ceiling prospects on his back, and no room at the major league inn in front of him. A change of scenery could be in order; if Moss stays healthy and continues to hone his command, he'll soon find that there is always room in the majors for a talented lefthanded starting pitcher.

8 - RHP Dan Curtis - Yup, yet another starting pitcher prospect. Curtis, 20, is a 1998 17th round pick who made major steps forward in 2000. The 6'3", 215, righthander relies on extreme precision low in the strike zone, as his fastball is just a touch above average velocity-wise. He also throws a curveball and a changeup, and owed most of his 2000 High-A success to his ability to mix the three and keep hitters off balance. He showed an aptitude for throwing strike one, retiring hitters early in the count, and consequently keeping his pitch counts down and lasting deep into ballgames. Double-A could be a challenge for Curtis, however, as he hasn't yet developed a true strikeout pitch, which could present trouble against the more polished hitters at that level. Still, considering how far Curtis has come over the past year, upper minor league success can't be ruled out. With all of the other higher-ceiling hurlers around him, the best bet is that Curtis will become a setup reliever or closer in the upper minors, and serve in a situational bullpen role upon his arrival in the majors, possibly in 2003.

9 - 3B Wes Helms - Once upon a time, the Braves thought that Helms, now 24, might push Chipper Jones off of the hot corner to a less demanding defensive position. That was many years and injuries ago, but Helms has now defied the odds and moved back onto the brink of crashing the Braves' roster. Helms is a 6'4", 230, righthanded hitter with a compact power stroke that also enables him to hit for a high average. He has not developed acceptable plate discipline, and therefore could be picked apart in an everyday big league role. Defensively, the rotator cuff surgery that cost him much of the 1999 season robbed him of his once superior arm strength, but he remains a solid defender at both infield corners who could be a valuable bench asset to the Braves or some other major league team in 2001.

10 - OF Ryan Langerhans - Langerhans, 20, is an extremely athletic outfield prospect with solid all-around tools, but his inability to develop a cohesive offensive game could prevent him from reaching the upper minors, let alone the major leagues. The 6'3", 195, lefthanded hitter has a substantial power/speed upside, but his penchant for burying himself in the count, often on bad pitches, made him an easy mark for High-A Carolina League hurlers last season. Defensively, Langerhans combines exceptional range and a strong throwing arm, and has the ability to play either center or right field as he advances. His relative youth gives the Braves cause for hope, he needs to, and should perform markedly better in a second High-A season in 2001. If all goes well, the Braves envision him as at best their future starting right fielder, or more likely as a valuable fourth outfielder.

OTHER PROSPECTS

RHP Winston Abreu - Abreu has a live arm and very good stuff. Control had been a bit of problem for him in the past but he seemed to correct that during the 2000 season. He had some arm problems and didn't pitch many innings, but the innings he did pitch were excellent. He pitched the most at Low-A Macon trying to get himself back on track and he struck out 48 batters in 28-plus innings while allowing just 11 hits and six walks. He was used as a reliever in 10 of his 11 appearances there as well as at the Double-A level for a few innings and might remain in the bullpen if he continues to have success in that role.

SS Wilson Betemit - Betemit is an raw talent who really knows what he's doing at the plate. He's just a teenager, but he's shown patience at the plate and the ability to hit well over .300 already. He's got better pop than you might expect for a teenage shortstop and he runs pretty well, though he's not polished as a basestealer just yet. He's got all the tools necessary to be a good defensive shortstop, but he's very inconsistent at this point and he makes a lot of unnecessary errors.

C Jean Boscan - Boscan is a bit of a wild swinger with some power potential. The strange thing about him is that he strikes out a ton and doesn't hit for much average, but has shown the ability to draw a fair number walks. Should he calm himself down at the plate, he could be a 15-20 home runs guy. Boscan's defense is good and his arm is very good.

LHP Derrin Ebert - Ebert is a soft-tossing lefthander who relies totally on pitch placement and changing speeds. He's been hit very hard at Triple-A and in his brief major league appearances, but he's still young enough to improve and make himself a big leaguer.

RHP John Ennis - Ennis had an outstanding season at Low-A Macon last year. He has good stuff and very good control to go with it, leading to his success. He allowed just 77 hits and 25 walks in 98-plus innings while striking out 105 batters. Opponents hit just .209 against him and he was able to get all of his pitches over the plate on a fairly consistent basis.

OF Damien Jones - Jones is a burner with some patience at the plate. He doesn't have much pop and isn't a great hitter for average right now, but his ability to get on base is decent and should get better as he gets older. He stole 44 bases last year at Low-A Macon and that was despite hitting just .268. His range in center field is excellent and he can run down balls he misjudges.

RHP Derrick Lewis - Lewis has a good sinking fastball and a good breaking pitch, but his control betrays him at times. When he's on, Lewis can be unhittable, though his control puts him in precarious spots from time to time. Even though his control is far from perfect, he did make strides in that area during the 2000 season at Double-A. He allowed just 146 hits over 163-plus innings while striking out 143 batters, but he walked 83. Another positive sign: he allowed just five home runs in those 163-plus innings.

2B Pat Manning - Manning is just a teenager, but his ability has already begun to show. He played full-season Low-A ball at the age of 19 and didn't embarrass himself. He has the ability to become a 20 home run hitter in the future and he's fairly patient for being so young. He's already a good defensive second baseman and as he gets stronger his offensive numbers will improve.

RHP Jason Marquis - Marquis could be the next addition to the Braves' rotation. He throws in the mid 90s and has a good slider, though he could stand to be more consistent with his control. Marquis has a good body with strong legs and his pitching style is somewhat similar to that of John Smoltz. He's still very young, only 22 years old, and he could be an outstanding pitcher in the very near future.

RHP Christian Parra - Parra, 22, posted awesome all-around numbers at High-A Myrtle Beach (17-4, 2.28, 98 hits allowed in 158 innings, 163/56 K/BB ratio), but there are multiple reasons to believe he might struggle at higher levels. First, he stands a massive 6'1", 255, and doesn't exactly reek athleticism. Secondly, neither the peak velocity on his fastball nor the bite of his breaking stuff are extraordinary. He did pick-apart Carolina League hitters with guile and just enough stuff, however, albeit as one of the older starters in his league. If he can keep it rolling in the upper minors in early 2001, move him way up on your list.

OF Justo Rivas - Rivas is a pretty good looking young hitter with the ability to get a lot better if he can become more selective. He doesn't have a lot of home run power at the moment and he doesn't really know how to run the bases all that well, but he has potential to become a threat in both areas. His 30 doubles at Low-A Macon indicate potential for home run power in the future.

RHP Tim Spooneybarger - Not only does Spooneybarger have a good name, he's got outstanding stuff. Last year at High-A Myrtle Beach, he had a 0.91 ERA and allowed just 18 hits and 19 walks over 49-plus innings while striking out 57. His plus control combined with his plus fastball give him a chance to be an outstanding relief pitcher as he moves up the ranks. He also started six games, so there is a chance he could wind up used in that capacity as well.

RHP Billy Sylvester - His name may not be as cool as Tim Spooneybarger's, but his stuff is right there. Sylvester is a hard thrower who is very tough to hit against. He had a 0.79 ERA last year at High-A and he allowed just 16 hits and 15 walks over 45-plus innings, striking out 48 batters. If he comes even close to that at Double-A next year, he'll be promoted before you can say "Spooneybarger."

CHICAGO CUBS
ORGANIZATIONAL GRID

	AAA	AA	HI-A	LO-A
1B	Julio Zuleta - R - 25 Alan Zinter - B - 32	Hee Seop Choi - L - 21 Scott Vieira - R - 26	Ron Walker - R - 24 Derrick Bly - R - 25	Luis Medina - R - 21
2B	Chad Meyers - R - 24 Keith Johns - R - 28	Franklin Font - R - 22	Tony Schrager - R - 23 Dennis Abreu - R - 22	Mike Dzurilla - R - 22 Tony Gsell - R - 23
SS	Augie Ojeda - B - 25 Tim Florez - R - 30	Jason Smith - L - 22	Nate Frese - R - 22	Jim Deschaine - R - 22
3B	Cole Liniak - R - 23 Shane Andrews - R - 28 Keith Luuloa - R - 25	Eric Hinske - L - 22	David Kelton - R - 20 Brent Sachs - R - 25	Ryan Gripp - R - 22
OF	Raul Gonzalez - R - 26 Tarrik Brock - L - 26 Roosevelt Brown - L - 24 Ross Gload - L - 24 Mike Stoner - R - 27	Jaisen Randolph - R - 21 Corey Patterson - L - 20 Jayson Bass - B - 24 Tydus Meadows - R - 23	Pete Fukuhara - R - 24 Gary Johnson - R - 23 Brandon Pernell - R - 23 Jorge Piedra - L - 21	Ben Johnstone - R - 22 Kevin Bass - B - 21 Pete Zoccolillo - L - 23 Bryan Warner - L - 25 Franklin German - R - 20
C	Jose Molina - R - 25 Mark Dalesandro - R - 32 Mike Mahoney - R - 27	Mike Amrhein - R - 25 Pee Wee Lopez - R - 23	Jeff Goldbach - R - 20 Brad Hargreaves - R - 22 Ryan Van Horn - R - 22	Matt Mauck - L - 21 Casey Kopitzke - R - 22 Chris Curry - R - 22
SP	Brian McNichol - L - 26 Phillip Norton - L - 24 Dave Zancanaro - L - 31 Jamie Arnold - R - 26 Ben Ford - R - 24 Mario Iglesias - R - 26 Mike Meyers - R - 22 Eric Newman - R - 27	Jeff Yoder - R - 24 Joey Nation - L - 21 Chris Gissell - R - 22 Doug Johnston - R - 22 Micah Bowie - L - 25 Ben Christensen - R - 22 Lindsay Gulin - L - 23 Nate Teut - L - 24	Mike Wuertz - R - 21 Ricardo Palma - L - 20 Steve Smyth - L - 22 Matt Bruback - R - 21 Juan Cruz - R - 19 David Noyce - L - 23	Ken Conroy - R - 21 Jeremy Gomer - L - 21 John Webb - R - 21 Aaron Sams - L - 24 Ben Shaffar - R - 22
CLOSER	Carlos Zambrano - R - 19	Courtney Duncan - R - 25 Jay Yennaco - R - 24 Chris Booker - R - 23	Matt Murphy - L - 21	Frangil Cordero - L - 19 David Bailey - R - 23 Oscar Montero - R - 22

CHICAGO CUBS

A very strong 1998 draft, featuring first round pick Corey Patterson, anchored the recent revitalization of the once-moribund Cubs' system. The future would be even brighter if top pitching prospect Jon Garland, a 1997 first rounder, hadn't been traded across town a couple of years back for nondescript middle reliever Matt Karchner.

With Mark Grace getting a little long in the tooth, minor league options at first base include Julio Zuleta and Hee Choi. Though Zuleta's minor league numbers are more impressive, he likely projects as no better than an undisciplined bench bat at the major league level. Choi, on the other hand, could well establish himself as an above average major league starter in the next few seasons. He has an exciting power upside, and should be ready in the next one to two years.

When the Cubs signed free agent Eric Young, they apparently decided that Chad Meyers lacks what it takes to be an everyday player in the major leagues. However, Meyers' excellent speed and baserunning instincts and his ability to play multiple defensive positions keeps him in line for a crack at a multipurpose backup role in Chicago. Franklin Font is a slick fielder who could also eventually settle in as a big league utilityman.

Utility prospects abound at shortstop, though a viable alternative to Ricky Gutierrez as the big league starter doesn't appear to be in the system. Switch-hitter Augie Ojeda has no glaring shortcomings, and acquitted himself well in a brief big league cameo in 2000. He's worthy of a backup job in the majors. Jason Smith has an intriguing power/speed upside, and is the most likely to break out as a starter candidate among this group. His lefthanded bat is also a plus. Jim Deschaine put up big Low-A numbers in 2000 as a 22-year-old. If he can jump a couple of levels and duplicate such performance in 2001, he could become a viable utility candidate.

Third base options are plentiful, a relief in a system that is still struggling to replace Ron Santo. Cole Liniak has no significant strengths or weaknesses, and has given the

Cubs no compelling reason to give him a lengthy trial as their big league starter. His window of opportunity is closing. Lefthanded hitter Eric Hinske projects as a major league backup at both infield corners, combining decent power and speed upsides. Dave Kelton's upside is much higher; he could evolve into a 30-homer hitter, though he needs to refine his swing a bit. Look for a major step forward in 2001 for the Cubs' likely future third sacker.

Outfield depth isn't great, but there's some quality talent at the top. Gary Matthews, Jr., didn't exactly shine in his trial as an outfield backup, and might not get another chance. Roosevelt Brown, a lefthanded hitter, has the bat to thrive in a backup role, but is no great shakes in the field. Corey Patterson, despite some 2000 Double-A struggles as a 20-year-old, is the real deal. The power/speed stud will start for the Cubs sometime in 2001, and will entrench himself as a star once he learns to take a pitch. Jaisen Randolph can flat out fly, and could evolve into a fine fourth outfielder if he continues his gradual offensive development. The Cubs had better get some production from these guys, as there's little or no help on the way from the Class A outfield crew. Jorge Piedra, a gaps slasher with an interesting power/speed upside, was added in the late-season Ismael Valdes deal, and offers some hope for the future.

Though Jeff Goldbach suffered through a subpar High-A season in 2000, he remains the Cubs' foremost catching prospect. He's a durable defender with a substantial power upside who has the ability to be at least a major league platooner, and quite possibly more.

A number of youthful hurlers will be banging on the Cubs' major league door over the next couple of seasons, and the law of averages suggest that at least a couple will stick. Carlos Zambrano, 19, and Ruben Quevedo, 21, represent the youngest, the most talented, and, quite possibly, the most ready. Zambrano has been used as a starter and reliever, and could be a staff ace someday. He's ready to help out the major leaguers in a complementary role. Quevedo got some big league chances in 2000, with mixed results. With improved conditioning, Quevedo can be a solid major league winner soon. Lefty Phillip Norton doesn't have a particularly exciting upside, but has a rubber arm and a feel for pitching. He could fit in as a swingman or situational lefty, if he improves his command. Righty Mike Meyers doesn't throw particularly hard, but is nasty when hitting his spots. His Triple-A struggles in 2000 suggest a limited, mid-rotation upside. Lefty Joey Nation and righty Chris Gissell are solid bets for big Triple-A seasons in 2001. All Nation needs is experience before he becomes a solid big league starter, while Gissell is a strikeout pitch away. Ben Christensen, the Cubs' 1999 first round draftee, had an excellent first full pro season in 2000. He's a future nine-inning horse who could crack the major league rotation by late 2001. His upside might be the highest of the bunch. Finesse hurler Mike Wuertz seems to be the type who will always extract the maximum from his relatively average skills. He could be a future major league swingman. Crafty lefty Ricardo Palma, 20, lacks the stuff of many of these guys, but youth is on his side. Double-A could be a daunting challenge for Palma in 2001. Keep an eye on hard-throwing righty Juan Cruz. With the most talented hurlers in the system a couple of levels ahead of him, he could advance briskly if he tames his wildness.

TOP TEN PROSPECTS

1 - OF Corey Patterson - Many observers were quick to paint Patterson's 2000 season at Double-A West Tennessee as a disappointment; they tend to forget that this was a 20-year-old kid competing against significantly older competition. So what if he's not Ken Griffey, Jr., this kid is still going to be darned good. Though he stands only 5'10", 175, Patterson possesses a 30/30 power/speed upside, hitting the ball with consistent authority to all fields. However, he has been limited by poor plate discipline; if Patterson could evolve into a 60-70 walk threat, he would magically become a .300-.320 hitter and long-term major league number three hitter. He has advanced basestealing technique for his age and experience level. Defensively, Patterson might never be a Gold Glover, but he outruns a lot of his imperfections and has a strong throwing arm. Look for Patterson to shove aside Damon Buford by late 2001. He won't dominate right away, but with improved plate discipline, and will evolve into an All-Star.

2 - 1B Hee Seop Choi - Choi, 21, certified himself as a top-shelf power prospect with a massive season split between High-A Daytona and Double-A West Tennessee. He also showed above average plate discipline, which allowed him to hit for a high average, and improved immensely defensively, to the extent that he was recognized as the best defensive first sacker in the High-A Florida State League by its managers. The 6'4", 235, first baseman impressively maintained, even enhanced his offensive productivity after his promotion to Double-A, a very strong indicator of future success at the major league level. Choi has clearly established himself as one of the best first base prospects in the minors, and conveniently, he'll be ready at about the time Mark Grace's decreased production becomes a true concern. Look for Choi to step in by Opening Day 2002, and eventually become one of the premier first sackers in the majors.

3 - RHP Carlos Zambrano - At the tender age of 19, Zambrano pitched the bulk of the 2000 season at the Triple-A level, where he was easily the youngest player in the Pacific Coast League. This 6'4", 220, righty is one of the hardest throwers in the minors, routinely reaching the upper 90s with his fastball. He has the makings of an above average breaking ball repertoire, including a hard curve plus a slider and changeup. However, the Cubs made an interesting move with Zambrano following his promotion to Triple-A, moving him to the bullpen for the first time in his professional career. They had expressed concern with the number of innings he had thrown at such a young age, and wanted to change the pace for awhile. Results were mixed, Zambrano was as difficult to hit as ever, but struggled mightily with his command. Zambrano's upside as a starting pitcher rivals that of nearly any other pitcher in the minors, and it appears odd that the Cubs are changing their approach so radically at this stage of the game. Look for Zambrano to start again at Triple-A in 2001, and earn a promotion by midseason. He could be the Cubs' future big league ace.

4 - RHP Juan Cruz - Cruz, 19, dominated at both Class A levels, overpowering hitters with a mid-to-upper 90s fastball plus an advanced slider and changeup for his age. He stands a lean, wiry 6'2", 155, but generates extreme power because of nearly flawless mechanics. He could become truly scary if he adds a little more juice as he physically matures. He pitched even better after a late promotion to High-A Daytona in the Florida State League, significantly enhancing his command. He also possesses a significant mean streak. He's effectively wild, and hitters are loath to dig in against him. It looks like he'll be arriving at the Double-A level early in 2001, way ahead of schedule. If he thrives immediately, he'll jump to the elite level among major league pitching prospects.

5 - RHP Ben Christensen - Christensen, 22, was the Cubs' 1999 first round pick, and will always be haunted by his intentional beaning of a player standing in the on-deck circle during a game in his final college season. The Cubs are convinced that this incident was an isolated one, and Christensen was on his best behavior in an excellent 2000 season split between High-A Daytona and Double-A West Tennessee. The 6'4", 210, righty combines a hard low-to-mid 90s fastball and a nasty slider. His command was impeccable last season; not only did he rarely walk hitters, even after the pivotal promotion to Double-A, he regularly kept the ball down in the strike zone and claimed the inside part of the plate for his own. Pitchers who maintain or improve their strikeout rate after rising to the Double-A level have a high incidence of eventual major league success: Christensen fits that profile. Christensen's upside might not match Zambrano's, but he's a much surer thing. He's a solid bet to be a long-term 200-inning horse near the top of the Cubs' rotation by 2002.

6 - RHP Ruben Quevedo - The Cubs heisted Quevedo, 21, from the Braves along with pitchers Joey Nation and Micah Bowie from the Braves for Terry Mulholland and Jose Hernandez in 1999. He has always ranked as one his level's youngest players as he has advanced through the ranks, and he showed flashes of brilliance in a major league trial last season. Quevedo throws a low 90s fastball with exceptional movement, and has a solid feel for his curve and changeup considering his age and limited experience level. His control is excellent, his mechanics smooth, and his mound savvy fairly advanced for a youngster. The 6'1", 225, righty appears to be developing a weight problem, however. He looks much older than he is, and runs the risk of becoming a serial muscle pull victim or a constant target of bunts by opposing hitters unless he takes control of the situation. Look for Quevedo to earn a spot in the Cubs' rotation from day one in 2001. Along with Zambrano and Christensen, the Cubs could have the equivalent of three aces in their rotation before too long.

7 - LHP Joey Nation - Nation, 21, could help make the deal in which he and Quevedo came over from the Braves the deal that turns around the Cubs' fortunes. The 6'2", 175, lefty was the Braves' second round draft pick in 1997, and he cruised through the lower end of the Braves' system on the strength of precision and aggressiveness, not raw stuff. Most pitchers with those traits find Double-A life quite hard, but Nation actually raised his game significantly at that level in 2000, striking out over a batter per inning at West Tennessee while averaging well over six innings per start. His fastball only reaches the upper 80s, but his curveball is exceptional and Nation's feel for setting up hitters and keeping them off balance, and off of the plate, sets him apart. Nation is headed for the major leagues by sometime in 2003, and should establish himself as a viable 200-inning mid-rotation horse.

8 - 3B David Kelton - Kelton, 20, has asserted himself as the most likely intermediate-term answer to the Cubs' longstanding third base problem thus far in his brief pro career. The 6'2", 190, righthanded hitter has a sweet swing and exudes power potential, though he has been limited by poor plate discipline and an inability to handle quality breaking pitches at this stage in his development. Still, about 40% of his hits have gone for extra bases in the spacious ballparks of the lower minors, if he works out the bugs, he could become a 30-homer force. Defensively, he is quite athletic, with an exceptional first step and above average range. His defensive development was set back by shoulder surgery in his senior year of high school, and he has logged some designated hitter and first base time in the pros as a result. The Cubs expect him to be ready to handle the everyday Double-A third base load in 2001, and exhibit at least average arm strength in the process. Kelton will take off if and when he learns to take a pitch: don't be surprised if 2001 is his breakout year. He projects as either a starting third baseman or productive corner infield bench bat in the majors.

9 - C Jeff Goldbach - Goldbach, 20, is a 1998 second round pick who suffered through a poor offensive season in 2000 at High-A Daytona, where he was one of the Florida State League's youngest regulars. The 6'0", 190, righthanded hitter had a quite productive Low-A season with the bat in 1999, but suffered from a loss of confidence in 2000. He had worked hard to improve his plate discipline in the former season, but gave back that year of progress in the latter, routinely allowing himself to be buried in the count, often on bad pitches. He'll likely develop into a low-average hitter with 20-homer power potential, an acceptable combination for a catcher. Defensively, Goldbach is fundamentally sound, has a strong throwing arm, and handles a pitching staff well. Goldbach might not be as good as he looked two years ago, but it would be foolish to give up on him based on last season's performance. He still has a solid chance to be the Cubs' catcher of the future, and could arrive by 2003.

10 - RHP Mike Meyers - Meyers, 22, is a 1997 26th round pick who fell on some hard times last season after rocketing to prominence the previous year. The 6'2", 210, righty knifed through High-A and Double-A ball in 1998 by varying speed and location and pitching to precise spots consistently. Meyers' fastball only reaches the upper 80s, and he therefore needs to able to throw his curve, his best pitch, and changeup to get ahead of hitters early in the count to be successful. In 1999, Meyers' command eluded him, and he found himself nibbling around the edges of the plate with all of his pitches, a no-no for a hurler with middling raw stuff. Meyers needs to make the mechanical and psychological adjustments necessary to get back to where he was in 1998 to have a chance to make a significant major league contribution. With the emergence of Zambrano, Christensen, Quevedo and possibly Nation as viable major league starter candidates, the Cubs might be content to see Meyers evolve into a situational relief candidate in the near term. That is well within Meyers' grasp provided he regains his take-charge approach on the mound.

OTHER PROSPECTS

OF Roosevelt Brown - Brown pounds Triple-A pitching, but he can't hit major league pitching because he's a wild swinger who can't hit breaking stuff. He's got pretty good power and could be a decent platoon or reserve outfielder if he'd simply take more pitches. His defensive skills are very average and he's not fast either.

SS Jim Deschaine - Deschaine is a shortstop prospect with some power and a good approach at the plate. His strike zone judgment thus far has been outstanding and he's got the size (6'0" 200) and power potential to move over to the hot corner if things don't work out at shortstop. He tore up Low-A for the Lansing Lugnuts, posting excellent power numbers, a high batting average, a fair number of steals while showing good patience at the plate.

RHP Ben Ford - Ford is a 6'7" righthander with an low to mid 90s fastball and an above average slider. Most of his time in the minors has been spent in the bullpen, but he was used as a starter for much of the 2000 season. Ford is a quality pitcher, but because he really only has two major league pitches he's best suited for relief work.

RHP Chris Gissell - Gissell is a 6'4" righthander with a 90 MPH heater and improving control. He needs to improve his offspeed pitches if he wants to pitch in the majors. He had a very nice season at Double-A, posting a solid ERA and pitched consistently well.

3B Ryan Gripp - Gripp has displayed the classic third base set of offensive skills at the low levels of the minors. He can hit for both average and power, which is due to his relative patience at the plate. Defensively he needs to work on consistency and he doesn't run all that well, but all he needs to do is continue hitting to keep moving up the ladder.

3B Eric Hinske - Hinske is a lefthanded hitting third baseman with good power potential. He strikes out way too much, but is patient and he comes up with a lot of extra base hits. He also runs well, though his defense could use work as well. He appears to be in line for a shot at the Cubs' third base job at some point in the near future.

3B Cole Liniak - Liniak is a solid player, but probably not an everyday major league player. He can hit near .300, but sacrifices his power to do so. If he can ever combine his 20 home run power with a good average, he'll get a shot. He's a very good defensive third baseman and could be a nice platoon player. His 2000 performance might have put him in the running for a shot at competing for a major league job this season.

OF Gary Matthews, Jr. - Matthews is too old to be considered a prospect, but he runs well and is an exceptional defensive player in the outfield. He isn't the hitter his dad Gary Sr. was, but as a switch-hitter he has some value to a big league team. If he can improve his discipline at the plate, Matthews could become a part-time starter in the majors.

2B Chad Meyers - Meyers is an unproven player with plenty of speed and the ability to get on base consistently. He can play more than just second base: he spent some time at third base and in the outfield over the past two seasons. He's not going to hit for power and probably won't contend for any batting titles, but by putting the ball in play and drawing walks he's a threat to steal 40-plus bases if he plays everyday.

SS Luis Montanez - Montanez was drafted in the first round by the Cubs in the 2000 draft and tore up the Arizona Rookie League after signing. He can hit for average, has better than average power for someone his age, he runs very well and can be spectacular defensively. He's inconsistent in the field, but he's fresh out of high school and that shouldn't be a problem in the future.

SS Augie Ojeda - Ojeda doesn't have much in terms of physical tools, but he is a hustler who is always a fan favorite. He's only about 5'6" and isn't much of a hitter, but he's a very good defensive shortstop and he's also got better than average speed. He'll never be a major league regular, but could be a solid utilityman.

OF Jaisen Randolph - Randolph is a switch-hitting outfielder with very little extra base power and virtually no patience. He puts the ball in play, but not with authority and even though he steals a lot of bases, he's not as effective as he could be. He covers a lot of ground in the outfield and should have no problems defensively as he moves up, but unless he really improves as a hitter he'll be stuck in the minors.

SS Jason Smith - Smith, 22, is an intriguing prospect with an unusual array of skills for a shortstop. However, he is exceedingly raw in certain facets of his game, and could easily become either a solid future major league starter or a long-term Triple-A fixture. Smith is an athletic 6'3", 190, lefthanded hitter with a 20/20 power/speed upside. The ball jumps off of his bat, but he hurts himself by swinging at just about anything that he can reach. He buries himself in the count regularly, and struggles greatly with quality breaking pitches. Defensively, his range is adequate for a shortstop, and he has a cannon for an arm. However, it's quite possible that he'll outgrow the position and eventually slide over to third base, where his current offensive package might not be sufficient to start in the majors. Smith needs to make major strides with the bat at Triple-A in 2001 to project as an eventual big league starter. More likely, he'll develop into an outstanding all-purpose utility prospect capable of adding a dimension to the Cubs' offensive attack.

RHP John Webb - Webb has a live arm and good control for someone with only a few games of experience above Low-A. He's not truly a strikeout pitcher, but he gets good movement on his pitches and isn't easy to hit against. He lasted more than six innings per start last year, which is also a good sign.

1B Julio Zuleta - Zuleta is a 6'5" power hitter with a chance to be a good run producer. He's made excellent strides at the plate over the last year and was rewarded with a spot in the Future Stars Game during the All-Star break. He's not exactly a defensive star, but he's not a butcher either. If Zuleta gets a shot, he could hit a lot of homers at Wrigley Field.

CINCINNATI REDS
ORGANIZATIONAL GRID

	AAA	AA	LO-A (Dayton)	LO-A (Clinton)
1B	D.T. Cromer - L - 29	Ron Wright - R - 24 Eric Welsh - L - 23	Casey Bookout - L - 23 James Matan - R - 24	Samone Peters - R - 21
2B	Jason Williams - R - 26 Jed Hansen - R - 27	Bobby Morris - L - 27	Jason Huth - B - 23 Joe Kilburg - L - 24	Mark Burnett - L - 23
SS	Chris Sexton - R - 28	Travis Dawkins - R - 21 Wilmy Caceres - B - 21	Ranier Olmedo - R - 19 Robbie Kison - R - 23	Andrew Beattie - B - 22
3B	Brandon Larson - R - 24 Tom Nevers - R - 28 Chris Saunders - R - 29	Drew Henson - R - 20	Kevin Baderdeen - R - 23 Randy Stegall - R - 25	Matt Dehner - R - 23 Josh Spoerl - R - 21
OF	Kimera Bartee - B - 27 Brady Clark - R - 26 Robin Jennings - L - 28	Ben Broussard - L - 23 Alejandro Diaz - R - 21 Andy Burress - R - 22 Stephen Larkin - L - 26 Jackson Melian - R - 20	Adam Dunn - L - 20 Blane Layton - L - 23 Austin Kearns - R - 20 Serafin Rodriguez - R - 21 Fernando Rios - R - 21	Jon Weber - L - 22 Omar Hurtado - R - 21 Chris Van Rossum - L - 26 Ryan Lundquist - R - 23
C	Jason LaRue - R - 26 Guillermo Garcia - R - 28 Mike Stefanski - R - 30	Corky Miller - R - 24 Brad King - R - 25	Braxton Whitehead - R - 24 Pat Cline - R - 25 Ed Sparks - R - 21	Francisco Rivera - L - 20 Bobby Cripps - L - 23
SP	Justin Atchley - L - 26 Steve Soderstrom -R- 28 Willis Roberts - R - 25 Vaughn Eshelman - L - 31 Terrell Wade - L - 27 Ed Yarnall - L - 24	Eddie Priest - L - 26 Brett Haring - L - 25 Arnold Gooch - R - 23 Chris Reitsma - R - 22 Lance Davis - L - 23 Jason Sekany - R - 24 David Gil - R - 22	Jose Acevedo - R - 22 Tim Birdsong - R - 23 Ty Howington - L - 19 John Curtice - L - 20 Travis Thompson - R - 23 Brian Reith - R - 22	John Darnell - L - 22 Paco Escamilla - L - 23 Scott Dunn - R - 22 John Koronka - L - 20 Jose Valdez - R - 21 Brad Salmon - R - 20 Jorge Cordova - R - 22 Darrell Hussman - R - 23 Ryan Mottl - R - 21
CLOSER	Rick Greene - R - 29 Joe Hudson - R - 29 John Riedling - R - 24	Bo Donaldson - R - 25 Ted Rose - R - 26	David Huggins - R - 24	Michael Neu - R - 22

CINCINNATI REDS

Just a couple of years ago, the Reds possessed one of the leanest farm systems around. Now, a combination of shrewd drafting with a focus on high-ceiling, high school talent plus the occasional blockbuster trade of a top veteran, like Denny Neagle, for prospects, has put the Reds among the top half in terms of talent quality.

Sean Casey had better be a long-term solution at first base, as there isn't much help on the farm. Low-A first sacker Samone Peters can hit them a long way when he makes contact, which isn't often. He could still put it together, but is incredibly raw.

Switch-hitter Wilmy Caceres, primarily a second baseman, is an intriguing utility prospect. He makes the plays, sprays the ball around with a touch of power and runs well. He's no threat to Pokey Reese, however.

Travis "Gookie" Dawkins remains the heir apparent to Barry Larkin despite a poor 2000 campaign. Dawkins has Pokey Reese-like skills, and might caddy for both major league incumbents as he continues to refine his exciting all-around ability. He could start elsewhere if he's dealt for pitching. Ranier Olmedo can play both middle infield positions, and held his own as a teenage Low-A starter in 2000. He too projects as a future utility prospect.

Third base was an organizational weak spot before the acquisition of Drew Henson from the Yankees in the Neagle deal. Few minor leaguers have Henson's power upside, but few minor leaguers also project as potential future starting NFL quarterbacks. The Henson soap opera likely has a few plot twists remaining, and the Reds will be watching.

The Reds' top outfield prospects are an elite group made even stronger by the acquisition of Jackson Melian in the Neagle deal. The oldest and arguably most limited of the group is lefthanded hitter Ben Broussard, a fairly one-dimensional power stud who can also play first base. He projects as a big-league platooner or power bat off of the bench. Lefty Adam Dunn and righty Austin Kearns look like sure future big league starters. Dunn runs incredibly well for a 240-pounder, and is a natural hitter with still untapped power. Kearns tapped into his power in 2000, and looks like a five-tool major league express at this point. Melian's raw skills might be even better than theirs, but his minor league performance has been much more uneven to date. Think Ruben Rivera when you think of this high-risk, high-reward prospect. Andy Burress is a decidedly lower level prospect, but could fit an as a righthanded major league bench bat with continued offensive development. Serafin Rodriguez is a speedy Low-A outfield prospect whose development has been stunted by injury woes. He too projects as a big league backup at best.

Catching help is not plentiful. Jason LaRue and Guillermo Garcia appear to be classic Quadruple-A players who excel at Triple-A but aren't big league timber. Lefthanded-hitting Low-A receiver Francisco Rivera bears watching. His offensive game has improved markedly, and he is a durable defensive presence who could someday be a major league platoon option.

A relatively lean minor league pitching arsenal was helped significantly by the acquisition of lefty Ed Yarnall and righty Brian Reith in the Neagle deal. Yarnall, widely expected to entrench himself as the Yankees' fifth starter in 2000, is a pretty fair bet to succeed in 2001 with the Reds. Conditioning, a shortcoming in 2000, is a key. Reith should quickly establish himself as one of the Reds' foremost prospects. His command is solid, and his ability to retire hitters early in the count is an asset. He could be a future 200-inning mid-rotation horse in the majors. Lefty Ty Howington, 19, the Reds' 1999 first round pick, has a high ceiling, but is far from a finished product. He's the Reds' only viable southpaw pitching prospect, and has the goods to become an ace. Mechanics and command are two keys. Righty Brandon Love, 20, a 1999 third round pick, doesn't have Howington's upside, but his development has been smoother to date. With improved command, he could slide into the middle of the Reds' rotation within two to three years. Righty Jose Valdez, 21, ranked among the toughest-to-hit Low-A Midwest League hurlers in 2000. The addition of a Reds' High-A affiliate in 2001 comes just in time for Valdez, who could become a viable starter prospect with improved command. Lefty John Koronka and righty Brad Salmon are two other 2000 Low-A hurlers with laudable command, but both likely lack the stuff to make material upward progress. Youth is on their side, however.

TOP TEN PROSPECTS

1 - OF Austin Kearns - Kearns, 20, is a strapping 6'3", 220, righthanded hitter with exciting all-around skills. Offensively, Kearns overmatched Low-A Midwest League hurlers last season, hitting for average and extreme power with excellent plate discipline. His outburst must be taken with a grain or two of salt, as the Reds' lack of a High-A affiliate forced him to remain at a level of competition that he had already mastered. Kearns has a compact stroke and quick hands, and drives the ball for extreme distance from gap to gap. He also runs surprisingly well for a big man. Defensively, Kearns is a natural right fielder with solid range and a howitzer arm that was recognized as the best outfield arm in the Midwest League by its managers. Kearns may require a slight adjustment period at Double-A in 2001, but should quickly jump back on the fast track to the majors. He's a possible future All-Star right fielder in the bigs, and should arrive to stay in late 2002.

2 - OF Adam Dunn - In Kearns, Jackson Melian and Dunn, the Reds corner the market on hyper-athletic, five-tool outfield prospects. Dunn, 20, stands 6'6", 235, and like Henson, is a former major college quarterback candidate (University of Texas). The 1998 second round pick is less polished as a power prospect than Kearns, but has better raw speed and certainly knows how to use it. Like Kearns, the lefthanded-hitting Dunn refuses to swing at bad pitches. However, Dunn also was sent back to Low-A Dayton for a second season because of the Reds' lack of a High-A affiliate, certainly padding his statistics a bit. Defensively, Dunn is not in the same class as Kearns or Melian, but his speed and athleticism compensate for some of the rough spots. Dunn also is a likely future major league starter, most likely in left field. Look for many of his Low-A doubles to become Double-A homers after an early adjustment period next season, and expect Dunn to slide into the Cincy lineup sometime in 2003.

3 - 3B Drew Henson - Henson, 20, was a key part of the return received from the Yankees in last season's Denny Neagle deal. The 6'5", 220, righthanded power hitter might be best known for moonlighting as the University of Michigan's quarterback. Henson is a top-notch power prospect with prodigious pop to all fields. However, he will likely need to make a long-term commitment to baseball in order to approach his maximum potential. At this stage in his development, Henson is overanxious at the plate, buries himself in the count, and struggles to hit quality breaking stuff. Defensively, Henson has solid lateral quickness and an excellent throwing arm, prior to his trade last season, Double-A Eastern League managers recognized him as the circuit's best defensive third baseman. Henson will likely make his long-term career decision within the next season. Baseball is the frontrunner at this point, and Henson should quickly blossom into a major league caliber player by the end of next season should he make that choice.

4 - OF Jackson Melian - Along with the aforementioned Henson, Melian was another key component of the package received from the Yankees in the Neagle trade. Melian, 20, is a raw five-tool prospect who evokes memories of former Yankee farmhand Ruben Rivera at a similar stage in development. The 6'2", 190, righthanded hitter is a superior athlete who hits the ball a country mile in batting practice, and ranks among the fastest minor leaguers around. However, poor plate discipline and inconsistency against quality breaking stuff have kept his power numbers down, and he hasn't yet found a way to incorporate his speed into his offensive game. Defensively, Melian is a natural center fielder with exceptional range and an above average throwing arm. Melian has always ranked among the youngest players at each successive level, but might need to make a return trip to Double-A and dominate to remain a potential impact prospect. Center field appears to be taken in Cincinnati, so a change of scenery, role, or position might be necessary for Melian to reach his ultimate major league potential.

5 - SS Gookie Dawkins - Believe it or not, Dawkins, who has seemingly been Barry Larkin's heir apparent forever, is still only 21 years old. Defensively, Dawkins is state-of-the-art, and has been for quite awhile. He evokes memories of a young Pokey Reese, covering expansive range because of excellent speed and an explosive first step. The 6'1", 180, Dawkins also has a high-octane throwing arm and a quick release. However, he has made no progress with the bat over the past year, and that will keep him off of the Reds' major league roster in the immediate future. Dawkins has hit the ball with more authority as he has physically matured, but his approach at the plate has become less disciplined. He needs to learn to hit the ball on the ground more often and trust his raw speed, which makes him a 30-plus stolen base threat. It's quite possible that Dawkins read more than a few of his own press clippings, and thought he had nothing left to prove in the upper minors after a fine 1999 season that culminated in a starting role on the Pan Am games team. The game humbled Dawkins a bit in 2000: look for him to bounce back and reassert himself as a future starting major league shortstop with a fine Triple-A season in 2001.

6 - LHP Ed Yarnall - 2000 was not the best of seasons for Ed Yarnall. It began pleasantly enough, with Yarnall practically being handed the fifth starter job for the World Champion Yankees early in spring training. It all headed south in a single one-inning, ten-run start this spring in front of George Steinbrenner. Though Yarnall, 24, eventually pitched well in stretches at the Triple-A level, he never escaped the Yankee doghouse, and moved to the Reds in the Neagle deal. The 6'3", 234, southpaw combines a 90 MPH fastball with a curveball and changeup, and is a rhythm pitcher prone to extended stretches of excellence as well as long slumps. The 1996 third round pick needs to watch his conditioning, as the slightest lapse in his mechanics causes his pitches to flatten out and become much more hittable. Yarnall will likely get another crack at a major league fifth starter role next season, and is about 50/50 to succeed. He should fit onto the Reds' staff as a swingman or situational reliever at the very least, and could evolve into a mid-rotation starter.

7 - LHP Ty Howington - In Howington, 19, the Reds possess a younger, harder-throwing version of Yarnall, with an arguably higher upside. The 6'5", 220, southpaw is exceedingly raw at this point, however, and struggled mightily in his pro debut at Low-A Dayton last season. Howington throws a low to mid 90s fastball and a hard curve, and is refining his changeup. His mechanics were inconsistent last season, leading to uneven command, high pitch counts, and relatively short stints on the mound. Despite his struggles, however, Howington kept his head and took the ball every fifth day, showing exceptional maturity for a teenager. The raw materials are certainly there, but Howington has a great deal of work to do before asserting himself as a can't-miss starting pitcher prospect. Look for him to achieve much more success in a second crack at Low-A ball in 2001. With some polish, he could evolve into a mid-rotation major league starter or a short reliever, depending on the diversity of his repertoire.

8 - RHP Chris Reitsma - Reitsma, 22, was the Red Sox' first round pick in 1996, and came to the Reds long with fellow pitcher John Curtice in the late August deal for Dante Bichette. A battery of injuries and poor control had caused the Red Sox to leave him unprotected from the Rule 5 draft, where he was claimed in 1999 by the Devil Rays. He didn't make the Tampa Bay roster out of spring training, and was returned to the Sox, where he promptly had his best pro season at Double-A Trenton. Now, the 6'5", 195, righty isn't going to develop into the top-of-the-rotation stud that he was once expected to become, but he just might become a mid-rotation finesse guy or a viable setup man. Reitsma's fastball peaks at around 90 MPH, but he changes speed and location well, and consistently keeps the ball on the low edges of the strike zone. He gets ahead of hitters, keeps his pitch count down, and consequently lasts deep into ballgames. Most impressively, he took a regular Double-A turn without incident for an entire season. Reitsma's career is back up off of the mat, and with a solid start at the Triple-A level in 2001, he could join the major league staff later in the season as a swingman or fifth starter.

9 - OF Ben Broussard - Broussard, 23, was the Reds' second round draft pick in 1999. He raced through three levels that year, showing power potential against the younger lower level hurlers he faced. However, the 6'3", 225, lefthanded hitter has struggled for over one full season now at the Double-A level. While Broussard certainly can drive a mistake fastball a long way, his bat speed isn't spectacular, and his power is his only tool that projects as above major league average. His plate discipline is above average, but his foot speed is only adequate, and he is quite green defensively in the outfield, as he was a regular first baseman in college at McNeese State. His early power barrage after being drafted caused many to lump him in with the Kearnses and Dunns as a Reds' starting outfielder of the future. Don't believe it, Broussard is much more likely to fit in as a power off of the bench in Cincinnati, but only if he shows material progress in 2001 at Triple-A.

10 - RHP Brian Reith - Reith, 22, was the last piece of the four-part package received from the Yankees for Denny Neagle. Though the 6'5", 190, righthander doesn't throw exceedingly hard, he can be an extremely tough customer when he is placing his upper 80s fastball plus his changeup and curveball for quality strikes on the edges of the zone. He could add 15 or 20 pounds of muscle with some weight room work, and that could give him the extra bite he needs to excel at higher levels. Reith is a bit old to not have dented the Double-A level. If he can't be an above average performer at that level at age 23 next season, than Reith will be a dark horse to ever be a front line major leaguer. Watch his Double-A strikeout rate next season, if it's above average, he'll likely contend for a swingman or middle relief role in the majors by sometime in 2003.

OTHER PROSPECTS

OF Andy Burress - Burress took a step backwards as a prospect during the 2000 season and with the Reds' depth of outfield prospects that's not a good thing. He doesn't have much power and needs to hit for average and steal bases to be effective. He hit just .250 at Double-A last year while only managing 15 steals in 29 attempts. He makes contact and draws an acceptable number of walks, but must improve as a hitter.

RHP Bo Donaldson - Donaldson is an extremely hard thrower who relies almost totally on his fastball. Control is a big problem with Donaldson, but if he makes some improvement in his ability to locate the fastball he could be in the majors quickly. He had 24 saves at Double-A last year and struck out 78 batters in 61-plus innings, but he also walked 48.

3B Brandon Larson - Injuries held Larson back when he was first brought into the Reds' system but he has fought his way back nicely. He is a bit old for a player who hasn't seen more than a few games above Double-A, but he has good power. He strikes out a lot and hasn't drawn many walks thus far in his career, but if he improves just a little bit in that area and field his position relatively well he'll earn a shot at big league time.

C Jason LaRue - LaRue is a good hitter with a little power. He's also solid behind the plate with an average throwing arm, but he works hard. If he can improve his patience, LaRue could be a double-digit home run guy as part of a lefty-righty catching platoon.

RHP Michael Neu - Neu is an aggressive closer with a low to mid 90s fastball and an excellent breaking pitch. He walks far too many hitters at this point of his career, but he was a successful closer at the Division I college level and has picked up his fair share of saves in the minors. He had 24 saves last year at Low-A while striking out a whopping 95 batters in just 69 innings. His 52 walks, however, were a bit of a problem.

1B Samone Peters - Peters has one thing going for him: raw power. He's 6'7" and more than 260 pounds and can drive the ball a mile, but he's a wild swinger who strikes out way too much. He whiffed 198 times in 456 at-bats at Low-A last year and he also made 22 errors at first base. In other words, he needs a lot of work.

RHP John Riedling - Riedling came into his own late in the 1999 season as a reliever and he continued that success with a strong 2000 campaign that saw him pitch in Cincinnati at the end of the year. He has a low 90s fastball that gets good movement and he throws a slider that's effective when he's ahead in the count. He could be a closer at some point in the future, but for now he looks like a nice setup man or middle reliever.

RHP Jose Valdez - Valdez has a live fastball and good raw stuff, though control is a problem. He held Single-A Midwest League hitters to a .206 average against him last year, but also yielded 40 walks in just 86 innings. If he can improve his breaking pitch and locate his fastball better, especially early in counts, he'll be fine.

COLORADO ROCKIES
ORGANIZATIONAL GRID

	AAA	AA	HI-A	LO-A
1B	Phil Hiatt - R - 31	Steve Goodell - R - 25	Justin Hemme - L - 24 John Lindsey - R - 23 Jerome Alviso - B - 24	Kevin Duck - L - 22 Augustin Sanchez - B - 21
2B	Brent Butler - R - 22 Aaron Ledesma - R - 29	Belvani Martinez - R - 21	Chone Figgins - B - 22	Miguel Vilorio - R - 20
SS	Juan Sosa - R - 24	Elvis Pena - B - 23 Brian Keck - R - 26	Juan Uribe - R - 20	Justin Lincoln - R - 21
3B	Scott McClain - R - 28	Javier Colina - R - 21	Matt Holliday - R - 20	Chris Warren - R - 23 Chris Moore - L - 23 Sam Smith - R - 21
OF	Chris Latham - B - 27 Carlos Mendoza - L - 25 John Cotton - L - 29 Shane Monahan - L - 25 Juan Pierre - L - 22	Jody Gerut - L - 22 Danny Ramirez - R - 26 Norm Hutchins - B - 24 Kevin Gibbs - B - 26 Mike Meggers - R - 29	Scott Seal - L - 24 Choo Freeman - R - 20 Luis Landaeta - L - 23 Kevin Burford - L - 22 Erik Johnson - R - 23	Dan Phillips - R - 21 Melvin Rosario - L - 21 Greg Catalanotte - B - 23 Jim Rinne - R - 23 Edmund Muth - R - 21
C	Mark Strittmatter -R- 31 Darron Cox - R - 32 Adam Melhuse - B - 28	Walt McKeel - R - 28 Jason Dewey - R - 23	Josh Bard - B - 22 Jay Jones - L - 25 Josh Pride - R - 21	Jeff Winchester - R - 20 Eric McQueen - R - 23
SP	Doug Linton - R - 34 Steve Bourgeois - R - 25 David Moraga - L - 24 Steve Ontiveros - R - 39 Aaron Small - R - 28	Shawn Chacon - R - 22 Mark DiFelice - R - 23 Josh Kalinowski - L - 23 Mike Porzio - L - 27 Ryan Seifert - R - 24 Robert Averette - R - 23 Randey Dorame - L - 21 Jason Jennings - R - 21	Justin Carter - L - 23 Luke Hudson - R - 23 Chuck Crowder - L - 23 Ryan Cameron - R - 22 Ryan Price - R - 22 Aaron Cook - R - 21 Chandler Martin - R - 26	Julio DePaula - R - 20 Ryan Kibler - R - 19 Enemencio Pacheco - R - 21 Chin-Hui Tsao - R - 18 Scott Dohmann - R - 21 Tom Stepka - R - 24
CLOSER	David Lee - R - 27 Craig House - R - 22	Travis Thompson - R - 25	Jase Wrigley - R - 24 Steve Matcuk - R - 24	Cam Esslinger - R - 23 Colin Young - L - 22 Rick Cercy - R - 23

COLORADO ROCKIES

A little over a calendar year ago, the Rockies' minor league system appeared to be on life support. Now, thanks to a couple of productive drafts, a key overseas signing or two, and trades of the likes of Dave Veres and Tom Goodwin for top-shelf prospects the organization has been revitalized. Prospect depth isn't the greatest, but prospect quality has significantly improved.

It's a good thing that the Rockies have Todd Helton in place for the next decade plus, as there are no viable first base prospects on the horizon.

Along with the recently acquired Jeff Frye and Todd Walker, Brent Butler is a candidate to step into the Rockies' second base job in 2001. He makes consistent authoritative contact, but lacks the quickness generally associated with middle infielders. His bat could be quite lethal in Coors Field's rarefied air, however. Belvani Martinez is speedier and less disciplined and powerful than Butler. He can also play a respectable shortstop, and could be a decent fit as a major league utilityman, a role in which his offensive weaknesses would be better masked. Chone Figgins has excellent raw skills, but needed a second High-A season to translate them into performance. He too projects as a possible major league backup down the road. Miguel Vilorio is another speedy second sacker with a lot of rough edges to his game. He might not have a single eyecatching tool that would put him in the hunt for a significant big league role.

The Rockies also have a stable of shortstop prospects set to put pressure on big league incumbent Neifi Perez. Juan Sosa has surprising pop or a shortstop and puts the ball in play regularly, but likely lacks the defensive upside to start in the majors. He's yet another utility candidate. Ditto Elvis Pena, likely the king of the Rockies' utility prospects. The switch-hitter plays both second base and shortstop well, and has matured into a solid on-base threat at the top of the order. Toss in big-time speed and you have the recipe for a near-term major league contributor. Juan Uribe is potentially much more than a utility prospect; he's a genuine threat to Perez. He can flat out pick it at

shortstop, and projects to have more power than the current major league starter. He could arrive sometime in 2002. Justin Lincoln has an intriguing power/speed upside for a shortstop, but his game has multitudes of raw edges. At 6'3", 200, he's also a pretty fair bet to outgrow the position.

Javier Colina leaped over a level to Double-A and from second to third base in 2000, and the transition proved difficult. Colina has the bat to contribute in the majors, but needs to develop patience to have a chance to get there. He's another utility candidate, who can play both the middle and corner infield spots. Matt Holliday is a power prospect whose longball numbers were down in the pitcher-friendly High-A Carolina League. Look for improvement in the smaller upper minor league parks, and watch Holliday possibly move into contention to succeed or supplement Jeff Cirillo in two to three years.

Outfield pickings are relatively slim. Jody Gerut and Juan Pierre are the closest to making major league contributions. Gerut is a gaps slasher who rarely strikes out who should become at least a productive 300 at bat per season contributor, and quite possibly much more. Pierre made major strides forward in 2000, and with the trade of Tom Goodwin, becomes a candidate to patrol center field for the Rockies sometime in 2001. He can flat out fly, and though he has very little power, he has honed an offensive package that should eventually be better than Goodwin's. 1998 first round pick Choo Freeman has been a major disappointment, showing little of the longball power expected of him. He'll get lots of chances, but it's not looking good. Lefty Kevin Burford and righty Dan Phillips have outside chances to develop into big league role players. Burford has a smooth line drive stroke with some power potential, and Phillips, an intriguing power/speed upside despite an utter lack of plate discipline.

Ben Petrick is the future, and the present, at catcher. He has the complete package, and should move in as a long-term starter, and future All-Star, in Colorado in 2001. 1999 third round pick Josh Bard is a slashing contact hitter with solid defensive skills who could eventually be a very strong backup to Petrick. Jeff Winchester has an intriguing power upside, but might need a position switch before threatening to reach the majors.

The Rockies have been trying to assemble a stable of pitching prospects since their inception, and only now do their efforts appear to be bearing fruit. Most of the help is a couple of years away, however. Lefty Randey Dorame, acquired from the Dodgers in the Goodwin deal, could be the first one on the scene. He's a finesse guy who will have to be infinitely precise to avoid getting rocked in Coors. The jury's out. Finesse righty Robert Averette has excelled in Double-A, but might not have a true out pitch against upper level hitters. He's far from a sure thing to stick in the bigs. Righty Shawn Chacon has great stuff, but questionable makeup has impeded his progress. He was a solid citizen, and a successful one, at Double-A in 2000, and might have the power to succeed in Colorado a la Pedro Astacio. Lefty Josh Kalinowski hit some speed bumps at Double-A in 2000, but retains the raw stuff to get the ball past higher level hitters. He might fit in best as a swingman or southpaw relief specialist in Colorado. Ryan Price nibbled in his first crack at Double-A hitters, setting his progress back. He looks like no better than a big league middle relief candidate at this point. Jason Jennings has the tools to be a long-term major league winner. At this stage, he still gives batters one eminently hittable pitch per at bat, which could get him burned initially in the upper minors. Ryan Cameron moved from the bullpen to the rotation at High-A Salem in 2000, with sometimes powerful results. A repeat performance at Double-A could put him on the major league radar screen. Chin-Hui Tsao is one of the very best pitching prospects in the game. He's good enough to put up sea level numbers in the mile high altitude, and could arrive via express by early 2002. He's a potential future staff ace. Aaron Cook is a finesse righty who could jump into the picture with a successful two-level jump to Double-A in 2001. Righty Julio DePaula can blow it by minor league hitters, and could become a solid starter candidate with improved command. More likely, he'll become a reliever and a possible future closer candidate. Righty Craig House is another possible closer, but he hasn't thrown many innings and has the motion of someone who isn't long for this game.

TOP TEN PROSPECTS

1 - RHP Chin-Hui Tsao - Tsao, 18, exploded onto the scene in his first professional season, striking out well over a batter per inning and exhibiting pinpoint control as the youngest player in a full season league. The 6'1", 180, righthander wowed South Atlantic League managers, who recognized him for having the best fastball in the circuit. He pushes the radar gun up into the mid 90s, and mixes in a hard slider and an improving changeup, both of which could develop into above average major league pitches. He has an advanced feel for pitching, setting up hitters well and working the corners like a veteran. Physically, the 6'1", 180, Tsao is basically a finished product, any additional velocity or movement will come from mechanical adjustment, not from growth. Tsao should explode through the minor leagues and contend for a rotation spot in Colorado in 2002. It will be interesting to see whether a top-shelf power pitcher like Tsao can flourish in Coors Field. The guess here is that he will.

2 - RHP Jason Jennings - Jennings, 21, was the Rockies' 1999 first round draft pick. The 6'2", 235, righthander has progressed rapidly, earning a promotion to Double-A Carolina by the end of 2000. Jennings fastball flirts with 90 MPH, but he consistently keeps it low in the strike zone and mixes it with a sharp slider and an improving changeup, all of which he can consistently throw for strikes on any count. Jennings is adept at throwing strike one, and his ability to maintain low pitch counts allows him to last deep into ballgames. The fact that none of his pitches projects as a true strikeout offering at higher levels, and that he has allowed about a hit per inning thus far in his pro career, suggests that Jennings is not a future top-of-the-rotation major leaguer. Jennings is right on schedule, and should contend for a spot in the Rockies' rotation by early 2002. Look for him to be a strong number two or three starter in Colorado over the long haul.

3 - LHP Randey Dorame - The Rockies stole Dorame, 21, from the Dodgers in the Tom Goodwin trade last July. The 6'2", 205, lefthander is a finesse hurler with a mid to upper 80s fastball, plus an above average curve and changeup. Dorame varies speed and control expertly, and his ability to consistently throw a quality strike one has allowed to pitch deep into ballgames throughout his pro career. He maintained his effectiveness, but not his strikeout rate, after being promoted to the Double-A level for the first time in 2000. He needs to fine tune his mechanics and develop a true strikeout pitch for use in the high altitude that awaits him at the Triple-A and major league levels in the Rockies' system. The predictable failure of Scott Karl in Colorado last year proved that the garden variety "crafty lefty" is dead meat in the mile-high Coors Field conditions. Dorame will have to evolve beyond his current form to achieve in those surroundings. Watch his strikeout/walk numbers carefully at Triple-A Colorado Springs in 2001: early success there could result in a quick promotion to the majors. He's got a chance to be a solid mid-rotation big league southpaw.

4 - 2B Brent Butler - Butler, 22, was drafted on the third round by the Cardinals in the 1996 draft, and came to Colorado in the trade that delivered Darryl Kile and Dave Veres to St. Louis. The 6'0", 180, righthanded hitter is a consistent line drive gaps hitter who should thrive in the Colorado altitude. Those huge gaps at Coors Field are tailor-made for his stroke, which could produce .300 averages and 50-double totals on a consistent basis. Butler rarely strikes out, but needs to develop a little better plate discipline. He projects to have no better than 15 homer power, and his foot speed is below average for a middle infielder, so he needs to be a .300-plus hitter to carve out a starting big league role with the Rockies. Defensively, Butler is solid but unspectacular, making all of the plays within his fairly average range and showing slightly above average arm strength. Butler has also played shortstop and third base, and his versatility could help him stick in Colorado as a utilityman should he prove unable to win the second base job. Look for him to battle Todd Walker for that job and possibly platoon with him in 2001. Butler is the better bet win the job over the long haul, and should be at least major league average.

5 - SS Juan Uribe - Uribe, 20, is a 6'1", 145, righthanded hitter who has a chance to press Neifi Perez for the major league shortstop job within a couple of seasons. Despite his rail-thin stature, Uribe hits the ball with substantial authority to the gaps. He could put up some interesting doubles and triples numbers once he reaches the high-altitude environments at the Triple-A and major league levels. Poor plate discipline is one flaw that he'll need to address before fulfilling his potential however. Defensively, he has well above average range and can make both the routine and spectacular play with some degree of consistency. His infield arm, rated as the best in the High-A Carolina League last season by its managers, ranks among the best in the minor leagues. Uribe is on track to be a big league starter, but his offensive development at upper minor league levels will be the key. Without improvement, he could be in for a big surprise at bat at the Double-A level in 2001. If all goes well, he'll duke it out

with Perez in 2003 spring training, and could move Perez over to second base.

6 - OF Juan Pierre - Pierre, 22, was one of the most improved players in the minor leagues last season, and he rode his success all the way into the major league lineup by the end of the summer after the trade of Tom Goodwin to the Dodgers. Actually, Goodwin is a good place to start when discussing the 6'0", 170, lefthanded-hitting Pierre - they're almost the same exact player. Both players have game-breaking speed, Pierre was recognized as both the fastest and best baserunner, and as the most exciting player in the Double-A Southern League by its managers last season. He did so after being aggressively promoted two levels ahead after hitting .320 at Low-A Asheville in 1999. Pierre is a slap hitter with no noticeable extra base power; like Goodwin. He's a fairly wild swinger who rarely walks but is difficult to strike out; like Goodwin. He covers a lot of ground in center field, but doesn't throw that well; like Goodwin. However, Pierre is only 22, and could still enhance his weak areas, while Goodwin never did so. Pierre will get a chance to win the Rockies' center field job in 2001. Don't expect him to be a quality leadoff hitter yet, but he could be evolve into one if he works hard on his plate discipline.

7 - OF Jody Gerut - Gerut, 22, was a 1998 second round draft pick out of Stanford. Like Brent Butler and major league incumbent third baseman Jeff Cirillo, he has "Made for Coors Field" stamped all over him. The 6'0", 190, lefthanded hitter is a line drive machine with consistent gaps power and is 20 steal threat because of decent speed and exceptional baserunning instincts. Put Gerut in a major league lineup with Todd Helton, Cirillo and Butler, and you could have four 50-double guys. He works deep counts, rarely strikes out, and pounces on the one hittable pitch per at bat that a pitcher tends to give. Defensively, Gerut is fundamentally sound, but lacks exciting range or above average arm strength; he's likely ticketed for left field in the major leagues. Gerut is on track for September 2001 arrival in the major leagues. He'll battle for a starting job the next spring, and would be a fine fourth outfielder during his apprenticeship period.

8 - RHP Shawn Chacon - Chacon, 22, is a talented 6'3", 195, righty with plenty of checks in both the plus and minus columns. He has a prototypical power pitcher's frame, a low 90s fastball and a hard overhand curve. His first crack at the Double-A level last season was a rousing success, his command was better than it had been at lower levels, allowing him to routinely pitch seven quality innings or more. He also maintained a strikeout per inning pace, a reliable indicator of future major league success. He does have some skeletons in his closet, however. He has a history of elbow trouble, was suspended late in 1999 for disciplinary reasons, and has shown a tendency to put on weight at times over the years. However, he was on his best behavior on all fronts in 2000, so an optimist would say he has matured. Chacon will pitch his home games in high altitude for the first time in 2001 at Triple-A Colorado Springs. If he can handle the adversity that will surely surface at times without regressing toward old bad habits, then Chacon could possibly still evolve into the top-flight major league power pitcher he was once expected to become.

9 - RHP Craig House - House, 22, exploded through three minor league levels and then into the major league bullpen by the end of his first full professional season in 2000. The 6'2", 195, 1999 12th round pick is a potential future closer who will ride his high-octane fastball and deceptive, but scary, delivery as far as they will take him. His fastball pushes the radar gun up to 100 MPH on occasion, and was recognized as the best heater in the Double-A Southern League last season by its managers. He often uses his late-breaking slider as a strikeout pitch, and has added a splitter to flesh out his arsenal. His motion, which will be quite an asset his first time around the league, could develop into his greatest enemy over time. It's hard to fathom how his grinding motion won't eventually spell major shoulder or elbow trouble for House. Poor command is also an issue, but not a major one if House is allowed to start innings rather then enter them with multiple runners on base. Look for House to thrive initially in an eighth or ninth inning role in Colorado. How he adjusts after the league makes its preliminary adjustments to him will determine whether he settles in as a long-term big league closer.

10 - OF Choo Freeman - The Rockies have to be getting a bit concerned about the slow offensive development of Freeman, 20, their 1998 first round draftee. The 6'2", 200, righthanded hitter was thought to have a legitimate 40/40 power/speed upside when drafted, with the power considered a sure thing and his speed considered to be a tool he would develop over time. After displaying acceptable power potential in 1999 at Low-A Asheville, Freeman completely misplaced his power stroke last season at High-A Salem. A big part of his problem has been subpar plate discipline. He has too often buried himself in the count, and his relative inability to hit quality breaking stuff has made him a sitting duck in 0-2 and 1-2 situations.

He needs to learn to work the count in the other direction and then pounce on the resulting fastballs. His baserunning development is on schedule. Defensively, Freeman has the speed to play a quality center field, but could outgrow the position and move to left, as his average throwing arm likely rules out right field. Freeman is a high-risk, high-reward prospect who could be a future major league star or a long-term Triple-A question mark, a la Derrick Gibson. Another year in neutral would make the latter case most plausible.

OTHER PROSPECTS

RHP Robert Averette - Averette is a control pitcher who has pretty average stuff. His fastball is good enough to get him by in the majors, but he has to locate it well. He does a nice job of keeping the ball low in the zone and getting ground balls: if he works the ball up he'll get hit hard. He only allowed 28 walks in 136-plus innings of work last year at Double-A and if he does that at Triple-A this year he'll be on his way.

OF Kevin Burford - Burford has a little bit of everything going for him. He can hit for average, he has extra base power with home run potential, he runs fairly well and he exhibits above average patience at the plate. The only thing he has to do now is prove himself against more experience pitchers at the Double-A level. If his home runs power develops, which the 40 doubles he hit last year suggests, he could be a valuable player for a team playing at high altitude.

RHP Ryan Cameron - Cameron has an above average fastball and he's a strikeout pitcher, but he'll have to improve his control as he moves up the ladder in the Rockies' system. His control isn't awful, but it needs to be better. He keeps the ball in the ballpark, which is a great sign in this organization, allowing just nine home runs over 160-plus innings at High-A last year. If he keeps that trend up, he'll become very popular with management.

OF Greg Catalanotte - Catalanotte is a switch-hitter with good power. He has the ability to be a 30 home run guy down the line, but he'll need to make more consistent contact to have success against older pitchers. He strikes out a ton, 149 times in 454 at-bats at Low-A last year, and that could be a problem. He didn't run much either, but that won't matter if he keeps hitting the long ball.

RHP Aaron Cook - Cook is a young pitcher with an idea of what he needs to do to get hitters out. His stuff is a little above average, but his control is just amazing. In 142-plus innings of work at Low-A last year he walked just 23 batters and threw only five wild pitches. That kind of command isn't commonplace at Low-A, so he's got something that most guys his age don't. He's gotten a fair number of strikeouts so far, but he's not a power pitcher and doesn't figure to keep racking up the whiffs as he advances.

RHP Julio DePaula - DePaula has an outstanding fastball but he makes too many mistakes at this point of his career. Someone who can overpower hitters like he can shouldn't allow as many hits or home runs as he did at Low-A last year. He gave up 151 hits and 16 home runs in 155 innings of work and that's against a lot of immature young hitters. He needs to get ahead in the count more consistently and exploit his ability to get the strikeout when he needs it. DePaula fanned 187 batters in those 155 innings, which is nearly 11 strikeouts per nine innings.

3B Matt Holliday - Holliday hasn't shown the long ball ability one might expect from a 6'4" 215 pound third baseman, but he's still only 20. He needs to be more aggressive and he needs to learn how to lift the ball into the air, both of which could come anytime. As long as he keeps making contact and holding his own at third base he'll keep advancing and the higher he goes in the Rockies' system the more likely he is to start hitting more homers.

LHP Josh Kalinowski - Kalinowski has an above average fastball, a decent change and a knee-buckling curveball that he uses to get strikeouts. His greatest weakness is control and in the Rockies' organization that will hold you back. Most of Colorado's young pitchers can get by as high as Double-A and still pitch well with control issues, but once they reach Triple-A and the majors throwing strikes becomes essential. Kalinowski must throw more strikes or he'll have a limited future with the Rockies, though a change of scenery may be to his benefit anyway.

2B Belvani Martinez - Martinez can run and he has good defensive skills, but he's a wild swinger who rarely takes a walk. Combine that with little physical strength and no power to speak of and you have the makings of a utility man. Should he decide to be more patient at the plate and to put his speed to better use he could be a prospect worth watching.

OF Carlos Mendoza - Mendoza can put the ball in play and he can really run, but he has no power at all. He hit .354 with 26 steals at Triple-A Colorado Springs but never got a callup to the majors last year, which is a bit odd. Even playing at a high altitude he didn't hit a single home run, which is clearly a drawback, but he could still help a Major League team in some capacity.

SS Elvis Pena - Pena is a good contact hitter who puts the ball in play, draws a fair number of walks and uses his speed extremely well. He struggled defensively last year after moving from second base to shortstop, but that's to be expected with that kind of a move. He has a chance to be a major league regular if he can continue hitting around .300 with 40-plus stolen bases, which is what he produced at Double-A during the 2000 season.

FLORIDA MARLINS
ORGANIZATIONAL GRID

	AAA	AA	HI-A	LO-A
1B	Nate Rolison - L - 23	Chris Norton - R - 29	Tony Lucca - L - 25	David Callahan - L - 20
2B	Amaury Garcia - R - 25 Casey Candaele - B - 39	Pablo Ozuna - R - 21	Jesus Medrano - R - 21	Kevin Hooper - R - 23
SS	Aaron Holbert - R - 27 Chris Clapinski - B - 28 Mendy Lopez - R - 25	Matt Erickson - L - 24 Joe Funaro - R - 27 Derek Wathan - B - 23	Drew Niles - B - 23	Luis Ugueto - B - 21
3B	Sean McNally - R - 27	Todd Betts - L - 27	Jose Santos - R - 22 Raul Franco - R - 24 Heath Honeycutt - R - 23	Kelley Washington - R - 20 Matt DeMarco - L - 20
OF	Luis Raven - R - 31 Manny Martinez - R - 29 Mike Gulan - R - 29 Derrick Gibson - R - 25 Julio Ramirez - R - 22	Cesar Crespo - B - 21 Jaime Jones - L - 23 Wynter Phoenix - L - 25 Ben Candelaria - L - 25	Willy Hill - L - 23 Chris Aguila - R - 21 Brett Roneberg - L - 21 Randy Rigsby - L - 23 Abraham Nunez - B - 20 Heath Kelly - R - 24	Matt Padgett - L - 22 Chip Ambres - R - 20 Francisco Ferrand - L - 20 Scott Goodman - L - 22 Kevin Perkins - R - 22
C	Sandy Martinez - L - 27 Alex Melconian - R - 25	Brandon Harper - R - 24 John Pachot - R - 25	Matt Treanor - R - 24 Jeff Bailey - R - 21 Dennis Anderson - R - 22	Matt Frick - R - 24 Stephen Morales - B - 22 Dominic Woody - R - 21
SP	Mike Drumright - R - 26 Jason Grilli - R - 23 John DeSilva - R - 32 Bronswell Patrick - R - 29 Sean Bergman - R - 30 Vladimir Nunez - R - 25 Joe Fontenot - R - 23	Brandon Leese - R - 24 Nate Bump - R - 23 Gary Knotts - R - 23 Scott Comer - L - 23 Kevin Olsen - R - 23	Aaron Akin - R - 23 Wes Anderson - R - 20 Hector Almonte - R - 24 Claudio Vargas - R - 21 Ryan Moskau - L - 22 Ryan Harber - L - 23	Josh Beckett - R - 20 Todd Moser - L - 23 Marc Sauer - R - 20 Gustavo Lopez - R - 21 Brad Farizo - R - 21
CLOSER	Joe Strong - R - 37 Mike Cather - R - 29	Bobby Rodgers - R - 25 Scott Henderson - R - 25 Geoff Goetz - L - 21	Blaine Neal - R - 22 Tim McClaskey - R - 24	Bryan Moore - R - 23 Brandon Bowe - R - 24

FLORIDA MARLINS

After dismantling their expensive World Championship club, the Marlins set out to assemble an array of inexpensive minor league talent. Their labors have produced an exciting young major league team, and an abundance of minor league prospects who are banging on the door. Some will stick around, and others will likely be dealt to add needed veteran pieces for near-term playoff runs.

Derrek Lee is likely set at first base for awhile in the majors, and isn't likely to be pushed soon by current Marlin farmhands. 6'6", 240, behemoth Nate Rolison could press for a backup major league role in 2001, and might be quite productive in a well-tailored role. He remains a promising sleeper to possibly earn a larger role. David Callahan could make some noise if he significantly refines his power stroke as he advances. He's had warning track power to date in the pros.

With Luis Castillo in place, it's going to be hard for solid prospects Amaury Garcia and Pablo Ozuna to carve out significant big league roles. Garcia has a solid power/speed upside for a middle infielder, and has been a high achiever in two consecutive Triple-A campaigns. He's likely no more than trade bait to the Marlins, but could be a big league starter given a change of scenery. Ozuna is an exciting prospect whose path to the majors might gather steam if he is moved back to shortstop, his natural position. He puts the ball in play with authority regularly, runs well, and has great defensive range. He projects as an above average major leaguer at either second base or shortstop within two years.

Ozuna is the only viable shortstop prospect in the system, and could move back there soon if Alex Gonzalez' struggles at the major league level continue.

Third baseman Mike Lowell is likely to remain virtually unchallenged from within the Marlins' system over the next couple of years. Kelley Washington, who also has some shortstop experience, is a solid athlete with power and speed potential, but has yet to develop a consistent batting stroke. He's an outside sleeper utility prospect.

Outfield prospect depth is relatively solid. The Marlins took a flyer on former Rockies' blue-chipper Derrick Gibson, who retains a massive power/speed upside. Unfortunately, his penchant for swinging at virtually every pitch hasn't changed, and is likely to keep him down on the farm. Julio Ramirez has the ability to be a leadoff hitter and starting center fielder in the majors, but has been slow to work on his shortcomings, particularly his poor plate discipline. 2001 needs to be a breakout year at Triple-A for Ramirez to retain his top prospect status and chance for a 2002 major league role. Cesar Crespo could be an exciting multipositional backup in the majors. He can play multiple infield and outfield positions, has sneaky power/speed potential, and will wait out a walk. Look for him in South Florida in 2002. Switch-hitter Abraham Nunez is the Marlins' best all-around position player prospect. He has a 30/30 power/speed upside, projects as a starting big league rightfielder, and will be banging on the Marlins' door in 2001 at age 21. He could be a future All-Star. 2000 High-A outfielders Chris Aguila and Brett Roneberg could be major league role players down the line. Aguila has a significant power upside and Roneberg is a pesky on-base threat. 1998 first round pick Chip Ambres has been plagued by nagging injuries during his short career, but looked good during the second half of 2000. He's a potential future major league leadoff man with a 20/30 power/speed upside. The Marlins need to see him produce over a full minor league season soon, however. Lefty hitter Francisco Ferrand has deceptive longball power for his size (5'10", 170) and could become a candidate for a complementary big league role if he maintains his current rate of progress.

The Marlins need to find out if Ramon Castro is their catcher of the present, and soon. He annually tears up Triple-A pitching, and seems to have the defensive skill set to cut it in the bigs. He'll likely be their man behind the plate in 2001. Jeff Bailey was once considered a solid all-around catching prospect, but injuries have rendered him a designated hitter for much of his pro career. He has solid power potential for a receiver, but needs to be behind the plate more to have a chance.

Even with the quick advancement to the majors of hurlers like Ryan Dempster, Brad Penny and A.J. Burnett, the Marlins have quite a few more quality pitching prospects remaining on the farm, particularly at the lower levels. Righty Jason Grilli has seen his confidence sapped by his ongoing struggles in the hitter-friendly Pacific Coast League, and is no longer a sure bet for major league success. He has all of the raw tools, but might be in line for a change of scenery if he doesn't break through soon. Nate Bump, like Grilli a highly regarded former Giants' prospect, also currently sees his prospects dimming. Bump never developed a strikeout pitch, and his location within the strike zone has deteriorated. He'll have a hard time fighting off the hordes of prospects gaining on him. Smooth 6'4", 175, righty Wes Anderson has a high power/control ceiling and should only get better as he physically matures. He looks like a future mid-rotation anchor in the majors. 6'3", 210, righty Claudio Vargas has very quietly blown the ball past Class A hitters during the last two seasons, and will certify himself a prospect with similar Double-A performance in 2001. His stuff isn't overwhelming, but Vargas has a knack for making hitters miss. He could eventually be a passable ninth or tenth man on a big league staff. 1999 first round pick Josh Beckett has a scary upside. His high 90s fastball, hard curve combination ranks among the minors' deadliest, and all he needs is innings before making a profound major league impact. Righty Marc Sauer is a thinking man's hurler who grew more effective as his 2000 Low-A season progressed. He's learning to retire lefties with his breaking stuff, and is a sleeper to eventually slip into the low end of the rotation in South Florida.

In righty Blaine Neal and lefty Geoff Goetz, the Marlins possess a pair of viable short relief prospects. Neal is a 6'5", 205, converted shortstop with a blazing fastball, while Goetz is a former first round Mets' draftee with a slight, 5'11", 163, build that masks sneaky power that is quite lethal once through the order.

TOP TEN PROSPECTS

1 - RHP Josh Beckett - Beckett, 20, was the Marlins' first round pick, and the second selection overall in the 1999 draft. Though the 6'4", 200, righthander was limited by an ongoing bout with shoulder tendinitis in his first pro season, he showed enough flashes of brilliance to show why the Marlins consider him a potential future ace starter in the big leagues. Beckett's feature pitch is an explosive mid to upper 90s fastball which was recognized as the best heater in Low-A Midwest League by its managers last season. He also throws a sharp curveball that functions as a second strikeout pitch. His control is quite exceptional for a young power pitcher, and once Beckett builds up some innings and hones his changeup into a viable third pitch, he will be on the express train to the major leagues. The Marlins need a 150-plus inning season from Beckett in 2001. If that happens, everything else will fall into place for this future big league star.

2 - 2B Pablo Ozuna - Ozuna, 21, is a 6'0", 160, switch-hitter who was acquired from the Cardinals in the Edgar Renteria deal. Speed is the central element of Ozuna's game. He's a line drive hitter who makes consistent contact and gets more than his share of leg hits. He hits the ball with sufficient authority to project as a 30 double man in the majors, but his tendency to expand his strike zone to an unacceptable size could hold his average down against top-shelf pitching. His basestealing technique has improved, but he still needs to learn to read catchers and analyze game situations better. Defensively, Ozuna covers acres of ground and has soft hands, but his arm strength is only average. He's a superb athlete who could fit into the Marlins' future as an all-purpose infield/outfield backup. He was a Midwest League All-Star shortstop in the Cards' system. Ozuna is a year away from the majors. If he can enhance his plate discipline and on-base skills, he could fit in as the Marlins' No. 2 hitter, either as their shortstop or as all-around roster insurance.

3 - OF Abraham Nunez - Nunez, 20, was part of the impressive haul received from the Diamondbacks in the 1999 Matt Mantei deal. Since coming over to the Marlins, the 6'2", 165, switch-hitter has been hampered by injuries, the most significant of which is a shoulder muscle tear that has limited him to designated hitter duty, and which still could require surgery. Nunez is a power/speed prospect who unfurled a 22 homer, 40 steal, tour-de-force at High-A High Desert as a 19-year-old Diamondback prospect in 1999. The ball explodes off of his bat, and natural physical development should add 15-20 pounds of muscle to his frame in the near term. He has excellent plate discipline for a youngster, which could enable him to evolve into .300 hitter with a 30/30 power/speed upside. Defensively, Nunez was a prototypical impact right fielder prior to the shoulder injury. If he can regain his arm strength, his combination of range and arm could make him a future Gold Glove candidate. Health is the key here; if Nunez can play 100-plus games in the field at a high level in 2001, he'll be ready to crack the big league lineup in 2002. He could be a future No. 3 hitter in the majors.

4 - RHP Wes Anderson - Anderson, 20, was a 14th round draft steal back in 1997. The 6'4", 175, righthander offers a winning combination of power and finesse, mixing a lively low to mid 90s fastball with an above average slider and a solid changeup, all of which he can throw for quality strikes consistently. However, Anderson has been limited by bouts with shoulder tendinitis in both 1999 and 2000, preventing him from earning late season promotions in both seasons. This in turn keeps him off of the extreme fast track for the future. Like Beckett, Anderson needs to remain healthy over a full season to show the Marlins the apex of his potential. Double-A looks like his 2001 destination: 150-plus innings of effectiveness will keep Anderson on schedule for a late 2002 or early 2003 big league debut. He looks like a future mid-rotation major league starter, but expected physical development and its effect on his stuff could push him higher.

5 - OF Cesar Crespo - Crespo, 21, is a 5'11", 170, switch-hitter who came to the Marlins from the Mets in the Al Leiter deal. This 1997 third round draftee falls short in raw tools. He runs quite well but doesn't grade out above average in any other area, but is one heck of a baseball player. Offensively, Crespo will take a walk, and he possesses surprising pop to the gaps for his size. He'll chase the high fastball on occasion, leading to relatively high strikeout totals for a top-of-the-order hitter. He's evolved into a prolific basestealer, due as much to his instincts and baserunning savvy as to his speed. Defensively, Crespo was originally a second baseman, but he was moved to the outfield to accommodate Pablo Ozuna at Double-A Portland last season. He has above average range at either position, but only an average throwing arm. Crespo's versatility and power/speed potential makes him a likely future major leaguer, most likely as an all-around 300 at bat multipurpose backup. A change of scenery might be in his best interests, as it's hard to see where he will fit in among the Luis Castillos and Ozunas in South Florida.

6 - OF Julio Ramirez - Ramirez, 22, is a gifted center field prospect whose development has stagnated over the last two seasons. The 5'11", 170, righthanded hitter has a 20/50 power/speed upside, but his pursuit of power at the expense of on-base skills has put him in a precarious position. Ramirez' only hope of starting in the majors is as a top-third-of-the-order hitter. At this point in his development, Ramirez still buries himself in the count too often on bad pitches to come close to being a .300 hitter, or a .350-plus on-base threat, prerequisites for batting in that region of the order. He still has difficulty handling quality breaking stuff, and has made little progress recently in that problem area. Defensively, Ramirez has well above average range and a fairly strong throwing arm. Defense comes fairly easy to him. If his offense comes around, he'd certainly rank among the top third of major league starting center fielders with the glove. The bat is the key, and Ramirez is clearly unready with it for the majors in 2001: not a good sign at age 23. The Marlins will give him one more year, and will then have to make a decision. It's not looking good for Ramirez at this point.

7 - 1B Nate Rolison - Rolison, 23, is a 1995 second round pick who finally made a quantum leap in production last season at Triple-A Calgary. The 6'6", 240, lefthanded hitter has gradually honed his power stroke over the years, increasing his power production while whittling down his strikeout total as he advanced through the system. He has improved his plate discipline to a respectable level, and the resulting additional fastballs thrown his way have made Rolison a more dangerous hitter. So dangerous, in fact, that Triple-A Pacific Coast League managers rated him the best power prospect in the circuit. The offensive bar is set exceedingly high for major league first basemen. Marlins' incumbent Derrek Lee showed flashes of brilliance in 2000 that gave Marlins' brass hope that he might be able to clear that bar. Chances are, however, that Lee will falter enough to give Rolison at least one chance to slip through the back door into his job. He'll have only that one chance, however, to start, and most likely will fit in as a viable major league bench bat in the near term.

8 - LHP Geoff Goetz - Goetz, 21, was part of the package received from the Mets for Mike Piazza. This 5'11", 163, lefthander could make the Marlins' one-week stewardship of Piazza worthwhile. It looked like his run to the majors might end before it began because of shoulder problems caused by his grinding pitching motion. His 2000 High-A campaign was a rousing success, however, and occurred with Goetz being utilized in a creative manner designed to preserve his health and build his arm strength. Goetz was used as a reliever every third day, and was limited to a 55-60 pitch count. His health was great, and his pitching better. He combined his low 90s heater and sharp curve, rated as the best breaking pitch in the Florida State League by its managers, into a dominating combination. He also smoothed out his motion and improved his changeup, likely paving the way for a eventual return to the rotation. Goetz will still need to be coddled a bit, but is now established as a future major leaguer, either as a mid-rotation starter or a dominant short reliever.

9 - C Ramon Castro - Castro, 24, appears to be in line for one last chance to be the Marlins' starting catcher. September 1999 was supposed to be his coming-out party, but Castro's poor hitting then, and again in both winter ball and spring training earned him a ticket back to Triple-A. The 6'3", 225, righthanded hitter made offensive strides last season, as he regularly used the entire field for the first time in his pro career. If he resists temptation to pull the ball, he could be a .270ish hitter with 15 homer power in the majors. He remains quite overaggressive at the plate, and is especially vulnerable to quality breaking stuff. Castro is a fine defensive receiver, combining a strong throwing arm with exceptional durability and solid game-calling skills. Pacific Coast League managers recognized him as the circuit's premier defensive receiver last season. Castro is no All-Star in waiting, but could still be a reliable 400 at bat catcher. If this chance doesn't work out, he could have a lengthy Chad Kreuter-ish career as a backup.

10 - OF Chip Ambres - Ambres, 20, was the Marlins' 1998 first round draft pick. He has the raw ability to evolve into a major league leadoff man, but recurring hamstring problems curbed his all-around game last season. The 6'1", 190, righthanded hitter has solid plate discipline for a youngster, but is often overmatched by quality breaking stuff and will swing through high fastballs on occasion. He has solid power to the gaps, but needs to hit the ball on the ground more often to take advantage of his speed. Once he gets past the hamstring woes, look for Ambres to put up some big stolen base numbers in the minors. Defensively, his raw speed overcomes some of his weaknesses, but he likely projects as a left fielder at higher levels because of average arm strength and his sometimes circuitous routes to fly balls. He needs to have a huge, healthy 2001 season to remain on the radar screen as a potential future big league starter.

OTHER PROSPECTS

OF Chris Aguila - Aguila is a good defensive outfielder with some offensive ability. He's has some extra base power right now and could turn into a double-digit home run hitter if he can improve his strike zone judgment. He also runs pretty well, though he's not a particularly slick basestealer. There is potential here, but he needs to learn how to be a professional hitter.

RHP Nate Bump - Bump is a solid pitching prospect without great stuff, but with good mechanics and a solid approach. He needs to be more fine with his control because he doesn't have the kind of fastball a pitcher needs to pitch from behind in the count. He could stand to be more aggressive with his 90 MPH fastball early in the count, which would allow him to last even longer in games than he currently does. Bump projects as a possible fourth or fifth starter should he reach the majors.

LHP Scott Comer - Comer is a crafty lefthander with outstanding control. He's still a little too easy for hitters to hit against, but if he can work the corners more effectively and get ahead in counts more often he can be effective. He has a good breaking ball and because he throws strikes there's a chance he could be turned into a lefthanded reliever should things not work out for him as a starter down the line.

OF Francisco Ferrand - Ferrand is a good looking hitter with some power. His numbers at Low-A Kane County don't jump off the page at you, but when you consider it's not a good hitter's league and the fact that he only played about half a season they look a little better. He had 12 home runs and 42 RBI in 257 at-bats, which isn't bad for the Midwest League. He doesn't run all that well and has some defensive issues, but he also has time to work those out.

RHP Joe Fontenot - Fontenot is a control pitcher who relies on changing speeds and hitting the corners. He's had some major league experience and could be a serviceable bottom of the rotation starter in the future. He hit a major bump in the road last year, missing the entire 2000 season due to injury. If he recovers physically, he'll need some time in the minors to get his feel for pitching back.

2B Amaury Garcia - In most organizations, Garcia would be a Top 10 prospect. That shows you two things: he's really good and the Marlins have a lot of good prospects. Garcia has everything you could want out of a second baseman. He hits for average, has some power, steals bases and plays excellent defense. He also played a few games in the outfield during the 2000 season, perhaps because Luis Castillo is entrenched at second base in the majors. He's ready for a major league job right now, he just needs an opportunity.

OF Derrick Gibson - Body by Bo Jackson, swing by Dave Kingman. That's the best way to describe Gibson's obvious physical talent and his lack of discipline at the plate. He's big, strong and very fast for someone his size, but he's pretty clueless at the plate. If he could just cut down on the whiffs a little bit and draw a few more walks, Gibson would be ready for the majors. He could be a Glenallen Hill-type player down the line.

1B Adrian Gonzalez - Gonzalez was the Marlins 2000 first round draft pick and he was regarded as perhaps the most polished high school hitter in the draft. He has a smooth stroke and he's very patient for someone so young. He hasn't shown much power with wood yet, but scouts feel it will come with time. He's got a chance to be one of the Marlins top prospects in a year or two.

RHP Nelson Lara - Not many pitchers throw harder than Lara, but he generally has little idea of where his pitches will end up. He is still young at 21 and could turn into a dominant major league relief pitcher if he ever gets his control issues ironed out. With a mid to upper 90s fastball, it's unlikely the Marlins will give up on him soon.

LHP Todd Moser - Moser was a high draft pick of the Marlins a couple of years ago and he's got a nice future in front of him. His stuff isn't great, but it's better than average and throws an incredible number of strikes. His fastball is around 90 MPH, at best, but he has a good breaking pitch and solid change to go with pinpoint control. He walked just 26 batters in 136-plus innings at Low-A Kane County last year while posting an impressive 2.83 ERA.

RHP Bobby Rodgers - Rodgers had struggled as a starter before the 2000 season, but he really came on strong at Double-A for the Marlins as a closer. He had 22 saves, struck out 58 hitters in 55-plus innings and held opposing hitters to a .194 average in the Eastern League. Control has also been an issue with Rodgers, and it still is, but it hurts him less as a reliever than it did as a starter. He's 25 now and could move up to the majors at some point during the 2001 season.

OF Brett Roneberg - Roneberg is a disciplined hitter with a smooth lefthanded stroke. He hasn't developed much power at this point, but if he can add a little muscle in the future he could reach double-digits. He's adept at drawing walks and rarely strikes out, but he needs to be more of a force at the plate because he lacks speed. Roneberg is solid defensively in the outfield and can also play first base. He gained some valuable experience playing for the Australian Olympic baseball team last September.

1B Jason Stokes - Stokes was projected as a first rounder this past June but he slipped because of his contract demands and because he was a threat to go to college. The Marlins took him anyway and signed him near the end of the Summer. Stokes is considered a big-time power prospect who could be a 30-40 home run guy in the future. He didn't get to play last year because he signed late, but he's got a chance to be a real impact prospect.

RHP Claudio Vargas - Vargas certainly has a lot going for him at the age of 21. He's got a live low 90s fastball that gets good sinking motion and he has phenomenal control for a young power pitcher. Combine that with the fact that he throws with a loose, easy motion and has a strong mound presence and you have a very good prospect on your hands. On many teams, Vargas would be a Top 10 prospect.

HOUSTON ASTROS
ORGANIZATIONAL GRID

	AAA	AA	HI-A	LO-A
1B	Mike Robertson - L - 29	Aaron McNeal - R - 22 Kevin Burns - L - 24 Charley Carter - R - 24	J.J. Thomas - R - 24	Brian Schmitt - L - 21
2B	Ryan Miller - R - 27 Tripp Cromer - R - 32	Keith Ginter - R - 24	Aaron Miles - L - 23	Johan Maya - B - 20 Jason Maule - L - 23
SS	Adam Everett - R - 23	David Matranga - R - 23 Cesar Morillo - B - 26	Jason Alfaro - R - 22 Felix Escalona - R - 21	Donaldo Mendez - R - 22
3B	Juan Bautista - R - 25 Brian Richardson - R - 24	Morgan Ensberg - R - 24	Royce Huffman - R - 23 Tyler Turnquist - R - 24	Jon Helquist - R - 19 Luis Dominguez - R - 20
OF	Omar Ramirez - R - 29 Marc Sagmoen - L - 29 Jim Betzsold - R - 27 J.R. Phillips - L - 30	Eric Cole - R - 24 Colin Porter - R - 24 Kyle Logan - L - 24 Jhonny Perez - R - 23	Michael Rosamond - R - 22 Luis Lopez - R - 22 Jesse Joyce - R - 24 Barry Wesson - R - 23 Kevin Jordan - R - 23	Jon Topolski - L - 23 Gavin Wright - R - 21 Derek Nicholson - L - 24 Jason Lane - R - 23 Alejandro Vasquez - L - 22 Mike Hill - R - 23
C	Raul Chavez - R - 27 Frank Charles - R - 31 Pedro Lopez - R - 31 Jerrey Thurston - R - 28	Carlos Maldonado - R - 21 Brandon Buckley - R - 23	Scott Chapman - R - 22	John Buck - R - 19 Danny Fatheree - R - 21 Brian O'Connor - R - 23
SP	Travis Driskill - R - 28 Brian Powell - R - 26 Kip Gross - R - 35 Mark Guerra - R - 28 Tony McKnight - R - 23 Jeriome Robertson - L - 23	Bryan Braswell - L - 25 Eric Ireland - R - 23 Tom Shearn - R - 22 Scott Navarro - L - 25 Kyle Kessel - L - 24 Roy Oswalt - R - 22 Wilfredo Rodriguez - L - 21	Brad Lidge - R - 23 Greg Miller - L - 20 Tim Redding - R - 22 Esteban Maldonado - R - 24 Mike Nannini - R - 19	Mike Gallo - L - 23 Travis Anderson - R - 22 Derek Stanford - R - 21 Carlos Hernandez - L - 20 Nick Roberts - R - 23
CLOSER	Rick Huisman - R - 31 Jose Cabrera - R - 28 Fernando Hernandez - R - 29	Doug Sessions - R - 23 Travis Wade - R - 24	Brandon Puffer - R - 24 Jacob Whitney - L - 24	Chris George - R - 22 Ryan Jamison - R - 22

HOUSTON ASTROS

A practice of spending most of their upper round draft picks on relatively low ceiling college talent has given the Astros a system full of teams with players two and three years older than their levels' average age. Position player depth is quite lean, though the Astros do have a few promising arms that could break onto the big league squad in the intermediate term.

Aaron McNeal is the club's lone legitimate first base prospect. He maintained a high offensive performance level despite making a daunting two-level jump to Double-A in 2000, though he still likely lacks the offensive upside to someday claim a starting major league job. He could have a future as a part-time bat off of a big league bench.

Sure, Keith Ginter was 24 when he torched the Double-A Texas League last season, but his power/speed/average exploits simply can't be ignored. He too is an unlikely big league starter, but could be an interesting all-purpose big league backup. Felix Escalona is a sleeper who needs to step forward in 2001. Decent extra base pop for a middle infielder is his biggest asset. If he learns a secondary position, he too could evolve into a utility candidate.

Shortstop prospect Adam Everett was a key part of the return from the Red Sox in the seemingly disastrous Carl Everett deal. He can flat out pick it at shortstop, but needs to become more than an afterthought to opposing pitchers at the plate to project as a big league starter. He has the raw ability, despite what his numbers say. Don't be surprised if Everett grows into the starting major league role sometime in 2001.

Among third base prospects, only Low-A Michigan's Jon Helquist offers much hope for the future. He struggled at the plate after a strong start in 2000, but projects as a high average hitter with some pop to the gaps who could blossom with physical development. He's a sleeper with a chance of becoming a major league contributor.

Outfield help is nearly nonexistent. 1999 first round pick Michael Rosamond has a high power/speed ceiling, but struggled to make contact against younger High-A hurlers last season. At this point, it's a longshot that he'll evolve into a big league starter, though he could help in a complementary role. Gavin Wright is a consistent line drive hitter with some gaps power and excellent speed who could develop into a candidate for a complementary big league role. That's all there is, folks.

There could be some catching help on the horizon, however. Former Mariners' prospect Carlos Maldonado, 21, is a durable receiver with a line drive bat who was one of the youngest Double-A receivers in 2000. He should contend for a share of the big league job as soon as 2002. Scott Chapman doesn't have imposing defensive skills, but he has a substantial power upside at the plate. He could evolve into a major league third catcher/bench bat possibility as he advances. John Buck has the best chance among Astro catching prospects to someday be an everyday player in the majors. He's smooth and durable behind the plate, and has made a quick adjustment to the wooden bat at the plate at age 19. Look for a breakthrough year from Buck in 2001, and his arrival as the Astros' starter by 2003.

Righthanded starting pitcher Wade Miller likely arrived in the majors to stay in the second half of 2000. He's a legitimate mid-rotation starter with a diverse repertoire featuring a mid 90s heater, good control and improved poise. The Astros acquired former top Giants' prospect Scott Linebrink for Doug Henry. Linebrink is a hard thrower who has been slowed by injuries, but he still possesses enough heat to project as a potentially solid situational righty in the majors. Up-and-down former top draftee Tony McKnight saw his stock drop last season in a poor Triple-A campaign. He couldn't make hitters miss, as his once excellent curve was missing in action. He's likely to be stampeded from behind by some talented hurlers in 2001. Righties Eric Ireland and Tom Shearn and lefty Jeriome Robertson might not be among them, however. They're finesse hurlers who excelled in Class A ball, only to become Double-A nibblers. All three are likely long-term upper minor leaguers. Former top draftee Brad

Lidge has been overpowering when healthy, but has been injured for about 80% of his pro career. Anything the Astros get from Lidge will be a bonus. Righty Roy Oswalt had a breakthrough Double-A season in 2000, showing superior command and surprising power. He now must be considered a legitimate major league mid-rotation possibility, and could arrive in late 2001. Lefty Greg Miller is a finesse hurler who also came from Boston in the Everett deal. Double-A will be a litmus test for the quality of his stuff, but his relative youth would make early struggles there tolerable. He could be a big league swingman down the road. Lefty Wilfredo Rodriguez is arguably the Astros' most talented pitching prospect. However, injuries and mechanical inconsistency caused a subpar 2000 season. He remains a potential top-flight major leaguer, but is now far from a sure thing. Watch those walk totals. Righty Tim Redding had his second straight dominant Class A season against younger hitters, and is ready for a challenge. If he can maintain his strikeout rate at higher levels, he'll be the next Oswalt. Righty Mike Nannini made it to High-A ball at age 19 in late 2000, a strong sign of future major league success. He's a finesse hurler who could use a little more movement on his pitches and better command within the strike zone, but is ahead of the game for his age. He'll advance a level per year, and could be a future mid-rotation major leaguer. Lefty Carlos Hernandez might be set to inherit the mantle of "top Astro pitching prospect" from Rodriguez. His stuff is downright nasty, and once he develops additional physical stamina, Hernandez could evolve into a No. 1 or No. 2 starter.

TOP TEN PROSPECTS

1 - RHP Roy Oswalt - Oswalt, 22, made a daunting two-level jump from Low-A to Double-A last season, and his excellent performance there certifies him as a viable big league starting pitcher candidate. On the surface, the 6'0", 170, righty wasn't a prime candidate to maintain, let alone dramatically improve his performance at the Double-A level, but substantially improved command made Oswalt one of 2000's breakout prospects. He combines a low 90s fastball and an excellent curve, both of which he can throw for quality strikes on any count. Double-A Texas League managers rated him as having the best control in the circuit. His ability to throw strike one allowed him to average seven innings per start at the Double-A level. Oswalt must continue to pitch to precise spots to achieve significant success, but he appears polished enough to at least contend for a bottom-of-the-rotation slot in Houston by mid 2002

2 - LHP Wilfredo Rodriguez - Rodriguez, 21, is a gifted lefthanded starting pitcher prospect whose 2000 season was laid to waste by a combination of shoulder tendinitis and hamstring problems. The 6'5", 210, southpaw never established mechanical consistency, and his control suffered as a result. The good news is that Rodriguez' top-shelf stuff appears to have emerged intact. He combines a mid to upper 90s fastball and a powerful curveball, and has the makings of a viable changeup. Rodriguez needs to recapture command of his pitches and reemerge as a complete game threat before making a play for a big league job. If he stays healthy for the duration in 2001, he'll be a solid bet to crash the Houston rotation in 2002. Rodriguez has the highest upside of a promising group of Astro starting pitching prospects, though his injury risk is high.

3 - LHP Carlos Hernandez - Hernandez, 20, is a smaller, but nearly as powerful version of Rodriguez. This 5'11", 160, southpaw generates surprising power from his slight frame, combining a low 90s fastball with a sharp curveball. There isn't a lot of finesse to Hernandez' game. He lacks a passable changeup at this point, and tends to go right after hitters with hard stuff. He tends to try to throw the perfect pitch too often, and consequently runs up high pitch counts and doesn't last deep into ballgames. Hernandez' mechanics are quite consistent, and leave open the possibility of him becoming a complete game threat despite his size. Look for Hernandez to continue to flesh out his repertoire at the High-A level in 2001. If he begins to average six to even seven innings per start without diminished effectiveness, he'll remain on track to be a quality starting pitching prospect, with a projected late 2003 big league arrival.

4 - C John Buck - Buck, 19, was a seventh round draft pick in 1998. The 6'3", 200, righthanded hitter took major strides forward in his first full-season opportunity in 2000 at Low-A Michigan. He has made a smooth transition to the wooden bat, building solid gaps power that should eventually translate into 20 homer production at higher levels. He has ranked among league leaders in doubles in both 1999 and 2000. He has advanced plate discipline for a youngster, and projects as an above average on-base threat for a catcher. Defensively, Buck is fundamentally sound and durable, combining a strong throwing arm with above average agility for a big man. Buck could be poised to make an explosive step forward in 2001, especially with the bat. Look for Buck to emerge as the Astros' catcher of the future, with a projected big league arrival date of late 2003.

5 - RHP Tim Redding - Redding, 22, was a draft steal, selected on the 20th round in 1997. He generates extreme power from his relatively unimposing 6'0", 180, frame, jacking his powerful fastball all the way up to the upper 90s on the gun. His heater was recognized as the best in the High-A Florida State League last season by circuit managers. He also greatly improved his command of his slider and curveball last season, at least delaying an anticipated shift into a short relief role. Redding won't crack Double-A until 2001 at age 23: not a great sign for future success in the majors as a starter. If he maintains his strikeout rate there, he could get to the majors quickly. The abundance of quality starting pitching prospects around him makes the bullpen his most likely eventual destination. He should reach the majors in early 2002.

6 - RHP Mike Nannini - Nannini, 19, was the Astros' supplemental first round pick in 1998. Despite always being one of the youngest hurlers at each successive minor league level, he has held his own performance-wise. He stands a mere 5'11", 175, but generates low to mid 90s peak velocity on his fastball, and also possesses a slider and changeup that could eventually become plus pitches. His mechanics are smooth, and his control is good; but sometimes too good. He's seemingly allergic to walking hitters, to the point where he will lay the ball down the middle of the plate when behind in the count. However, he is a tough competitor with the savvy and mental toughness to work out of most of the jams he creates for himself. He might need a couple of cracks to master Double-A, but Nannini is a solid bet to eventually become a major league mid-rotation starter. He'll be ready by late 2003.

7 - 2B Keith Ginter - OK, Ginter is 24, and hasn't played above the Double-A level, so he doesn't meet my standard definition of "prospect". When a middle infielder dominates with the bat the way Ginter did at Round Rock in 2000, however, you make some exceptions. The 5'10", 190, 1998 10th round draft pick showed a complete offensive package, working the count and hitting for average with power to all fields. Though his speed is only a bit above average, Ginter is an instinctive baserunner who would carve out 15-20 steals per season as a full-time major leaguer. Defensively, Ginter's range and arm are ordinary, but he's a dogged worker who will extract every last bit from his raw ability. He's nearly a finished product, and remains a longshot to succeed Craig Biggio as the full-time second baseman, but Ginter is a good bet to be a vital bench bat for the Astros within a season and a half.

8 - 1B Aaron McNeal - McNeal, 22, is a 1995 27th round draftee who exploded onto the map with a 38 homer, 131 RBI season at Low-A Michigan in 1999. Though McNeal's power numbers dropped precipitously in 2000 after a two-level jump to Double-A Round Rock, improvement in other areas has maintained, and maybe enhanced his prospect status. The 6'3", 230, righthanded hitter has come this far without learning to pull the ball consistently; most of his power is to the opposite field. He hits the ball where it's pitched with authority, but Astros' brass would love to see him turn and fire on pitches on the inside half of the plate. To reach his potential, he will also need to develop better plate discipline. He has come a long way with the glove, once quite unathletic, he has become nimble enough around the bag to be named the best defensive first sacker in the Texas League last season by circuit managers. McNeal is no threat to Jeff Bagwell, but he should be an attractive bat and glove off of the Astros' bench by sometime in 2002.

9 - C Carlos Maldonado - Maldonado, 21, is a former Mariners' farmhand who very quietly had a fine 2000 season as one of the youngest full-time Double-A catchers. The 6'2", 185, righthanded hitter lacks extra-base power, but is content to spray the ball to all fields. He will take a pitch, and puts the ball into play quite consistently. Like McNeal, Maldonado made a two-level jump in 2000 without a significant drop off in performance. He has shown no signs of developing a power stroke, but at his size, there's always hope. Maldonado is a reliable defensive receiver, combining durability with slightly above average arm strength and good agility. Maldonado is not a likely future big league starter, but he appears to be on track to become a viable backup. Look for him to make that jump by sometime in the 2002 season.

10 - RHP Scott Linebrink - Linebrink, 23, is a former Giants' prospect, acquired last summer for Doug Henry, who was selected on the second round of the 1997 draft. The 6'3", 185, righthander was sidetracked in 1999 by shoulder surgery, and now projects as a reliever instead of a starting pitcher prospect. Pitching out of the bullpen has enabled Linebrink to limit his repertoire to his low to mid 90s fastball and a nasty splitter. He threw both for strikes with regularity last season at the Triple-A level, though his overall numbers were ruined by poor pitching with men on base. If Linebrink can show consistent mechanical form, he can evolve into a fine major league situational reliever. Look for Linebrink to earn a bullpen job in Houston in 2001, and possibly move into a meaningful setup role by season's end.

OTHER PROSPECTS

OF Eric Cole - Cole is a 20-20 hitter already, possessing both above average power and speed. He's also a productive RBI man who doesn't strike out all that much (98 times in 543 at-bats at Double-A) when you consider that he also hit .291 with 46 doubles and 22 home runs. All he needs to do is maintain that kind of production at Triple-A next year and he'll be a legit prospect.

3B Morgan Ensberg - If Chris Truby doesn't work out at third base for the Astros, Ensberg could enter the picture by the end of the 2001 season. He's a steady fielder at third base and he's a legit hitting prospect. He's got power, patience and the ability to hit .300 or better. At Double-A last year he hit .300 with 28 homers, 90 RBI and 92 walks.

2B-3B Royce Huffman - Huffman is a good-looking hitter who plays two infield positions relatively well. He doesn't have much home run power at this point, but he has gap power and is a good average hitter. He's also shown excellent patience at the plate, drawing 84 walks while striking out just 49 times at High-A last year. He also runs well and is a skilled basestealer, swiping 31 bases in 35 tries in 2000.

RHP Eric Ireland - Ireland is a pitcher in the true sense of the word. He only throws in the upper 80s, but he's got outstanding control and he changes speeds well. He does a fine job of working ahead early in the count and using his breaking stuff to coax groundball outs. He has been able to pick up his fair share of strikeouts so far in the minors, but that will probably change the higher up he goes. His consistency will give him a strong shot at major league time in the near future.

1B-OF Jason Lane - Lane is a young power hitter with a good idea of what he needs to do at the plate. His patience is pretty good for someone playing at Low-A and he doesn't strike out much for a home run hitter. Last year he hit .299 with 38 doubles, 28 home runs and 104 RBI which was outstanding for the Midwest League. He struck out just 91 times in 511 at-bats and drew 62 walks. Those are encouraging numbers for someone so young.

RHP Brad Lidge - Lidge is an flame thrower who is improving his control as well as working on his secondary pitches. He's been able to blow Single-A hitters away with his fastball when he gets it over the plate, but he'll need more than just the fastball when he begins facing Double-A and Triple-A players. He had a 3-to-1 strikeout to walk ratio last year and if he keeps that up he'll be in the majors in no time. If things don't work out for him as a starter, he's got the perfect arm for the closer's role.

LHP Tony McKnight - McKnight is a hard throwing lefty with pretty good control and a good curveball. His fastball is straight, which is part of the reason he doesn't get many strikeouts. Unless he improves his changeup or starts making hitters miss more often, McKnight could have trouble getting good hitters out.

LHP Greg Miller - Miller is a young lefty with good control that does a nice job of keeping hitters off balance. He's got a good fastball with movement and he spots it well, which prevents hitters from getting really good swings against him. He's got a solid breaking pitch as well, though he could turn into the kind of pitcher who allows a few home runs down when he begins facing older, stronger hitters in the future.

LHP Jeriome Robertson - Robertson is a finesse pitcher who changes speeds well and throws strike one consistently. His fastball has some movement and at times it surprises hitters because he really sets it up well with his curve and change. Things will surely be tough for him against more experienced hitters, but he's smart enough to adjust eventually and he has a solid chance at making it to the majors in some capacity.

RHP Tom Shearn - Shearn has a live fastball in the low to mid 90s and he's got a bit of a funky motion that makes him difficult to settle in against. He also has a sharp breaking ball and when he's working ahead in the count he can be unhittable. He's been a starter to this point in his career, though his stuff would suit him well in short relief if things don't work out for him as a starter.

LOS ANGELES DODGERS
ORGANIZATIONAL GRID

	AAA	AA	HI-A (San Bernardino)	HI-A (Vero Beach)
1B	Kevin Grijak - L - 29	Glenn Davis - B - 24 Robb Gorr - R - 23	Pete Paciorek - B - 24	Cliff Wren - R - 23 Hunter Bledsoe - R - 24 Brett Illig - R - 22
2B	Hiram Bocachica - R - 24	Rich Saitta - R - 24	Michael Collins - R - 23	Ismael Gallo - L - 23 Jim Goelz - R - 24
SS	Shawn Gilbert - R - 35 Mike Metcalfe - B - 27	Eric Riggs - B - 23 Kip Harkrider - L - 24	Joe Thurston - L - 20	Jorge Nunez - R - 22
3B	Jeff Branson - L - 33 Adam Riggs - R - 27	Luke Allen - L - 21 Mike Berry - R - 29	Jimmy Gonzalez - R - 21 Ramon Ruiz - R - 24	Ricky Bell - R - 21
OF	Chris Ashby - R - 25 Tony Mota - B - 22 Dante Powell - R - 26 Curtis Pride - L - 31	Chin-Feng Chen - R - 22 Ramon Moreta - R - 24 Nick Theodorou - B - 25	Lamont Matthews - L - 22 Jesus Feliciano - L - 21 Max Mejia - R - 22 Darron Ingram - R - 24 Sandy Vasquez - R - 23 Ryan Jaroncyk - B - 23	Bubba Crosby - L - 23 Jeff Auterson - R - 22 Jason Herrick - L - 26 Brian Ralph - L - 24
C	Angel Pena - R - 25 William Duplissea - R - 22	Geronimo Gil - R - 24 Mike Figga - R - 29	John Hernandez - R - 20 David Ross - R - 23	Will McCrotty - R - 21 Ryan Kellner - R - 22
SP	Mike Judd - R - 25 Robinson Checo - R - 28 Heath Murray - L - 27 Chris Michalak - L - 29 Trever Miller - L - 27 Jeff Williams - L - 28	Allen Davis - L - 24 Luke Prokopec - R - 22 Adrian Burnside - L - 23 Ben Simon - R - 25 Victor Alvarez - L - 23 Geoff Edsell - R - 28 Hal Garrett - R - 25	Lance Caraccioli - L - 22 Phil Devey - L - 23 Carlos Garcia - R - 21 Eric Junge - R - 23 Hong-Chih Kuo - L - 18 Scott Martin - R - 22 T.J. Nall - R - 19 Mike Fischer - R - 23 Rick Roberts - L - 21	Marcos Castillo - R - 21 Steve Colyer - L - 21 Randy Hadden - R - 22 Adam Williams - L - 21 Lino Urdaneta - R - 20 Tim Harrell - R - 24 Carlos Ortega - L - 21
CLOSER	Chad Ricketts - R - 25 Ricky Stone - R - 25 Al Reyes - R - 29	Maximo Regalado - R - 23 Brent Husted - R - 24	Elvis Correa - R - 21 Jon Berry - R - 22 Dwayne Jacobs - R - 23	Bill Everly - R - 25

LOS ANGELES DODGERS

The Dodgers are no longer the talent factory that they were throughout the 70s and much of the 80s. Other clubs have followed the Dodgers' trailblazing leads into the Caribbean and Latin American regions, and the Dodgers can't seem to resist the temptation of trading their best prospects for veteran help for often futile stretch drives.

There are no in-house competitors for Eric Karros' major league first base job. 1997 first round draftee Glenn Davis has seemingly stagnated at the Double-A level, and at age 24, hopes for him reaching his power potential dim each day. He seems destined to be a career minor leaguer.

Second baseman Hiram Bocachica has been a perennial prospect in the Expos' and Dodgers' systems for more than a half decade. He fell off of the fast track for a couple of years, and is no longer the five-tool stud he once appeared to be. He does have a ton of pop for a middle infielder, however, and should arrive in the majors as at least an effective multipurpose backup sometime in 2001.

The Dodgers have some promising shortstop prospects in their low minors. Joe Thurston is a scrappy slap hitter that runs well and does all of the little things. He lacks a single eyecatching tool that would make him a surefire big league starter, but should cut it as a utilityman in the majors at the very least. Jorge Nunez came over from the Blue Jays in the Raul Mondesi deal. He has an exciting power/speed upside for a middle infielder, but is sometimes erratic in the field. He's a bit old to just be reaching the Double-A level, and needs to have a breakout season now to have a chance to blossom into a big league star. Most likely, he too will be a complementary big league contributor.

Luke Allen is a promising offensive prospect with a 20/20 power/speed upside who will likely need to move from third base to the outfield to start in the majors for the Dodgers. His lack of power development in his second Double-A season was a bit disappointing, but Allen remains a viable candidate to contribute in the majors by 2002. Jimmy Gonzalez is a speedy slap hitter that can play second and third base, making him an attractive candidate for an eventual big league utility role. He'll advance a level per season, and could be a big league factor in 2003. 6'2", 180, righthanded hitter Ricky Bell has power potential, but has yet to tap into it in a pair of Double-A campaigns. He too can play multiple infield positions, and could surface as a future big league utility candidate.

There isn't a whole lot of outfield help on the horizon. Tony Mota overachieved for a couple of seasons prior to 2000, but neither his power nor speed potential has blossomed as the Dodgers had hoped. Even the hitter-friendly Pacific Coast League ballparks didn't perk up Mota last season. He now projects as no better than a backup major league outfielder. Chin-Feng Chen also misplaced his power stroke for much of 2000, but remains the club's foremost outfield prospect, and the most likely to eventually start in the majors. He runs very well for a big man, and is a prime candidate for a big Triple-A season in 2001. He'd better if he wants to reach his major league ceiling. Jesus Feliciano is a slight 5'11", 150, lefthanded hitter that makes consistent contact and runs well, but he needs to hit the ball with more authority to avoid being physically overmatched by higher level pitching. He's a sleeper at best to make the majors. 1998 first round pick Bubba Crosby was expected to be an impact power/speed prospect, but his power hasn't translated to the wooden bat. He turned 24 late last season, and hadn't yet made Double-A. His chances of making a major league impact are slim to none.

Angel Pena, once thought to be the club's catcher of the future, will now be fortunate to be their Triple-A catcher of the present. His lack of work ethic during key formative minor league seasons has cost him dearly. He retains a decent power stroke, but has fallen short of expectations in all areas. John Hernandez is a durable defensive receiver, but appears to lack the offensive tools to move significantly higher up the ladder. He's a sleeper for a major league backup role at best.

There isn't a lot of major league pitching help on the horizon. Mike Judd has had a couple of major league cameo appearances, but hasn't stuck. His stuff hasn't translated into recent success as a starter, though he might benefit from a shift to the bullpen, where hitters might only get a single look at him. He's a middle relief prospect at best for major league purposes. Luke Prokopec was brilliant in a second crack at Double-A hitters, consistently throwing his lively low 90s heater to precise spots regularly. He has a solid chance to develop into a mid-rotation starter in the majors, arriving by Opening Day 2002. Adrian Burnside is a late-blooming 6'4", 190, lefty that has become more effective at each successive minor league level. His command still needs work, but he now must be considered at least a relief specialist candidate with the possibility of remaining in the hunt for a low-rotation big league starting spot. Hong-Chih Kuo, at the tender age of 18, struck out seven in three perfect innings in his minor league debut in 2000 at High-A San Bernardino. Then he ruined his elbow. He'll likely return in 2000, and could emerge as an ace starter prospect if he regains all of his stuff. T.J. Nall is another hurler who was injured for most of 2000 after a promising High-A start. He's no Kuo, but he's got big league stuff and a mid-rotation upside. Marcos Castillo is a finesse righty who has allowed over a hit per inning in two High-A seasons. It's a solid bet that higher level hitters will tear into Castillo if he doesn't significantly fine-tune his command. He's a sleeper at best to make a big league impact. Steve Colyer was a 1997 second round pick, but he hasn't been able to match his great stuff with consistent command thus far in his pro career. He needs to show something soon, or else won't thrive in the upper minors, let alone reach the majors.

Elvis Correa is the most promising relief prospect in the system, combining live stuff with greatly enhanced command. He's not a likely closer prospect, but could evolve into a two-inning setup man at higher levels, and possibly in the majors.

TOP TEN PROSPECTS

1 - OF Chin-Feng Chen - Chen, 22, suffered through a down season power-wise at Double-A San Antonio, but remains the most complete batting prospect in the Dodgers' system. The 6'1", 189, righthanded hitter makes hard contact to all fields, but simply didn't get the ball into the air enough last season to approach his 1999 total of 31 homers. Expect him to level off somewhere between his 1999 and 2000 power totals; he could be a .300 hitter with 20 homer power in the bigs. Chen will take a pitch, but will also swing through his share of high fastballs. He also runs extremely well and possesses fairly advanced basestealing technique. Defensively, Chen has above average range but his relatively weak throwing arm will likely limit him to left field in the majors, which could be a problem if Gary Sheffield sticks around. Look for Chen to drive the ball for distance more regularly at the Triple-A level in 2001, and then compete for at least a supporting major league role the following season.

2 - RHP Luke Prokopec - Prokopec, 22, has been on quite a rollercoaster the past two seasons, and is now again on the upswing. The 5'11", 166, righty was smoked in his first opportunity at the Double-A level in 1999, largely due to his inability to control his slider due to a finger injury on his pitching hand. He had no such problems in his second chance there last season, dominating Texas League hitters with his 90 MPH fastball, his reborn slider, rated the best breaking pitch in the circuit by its managers, and a solid curveball, all of which he can consistently throw for quality strikes. Even when he struggled in 1999, Prokopec rarely walked anyone, and he can dominate with precision when painting the corners. Prokopec's slight frame makes him an unlikely candidate to become a nine-inning pitcher; he's completed just one game in his four-year pro career. Prokopec could evolve into a fine mid-rotation starter in the majors, but might be even better suited for a short relief role, either as a setup man or closer. He's a year away.

3 - SS Joe Thurston - Thurston, 20, is a 1999 fourth round draft pick who has made a quick, positive impression in his brief pro career. The 5'11", 175, lefthanded hitter was an all-around standout in his first full pro season at High-A San Bernardino in the California League. He makes consistent contact to all fields, works the count well, has surprising extra-base pop to the gaps for his size, and causes major disruption on the bases with his excellent speed, aggressiveness and baserunning savvy. Defensively, Thurston has exceptional range and first-step quickness, but his arm strength is average and his aim often erratic. A move to second base is a distinct possibility as Thurston rises through the chain. He plays the game with a contagious enthusiasm that California League managers certainly noticed, as they rated him the circuit's most exciting player. Thurston projects as a future catalyst at the top of a major league order. He should be ready to compete for a starting middle infield job in Los Angeles by Opening Day 2003 at the latest.

4 - 3B Luke Allen - Allen, 21, was a major find as a non-drafted free agent in 1996. The 6'2", 208, lefthanded hitter has always ranked among the youngest players at each successive minor league level, and has always performed commendably with the bat. His second Double-A campaign has to be classified as at least a mild disappointment. His power numbers and batting average both sagged a bit, though he made more consistent contact and showed more patience at the plate. The Dodgers envision him as a .280 hitter with a 25/15 power/speed upside. Defensively, Allen is a bit shaky on the routine play at third base, though he did show some progress last season. His range isn't particularly exciting, but his arm strength ranks among the minors' best. Texas League managers recognized him for having the best infield arm in the circuit. With Adrian Beltre in place at third base at the major league level, Allen will need to move to the outfield to have a future as a starter in Los Angeles. He'll be ready to contend for a starting job somewhere in the majors in 2002.

5 - LHP Hong-Chih Kuo - It's a tribute to Kuo's immense talent that he ranks this high on this list after pitching only three innings in 2000 after undergoing Tommy John elbow ligament transplant surgery. Those three innings were kind of impressive, however, as Kuo, 18, hurled three perfect High-A frames, striking out seven. The 6'0", 187, southpaw relied heavily on his high 90s fastball prior to the injury. If he doesn't get the heater back, his future is questionable, as his curveball and changeup were basically for show at the time of the injury. All bets are off on Kuo until his rehabilitation is complete, and he again competes against full-season league hitters. He could be a future major league staff ace, but at this point it's at least as likely that he'll go down as one of the all-time unluckiest injury cases in the game's recent history. At best, he's three years away.

6 - 2B Hiram Bocachica - Bocachica, 24, has had about nine lives as a prospect. Once a strong number two to Vladimir Guerrero in the Expos' system, the 5'11", 165, righthanded hitter bottomed out in 1998, when he was included in the Carlos Perez deal and was temporarily moved from second base to center field because of major defensive struggles. Bocachica is back at second base now, and has been much more consistent on the routine play than in the past. His offensive game has never been in question. Bocachica has surprising power for his size, and has a compact stroke that should also make him a candidate to bat .300 at the major league level. He needs to tone down his aggressiveness at the plate a bit to be a credible major league top-of-the-order hitter. Bocachica's long and winding road to the major leagues should culminate in a roster spot in Los Angeles in 2001. He could push Mark Grudzielanek for the starting second base job, and should at least steal an all-purpose utility role, in which he should be quite effective.

7 - SS Jorge Nunez - Nunez, 22, was a key add-on to the Dodgers' haul in the Shawn Green/Raul Mondesi deal following the 1999 season. The 5'10", 158, righthanded hitter played second base in the Jays' system in 1999, but was moved to shortstop last season because of his strong, accurate throwing arm that was recognized as the best infield arm in the High-A Florida State League by its managers. Offensively, Nunez suffered through an uneven campaign last year, not a good sign for a 22-year-old yet to face Double-A opposition. He has substantial gaps power for his size, but too often buries himself in the count, and consequently doesn't see enough fastballs to do any real damage. Even the relatively minor jump from Low to High-A resulted in a major drop off in performance; wait until he gets a load of Double-A pitching. His speed is legit, Nunez accelerates explosively and has a polished basestealing approach. Nunez needs to make a major offensive advance next year to remain a candidate for future big league starting duty. It's more likely that he'll evolve into an all-purpose middle infield backup and speed resource off of the bench. He could arrive sometime in 2003.

8 - LHP Adrian Burnside - Burnside, 23, is a 6'4", 190, southpaw who has quietly evolved into a sleeper prospect with an outside chance of eventually entering the major league rotation. Burnside is the stereotypical crafty lefty, possessing a mid to upper 80s fastball, plus a curve and changeup, and he keeps all of his pitches on the lower edges of the strike zone consistently. He keeps hitters off balance by varying speed and location consistently, and is just wild enough to keep batters from digging in against him. He needs to throw strike one more consistently, as his pitch counts have been high, preventing him from averaging even six innings per start in a season. His best bet for major league success would be in a swingman or middle relief role. Look for Burnside to contend for one of the last spots on the Dodgers' staff by 2002, and possibly fashion an extended career in such a complementary role.

9 - RHP Marcos Castillo - Castillo, 21, is a finesse hurler whose eventual upside will quite possibly be determined by his initial performance at the Double-A level in 2001.

The 6'2", 172, righty has fairly average stuff, including a mid to upper 80s fastball, curve and changeup. His pitches sometimes catch a bit too much of the plate. He has allowed over a hit per inning thus far in his pro career. However, he throws strike one consistently, and the ensuing low pitch counts enabled him to average nearly seven innings per start in 2000 at High-A Vero Beach, a major improvement from previous seasons. The Dodgers hope that Castillo adds some muscle to his frame, and some velocity and/or movement as a result. Watch that strikeout/walk ratio carefully at Double-A in 2001, if it holds up, then Castillo could jump higher on this list and become a solid candidate for a future rotation slot. More likely, he could evolve into a rubber-armed bullpen righty capable of being utilized in a variety of roles. He's at least two years away from the majors.

10 - OF Tony Mota - Mota, 22, took a few steps backward with an unexciting Triple-A season in 2000. The 6'1", 170, switch-hitter is a line drive hitter who appeared to be developing substantial gaps power in 1999 at Double-A San Antonio, but it evaporated last season. Mota puts the ball in play consistently to all fields, but his dangerous low-power, low-plate discipline combination comes nowhere near the high offensive threshold set for starting major league outfielders. Defensively, Mota has good range and adequate arm strength, and can play any of the three outfield positions in a pinch. Mota will have to at least recapture some of his 1999 extra-base power to eventually claim even a complementary big league job. Look for him to bounce back a bit in a second Triple-A campaign, and then get a midseason crack at such a role in Los Angeles.

OTHER PROSPECTS

1B Glenn Davis - The switch-hitting 25-year-old brother of Padres catcher Ben Davis has spent more than two years at Double-A El Paso, and Glenn's performance has fallen off each year. In 113 games last season, he batted just .207-9-40. There was little improvement in his strikeout/walk ratio. A first-round pick in 1997 out of Vanderbilt, Davis is a good defensive first baseman who has played in left field.

SS Milko Jaramillo - Another switch hitter, Jaramillo began the season at High-A San Bernardino. But after batting just .190, he finished the year in short-season ball. He's just 21 years old, and hasn't developed any power. However, he stole 21 bases in 85 games.

3B Jimmy Gonzalez - The 22-year-old didn't improve at bat in his second season at San Bernardino, but he did boost his stolen bases from nine to 30. Gonzalez is a very aggressive batter who rarely walks or strikes out. He has also played second base and shortstop, but is not a good defender.

OF Lamont Matthews - After Matthews slugged 30 home runs at Oklahoma State in 1999, the Dodgers drafted him in the 10th round. The righthanded batter quickly adjusted to wooden bats. His 2000 season included 24 homers and 90 RBI at San Bernardino, but he batted just .245. Matthews did show speed, with 12 stolen bases and 13 triples. He has a long swing that resulted in 170 strikeouts.

OF Bubba Crosby - The Dodgers envisioned Crosby as a latter-day Lenny Dykstra, but he hasn't developed much power in three pro seasons. Neither has he shown the patience to draw walks, nor that he's more than a left fielder defensively. A first-round draft pick out of Rice in 1998, Crosby spent most of last season at High-A Vero Beach, where he batted .266-8-51 and stole 27 bases.

C Angel Pena - The 26-year-old is an enigma. He spent some time with the Dodgers in 1998 and '99, but didn't hit. Then Pena showed up at spring training in 2000 weighing 262 pounds. Back at Triple-A Albuquerque, he regained his stroke to bat .308-17-61. He once was considered a good defensive catcher, but now only his arm is above average. Pena didn't have a chance to play in LA last season because of a torn ligament in his left hand.

RHP Mike Judd - A .500 pitcher in three seasons at Albuquerque, Judd also has pitched in the majors during each of the last four years. In 2000, his strikeout/walk radio struggled in Triple-A and he was hammered in his only start for the Dodgers. The 25-year-old throws a mid 90s fastball and a slurve, but has only an average changeup. His limited repertoire may make him a better candidate for the bullpen. Baserunners can steal on him easily.

RHP Robinson Checo - At 29, Checo may be too old to be considered a prospect. But he pitched well in 2000 at Albuquerque (8-3, 3.63, 85 strikeouts and just 33 walks). The 6'1", 185-pound Checo throws a mid 90s fastball, a slider and a splitter he uses as a changeup. He's effective as long as he keeps his pitches down.

RHP Randy Galvez - After undergoing Tommy John surgery in 1999, Galvez returned to go 4-4, 5.12 at Double-A San Antonio. He had very little power, and was hit pretty hard.

LHP Steve Colyer - He increasingly was used as a reliever last season at High-A Vero Beach (5-7, 5.96). The 22-year-old has a mid 90s fastball and a good overhand curve, but he needs to develop a changeup to be effective as a starter. Colyer's desire has been questioned, but he did work to lose 30 pounds after the 1997 second-round draft pick signed a contract in '98.

RHP Carlos Garcia - After pitching for two years in Mexico, the 23-year-old Garcia returned to the Dodgers organization at San Bernardino in 2000. More a craftsman than an overpowering pitcher, he compiled a 14-7 record and 2.57 ERA. He has grown two inches and gained 30 pounds since signing with LA in 1996. His work ethic carried over into learning English as quickly as he could last season.

RHP Lino Urdaneta - He has had two remarkably similar seasons at Vero Beach — both 5-4 in 27 appearances, with five starts and ERAs on either side of 5.00. The 21-year-old has shown little strikeout ability.

MILWAUKEE BREWERS
ORGANIZATIONAL GRID

	AAA	AA	HI-A	LO-A
1B	Kurt Bierek - L - 27 Kevin Barker - L - 24	Bucky Jacobsen - R - 24	Nick Caiazzo - R - 25	Hector Garcia - R - 20 Eduardo Figueroa - L - 23
2B	Marcos Scutaro - R - 24 Norberto Martin - B - 33 Jeff Pickler - L - 24	Mickey Lopez - B - 26	Chris Patten - R - 21	Steve Scarborough - R - 22
SS	Santiago Perez - B - 24 Brandon Cromer - L - 26	Wellington Sanchez - R - 23 Mark Ernster - R - 22	Frank Jaramillo - L - 23 Chris Rowan - R - 21	Bill Hall - R - 20
3B	Jose Fernandez - R - 25	Lou Collier - R - 26 Josh Klimek - L - 26	Jeff Deardorff - R - 21 Jeff Kenney - R - 22	Nick Frank - R - 24 Frank Alfieri - R - 23
OF	Brad Tyler - L - 31 Damon Hollins - R - 26 Chris Jones - R - 34 Lyle Mouton - R - 31 Mark Sweeney - L - 30	Toby Kominek - R - 27 Chad Green - B - 25 Jared Mathis - R - 24 Scott Krause - R - 26 Scott Kirby - R - 22 Bobby Darula - L - 25	Mark Cridland - L - 24 Jason Fox - B - 23 Jon Macalutas - R - 25 Derry Hammond - R - 20	Ryan Knox - R - 22 Frank Candela - R - 21 Will Ford - L - 23 Erickson De la Cruz - R - 21
C	Creighton Gubanich - R - 28 Kevin Brown - R - 27	Brian Moon - B - 22 Lance Burkhart - R - 25 Robinson Cancel - R - 24	Obispo Brito - R - 22 Matt Ceriani - R - 23	Eliezer Alfonzo - R - 21 Ryan Bordenick - R - 24
SP	Allen Levrault - R - 22 Everett Stull - R - 28 Kane Davis - R - 25 Horacio Estrada - L - 24 Tim Harikkala - R - 28 Ben Sheets - R - 21 Derek Lee - L - 25	Al Hawkins - R - 22 Travis Smith - R - 27 Jose Garcia - R - 22 James Johnson - L - 23 Nick Neugebauer - R - 19 Kyle Peterson - R - 24	Jason Childers - R - 25 Paul Stewart - R - 21 Matt Childers - R - 21 Jose Mieses - R - 20 Jaron Seabury - R - 24	Jeff Robinson - R - 23 Chris Simonson - R - 23 Kevin Grater - R - 22 Luis Martinez - L - 20 Matt Parker - R - 21 Dave Pember - R - 22 J.M. Gold - R - 20
CLOSER	Bob Scanlan - R - 33	Mike Rossiter - R - 27	Jack Krawczyk - R - 24 Fontella Jones - R - 25	Gene Altman - R - 21 Dan Mathews - R - 24

MILWAUKEE BREWERS

Years of neglect have reduced the Brewers' system to a wasteland at the higher levels, though the drafting of a couple of potentially dominant starting pitcher prospects in the last couple of years offer some hope for an impending organizational turnaround.

Only Low-A first base prospect Hector Garcia has a major league upside at that position. Significant physical development of his 6'3", 165, frame lies ahead, and that combined with an improvement in plate discipline could propel him upward. He has a long way to go before he can be considered a top prospect, however.

Chris Patten is the organization's lone promising second base prospect. He drives the ball to the gaps with some regularity, and is an adequate baserunner and defender. He might need to learn a secondary position to help him evolve into a major league utility prospect.

Santiago Perez got an audition in the majors when starter Mark Loretta was sidelined with a broken toe. He has the raw tools to succeed, combining power and speed potential with solid defensive range, but his poor plate discipline will likely hold him back. He likely will reside at the Triple-A level for awhile, and possibly make the Brewers as an infield backup. 1999 sixth round pick Mark Ernster made a bold step forward in his first full pro season, winding up as the regular Double-A shortstop. He puts the ball in play, makes all the plays, and helps win ballgames. Look for Ernster, who can play both middle infield positions, to win a spot as a Milwaukee utilityman in 2002. Bill Hall has a solid offensive package, combining gaps power and speed, for a shortstop, but has multiple rough edges. His upside might be higher than Ernster's, but Hall has much work ahead of him. He's a sleeper prospect at best.

Third base prospect Scott Kirby hit a brick wall when he ran into Double-A pitching last season. He has a sizeable power upside, but hasn't made consistent contact or done a passable job defensively at either infield corner or in the outfield. He needs to substantially upgrade his performance in 2001 to remain on the Brewers' radar screen. His chances of making a major league impact are diminishing. Jeff Deardorff has a decent power upside, but like Kirby, struggles to make consistent contact. His 2001 Double-A performance will determine whether he's any better than Kirby. Deardorff has an outside shot to be a major league backup at both infield corners.

Future outfield help is nearly nonexistent. Derry Hammond has a massive power upside, but can't resist bad pitches, and is therefore a constant strikeout threat. He's a high risk, high reward prospect with a 5% chance of being a solid major leaguer, and a very high possibility of never excelling in the upper minors. Cristian Guerrero is an exciting, multi-skilled outfield prospect who couldn't cut it in full season ball last season because of poor plate discipline. He's still a baby, and is likely to fare much better this time around. Plus, the bloodlines are good; he's Vladimir's brother. Keep an eye on the Brewers' best position player prospect, a potential future big league starter.

There is no viable major league catching prospects in the Milwaukee organization.

Things are a bit brighter on the pitching front. Allen Levrault, a strapping righthander with a heavy fastball, got his first crack at the majors in 2000. His relatively limited repertoire and bulldog mentality suggest a future as a major league setup man or closer. He'll reach Milwaukee to stay in 2001. Ben Sheets is the surest thing in the Brewers' system, and isn't far from the majors. He has a mature approach, a diverse repertoire, and maturity beyond his years. He's a likely major league number two starter, and should arrive to stay sometime in 2001. Jose Garcia was once considered the premier pitching prospect in the system, but recurring elbow woes have set him back. His command was uneven at Double-A Huntsville last season, though he did show flashes of excellence. An injury-free 200 inning Triple-A season in 2001 would put him back in the Brewers' major league plans. Nick Neugebauer, 19, is one scary prospect, in a lot of ways.

The 6'3", 225, righty is utterly unhittable, but his wildness is legendary, and his conditioning a major worry. He could be a major league star, or could blow his arm out tomorrow. Bet on the former. 6'5", 225, righty Paul Stewart has the potential to develop into a major league horse, but hasn't yet been able to locate a true out pitch. He failed in a Double-A audition last season, which isn't a positive sign for his future. He'll toil in the upper minors for awhile. 1998 first round pick J.M. Gold has been detoured by arm problems, and all bets are off regarding his future until he proves his health in 2001. The Brewers still hope that he can mature into a top-of-the-rotation starter, but he has clearly fallen behind Neugebauer and Sheets for now. Keep an eye on righty Jose Mieses, a finesse hurler with an innate feel for pitching. Double-A will be a key litmus test, and success there might suggest an eventual mid-rotation spot in the majors.

Gene Altman came over from the Reds during the 2000 season, and quickly asserted himself as a viable relief prospect. He has above average peak velocity and a strong two-inning arm, but needs to work on his command. He's got an outside shot to eventually emerge as a big league middleman.

TOP TEN PROSPECTS

1 - RHP Ben Sheets - Sheets, 21, was the Brewers' first round draft pick, and the 10th overall selection, in the 1999 draft. The 6'2", 195, righthander was brilliant at both Double-A Huntsville where Southern League managers recognized him as the circuit's best pitching prospect, and Triple-A Indianapolis. Sheets is one of the most polished pitching prospects in the minor leagues, combining a lively low to mid 90s heater with his out pitch, a killer curve that falls off of the table. His changeup also could be an above average major league pitch. His command of all of his pitches is excellent, and he has an advanced feel for setting up hitters. Sheets is also a dogged competitor who has never had an arm injury of any type, a rarity for any recent Brewers' pitching prospect. Sheets is as close to a sure thing as they come. He's a future nine-inning horse who should move into the major league rotation, and stay at or near the top of it for a very long time.

2 - RHP Nick Neugebauer - Neugebauer, 19, is a 1998 second round draft pick who has put up some of the scariest pitching numbers in the game over the last two seasons, most recently at Double-A Huntsville, where he

was the Southern League's youngest competitor after a late-year promotion. Unfortunately, his numbers scare both the opposition and his parent club. The 6'3", 225, righty struck out about a batter and a half per inning last season, but amazingly also walked over a batter per inning. Incredibly, more than half of the batters who faced Neugebauer last season either walked or struck out. His best pitch is an overpowering high 90s fastball that was rated as the High-A California League's best heater by circuit managers. He also throws a hard slider plus a passable curve and changeup. Obviously, command is the key for Neugebauer. If he can refine his mechanics a bit, he'll lessen the strain on his arm and become a potential monster. Right now, he's so wild that he's not even a five-inning guy. If he stays healthy, he'll become a major league star. With improved command, he and Sheets will form a lethal one-two punch. Without it, he could be an impact big league closer. Neugebauer is a good bet to crash the majors in 2002.

3 - OF Dave Krynzel - I don't make it a habit to include rookie ball players in organizational Top Tens, but both Krynzel's talent and the Brewers' overall lack of it force me to make an exception. Krynzel, 18, was off to a good start at Ogden in the Pioneer League before his season was prematurely ended by a torn thumb ligament. The 6'1", 180, lefthanded hitter was batting .359 with gaps power and excellent speed in his first 131 pro at bats before the injury. He projects as a leadoff-hitting center fielder with 15-20 homer power and 50 steal speed. His plate discipline is fairly advanced for a youngster, and he has the range to be a well above average defender. The Brewers hope that there will be no lingering effects from his injury, and that he'll be ready for full-season league duty next April. Krynzel might not crack the majors until 2004 or so, but his selection hopefully marks a change in organizational focus towards high-ceiling, high school prospects.

4 - OF Cristian Guerrero - Here's another rookie leaguer on the Brewers' list. Guerrero, 19, has great bloodlines; he's the brother of Vladimir. The 6'4", 198, righthanded hitter has a huge power/speed upside, and could develop light-tower power with expected natural physical development. He failed miserably in an early 2000 Low-A trial due to extremely poor plate discipline, but put it all together with Ogden in the rookie level Pioneer League. He worked the count regularly, and laid waste to the additional fastballs he saw. He runs quite well, and has advanced basestealing technique for a youngster, making him a potential 40/40 guy if all goes according to plan. He is a natural right field prospect, combining above average range with an exceptionally strong throwing arm. None of it matters, however, if he can't discipline himself at the plate against the more polished full-season league hurlers. Bet on Guerrero taking a major step forward in 2001 in Low-A ball. He could be a fast-tracker, and might be ready for the majors by sometime in 2003.

5 - RHP Jose Mieses - Mieses, 20, is an intriguing 6'1", 165, righthander who overmatched Low-A Midwest League hitters in 2000. His fastball is nothing special, tooling along in the mid to upper 80s, but he has a pair of excellent breaking pitches that he can use as out pitches against both lefties and righties. His palm ball is his most consistent pitch, and his curve is also above average. Both of them make his fastball look a lot harder than it is, and he has an advanced feel for mixing all of them to keep hitters off balance. Mieses gets ahead of hitters and retires them early in the count quite often. He was recognized by Midwest League managers for having the circuit's best control and averaged nearly seven innings per start last season as a result. It's always questionable whether Low-A finesse hurlers can get the ball past upper level hitters, but Mieses appears to have enough pluses in his favor to get the job done. He's a likely future mid-rotation starter in Milwaukee who should be in the 2003 Opening Day rotation.

6 - SS Santiago Perez - Perez, 24, is a switch-hitting shortstop prospect who received a major league audition in 2000 due to the broken foot suffered by incumbent Mark Loretta. The 6'2", 170, Perez has exciting all-around skills, including a live line drive bat with substantial gap power for a middle infielder plus well-above average raw speed and solid basestealing technique. Though he isn't quite as much of a wild swinger as he used to be, he still strikes out too much and walks too little to bat neat the top of a big league order. He covers quite a bit of ground in the field and has a well above average arm strength, but has always been maddeningly inconsistent on the routine play. It doesn't appear that Perez will unseat Loretta in Milwaukee anytime soon, so he will need a change of scenery to start in the majors, or will need to learn another position or two to serve as a backup with the Brewers. Bet on the latter: he could add a much-needed offensive dimension to the Brewers' bench in 2001.

7 - RHP Allen Levrault - Levrault, 22, is a hulking 6'3", 230, righthander who was drafted on the 13th round in 1996. He has been used both as a starter and short reliever in his pro career, and while he is seemingly better suited to the latter role because of his relatively thin repertoire, he has been more successful in the former. Levrault features a low 90s fastball and a deceptive changeup, but has never sufficiently developed his curve ball into an adequate third pitch. His mechanics were inconsistent at times last season, causing his fastball to straighten out and also negatively affecting his control. Levrault would likely benefit from being used in a consistent manner at the Triple-A level next year. He could quickly evolve into a durable middle reliever who could be used in two-inning doses two or three times a week. If he doesn't iron out his mechanics soon, however, Levrault could find himself marooned at the Triple-A level for quite a while.

8 - RHP J.M. Gold - Gold, 20, was the Brewers' 1998 first round pick and the 13th overall selection in the draft. He would rank much higher on this list, but underwent Tommy John reconstructive elbow surgery early last season. The 6'5", 225, righthander combined a hard mid 90s fastball and a power curve prior to his injury, which wasn't a surprise to many because of his awkward mechanics. He'll be building everything up from the ground floor once he is fully rehabilitated, and his lack of precision prior to the injury raises questions as to whether he'll ever reach his considerable potential. If Gold pitches pain-free at the High-A level in 2001, it will again be safe to discuss a possible major league future. However, it appears to be a longshot at best that Gold will evolve into the top-of-the-rotation starter the Brewers envisioned when they expended a premium draft pick on him. At best, he'll enter the big league picture in 2003.

9 - RHP Jose Garcia - Garcia, 22, was the Brewers' second round draft pick in 1996. The 6'3", 200, righthander was a premier prospect before missing all of 1999 with an elbow injury. He took a regular turn for the first couple of months of the 2000 season before he was again shut down. When healthy, Garcia popped a lively low 90s heater and a hard curveball, though he often battled inconsistent mechanics and relatively poor command. He was the type of raw but talented hurler who simply needed to pitch a whole bunch of innings to find himself. The last two seasons now represent little more than a lost opportunity. Garcia's upside is sufficiently high for him to remain on this list even though the likelihood of him reaching his potential continues to diminish. If Garcia can regain his health and his stuff in the near term, his quickest way to the majors could be as a short reliever, a role in which he can fall back on with as few as two pitches. If he's healthy in 2001, he could help out in a complementary role in Milwaukee in 2002.

10 - OF Scott Kirby - Kirby, 22, has come a long way since being drafted on the 30th round back in 1995. The 6'2", 190, righthanded hitter is a fairly one-dimensional prospect, a slugger who struggled mightily in his first shot at the more polished Double-A hurlers in 2000. Defensively, he has proven himself incapable of playing both third and first base due both to his lack of mobility and questionable footwork, and now projects as a left fielder. Kirby can drive a mistake fastball for extreme distance, and is willing to take a pitch, but he becomes an easy mark when falling behind in the count, often getting himself out on outside breaking pitches or high fastballs. Kirby's bat is his only ticket to the bigs, so major improvement will be expected in 2001 at either Double or Triple-A. At best, Kirby will surface as a major league bench bat, with an arrival date of late 2002.

OTHER PROSPECTS

RHP Jason Childers - If his performance at High-A Mudville last year was any indication of how good this kid can be, the Brewers will have a fine pitcher on their hands shortly. He's a power pitcher who is adept at striking hitters out and he's also got very good control. For a young strikeout pitcher to also maintain a low walk total is just great. He struck out 177 batters in 157-plus innings last year while allowing just 140 hits and 54 walks.

OF Mark Cridland - Cridland has above average power and speed, but he's not a polished hitter. He could stand to be more patient and would also benefit from being a better situational hitter. He was a 20-20 guy last year at High-A, but he only hit .260 and only drove in 66 runs. With a little fine tuning he could become an offensive force.

OF Bobby Darula - He only managed half a season at Low-A Beloit last year, but his offensive output was tremendous. He's an extremely good hitter with some speed, but very little home run power at the moment. He's very patient and if he can hit as well this year as he did last year, Darula will start showing up on prospect lists everywhere. He hit .384 with three home runs, 43 RBI and 16 steals in just 71 games, drawing 44 walks and striking out just 25 times.

OF Chad Green - Green just doesn't get it. He has all the speed in the world and he could be a fantastic leadoff man if he would just learn how to be more patient at the plate. He strikes out a lot, rarely walks and has minimal power, which is too bad because he can really go get fly balls in the outfield. He's a fourth outfielder at best right now.

RHP Al Hawkins - Hawkins has a good arm and a respectable breaking pitch but control has held him back. During the 2000 season he made some improvements in that area and if he keeps it up he could become a decent starting pitcher. He's not overpowering and he gives up some long balls, but there is ability present in him.

1B Bucky Jacobsen - Jacobsen is a good young hitter with power and patience. He's about average defensively as a first baseman, but his defense isn't what the Brewers care much about. In half a season of Double-A ball last year he hit 18 home runs, drove in 50 runs and drew 51 walks while striking out 69 times. If he keeps that kind of production up he'll be knocking on the door very soon.

RHP Jeff Robinson - Robinson has an above average fastball that can be overpowering at times, but he's got control problems. Not only does he have problems with walks, but he falls behind in the count quite often and winds up giving up home runs when he gives in with the fastball. At Low-A last year, 10 of the 63 hits he gave up were home runs. He did strike out 88 batters in 82-plus innings, but also walked 43 batters.

RHP Paul Stewart - Stewart has a very good fastball and is capable of racking up strikeouts, as evidenced by his 9.3 strikeouts per nine innings last season at High-A. He's got control problems and he needs work on his offspeed pitches, but there is plenty of time for that.

MONTREAL EXPOS
ORGANIZATIONAL GRID

	AAA	AA	HI-A	LO-A
1B	Talmadge Nunnari - L - 25	Shawn Gallagher - R - 23	Thomas Pittman - R - 20 Mark Thomas - L - 24	Richard Lane - L - 20 Jon Palmieri - R - 23
2B	Jamey Carroll - R - 25 Kary Bridges - L - 28 Jason Camilli - R - 24	Henry Mateo - B - 23	Tootie Myers - R - 21 Randy Meadows - R - 23	Bret Boyer - R - 19 Lou Melucci - R - 22
SS	Dave Post - R - 26	Josh Reding - R - 23	Albenis Machado - B - 21	Brandon Phillips - R - 19
3B	Michael Barrett - R - 23 Jarrod Patterson - L - 26	Scott Zech - R - 26 Garrett Osilka - R - 22 Brian Sherlock - R - 24	Scott Hodges - L - 21	Josh McKinley - B - 20 Felix Lugo - B - 19
OF	Milton Bradley - B - 22 Pat Lennon - R - 32 Trace Coquillette -R- 26 Kenny James - B - 23 Brad Wilkerson - L - 23	Jeremy Ware - R - 24 Dan McKinley - L - 24 Noah Hall - R - 23	Matt Cepicky - L - 22 Ron Calloway - L - 23 Valentino Pascucci - R - 21 Matt Watson - L - 21	Wilken Ruan - R - 20 Martires Castro - R - 23 Andres Espinoza - R - 21 Clyde Williams - L - 20
C	Brian Schneider - L - 23 Chris Snusz - R - 27 Sean Mulligan - R - 30	Yohanny Valera - R - 23 Jaime Malave - R - 25 Scott Sandusky - R - 23	Jose Carreno - R - 22 Scott Ackerman - R - 21	Todd Johannes - R - 23 Brian Preston - R - 23 Todd Kasper - L - 23
SP	Brent Billingsley - L - 25 Shayne Bennett - R - 28 Scott Mitchell - R - 27 Brad Rigby - R - 27 Joey Eischen - L - 30 Jeremy Powell - R - 24	T.J. Tucker - R - 21 Troy Mattes - R - 24 Bryan Hebson - R - 24 Bran. Agamennone -R- 23 Donnie Bridges - R - 21 Chuck Crumpton - R - 23 Brian Matz - L - 25	Jorge Julio - R - 21 Ron Chiavacci - R - 22 Mark Mangum - R - 21 Ryan Becks - L - 24 Jeremy Salyers - R - 24 Ed Klepacki - R - 22 Trevor Wamback - R - 23 Justin Wayne - R - 21	Cristobal Rodriguez - R - 21 Pat Collins - R - 22 Eric Charron - R - 21 Eric Good - L - 20 Clifton Lee - L - 21 Luke Lockwood - L - 18 Ben Washburn - R - 21
CLOSER	Guillermo Mota - R - 26 Pat Flury - R - 27	Jim Serrano - R - 24 Derrick DePriest - R - 21	Kris Tetz - R - 21 Julio Perez - R - 21	Chris Humrich - R - 22

MONTREAL EXPOS

The vaunted Expos' organizational prospect machine ain't what it used to be. Only the stockpile of first round picks they tend to accumulate as a result of regularly allowing veteran free agents to escape Montreal keeps the talent base at a respectable level. Pitching depth in particular has thinned considerably.

Fernando Seguignol has had a couple of extended trials in the majors, and though he has a high power upside, his swing is long and has many holes. He could be a major league fit as a 300 at-bat backup at both first base and in the outfield. Massive 6'4", 270, righthanded hitter Thomas Pittman has waffled between playing baseball and going to college to play football. His subpar High-A 2000 season just might drive him back to the gridiron. He has excellent power potential, but needs to dedicate himself fully to this game, and improve his conditioning, to have a significant chance of reaching it. Keep an eye on 6'3", 195, lefthanded hitter Richard Lane. He's shown a consistent line drive bat to date, and could make a serious upward move if his power stroke develops. If Pittman leaves, Lane could be a major beneficiary. He's a sleeper for now.

Second base prospect Tootie Myers has a solid power/speed package for a middle infielder, but his game has numerous rough edges. Plate discipline is the largest issue. Myers could be a major league contributor in a couple of years if he develops it. 1999 seventh round pick Bret Boyer, 19, is a sleeper to watch. He can play either middle infield position and is an excellent baserunner. He has much to prove with the bat, however, before a major league future can be projected.

The Expos possess solid organizational depth at shortstop. Tomas De la Rosa made it to the majors in 2000, and has the defensive polish to eventually earn a permanent backup role there. He's unlikely to hit much against major league hurlers, but his decent speed and ability to make contact are mitigating factors. Switch-hitter Albenis Machado is an extremely patient batter with no power and decent speed who, like De la Rosa, projects as a possible future major league backup. Brandon Phillips, 19, has a much higher upside, and should mature into the Expos' shortstop of the future. He hit the wall physically in his first full pro season in 2000, but not before showing flashes of offensive and defensive excellence at Low-A Cape Fear. He has at least a 20/20 power upside, and moves well in the field. He's a keeper.

Third baseman Scott Hodges lacks a single defining tool, but his lefthanded line drive bat has produced scores of Class A doubles that could become upper level homers. He has a chance to evolve into a major league contributor, and maybe even a starter. Josh McKinley was a 1998 first round pick more because of his signability rather than his skills, but he has made major strides on the field. The 6'2", 190, switch-hitter has worked hard to build his athleticism, and now has 20 homer/30 steal potential. Another year of similar development could mark him as the Expos' future third sacker.

Outfielder Milton Bradley arrived to stay in the majors last July. Though his personality is either misunderstood or misguided depending on whom you ask, his level of effort is consistently high on the field, and his skills are impeccable. This kid was born to be a star. 1998 first round pick Brad Wilkerson, 23, made major strides last season, leading all of organized ball in doubles. He's a patient lefthanded hitter who has learned to pounce on the most hittable pitch of each at bat, and could ride his bat into the big league lineup sometime in 2001. If Bradley or Peter Bergeron falter, Wilkerson will be ready, and should at least be a productive fourth outfielder in the bigs. A handful of Class A outfield prospects have specific traits that could propel them into future battles for major league backup spots. 1999 draftees Matt Cepicky (fourth round) and Valentino Pascucci (16th) were productive at High-A Jupiter in their first full pro seasons. Cepicky has gaps power and solid basestealing ability, and Pascucci is a 6'6", 225, righthanded hitter who could mature into a longball bomber. Both are raw, but have a chance to make the show in supporting roles. Wilken Ruan can flat out fly, and hit the ball with much more authority last season than in 1999. He's still quite undisciplined at the plate, but might evolve into a credible major league fourth outfielder candidate.

Brian Schneider, the Expos' foremost catching prospect, got his first taste of the majors last season. He's solid but unspectacular across the board, but should be able to move into a platoon role in the majors within a year or so. He projects as a lefthanded-hitting Chris Widger, at best. Keep an eye on Scott Ackerman, who possesses exceptional offensive skills for a receiver. If his defense can catch up to his bat, he could emerge as a candidate for big league time a couple of years from now.

T.J. Tucker, 21, is the Expos' most advanced pitching prospect. While his control is good and his mechanics are solid for his size (6'3", 245), he needs to develop a true strikeout pitch to reach his potential. Once he does, he should quickly slide into the middle of the Expos' big league rotation. 1997 first round draftee Donnie Bridges has made major strides. The 6'4", 195, righty maintained a solid strikeout rate after a promotion to Double-A in mid 2000, and showed the rare ability to complete games. He may have passed Tucker on the depth chart, and could reach Montreal in 2001. The two prospects' ceilings are similar. Righthander Jorge Julio made little progress in his second High-A season in 2000. His inability to locate the ball precisely within the strike zone makes him quite hittable and unlikely to experience significant upper minor league success soon. He's got the ability, but must make a move now. Former top Rockies' draftee Mark Mangum had a poor strikeout rate at High-A Jupiter last season, not a particularly positive sign for his future. Significant development of his 6'2", 165, frame would give him a shot at gaining the movement on his pitches needed for him to make a run at the majors. Righty Shane Arthurs is a finesse hurler who took some steps backward in his second Low-A season in 2000. Mechanical adjustments will be necessary for him to succeed at higher levels. 1998 draftees Ed Klepacki and Ron Chiavacci, both 22, were a bit old to still be Class A hurlers in 2000, but showed the command and polish necessary to be considered for major promotions in 2001. Neither is a sure thing to reach the majors, but both have the potential to make it in limited roles.

Julio Perez is a hard thrower who was a dominant Low-A closer last season. He has a two-inning arm, and could project as a future situational reliever in the majors with further development.

TOP TEN PROSPECTS

1 - OF Milton Bradley - Bradley, 22, was a second round draft pick in 1996. The 6'0", 170, switch-hitter is a multi-talented outfield prospect with 30/30 power/speed skills whose minor league career has had spectacular highs and lows. On the plus side of the ledger is the two-out, bottom-of-the-ninth grand slam that won the 1999 Double-A Eastern League title. On the negative side are the disciplinary problems and the sullen attitude that can either be seen as a single-minded focus on reaching the majors or as a divisive clubhouse presence. Bradley has a quick bat and substantial line drive power to both gaps. His plate discipline is poor at this stage, but an improvement in that area would likely lead to much higher home run totals because of the additional fastballs he would see. Defensively, Bradley is a greyhound in center field with a plus arm that would be wasted in left field. Look for Bradley to play center, moving Peter Bergeron to left in 2001. If he learns to take a pitch, Bradley will make an immediate impact in 2001, and could eventually be a star. If not, Bradley's attitude will be tested, and could become a negative factor.

2 - SS Brandon Phillips - Phillips, 19, was drafted on the second round in 1999. The 5'10", 170, righthanded hitter got off to a brilliant start with the bat last season, but hit a physical wall down the stretch at Low-A Cape Fear. Despite his relatively small stature, the ball jumps off of Phillips' bat, giving him the potential to both hit for average and drive 15-20 homers per year. He might have to cut down his focus on the power to develop the on-base skills he needs, however. His plate discipline needs a bit of work, but is acceptable for his age and experience level. At this point, he buries himself in the count too often, and then chases bad pitches, racking up high strikeout totals. His speed is a prime weapon, and he knows how to use it. It makes him an above-average basestealer with exceptional defensive range. He also has soft hands and a strong arm, and his overall defensive package was good enough for him to be recognized as the best defensive shortstop in the Low-A South Atlantic League, as one of its youngest competitors. He's a solid bet to be a future big league starter, and a potential 20/20 guy at a position not known for such players, at least in the National League. He could arrive in late 2003.

3 - RHP Donnie Bridges - Bridges, 21, is a late-blooming pitching prospect who was drafted in the first round in 1997. After struggling through his first three pro seasons, Bridges took off at the Double-A level in 2000. Pitchers who enhance, not just maintain, their strikeout rate and overall performance level there have a high probability of future big league success. The 6'4", 195, righty has a diverse four-pitch repertoire featuring a mid 90s fastball and a plus slider which he uses as his out pitch against lefties. He also has a solid curve and is working on a changeup. He consistently threw strike one last year, and averaged nearly seven innings per start thanks to the resulting low pitch counts. He's a strikeout pitch away from developing into a scary top-of-the-rotation prospect. His prototypical pitchers' frame could accommodate 10-15 pounds of muscle that could give his pitches that extra juice. Bridges could get a midseason audition in 2001 should he get off to a big Triple-A start. He'll eventually settle in as at least a mid-rotation starter in Montreal.

4 - OF Brad Wilkerson - Wilkerson, 23, was a supplemental first round draft pick in 1998. The 6'0", 190, lefthanded hitter blossomed offensively at both Double-A Harrisburg and Triple-A Ottawa last season, and was recognized as the best batting prospect in the Eastern League. Wilkerson uses a patient approach and a quick, compact stroke that translates into above average power to the gaps. He appears to be evolving into a .280ish hitter with 40 double, 20 homer, 100 walk potential; numbers that would look good in the upper third of the Expos' batting order. He runs fairly well, but is not a particularly aggressive baserunner. He has solid outfield range and a plus throwing arm, making him a viable major league right field prospect; though that position is kind of taken in Montreal. Wilkerson could be ready to help at the major league level from the get-go in 2001, but it doesn't appear that a full-time job is available. Look for him to be quite effective in a part-time, fourth outfielder role, and he could get a full-time shot if either Peter Bergeron or Milton Bradley falter.

5 - RHP T.J. Tucker - Tucker, 21, was a supplemental first round draft pick in 1997. The 6'3", 245, righthander rocketed through the system in a brilliant 1999 campaign, and reached the majors briefly in 2000 in a relatively unexciting Double-A season. Tucker is a precise control hurler who features a low 90s fastball, a hard curve and an average changeup. His mechanics are quite solid for a big man, and his ability to pitch ahead in the count keeps his pitch counts down and his innings per start average over six innings. However, conditioning is a significant concern. Tucker has some extra pounds on him, and they have caused to wear down late in seasons and made him susceptible to nagging, though relatively minor injuries.

His quick rise through the minors gives him the luxury of some time to work through his physical issues, but the Expos need to see a meaningful step forward in 2001. Tucker can earn a spot in their rotation by late 2001, and given physical refinement, should be a lock by 2002. He projects as a 200 inning horse who could fit snugly into the middle of the Expos' major league rotation for years to come.

6 -C Brian Schneider - Schneider, 23, was the Expos' fifth round draft pick in 1995. The 6'1", 185, lefthanded hitter made strides at bat and in the field last season, earning some major league time in the process. Offensively, Schneider has a quick bat and above average power potential for a catcher. He could be a 20 homer guy in the majors. His over aggressiveness at the plate needs to be toned down quite a bit. At this point, he projects as a .250 hitter at best at the major league level. Defensively, Schneider is quite agile and is smooth mechanically. He doesn't have top-grade arm strength, but his quick release compensates to a large extent. With Chris Widger out of the Expos' picture, Michael Barrett and Schneider remain as viable major league catching alternatives. Schneider will either back him up or be the regular Triple-A receiver in 2001. Over the long haul, he projects as either an adequate big league starter or as a top-notch backup or platooner.

7 - 3B Josh McKinley - McKinley, 20, was the Expos' first round draft pick in 1998. He was selected that high based on signability as much as talent, but did make significant strides on the field last season. The 6'2", 190, switch-hitter was moved from shortstop to third base, a position much better suited to his skills, which emphasize first step quickness over the extreme lateral movement required at shortstop. Offensively, McKinley faded after a strong start at Low-A Cape Fear last season, but showed a live bat with substantial gaps power who could evolve into a 40 double, 15 homer package as he matures. McKinley is an extremely aggressive baserunner, and has studied pitchers extensively, improving his basestealing success rate to an acceptable level. He still needs to smooth out his offensive and defensive games, but McKinley served notice for the first time in 2000 that he just might have a major league game. If he can reach the Double-A level by the end of 2001, he'll certify himself as a potential future major league starter. At the very least, McKinley could be a multi-skilled all-purpose reserve in the majors, and could arrive by late 2003.

8 - OF Wilken Ruan - Ruan, 20, is an exciting speed prospect who could evolve into a major league leadoff man if he can add substantial discipline to his game. The 6'0", 160, righthanded hitter significantly improved all aspects of his game in a second year at Low-A Cape Fear. He made consistent, authoritative line drive contact, with surprising extra-base pop to the gaps. His speed is game-breaking and disruptive, and Ruan learned to use it much more efficiently last season. He is a wild swinger at this stage in his development, and his on-base percentage won't likely be high enough at upper minor league levels for him to remain a leadoff man unless he learns to take a pitch. Defensively, Ruan has above average range, and a very strong and accurate throwing arm that qualifies him to play either center or right field. Ruan will have to venture above Low-A ball in 2001, and his offensive performance at higher levels will dictate how far he can go. The best guess is that Ruan will eventually become a part-time major league outfielder because of his speed and defense. Much work with the bat will be necessary for him to lead off in the bigs.

9 - 3B Scott Hodges - Hodges, 21, was one of a bevy of 1997 Expos' first round draftees. After a fairly silent beginning to his minor league career, the 6'0", 185, lefthanded hitter began to break out last season at High-A Jupiter, He has a compact line-drive stroke, and is showing signs of developing 40 double, 20 homer power. He puts the ball in play fairly consistently for a powerful hitter, and has made some strides with regard to plate discipline. Hodges has average speed, but has been known to be an overaggressive baserunner at times. Defensively, he has soft hands, well above average range and a strong throwing arm, and should remain at the position as he advances. Hodges and McKinley are comparable prospects. Hodges might be a little more complete right now, but might lack McKinley's all-around upside. Hodges' offensive performance at the Double-A level could be telling. If some of his High-A doubles become Double-A homers, a distinct possibility, then Hodges could shoot way up on this list and become the Expos' third baseman of the future, with a possible major league arrival date of late 2002.

10 - 1B Thomas Pittman - Pittman, 20, was a supplemental first round draft pick in 1997. The 6'4", 270, righthanded hitter remains on this list solely because of his youth and power potential, as his 2000 High-A season was beyond dismal, and could spell the impending end of his dalliance with the sport of baseball. Pittman was a highly sought football prospect, and was on the verge of heading off to

Auburn after the 1999 season only to be convinced to give baseball another try. He went backwards in all respects at High-A Jupiter, totally misplacing his power stroke and getting himself out too often on bad pitches. He's not a good breaking ball hitter at this point, and his wild-swinging ways have ensured him a steady diet of the same. He's a solid athlete who moves well in the field for his size, but his bat will determine how far he advances. If Pittman elects to continue his baseball career, 2001 will be a watershed season. If he does not show major power progress in a second High-A campaign, his window of opportunity will start to close. Pittman has the goods to be a major league first baseman (by late 2003), but an awful lot will have to break right for him to get there.

OTHER PROSPECTS

RHP Shane Arthurs - His stuff isn't inspiring, but his control and composure leave open the possibility for improvement. He's also very young and needs to fill out, which could take his fastball from the upper 80s into the lower 90s. He still makes too many mistakes in the strike zone and he'll need to correct that flaw as he advances.

OF Matt Cepicky - Cepicky has shown very good speed and the ability to make contact, but it would be in his best interest if he were to be more patient and drew more walks. For a big guy (6'2" 215) he hasn't shown much home run power so far, but that can be expected to come soon. A move up to Double-A would make sense given his success at single-A Jupiter in 2000. He could wind up being one of the Expos' best hitting prospect before long.

RHP Ron Chiavacci - Chiavacci is a big, strong righthander who throws reasonably hard and has good control. He's a power pitcher who gets a fair number of strikeouts and he keeps the ball in the ballpark. He's just 22 years-old and should advance to Double-A this season, which would be a nice test for him.

SS Tomas De La Rosa - De La Rosa is a slick fielding shortstop who isn't much of a hitter just yet. He's pretty young at 22, so there is time for him to learn. He runs fairly well and makes a lot contact, though it's not always solid contact. He can more than handle himself at shortstop, but he won't have a shot at regular time in the majors unless he makes some major improvements at the plate.

LHP Josh Girdley - Girdley has a 90 MPH fastball and a potentially dominant curveball. He should advance quickly because he has sound mechanics and knows what he's doing out on the mound. Within a year or two he'll be one of the Expos' top prospects.

RHP Ed Klepacki - For a young pitcher, Klepacki has excellent control. He gives up his share of hits and definitely isn't overpowering, but by keeping the walks to a minimum allows him to be very effective. He allowed just two home runs in 83 innings last year at Low-A and if he can continue to keep the ball in the park as he advances he'll be in great shape.

SS Albenis Machado - Machado is a good defensive shortstop with tremendous patience at the plate. He's shown the ability to walk more than he strikes out and despite a .245 average at High-A last year, his 79 walks allowed him to get on base at a .363 clip. He doesn't have any power and isn't adept at stealing bases, but his ability to draw walks, make contact and his above average speed give him a shot at reaching the majors some day.

2B Henry Mateo - Mateo is a good middle infielder who can hit a little bit and run like the wind. He could stand to cut back on the strikeouts, but he has demonstrated the ability to carry a decent batting average and he draws a fair number of walks. He's not a home run hitter, but his speed gets him plenty of doubles and triples. He has 40-50 stolen base potential and is a good, though at times inconsistent, defender at second base.

2B Tootie Myers - Myers has tools, but he needs refining. He needs to be much more patient at the plate, which would allow him to make more consistent contact. He doesn't have a lot of power, but with added patience he could manage double-digit home runs and 20-30 doubles. His defense is erratic and needs work as well. He's still young and has time to work on his weaknesses, so there is reason to keep an eye on him.

OF Val Pascucci - At 6'6" and 225 pounds, Pascucci has all the physical talent he'll ever need, it's just a matter of polishing his skills. He hasn't learned how to lift the ball into the air consistently just yet, but his moderate home run total combined with all the doubles he's hit indicate future power. He runs well for a big man and knows what he's doing at the plate, but needs work in the outfield. A big man with above average patience is definitely worth noting.

1B Fernando Seguignol - Seguignol is a switch-hitter with big-time power who needs a place to play in the majors. He strikes out a ton, but has improved his ability to hit for average to go along with his 30-plus home run potential. He's not good enough defensively to play left field, so he'll have to stay at first base.

RHP Luis Torres - At 6'5" and just about 200 pounds, Torres is the kind of kid who can add a couple of miles per hour to his 90 MPH fastball as he matures. His control is decent right now, but his secondary pitches need work. He's not a top prospect, but he's definitely worthy of keeping an eye on.

RHP Ulmer Urbina - Like his brother Ugueth, Ulmer has a big-time fastball. He spent last season pitching in relief at short season Vermont and he did reasonably well, though his ERA wasn't what you might expect. If he can develop a consistent second pitch like his brother did, Ulmer could be a good reliever in a few years.

NEW YORK METS
ORGANIZATIONAL GRID

	AAA	AA	HI-A	LO-A
1B	Jorge Toca - R - 25 Mark Johnson - L - 32	Bryon Gainey - L - 24 Dan Held - R - 29	Earl Snyder - R - 24 Pat Burns - B - 22	Craig Brazell - L - 20
2B	Mitch Simons - R - 31	Ty Wigginton - R - 22 John Tamargo - B - 25 Gavin Jackson - R - 26	Bobby Hill - L - 21 John Dorman - R - 26	Jason Brett - R - 23 David Abreu - B - 21
SS	Kevin Baez - R - 33 David Lamb - B - 25	Gabby Martinez - R - 26	Gil Velazquez - R - 20	Ruddi De la Cruz - R - 20 Brian Shipp - R - 21
3B	Maurice Bruce - R - 25 Matt Franco - L - 30	Junior Zamora - R - 24	Rodney Nye - R - 23	Pat Deschenes - L - 22 Eric Guyton - R - 23
OF	Ryan McGuire - L - 28 Todd Dunn - R - 29 Chris Sheff - R - 29 Timoniel Perez - L - 23	Allen Dina - R - 26 Alex Escobar - R - 21 B.J. Huff - R - 24 Brian Cole - R - 21	Endy Chavez - L - 22 Robert Stratton - R - 22 Juan LeBron - R - 23 Juan Moreno - R - 24	Prentice Redman - R - 20 Marvin Seale - B - 21 Brian Jenkins - R - 21
C	Vance Wilson - R - 27 Alan Probst - R - 29	Jimmy Gonzalez - R - 27 Jason Phillips - R - 23	Sammy Rodriguez - R - 24 Ryan Bennett - R - 25 Andrew Thompson - L - 26	Steve Elzy - R - 22 Bubba Casteneda - R - 21 Javier Ochoa - R - 21
SP	Grant Roberts - R - 22 Bobby Jones - L - 28 Dennis Springer - R - 35 Willie Banks - R - 31 Mark Corey - R - 25 Tyler Walker - R - 24	Dicky Gonzalez - R - 21 J.D. Arteaga - L - 25 Marino Cota - R - 23 Pablo Ochoa - R - 24 Pat Strange - R - 19	Nick Maness - R - 21 Jason Saenz - L - 23 Rene Vega - L - 23 Andy Cook - R - 23 Jason Roach - R - 22	Ken Chenard - R - 21 Frank Graham - R - 21 Jeremy Griffiths - R - 22 Justin Dunning - R - 23 Greg Halvorson - R - 23 Joe Cole - R - 22 Jake Joseph - R - 22
CLOSER	Eric Cammack - R - 24 Lariel Gonzalez - R - 24	Jerrod Riggan - R - 26 Corey Brittan - R - 25 Juan Aracena - R - 23	Heath Bell - R - 22	Jose Nunez - L - 21 Robert Weslowski - R - 21 Scott Polk - R - 23

NEW YORK METS

It's a cliché, but it's true. Sometimes, the best trades you make are the ones that you don't make. The Mets tried to get Barry Larkin in a deal that would have cost them top prospect Alex Escobar, among others. After they were spurned by the Reds' shortstop, however, they were able to acquire Mike Bordick from the Orioles in exchange for a package that included only one viable prospect, pitcher Lesli Brea. The Mets system as a result remains somewhat lean in quality, but respectable in terms of the quality of its top prospects.

At first base, Jorge Toca has fallen off of the fast track to the major leagues. He's listed at 25 years old, which might be a bit low, and hasn't developed the plate discipline that would allow him to take full advantage of his natural longball power. He's a big league bench bat at best. 6'3", 185, lefty Craig Brazell found out the hard way that full-season leagues are a big step up from rookie ball. He has a solid power upside, but like Toca, needs to take pitches and work deep counts to see more fastballs. He's a big league longshot at this point.

At second base, Ty Wigginton is the closest thing to a true prospect. He has a solid power upside for a middle infielder, but poor plate discipline and inconsistent defensive mechanics could hold him back. He's certainly no Edgardo Alfonzo, but could eventually be a candidate for a bench bat role in the majors.

Shortstop Gil Velazquez is a reliable defender, but needs to develop a semblance of an offensive game to continue to forge ahead. At 6'2", 170, there's got to be some power in there somewhere. He is a big league longshot at this point. Enrique Cruz, only 18, fizzled in a stint as Low-A Capital City's shortstop last season, and was then shifted to third base in rookie ball. He has a substantial power/speed upside that would be particularly appealing at shortstop, but he needs to learn to take a pitch. If he can star in a full-season league job in 2001, he'll be on target for a future starting infield job at either position.

Cruz is the best bet among Mets' prospects to emerge as a major league third baseman.

Outfield prospect depth is weak, but the quality of two of the remaining prospects is spectacular. Center field prospect Alex Escobar has overcome back and shoulder injuries, and is back on the fast track to the major leagues. He's a pure power/speed prospect with 30/30 potential. Sometime in 2001, he's a likely bet to emerge as a Mets' regular, and should eventually become a star. Brian Cole might not have Escobar's raw ability, but he has outshone his organization-mate on the field over the past two seasons. The 5'9", 172, center fielder has shocking raw power for his size, and is among the best basestealers in the minors. He could shove Escobar over to right field, and also shapes as a future big league stalwart. Cole's two 2000 High-A outfield partners, Endy Chavez and Robert Stratton, have individual skills that could be parlayed into major league backup jobs. Chavez makes consistent line drive contact and runs well, and Stratton can drive mistake fastballs for serious distance. Neither projects as a big league starter, and both have lots of work ahead to simply make the majors. 6'3", 185, righthanded hitter Prentice Redman has decent gaps power, a good eye and plus speed, and could move onto the major league radar screen if he develops a power stroke. Switch-hitter Marvin Seale can flat out fly, and showed a surprisingly consistent line drive bat with gaps power in his first full pro season. Both Redman and Seale project as no better than future big league role players at this point.

Jason Phillips, a contact hitter with a budding power bat, is the Mets' best catching prospect. At best, he shapes up as a major league bench option down the road.

As with the outfielders, starting pitcher depth is just average, though the quality of the front-liners is very solid. Righthander Grant Roberts has struggled to rebound from elbow problems, and no longer appears to be a front-of-the-rotation prospect. He hasn't developed a true out pitch to complement his low 90s fastball, especially against lefties. He'll get a chance to crack the bottom end of the Mets' rotation in 2001, but might not be ready just yet. At 5'11", 170, and possessing only an average fastball, righty Dicky Gonzalez doesn't look like your typical starting pitcher prospect. He just keeps getting hitters out, and getting the ball past them. He's likely to make the Mets by 2002 as either a bottom-end starter or a two-inning arm out of the pen. Pat Strange has been rocketing through the Mets' system, and has an outside chance to reach the Big Apple in 2001 at age 20. The 6'5", 240, righthander possesses powerful stuff and exceptional command, and could thrive in the majors as either a frontline starter or a closer. Bet on the former. Righty Nick Maness lacks the stuff of the aforementioned hurlers, but his prototypical 6'4", 195, frame and his feel for pitching holds open the possibility for a near-term breakout. His Double-A campaign in 2001 will determine how far he can go. He's a big league sleeper at this point. 6'3", 175, righty Ken Chenard had an excellent Low-A season in 2000. With natural physical development and improved stamina, Chenard could get the ball past upper level hitters and develop into a major league option as a swingman or bullpen righty. 6'7", 233, righty Jeremy Griffiths has superb mechanics for his size, and with improved command within the strike zone, could evolve into a major league mid-rotation option.

Righthanders Eric Cammack and Lariel Gonzalez have at times excelled as minor league closers, and could evolve into viable big league middle relievers or setup men. Cammack's fastball isn't overpowering, but he changes speeds well and has historically fared well against lefthanded hitters. He'll likely be on the Mets' 2001 staff. Gonzalez' fastball is harder, and his upside a bit higher than Cammack's. However, his mechanics and command have wavered, 2000 included. 2001 could be a make-or-break year for the former Rockies' prospect.

TOP TEN PROSPECTS

1 - OF Alex Escobar - Escobar, 21, bounced back with a strong Double-A season after missing virtually all of 1999 with shoulder and back injuries. The 6'1", 185, righthanded hitter was healthy from start to finish, and quickly regained his status as one of the top all-around prospects in the game. His power/speed combination is quite possibly the best in the minors. With improved plate discipline, Escobar could be a perennial 30/30 man in the major leagues. The ball explodes off of his bat, and his combination of on-base and power skills makes him a natural for the No. 3 spot in a major league batting order.

Defensively, he has above average range for a center fielder, and a strong throwing arm who would play in either center or right field. Double-A Eastern League managers recognized Escobar's array of skills, citing him as the circuit's most exciting player. Escobar is a solid bet to earn an everyday job with the Mets sometime in 2001, quite possibly by Opening Day. He might scuffle at first, but once he learns to take a pitch, he'll be a star.

2 - RHP Pat Strange - Strange, 19, was the Mets' second round draft pick in 1998. The 6'5", 240, righthander is an amazingly complete pitching prospect for his age. He has a diverse repertoire, featuring a lively low 90s heater, an excellent slider, a couple of different types of changeups, and a curveball. He has an advanced knack for setting up hitters, is uncannily precise, and because of his size and smarts, should develop into a nine-inning hurler. Before being promoted to Double-A Binghamton, Strange dominated the High-A Florida State League, where he was recognized by circuit managers as the best pitching prospect. After his promotion, Strange nibbled around the edges of the plate in his early Double-A starts, showing impressive stuff while too often working from behind in the count. Strange will likely start 2001 back at Double-A, where he should emerge as a staff anchor. He has a chance to be truly special: a power/control pitcher likely to entrench himself as a big league starter at age 21 in 2002. Strange is a future staff ace.

3 - OF Brian Cole - Cole, 21, has made lightning-quick progress through the Mets' system since being selected on the 18th round of the 1998 draft. The smallish 5'9", 172, righthanded hitter has surprising extra-base power for his size, and is capable of 40 double, 20 homer, 40 steal seasons should his development proceed smoothly. However, for Cole to reach his potential, he will need to significantly enhance his on-base skills and develop into a top-of-the-order hitter. At present, Cole's poor plate discipline is a major drawback. Witness his major struggles at the plate after being promoted to Double-A Binghamton in mid-2000. He batted well below .200 in his first month there, walking only three times. Prior to that promotion, Cole tore apart the High-A Florida State League, where he was rated the fastest baserunner and most exciting player in the circuit by its managers. Defensively, Cole has the range to be an above average center fielder, but both his subpar arm strength and the presence of Alex Escobar could conspire to keep him in left field. The Mets would love for Cole to be their future everyday leadoff man, and he could be just that by sometime in 2002. At worst, he could be an effective fourth outfielder and bench bat.

4 - RHP Grant Roberts - Roberts, 22, was the Mets' 11th round draft pick in 1995. The 6'3", 205, righthander appeared to be on a rocket ship to the major leagues before undergoing elbow surgery in 1998, and simply hasn't been quite the same pitcher since. His stuff seems to be all the way back. He combines a live low 90s fastball with a slider and curveball, and needs to keep his pitches low in the strike zone to experience consistent success. Inconsistent location, in fact, is what has plagued Roberts over the past year and a half. He has allowed over a hit per inning over that stretch, as his strikes have caught too much of the plate. Also, hitters are now fouling off pitches they might have missed before the injury, as a little bit of movement appears to be missing in action, quite possibly due to mechanical inefficiencies. Roberts was torched in a mid-season major league start, but will get more chances. He needs to dominate Triple-A hitters for a period in 2001 before getting his next opportunity. Look for him to eventually settle in as a Bobby Jones-ish mid-rotation starter in New York.

5 - OF Timoniel Perez - How's this for an out-of-nowhere success story. Perez, 23, played anonymously in Japan prior to last season, and then proceeded to tear apart Triple-A International League pitching in 2000, likely edging his way into the Mets' long-term outfield plans alongside Alex Escobar and Brian Cole. The 5'9", 167, lefthanded hitter slaps the ball to all fields, showing surprising gaps power for his size and rarely striking out. He'll need to improve his plate discipline to project as a major league leadoff man, but that's likely the final offensive frontier. He runs extremely well, though he still needs to more efficiently incorporate his speed into his overall offensive package. Defensively, Perez possesses exceptional range in center field and passable arm strength. He certainly has caught the eyes of Mets' brass, to the extent that they were able to confidently include 1998 first round pick Jason Tyner in the deal with Tampa Bay that brought Rick White and Bubba Trammell to the New York. Perez has a future with the Mets, either as a leadoff-hitting center fielder or as a multifaceted fourth outfielder. He could stick with the club out of spring training in 2001.

6 - RHP Dicky Gonzalez - Gonzalez, 21, was a 16th round draft pick in 1996. The onetime skinny soft-tosser has grown substantially to 5'11", 170, and his fastball's peak velocity has increased significantly to about 90 MPH. The Mets have advanced the extreme control pitcher at an intelligent pace, with Gonzalez arriving at the Double-A level at precisely the time his stuff was able to handle the move. He impressively maintained his strikeout rate of nearly one per inning at Double-A Binghamton last season, and did so while pitching ahead in the count consistently, and walking as few batters as ever. Gonzalez mixes his fastball with an above average changeup and an improving curve and slider. He sets up hitters well, and spots his fastball so that it appears to be much faster than it is. He has smooth mechanics and has never failed to take the ball on his scheduled day as a pro. Gonzalez could become a potential ace if one of his breaking pitches develops into a true strikeout pitch against lefties. More likely, the control artisan will continue to evolve into a reliable, 200 inning major league mid-rotation starter, with a 2002 arrival date.

7 - 3B Enrique Cruz - Cruz, 18, is an extremely talented but raw prospect who could eventually develop into a potent power hitter and exceptional defensive player. The 6'1", 175, righthanded hitter started 2000 in Low-A Capital City's lineup as a shortstop, but proved unready with the bat and glove. His plate discipline was poor, and he consequently got himself out on a regular basis. Defensively, he was inconsistent on the routine play, battling poor footwork. Though his selectivity at the plate continued to be an issue after his return to rookie ball, Cruz showed more frequent flashes of his undeniable all-around skills. He has lightning-quick bat speed, and can drive the ball for extreme distance to all fields. He has much natural physical development ahead, and could develop 30-plus homer power in the process. His speed is above average, and Cruz showed signs of developing an aggressive mindset on the bases in rookie ball. Defensively, third base suits him better physically. What was average quickness for a shortstop, is now exceptional at his new home. He could be a major league starter in 2004 or so, but much work is ahead. Jot down his name for the future, and watch those homer totals as he rises through the system.

8 - 2B Ty Wigginton - Wigginton, 22, was a 17th round draft pick in 1998. The 6'0", 190, righthanded hitter has overcome his lack of a draft pedigree to become a candidate for a significant big league role on the strength of two consecutive excellent offensive seasons in which he displayed substantial home run power for a middle infielder. His complementary skills aren't great. Wigginton's plate discipline is quite poor, his raw speed is average and his baserunning instincts quite ordinary, and neither his defensive range nor arm strength raises eyebrows. Still, Wigginton could emerge as a strong contender for an all-purpose reserve role in New York by 2002 should he learn to play another position or two. Otherwise, lesser major league clubs that do not have an incumbent second baseman like Edgardo Alfonzo in place might be willing to trade for Wigginton and give him a chance to prove his mettle at the game's ultimate level as a starter. Watch those strikeout/walk numbers carefully; they'll tell you when Wigginton's bat is ready.

9 - 1B Jorge Toca - Toca, who is either 25 or 29, depending on whom you believe, suffered through a subpar Triple-A season in 2000 that calls into question his ability to be a viable major league power hitter. The 6'0", 190, righthanded hitter has little more than a substantial power upside to fall back upon. He does not run well, is adequate at best with the glove, and most importantly, has extremely poor plate discipline. Toca has never met a pitch that he didn't like, and as a result finds himself buried in the count quite often, being fed a steady diet of breaking pitches out of the strike zone. It's highly unlikely that Toca will ever meet the high offensive standards set for starting major league first basemen, though it's quite possible that he could make the Mets as a righthanded bat off of the bench in 2001.

10 - OF Robert Stratton - Talk about one-dimensional prospects. Stratton, 22, was the Mets' first round draft pick in 1996. The 6'2", 220, righthanded hitter has extreme raw power to all fields. He was recognized as the High-A Florida State League's best power prospect last season by circuit managers. However, it isn't a good sign when a first round pick fails to reach the Double-A level by age 22, after spending five seasons in pro ball. Stratton's complementary skills are nearly nonexistent. He's a low average hitter who is a strikeout machine, a wild swinger who struggles against the most rudimentary breaking stuff. Defensively, calling Stratton an outfielder is being gracious. He's a designated hitter who gives it the old college try in left field. Power like this simply doesn't grow on trees, however, so Stratton will be given many chances. Look for him to eventually gravitate into an American League team's system, and creep towards the majors as a DH prospect. He could make it to the majors in a supporting role by 2003.

OTHER PROSPECTS

LHP J.D. Arteaga - Arteaga has an average fastball that he spots well, a good overhand curve and a solid changeup in his repertoire. He lets opposing hitters put the ball in play and does a reasonably good job of getting ground ball outs. He hasn't had a chance to prove himself above Double-A yet, so that will be his task this year. He could either start or relieve at the major league level, though he'd probably be more effective coming out of the bullpen.

RHP Eric Cammack - Cammack has been a very good minor league reliever for years now. He doesn't have the raw stuff to be a major league closer, but should be a serviceable middle man or setup man sometime soon. He had some problems with walks last season, though they didn't hurt him as much at Triple-A as they did in his short stint with the Mets.

RHP Ken Chenard - Chenard has a very strong arm and is tough on opposing hitters, but his control needs quite a bit of work. He made 21 starts at Low-A last year, but averaged less than five innings per start because of high pitch counts. He did manage 112 strikeouts in 94 innings, but his 48 walks was a lot. The league hit just .219 against him, so if he can throw strikes more consistently in the future, he could be a good one.

RHP Lariel Gonzalez - Gonzalez has an outstanding fastball that routinely reaches the mid 90s, but he's had plenty of control problems so far in his career. He falls behind in counts a lot, which leads to more hits than you might expect against someone with his velocity, but he's got the potential to improve quickly. If he can refine his number two pitch and get ahead with the heater he'll be in the Majors shortly.

RHP Nick Maness - Manses has the size (6'4" 195) and long arms teams like in their starting pitchers. His fastball isn't the greatest in the world, but it is very lively. He can be extremely tough to hit against as evidenced by the .223 opponents' average he allowed at High-A last year. With some more physical maturation and a little refinement of his offspeed stuff, Maness could be pretty good.

RHP Jerrod Riggan - He's too old to truly be considered a top of the line prospect, but the Mets thought enough of him to send him to the Arizona Fall League this past Fall. He can be virtually unhittable when he's on, which was quite often last season. At Double-A Binghamton he went 2-0 with a 1.11 ERA and 28 saves in 65-plus innings of work. He gave up just 43 hits and 18 walks, less than a baserunner per inning, and struck out 79. He could figure into the Mets' bullpen picture sometime in the near future.

OF Marvin Seale - Seale is a switch-hitting speedster who needs to reign himself in a bit. He was able to manage a respectable .291 batting average at Low-A Capital City last year, but his 125 strikeouts were alarming for someone with little power. He'll need to cut back a lot on the whiffs and draw some more walks to take full advantage of his outstanding speed. He stole 52 bases during the 2000 season and he could keep that up as he advances if he can get on base consistently.

1B Earl Snyder - Snyder won't show up on many prospect lists, but his production at High-A during the 2000 season cannot be ignored. He showed excellent power, especially for the Florida State League, hitting 25 home runs and also pounding out 36 doubles. He proved to be a good RBI man as well, driving in 93 runs. On the down side, he strikes out a lot and has been much older than his competition so far in the minors. He was 23 last year playing at Single-A. He has much to prove, but his power makes him worth watching.

RHP Tyler Walker - Walker has a live arm and reasonably good control, but he's a little old to have not seen Triple-A yet. He posted strong numbers at Double-A last year, allowing opponents to hit just .190 against him, but he was repeating that level. He needs to show something at Triple-A this year to make himself a legit prospect.

PHILADELPHIA PHILLIES
ORGANIZATIONAL GRID

	AAA	AA	HI-A	LO-A
1B	Gene Schall - R - 30 Chris Pritchett - L - 30	Gary Burnham - L - 25	Bob Van Iten - L - 23	Nate Espy - R - 22
2B	David Newhan - L - 26	Jason Knupfer - R - 25 Brian Harris - B - 25	Sergio Nunez - R - 25 Uriel Casillas - R - 24	Brian Hitchcox - L - 21
SS	Jimmy Rollins - B - 21	Nick Punto - B - 22	Anderson Machado - B - 19	Julio Collazo - R - 19 Ambiorix Reyes - B - 21
3B	Dave Doster - R - 29 Tomas Perez - R - 26	Pete Rose, Jr. - L - 30 Rusty McNamara - R - 25	Matt Bryant - R - 24 Jeff Terrell - L - 25 Tom Batson - R - 23	Buzz Hannahan - R - 24 Juan Richardson - R - 19
OF	Kenny Woods - R - 29 Reggie Taylor - L - 23 P.J. Forbes - R - 32 David Francia - L - 25	Jason Michaels - R - 24 Eric Valent - L - 23 Aaron Royster - R - 27 Carmine Cappuccio - L - 30 Josue Perez - B - 22	Carlos Duncan - R - 23 Jason Johnson - R - 22 Alejandro Giron - R - 21 Skip Kiil - R - 26 Brian Bush - R - 22	Marlon Byrd - R - 22 Shomari Beverly - R - 22 Jorge Padilla - R - 20 Jay Sitzman - L - 22 Aaron Merhoff - R - 24 Dan O'Neill - R - 23
C	Gary Bennett - R - 28 Fausto Tejero - R - 31 Cesar King - R - 22 Clemente Alvarez - R - 32	Johnny Estrada - B - 24 Andy Dominique - R - 24	Jeremy Salazar - R - 23 Jerry Valdez - R - 26 Eric Schreimann - R - 25	Russ Jacobson - R - 22 Jeremy Deitrick - R - 23 Kevin Sullivan - R - 21
SP	Mark Brownson - R - 25 Evan Thomas - R - 26 Shane Bowers - R - 28 Amaury Telemaco - R - 26 Dave Coggin - R - 23 Nelson Figueroa - R - 26	Jason Brester - L - 23 Kris Stevens - L - 22 Brandon Duckworth - R - 24 Geoff Geary - R - 23 Mark Rutherford - R - 25 Jimmy Osting - L - 23 Jason Kershner - L - 23 John Sneed - R - 24	Brad Baisley - R - 20 Greg Kubes - L - 23 Franklin Nunez - R - 23 Carlos Silva - R - 21 Bobby Sismondo - L - 23 Adam Walker - L - 24 Ken Westmoreland - R - 25	Frank Brooks - L - 21 Brett Myers - R - 19 Martire Franco - R - 18 Ryan Madson - R - 19 Franklin Perez - R - 19 Brad Pautz - R - 23
CLOSER	Kirk Bullinger - R - 30 Manny Barrios - R - 25 Steve Schrenk - R - 31	Doug Nickle - R - 25 Blas Cedeno - R - 27 John Daniels - R - 26	Cary Hiles - R - 24 Jeremy Wedel - R - 23	Mark Outlaw - L - 23 Justin Fry - R - 23 Elio Serrano - R - 21

PHILADELPHIA PHILLIES

Based on their gaudy 2000 organizational winning percentage, Phils' brass would have you believe that they have emerged as one of the top producers of minor league talent in the game. While they have certainly advanced from their rock-bottom days of just a few years ago, the Phils are just beginning to approach major league average with regard to prospect quality and quantity.

Most of the Phils' minor league first basemen are years older than their leagues' average age. The only legitimate prospect is Nate Espy, who strafed Low-A South Atlantic League pitching last year. However, he did so in his second tour of the league, and at 22, as one of its older players. If he does the same at Double-A in 2001, then believe. For now, pencil him in as a future big league backup.

Marlon Anderson couldn't hold the major league second base job, so he showcased his line drive bat and basestealing ability at the Triple-A level last season. The Phils aren't sold on his defensive reliability, but he's got to be better than Mickey Morandini, right? 1999 25th round pick Brian Hitchcox is a spray hitter with decent speed who has an outside chance to evolve into a utility candidate.

The Phils do have some possibilities at shortstop. Jimmy Rollins, 21, the Phils' 1996 second round pick, should compete for the starting big league job in 2001. He's a reliable defender, and hits the ball with surprising authority for his 5'8", 160, frame. He could be a reasonable number two hitter down the road, and is of near-term value at the major league level. Switch-hitter Nick Punto's raw skills aren't inspiring, but his fire and zest for the game sure are. He runs the bases well, takes pitches and does all of the little things, and should be a serviceable big league utilityman. He's a poor man's Larry Bowa. Anderson Machado, 19, showed flashes of brilliance last season at High-A Clearwater. He has great speed and an immense defensive upside, and should eventually develop a bit of power. Look for a breakout season from the man who should eventually slide Rollins over to second base. Julio

Collazo is another highly talented, but very raw, shortstop who was a bit overmatched last season at Low-A Piedmont. Expect a step forward in 2001, though it's way too early to project a big league future.

The Phils better hope that Scott Rolen sticks around awhile, because there is no third base hope in the system.

With Doug Glanville getting on base at barely a .300 clip in 2000, why didn't multi-talented center field prospect Reggie Taylor merit a look? Taylor, contrary to popular belief, is not a leadoff prospect, but he has substantial extra base power, great speed, and is an exceptional defender. His plate discipline is poor, but he's a starting-quality major league center fielder, though the Phils might not realize it. Lefthanded hitter Eric Valent, 23, put up solid Double-A numbers, but at his age, and with his first round draftee pedigree, he darn well should have. Valent hasn't been challenged enough, and is no longer projected as a big league starter as a result. He should be a decent major league fourth outfielder in a couple of years. Josue Perez, 22, is another prospect who put up deceptively good numbers against much younger competition last season at High-A Clearwater. He has less power and speed potential than Taylor, but is almost as good a defender. Perez should also someday be an extra man in Philadelphia. Alejandro Giron is a sleeper prospect with a consistent line drive bat, and has started to develop gaps power. With a little more plate discipline, he too could evolve into a viable backup major league outfield candidate within two years. 1999 10th round pick Marlon Byrd, 22, also put up excellent power/speed numbers against much younger pitching at Low-A Piedmont. He does have a 20/20 power/speed upside, but he'll have to fine-tune his 5'11", 225, frame. He's yet another future major league backup candidate. Jorge Padilla, 20, has arguably the highest power upside in the system. The 6'2", 210, righthander has made strides towards improving his plate discipline, but still has a ways to go. He's a high-risk, high-reward prospect who could eventually start in the majors.

The Phils are hoping that they can revitalize the career of former top Ranger catching prospect Cesar King. He possesses fine defensive technique, but his bat and conditioning have held him back. He certainly can give Tom Prince and Gary Bennett a run for the major league backup job in 2001, however. 1999 third round pick Russ Jacobson, 22, has a substantial power upside for a catcher, and is a durable receiver. However, he too played against much younger competition last season at Piedmont, so it's tough to put too much stock into his numbers. Pencil him in as a future big league backup for now.

Pitching depth is a bit thin in the upper minors, but there's a bit more hope down low. Lefty Jason Brester totally lost touch with home plate at Double-A Reading last season, a no-no for a hurler without a killer fastball. With some significant mechanical fine-tuning, Brester could surface as a candidate for a situational bullpen role in the majors. Lefty Kris Stevens' once-promising career has been derailed by injuries. He needs to prove his health over a full season before reentering the Phils' plans. Brandon Duckworth overpowered Double-A hitters last season: at age 24, of course. However, the 6'2", 185, righty has solid control and a convincing mound presence, and could eventually help a major league staff in a supporting role. Geoff Geary is a finesse righty who almost never walks a batter. However, his stuff is so hittable that he has nearly no chance to make the majors. Righty Dave Coggin, 23, a former first round pick, was surprisingly not mauled in his first crack at the majors. Though the 6'4", 195, righty has four seemingly solid pitches, none of them make hitters miss. He'll get another chance to stick in the majors, but needs to be significantly better than the first time. Righty Brad Baisley, 20, has the highest upside of the Phils' starting pitcher prospects. He stands 6'9", 200, and combines his power repertoire with surprisingly sound mechanics for his size. If he puts nagging injuries behind him, he'll be ready for a true breakout season in 2001. He could be a future number one or two starter in the majors. Righty Carlos Silva made the Futures Game last season. That tells you more about the paucity of top-flight talent in the chain than it does about Silva's ability. Silva has great control, but is eminently hittable, and could get carved up at Double-A in 2001. He's unlikely to make a significant big league impact. Lefty Frank Brooks, 21, a 1999 13th round pick, was a pleasant surprise at Low-A Piedmont last season. His command was excellent, and his durability was arguably the best in the system. He might not have the stuff to similarly excel at higher levels, however. He remains a sleeper with an outside chance to make the majors as a starter. 1999 first round pick Brett

Myers showed flashes of brilliance at Piedmont, and has the raw tools to someday be a solid power pitcher in the majors. First, he needs to tweak his mechanics to get a bit more movement on his pitches. His upside approaches Baisley's. So does that of righty Ryan Madson, a 1998 ninth round selection. His initial crack at a full season league was a rousing success, as he combined power with solid command at Piedmont. His 6'6", 180, frame should fill out and give his stuff a bit more juice, making him a potential future number two or three starter in the majors. At age 18, righty Martire Franco did well to keep his head above water at Piedmont. In 2001, more will be expected. Expect to see his strikeout rate rise, with Franco's stock rising in tandem. He too could someday join a big league rotation.

Doug Nickle, 25, has a lively mid 90s heater, a darting knuckle-curve and good control. Why then, was he mired at Double-A Reading for all of 2000 at his age? Despite his dogged closer mentality, he won't serve in that role in the bigs, where he'll possibly be an effective middleman. Keep an eye on righty Franklin Perez, 19. His control has improved greatly, and he could add velocity to his average fastball with natural physical development of his 6'2", 175, frame.

TOP TEN PROSPECTS

1 - SS Jimmy Rollins - Rollins, 21, was the Phils' second round draft pick in 1996. The undersized 5'8", 160, switch-hitter got off to a miserable start last season at Triple-A Scranton-Wilkes Barre, but a second-half surge resulted in an excellent all-around year for one of the youngest everyday players in the International League. Rollins makes consistent contact, and hits the ball with significant authority to the gaps for a player of his size. He needs to improve his plate discipline a bit to become a good fit in the first or second spot in a major league batting order. He has well above average raw speed, but needs to study pitchers and get better jumps to improve his basestealing success rate. Rollins' offensive upside is likely a bit higher than Machado's, but he isn't quite as spectacular in the field. He has above average lateral quickness and a quick release, though he lacks overwhelming arm strength. Rollins will likely be the Phils' starting shortstop in 2001, and could rank among NL Rookie of the Year candidates. He could slide over to second base a couple of years down the road if Anderson Machado develops as expected.

2 - RHP Brett Myers - Myers, 19, was the Phils' first round draft pick in 1999. The 6'4", 210, righthander was one of the youngest hurlers to take a regular turn in the Low-A South Atlantic League last season. Myers throws a mid 90s fastball, a powerful curve and a decent changeup. His mechanics tend to be a bit inconsistent. Improvement in that area should add some movement to his pitches and bring his strikeout rate closer to a batter per inning. He's a durable horse who should eventually develop into a consistent complete game threat. His control is quite good for a power pitcher, and should help him thrive after the all-important jump to Double-A, which could take place in late 2001. Myers was known for his cockiness after being drafted, and has toned it down to the level of extreme confidence. He has matured both on and off the mound over the past year, and should eventually graduate into the top end of the Phils' major league rotation. If he ups his whiff rate a bit in 2001 at High-A Clearwater, Myers will be on track for a 2003 Phillies' debut.

3 - SS Anderson Machado - Machado, 19, was signed as a free agent out of Venezuela in 1998, and has rapidly evolved into arguably the Phils' best position player prospect. The 5'11", 165, switch-hitter was one of the youngest everyday players in the High-A Florida State League last spring, making his rather pedestrian offensive performance acceptable. His swing is a bit long at this point, and its slight loop results in too many lazy fly balls. Machado has a touch of gaps power, and could eventually become a 30 double, 10 triple, 10 homer guy. His plate discipline is fairly advanced for a youngster, and continued improvement could make him a viable leadoff or No. 2 hitter down the road. He's an aggressive baserunner with above average speed, and isn't afraid to get his uniform dirty. Machado shines with the glove. His range is spectacular, and he has a quick release and above average arm strength. Florida State League managers recognized him as the best defensive shortstop prospect in the circuit. Machado could be a future big league All-Star if his offensive game blossoms, at worst, he'll be a big league No. 8 hitter and Gold Glove candidate, who should arrive in the majors by Opening Day 2003.

4 - RHP Brad Baisley - Baisley, 20, was the Phils' second round pick in 1998. He appeared poised to have a massive season at High-A Clearwater based on a handful of impressive early starts, but lost a couple of months due to a bout with shoulder tendinitis. The 6'9", 205, Baisley obviously evokes images of a righthanded Randy Johnson because of his imposing physical stature. He throws a low 90s heater plus an above average curveball, and though he

also possesses above average command, he remains raw in a number of respects. He needs to be more consistent mechanically, currently, Baisley's fastball is a bit straight, and is left out over the plate too often. It's incomprehensible that a player with such size and stuff allowed over a hit per inning in High-A ball last season. He also needs to develop a representative changeup, especially for use against lefthanded hitters. Baisley still has much physical development ahead, and the velocity he might add could make him quite scary. He's much more polished than Randy Johnson was at a similar age, and has an excellent chance of developing into the Phils' next ace. He'll arrive by late 2002.

5 -OF Reggie Taylor - Taylor, 23, was the Phils' first round draft pick in 1995. Though the start of his season was delayed by a left (non-throwing) shoulder dislocation in winter ball, the 6'1", 178, lefthanded hitter rebounded to post a fine all-around season at Triple-A Scranton-Wilkes Barre. One problem remains, however, if the Phils still project Taylor as a future leadoff man, they are likely to be frustrated. Taylor is a free swinger who has walked in less than 5% of his professional plate appearances. His single-season high walk total is 30 at High-A Clearwater in 1997, in 575 plate appearances. If the Phils are looking for a number five or six hitter, though, Taylor could be the guy. He has lightning-quick bat speed, and has developed substantial gaps power over the years. He could be a 30 double, 20 triple, 20 homer guy in the majors. He has explosive speed on the bases, but needs to pick his spots a little better and improve his basestealing success rate. Defensively, Taylor is scintillating, combining expansive range with a strong throwing arm that was rated the best in the International League by circuit managers last season. Earth to the Phils; Reggie Taylor is a better player today than Doug Glanville, in all respects. He's no leadoff man, but then again, neither is Glanville. At the very least, Taylor will be a fourth outfielder in Philly in 2001.

6 - RHP Ryan Madson - Madson, 19, was the Phils' ninth round draft pick in 1998. The Phils, who have focused on college players in the upper rounds of recent drafts, should take note of the development of high-schooler Madson. He struggled early on in rookie ball, but now has an exceptional Low-A season under his belt at 19, while college pitchers who progress similarly are 23 by the time they're on their feet, and are non-prospects. The 6'6", 180, righthander throws a live low 90s fastball and a sharp curve, and his slider and changeup have developed into viable complementary offerings. Madson also made significant strides mechanically last season, developing well above average command within the strike zone, and lasted deep into ballgames because of his ability to throw strike one with regularity. Madson lacks the upside of Baisley or Myers, but might have less to work on those two top-shelf prospects. He should rise through the system at a rate of one level per season, and be in position to join the Phillies in 2004. His Double-A performance in late 2001 or early 2002 will dictate whether he is either a mid-rotation prospect or something more special.

7 - OF Jorge Padilla - Padilla, 20, was the Phils' third round draft pick in 1998. The 6'2", 210, righthanded hitter showed substantial improvement in his second crack at the Low-A South Atlantic League. Though he remains a very undisciplined hitter, Padilla began to tap into his immense power potential last season. He has a natural power stroke, and is capable of driving the ball for extreme distance from gap to gap. Continued improvement of his plate discipline would increase the number of fastballs he sees, and cause his homer output to double. Defensively, Padilla's outfield range is just average, but he has a strong throwing arm. He could fit in at either outfield corner at the major league level, but left field is the best bet. If Padilla cuts his strikeout/walk ratio to 2:1 in 2001 at High-A Clearwater, then his power numbers will continue to increase, and he'll remain on track to potentially start in Philadelphia by 2004. He could be a 30 homer guy in the majors.

8 - OF Eric Valent - Valent, 23, is a 1997 supplemental first round draft pick who has been advanced through the system at a glacial pace. The 6'0", 191, lefthanded hitter is likely capable of more production than he has shown, most recently at Double-A Reading, but the absence of a challenge has likely held him back. Valent has solid knowledge of the strike zone and above average power potential, but has a tendency to attempt to pull outside pitches. Combined with his average, at best, speed, this makes him a constant double-play threat. If he learns to take the outside pitch to left field with some consistency, Valent could evolve into a .280-.300 hitter with 25 homer power and have a chance to start in Philly. Defensively, he has adequate range for a corner outfielder, and enough arm strength to play right field. If he had been challenged throughout his pro career, he'd be ready for the majors now. Instead, it will be off to Triple-A at age 24 in 2001. Valent will likely become a productive fourth outfielder for the Phils in 2002, and could start in left or right if anything happens to Pat Burrell or Bobby Abreu.

9 - OF Josue Perez - Perez, 22, was signed to an $825,000 free agent contract by the Phils in 1999 after it was ruled that he had illegally signed his original pro contract with the Dodgers. The 6'0", 180, righthanded hitter is a line drive hitter with a bit of gaps power who will need to significantly enhance his plate discipline to have a chance to develop into the top-of-the-order batter that the Phils envision. Perez' raw speed is well above average, but he needs to utilize it more efficiently. He needs to get better jumps and read pitchers better to become a true basestealing threat. Defensively, Perez' game is quite advanced. He gets excellent jumps on fly balls, has exceptional range in center field, and an above average throwing arm. Perez is not Reggie Taylor's equal as an overall prospect, but has a better chance of developing into a big league leadoff man. Perez should become at least a defensive replacement and backup outfielder at the major league level, and could arrive in late 2002. Watch his walk and extra-base hit totals carefully.

10 - SS Nick Punto - Punto, 22, was drafted on the 21st round in 1998. The 5'10", 170, switch-hitter is a Mickey Morandini play-alike. Before you scoff, consider that Morandini, who played shortstop in the minors, has made quite a bit of money in this game for the better part of a decade at the major league level. Punto puts the ball in play with consistency, will take a walk, slaps the ball to all fields, and is a fairly prolific basestealer, more because of technique than raw speed. He's a dirty uniform guy with only a little pop to the gaps, who must hit the ball on the ground more often to have a chance of surviving offensively in the major leagues. Defensively, Punto is sure-handed within his average range, and compensates for a lack of overpowering arm strength with a quick release. Look for Punto to get some reps at other infield positions at the Triple-A level in 2001 in preparation for his likely future as an all-purpose infield backup for the Phils, beginning in 2002. The Phils would be thrilled if they could get a Morandini-like career from Punto.

OTHER PROSPECTS

2B Marlon Anderson - Anderson is a fine a hitter with some extra base and home run power as well as very good speed. His erratic defense led to his return to Triple-A for the 2000 season even though he spent the entire 1999 season with the Phillies. He improved his defense last year and should be the leading candidate to start at second base for the Phillies this year if the organization doesn't keep him in the dog house.

RHP Nelson Figueroa - He is a 26-year-old control/finesse pitcher who has been traded twice in the last three years. In 2000, he was one of four players the Phillies obtained from Arizona for Curt Schilling. Figueroa has spent parts of the last three seasons at Triple-A Tucson. Between there and the Phils' Scranton farm, Figueroa was 13-7. He was 0-1 in three starts for the Diamondbacks. The slim 6'1" righty can throw four pitches for strikes, but he is around the plate so often that he gives up lots of home runs. He can become a number four or five starter.

OF Marlon Boyd - Boyd is an outstanding offensive player with power, speed and the ability to hit for average. He does strike out quite a bit, but for someone who produces like he has so far that won't make any difference. He hit .305 with 29 doubles, 13 triples, 17 home runs, 93 RBI and 41 steals at Low-A Piedmont last year. Normally a stat line won't show up in a scouting report, but it's hard not to be impressed by his production.

LHP Jason Brester - Brester has a live arm and a good breaking pitch, but for some reason his control was a big problem last year at Double-A, a level he was repeating from the year before. He has the stuff to be a major leaguer, though probably not a starter.

LHP Frank Brooks - Brooks has a chance to be pretty good in a couple of years. He's got good stuff, he throws strikes and he has the ability to strike hitters out when the situation is right. He's not overpowering, but does have a good fastball and a solid breaking pitch. He hit quite a few batters with pitches last year, which indicates that he's aggressive on the inside part of the plate.

RHP Mark Brownson - Brownson doesn't have great raw talent, but he does have an outstanding curveball at his disposal. He must work ahead in the count consistently to be successful because if he's throwing 2-0 or 3-1 fastballs he's getting hit hard. Brownson may not turn into a consistent major league starter, but could find a role as a reliever if that is the case.

RHP Brandon Duckworth - Duckworth is a bit of a sleeper prospect. He dominated the Double-A Eastern League last year and was considered one of the top five pitching prospects in the league, but because he only has an average fastball he's not considered a top of the line starter. He has an outstanding curveball and a solid changeup to go with good control and an abundance of composure. He moves his pitches around well and knows what he's doing out on the mound.

1B Nate Espy - Espy is an outstanding young hitter with power and patience. He hit .321 with 32 doubles, 21 home runs and 87 RBI while walking 101 times. That kind of production from such a young player isn't very common.

OF Alejandro Giron - Giron has the tools to be an offensive threat, but he must be more patient at the plate. His home run power didn't improve at High-A last year because of his lack of discipline, but the 30 doubles he hit demonstrate potential for more power in the future. He runs well, though he's not a great basestealer just yet, and could be a 20-20 man if he can learn what it means to take a pitch here and there.

C Russ Jacobson - Jacobson is a solid defensive catcher with exceptional power for such a young player. His patience is not what the Phillies would like and he strikes out quite a bit, but as long as he hits home runs and plays good defense it won't hold him back. The Phillies already have Mike Lieberthal at the major league level, but given his injury history and the fact that Jacobson still needs a couple of years time to develop.

2B-3B Rusty McNamara - McNamara put up really nice offensive numbers at Double-A last year, but he was repeating that level and should have shown that kind of improvement. He was considered a third baseman in past seasons, but played second, third and outfield during the 2000 season. He's got some pop, he makes consistent contact and showed he could drive in some runs as well. He doesn't run much and doesn't have a defined position, but his versatility and his bat could get him to the majors.

OF Jason Michaels - Michaels isn't a big-time prospect because he hasn't developed any power so far, but he's a good hitter with some power potential. He has managed to reach double-digits in home runs while pounding out a bunch of doubles, a sign of potential power. The one thing he lacks as a hitter is patience. If he ever becomes more selective at the plate, his batting average and power numbers will improve. He's also a good outfielder with the ability to play all three spots.

LHP Jimmy Osting - The Phillies got him, along with Bruce Chen, in the deal that sent Andy Ashby to Atlanta. Chen had a big impact at the major league level last year and Osting could soon join him there. His raw stuff isn't great, but he can be reasonably compared to Bruce Chen, using a slightly above average fastball, a curve and a change to go with good control. Osting had plenty of success at the Double-A level during 2000, so a move up to Triple-A seems like it would make sense.

PITTSBURGH PIRATES
ORGANIZATIONAL GRID

	AAA	AA	HI-A	LO-A
1B	Alex Hernandez - L - 23	Eddy Furniss - L - 24 Lee Evans - B - 22	Carlos Rivera - L - 22 Dan Meier - L - 22	Jeremy Cotten - R - 19 Matt Schneider - L - 22
2B	John Wehner - R - 33	Rico Washington - L - 22 Rob Mackowiak - L - 24	Jonathan Prieto - B - 20	Josh Bonifay - R - 21
SS	Abraham Nunez - B - 24 Jason Wood - R - 30	Jack Wilson - B - 22	Victor Gutierrez - R - 22 Ambioris Cleto - R - 20	Jose Castillo - R - 19
3B	Luis Figueroa - R - 26	Kevin Haverbusch - R - 24	Rolando Segura - R - 21 Luis Lorenzana - R - 21	Deivi Perez - R - 20 James Langston - B - 22
OF	Ray Montgomery - R - 30 Tike Redman - L - 23 Brent Brede - L - 28 Chad Hermansen - R - 22	Adam Hyzdu - R - 28 Garrett Long - R - 23 Derrick Lankford - L - 25 Darren Burton - B - 27 Jayson Bass - B - 24 Shaun Skrehot - R - 24 Keith Williams - R - 28	B.J. Barns - L - 22 Paul Weichard - B - 20 J.J. Davis - R - 21 Jay Hobbs - L - 25 Justin Martin - B - 24 Tracy Sanders - L - 30	Antonio Alvarez - R - 21 Jeremy Harts - B - 20 Jovanny Sosa - R - 20 Jason Landreth - R - 24 Aron Weston - L - 19
C	Tim Laker - R - 30 Craig Wilson - R - 23	Humberto Cota - R - 21	Yamid Haad - R - 22 Jeremy Sickles - R - 22	J.R. House - R - 20 Ronny Paulino - R - 19 Jose Hernandez - R - 19
SP	Jose Parra - R - 27 Travis Baptist - L - 28 Paul Ah Yat - L - 25 Sam McConnell - L - 24 Brian O'Connor - L - 23 Fred Rath - R - 27 Dan Serafini - L - 26	Steve Sparks - R - 25 John Grabow - L - 21 Joe Beimel - L - 23 Aaron France - R - 26 Wilson Guzman - L - 22	Clint Johnston - L - 23 Jason Haynie - L - 26 Franklin Bravo - R - 21 Kevin Pickford - L - 25 Geraldo Padua - R - 23 Mike Gonzalez - L - 22 Jose Lopez - R - 20 Neal McDade - R - 24 Larry Wimberly - L - 24	Jeff Bennett - R - 20 David Williams - L - 21 Bobby Bradley - R - 19 Luis Torres - R - 20 Greg Dukeman - R - 21 Justin Reid - R - 23 Landon Jacobsen - R - 21
CLOSER	Cory Bailey - R - 29	Brian Smith - R - 27 Brad Guy - R - 24 Matt Duff - R - 25	Tony Pavlovich - R - 25 Clint Chrysler - L - 24	Mike Bumatay - L - 20

PITTSBURGH PIRATES

Just as their farm system was beginning to thin out at the top end, the Pittsburgh Pirates reloaded at the bottom with a superb 1999 draft supplemented by the maturation of some youthful international free agent signees. If Pirates' fans are willing to wait a couple more years, payoff time could finally arrive.

Jeremy Cotten, 19, is the Bucs' foremost first base prospect. The 6'3", 226, righthanded hitter has a substantial power upside, but will need to monitor his conditioning closely to approach it. He has the ability to someday start in the major leagues, but has much to accomplish before doing so.

Rico Washington toiled at catcher, then third base and now second base in the last two seasons. He has a great eye at the plate, with a bit of gaps power. His versatility will get him to the major leagues, possibly by late 2001, but he will need to improve either his fielding or power stroke markedly to clinch a starting spot. Switch-hitter Jonathan Prieto is a spray hitter with decent speed and solid defensive ability. He doesn't have the bat for the majors, and will need to learn another position to have a chance to make it as a utilityman. Josh Bonifay has good power for a middle infielder, but needs to make a two-level jump and sustain his production in 2001 to be considered a viable prospect.

Jose Castillo, 19, is a multi-talented shortstop prospect who could eventually blossom into a major league star. He has an exciting power/speed upside for a middle infielder, and his speed makes him an above average baserunner and defender. Plate discipline is an issue, but for his age, he's extremely advanced. He's a couple of years away. The Bucs also added Jack Wilson, a former Cards' shortstop prospect, in a deadline deal for reliever Jason Christiansen. Wilson is a heady line drive hitter who gets his uniform dirty on a daily basis. He's a solid bat to eventually become a solid part-time big league contributor.

Kevin Haverbusch has a live line drive bat and can play multiple defensive positions, but has been marooned at the Double-A level for a while now. He still could develop into a viable big league backup, but it doesn't appear that it will happen in Pittsburgh.

Tike Redman got a brief glimpse of the major leagues in 2000, but didn't acquit himself too well during the regular Triple-A season. He's a smooth defensive outfielder who should be a decent top-of-the-order threat, but poor plate discipline has kept his on-base percentage down. He runs well and can play multiple outfield positions, and could fit as a deep major league reserve in 2001. Six-year minor league vet Garrett Long has good power and solid plate discipline, and his ability to play first base and the outfield make him a sleeper to snare a big league reserve job in the near term. Switch-hitter Paul Weichard, 20, has great speed and solid all-around tools, but hasn't been able to reach first base enough to project as a future major leaguer. Youth is on his side. J.J. Davis has massive power potential, but has been slow to address his primary weakness, poor plate discipline. The 6'6", 230, 1997 first round pick might be one of those players whose performance will improve as he rises through the ranks. 2001 will be a telling year that will likely determine whether his selection was a boom or bust.

The real fun went on at Low-A Hickory in 2000. Tony Alvarez, 21, emerged as an exciting power/speed phenomenon. He too needs to work on his plate discipline, but a successful two-level jump in 2001 would mark him as a likely future big league starter. Switch-hitter Jeremy Harts is a raw power/speed prospect whose plate discipline is arguably worse than Alvarez'. He could make a major step forward in High-A ball in 2001. Jovanny Sosa, 20, can hit the ball a mile, and took baby steps forward in his approach at the plate last season at Low-A Hickory. If the 6'2", 207, righthanded hitter can hit for a passable average at a higher level next season, he'll be on track to someday contribute at the big league level. Lefthanded hitter Aron Weston is the baby of the group at 19, and has game-breaking speed and a consistent line drive bat. The 6'5", 173, 1999 third round draftee could also add power as he physically matures and might someday be a fixture in the upper portion of the major league lineup.

Craig Wilson is a hitter first and a catcher second, but his power bat just might earn him a supporting role in the major leagues soon. His ability to also play first base enhances his value. He'll battle Keith Osik for the big league backup job in 2001. Humberto Cota has the all-around ability to be a starting major league catcher, and might be ready in a year. He's extremely durable and possesses solid defensive skills, and could evolve into a .270 hitter with 10-15 homer power. If Jason Kendall isn't inked to a long-term deal, Cota will likely succeed him in Pittsburgh. Lee Evans, 22, has a surprising power/speed package for a catcher and is an impressive athlete, but his inability to crash Double-A by now isn't a promising sign. He could emerge as a future candidate for a major league backup role with a strong 2001 campaign in the upper minors. 1999 fifth round pick J.R. House was one of the top breakout prospects of 2000. The 6'2", 215, righthanded hitter made a smooth transition to the wooden bat, hitting for average and power in the Low-A South Atlantic League. Defensively, first base might be the best fit, though he's decent behind the plate. He'll be a major league starter, and possibly a star, down the road. Ronny Paulino, 19, stands a durable 6'3", 190, and has swung a consistent line drive bat thus far in his brief pro career. House is keeping him in the shadows for now, but if Paulino proves able to carry the full-time catching load somewhere in the system in 2001, he too will certify himself as a future big leaguer.

Most of the real pitching action went on at the bottom end of the Pirates' system in 2000. Their best upper minor league pitching prospect is lefty John Grabow. He held his own despite making a daunting two-level jump to Double-A Altoona in 2000. He needs to be a bit more aggressive early in the count for him to approach the lofty strikeout totals he posted in the lower minors. His lack of a big-time heater might limit him to a swingman role in the majors. He could arrive by 2002. Lefty Wilson Guzman, 22, thrived after being shifted from the bullpen to the rotation. The 5'11", 199, southpaw has precise command that offsets relatively ordinary peak velocity. He averaged seven innings per start down the stretch at the Double-A level, a strong indication that he could eventually be used in a variety of major league roles. Bobby Bradley, 19, the Pirates' 1999 first round pick emerged as one of the best pitching prospects in the game last season. He completely

overmatched Low-A hitters with his diverse, powerful repertoire and ability to consistently throw quality strikes. He's on the express train to the majors, and should arrive in early 2002. Righty Luis Torres, also 19, struggled through an uneven Low-A season, but likely has the best fastball in the system. He needs some mechanical tweaking and must build strength, but he still projects as a solid future major leaguer, either as a mid-rotation starter or closer. Lefty David Williams and righty Jeff Bennett filled out a superior Low-A rotation. They were drafted on the 17th and 19th rounds, respectively in the 1998 draft, but now must both be seen as potential future major league contributors because of their respective solid approaches on the mound plus expert command, offsetting their relatively average stuff. If either can make a Double-A impact in 2001, their potential eventual major league roles could expand.

TOP TEN PROSPECTS

1 - RHP Bobby Bradley - Bradley, 19, the Pirates' 1999 first round draft pick, appeared set to rack up historic numbers at Low-A Hickory after a dozen brilliant starts (8-2, 2.14, 115/21 K/BB in 80 IP), but was shut down in midseason with a sprained elbow ligament. The 6'1", 170, righthander combines a live low 90s fastball and an overpowering curveball that was rated the best breaking pitch in the South Atlantic League by its managers. In fact, it might already be one of the best in all of pro ball, including the majors. Bradley fills out an impressive repertoire with a slider and changeup, both of which could also become plus pitches. Bradley's command and mound presence are also exceptional for a young pitcher. He throws all of his pitches to precise spots consistently, and his ability to get ahead of hitters and keep his pitch count down suggests that he'll be a complete game guy down the road. If he's healthy, that is. Bradley needs to come back 100% healthy in 2001 to stay on the fast track. If he dominates right away, he'll be on track for early 2003 entry into the Pirates' rotation, which he will eventually lead.

3 - SS Jose Castillo - Castillo, 19, exploded onto the scene with an excellent all-around season at Low-A Hickory in the South Atlantic League. The 6'0", 180, righthanded hitter has a live line drive bat with substantial gaps power for a middle infielder, and appears to be rapidly adding strength as he physically matures. His plate discipline needs quite a bit of work, however, for him to be able to perform similarly at higher levels. He's not a speedburner, but has above average speed and excellent baserunning instincts that make him a high-percentage 20 steal threat. Defensively, Castillo's range is a bit above average, but his powerful arm, rated the best infield arm in the South Atlantic League by its managers, is clearly his foremost tool. He needs to become more consistent on the routine play, but so does every other teenage shortstop prospect on the planet. It is possible that Castillo will eventually outgrow shortstop and slide over to third base, where his relative offensive worth would diminish a bit. Regardless, Castillo is a high-ceiling power/speed prospect who projects as a future major league standout, and could arrive in late 2003.

2 - C J.R. House - House, 20, was the Pirates' fifth round draft pick in 1999. The 6'2", 215, righthanded hitter adjusted to the wooden bat with ease, hitting for extreme average and power in the Low-A South Atlantic League, though his season was shortened by a bout with mononucleosis. House has considerable raw physical strength, and generates extreme power to all fields with his short, compact stroke. He hit breaking pitches much better last year than he had in rookie ball, and his batting average exploded upward as a result. A naturally aggressive hitter, House needs to be more patient early in the count, or else could be taken advantage of by the more polished upper level hurlers. Defensively, House is a hard-working, athletic catcher, but likely lacks the arm strength necessary to remain at the position much longer. Plus, the Pirates don't want to dampen his offensive performance with the physical demands of catching every day. Look for House to move to first base for good fairly soon. House might be challenged with a two-level jump to the Double-A level in 2001. If he maintains his offensive output, he'll be on track for an everyday job in Pittsburgh by Opening Day 2003.

4 - OF Tony Alvarez - Alvarez, 21, is an interesting power/speed prospect who exploded onto the scene with an excellent all-around campaign at Low-A Hickory. The 6'1", 202, righthanded hitter is extremely aggressive in all facets of the game. He's a fairly wild swinger with a quick bat and substantial gaps power to all fields. He could evolve into a 25-30 homer threat if he learned to work deeper counts and saw more fastballs as a result. Currently, he too often gets himself out on bad breaking pitches. Alvarez runs fairly well, but isn't as speedy as his prolific basestealing totals would suggest. He's an instinctive baserunner who reads pitchers well and gets good jumps on a consistent basis. Defensively, Alvarez was moved from third base to the outfield, his likely long-

term home, last season. Though a case could be made or him playing any of the three outfield spots down the line, it's most likely that he'll wind up in an outfield corner. Alvarez could be challenged with a two-level jump to Double-A in 2001. If he can handle that without a significant decrease in production, then he's on his way to a starting big league role by sometime in 2003. At worst, he projects as a multi-positional part-time major leaguer, playing both outfield and infield positions.

5 - OF J.J. Davis - Davis, 21, was the Pirates' first round draft pick in 1997. The 6'6", 230, righthanded hitter clearly has the raw ability to reside at the very top of this list, but his inability, or unwillingness, to develop even a modest level of plate discipline has dropped his stock. Davis has raw power, and is capable of driving tape-measure homers to any part of the field. High-A Carolina League managers recognized him as the circuit's premier power prospect despite his uneven 2000 campaign. However, he routinely expands his strike zone to an unacceptable size, going after high fastballs and outside breaking balls on a regular basis. He struck out in nearly 40% of his at bats last season, way too high for someone not delivering Russell Branyan home run totals. Davis runs well, but has never fully incorporated his speed into his offensive game. Defensively, he has more than adequate range for right field, and above average arm strength. Davis needs to smooth out the rough edges in his game in the near-term to reach his ultimate potential, but has shown little sign of doing so. 2001 is a pivotal year for this potential future middle-of-the-order fixture.

6 - C Humberto Cota - Cota, 21, was acquired from the Devil Rays in 1999 in the Jose Guillen deal. The 6'0", 175, righthanded hitter is a polished defensive receiver, but lacks overpowering arm strength. He moves well behind the plate, is extremely durable, and controls the running game despite his average arm strength. He gets rid of the ball quickly and is a commanding field presence. Cota has significant offensive potential for his position, but his progress has been limited by poor plate discipline. He has a live line drive bat with 30 double, 10 homer power, but would have trouble hitting .230 in the majors today because of his penchant for burying himself in the count on bad pitches. He runs quite well for a catcher, though he isn't a significant stolen base threat. Cota's future in Pittsburgh hinges on the status of Jason Kendall, whom the Pirates might not be able to afford for much longer unless their new stadium is a rousing success. If Kendall goes, Cota will get his job in 2002, and projects as at least an average all-around big league starter.

7 - OF Aron Weston - Weston, 19, is a bundle of potential who was drafted in the third round in 1999. The 6'5", 173, lefthanded hitter has as much basestealing potential as any minor league outfielder, combining outstanding raw speed with solid baserunning instincts for a youngster. Though he has yet to show a power stroke in his brief pro career, Weston is far from a finished product physically, and could add another 20 pounds or so of muscle mass. At this point, he's a tweener who doesn't make consistent enough contact to be a top-of-the-order hitter, and doesn't show enough power to be a middle-of-the-order threat. For now, the Pirates will just run him out there and see which of his traits develop more fully. Defensively, Weston has enough range to play a credible major league center field, but needs to run more consistent routes to fly balls. His arm strength is adequate. Weston might return to Low-A ball in 2001, but would likely play his way out of there quickly. He won't get to the majors before 2004, and much needs to happen for him to get there. Keep an eye on his all-around numbers to determine whether he becomes merely a speed player (most likely), a power/speed stud (not that likely) or a power prospect (least likely).

8 - LHP John Grabow - Grabow, 21, was drafted on the third round in 1997. The 6'2", 189, southpaw made a daunting two-level jump to Double-A Altoona last season, and though he wasn't terribly effective, lived to tell about it. Though his mainstream stats were poor, his ability to put up a 2:1 strikeout/walk ratio as one of the younger hurlers at that level speaks well for his future. Grabow's fastball only reaches the upper 80s, and he needs to place it precisely and mix it well with his curve and changeup on the edges of the strike zone to be effective. His 164/32 Low-A strikeout/walk ratio in 156 1/3 innings in 1999 is living proof that he can do it if he maintains a consistently aggressive approach. He's about fully developed physically and therefore unlikely to add peak velocity, so his improvement will likely come via experience and the added confidence upper level success brings. Look for Grabow to fare much better in a second tour of the Eastern League in 2001, and possibly advance to Triple-A late in the year. Grabow is a potential future major league mid-rotation guy who should arrive in late 2002. At worst, he might develop into a situational bullpen lefty.

9 - OF Jovanny Sosa - Sosa, 20, is a high-ceiling power prospect who made significant strides in his second season at Low-A Hickory. The 6'2", 207, righthanded hitter has explosive power from gap-to-gap, but needs to learn to work the count better in order to see more fastballs and maximize his output. Though his strikeout/walk ratio changed little from 1999 to 2000, he made impressive strides in selecting the appropriate pitches to chase in an at bat, and raised his batting average significantly. However, he will need to make substantial further strides, or else risk being eaten up by higher level hurlers, with their superior command and more diverse repertoires. He needs to maximize his power output, as that is his only noticeable tool. His speed, defensive range and throwing arm are all average at best, and are likely to limit him to left field as he advances. Sosa has about a 10% chance to evolve into a major league home run force, more likely, he'll become a major league power bat off of the bench, and could arrive in 2004.

10 - SS Jack Wilson - Wilson, 22, was the Cards' 1998 ninth round draftee, and was acquired by the Pirates at last year's trading deadline for lefthanded reliever Jason Christiansen. The 6'0", 170, switch-hitter is a scrappy player who gets the most out of fairly ordinary tools. Offensively, he's a line drive hitter with a bit of gaps power who rarely strikes out. However, he needs to improve his subpar plate discipline or else run the risk of being buried in the No. 8 hole in the batting order at higher levels. Though he lacks explosive speed, he is an intelligent baserunner who studies pitchers and gets above average jumps. Defensively, Wilson has only slightly above average range, but has a plus arm and is extremely consistent on the routine play. Prior to his trade last season, Double-A Texas League managers recognized him as the best defensive shortstop prospect in the circuit. Wilson is a solid Triple-A season away from contending for the starting major league shortstop job in Pittsburgh. Though he doesn't project as a future All-Star, he could be a solid long-term solution at the position. At worst, he'll be a useful utilityman in the majors.

OTHER PROSPECTS

RHP Bronson Arroyo - Arroyo doesn't have the stuff of a top of the rotation starter, but he could be a nice fourth or fifth starter with just a little more work. He has an average fastball and average offspeed stuff, but he gets by because he keeps the ball down in the zone and he throws strikes. He's still relatively young at 23, especially since he spent half of last season at Triple-A, and he could reach the majors shortly.

C Lee Evans - Evans has good speed and a little pop for a catcher. He's not a power hitter, so to speak, but he does have the ability to reach double-digits in both home runs and steals. He also strikes out quite a bit and could stand to be more relaxed at the plate. His defense is acceptable behind the plate and he can also play some first base.

1B Eddy Furniss - Furniss has power potential, though you wouldn't know it by looking at his numbers from last year. He experienced some growing pains in terms of hitting the long ball in his first shot at Double-A, but he can still be a 25-30 home run guy in the future. The other thing Furniss has going for him is good knowledge of the strike zone. He needs some work, but he can make big strides this year.

3B Kevin Haverbusch - At 24 years-old, Haverbusch is at a crossroads in his career. His performance at the Single-A level a few years ago opened eyes and he demonstrated the ability to be a good hitter with some power potential. The 2000 season set him back a bit as he played just 43 games, batting .279 with five home runs and 18 errors at third base. He must have a big year in 2001 to reopen some eyes.

1B-OF Alex Hernandez - Hernandez looks like he can be a pretty good hitter if he can improve his patience. He's not an incredibly powerful hitter, but he does have double-digit home run ability and he hits a lot of doubles. He doesn't walk a lot and strikeouts are a problem for him when he faces older pitchers, but he does have a little speed. He also has a nice looking swing and he could be a late bloomer along the lines of Luis Gonzalez.

LHP Sam McConnell - McConnell is a finesse pitcher who could also be called a "crafty lefthander." He barely throws hard enough to break a pane of glass, but he throws strikes, moves the fastball around and has a good curveball. He shredded the Double-A Eastern League during the first half of the 2000 season and struggled after a promotion to Triple-A but that's not a big surprise. He needs to learn the league before having success and he will probably struggle in his early major league appearances. He's not a top of the rotation guy, but could work out as a serviceable fourth or fifth starter.

OF Tike Redman - Redman can really run, but he's got a bit of work to do as a hitter. Against Triple-A hitters last year his ability to draw walks dropped off and he was unable to get on base consistently. He has some gap power, but someone without home run power needs to find ways to get on base more often. He also struggled on the bases, getting thrown out attempting to steal 18 times in 42 tries. He'll need to have a much better year in 2001 if he wants a shot at the majors in the near future.

RHP Justin Reid - Reid has a live arm, excellent control and knows what he's doing out on the mound. Sally League hitters managed just a .223 average against him last year and he struck out 176 while walking just 30 in 170 innings. He may not continue to rack up strikeouts at that kind of a pace when he gets to the upper levels, but anyone who embarrasses hitters like he did in 2000 deserves to be noticed.

2B Rico Washington - Washington has played catcher, third base and second base over the past three seasons. It looks like second base will be his future home and he should show improvement once he settles in. Washington has good gap power right now with the ability to develop a little more home run power in the future. He has demonstrated above average patience at the plate and if he can just refine his hitting a little he can be pretty good.

LHP Dave Williams - The 21year-old lefty is a power pitcher with a live fastball and good breaking pitch. He's been able to punch out Low-A hitters at an extremely high pace (10.2 per nine innings) and he's also been able to throw strikes consistently. For someone his age to have the ability to strike hitters out without walking a lot of batters is commendable.

C Craig Wilson - Wilson has a lot of power for a catcher and considering that he's just 23 years old, he probably has quite a bit of major league time in his future. He'll need to improve his defense, including his ability to catch potential basestealers, if he wants to play regularly in the majors, but if he continues to hit for power he can at least play part-time. He strikes out a lot and doesn't walk much, but 33 home runs at Triple-A is hard to ignore, especially from a catcher.

ST. LOUIS CARDINALS
ORGANIZATIONAL GRID

	AAA	AA	HI-A	LO-A
1B	Larry Sutton - L - 30	Mike Mitchell - L - 27 Eddie Pearson - B - 26	Troy Farnsworth - R - 24 Billy Deck - L - 23	Chris Duncan - L - 19 Travis Bailey - R - 23
2B	Stubby Clapp - B - 27	Alex Eckelman - R - 25 T.J. Maier - R - 25	Rob Macrory - R - 25 Bo Hart - R - 23	Danilo Araujo - R - 23 Chase Voshell - R - 21
SS	Luis Garcia - R - 25 Pablo Martinez - B - 31	Jason Woolf - B - 23 Nate Tebbs - B - 27	Jason Bowers - R - 22 Damon Thames - R - 23	Ramon Carvajal - B - 19
3B	Lou Lucca - R - 29	Chris Haas - L - 23	Albert Pujols - R - 20 Ryan Darr - R - 22 Jose Nunez - R - 21	Gustavo Escobar - R - 20
OF	Ernie Young - R - 30 Mark Little - R - 27 Darrell Whitmore - L - 31 Steve Bieser - B - 32 Thomas Howard - B - 35 Juan Munoz - L - 26	Cordell Farley - R - 27 Luis Saturria - R - 23 Bill Ortega - R - 24 Andy Bevins - R - 24 Joe Secoda - R - 22	Esix Snead - B - 24 Troy McNaughton - L - 25 Miguel Diaz - R - 22 Darren Dyt - L - 24 Brandon Copeland - R - 23	Johnny Hernandez - B - 20 Tim Lemon - R - 19 Charles Williams - B - 22 Covelli Crisp - B - 20
C	Rick Wilkins - L - 33 Keith McDonald - R - 27	Matt Garrick - R - 24 David Benham - R - 24	Kevin Nykoluk - R - 25 Jovany William - R - 23	Greg Clark - R - 23 Gabe Johnson - R - 20
SP	Luther Hackman - R - 25 Mark Thompson - R - 29 Britt Reames - R - 26 Bud Smith - L - 20 Clint Weibl - R - 25	Chad Hutchinson - R - 23 Patrick Coogan - R - 24 Jason Karnuth - R - 24 Adam Benes - R - 27 Lance Franks - R - 24 Otoniel Lanfranco - R - 23 Josh Pearce - R - 22	Steve Stemle - R - 23 Les Walrond - L - 23 Chance Caple - R - 21 Cristobal Correa - R - 20 Ryan Christenson - R - 23 B.R. Cook - R - 22	Cheyenne Janke - R - 23 Kevin Sprague - L - 23 Nick Stocks - R - 21 Trevor Sansom - R - 24 Shaun Stokes - R - 21 Franklin Tejada - R - 20
CLOSER	Gene Stechschulte - R - 26 Rick Heiserman - R - 27	Corey Avrard - R - 23 John Ambrose - R - 25	Jason Marr - R - 24	Scotty Layfield - R - 23 Chad Yates - R - 23

ST. LOUIS CARDINALS

The Cards have adopted a "win now" organizational strategy with a focus upon drafting high-ceiling, supposedly unsignable prospects like Rick Ankiel, J.D. Drew and Chad Hutchinson, and then advancing them to the majors as quickly as possible. On the whole, this approach has served them well, but has left the system light in terms of prospect quantity.

Chris Haas is a power prospect who has seemingly stalled at the Triple-A level. He has a legitimate power bat and a decent eye, but doesn't meet the high offensive standards set for major league corner infield starters. He's no threat to the Mark McGwires and Fernando Tatises of this world, but his ability to play both corners gives him a chance to stick in the majors as a backup. Keep an eye on 1999 first round pick Chris Duncan, a 6'5", 210, lefthanded hitter who showed some gaps power at Low-A Peoria. Some of his doubles should evolve into homers as Duncan, 19, advances. He's a sleeper to make a big move in 2001.

At second base, switch-hitter Ramon Carvajal, 19, is the only player with even a remote chance of making a big league impact. He runs well and has a bit of gaps power, but would have to dramatically enhance his offensive game and also learn another position to have a chance of being a backup in the majors.

Shortstop Jason Woolf was once considered the Cards' shortstop of the future, but his development has slowed in recent seasons. The 6'1", 170, switch-hitter's offensive game hasn't developed as expected, though he does have good speed and plate discipline and once appeared to have power potential. He has a cannon arm, which remains his best hope to get noticed for a big league bench spot. He's a big league longshot.

Third baseman Albert Pujols established himself as a legitimate candidate to eventually start in the majors with a fine Low-A season. He makes consistent contact, and has potentially explosive, Fernando Tatis-like power. He might be ready for a bold two-level jump in 2001, and will challenge for a major league job by late 2002.

2000 Double-A regulars Luis Saturria, 23, and Bill Ortega, 24, are the Cards' most advanced outfield prospects. Saturria is a lithe, 6'4", 165, righthanded hitter with a 20/20 power/speed upside. His plate discipline is poor, however, he'd be little better than a .200 major league hitter today. At best, he's a future big league backup. Ortega has a higher upside, but was a little old to just be reaching the Double-A level last season. He's a natural hitter who smokes line drives to all fields, and has 15 homer power. He's unlikely to evolve into a big league starter, but is an excellent bet to be a valuable big league backup quite soon. 1998 second round pick Tim Lemon, 19, has exceptional tools, but is quite raw. The 6'1", 180, righthanded hitter too often retires himself on bad pitches at this stage. Youth is on his side, but significant progress must be made in 2001 for him to considered a viable prospect.

The Cards have no quality catching prospects.

Righthander Luther Hackman, 25, is a bit old to be considered a true prospect, but his ability to keep his hard fastball low in the strike zone gives him a chance to be a serviceable major league middleman. Lefthander Robert "Bud" Smith, 20, has surpassed Chad Hutchinson as the Cards' best pitching prospect. The 6'0", 170, southpaw doesn't have a top-shelf fastball, but he keeps hitters off balance and places the ball expertly. His strikeout rate actually improved when he reached Double-A, an indicator of future big league success. He'll reach the majors by early 2002 at the latest, and will stay awhile. Hutchinson, 23, slid backward because of poor command last season, His raw stuff is at times overpowering, but it simply takes him to too many pitches to get through innings. He has the stamina to be a major league starter, but might not have the consistency. A shift to short relief could help. 1999 first rounder Chance Caple, 21, showed excellent command at High-A Potomac, but needs to develop a true strikeout pitch to reach his potential. The 6'6", 215, righty also needs to toughen up a bit with men on base. He has a major league mid-rotation upside. 6'1", 175, righty Cristobal Correa, 20, has a smooth motion and places the ball on the edges of the strike zone quite regularly. If he experiences Double-A success in 2001 at age 21, he'll start to work his way into the Cards' plans for their future rotation. The Cards advanced 1999 second round pick Josh Pearce, 22, rapidly in his first full pro season. His limited repertoire held his strikeout rate down at Double-A Arkansas, but he could make upper level noise if he improves his breaking stuff. He too might be suited for a shift to the bullpen in the intermediate term. 1999 first round pick Nick Stocks, 21, was a bit of a disappointment at Low-A Peoria. His stuff was simply too good for him to allow a hit per inning at that level at that age. His command is good, but he needs to generate more movement on his fastball and curve and learn to change speeds better. His upside parallels Caple's, but Stocks has fallen behind for now.

TOP TEN PROSPECTS

1 - 3B Albert Pujols - Pujols, 20, was the Cards' 13th round draft pick in 1999. The 6'3", 210, righthanded hitter didn't play pro ball in 1999 after holding out for a higher bonus, and then paid off in a big way with a spectacular season at Low-A Peoria. He displayed excellent all-around offensive skills, making consistent contact and driving the ball for distance to all fields. Once he begins to work the count a little better, he could blossom into a legitimate triple crown threat at higher minor league levels, and a future .300-30-100 major league force. Defensively, Pujols possesses exceptional first-step quickness, above average range and a cannon-like throwing arm. Midwest League managers certainly were wowed by Pujols' performance, recognizing him as the best batting prospect, best defensive third base prospect, and best infield arm in the circuit. Pujols could be ready for a Double-A challenge in 2001. He'll likely by ready to challenge for the Cards' third base job in 2003, and could develop into a future All-Star caliber performer.

2 - LHP Bud Smith - Smith, 20, was the Cards' fourth round draft pick in 1998. The 6'0", 170, southpaw evokes images of a young Tom Glavine, combining deceptively good stuff with impeccable command and a steely mound demeanor. Smith has knifed through the Cards' system quickly, dominating at each level, even in a handful of late 2000 starts at Triple-A Memphis. He combines a 90 MPH fastball with an above average curveball and changeup, and consistently gets ahead of hitters by throwing all of the above on the corners. Smith maintains low pitch counts and figures to be a complete game threat in the major leagues despite his lack of size. Last season, he became the first Texas League pitcher in 39 years to throw a pair of no-hitters in the same year, no small feat, especially for a control pitcher. The Cards are pretty well set for major league starting pitching, so there's no need to rush Smith. He'll start 2001 back at Triple-A, but will be ready if anyone falters. He projects as a strong number two or three starter over the long haul in St. Louis.

3 - RHP Chad Hutchinson - Hutchinson, 23, was the Cards' second round pick in 1998, a former Stanford quarterback lured away to baseball by first round money. The 6'5", 220, righthander was once considered among the foremost pitching prospects in the game, but he slid backward last season due to a total loss of control, especially at Triple-A Memphis early in the year. Hutchinson relies primarily on hard stuff; his fastball routinely reaches the mid 90s, and is mixed with a hard slider that is almost as fast as some pitchers' heaters. He was unable to throw either pitch for strikes early in the count with any level of consistency last season, largely due to mechanical imperfections. Even after he was sent back to Double-A Arkansas, a level that a player of his pedigree should have mastered by now, Hutchinson racked up high pitch counts and struggled to keep his club in the game for five innings. To excel as a starter, he will need to both significantly enhance his command and probably add a third, slower pitch. However, he would seem to be a natural for a shift to the bullpen, where his fastball/slider combo could make him a lethal once-around-the-order closer. It could all come together fast for Hutchinson in that role and a 2001 advance to the bigs can't be ruled out.

4 - OF Bill Ortega - Ortega, 24, is a Cuban defector signed by the Cards as a free agent in 1997. The 6'4", 205, righthanded hitter put it all together with the bat last season at Double-A Arkansas, learning to pull inside pitches for distance for the first time in his career. Ortega has a picturesque swing and makes authoritative line drive contact to all fields. He rarely strikes out, and his new found power potential fills out a high-impact package. He does have a tendency to swing at bad pitches, and won't hit .300 at the major league level unless he improves his patience. He has average speed, but is no threat as a basestealer. Defensively, Ortega has better than adequate range for a right fielder, plus a strong throwing arm, and was recognized as the best defensive outfield prospect in the Texas League by its managers. Ortega, whose fine 2000 season was shortened by a wrist injury, has always been a bit old for his level, and might be ready for a challenge. Don't be surprised if he finds himself in the outfield rotation in St. Louis by midseason. He'll be a solid platooner in the short term, and could evolve into an everyday .300 hitter.

5 - RHP Cristobal Correa - Correa, 20, is a Venezuelan 1998 free agent signee who came out of nowhere to shine as one of the younger regular starting pitchers in the High-A Florida State League last season. The 6'1", 175, righthanded hurler combines a live high 80s fastball with a sharp curveball that was rated as the best breaking pitch in the circuit by FSL managers. His changeup is improving, and could develop into an out pitch against lefties. Correa has a tendency to try to throw the perfect pitch every time, leading to relatively high pitch counts and walk per inning totals. He's almost fully physically developed, and won't add much more peak velocity. However, experience and mechanical fine-tuning should result in more first-pitch strikes and lower walk totals as he develops. At best, Correa could evolve into a mid-rotation starter with an estimated major league arrival date of mid 2003. If his repertoire doesn't sufficiently widen, he could be an effective situational reliever.

6 - RHP Chance Caple - Caple, 21, was the Cards' first round draft pick in 1999. The 6'6", 215, righthander combines a low 90s fastball with a potentially above average curveball and changeup, and consistently throws all of his pitches for strikes. However, there are issues that need to be addressed for him to approach his significant potential. His mechanics are fairly uneven; his fastball's peak velocity can swing wildly from start to start, and none of his pitches move very much. He is not a particularly good pitcher with men on base. Approximately 40% of the runners who reached base against him scored last season. Caple needs to be more aggressive on the mound, and needs to develop one of his breaking pitches into a true out pitch against lefties in order to make a major move. Caple will likely start 2001 at the Double-A level, and will struggle there unless he addresses his shortcomings. He'll eventually get it together, and could slide into the low end of the Cards' rotation by early 2003.

7 - RHP Nick Stocks - Stocks, 21, was the Cards' supplemental first round draft pick in 1999. Thought to be a polished college prospect who would rifle through the system, the 6'2", 185, righthander instead struggled at times as one of the older pitching prospects in the Low-A Midwest League. His stuff is solid. He combines a low 90s fastball with a hard curve, and is developing his changeup into a viable third pitch. He rarely walks hitters, but like Caple, often catches too much of the plate with his

strikes, and mystifyingly struggles with men on base. With his all-around package, Stocks should have owned the Midwest League last season. Don't be surprised if the Cards challenge him with a two-level jump to Double-A in 2001 to see if he can step back onto the fast track. Stocks is yet another potential future mid-rotation major league starter creeping through the Cards' system. He too could be ready by the end of 2003.

8 - 1B Chris Duncan - Duncan, 19, was also a Cards' supplemental first round draft pick in 1999. The son of Cards' pitching coach Dave Duncan, the 6'5", 210, lefthanded hitter was one of the youngest everyday players in the Low-A Midwest League last season. He overcame a slow start to put up respectable all-around offensive numbers in his first full pro campaign. Duncan showed exceptional power to the gaps at Peoria, which should translate into 20-plus homer totals at higher levels as he physically matures and improves his approach at the plate. Currently, Duncan swings at almost everything, cutting down the number of fastballs he sees and minimizing his batting average and power output. Defensively, Duncan moves pretty well for a big man and projects as an above average first baseman. It remains to be seen whether Duncan will be able to meet the high offensive standards set for starting major league first sackers. If he can bat .280 with 15 homers and an improved strikeout/walk ratio at the High-A level in 2001, he'll be on track for a crack at the big league job in 2004.

9 - OF Luis Saturria - Saturria, 23, has exciting raw skills, but has been fairly slow to address the weaker areas of his game. The 6'2", 165, righthanded hitter can flat out fly. He was recognized as the fastest baserunner in the Double-A Texas League by its managers last season. Saturria also possesses well above average extra-base power for his size. However, he has not been able to fully incorporate his speed into his offensive game - he's never stolen more than 26 bases in a season, and his career success rate is below 70%. Saturria is a dead fastball hitter with relatively poor plate discipline, which isn't exactly the formula for upper level success. He's a fairly easy mark for quality breaking stuff, and showed only marginal improvement in his offensive approach in his second Double-A campaign last year. Saturria has well above average defensive range and arm strength, and would be a fit in either center or right field at the major league level. It's unlikely that he'll polish his offensive game enough to be an everyday major leaguer, but his breadth of skills will likely make him a useful backup outfielder in the bigs. He could arrive in 2002.

10 - OF Tim Lemon - This is purely a play on potential. Lemon, 19, is a raw power/speed prospect who has done himself in thus far in his pro career by swinging at virtually every pitch thrown to him. The 6'1", 180, righthanded hitter has shown the ability to drive a mistake fastball a long way, but has rarely given opposing pitchers the opportunity to make that mistake. He has well above average speed, and his approach on the bases improved somewhat last season after a brutal 16 for 32 stolen base performance in rookie ball in 1999. The 1998 second round draft pick is the nephew of former major league standout Chet Lemon, so he'll have a seasoned ear to chew on during the offseason. It's just a hunch, but don't be surprised if Lemon fares much better in a second Low-A season in 2001. He's a sleeper prospect who could be banging on the major league door by late 2004, where he could be an interesting part-timer or bench player.

OTHER PROSPECTS

OF Andy Bevins - Bevins has outstanding power and is becoming a much better hitter quite rapidly. Strikeouts have been a problem for him throughout his career, but if he hits 25-plus home runs and drives in runs the Cardinals will deal with the whiffs. He doesn't run particularly well and isn't know for his defense in the outfield, but he's a power hitter and that will get him chances, especially if he hits over .300 as he did at Double-A last year.

1B-3B Troy Farnsworth - Farnsworth is a power prospect who strikes out a ton. He has very little patience and is probably much better off at first base than at third. If he can be more disciplined at the plate 30-plus home runs would be a realistic goal. Last year at High-A he hit 23 homers and drove in 113 runs.

3B Chris Haas - Haas has plenty of power and a strong arm, but the rest of his game lags behind. He's an impatient hitter who strikes out a ton and who struggles against more experienced pitchers. He spent a large part of the 2000 season back at Double-A, which has to be considered a bad sign after he had spent a good bit of time at Triple-A before. Unless he makes significant progress as a hitter soon, Haas may wind up stuck in the minors.

RHP Britt Reames - Reames came on very strong near the end of the 2000 season and performed so well with the Cardinals in September that they kept him on their playoff roster. He has a chance to be either a starter or reliever over the long haul, but he's been a starter to this point in his career. Reames has a low to mid 90s fastball that really moves and he has a good, hard slider. He was never intimidated by major league hitters during the regular season and he was one of the Cardinals' most effective pitchers in the post-season. It wouldn't be a surprise if he were to wind up in the Cardinals' rotation in this year.

OF Esix Snead - Snead, 24, is a switch-hitter who runs like the wind. He stole 109 bases at High-A last year, but was older than most players in the league and will have to prove he can do that against better catchers. The thing that makes him worth noting, other than his phenomenal speed, is his patience at the plate. He drew 72 walks and got on base at a .340 clip despite a .235 batting average. If he can become a little better hitter, he'll have a major league future, even if it is as a fourth outfielder.

LHP Les Walrond - Walrond, 23, performed exceptionally well at High-A last year and that's not surprising given his age and his above average stuff. He has a live arm and he throws strikes; always a good combination. He struck out 153 batters in 151 innings last year, allowing 134 hits and 54 walks during the 2000 season.

RHP Clint Weibl - Weibl has been slow to develop, but a strong season at Triple-A last year makes him a candidate for major league duty in the near future. He's not overpowering, but has an above average fastball, and he's got above average control as well. He moves his fastball around well and his pitches have life to them as evidenced by the fact that Triple-A PCL hitters only batted .226 against him.

SS Jason Woolf - Woolf has all the physical tools he'll ever need to be a successful major league shortstop, but he hasn't figured out how to best put them to use just yet. He's got some pop in his bat and excellent speed, but he's not able to get on base enough to make good use of it. Defensively, Woolf has a tremendous arm and decent range, though he lacks consistency. He's still young and has a high upside, but he needs to show something this year.

SAN DIEGO PADRES
ORGANIZATIONAL GRID

	AAA	AA	HI-A	LO-A
1B	Gabe Alvarez - R - 26 John Scheschuk - L - 23	Kevin Eberwein - R - 23 Ricky Magdaleno - R - 25	Graham Koonce - L - 25	
2B	Ralph Milliard - R - 26	John Powers - L - 26 Robbie Kent - R - 26	Jason Dunaway - R - 23 Clay Snellgrove - R - 25 Ben Risinger - R - 22	Brian Ward - R - 22
SS	Kevin Nicholson - B - 24	Julius Matos - R - 25	Cristian Berroa - B - 21	Jason Moore - B - 22 Cesar Saba - B - 18
3B	Greg LaRocca - R - 27 Alex Pelaez - R - 24	Sean Burroughs - L - 19	Shane Hopper - R - 24 Bryan Schmidt - R - 25	Troy Schader - R - 23
OF	Ryan Radmanovich - L -28 John Curl - L - 27 John Roskos - R - 25 Ethan Faggett - L - 25 Dan Fraraccio - R - 29	Ryan Balfe - B - 24 Pete Tucci - R - 24 A.J. Leday - R - 27	Al Benjamin - R - 22 Jeremy Owens - R - 23 John Adams - R - 23	Todd Donovan - R - 21 Vince Faison - L - 19 Shawn Garrett - B - 21 Bobby Scales - B - 22 Ben Johnson - R - 19 Nick Day - R - 21
C	George Williams - B - 31 Steve Soliz - R - 29 Mark Strittmatter - R - 31	Wilbert Nieves - R - 22 Tim DeCinces - L - 26	Sean Campbell - L - 23 Darren Bush - L - 26 Josh Loggins - R - 23 Jon Stone - B - 21	Jake Huff - R - 22 Tony Cosentino - R - 21 Jarrod Bitter - R - 21
SP	Buddy Carlyle - R - 22 Junior Herndon - R - 21 Rodrigo Lopez - R - 24 Will Cunnane - R - 26 Tom Davey - R - 26 Mike Saipe - R - 26 Brian Lawrence - R - 24	Brian Doughty - R - 25 Jason Middlebrook - R - 25 Wascar Serrano - R - 22 Rick Guttormson - R - 23 Doug Dent - R - 23 Mike Bynum - L - 22	Ben Howard - R - 21 Jason Shiell - R - 23 Steve Watkins - R - 21 Omar Ortiz - R - 22 Blair DeHart - R - 22 Johnny Hunter - R - 25	Gerik Baxter - R - 20 Jacob Peavy - R - 19 Travis Devine - R - 20 Roger Luque - L - 20 Chris Rojas - R - 23 Dennis Tankersley - R - 21
CLOSER	Brandon Kolb - R - 26 Jayson Durocher - R - 25	Angel Aragon - R - 26 Isabel Giron - R - 22	Jeremy Fikac - R - 25	John Trujillo - R - 24

SAN DIEGO PADRES

In Sean Burroughs, the Padres possess that rare player who single-handedly makes the minor league system a productive one. The Padres also are quite deep in starting pitching at the lower levels, though they lack a true ace prospect.

John Roskos has torched Triple-A pitching over the last two seasons, but has fallen way short in brief major league trials. His ability to hit for power and average and play catcher, first base and outfield respectably should continue to provide major league bench opportunities. Kevin Eberwein has 20-plus homer power and has marginally improved his plate discipline, but likely lacks the bat speed to be a productive major leaguer. He could get into the mix for a corner infield reserve spot within the next two seasons.

Nothing is going on prospect-wise at second base. Bret Boone better last awhile.

Kevin Nicholson's excellent Triple-A start earned him a major league trial in 2000. He has no single defining skill, but does everything a bit better than average, combining line drive gaps power, speed and solid defensive ability. The Padres would like him to learn second base in addition to shortstop and fill a utility role in 2001. Switch-hitter Cristian Berroa, 21, has a higher upside than Nicholson. Berroa runs well, and complements decent range with a cannon-like throwing arm. Berroa must become more patient at the plate and hit the ball with more authority to eventually start in the bigs. Keep an eye on switch-hitter Cesar Saba, 18, who hits the ball with significant authority considering his age and slight 6'0", 160, frame. He could break out in 2001 and establish himself as a potential future starter.

Burroughs is the Padres' future at third base, and a big part of their future, period. Burroughs, 19, is well beyond his years in most respects. He is a disciplined hitter who is a better baserunner than his speed would suggest, and has worked hard to be a solid fielder. He's a natural line drive hitter, and home run power should develop as he begins to play against players closer to his age. Two years from now, at the most, he'll begin a long, All Star career.

Like Roskos, lefthanded-hitting outfielder Mike Darr continuously carves up Triple-A pitching, only to struggle in the majors. The guess here is that Darr will assume Tony Gwynn's job in 2001 and begin to fulfill his promise. He's a potential perennial .300 hitter with 15 homer power, and should make big league noise right away. Former Expos' prospect Al Benjamin has a line drive bat with power to the gaps plus decent speed, and could evolve into a major league backup outfielder prospect with development of adequate plate discipline. 1999 first round pick Vince Faison, 19, struggled through a poor Low-A season in 2000. He runs quite well, and the ball jumps off of his bat when he makes contact, but poor plate discipline and an inability to handle quality breaking stuff currently limits him. He needs to take a major step forward in 2001 to retain his status as a potential future major league impact player. The Padres stole outfield prospect Ben Johnson, 19, a 1999 fourth round pick, from the Cards in the Carlos Hernandez deal. Johnson has a possible 30/30 power/speed upside, and an advanced feel for the strike zone for his age. He's way ahead of Faison at this stage, and could someday be a major league star. 1999 eighth round pick Todd Donovan has exceptional speed, but lacks power at this stage in his development. He could evolve into a candidate for a backup role in the majors down the line.

The Padres hope that Ben Davis finally assumes their catching job in 2001. His defensive upside is substantial, and though he has worked hard to add strength and improve his plate discipline, he hasn't advanced similarly at bat. Still, he should be an above average big league receiver, and still has a chance to star. Wilbert Nieves, 22, has adequate skills across the board, and is a consistent line drive contact hitter and durable receiver. He projects as a contender for the backup catcher job in San Diego within two years.

In lefty Buddy Carlyle, 22, and righty Junior Herndon, 21, the Padres possessed two of the younger Triple-A starters last season. Both are finesse hurlers who could battle for the fifth starter role in San Diego in 2001. Herndon's stuff is a little better though he lacks a true strikeout pitch, and Carlyle has better control, though he tends to leave his adequate fastball out over the plate too often. Righty Wascar Serrano, 22, has a low 90s heater and a diverse repertoire, and has a chance to evolve into a mid-rotation starter in the majors. He needs to add a little bulk and improve his command before getting there, however. 1998 17th round pick Brian Lawrence, 24, lacks a top-shelf fastball, but has excelled at the Double-A level and below because of exceptional command. He now must be considered a near-term candidate for a fifth starter or swingman role at the major league level. He could be the next Brian Tollberg. 1999 first round draftee Mike Bynum, 22, excelled in the hitter-friendly High-A California League, and could be ready for a major move in 2001. The 6'4", 200, lefty is death to southpaw hitters, and probably has the highest upside of Padre pitching prospects. He'll be up by 2002. 6'2", 190, righty Ben Howard has a chance to be a successful power pitcher in the upper minors and maybe even higher, but his inability to throw strikes consistently is a major problem. A shift to short relief could be a boon for Howard. 1998 16th rounder Steve Watkins has added velocity in his brief pro career, and now could make a strong upward move if he improves his command. He remains a darkhorse for significant major league success at this point, however.

Omar Ortiz, 22, was a 1999 first round pick, but struggled due to poor control last season at High-A Rancho Cucamonga. He has the ability to be an upper minor league power hurler, but needs to make a significant upward move in 2001 to project as a potential future big league starter. Righthander Gerik Baxter, 19, is a 1999 first rounder who has accomplished quite a bit considering his tender age. He's a prototypical power pitcher with solid control, once he learns to get hitters out earlier in the count and last deeper into ballgames, he could become a top-of-the-rotation prospect. 1999 15th round pick Jacob Peavy, 19, has been spectacular in his brief pro career. The 6'1", 180, righty lacks overpowering stuff, but he changes speeds well, navigates the corners expertly, and has smooth mechanics. He could fit into the San Diego staff in a variety of roles within two to three seasons. Keep an eye on 1999 fourth rounder Travis Devine, 20, a 6'5", 190, righty with a smooth delivery. He needs to find a strikeout pitch, and natural physical development will aid him in his search. He could break out in 2001.

Hard-throwing lefty Cliff Bartosh, 20, benefited from a switch to the bullpen at Low-A Fort Wayne last season. He has a strong two-inning arm and could evolve into a viable setup relief candidate at higher levels.

TOP TEN PROSPECTS

1 - 3B Sean Burroughs - Burroughs, 19, was the Padres' first round draft pick and the ninth overall selection in the 1998 draft. The 6'1", 195, lefthanded hitter has rocketed through the Padres' system, and spent a full season as the youngest competitor in the Double-A Southern League last year. Burroughs ranks among the most polished teenage hitters ever. He consistently makes authoritative contact to all fields, and possesses advanced plate discipline. Though most of his extra-base power is to the gaps as of now, he's a sure bet to develop 25-plus homer power as he physically matures and gets closer in age to the pitchers he faces. Though he doesn't run particularly well, Burroughs is a smart, aggressive baserunner who will steal 10 bases per season on instinct alone. Defensively, he has worked hard to improve his footwork, and possesses decent range and a strong throwing arm. Burroughs was one of the centerpieces of the 2000 Olympic team as its youngest member. This guy is the real deal, and should be a long-term big league star and one of the best players of his generation. Expect him to get the call to San Diego sometime in 2001, especially if the Padres do not contend.

2 - OF Ben Johnson - Johnson, 19, was acquired from the Cardinals in the 2000 trading deadline deal for catcher Carlos Hernandez. The 6'1", 200, righthanded-hitting outfield prospect was the Cards' fourth round draft pick in 1999, and could go down as one of the most egregious deadline steals in recent memory. Johnson is a raw power/speed prospect who showed flashes of his exciting all-around skills as one of the youngest regulars in the Low-A Midwest League last season. He's an excellent athlete who was a high school football standout in Tennessee. He's strong enough to drive the ball for extreme distance to all fields, and fast enough to be a significant stolen base threat and cover a lot of ground at either outfield corner. Though he does have a tendency to swing through high fastballs, his concept of the strike zone is fairly advanced for a teenager. The only flaw in his superb all-around package is an average throwing arm that might limit him to left field at upper levels. Johnson is a prime candidate for a breakout 2001 season, and should contend for a starting job in San Diego by late 2003. He's a good bet to eventually reside somewhere in the heart of their major league lineup.

3 - LHP Mike Bynum - Bynum, 22, was a Padres' supplemental first round draft pick in 1999. The 6'4", 200, southpaw was surprisingly assigned to High-A Rancho Cucamonga for most of late season, where he predictably dominated the younger hitters at that level. He struck out over a batter per inning there and showed decent command, and was rated the best pitching prospect in the circuit by league managers. Bynum's out pitch is an extremely nasty slider, which was been compared to Hall of Famer Steve Carlton's by more than one observer. Bynum's fastball routinely reaches the low 90s, and he has honed his changeup to the point that it can be considered a viable third pitch. Mechanics are the key for Bynum. When he throws his fastball for quality strikes on the corners, he often dominates. However, he struggled in early Double-A outings after a late-season promotion due to inconsistent command of his fastball, particularly early in the count. Don't get overly excited by Bynum's 2000 High-A dominance, it's simply what he was supposed to do at that level. For Bynum to project as an ace major leaguer, he'll need to carve up Triple-A Pacific Coast League hitters early in 2001, no easy task. He'll most likely slide in as a solid mid-rotation starter in San Diego, and will arrive sometime in 2001.

4 - RHP Jacob Peavy - Peavy, 19, was an outright steal in the 15th round of the 1999 draft. The 6'1", 180, righthander lacks overwhelming peak velocity, but has a diverse four-pitch repertoire and can throw quality strikes with any of his pitches on any count. Peavy's heater only reaches the upper 80s, but it seems much faster compared to his curve and changeup, both of which he often uses to get ahead in the count. His mechanics are very solid, and his pitches have exceptional movement as a result. Peavy was slowed at the beginning of the 2000 season by a bout with viral meningitis, but quickly made his mark as one of the youngest starters in the Low-A Midwest League, where he was recognized as the best starting pitcher prospect by circuit managers. He is basically a five or six-inning pitcher at this stage in his development, and might not develop the physical stamina to become a 200-plus inning horse, possibly limiting him to a mid-rotation starting or situational short relief role. He could reach Double-A sometime in 2001. His performance there will dictate the height of his upside. Peavy should get to San Diego sometime in 2003 and be a significant major league contributor.

5 - RHP Wascar Serrano - Serrano, 22, is a 1995 free agent signee from the Dominican Republic who has blossomed over the last two seasons. The 6'2", 178, righty is equal parts power and control, and possesses a diverse four-pitch repertoire featuring a low to mid 90s heater and improving breaking stuff. He maintained a solid strikeout rate in his Double-A debut last season, largely due to his ability to use his slider and changeup effectively against lefthanded hitters. He's deadly against righties, both because of his stuff and his deceptive delivery. Serrano could still add a bit more bulk as he matures and evolve into a true power pitcher. Right now, he's basically a six-inning hurler despite his ability to consistently throw strike one and keep his pitch counts down. If he develops stamina and handles the jump to the hitter-friendly Pacific Coast League well, he was carved up there in a couple of starts last season, Serrano could arrive in San Diego by the end of 2001 and reside in the middle of their rotation for many years.

6 - RHP Junior Herndon - Herndon, 21, was the Padres' ninth round draft pick in 1997. The 6'1", 190, righthander has always been one of his levels' youngest prospects, most recently at Triple-A Las Vegas last season. Herndon has always relied on precise control for success, but pitched quite tentatively last year, and his overall numbers suffered as a result. Herndon's fastball reaches around 90 MPH, but is quite straight and is not a strikeout pitch. He throws a slow curve that can be quite effective against righthanded hitters, but his changeup has not evolved to the point where it can be considered a true out pitch against lefties. You can usually tell when within a couple of batters whether or not it will be Herndon's night. If he's aggressively painting the corners with all of his pitches, Herndon can spin a low pitch count complete game. If not, well, it's going to be a lengthy nibblefest. He's likely fully physically developed, so mechanical adjustments are the only way for Herndon to improve his stuff. He remains quite young, so the Padres will chalk up 2000 in the learning experience category. He could be a midseason callup into the rotation in 2001, and projects as either a low-end starter or situational bullpen righty in San Diego.

7 - RHP Gerik Baxter - Baxter, 20, was a Padres' first round draft pick in 1999. The 6'2", 185, righthander quite possibly has a higher upside than Peavy or Herndon, but has more to do to reach his ultimate potential. Baxter possesses a potentially lethal three-pitch combination including a low to mid 90s fastball, a nasty curve and a passable changeup. He's a bit inconsistent mechanically, but can be quite overpowering when he's in a rhythm and is getting ahead of hitters. He tends to try to make the perfect pitch too often, and finds himself racking up high pitch counts and exiting games after five or six innings; he has yet to complete a game as a pro. Baxter is the type of pitcher who should maintain a high strikeout rate after his advance to the Double-A level, which might happen by the end of 2001. The Padres will be patient with Baxter, allowing him to build the stamina and mound savvy that could lead to a mid-rotation role in San Diego, quite possibly by sometime in 2003.

8 - OF Vince Faison - Faison, 19, was yet another Padres' 1999 first round draft pick. The 6'0", 180, lefthanded hitter has unquestioned raw skills, but was quite over-matched at the plate as one of the youngest regulars in the Low-A Midwest League last season. Faison has light-ning-quick bat speed and surprising power potential for his size, but is hyper-aggressive at the plate, often burying himself in the count on bad pitches. He has a weakness for both outside breaking stuff and high fastballs, a no-no for a guy who wants to make a living as a top-of-the-order hitter. Faison has top-of-the-line speed, and his baserunning instincts are quite advanced for his age. If he learns how to get on first base, he could quickly evolve into a 50 steal threat. Defensively, his speed compensates for some fundamental shortcomings, and his arm is strong enough for him to remain in center field as he advances. This exceptional athlete concentrated on football in high school, and should be ready to take off in 2001. He might not become the leadoff man once envisioned by the Padres, but could be a No. 6 hitter in their major league lineup in 2004 if all goes well.

9 - OF Mike Darr - Darr, 24, was the Padres' second round draft pick in 1994. The 6'3", 205, lefthanded hitter has long been one of the club's most highly touted prospects, and received a lengthy look in the majors last season after the injuries to future Hall of Famer Tony Gwynn. Talent-wise, Darr projects as a poor man's Gwynn in most respects. He's a consistent line drive machine who has learned to make regular contact after swinging through too many pitches early in his career. He's an aggressive hitter who doesn't walk as often as other top-of-the-order hitters, but should hit for a high enough average to compensate for his impatience. Like Gwynn, Darr could probably be a power hitter if he felt like it, but instead projects as a 30 double, 10 homer guy. Speed-wise, he's not a major stolen base threat, but runs well enough to bat second in the order and play a representative right field. His arm strength is well above average. Darr's

major league performance to date has been inconclusive. He'll never have a better chance to leave spring training with the starting right field job than he will in 2001. Look for him to win it, and settle in as a solid .290 hitter in the intermediate term.

10 - RHP Buddy Carlyle - Carlyle, 22, is a former Reds' prospect who came to San Diego in a deal for the immortal Marc Kroon. The 6'3", 175, righthander has been one of the younger Triple-A Pacific Coast League starting pitch-ers for two seasons now, but his extremely good control has yet to win out over his lack of raw stuff, causing him to consistently struggle. Carlyle's fastball only reaches the mid to upper 80s, and he mixes it with a curveball and changeup. Though he throws all of his pitches for strikes and varies speed well, Carlyle has a tendency to catch too much of the plate with his strikes, and has yet to develop a true out pitch against lefthanded hitters. The Padres moved starting pitchers up and down from San Diego to Las Vegas often prior to the September roster expansion last year, and Carlyle was a notable omission despite the fact that he got a brief glimpse of the majors in 1999. It doesn't appear that Carlyle figures too prominently in the club's future plans, especially with the emergence of the Bynums, Peavys, Serranos and Baxters. Carlyle could still latch on in San Diego as a swingman as early as 2001, but a change of scenery would likely do him good.

OTHER PROSPECT

SS Cristian Berroa - Berroa is a switch-hitting shortstop with a little pop and above average speed. He's still inconsistent at shortstop, but he has the physical tools necessary to have success as a fielder. He doesn't strike out a lot and he almost never walks, so it's safe to say he can put the ball in play. If he could be a little more patient at the plate, Berroa could hit closer to .300 and be more of a threat on the bases than he already is.

C Tim DeCinces - DeCinces, the son of former major league third baseman Doug DeCinces, has good power for a catcher and an outstanding eye at the plate. His defensive skills need work, as is the case with most young catchers, but his bat is his strength right now. He hit 11 home runs and drove in 44 in just 207 at-bats at Double-A last year. He drew 42 walks and whiffed just 28 times, a sign that he could be ready to make a move this year.

RHP Jeremy Fikac - Single-A closers generally don't show up on prospect lists or in prospect books, but Fikac performed well enough last year to make people take notice. He has an excellent arm to go with outstanding control and he proved he was more than capable as a reliever by posting a 1.80 ERA and 20 saves over 75 innings of work. He gave up just 46 hits and 24 walks while striking out 101 batters, which is more than 12 per nine innings of work.

OF Shawn Garrett - Garrett is a switch-hitter with power potential and the ability to make consistent contact. He's not a home run hitter at this point of his career, but with some work in the weight room and some natural maturation he could turn some of the doubles he hit last year into home runs. In addition to playing in the outfield, Garrett also demonstrated the ability to play first base and third base as well.

RHP Ben Howard - Howard has a fantastic arm and he could be the kind of pitcher who could dominate hitters if he could simply get the ball over the plate. High-A California League hitters managed to hit just .227 against him and he averaged 12.6 strikeouts per nine innings last year, but he also walked 111 batters in 107-plus innings. Needles to say, Howard is a work in progress.

1B Graham Koonce - Koonce is a little old to have not played about High-A, but his set of offensive skills are worth noting. He's a very good hitter with tremendous patience at the plate and he's got some power. Last year at High-A Rancho Cucamonga he hit .295 with 40 doubles, 18 home runs and 93 RBI. What makes those numbers even more impressive is the fact that he drew 107 walks. Another year like that at Double-A and he could be on his way.

RHP Brian Lawrence - Lawrence doesn't have the greatest arm in the world, but it's good enough when combined with his well above average control and his aggressiveness. Double-A Southern League hitters batted just .216 against him and he allowed just 28 walks in 125-plus innings while fanning 119 batters.

RHP Rodrigo Lopez - Lopez has a good arm, consistently reaching the low 90s with his fastball, but he makes quite a few mistakes. He needs to work on getting ahead of hitters with the first pitch and then focus on making good pitches. He throws too many hittable fastballs when he's behind in the count and that haunts him.

RHP Omar Ortiz - Ortiz, much like Ben Howard, has a very good arm but lacks. He had 97 strikeouts in 99 innings at High-A last year, but also allowed 111 hits and 81 walks, which is quite ridiculous. His raw ability is fine, but he's got to get himself under control and start getting his fastball over the plate early in the count.

OF Jeremy Owens - There isn't anything that Owens can't do on a baseball field, except make consistent contact. Owens reached double-digits in doubles, triples and home runs last year and he stole 54 bases. It's not often that kind of extra base power and speed are combined. If he were to cut down on the strikeouts (183 in 570 at-bats last year at High-A) he could push his home run totals into the 20's and perhaps even steal a few more bases. He's raw but quite gifted.

1B-OF John Roskos - Roskos can mash, but because he's with a National League team it's difficult to find a place for him to play. He's a decent first baseman, but the Padres already have Ryan Klesko there, and he's a below average left fielder. Roskos combined the ability to hit for average and power, good strike zone judgment and a knack for driving in runs. He should have a major league job at some point before the end of the 2001 season, though he would be best served in the American League where he could DH.

RHP John Trujillo - Yet another Single-A closer to keep an eye on, Trujillo was absolutely dominant at Low-A Fort Wayne last year, putting up a 1.33 ERA and notching 42 saves. The Midwest League hit just .154 against him in 74-plus innings, during which he struck out 85 batters and walked just 25. His live arm, along with this kind of performance, should garner him some attention in the future.

OF Pete Tucci - Tucci has a lot of raw power, but he's a wild swinger who needs to calm down at the plate. He's begun to show the ability to steal some bases and if he could ever become a more professional hitter he could hit 30-plus home runs with double-digit steals. Right now he's a long way from being able to handle major league pitching, as evidenced by his .216 average and the 147 strikeouts he posted in 476 at-bats at Double-A last year.

RHP Steve Watkins - Last year, the Padres High-A Rancho Cucamonga team was littered with young pitchers who have outstanding arms, but who also have control problems; Watkins was one of them. The league batted just .216 against him and he struck out nearly 10 batters per nine innings, but he also allowed 90 walks in 151 innings. His control problems weren't as severe as those of Ben Howard and Omar Ortiz, but they were pretty bad.

SAN FRANCISCO GIANTS
ORGANIZATIONAL GRID

	AAA	AA	HI-A (San Jose)	HI-A (Bakersfield)
1B	Damon Minor - L - 26	Sean McGowan - R - 23 John Summers - B - 23	Matt Keating - L - 21	Jeremy Luster - B - 23 Tim Flaherty - R - 23
2B	Edwards Guzman - B - 23	Travis Young - R - 25	Joe Jester - R - 21 William Otero - R - 23	Ryan Luther - R - 23 Marco Pernalete - B - 21 Paul Turco - B - 23
SS	Juan Melo - B - 23 Nelson Castro - B - 24	Cody Ransom - R - 24	Carlos Mendoza - B - 20	Carlos Campusano - R - 24
3B	Pedro Feliz - R - 23	Tony Zuniga - R - 25 Raul Marval - R - 24 Tony Torcato - L - 20	Josh Cook - R - 22	Julio Cordido - R - 19
OF	Terrell Lowery - R - 29 Mike Byas - B - 24 Josh Tyler - R - 26 Jeff Ball - R - 31 Mike Glendenning - R - 23 Jalal Leach - L - 31	Doug Clark - L - 24 Chris Magruder - B - 23 Jeff Allen - R - 24 Jake Messner - L - 23	Ryan Pini - L - 23 Alex Fajardo - R - 24 Clay Greene - R - 25 Scott Daeley - R - 23 Pedro Mota - L - 22	Carlos Valderrama - R - 22 Arturo McDowell - L - 20 Brett Casper - R - 24 Kevin Tommasini - R - 25
C	Gius. Chiaramonte -R- 24	Yorvit Torrealba - R - 21 Matt Priess - R - 25	Sammy Serrano - R - 23 Mike Wright - R - 24 Anthony Turco - L - 22	Guillermo Rodriguez - R - 22
SP	Ryan Jensen - R - 24 Michael Riley - L - 25 Miguel Del Toro - R - 28 Jeff Andra - L - 24 Brian Knoll - R - 26 Jim Lynch - R - 24 Joe Nathan - R - 25 Chad Zerbe - L - 28	Ryan Vogelsong - R - 22 Kurt Ainsworth - R - 21 Kevin Joseph - R - 23 Luis Estrella - R - 25 Edwin Corps - R - 27 Ryan Cox - R - 22 Jake Esteves - R - 24	Joe Horgan - L - 23 Jeremy Cunningham - R - 21 Jeff Verplancke - R - 22 Jerome Williams - R - 18 Chris Jones - L - 20	Tony Coscia - R - 25 Vance Cozier - R - 22 Kevin Vent - R - 23 Tom Miller - L - 24 Danny Prata - L - 21
CLOSER	Robbie Crabtree - R - 27 Ben Weber - R - 30 Steve Connelly - R - 26	Randy Goodrich - R - 23	Todd Ozias - R - 23	Jason Bullard - R - 31 Manny Bermudez - R - 23 Jon Valenti - R - 26

SAN FRANCISCO GIANTS

In recent seasons, the Giants have traded many of their best prospects for veteran help for often futile stretch drives. They are left with an adequate major league club from which manager Dusty Baker squeezes every last drop of production, and a rather weak minor league system behind a handful of top-shelf prospects, including third baseman Tony Torcato and pitchers Kurt Ainsworth and Jerome Williams.

There's very little going on within the system at first base. Only 6'6", 235, Sean McGowan has substantial talent, and at age 23, he has yet to play Double-A ball. His ability to hit for average and his largely untapped power potential does make him a threat for an eventual backup major league role.

1999 seventh round pick Joe Jester, 21, is a scrappy overachiever with top-of-the-order batting skills. He has little power, but has a great eye and runs well. His ability to play both middle infield positions makes him a future major league utility candidate. Switch-hitter Marco Pernalete is similar to Jester in many respects, but has a lower offensive upside. He's a longshot to make a significant major league impact.

Juan Melo continues to bounce from organization to organization, but remains a multi-skilled offensive and defensive player who could back up at second and third base as well as shortstop in the majors. He has a substantial power/speed package for a middle infielder, and his once suspect work ethic is greatly improved. He'll likely make a big league dent in 2001. Carlos Mendoza, 20, is a slick fielder whose offensive development was aided by a demotion to High-A San Jose last season. The 6'0", 175, switch-hitter runs well, but will have to evolve into a .270ish hitter to project as a big league starter. More likely, he'll be a future big league part-timer.

Third baseman Pedro Feliz has a 20 homer power upside, but wouldn't likely reach it at the major league level because of poor plate discipline. He's made zero progress in that area in his seven-year pro career, and as a result

seems destined for more years in the upper minors. Tony Torcato, 20, represents the Giants' future at the hot corner. He is one of the purest hitters in the minors, and could contend for big league batting titles once he learns to take a pitch. He has 40 double, 20 homer power, and is two years at most away from inheriting the major league job. Keep an eye on Julio Cordido, 19, a 6'1", 192, righthanded hitter with 25/15 power/speed potential. He could put up excellent numbers in a second High-A season in 2001 and propel himself into the Giants' plans.

Outfield pickings are quite slim. Mike Byas is a solid defensive outfielder with good speed and excellent plate discipline, but he would likely be overpowered by major league pitching. At best, he fits in as a fourth or fifth outfielder at the big league level. At ages 24 and 23, respectively, Doug Clark and Chris Magruder are a bit old to have yet to reach Triple-A. Clark has some offensive potential, and Magruder plays an effective center field, but both to appear to lack the power/speed skills required to make significant major league impacts. Arturo McDowell, 20, a 1998 first round pick, has to this point been unable to make consistent, authoritative contact against professional pitching. He's a solid defensive outfielder who could evolve into a prolific basestealer, but appears to need a third High-A season; not a very good sign. Youth remains on his side, however. Carlos Valderrama, 22, has been in the Giants' system since 1995, and finally made a full-season roster last season. The 5'11", 175, righthanded hitter showed a consistent line drive bat with a bit of gaps power plus excellent speed, and could be working his way into the mix for a future outfield backup job in San Francisco.

Giuseppe Chiaramonte, 24, could make a run at the major league backup catcher spot in 2001. He's a durable, if somewhat slow receiver with a power stroke at the plate. If his bat speed is sufficient to hit major league pitching in the spring, he could stick. Edwards Guzman can play multiple positions, including catcher, which could be his ticket to a major league 25th man spot. The former 50th round got a brief, unexciting big league look back in 1998.

Yorvit Torrealba, 21, is a sleeper prospect with no significant weaknesses nor exciting strengths. He's a reliable line drive hitter with some gaps power, and proved to be a solid, durable defender at Double-A Shreveport last season. He too could be major league backup within two seasons. Sammy Serrano, 23, played his way out of the Giants' plans with a poor High-A season. The 1998 second round pick was lost at the plate, and his defensive skills weren't good enough to compensate. 2001 could be his last shot. Keep an eye on Guillermo Rodriguez, who has an interesting power/speed upside for a catcher. If he establishes himself at the Double-A level in 2001, he too could have a big league future as a backup.

Pitching prospect quantity is a bit lean, but the quality of the Giants' best minor league hurlers is unquestioned. The two leaders are Kurt Ainsworth and Jerome Williams. Ainsworth, 21, is a 6'4", 181, righty who is exceptionally polished considering his age and inexperience as a professional. He sets up hitters well and can put them away with a mid 90s heater. He has Tommy John surgery in his history, but still appears a good bet to evolve into a nine-inning top-of-the-rotation starter in the majors. He should arrive sometime in 2001. Williams performed admirably as an 18-year-old High-A starter, overpowering California League batters with his lively low 90s heater. Once he spruces up his breaking stuff, the 6'3", 190, righty could get scary. The Giants will try to be patient with him, but Williams is a potential future ace who could make the majors at age 20 or 21. 1998 fifth round draftee Ryan Vogelsong, 22, adjusted well in his first full Double-A season, though he left his low 90s heater out over the plate too often. Vogelsong's solid control and relatively limited repertoire could make him a better fit for the bullpen as he advances. He could be a major league setup man. 1998 first rounder Chris Jones, 20, could not find the plate at High-A San Jose last season. The 6'4", 200, lefty has youth on his side, and if he can get his mechanics straightened out in the near term, could still develop into a major league caliber starter. 2001 is a key year. 1999 draftees Jeremy Cunningham (fourth round) and Jeff Verplancke (11th round) took regular High-A turns in their initial full pro seasons, albeit with little success. Both have prototypical pitchers' frames, and Verplancke in particular has a live fastball. Both will expected to perform much better in High-A reprises in 2001.

TOP TEN PROSPECTS

1 - RHP Jerome Williams - Williams, 18, was the Giants' supplemental first round draft pick in 1999. The 6'3", 180, righthander had a brilliant initial full season in the pros, often dominating High-A California League hitters as one of that circuit's youngest players. Williams has already picked up velocity on his fastball since being drafted, now reaching the low 90s on a regular basis. He's a solid bet to pick up even more, and could be pushing it into the upper 90s before long. Williams also throws a curve, slider and changeup, and improved his mastery of all of those pitches last season. His mechanics are quite consistent, and his command within the strike zone quite precise, especially for such a youngster. He has the size, stamina and mound savvy to evolve into a nine-inning horse in the majors. If Williams can maintain or enhance his strikeout rate upon his promotion to the Double-A level in 2001, then watch out. He's one of the most advanced teenage pitching prospects to hit the scene in recent years, and could be a future staff anchor in San Francisco. He could make it to the majors sometime in 2002.

2 - 3B Tony Torcato - Torcato, 20, was the Giants' first round draft pick in 1998. The 6'1", 195, lefthanded hitter has one of the sweetest swings in the minor leagues. He effortlessly drives the ball deep to both gaps, and many of his High-A doubles will likely become upper level homers as he physically matures and continues to hone his swing. Torcato has slightly above average foot speed, and showed new found aggressiveness on the bases last season at High-A San Jose. Defensively, he has served quite a bit of time in the designated hitter role during his pro career, as his right throwing shoulder has been operated on twice, including an arthroscopic procedure late last summer. Torcato projects as an adequate third base defender, with relatively soft hands and a quick first step. The Giants expect his arm strength to bounce back, but he could wind up at first base if it doesn't. No matter what, Torcato will certainly eventually fill the number three spot in the Giants' order because of his .320-25-110 offensive upside. He could arrive by late 2002, and projects as a potential future All Star.

3 - RHP Kurt Ainsworth - Ainsworth, 21, was the Giants' first round draft pick in 1999. The 6'4", 181, righthander got off to an excellent start at Double-A Shreveport but stumbled down the stretch due to fatigue as well as nagging injuries that included a broken middle finger and a bruised elbow, both on his non-pitching arm, and both the result of being hit with line drives. In addition, Ainsworth underwent Tommy John elbow surgery in college, but has shown no ill effects as a pro. His diverse repertoire includes a low 90s fastball, a sharp slider and an improving changeup. His mechanics are quite smooth, but Ainsworth has a tendency to nibble around the edges of the plate, too often trying to throw the perfect pitch. That trait often causes him to fall behind in the count and incur high pitch counts, leading to relatively short stints. Throwing strike one more consistently, plus the natural maturation of his lanky frame should enhance his durability and allow him to develop into a 200-inning major league horse. The 2000 Olympian might start 2001 at the Triple-A level, but should get to the majors quickly. He could settle in as a number two or three starter with the Giants over the long haul.

4 - SS Carlos Mendoza - Mendoza, 20, was signed by the Giants' as a 16-year-old free agent out of Venezuela. The 6'0", 175, switch-hitter spent all of 1999 at the Double-A level, where he was physically overmatched by the much older pitchers, though he showed a promising glove. The Giants slid him back a level to High-A San Jose in the California League in 2000, allowing him to get his offensive game on solid footing, as he became more consistent defensively. Mendoza has greatly improved his plate discipline, and was a fairly consistent line drive hitter with a bit of gaps power last season. Despite his demotion, he remained one of the younger starters at his level last season, and began to incorporate his above average speed into his offensive game for the first time. Defensively, Mendoza moves gracefully, and possesses well above average range and a strong throwing arm. Like most young shortstop prospects, Mendoza needs to become more consistent on the routine play. His second crack at Double-A pitching should go much better in 2001. Look for Mendoza to be ready to challenge Rich Aurilia for the major league shortstop job in 2003. He'll likely be a bottom-of-the-order hitter, and at worse would fit in as a utilityman or defensive replacement.

5 - OF Arturo McDowell - McDowell, 20, was one of three Giants' first round draft picks in 1998. The 6'1", 175, lefthanded hitter is a raw, unpolished gem who needs to build his all-around game around his blazing speed. McDowell remained lost offensively in his second High-A season, again batting in the low .200s with fairly minimal extra base power. On the plus side, McDowell's plate discipline improved, though his long swing led to an unacceptably high strikeout total for a spray hitter. To become a passable top-of-the-order threat, McDowell

must be content to simply slap the ball on the ground and take advantage of his wheels. He improved his basestealing success last season, as he learned to read pitchers and get better jumps. Defensively, McDowell is a greyhound who covers a lot of ground in center field, though his arm strength is just average. It's pretty rare for a legitimate prospect to spend three consecutive years at the same level, but that could be McDowell's fate. Look for him to bust into Double-A sometime next year, and contend for a major league role in mid 2003. Development of his ground ball stroke at the plate will determine whether McDowell is a future big league leadoff man or extra man, for now, bet on the latter.

6 - 3B Pedro Feliz - Feliz, 23, was signed as a free agent out of the Dominican Republic in 1994 at age 16. The 6'1", 180, righthander wandered about the Giants' system without real effect until last season, when he went on a power rampage at Triple-A Fresno. Feliz had previously shown glimpses of power potential, but it was usually obscured by his overaggressive ways at the plate. He walked all of 79 times in 2009 plate appearances in his first six pro seasons. Though he didn't walk much last season either, Feliz did learn to lay off of bad pitches early in the count, particularly low and outside sliders, his Achilles' heel in previous campaigns. He did a much better job of pouncing on the most hittable pitch of individual at bats last season, and posted career-best power numbers. Defensively, Feliz has soft hands, a strong arm and above average lateral range. Triple-A Pacific Coast League managers recognized him as the circuit's best defensive third base prospect last season. Feliz is out of options, and could be given a chance to break north with the Giants in 2001. He could be a solid righthanded platoon partner for Bill Mueller, and would also provide defensive support off of the bench. He'll need to continue to improve his plate discipline to cut it offensively in the majors.

7 - SS Juan Melo - To put it mildly, Melo, 23, has been around. The 6'1", 180, switch-hitter has bounced from the Padres to the Blue Jays to the Reds to the Yankees to the Giants in the last season and a half. His highs are high and his lows are low. He's been released for having a questionable work ethic, and been lauded by none other than Joe Torre for having an excellent spring training camp with the Yankees in 2000, almost breaking north with the club. Melo's raw tools are unquestioned. He has a decent power/speed upside for a middle infielder, driving the ball to the gaps and beyond with regularity, and running the bases well, though not stealing at a prolific pace. He's a wild swinger who has been prone to extended slumps in the past, however, and the holes in his swing would surely be exposed in a significant big league role. Defensively, Melo moves well for a big man and has a strong enough arm to play shortstop or third base well. He's athletic enough to also play second base and the outfield, and could be a superb 25th man on a big league roster. His weight has been known to fluctuate in the past, but was in check last year. Sooner or later, Melo is going to help someone in the major leagues. It might as well be the Giants, in 2001, as a utilityman.

8 - 2B Joe Jester - Jester, 21, was the Giants' seventh round draft pick in 1999. The 5'10", 180, righthanded hitter might be a little low on raw tools, but is a top-of-the-order sparkplug who does the little things well and always seems to have a dirty uniform. Jester is a consistent line drive hitter with a bit of power to the gaps. He works the count to the edge in most at bats, often fouling off lots of pitches and drawing plenty of walks. His speed is only a bit above average, but his exceptional baserunning instincts have made him a run-scoring machine thus far in his pro career. Defensively, he is fundamentally sound and reliable on the routine play, though he lacks highlight-film range or arm strength. He can play either middle infield position respectably, and is likely to add other positions to his resume as he advances through the system. Jester is a winning ballplayer who seems destined to be an effective all-purpose major league backup, with a likely arrival date of 2003.

9 - RHP Ryan Vogelsong - Vogelsong, 22, was drafted on the fifth round in 1998. The 6'3", 195, righthander combines a low 90s fastball with a slider and changeup, and impressively maintained a strikeout rate of about a batter per inning in his first full Double-A season in 2000. He lacks a true out pitch against lefthanded hitters, and has struggled to last six innings or more in Double-A starts because of inconsistent command, particularly early in the count. In his current form, he could be a natural fit as a situational, once-around-the-order bullpen righty. However, Vogelsong still could add 10 to 15 more pounds of muscle to his frame, which could add a bit of velocity to his heater and make him a true power pitcher. One word of caution; Vogelsong was dogged by injuries in college, though he's been fairly healthy as a pro. If he gets off to a solid start at the Triple-A level in 2001, Vogelsong could be promoted to the majors at some point. Look for him to establish himself as a viable big league swingman or middle reliever shortly thereafter.

10 - OF Mike Byas - Byas, 24, was the Giants' 15th round pick in 1997. The 6'0", 170, switch-hitter might be a dinosaur in today's power-oriented style of play. He's a slap hitter with virtually no extra-base power, but possesses exceptional plate discipline, speed, baserunning instincts and defensive ability. Triple-A Pacific Coast League managers recognized him as the fastest baserunner in the circuit, and he is generally considered one of the premier defensive outfielders in the Giants' system, combining above average range and arm strength. Byas still needs to read pitchers better in order to get quicker jumps and improve his basestealing success rate. He is basically a slightly older version of the Devil Rays' Jason Tyner, who hasn't homered since high school. We're talking about a guy with a career .300 slugging percentage as a pro, folks. There is no room for such a punchless player to start in the majors in this day and age. However, Byas can play any of the three outfield positions well, and might fit in better with the Giants than he would with any other club in baseball. He could be a fourth or fifth outfielder, defensive replacement, pinch-runner, etc. in San Francisco in 2001 and beyond.

OTHER PROSPECTS

1B Sean McGowan - He came back from foot surgery to have an excellent year as a run producer at High-A San Jose (.327-12-106) and Double-A Shreveport (.348-0-12). It didn't seem to hurt the 23-year-old McGowan to stay at Boston College for four years; he was a third-round draft pick by the Giants in 1999. At 6'6" and 240 pounds, he should develop more power. He improved his strike-zone judgment significantly. He has good hands, but needs to improve his footwork at first base.

SS Cody Ransom - Good defense may not be enough to get Ransom to the majors. At Shreveport, he batted just .200-7-47 and stole nine bases. In addition, he struck out a whopping 141 times.

3B Pedro Feliz - His seventh pro season concluded with a Sept. 1 callup to San Francisco. The 23-year-old righthanded batter earned it by setting a Triple-A Fresno record with 33 home runs while batting .298 and driving in 105 runs. The Dominican made a breakthrough by laying off pitches that break out of the strike zone. He needs great defensive improvement; the Giants sent him to the Arizona Fall League to work on it.

3B Julio Cordido - The defensive prospect is the 20-year-old Cordido. The Venezuelan batted .252-10-64 with 13 stolen bases. If he can develop better bat speed as he matures, the 20-year-old can show more power.

OF Chris Magruder - The 23-year-old became a poster boy for leading-hitting center field prospects in his second season at Double-A Shreveport. The switch-hitting Magruder walked about as often as he struck out and stole 19 bases. The second-round draft pick in 1998 out of the University of Washington is a strong-armed defender with sure hands. The downside was that his power numbers were down in a .282-4-39 season, but he showed power to the gaps with 33 doubles.

OF Doug Clark - A football player at the University of Massachusetts, Clark signed as a seventh-round draft pick in 1998. Because he played four college seasons, he's already 25 years old. He hasn't been past Double-A — he batted .272-10-75 and stole 12 bases at Shreveport in 2000 — so he's a marginal prospect. He projects as a backup outfielder, and his arm may limit him to left field. He strikes out too often (102 times last year) for a spray hitter.

OF Mike Glendenning - The 24-year-old is an all-or-nothing hitter, probably best qualified as a DH because his defense is questionable. In 4 1/2 pro seasons, he has hit 112 home runs, with power to all fields. Last year, he started .261-16-54 at Shreveport and batted just .198-6-18 after a promotion to Fresno. Glendenning was a 10th-round pick in 1996.

OF Carlos Valderrama - A righthanded batter, Valderrama is a major basestealing threat. As High-A Bakersfield's left fielder, the 23-year-old stole 54 bases while batting .315-13-81. If he cuts down his strikeouts, he could be a major top-of-the-order prospect with some power.

C Giuseppe Chiaramonte - One of Chiaramonte's strong points is willingness to learn. He improved his strike-zone judgment and saw his power output increase to 24 homers and 79 RBI at Fresno. He was in familiar surroundings; he was a fifth-round draft choice in '97 out of Fresno State. He matched his career average of .255 in 2000. He also has worked with Doug Mirabelli to improve his defense, especially his throwing.

C Edwards Guzman - The Giants moved him from third base to catcher. The 24-year-old hasn't hit with much power. Guzman batted .280-6-52 in his third year at Fresno. The lefthanded batter is so aggressive at the plate that he rarely walks or strikes out. He'll have to improve his catching skills to have a significant major league career.

C Yorvit Torrealba - A good defensive catcher, Torrealba batted .286-4-32 at Shreveport. The righthanded batter hasn't done much with his bat in two Triple-A trials, and he has little power. He's just 22, so if his batting skills can approach his defense, he can be an everyday catching prospect.

C Sammy Serrano - A shoulder injury shortened Serrano's season to 38 games at High-A San Jose, where he batted just .182-2-17. The 24-year-old should be able to rebound from a wasted season. A second-round pick out of Stetson University in 1998, he has hit for average in the past. He can hit the ball to the gaps, but needs to improve his strike-zone judgment. Behind the plate, poor footwork has minimized the impact of his strong arm.

RHP Kevin Joseph - After a disappointing 3-11, 5.17 season at Shreveport, Joseph went to the Arizona Fall League. Even though Joseph is 6'4" and 200 pounds, he is a breaking-ball pitcher with a fastball that reaches only the high 80s.

LHP Chris Jones - The Giants' first-round draft choice in 1998 had a disastrous second season at San Jose. The 21-year-old couldn't throw strikes. He walked 85 batters in 61 1/3 innings, and had to be taken out of the rotation. He finished the year 3-6 with a 10.71 ERA. When San Francisco took him, it expected he would add muscle to a 6'3", 185-pound frame and add velocity to a high-80s fastball. He also has a good curve, but has to learn to throw both pitches over the plate.

ANAHEIM ANGELS
ORGANIZATIONAL GRID

	AAA	AA	HI-A	LO-A
1B	Larry Barnes - L - 25	Jeff Guiel - L - 26 Juan Rodriguez - B - 25	Robb Quinlan - R - 23 Bill Mott - L - 24 Jim Scharrer - R - 23	Casey Kelley - L - 23 Peter Orgill - L - 23 Greg White - R - 24
2B	Keith Johnson - R - 29	Chuck Abbott - R - 25	Alfredo Amezaga - R - 22 Bien Encarnacion - B - 22	Francisco Duran - R - 21 Miguel Ortiz - L - 21
SS	Brett King - R - 27	Jay Hood - R - 23	Brian Specht - B - 19	Josh Shaffer - L - 20
3B	Jamie Burke - R - 28 E.J. t'Hoen - R - 24	Jason Huisman - R - 24	Mike Christensen - R - 24	Del Lindsey - R - 22
OF	Darond Stovall - B - 27 Juan Tolentino - R - 24 Nate Murphy - L - 25 Dwayne Hosey - B - 33 Scott Morgan - R - 26 Edgard Clemente - R - 24 Chris Hatcher - R - 31	Jeb Dougherty - R - 24 Darren Blakely - B - 23 Derick Urquhart - L - 24 Nathan Haynes - L - 20 Gary Johnson - L - 24	Elpidio Guzman - L - 21 Rich Stuart - R - 23 Ariel Delgado - L - 23 Marcus Knight - B - 21	Mike O'Keefe - L - 22 Scott Bikowski - L - 23 Brian Seever - R - 23 Chip Gosewisch - R - 23 Chris Hills - R - 22
C	Bryan Graves - R - 25 Shawn Wooten - R - 27	Bret Hemphill - B - 28 Kevin Lidle - R - 28	Norberto Lopez - R - 23 Jason Hill - R - 23 Angel Diaz - R - 23	Tom Gregorio - R - 23 Anthony Doudt - R - 23 Chris Barski - L - 22
SP	Scot Shields - R - 24 Steve Green - R - 22 Elvin Nina - R - 24 Jeremy Callier - R - 24 Shad Williams - R - 29	Paul Morse - R - 27 Matt Beaumont - L - 27 Steve Fish - R - 25 Ryan Cummings - R - 24 Jacob Brooks - R - 22 Sean Brummett - L - 22 John Lackey - R - 21 Matt Lubozynski - L - 23	Doug Bridges - L - 23 Brandon Emanuel - R - 24 Jeff Hundley - L - 23 Wes Crawford - L - 23 Mario Mendoza - R - 21 Alex Lontayo - L - 24 Phil Wilson - L - 19 Francisco Rodriguez -R- 18	Dusty Bergman - L - 22 Julian Harris - L - 22 Vince LaCorte - R - 21 Chad Berryman - R - 23 Aaron Franke - R - 20 Heath Timmerman - R - 22
CLOSER	Lou Pote - R - 28 Eric Weaver - R - 26	Rich Kelley - L - 30	Ben Grezlovski - R - 23	J.T. Harris - R - 24

ANAHEIM ANGELS

The Angels' insistence on drafting college talent almost exclusively has provided them with full-season team rosters chock full of players two and three years older than their leagues' average age. The system is nearly totally devoid of position player talent, and only a couple of shrewd early round 1999 draft selections have kept pitching depth respectable.

Mo Vaughn had better last a while in Southern California, as only Triple-A first sacker Larry Barnes has an appreciable chance of reaching the major leagues at his position. Even then, Barnes' doesn't likely meet the high power thresholds required of starting big league corner infielders, and will likely function as an extra major league bat.

At second base, the Angels' two upper minor league clubs featured a pair of falling stars in Trent Durrington and Chuck Abbott, who both combine fairly solid tools with obvious weaknesses that they have been unable to address. The Angels' best hope at this position is teenager Carlos Gastelum, who kept his head above water in a limited role at High-A Lake Elsinore.

At shortstop, the Angels possess little more than fringe utility prospects Justin Baughman, Keith Luuloa and Keith Johnson. They're all too old to be considered genuine prospects, but each can play at least two positions and possesses at least one major league caliber tool.

In the outfield, the Angels noticeably lack prospects with high power or speed upsides, with very few exceptions. Double-A center fielder Nathan Haynes, 20, is the rare Angel prospect who was significantly younger than his level's average age last season, but he has not experienced significant on-field success to date. Lefthanded hitter Elpidio Guzman, 21, was one of the brightest lights in the system in 2000 at High-A Lake Elsinore, and might be the only Angels' outfield prospect with a significant chance of someday starting in the bigs. Former Cubs' prospect Gary Johnson torched the High-A California League in the first half of 2000, and might evolve into a spare major

league bat if all goes well. Even the system's Low-A Cedar Rapids outfield was loaded with players a year or more removed from college ball, indicating that the barren state of the Angels' system isn't about to change anytime soon.

At catcher, switch-hitter Bret Hemphill showed some power potential at Triple-A Edmonton last season, but defensive struggles have impeded his progress. It's a good thing for the Angels that Bengie Molina emerged as a successful major leaguer in 2000, as no other prospects appear on the horizon.

The outlook is a bit better on the mound. Ramon Ortiz and Seth Etherton showed flashes of ability at the major league level, but mostly toiled at the Triple-A level in 2000. Ortiz' upside is a bit higher, but his injury risk is quite great as well. Etherton is solid in all respects and should settle in as a mid-rotation guy before long. Righty Matt Wise might be in line for the same major league struggles in 2001 that the aforementioned two hurlers faced last season. He throws strikes, but needs an out pitch. Steve Green is closing fast, and might race to the head of this class with a strong start in 2001. He's a rare Angels' high school signee, and has made significant progress each season. If the Angels' have a top of the rotation starter in their system, he likely currently resides in the lower levels. Righty Francisco Rodriguez is the leading candidate at this point. He dominated at times as one of the younger High-A California League prospects. 1999 second round pick John Lackey is one of the more pedigreed prospects in the Angels' system, and could generally be counted upon for seven competitive innings per start in his first full pro season in 2000. Another rare high school draftee, Phil Wilson, is likely the best lefthanded starter prospect in the system, and should advance quickly.

The Angels' system produced a couple of significant major league contributors last season in catcher Bengie Molina and pitcher Scott Schoeneweis. Besides the aforementioned Ortiz and Etherton, righthander Brian Cooper and lefthanded Jarrod Washburn also had extended tours of duty in the major league rotation. Despite the overall dearth of talent in the Angels' system in recent years, the club must be commended for getting most of their legitimate talent: Troy Glaus, Darin Erstad, Garrett Anderson, etc., to the major leagues quickly.

TOP TEN PROSPECTS

1 - RHP Francisco Rodriguez - Rodriguez, 18, has by far the highest upside among Angels' prospects. The 6'0", 165, righthander could develop four above average major league pitches. The best among the group are an explosive upper 90s heater and a sharp slider that both could strike out major league hitters today with some consistency. However, youth and injury risk could combine to prevent him from fulfilling his potential. His 2000 season was marred by a bout with shoulder tendinitis plus a strained pitching elbow; neither injury was considered serious, but both prevented him from accumulating much needed game experience. As advanced as Rodriguez' stuff is, his ability to set up hitters is virtually unproven. The Angels need 150 innings from Rodriguez in 2001. If any of them are effective Double-A innings, then he will be on track to become a future major league ace.

2 - RHP John Lackey - Lackey, 21, has progressed rapidly since being drafted on the second round in 1999. After struggling through a poor 1999 rookie ball season characterized by bouts of wildness, Lackey blossomed in his first full professional season, rocketing through three levels and establishing himself as a solid Double-A hurler by season's end. The 6'6", 205, righthander is not a flamethrower, his heater tops out around 90 MPH, though he could add some juice as he fills out. He has worked hard to expand his repertoire, improving his curve ball significantly and adding a passable changeup. He impressively maintained his strikeout rate after his midsummer promotion to Double-A, a solid indicator of future success. One year ago, it would have been silly to expect Lackey to advance as far as he has this quickly. Though he's likely to encounter more obstacles in the next year, it now appears that Lackey has a major league future, quite possibly as a long-term mid-rotation starter.

3 - RHP Phil Wilson - Wilson, 19, is a 6'7", 210, righthander selected by the Angels on the third round of the 1999 draft. He was one of the youngest Low-A Midwest League hurlers last season, and he quickly established himself as a durable staff anchor at Cedar Rapids. He has quickly assembled a diverse four-pitch repertoire including a low 90s heater, a splitter, plus a curveball and changeup that have largely been developed over the past year. His size should act as an advantage on several fronts. He's quite an intimidating sight to right-handed hitters, and his frame still has room to accommodate more muscle, which could serve to gas up his fastball. His mechanics are quite refined for a youngster, and Wilson could be poised to make a major move once he develops a true strikeout pitch. 2001 could be a breakout year.

4 - OF Nathan Haynes - In a system filled primarily with low-ceiling college draftees much older than their levels' average age, prospects like Haynes, 20, are welcome relief. The 5'9", 170, center field prospect is a raw speed and defense prospect whose bat is lagging behind the rest of his game. The 1997 A's number one pick came over to Anaheim in the Randy Velarde deal, and has always ranked among the younger prospects at each successive minor league level. He was physically overmatched by the best Double-A pitchers last season, often getting himself out on bad pitches. He needs to take more pitches and hit more grounders to become a legitimate top of the order threat, as his power ceiling is low. He is a high quality defender in center field, and an extremely fast runner with fine basestealing technique. He'll likely fare much better in a second Double-A season in 2001, a pivotal year that will determine his eventual upside.

5 - OF Elpidio Guzman - Guzman, 21, is a bit more polished and has more diverse skills than Haynes, but is a year older and a level behind him. This 6'2", 166, lefthanded hitter is the closest thing to a true power/speed prospect in the Angels' system. Most of his power is to the gaps at this point, but normal physical development could lead to 20-25 homer power. Guzman steals more bases than Haynes despite possessing a little less raw speed, for the simple reason that he reaches base more often. Defensively, Guzman isn't as smooth as Haynes, but has a better throwing arm and has the power potential to be considered in a corner outfield slot. Guzman and Haynes are likely to toil side by side at the Double-A level next year. Don't be surprised to see the younger Haynes nudge ahead. Both could eventually be in the Angels' major league lineup by 2003.

6 - SS Brian Specht - Specht, 19, is an interesting prospect who has landed in an ideal situation in the shortstop-poor Angels' system. The 1999 ninth round pick signed too late to be placed on a minor league roster that season, and it turned out to be his biggest break ever. By early 2000, a hole opened for Specht at High-A Lake Elsinore, making him one of the very few current minor leaguers to make his minor league debut at that level. He stepped right in and became a consistent line drive hitter and on-base threat against the older California League hurlers. The switch-hitter lacks eye-catching tools, but is fundamentally sound in all respects, and has an innate feel for the game. Once he learns to make more consistent contact against quality breaking stuff, he'll evolve into a potential No. 2 hitter in a major league lineup. He's not a likely future All-Star, but could plug in the shortstop hole in Anaheim for quite a while.

7 - RHP Steve Green - Very quietly, this 1997 10th round draftee was worked his way to the doorstep of the major leagues. Green, 22, is a 6'2", 195, righthander who lacks an overwhelming fastball, but has succeeded because of an ability to vary speed and location expertly. He did have enough juice to maintain a respectable strikeout rate after being promoted to Double-A in late 1999 and again in the first half of 2000, though he did struggle in early Triple-A outings. He also impressed in the 1999 Pan Am Games, where he was an effective starting pitcher for the Canadian National Team. Green lacks the raw ability of such predecessors as Ramon Ortiz, Seth Etherton or Jarrod Washburn, but is a bulldog competitor who should extract the maximum from his abilities. Look for him to earn a few big league starts in 2001. He has put himself in line for a fifth starter/swingman role there for the near future.

8 - RHP Matt Wise - Wise, 24, is a 1997 sixth round pick who relies on finesse and location to retire upper minor league hitters. The 6'4", 190, righthander has routinely walked two batters or less per nine innings at each successive minor league stop, but his inability to develop a true strikeout pitch, particularly against lefthanded hitters, could prove his undoing at the major league level. Wise did get a brief opportunity to start in the majors last season, and the early returns were mixed. Wise has some significant pluses. In addition to his allergy to walks, Wise generally lasts deep into games because of his ability to retire hitters early in the count, thereby maintaining low pitch counts. It's uncertain whether his act will play in a major league rotation, but Wise likely has the finesse and smarts to earn a near-term complementary big league role as a swingman or situational bullpen righty.

9 - OF Gary Johnson - Sleeper alert. Johnson, 24, was a 1999 19th round pick who had spent the previous two years on a Mormon mission. The 6'3", 210, switch-hitter came back swinging, tearing up the High-A California League in early 2000, making the All-Star team before a midseason advance to Double-A. He overmatched the much younger California League competition, showing a high power/speed upside plus exceptional patience at the plate. The power bat might be for real, but many of the other totals were due to his advanced age and maturity compared to his peers. He was much less eyecatching after his promotion, despite the fact that he still ranked as one of the Eastern League's older players. Johnson's power potential could make him an eventual asset in a complementary role in the majors, either as a platooner or bench player. It's almost impossible for all but the greatest prospects to lose two key developmental years and still reach their full potential.

10 - 1B Larry Barnes - Barnes, 25, is at best a marginal major league prospect, but the talent level in the Angels' system takes a dive at this point on this list. This 6'1", 195, lefthanded hitter has a 15-20 homer bat and fairly interesting complementary skills for a first baseman. He runs quite well, fairly routinely putting up impressive stolen base and/or triples totals in his six-year minor league career. Defensively, he's no Gold Glover, but is fairly adept around the bag. In no way does Barnes meet the high offensive standards required for starting major league first basemen, but his combination of the aforementioned skills plus above average plate discipline might make him a bench player at the major league level. He doesn't look like a fit given the Angels' current personnel, so Barnes might need a change of scenery to make the majors.

OTHER PROSPECTS

2B-SS Alfredo Amezaga - Amezaga isn't a great hitter and he has almost no power, but he can fly on the base paths. He stole 73 bases at High-A last year and because he draws a fair number of walks, he can be an offensive weapon. He's more adept at playing second base than shortstop, but the ability to play both middle infield spots combined with his speed should keep him moving up the ladder.

2B Justin Baughman - Baughman's primary weapon is speed. He runs extremely well and is a good basestealer, but he needs to improve as a hitter. He has patience and makes consistent contact, but he has almost no power at all, rarely hitting even doubles or triples despite his outstanding speed. He was a shortstop at one time, so his versatility and speed could earn him a major league job even if his hitting doesn't come around.

OF Darren Blakely - Blakely has the power and speed to be a major league outfielder, but he's a wild, undisciplined hitter. He made the Double-A Eastern League All-Star Game in 2000, but his offensive numbers weren't what you would expect from someone of that standing. He hit just .237 and struck out 136 times while walking only 30 times. If he can improve his patience even just a little bit, he could be a 20-20 threat and could bump his average up 30-40 points.

OF-DH Bill Mott - Mott is a good looking lefthanded hitter with some pop, speed and excellent strike zone judgment. The problem is his defense. He played just nine games in the field at High-A during the 2000 season. Designated hitters aren't usually mentioned in prospect reports, but someone who gets on base at a .400 clip or better with speed and extra base power is worth watching.

RHP Scot Shields - Shields isn't a top prospect, but he has very good stuff. His problem is control. He's a strikeout pitcher with a very live fastball, but walks and wildness within the strike zone hurt him at Triple-A last year. He was close to a callup early in the season after he got off to a good start, but then hit the skids. He had 156 strikeouts in 163 innings at Triple-A, but his 82 walks were a major hinderance.

C Shawn Wooten - Wooten came out of nowhere during the 2000 season to place himself on the map in the Angels' system. He's shown that he can hit for both average and power at the Triple-A level and he's also able to play first and third base. His defensive skills may not be the greatest, but if he continues to hit like he did last year when he hit .353 with 11 home runs in just 66 games at Triple-A, he'll land in the majors in some capacity.

BALTIMORE ORIOLES
ORGANIZATIONAL GRID

	AAA	AA	HI-A	LO-A
1B	Tommy Davis - R - 27 Calvin Pickering - L - 23	David Gibralter - R - 25	Frank Figueroa - R - 23	Wes Rachels - R - 24 Doug Gredvig - R - 21
2B	Jerry Hairston - R - 24	Eddy Garabito - B - 21 Richard Paz - R - 22	Joey Hammond - R - 23	Willie Harris - L - 22
SS	Jesse Garcia - R - 26	Ed Rogers - R - 18	Brian Roberts - B - 22 Eddy Martinez - R - 22	Gary Cates - R - 19
3B	Francisco Matos - R - 30 Carlos Casimiro - R - 23	Jose Leon - R - 23 Rick Short - R - 27	Maikell Diaz - R - 20	Napolean Calzado - R - 20
OF	Jose Herrera - L - 27 Wady Almonte - R - 25 Wayne Kirby - L - 36 Darryl Brinkley - R - 31 Karim Garcia - L - 24	Darrell Dent - L - 23 Darnell McDonald - R - 21 Larry Bigbie - L - 22 Ntema Ndungidi - L - 21	Tim Raines, Jr. - R - 20 Roberto Rivera - R - 23 Craig Daedalow - R - 24 Keith Reed - R - 21	Matt Riordan - R - 22 Mamon Tucker - R - 20 Ray Cabrera - R - 21 Steve Salargo - R - 23 Antoine Ide - R - 21
C	Mike Kinkade - R - 27 Willie Morales - R - 27 Adan Amezcua - R - 26	Fernando Lunar - R - 23	Jayson Werth - R - 21 Tom McGee - R - 25 Alfredo Leon - R - 20	Jon Kessick - R - 22 Mike Seestedt - R - 22
SP	Javier Delahoya - R - 30 Josh Towers - R - 23 Rick Krivda - L - 30 Luis Rivera - R - 22 Mark Nussbeck - R - 26 Jay Spurgeon - R - 23	Rick Bauer - R - 23 Sean Douglass - R - 21 Juan Guzman - R - 22 Matt Snyder - R - 25 Matt Riley - L - 20 Lesli Brea - R - 21 Juan Figueroa - R - 21	Matt Achilles - R - 23 Steve Bechler - R - 20 John Stephens - R - 20 Jacobo Sequea - R - 18 Mike Paradis - R - 22	Sonny Garcia - R - 23 Jancy Andrade - R - 22 Erik Bedard - L - 21 Richard Stahl - L - 19 Randy Perez - L - 20
CLOSER	Sean Maloney - R - 29	Aaron Rakers - R - 22	Derek Brown - R - 23	Pat Gorman - R - 22 Terry Plank - R - 22 Travis Fleming - R - 23

BALTIMORE ORIOLES

Very quietly, the Orioles' system has evolved from one of the game's leanest to one of its strongest in just a few short seasons. An increasing focus on high-ceiling high school talent in the draft and an expansion of scouting efforts into relatively uncharted areas such as Australia and Zaire (that's right, Zaire, home of outfield prospect Ntema Ndungidi) have played important roles.

Calvin Pickering's weight problems appear likely to deny him a crack at a full-time major league job anytime soon, though his power ceiling remains virtually limitless. He's all there is in the system, so the O's might be investigating the free agent or trade markets to replace Will Clark.

Jerry Hairston, 24, remains the heir apparent to Delino DeShields at second base despite an injury-plagued 2000 season. His tools are just above average across the board, but Hairston knows how to play the game. Switch-hitter Eddy Garabito runs well and strikes the ball with authority for his size (5'8", 170), but will likely have to learn another position to fit in as a major league utility candidate. At 5'8", 130, there are no smaller prospects out there than Richard Paz, a scrappy top-of-the-order type with decent speed. He can also play third base, making him a viable utility prospect, assuming that upper level hurlers don't simply blow the bat out of his hands.

Their shortstop depth is solid. The ball jumps off of shortstop prospect Ivanon Coffie's bat, but the lefthanded hitter has needed a second attempt to solve each successive minor league level. His ability to play middle and corner infield spots could make him a deep major league reserve in 2001. Brian Roberts is a 1999 first rounder with a high defensive upside, but rather unexciting offensive skills. Such players are becoming extinct at the big league level, so Roberts had better hit to project as a future starter. Eddy Martinez, 22, never evolved into the defensive stud once envisioned, but has made great strides with the bat. He could get a major league shot as a backup before Roberts. Keep an eye on Ed Rogers, an 18-year-old with speed to burn and a live line drive bat. He's got the highest upside of the group, and could make one or more

of the aforementioned shortstop prospects expendable with a big 2001 season.

There are no prospects ready to inherit third base from Cal Ripken at this point. Down the road, Napolean Calzado, 20, could be an interesting option. The 6'3", 165, righthanded hitter has an intriguing power/speed upside, and has quite a bit of physical development in his future. The O's also landed Jose Leon from the Cards in the Will Clark deal. Leon has decent power potential, but has yet to develop plate discipline in his seven year pro career. He'll likely linger in the upper minors for the foreseeable future.

Orioles' outfield prospect depth is substantial, but most of the marquee names won't be ready for at least another year or two. Luis Matos, 21, was the first to get a crack at the majors, and will be back to stay before long. He has learned to make much more consistent contact, and retains the power/speed upside necessary to potentially propel him into a significant big league role. He needs a full Triple-A year in 2001. The evolution of Darnell McDonald, 21, has been slower than anticipated. The 1997 first round pick has all the tools, but he has yet to deliver on his power/speed potential. The meter's running and barring major 2001 progress, he could go down as a disappointment. Ntema Ndungidi, 21, improved as much as any minor leaguer in 2000, going from overmatched to dominant in a single season, combining power, speed and patience in high doses. He could be the Orioles' future major league leadoff man. Tim Raines, Jr., was one of the minors' most prolific basestealers last season, but his inability to steal first base will likely hold him short of a significant big league career. 6'4", 190, Larry Bigbie, a 1999 first rounder, is yet another power/speed prospect. He has been slow to adjust to the wooden bat, however, generating subpar power thus far in his pro career considering his size and pedigree. Keith Reed, 21, is another exciting power/speed guy, and could become pretty scary once he learns to take a pitch. The 6'4", 215, righthander could turn out to be the superior power hitter of this group. Mamon Tucker, 20, is a patient spray hitter with the body

(6'3", 190) of a run producer. He's a sleeper who could have a breakthrough year in 2001.

Jayson Werth, 21, represents the Orioles' future at catcher. The 6'6", 191, righthanded hitter suffered through a subpar 2000 season, but possesses a unique package of speed, defense and power potential for a receiver. Look for a solid rebound in 2001, and an eventual starting job in the majors.

Matt Riley, 20, remains an exceptional prospect, but a combination of injuries and bad behavior derailed him from the fast track in 2000. The best guess here is that he'll bounce back in 2001 as he finally grows up. Luis Rivera, 22, pitched very well in a short big league cameo appearance last year, and projects as either a starter, setup man or closer for the Orioles in the near term. He's had blister problems over the years, but that's his only wart. Josh Towers is a precise finesse hurler who could be a fit as a swingman or situational reliever in the majors in the near term. 5'11", 165, lefthander John Parrish, 22, surprised with a solid Triple-A campaign in 2000. His southpaw status and ability to notch a key strikeout could make him a viable extra man on a big league staff. Juan Figueroa, 21, was the most promising of the three arms received from the White Sox in the Charles Johnson/Harold Baines deal. The 6'3", 150, righty has fairly precise control, but will need to add velocity as his lean frame develops to become a mid-rotation major league prospect. The Orioles also landed righty Lesli Brea from the Mets in the Mike Bordick deal. Brea, 21, can really rush it up there for his size (5'11", 170), but his limited repertoire and spotty command make him a better fit for short relief than the rotation. Sean Douglass, 21, is a finesse righty who could add power as his 6'6", 200, frame develops, making him a potential mid-rotation guy in the majors. The Orioles jumped Juan Guzman, 22, over a level to Double-A in 2000, where he was a strikeout pitch away from potentially significant success. Watch his strikeout numbers in the upper minors in 2001 to assess his upside.

The lower minors are teeming with pitching prospects. Australian John Stephens, 20, doesn't have an A-list fastball, but still has a substantial power/control upside. Look for him to break onto everyone's top prospect lists in 2001, about three years late. Jacobo Sequea is only 18, but is already a three-year full season league veteran. He's made slow, steady progress, but it's about time he tasted some success to certify his top prospect status. 2001 is a key season for Sequea. Steve Bechler, 20, has looked quite ordinary next to teammate Stephens over the past two seasons, but can be downright dominant over short stretches. He could evolve into a major league mid-rotation guy, but needs to make a quantum leap in performance soon. 1999 first round pick Mike Paradis, 22, has not advanced as quickly as hoped, and has clearly been passed by another 1999 first rounder, 19-year-old lefty Richard Stahl. The 6'7", 185, Stahl could become a top of the rotation prospect once he refines his control. 1999 sixth round pick Erik Bedard, 21, has sneaky stuff, can start or relieve, and appears poised to squeeze the most from his potential. Finesse lefty Randy Perez, 20, has impeccable command, but might prove quite hittable against higher level hitters.

TOP TEN PROSPECTS

1 - RHP Luis Rivera - The Orioles conducted a full-blown clearance sale at the trading deadline last season, receiving mostly a group of older, mid-range prospects in return. Rivera, 22, is a welcome exception, a true top-shelf pitching prospect received from the Braves in the B.J. Surhoff deal. Of course, Rivera brings with him a lengthy injury history. He suffered from recurring blisters on his pitching hand in 1999, and battled tendinitis and a sore rotator cuff in 2000. When healthy, Rivera has proven able to overpower hitters, even at the major league level. Rivera's fastball routinely reaches the upper 90s, and his curveball is also a plus pitch. He has solid control and smooth, consistent mechanics for a young power hurler. Improved command of his changeup might make Rivera an upper-rotation starter prospect, without it, he could still be a dominant short reliever. He'll likely land a key role on the 2001 Orioles' staff.

2 - LHP Richard Stahl - Stahl, 19, was one of an amazing seven 1999 Orioles' first round picks. The 6'7", 200, lefthander was one of the youngest hurlers in the Low-A South Atlantic League, and for much of the season, one of its most effective. Stahl combines a mid 90s fastball with a developing curve and changeup, all of which could become strikeout pitches once he enhances his command. At this stage, Stahl too often tries to make the perfect pitch, falls behind in the count, and is fortunate to last five or six innings per start. However, compared to other tall, lanky southpaws, like Randy Johnson, Stahl is pretty far along for his age. Stahl could begin the 2001 season back at Low-A Delmarva, and should dominate. By 2003, Stahl will be banging on the big league door, and has a chance to become a top-of-the-rotation ace soon afterward.

3 - RHP John Stephens - What does this guy have to do to get some respect? Every year, this 6'1", 175, righthander puts up amazing strikeout/walk numbers and minuscule ERA's, and averages well over six innings per start, but doesn't wind up on anybody's top prospect lists. Except for this list, that is, where he's a regular. Stephens' fastball only reaches the upper 80s, but he consistently keeps it on the low edges of the strike zone, and mixes it well with a variety of breaking pitches. His control ranks among the very best in the minors, and was recognized as the best in the High-A Carolina League in 2000 by its managers. Double-A will be a key hurdle for Stephens. If he can keep his strikeout rate around one per inning there, then this 20-year-old will be on the express route to the major leagues. Expect him to get the job done at Double-A in 2001, and enter the big league rotation by late 2002. He's a likely future No. 2 or 3 starter in the major leagues.

4 - C Jayson Werth - Werth, 21, has an unusual array of skills for a catcher, especially for a 6'6", 190, catcher. His most advanced tools are his speed and plate discipline, which could make him a passable number one or two hitter once he regains the line drive stroke that abandoned him last season. Werth scuffled through a poor offensive season in the Double-A Eastern League, but did begin to show signs of developing the power to the gaps that has long been expected of him. He has the potential to develop into a .300 hitter with a 20/20 power/speed upside down the road. Defensively, Werth lacks exceptional arm strength, but moves well behind the plate and gets rid of the ball quickly. Look for the 1997 first round pick to improve in all facets of the game in 2001 at the Triple-A level, and possibly get a taste of the majors by midseason. If Werth makes up for the offensive ground he lost in 2000, he still could project as an above average big league receiver, and a potential eventual All Star.

5 - OF Keith Reed - Reed, 21, is yet another of the Orioles' seven 1999 first round draft picks. This 6'4", 215, righthanded hitter has substantial power potential, above average raw speed (though he isn't much of a basestealer), plus the arm strength and range to be an above average right fielder. His approach at the plate could use some work. He played his high school and college (Providence) ball in the Northeast, and therefore hasn't had as many repetitions as most prospects. At this stage in his development, Reed tends to be overanxious on breaking pitches, often bad ones. Reed is a dead fastball hitter who would benefit greatly from working deeper counts. Reed needs to experience Double-A success in 2001 at age 22 to project as an eventual major league

starter. He could either become a 30-homer big league stud or a useful power bat off of the bench, and should arrive by late 2002.

6 - OF Ntema Ndungidi - Here's a prime nominee for the Most Improved Minor Leaguer award for 2000. In 1999, Ndungidi, 21, went homerless with only 18 doubles and five triples in 497 Class A at bats. Last season, he blossomed as an on-base and power threat at High-A Frederick, earning a spot on the Carolina League All-Star team and a late season promotion to Double-A Bowie. The 6'2", 165, lefthanded hitter has always possessed above average plate discipline, but in 2000 he finally developed long-expected extra-base power. He projects as a 15/15 power/speed guy at higher levels, and has the defensive ability to play all three outfield positions. He might not have a high enough upside in any single area to be an everyday major leaguer, but should fit in as a productive fourth outfielder at the major league level, with an estimated arrival time of early to mid 2002.

7 - SS Ed Rogers - Here's a deep sleeper. Rogers, 18, is a 6'1", 165, righthanded hitter with a consistent line drive stroke and excellent raw speed. He could develop 10-15 homer power as he matures, and might be a consistent source of 30-40 steals per season as he advances. Development of plate discipline will be the key for Rogers to unlock his offensive potential. Defensively, Rogers has played both shortstop and third base. He might not have the defensive skill required to play shortstop at higher levels - a shift to third base would raise the bar offensively for Rogers. He looks like at least a future all-purpose infield backup with a diverse offensive game, and possibly quite a bit more. Rogers will likely be the everyday High-A shortstop in 2001, and will likely need a year at each level before competing for a big league job by 2004.

8 - 2B Jerry Hairston - Hairston, 24, might have been a prime beneficiary of the Orioles' late 2000 housecleaning at the major league level, but early-season shoulder surgery had him in rehabilitation mode at the trading deadline. This 5'10", 172, righthanded hitter lacks a single stand out tool, but is a gritty gamer with average skills across the board. He works deep counts, slaps the ball to all fields with a bit of gaps power, and is a savvy baserunner who is good for 15-20 steals per season despite ordinary raw speed. Defensively, Hairston is surehanded, consistently making the routine play and the occasional spectacular one. Triple-A International League managers recognized him as the circuit's best defensive second baseman last season. Hairston is not likely to be an above average major league starter, he's a pretty fair bet to struggle in that role in 2001. Over the long haul, he'd be best utilized as a 300 at-bat platooner or situational reserve.

9 - RHP Jacobo Sequea - Sequea, 18, has been creeping onto these Top Ten lists for a while now because of his extreme youth relative to his level of competition. Pretty soon, however, Sequea will need to begin dominating someone, at any level, to remain listed. The 6'0", 175, throws a hard low 90s heater and a decent curveball, and has solid control for his age. However, he has yet to become a true strikeout pitcher because of the lack of sharp movement on his heater, and of a consistent changeup. Inability to consistently get ahead of hitters has also been a problem, the resulting high pitch counts usually require Sequea to exit before the end of the sixth inning. Additional physical development isn't likely to be forthcoming, so Sequea must work with what he has. 2001 is a pivotal season, look for Sequea to finally overmatch High-A Carolina League hitters next season and begin to make towards an eventual mid-rotation slot in Baltimore.

10 - LHP Matt Riley - Riley was set to remain at the top of this list despite a woeful 2000 season, but then underwent an elbow ligament transplant that will cost him all of 2001. It's a testament to Riley's enormous raw talent that he remains on this list despite all of the adversity, much of it self-inflicted, that he has encountered in the past year. Riley, 20, was a favorite to earn a fifth starter job in Baltimore entering 2000 spring training, but quickly discounted himself by reporting late for workouts and becoming a general discipline problem. After reporting to the minor leagues, he endured multiple injury problems, among them a strained rotator cuff and sore biceps in his pitching arm. Afterwards, his mechanics were a mess at Double-A Bowie, where he alternated between missing the plate by a mile and catching too much of it. The 6'1", 205, lefthander hopefully learned a lot in 2000, and can now get down to the business of honing his powerful repertoire, which includes a mid 90s fastball, an overhand curve and a passable changeup, all of which he threw consistently for quality strikes prior to last season. It's wait 'til 2002 for Riley, but he could still be special if he gets healthy and grows up.

OTHER PROSPECTS

RHP Steve Bechler - Bechler is very polished for a young pitcher and he has the makeup to go a long way. His numbers haven't been overwhelming to this point in his career, but he has demonstrated the ability to throw strikes and punch hitters out at an above average pace. What he needs to do next is throw fewer hittable pitches and more "pitchers' pitches," so to speak.

LHP Eric Bedard - Bedard looked great last year and he could emerge soon as one of the Orioles better pitching prospects. He's combined the ability to throw strikes consistently with the ability to punch hitters out and the ability to keep hit totals against him to a minimum. He has a live arm and a good breaking ball and he's someone to watch as he moves up the ranks in the minors.

OF Larry Bigbie - Bigbie is a good hitter who has a chance to get a lot better in a hurry. He hasn't shown much power to this point of his career, but he has demonstrated an ability to hit for average and better than average speed on the bases. If he can develop some power, he'll begin to advance quickly.

3B Napolean Calzado - Calzado has potential, but he needs to sand down the rough edges a bit. He's inconsistent defensively, though the potential for success is definitely there. As a hitter, Calzado makes a lot of contact and should develop some more power as he becomes more disciplined at the plate. He also runs well too, though he's not a particularly skilled baserunner just yet.

RHP Sean Douglass - Douglass isn't an overpowering pitcher, but when he spots his pitches well he's effective. There's a chance he may struggle against older, more experienced hitters, so his progress between 2000 and 2001 will be key. He's only 21 and he still has plenty of time to finish fine tuning his skills, especially considering he's already had some success at Double-A.

2B Eddy Garabito - Garabito is a scrappy infielder with some speed who also happens to be a switch-hitter. He doesn't have much home run power and his discipline at the plate took a step back in 2000, so he'll have to really improve as a hitter to be a serious prospect. He may wind up being a utilityman if he can demonstrate the ability to play multiple positions.

2B Willie Harris - Harris is an intriguing player because of his speed and because of his outstanding patience at the plate. He's not a great hitter right now, but he's got some pop in his bat as evidenced by the 43 extra base hits he had last year, and he's able to play shortstop and outfield in addition to second base. Perhaps his most impressive quality is his ability to draw a walk (89 walks to 89 strikeouts in 2000), which should allow him to be a stolen base threat even when he's not hitting.

SS Eddy Martinez - Martinez is a 22 year-old shortstop with good defensive skills and the ability to put the ball in play. He has no power and is an average baserunner, which places him well behind Brian Roberts in the Orioles' system. If he shows well at the upper levels, he could turn himself into a valuable player, but he must improve his patience at the plate and his baserunning skills.

OF Darnell McDonald - He has all the physical talent he'll ever need, but McDonald hasn't really learned how to hit at this point. He has outstanding speed, though his baserunning skills aren't the greatest, and he has power potential. The problem is that he's not developing the ability to drive the ball consistently and he doesn't make consistent enough contact to be successful against good pitchers. Defensively, McDonald is good enough to play either center field or right field.

RHP Mike Paradis - Paradis has about as much upside as any pitcher in the Orioles' system. He has a low 90s fastball that moves and a good breaking pitch, but his control has been problematic so far. If he can work ahead in the count more often in 2001, he could move up a level or two during the season because of his college experience and his raw talent.

2B Richard Paz - Paz is a good contact hitter with just a touch of pop in his bat, not home run power, just some extra base pop. He actually spent some more time at Single-A during the 2000 than you would have thought he would heading into the season and that's probably a bad sign. His defense is solid, but he'll have to hit more to make himself a legit prospect.

LHP Randy Perez - Perez, much like Bedard, combines the ability to strike people out with good control. He's not overpowering, though he does have a pretty good arm, but he spots pitches well and knows exactly what he's doing out there on the mound. If he can maintain his composure against more experienced hitters and keep working ahead in the count, hell be successful.

1B Cal Pickering - Pickering is a hulking first baseman (6'5" 285) who elicits memories of Cecil Fielder. He has a lot of power, but has had trouble with strikeouts at the Triple-A level. Defensively, Pickering isn't bad for a really big man, but he's also not very good by major league standards. If he doesn't improve his discipline at the plate and start hitting against older pitchers, he'll be stranded forever in the minors.

OF Tim Raines, Jr. - Like his father at the same age, Rock, Jr. can absolutely fly. He isn't a particularly good hitter right now and he has minimal home run power, but he has shown a pretty good eye at the plate and can cover a lot of ground in the outfield. He's young and has a lot to learn, but a good year at the plate in 2001 and he could start to creep into some top prospects lists.

SS Brian Roberts - At this point, Roberts may be the Orioles' shortstop of the future. He's a good fielder who can hit for average and steal a lot of bases. The lack of power won't be an issue as long as he continues hitting .300 or better with speed. The real test for him will come when he begins facing Double-A and Triple-A level pitchers. If he can hit against them, his future will be bright.

LHP B.J. RYAN - Ryan is a hard-throwing lefthander with a chance to be a very good late-inning reliever. He throws a low 90s fastball and a hard slider, though his control was a big problem in 2000. At 6'6" and 230 pounds, Ryan can be intimidating and when he throws strikes he's very effective. The 24 year-old isn't really a top prospect and probably won't put up big numbers in terms of saves or wins, but he should be a valuable member of a major league bullpen for some time.

RHP Josh Towers - Towers doesn't have great stuff, but managers in the Triple-A International League voted Towers as the pitcher with the best control in the league. He spots all of his pitches well and he's able to keep his team in games by making hitters put the ball in play. He could be similar to Bob Tewksbury at the major league level if things break his way.

BOSTON RED SOX
ORGANIZATIONAL GRID

	AAA	AA	HI-A	LO-A
1B	Dernell Stenson - L - 22 Morgan Burkhart - B - 28	Shea Hillenbrand - R - 24 Juan Diaz - R - 24	Mike Dwyer - L - 22	Luis Garcia - R - 21
2B	David Eckstein - R - 25	Angel Santos - B - 20 Jorge DeLeon - R - 25	Carlos Leon - B - 20	Patrick Santoro - R - 21 Joe Kerrigan - L - 22
SS	Lou Merloni - R - 29 Andy Sheets - R - 28	Aaron Capista - B - 21	Alex Ahumada - R - 21	Jon Anderson - B - 23 Freddy Sanchez - R - 21
3B	Freddy Garcia - R - 27 Wilton Veras - R - 22	Tony DeRosso - R - 24 Les Dennis - R - 27	Juan Espinal - R - 25	Chaz Terni - R - 21 Brady Williams - R - 22 Steve Minus - R - 23
OF	Michael Coleman -R- 24 Jim Chamblee - R - 25 Garey Ingram - R - 29 Curtis Pride - L - 31 Donnie Sadler - R - 25 Julio Vinas - R - 27	Virgil Chevalier - R - 26 Rontrez Johnson - R - 23 Jess Graham - L - 24 Marc Lewis - R - 25 Garry Maddox - L - 25	Brian Wiese - R - 22 Tonayne Brown - R - 22 Angel Mendoza - R - 21 Danny Haas - L - 24 Mark Fischer - R - 24 Mike Robertson - L - 29	Lew Ford - R - 23 Chris Warren - R - 23 Carlos Rodriguez - R - 23 Kenichiro Kawabata - B - 21
C	Tim Spehr - R - 34 Angelo Encarnacion -R- 27	Steve Lomasney - R - 22 Damien Sapp - R - 24 Luis Rodriguez - R - 26	Rodolfo Pena - R - 21 Andrew Riepe - R - 23 Jeff Waldron - L - 23	Andrew Larned - R - 24 Kregg Jarvais - R - 23
SP	Sun Woo Kim - R - 22 Tomokazu Ohka - R - 24 Dan Smith - R - 24 Juan Pena - R - 23 Jared Fernandez - R - 28 Paxton Crawford - R - 22	Brian Barkley - L - 24 Justin Duchscherer - R - 22 Jin Ho Cho - R - 24 Marty McLeary - R - 25 Rob Radlosky - R - 26 Nerio Rodriguez - R - 27	Josh Hancock - R - 22 Casey Fossum - L - 22 Josh Garrett - R - 22 Tommy Darrell - R - 23 Bryan Eversgerd - L - 31	Brad Baker - R - 19 Eric Glaser - R - 22 Wilfredo Ledezma - L - 19 Anastacio Martinez - R - 19 Rick Riccobono - R - 20 Jerome Gamble - R - 20
CLOSER	Tim Young - L - 26 Rob Stanifer - R - 28 Sang-Hoon Lee - L - 29	Jeff Taglienti - R - 24	Josh Belovsky - R - 25	Bryan Leach - R - 22 Lance Surridge - R - 23

BOSTON RED SOX

The Red Sox possess substantial pitching depth, but lack a top-shelf pitching prospect likely to someday slide behind Pedro Martinez in the rotation. Conversely, position player depth isn't particularly exciting, but led by catcher Steve Lomasney and first baseman Dernell Stenson, their top prospects are of high quality.

Stenson, 22, remains the Sox' first baseman of the future despite an uneven last season-and-a-half. Look for the lefthanded power hitter to claim at least part of the major league job sometime in 2001 and evolve into a solid big league power source. Shea Hillenbrand's ability to play catcher as well as first base plus his live bat make him a possible future bench asset in the majors. Keep an eye of 2000 Low-A first sacker Luis Garcia, a budding power source who will need to sharpen his plate discipline to similarly produce at higher levels.

In Angel Santos and Carlos Leon, both 20, the Sox possess a pair of prospects who could evolve into future major league starters. Santos is a switch-hitter who already has Double-A season under his belt, and has solid gaps power and speed. Leon, also a switch-hitter, has a bit less power but makes more contact and is more consistent than Santos. The race is on to succeed the Jose Offermans and Jeff Fryes of this world.

With Nomar Garciaparra in place, the Sox could afford to trade Cesar Saba, their only frontline shortstop prospect, for Ed Sprague, leaving Aaron Capista and Alex Ahumada behind. Capista, a switch-hitting 1997 No. 2 pick, simply hasn't developed offensively. His glove could eventually propel him into a big league utility role. Ahumada has shown flashes of power at times in his pro career, but in most respects is a poor man's version of Capista.

There is nothing going on at third base in the minors now that Wilton Veras is in the majors, so the hot corner could be an offseason priority in the trade and free agent markets if John Valentin doesn't mend completely.

The injury and immaturity-plagued Michael Coleman remains the Sox' most talented outfield prospect, but may have finally run out of chances to earn a full-time job in Boston. His power and speed upsides remain high, but Coleman has been slow to iron out the rough edges of his game. At 25, Jim Chamblee might be a bit old to be considered a true prospect, but his ability to play the outfield and second base plus his power potential makes him a big league extra man candidate. Rontrez Johnson is an interesting top-of-the-order prospect who might not do any one thing well enough to start in the majors, but could emerge as a fourth outfielder candidate. 2000 High-A outfielders Brian Wiese (power), Tonayne Brown (speed) and Angel Mendoza (hitting for average) all have a solid tool or two, but none are likely to emerge as top-shelf prospects.

Catcher Steve Lomasney is arguably the Sox' best all-around prospect. His offensive game is stuck in neutral as he continues to struggle to make consistent contact, but his power upside and defensive skill make it likely that he'll challenge Jason Varitek for playing time in 2001. Only Rodolfo Pena, 21, a solid defensive receiver, has a shot to reach the majors among the Sox' other catching prospects.

The Sox possess a bevy of starting pitching prospects, but none have marked themselves as sure bets for big league stardom. Their Far Eastern connection of righties Tomokazu Ohka, Sun Woo Kim and Jin Ho Cho remain poised on the cusp of the major leagues, but appear no more ready than a year ago. Ohka overwhelms minor league hitters but has fallen short in big league trials, and Kim and Cho make too many mistakes over the middle of the plate. The oft-injured Juan Pena certainly has the ability to make some noise if healthy, but that's a big if. Righty Paxton Crawford held his own in a brief big league trial last season, marking himself as a near-term mid-rotation starter candidate. His stuff isn't great, but Crawford knows how to pitch. Justin Duchscherer is a slightly watered down version of Crawford, rarely walking hitters but often getting hurt on offerings catching too much of the plate. He could evolve into a big league swingman candidate. Former top pick Chris Reitsma, briefly out of the system after being selected in the Rule 5 draft, is reclaiming his prospect status. A solid Triple-A season in 2001 could place him in a battle for a mid-rotation spot the following year. John Curtice's once promising career appears to be in jeopardy, thanks to a combination of injury, poor conditioning and subpar control. His upside remains high, but his chances of reaching it dwindle daily. Lefty Casey Fossum was a disappointment at High-A Sarasota last season, but is a strikeout pitch away from making a serious move. He could break out to the upside in 2001. 1999 first round Brad Baker could have the brightest future of any Sox pitching prospect. He has exceptional control and an advanced feel for pitching for a teenager. His transition to Double-A ball in late 2001 or early 2002 will be telling. Lefty Wilfredo Ledezma is a raw power pitcher who could make a serious move if he fills out his lean frame or significantly enhances his command. He's a sleeper to watch.

TOP TEN PROSPECTS

1 - 1B Dernell Stenson - Most of the Sox' other top-shelf prospects also had subpar seasons in 2000, so Stenson, 21, remains atop this list despite underachieving in his second season at Triple-A Pawtucket. The 6'1", 230, lefthanded hitter can drive the ball for distance to all fields, but too often tries to pull the ball, and is also prone to getting himself out on bad pitches. His conditioning has been spotty, and his defensive development slow. When the Red Sox were crying out for offensive production during the second half of the 2000 season, it spoke volumes when they dealt for the likes of Ed Sprague and Rico Brogna to fill out their lineup instead of summoning Stenson. 2001 is a pivotal season for him; if he does not win the first base job, he could be used as trade bait to obtain pitching support for Pedro Martinez.

2 - C Steve Lomasney - Lomasney, 22, suffered through a disappointing offensive campaign at Double-A Trenton, but still remains the Sox' likely catcher of the future. He has 20-plus homer power potential, and well above average foot speed for a catcher, but was limited by extremely poor plate discipline and an inability to hit quality breaking pitches. Defensively, the 6'0", 195, Lomasney has the whole package. He moves quite well, has a strong arm with a quick release, and an excellent feel for handling pitchers. The Sox still hope that Lomasney can evolve into an All-Star caliber receiver with a strong

all-around game. At this point, however, there's a strong possibility that Lomasney could become a good-field, little-hit catcher at the major league level, a .230 batter with 15 homer power, unless he learns to hit breaking stuff.

3 - RHP Paxton Crawford - Crawford, 22, is a 6'3", 193, righthander who excelled in the upper minors and held his own in a brief major league trial last season, despite a lack of overpowering stuff. In fact, Crawford would likely have pitched the last two months in Boston if not for a freak incident in which he gashed his back rolling out of bed onto a drinking glass. His fastball occasionally reaches 90 MPH, but it moves sharply, and Crawford can place it on the low corners at will. He also has an above average curve and a decent changeup, and mixes his pitches well. Crawford is the rare prospect who pitches better at each successive minor league level. He sets very high standards for himself, and tends to reach them. Look for Crawford to step into the Sox rotation from Day One, next year, and eventually become a solid number two or three starter.

4 - RHP Brad Baker - The Sox love to draft local high schoolers in the early rounds, and this 1999 first rounder has quickly justified his selection. The 6'2", 180, righthander is quite polished for a 19-year-old - he mixes his low 90s heater with a hard curve and a decent changeup, which he added to his arsenal last season. He sets up hitters well, varying speed and location like a veteran. He did show signs of tiring late in the year, which is quite normal for a northeastern US prospect more accustomed to playing a fairly short season. Baker was limited to a strict pitch count in 2000, and averaged only five innings per start. Look for him to be stretched out to seven innings more often at the High-A level in 2001. Baker needs to develop a true out pitch for use against upper level hitters and, with work, his curve should be that pitch. Baker could be a future mid-rotation presence in Boston, and could arrive by late 2003.

5 - RHP Sun-Woo Kim - Kim, 22, is the most gifted of the Sox' group of Far Eastern pitching prospects. He's a feisty 6'2", 180, righthander who combines a low 90s fastball and a changeup, plus a slider and curve that have both been slow to develop. He has the stuff to become a solid starting pitcher, but often outwits himself and lets hitters beat him on his third or fourth best pitch. His control is good, sometimes too good. He often leaves his fastball out over the plate, with predictable results. Kim might be best suited for a shift to the bullpen, where he could rely more heavily on his two best pitches. He has the mindset for that role, he has feuded with his Far Eastern organization-mates, particularly Tomokazu Ohka. Look for Kim to potentially make the Opening Day major league roster as a middle reliever, his likely destination for the long haul.

6 - 2B Angel Santos - This 5'11", 185, switch-hitter is an impressive offensive prospect whose defensive versatility should help him carve out a long-term major league role. After an exceptional 1999 Low-A season featuring 47 extra-base hits and 25 steals, Santos, 20, was challenged with a two-level jump to the Double-A Eastern League, and performed quite well. He hit for a respectable average with some power to the gaps, and above average speed. After splitting 1999 between second base, shortstop and third base at Low-A Augusta, Santos focused primarily on second base last season. His range is above average, and his throwing arm solid. Santos needs to improve his plate discipline a bit, but could develop into a .280 hitter with a 15/15 power/speed upside as a major leaguer. At the very least, he'll be a solid all-purpose infield backup, and he could be much more. He'll arrive in the majors in early 2002.

7 - LHP Casey Fossum - Fossum, 22, is an undersized 6'0", 160, southpaw who performed unevenly against younger High-A Florida State League competition last season. On one hand, he unfurled a very impressive strikeout/walk ratio and pitched a no-hitter; on the other hand, he allowed over a hit per inning and averaged just over five innings per start. Fossum combines a low 90s heater and a sharp slider, but lacks a true quality offspeed pitch, as his two best pitches are similar in velocity. He has sound mechanics and is in control on the mound, but appears to be too hittable to project as a future major league starter. His attributes could eventually translate into major league success out of the bullpen as a fine two-inning setup man, or even as a closer. Watch his strikeout rate, and his role in 2001 at Double-A Trenton. Fossum could arrive in the majors by late 2003.

8 - RHP Chris Reitsma - Reitsma, 22, was the Red Sox' first round pick in 1996, but only a year ago, his career in the organization appeared to be over. A battery of injuries and poor control had caused the club to leave him unprotected from the Rule 5 draft, where he was claimed in 1999 by the Devil Rays. He didn't make the Tampa Bay roster out of spring training, and was returned to the Sox, where he promptly had his best pro season at Double-A Trenton. Now, the 6'5", 195, righty isn't going to develop into the top-of-the-rotation stud who the Sox once envisioned, but he just might become a mid-rotation finesse guy or a viable setup man. Reitsma's fastball peaks at around 90 MPH, but he changes speed and location well, and consistently keeps the ball on the low edges of the strike zone. He gets ahead of hitters, keeps his pitch count down, and consequently lasts deep into ballgames. Most impressively, he took a regular Double-A turn without incident for an entire season. Reitsma's career is back up off of the mat, and with a solid start at Triple-A Pawtucket in 2001, he could join the major league staff later in the season as a swingman or fifth starter.

9 - 2B Carlos Leon - Leon, 20, is a 5'10", 169, switch-hitter who made major strides with the bat last season at High-A Sarasota. He's a spray hitter with very little extra base pop, but he makes consistent line drive contact and will take a walk. His speed is only a little bit above average, but he's a savvy baserunner who should be able to steal 15-20 bases per season as he advances. He is a one-position player at this point, plus his rather narrow offensive game makes him a tough sell for a future significant major league role. He makes the plays at second base, but lacks the above average range or throwing arm that would qualify him for other positions. Leon will have to continue to hit over .300 as he advances to stay in the major league hunt. His performance against the more advanced Double-A hurlers in 2001 will be telling. He could arrive in late 2003.

10 - RHP Tomokazu Ohka - Ohka, 24, has proven beyond a shadow of a doubt that he can overmatch Triple-A batters. Unfortunately, he might have also proven that he cannot handle major league hitters. Yes, he could well be that most common of species; the Quadruple-A player. The 6'1", 180, righthander possesses a low 90s heater, and mixes it with a splitter and a changeup that was recognized as the International League's best breaking pitch by its managers. None of those offerings are true strikeout pitches, but he has succeeded against Triple-A competition by placing the ball on the edges of the strike zone consistently. However, he doesn't appear to believe he belongs in the majors. He has pitched quite timidly in his opportunities, and when he catches too much of the plate with any of his pitches, disaster often ensues. Some observers feel that Ohka lacks the fire to achieve at the game's ultimate level. He might be out of chances in Boston, but could snag a low-rotation role in the majors if he gets a change of scenery.

OTHER PROSPECTS

OF Rick Asadoorian - Asadoorian has tremendous potential, combining the ability to become a power hitter with excellent speed and defensive skills. He's still extremely young and needs to become more patient at the plate, but his upside is seemingly unlimited.

SS Aaron Capista - At this point, Capista is nothing more than a slick fielder struggling to learn how to be an offensive threat. His defensive skills should be more than good enough if he ever learns what he's doing at the plate. Right now he doesn't have any power and hasn't made his presence felt on the bases, which means he's destined for bench jobs unless he improve as a hitter.

OF Michael Coleman - Coleman is definitely a "tools player," the problem is that he's more likely to act like a tool than to put his skills to work. His attitude and lack of discipline have kept him from advancing the past couple of years and unless he changes the way he plays the game, he'll be stuck at Triple-A. He has what it takes physically to be a power/speed man in the majors, but will he ever get it mentally?

LHP Casey Fossum - Fossum is a very polished pitcher with excellent command and above average stuff. His fastball isn't outstanding, but he has a good curve and a solid changeup. He's really overmatched Single-A hitters to this point and needs to be tested in 2001. If he performs well early on, expect the Sox to promote him aggressively.

1B Luis Garcia - Garcia is a good looking power prospect with an idea of what it takes to be a good hitter. He's not there yet, but he has shown the inclination to draw a few walks here and there despite his propensity for striking out. As he matures and gets stronger, Garcia could improve on his 20 home runs at Low-A from last season.

1B-3B Shea Hillenbrand - The one thing Hillenbrand can definitely do is hit. He was a subpar catcher, but the Sox have since moved him to the corner infield spots. If he develops just a touch more power, he could be a good major leaguer. He's not a patient hitter, but at the same time he rarely strikes out. He could wind up being a lot like Greg Colbrunn if he hits the weights a little.

RHP Bryan Leach - Normally Single-A closers don't get much attention, but it's hard to ignore the numbers Leach put up during the 2000 season. He saved 40 games and struck out nearly 11 batters per nine innings and allowed just 65 total baserunners in 72-plus innings. He's a strikeout pitcher who throws strikes, which should serve him well should he continue that trend.

LHP Sang-Hoon Lee - Lee proved last year that he's too good for Triple-A hitters and a role as a lefthanded setup man in the majors seems to be coming. He throws strikes, has good offspeed stuff and a good enough fastball to get by. It's unlikely he'll be a star, but good lefthanded relievers are very valuable these days.

OF Angel Mendoza - Mendoza runs well and is a good outfielder, but he has a lot to learn as a hitter. He hasn't shown much power and isn't patient at all, so he must hit for a high average to keep progressing, which he didn't do in 2000.

RHP Juan Pena - Pena is a good pitcher, but arm problems kept him out of the 2000 season. He's not overpowering even when he's healthy, but he throws strikes and has a plus curveball that has enabled him to get his share of strikeouts over the years. He may have trouble regaining confidence in the curve when he first comes back from surgery, but long-term he could still be a solid major league pitcher.

OF Carlos Rodriguez - Rodriguez has demonstrated tremendous offensive potential so far, but must improve his pitch selection to continue putting up good numbers against older pitchers. He has above average power and speed to go along with the ability to consistently drive in runs, but he must draw more walks. He needs a fair amount of time before he can be considered major league material, but the tools are there.

CHICAGO WHITE SOX
ORGANIZATIONAL GRID

	AAA	AA	HI-A	LO-A
1B	Jeff Liefer - L - 25	Eric Battersby - R - 24	Matt Berger - R - 25 Brandon Hyde - R - 26	Casey Rogowski - L - 19
2B	Liu Rodriguez - B - 23	Jackie Rexrode - L - 21 Danny Bravo - B - 23 Jose Alguacil - B - 27	Kevin Connacher - R - 25 Danny Sandoval - B - 21	Nilson Teilon - R - 19 Tommy Nicholson - L - 21
SS	Mike Caruso - L - 23	Jason Dellaero - B - 23	Luis Suarez - R - 21	Lenin Solorzano - R - 20
3B	Brad Seitzer - R - 30 Brandon Moore - R - 27 Craig Wilson - R - 29	Joe Crede - R - 22	Ryan Hankins - R - 24 Tim Hummel - R - 21	Juan Santamarina - L - 20 Jason Aspito - R - 21
OF	Scott Lydy - R - 31 Steve Gibralter - R - 27 Desi Wilson - L - 31 McKay Christensen - L - 24 Jacob Brumfield - R - 35 Jeff Inglin - R - 24 Rod Myers - L - 27	Rick Prieto - R - 27 Aaron Rowand - R - 22 Adam Johnson - L - 24 Ryan Long - R - 27	Brett Caradonna - L - 21 Terrell Merriman - L - 22 Mario Valenzuela - R - 23 Marcellous Manuel - L - 24	Chad Durham - R - 22 Spencer Oborn - R - 22 Rolando Garza - R - 20 Jason Fennell - B - 22
C	Jimmy Foster - R - 28 Dave Toth - R - 30 Josh Paul - R - 25	Mel Rosario - B - 27 Chris Heintz - R - 25	Tony Garcia - R - 22 Jonathan Acevas - R - 22	Wally Rosa - R - 19
SP	Jason Secoda - R - 25 Carlos Chantres - R - 24 Kip Wells - R - 23 Aaron Myette - R - 22 Mark Roberts - R - 24	Josh Fogg - R - 23 Rocky Biddle - R - 24 Matt Ginter - R - 22 Jon Rauch - R - 21 Dan Wright - R - 22	Eric Fischer - L - 20 Geronimo Mendoza - R - 22 Rob Purvis - R - 22 Edwin Almonte - R - 23 Mitch Wylie - R - 23 Gary Majewski - R - 20	Jason Stumm - R - 19 Dennis Ulacia - L - 19 Josh Stewart - L - 21 Brian West - R - 19 Kris McWhirter - R - 21
CLOSER	Joe Davenport - R - 24 Chad Bradford - R - 25 Scott Eyre - L - 28	Marty Weymouth - R - 22 Matt Guerrier - R - 21 Jesus Pena - L - 25	David Sanders - L - 20	Joe Curreri - R - 23 Andre Simpson - R - 20

CHICAGO WHITE SOX

The White Sox' minor league pitching depth is the envy of other major league clubs, any one of six to eight Sox hurlers could eventually wend their way into the upper half of major league rotations. Though position player depth isn't nearly as strong, players like third baseman Joe Crede and outfielders McKay Christensen and Aaron Rowand could be of some use at the major league level before long.

With Frank Thomas and Paul Konerko in place at the major league level, not much near-term help is needed. Jeff Liefer's power bat could be attractive as trade bait or as a short-term injury fill-in at the major league level. 2000 Low-A first sacker Casey Rogowski, 19, could become interesting if he develops a power swing to go with his 6'2", 220, frame, but he hasn't shown any such signs to date.

At second base, Liu Rodriguez is a contact-hitting major league middle infield utility candidate. Jackie Rexrode is a speedster who gets on base constantly, but his total lack of extra base power and his defensive limitations paint an uncertain big league future. Nilson Teilon, 19, has an intriguing power upside for a young middle infield prospect, and is a sleeper to bust out to the upside in 2001.

Shortstop possibilities abound, but question marks are attached to all of them. Mike Caruso has already gotten his major league chance, and his spray-hitting bat plus many defensive questions suggest an uncertain future in Chicago. Jason Dellaero has a cannon arm and a number one draftee pedigree, but his offensive game has gone nowhere. His major league future is suspect, but his defensive upside is high. Luis Suarez is a future utility candidate who swings at everything and has little extra base power, but makes the routine play consistently. Keep an eye on sleeper Danny Sandoval, a slap hitter who consistently puts the ball in play and runs like the wind. Next to Dellaero, Sandoval has the best chance of making a big league impact at this position.

Joe Crede represents the White Sox' future at third base. All of his tools are a bit above average, and he projects as a solid, if not a star, AL third baseman over the next decade. His future could arrive sometime in 2001.

The Sox don't possess an abundance of minor league outfield talent, but McKay Christensen and Aaron Rowand could offer near-term support. Christensen, 24, is a former top Angels' draftee who runs extremely well and plays a solid defensive center field. He could challenge Chris Singleton for the major league job in the spring. Rowand possesses a solid gaps power/speed combination, but needs to tone down his aggressiveness at the plate to reach his power upside. He's a year away from challenging for a supporting big league role. Jeff Inglin is a line drive-hitting overachiever with a solid concept of the strike zone that could earn a major league cup of coffee as a backup outfielder. Terrell Merriman, a 1998 34th round pick, possesses an intriguing blend of power, speed and patience, and could creep into the hunt for major league playing time with a strong 2001 season.

The Sox don't have a lot of help on the way at catcher. Only 2000 Low-A receiver Humberto Quintero, 20, who possesses solid defensive skills and fine speed for a receiver, showed significant promise for the future last season.

Pitching depth is substantial. Some of these guys will make it with the Sox, and others will be packaged to bring marquee offensive talent to Chicago. Jon Garland, 20, is the real deal, and showed flashes of brilliance at the major league level at an even younger age than Rick Ankiel. He'll be a contributor from Day One in 2001, and should be a star soon. Lorenzo Barcelo has impeccable control, but might not have the out pitch required for him to make the big league rotation. In other systems, he'd have a shot; here, he has to get in line. Aaron Myette, not long ago considered by many to be the best of this strong group, has been slowed by injuries, but should soon join the Chicago rotation. If he hones his control, he could approach the Garland level. Josh Fogg is a workhorse who lacks

Garland and Myette's raw stuff, but his fine command and ability to last deep into ballgames serves him well. He could either start or pitch in middle relief in the majors. He could be the Sox' Ramiro Mendoza. Lefty Mark Buehrle, 21, also got a brief shot at the majors in 2000. He fills their need for a second lefty in the rotation behind Jim Parque, and evokes memories of a young Tom Glavine. Look for him to fit snugly into the back end of the Sox' 2001 rotation. 1999 first round pick Matt Ginter might be a bit more raw than Buehrle or Fogg, but his upside is likely higher. Ginter will likely be afforded a full year in the Triple-A rotation in 2001, but will be banging on the door shortly thereafter. Lean righthander Juan Figueroa overmatched High-A hitters in 2000, but might not have the raw stuff to get it done at higher levels. He'll have a hard time standing out in this group. 6'10" righthander Jon Rauch, a 1999 third round pick, showed exceptional mechanics for his size last season, and could evolve into a top-shelf major league starter. Double-A success in 2001 would mark him for potential stardom.

In most organizations, 22-year-old High-A righties Rob Purvis and Dan Wright would be heralded pitching prospects. In this system, these talented starters will need to bust it to continue to advance at a level per year pace. 1999 first round pick Jason Stumm, 19, is quite raw, but has the stuff to be a fine big league power pitcher. The Sox will have the luxury of bringing him around gradually given their pitching surplus. Fellow 1999 first round draftee Brian West, 19, stands a robust 6'4", 230, and could become a premium prospect once he develops a true strikeout pitch. Lefty Dennis Ulacia, also 19, has exceptional ability, but his mechanics were a mess last season. He'll need another Low-A season, and could be a breakthrough sleeper in 2001. Gary Majewski needs to work on his control, but his heavy heater has been hard for pro hitters to handle thus far in his brief pro career. He too will have a hard time standing out in this bunch.

TOP TEN PROSPECTS

1 - RHP Jon Garland - There are a number of things that set Garland, 20, apart from garden variety pitching prospects. After arriving in the majors last summer, the 6'6", 205, righty ranked as the youngest player in the majors, even younger than the Cards' Rick Ankiel. Previously, his tour de force at Triple-A Charlotte in the International League resulted in him being recognized as the best pitching prospect in that league by its managers. He also has the cachet of being drafted in the first round by one

Chicago team (Cubs, in 1997) and now emerging as a surefire pitching star for the other, after being acquired in a laughable 1998 stretch run deal for Matt Karchner. Despite his major league struggles in 2000, Garland is a premium prospect. His arsenal includes a darting, low-to-mid 90s sinking fastball that evokes images of Kevin Brown, an excellent curveball, a fine slider and an improving changeup. He has a shot to be his generation's Greg Maddux, who struggled similarly early in his career, before also being dealt by the Cubs. Look for a major step forward in 2001 from the White Sox' next ace.

2 - RHP Jon Rauch - Rauch, 21, is an enormous 6'10", 230, righthander who dropped to the third round of the 1998 draft due to a bout with viral meningitis and to questions about his work ethic. Rauch is totally healthy, and has exposed those concerns about his makeup as unfounded. Rauch has been excellent over the past two seasons. In 2000, he was recognized as the best pitching prospect in the High-A Carolina League by its managers. At his size, one might expect Rauch to merely be a raw flamethrower with a vague idea of the strike zone. That couldn't be farther from the truth. Rauch's mechanics and control are impeccable for his size and his age, and his professional success is as linked to his deceptive motion, nasty overhand curve and improving changeup as it is to his lively low 90s fastball. Rauch's ability to maintain his high standard of performance at the Double-A level after his late 2000 performance also speaks well for his future. Rauch could arrive in Chicago by the end of 2001, and will assume a prominent role beside Garland in their rotation for a decade or more.

3 - RHP Aaron Myette - Myette, 22, has taken some steps backward over the past season or so, but in terms of talent, is right there with the first couple of guys on this list. The 6'4", 195, righthander rocketed through the lower levels of the minors after being drafted on the first round in 1997, but his development has stagnated over the past two seasons as he has failed to significantly improve any of his secondary pitches. His fastball reaches the low 90s, and he possesses a diverse four-pitch arsenal including a curve, slider and changeup. He has a prototypical pitcher's frame, and should add additional velocity as he physically matures and fine tunes his mechanics. His 2000 Triple-A season was a mixed bag. He proved himself as a durable hurler who could keep his team in ballgames consistently over seven-inning stretches, a valuable commodity. However, he rarely dominated, his strikeout rate declining a bit from previous years. Myette should be ready to make a big league contribution in 2001, and will likely beat

Rauch to the majors. Look for him to become a valuable 200-inning mid-rotation horse in Chicago.

4 - 3B Joe Crede - Crede, 22, has made it all the way back from foot surgery which had sharply curtailed his effectiveness in portions of both 1998 and 1999. The 1996 fifth round pick is a well-rounded prospect with the ability to hit for a high average with 20-homer power, and above average defensive range and a strong arm at third base. Double-A Southern League managers voted him the best batting prospect and defensive third baseman in the circuit. His plate discipline, which will never be his strongest suit, has improved quite a bit, showing that he is a player willing to work on his weaknesses. At 6'3", 190, the strapping righthanded hitter is likely to add more muscle and become a 30-homer threat at the major league level. This isn't Scott Rolen we're talking about here, but it is a future above average starting major league third baseman. At the latest, he'll be in place by Opening Day 2002.

5 - RHP Jason Stumm - The White Sox, a brilliant young offensive club already at the major league level, obviously have an embarrassment of pitching riches on the way through the minor leagues. Stumm, 19, is a gifted 6'2", 210, righthander who likely possesses the best fastball in the White Sox' system, though he isn't nearly as polished as some of the other hurlers in the chain. At this point, Stumm is too reliant on his mid 90s heater, but it should act as a solid starting point from which to develop his slider and changeup from their current rudimentary level. Stumm averaged only five innings per start last season, largely due to high pitch counts generated by his tendency to try to throw the perfect offering on nearly every pitch. His command, an area of concern in his first pro season, was much improved in 2000, and his control is now quite good for a teenage power pitcher. It must be remembered that Stumm was one of the youngest pitchers in the Low-A Midwest League last season, and that more than his mediocre mainstream statistics offers information about his future. Look for him to continue to put it together at the High-A level in 2001, possibly having a Rauch-like breakthrough season. Stumm, like the others, will be a future major league stalwart.

6 - LHP Mark Buehrle - Buehrle, 21, is the first lefthanded pitcher on this list, and certainly is the least pedigreed, with the least raw ability. However, this 6'2", 195, southpaw might be the most polished, who has derived the most from the skills he does possess. This 1998 38th round draftee navigated the daunting two-level jump from Low-

A in 1999 to Double-A in 2000 with relative ease, and wound up spending the better part of his late summer in a major league pennant race in Chicago. Control is the essence of Buehrle's game. Double-A Southern League managers credited him for having the best control in the circuit, and he was able to average well over seven innings per start because of the low pitch counts he maintained. His fastball only reaches the upper 80s, and he completes a diverse repertoire with a curve, slider and changeup, all of which he throws for quality strikes consistently. It remains to be seen whether Buehrle can get the ball past major league hitters in tight spots. It's clear, however, that he will be a key component of near-term Sox' pitching staffs. Look for him to start for the next season or two, and then possibly slide into a lefty specialist bullpen role as the Rauchs and Stumms arrive in town.

7 - RHP Matt Ginter - Yup, there's more top pitching talent to discuss. Ginter, 22, is a 1999 first round draftee who quickly stepped in as a top-shelf Double-A starter in his first full season of professional baseball. The 6'2", 220, righthander doesn't have the power of Stumm, the control of Buehrle, or the diverse repertoire of Rauch, but he isn't far from their equal in any of those areas. Ginter's fastball routinely reaches the low 90s, and he consistently keeps it low in the strike zone, a la Garland. He uses his slider as out pitch against both lefties and righties. Like Buehrle, Ginter consistently gets ahead of hitters, often allows them to retire themselves early in the count, maintaining low pitch counts and lasting deep into ballgames as a result. With all of the starting pitching talent surrounding Ginter, it will be a challenge for him to crack into the major league rotation soon. He could be an excellent two-inning setup man during his apprenticeship at the major league level, and could eventually graduate into a mid-rotation role.

8 - OF Joe Borchard - Borchard, 21, was the White Sox' first round draftee in 2000, and advanced all the way to Double-A after signing a lucrative major league contract. The 6'4", 195, switch-hitter was a power hitter extraordinaire, and a football quarterback, at Stanford but didn't make a particularly smooth adjustment to the wooden bat the first time around in the pros. Focusing totally on baseball should speed his development, particularly with the bat. Defensively, he's a natural right fielder with decent range and explosive arm strength. He'll need to learn to work deep counts to see the fastballs he'll need to maximize his power output, and at his age will need to put it together quickly to become an elite prospect. He'll likely start 2001 at the Double-A level, and is a candidate to break out to the upside early in the season.

9 - RHP Brian West - West, 19, was yet another Sox' minor league hurler who flourished as one of his level's youngest players in 2000. The 6'4", 230, righthanded pitcher is a fine athlete who chose baseball over a scholarship to play defensive end at Texas A&M. He possesses a low-to-mid 90s fastball and a pretty raw breaking pitch arsenal at this point, but his potential is significant. He proved to be a durable staff anchor at Low-A Burlington last season, but his lack of a true offspeed pitch prevented him from racking up impressive strikeout totals. A little tweaking of his mechanics will also likely serve to add movement and maybe a bit of velocity to his fastball. Of this extraordinarily deep group of starting pitchers, West and Stumm are the farthest from the major leagues, and neither is likely to make the majors to stay before late 2003. Their upsides, however, are high. West could have a breakthrough 2001 season, and is a likely future major league mid-rotation starter.

10 - RHP Dan Wright - How about one more pitching prospect for the road? Wright, 22, is a 1999 second round pick with an intriguing skill set, including a lively mid-90's fastball, a hard curve, and a prototypical 6'5", 215, pitcher's build. However, he has not achieved significant success for a few years now, including his last two college seasons at Arkansas, when he went a combined 2-15. He allowed over a hit per inning last season at High-A Winston Salem, but did average nearly seven innings per start. His command is solid, with a low walk rate mitigated somewhat by his tendency to at times leave the ball out over the middle of the plate. At his age, the Sox will be looking for a breakout season at the Double-A level in 2001. If he doesn't make significant progress as a starter, he could have a future as a two-inning, once-around-the-order setup reliever.

OTHER PROSPECTS

RHP Lorenzo Barcelo - The fact that Barcelo isn't in the Top 10 should tell you what kind of system the White Sox have right now. He's got a world of potential and has already picked up a fair amount of major league experience. Barcelo throws in the mid 90s with pretty good control and has the ability to be a starter or a closer, though given the Sox' depth in terms of starting pitchers he seems likely to wind up in the bullpen.

RHP Rocky Biddle - Biddle put on a strong showing at Double-A during the 2000 season and made four major league starts late in the season. He's got a low 90s fastball that moves a little and a decent breaking pitch, but he doesn't seem like top of the rotation material. He'll be hard pressed to beat out the White Sox' other pitching prospects, but he could be used in a trade to fill other holes.

SS Mike Caruso - Caruso looks like he could be a one-year wonder. His hitting skills, never all that great, have declined over the past season two seasons and his defense at shortstop is still below average. Speed is his primary weapon and he only stole five bases at Triple-A last year, which is a bad sign. He's still young and if he can demonstrate the ability to play multiple positions, he's been tried at second base and in the outfield, there may still be some kind of major league future for him.

RHP Carlos Chantres - Chantres isn't considered one of the White Sox' best pitching prospects, but all he did last year was go 10-4 with a 3.53 ERA at Triple-A. He's done a fine job of keeping the ball in the park and even though he's not a strikeout pitcher, per se, he is very tough to hit against. Chantres' control is above average, as is his fastball, and even if he doesn't wind up in the White Sox' rotation he could be valuable trade bait or he could be used in relief.

OF McKay Christensen - Christensen is an excellent center fielder with tremendous speed, but he still has a bit to learn as a hitter. He doesn't look like he'll ever develop power, but with improved patience at the plate he could still be a major league regular. He has the physical tools to be a solid leadoff man in the Brett Butler mold, but he needs to hit for a higher average and draw more walks.

SS Jason Dellaero - Once considered the White Sox potential shortstop of the future, Dellaro has regressed badly over the past year. His strikeout total was astronomical at Double-A (142 whiffs in 438 at-bats) last year and he hit well under .200. He's decent defensively, but another year at the plate like 2000 could find him out of baseball.

RHP Josh Fogg - Fogg is another guy who could be in some teams' Top 10 lists, but not with the White Sox. He has a low 90s fastball, a solid breaking pitch and very good control to his credit. He's been very tough on Single-A and Double-A hitters so far and if that translates into success at Triple-A next year the Sox will have another major league arm to use or to trade. A move to the bullpen wouldn't be out of the question.

1B-OF Jeff Liefer - For all of the offensive strengths of the White Sox' major league lineup, Lifer has something they desperately need; lefthanded power. He strikes out a lot, doesn't walk an incredible number of times and isn't especially good defensively, but he can hit the long ball. If given an opportunity, Liefer could hit 25-30 home runs over a full major league season.

RHP Gary Majewski - Majewski has great stuff and has been excessively difficult to hit against in the minors. At Low-A last season, he allowed just 83 hits in 134-plus innings while striking out 137 batters. Those are absolutely remarkable numbers and it's also interesting to note that while his walk total wasn't high, he hit a lot of batters demonstrating his aggressiveness and his willingness to pitch inside. He's got a high upside and he could emerge as a top prospect in 2001.

OF Terrell Merrimen - Merrimen has some power and some speed, but perhaps more impressive than those two qualities is his discipline at the plate. He drew 94 walks at Single-A last season despite hitting just .232, leaving hope for improvement. He's a switch-hitter with the ability to steal 30-40 bases and hit 10-20 home runs a season, which is a nice combination.

RHP Rob Purvis - It's hard to believe, but Purvis is yet another good White Sox' pitching prospect. He's got a good, live fastball and above average breaking pitch, though control is a bit of a problem at this point. He's been able to pitch around his control problems against Single-A hitters, but that may not be the case as he moves up. Purvis has a good upside and if he can locate better he'll be fine.

2B Jackie Rexrode - Rexrode has excellent speed and outstanding strike zone judgment, which could lead to a spot at the top of a major league order at some point in the near future. He has no power at all, but he makes a lot of contact and knows how to get on base and make things happen. His defense has been inconsistent in the minors and that will have to change if he ever wants to play everyday in the majors.

OF Aaron Rowand - Rowand, 22, was the White Sox' 1998 first round draftee. The 6'1", 200, righthanded hitter is a bit above average in all respects, a potential high-average hitter with a 30/20 power/speed upside, plus above average defensive ability. He shone defensively last season, showing improved range and being recognized for having the strongest throwing arm in the Double-A Southern League by its managers. However, subpar plate discipline prevented him from dominating offensively last season, and will continue to do so against higher level pitching if not addressed. If Rowand were to work deeper counts, he'd see plenty more fastballs, and could develop into the 30-homer force he is capable of becoming. 2001 will be a key minor league season for Rowand, one that will tell whether he is a future productive major league middle-of-the-order hitter, or merely a useful future fourth outfielder and power bat off of a major league bench.

2B-OF Nilson Teilon - Teilon has a fair amount of power for someone so young, but he needs to improve his overall approach at the plate. He's not shown he can hit for much average at this point, he strikes out a lot and doesn't walk very often either. Teilon also hasn't shown much ability on the basepaths, so he's got some things to work on.

RHP Danny Wright - Wright might have the best pure fastball of anyone in the White Sox' system. He throws in the mid to upper 90s, but lacks control and a solid second pitch. He's working on some other pitches, but he might be best suited for relief work in the future because of his limited repertoire. His fastball, however, makes him an ideal candidate for the closer's role.

CLEVELAND INDIANS
ORGANIZATIONAL GRID

	AAA	AA	HI-A	LO-A
1B	Danny Peoples - R - 25	Billy Munoz - L - 24	Byron Ewing - R - 22	Curtis Gay - L - 22 Kyle Moyer - L - 19
2B	Jeff Patzke - B - 26	Scott Pratt - L - 23	Luis Gonzalez - R - 21	Omar Moraga - L - 23 Oscar Garcia - R - 19
SS	John McDonald - R - 25	Zach Sorensen - B - 23 Brian Whitlock - R - 25	Victor Rodriguez - R - 23	Jhonny Peralta - R - 17 Steven Lowe - R - 23 Maicer Isturiz - B - 19
3B	Jeff Manto - R - 35 Bill Selby - L - 30	Mike Edwards - R - 23	Corey Erickson - R - 23 Simon Pond - L - 23 Marques Esquerra - B - 24	Nate Grindell - R - 23
OF	David Roberts - L - 28 Mark Budzinski - L - 26 Chan Perry - R - 27 Russell Branyan - B - 24 Mark Whiten - B - 33	Jon Hamilton - L - 22 Chad Whitaker - L - 23 Scott Hunter - R - 24 Jason Fitzgerald - L - 24 Osmany Santana - L - 23	Jesus Hernandez - L - 23 Brian Benefield - R - 23 Tyler Minges - R - 20 Tom Bost - L - 24 Eric Johnson - R - 22	Jorge Moreno - R - 19 Alex Requena - B - 19 T.T. Gallaher - R - 22 Travis Santini - R - 19
C	Jesse Levis - L - 32 Bobby Hughes - R - 29 Chris Coste - R - 27	Mandy Romero - B - 32 Jeff DePippo - R - 24 Jim Rickon - R - 24	Casey Smith - R - 23 Matt Curtis - B - 25 Rusty Puffinbarger - R - 23	Edgar Cruz - R - 21 Victor Martinez - B - 21
SP	Jim Brower - R - 27 Willie Martinez - R - 22 Chris Clemons - R - 27 Tyler Green - R - 30 Chris Haney - L - 31 Tim Drew - R - 21	Frankie Sanders - R - 24 Jamie Brown - R - 23 Rob Pugmire - R - 21 Mike Bacsik - L - 22 Danys Baez - R - 22 Zach Day - R - 22 Joe Roa - R - 28 C.C. Sabathia - L - 19	Alberto Garza - R - 23 Matt White - L - 22 Mike Spiegel - L - 24 Steven Cowie - R - 23 Ryan Drese - R - 24 Wilson Sido - R - 24 Jay Sirianni - L - 24 Jason Stanford - L - 22	Devin Rogers - R - 21 Shane Wallace - L - 19 Kyle Denney - R - 22 Adam Barr - L - 19 Anthony Marini - L - 23 Phil Rosengren - R - 23
CLOSER	Chris Nichting - R - 34	Martin Vargas - R - 23 Ernie Delgado - R - 24 Roy Smith - R - 23	Jarrod Mays - R - 25 Dario Veras - R - 27 Jose Colon - R - 22	Ted Sullivan - R - 23 Rick Matsko - R - 23

CLEVELAND INDIANS

For most of the 1990s, the Indians' farm system was the envy of their major league brethren. The decade came and went without a World Championship, however, an elusive title that enticed the club to trade the Sean Caseys, Brian Gileses, Enrique Wilsons, Richie Sexsons, etc. in pursuit of it. Position player depth is quite thin at this point, but the Indians now for once possess a relative abundance of starting pitching prospects who are likely to begin to advance to the majors in 2001.

It took a while, but 1996 first round draftee Danny Peoples, 25, finally appears to be maturing into a near-term big league contributor. His power bat is his only plus tool, but the late 2000 wave of player movement may have opened a 2001 bench spot for him. He could be a poor man's Richie Sexson in a part-time role. He's the only viable first base prospect on the horizon.

With Roberto Alomar in place, only utility spots are available to the Indians' second base prospects. Marcos Scutaro is a scrappy offensive player who can also play a representative third base, giving him a competitive advantage for a 25th man slot. Scott Pratt runs well and can play defense, but his monopositional nature works against him. Luis Gonzalez has youth on his side, but lost a year of offensive development with a poor High-A season in 2000. His defensive upside is the highest of the bunch.

Switch-hitter Zach Sorensen makes contact and runs well, and likely could play second base as well as shortstop, making him a fringe big league utility contact despite his light-hitting ways. Jhonny Peralta has a chance to someday succeed Omar Vizquel at shortstop. He's one of the youngest players in organized ball, has exceptional plate discipline for a youngster, and can pick 'em in the field. Once he starts to hit with more authority, watch out.

Mike Edwards is the only viable third base prospect on the horizon, but he lacks a single stand out tool to build upon. He could be a long-term Triple-A fixture or major league bench bat.

It seems like only yesterday that the Indians' system was so deep in outfielders that Alex Ramirez, since being moved to the Pirates, would hit 30 homers but remain marooned in Buffalo on an annual basis. Things have thinned out a bit, however. Jon Hamilton is a well-rounded lefthanded hitter who lacks a significant flaw in his game. He could evolve into a viable major league platooner or fourth outfielder, and could arrive by 2002. Chad Whitaker has a power stroke, but his progress in all areas has been too slow for him to be considered likely to make a big league impact. Tyler Minges has the all-around ability to make a run at a major league role, but was physically overmatched at the plate in the High-A Carolina League in 2000, setting his progress back. The Indians' best long-term outfield prospects resided at Low-A Columbus in 2001. Jorge Moreno has a substantial power/speed upside, but still needs a lot of at bats before entering the big league radar screen. Alex Requena ranks among the fastest players in the minors, but significant physical development will be necessary for him to become a threat to upper level hurlers. Both Moreno and Requena have the raw goods to start in the majors someday, however.

Not a lot of catching help is on the horizon. Edgar Cruz was once considered a blue-chipper, but his offensive progress has stagnated at the Low-A level for three seasons now, making him a longshot to reach his considerable potential.

The Indians almost surely will add an impressive young arm or two to their major league rotation in the next season. Righthander Willie Martinez, once considered their foremost pitching prospect, probably won't be the guy, however. His command has wavered in recent seasons, and he hasn't located a true strikeout pitch. He'll remain a midseason reinforcement at best until he does so. C.C. Sabathia is quite possibly the single best starting pitcher prospect in the game. No lefty throws harder, and his command and breaking pitch repertoire are solid as well. He'll crack the rotation in 2001, and should emerge as the staff ace before long. Righty Jamie Brown has great control, but is still searching for a strikeout pitch. He looks more like a swingman or middle relief candidate at the major league level. Tim Drew got a couple of cracks at major league opposition in 2000, and clearly wasn't ready. He too might be best suited to facing major league hitters one time around the order as a setup reliever after a bit more seasoning. Rob Pugmire has the makings of a major league mid-rotation finesse righty, but has been dogged by injuries. The Tribe needs to see an injury-free upper minor league season from Pugmire before they pencil him into their plans. Lefty Mike Bacsik is a control pitcher who has quietly worked his way into the hunt for a southpaw specialist role in the majors. His soft-tossing act likely won't work in a big league rotation over the long haul. The Indians spent a ton of money importing righthander Danys Baez. After a slow start, he righted himself at the Double-A level, leaving indications that he could be a 200-inning anchor in the major league rotation within a couple of years. He needs to establish a true strikeout pitch first.

The Indians added further pitching depth with the acquisition of righties Jake Westbrook and Zach Day from the Yankees in the David Justice deal. Westbrook has gotten the most ink, and got a little major league experience under his belt at a very young age, but will reside squarely on the major league fringe until he starts making hitters miss. He lacks a true out pitch. Day's upside is higher, but he's battled injury problems and has yet to make a Double-A impact. The next year will be pivotal, but Day certainly has major league mid-rotation material. Keep an eye on finesse lefty Shane Wallace. He could be a solid upper minor league starter with improved command within the strike zone, and youth is on his side.

Keep an eye on Class A closer prospect Miguel Jauregui. He's got the arm strength to last two or three innings per outing, and laudable power and command. Watch his upper minor league performance before getting too excited, however.

TOP TEN PROSPECTS

1 - LHP C.C. Sabathia - Sabathia, 19, is a massive 6'7", 235, lefthander who ranks among the foremost pitching prospects in the minor leagues. His feature pitch is an overpowering fastball that pushes 100 MPH on the gun, and he mixes it with an improving curveball and a passable changeup. His mechanics are fairly consistent for someone of his age and size, and his command is

gradually improving. He was recognized as the best pitching prospect, with the best fastball in the Double-A Eastern League (as one of the circuit's younger hurlers) by its managers. Pitching prospects like this simply do not come around every day. He is a future number one stud who the Indians will not be able to keep on the farm much longer. Look for Sabathia to earn a job in the Indians' rotation in early 2001, and expect him to head up their rotation in fairly short order.

2 - RHP Danys Baez - The once-loaded Indians' system sure has taken a hit in recent seasons, as Sabathia is the only sure thing left. Baez, 22, was signed as a free agent out of Cuba in 1999, and as it was for many other recently signed Cuban expatriates, his first year was quite a rollercoaster. Many expected the 6'4", 225, righty to quickly step into a significant major league role, but those were clearly unrealistic expectations. After enduring some growing pains, however, Baez evolved into a fairly consistent hurler at the Double-A level by season's end. In other words, he's about where Livan Hernandez was at a similar stage in development. Baez is a prototypical power pitcher with a mid 90s fastball and a powerful curveball. His mechanics and command are quite polished for his age, and with the addition of a better changeup, Baez could emerge as a strikeout per inning pitcher. He suffered from a tender elbow for part of 2000, but appears to be healthy now. The Indians would love to see Baez join their rotation by the end of 2001. If he stagnates as a starter, Baez could develop into an overpowering reliever. Either way, Baez will be ready to help out in a complementary role in Cleveland quite soon.

3 - SS Jhonny Peralta - Peralta, 19, more than held his own as one of the younger players in the Low-A South Atlantic League. His defense is ahead of his offense at this point. Peralta has exceptional range thanks to impressive lateral quickness, plus a quick release and an extremely strong throwing arm. The 6'1", 185, switch-hitter needs plenty of polish at the plate, but already possesses solid plate discipline and shows flashes of his ability to drive the ball with authority to the gaps. Though he runs well, his inexperience and lack of aggressiveness on the bases makes him a subpar basestealing threat at this point. Don't be surprised if Peralta takes major steps forward in 2001, particularly with the bat. Peralta has a solid chance of eventually replacing Omar Vizquel in the Indians' lineup. If he can be a productive Double-A player by opening day 2002, he'll be a solid bet for future major league success.

4 - RHP Tim Drew - Drew, 21, is a 1997 first round draft pick who was rushed to the major leagues for a while in 2000 due to the spate of injuries suffered by members of the Indians' major league staff. The 6'1", 195, righthander throws a 90 MPH fastball that moves sharply, and his out pitch is a late breaking slider. He needs to significantly improve his changeup to become a solid upper minor league starter, let alone a viable major leaguer. Drew rarely walks hitters, but his inability to make upper minor league hitters miss is becoming a cause for concern. He needs pinpoint precision to be effective because of his lack of a true out pitch, especially against lefties. He's still quite young, and has an advanced feel for pitching for his age. The Indians believe it's only a matter of time before he tastes significant success. 2001 will be a key year for Drew, and he will likely spend it at the Triple-A level. If he doesn't cut it as a mid-rotation starter within two years in Cleveland, he could be a fit as a situational righty out of the bullpen.

5 - RHP Rob Pugmire - Pugmire, 21, is a talented prospect who has suffered from myriad injury troubles since being drafted in the third round in 1997. The 6'3", 205, righty has a low 90s fastball plus a curveball and changeup, and has smooth mechanics and well above average control. He was set back by losing the 1998 season to a severe back injury, but appeared to be on the fast track after a fine 1999 season split between both Class A levels. However, a frayed labrum delayed the start of his 2000 season, and as a result he didn't get an extended opportunity to prove he belonged at the Double-A level. Pugmire, despite his lively stuff, is not a strikeout pitcher, and will need to consistently navigate the edges of the strike zone at upper levels to excel. If everything breaks right, Pugmire could still evolve into a reliable major league mid-rotation starter. He needs to be successful and healthy over a full minor league season real soon to ensure that he will ever get his chance. 2001 is a pivotal year for Pugmire.

6 - 1B Danny Peoples - Peoples, 25, is a late-blooming 1996 first round draftee who finally showed signs of developing all-around offensive skills who could be of use in a complementary major league role. The 6'1", 207, righthanded hitter improved his plate discipline last season, and as his walk total rose, his strikeout total decreased, he saw more fastballs and hit for a higher average than ever before, without sacrificing home run power. It's unlikely that Peoples has the raw bat speed to be a true slugger at the major league level, but he could be quite useful in a 300 at bat role. Though he's not a particularly graceful athlete defensively, his ability to hold his own at first base, third base and left field also enhances his chances of sticking with the Indians in 2001. Peoples resides squarely on the major league fringe, and will likely never have a better chance to crack the Indians' big league roster than he will this season.

7 - OF Alex Requena - Speed thrills. Requena, 19, is a 5'11", 155, switch-hitter signed out of Venezuela in 1998 whose speed is by far his most advanced tool. Low-A South Atlantic League managers recognized him being both the fastest and best baserunner in the circuit last season. He reads pitchers quite well considering his age and experience level, and should remain a 40-plus stolen base threat as he advances through the minors. That is, if he can get on base at higher levels. Requena does not hit the ball with authority, he's a slap hitter who too often slaps the ball weakly in the air. He'd likely struggle to bat .230 in the upper minors at this point. Requena does not excel defensively, sometimes taking circuitous routes to fly balls, but outruns a lot of his mistakes. He has a solid throwing arm, and could play right field at higher levels. His improvement with the bat will determine his eventual upside, he could be a future big league leadoff man, or could struggle to start at Double-A. Most likely, he'll be a big league role player.

8 - OF Jorge Moreno - Moreno, 19, is an interesting power/speed prospect who showed flashes of brilliance at Low-A Columbus last season as one of the younger players in that circuit. The 6'0", 175, righthanded hitter hits the ball with consistent authority to the gaps and beyond, and could evolve into a 25/20 power/speed threat as he advances. Despite his youth, his frame is nearly fully physically developed, precluding any hopes for explosive offensive development beyond that level. Another limiting factor is his inability to handle quality breaking stuff at this stage in his development. He struck out in about a third of his at bats last season, often on pitches outside the strike zone. Still, Moreno is a sleeper to watch in 2001. At best, he could evolve into a starting corner outfield candidate in the majors within three seasons, but more likely will have to carve out a complementary bench bat role.

9 - RHP Zach Day - Day, 22, came over from the Yankees along with fellow pitching prospect Jake Westbrook in the David Justice deal. The 6'4", 185, righthander was injured for most of the 1999 season and lost his place in the long line of top-shelf Yankee pitching prospects. Day is not a power pitcher, but could add a bit of velocity and movement to his upper 80s heater if he added 10 to 15 pounds of muscle. His mechanics are true, and when Day is hitting his spots, his ability to change speed and keep hitters off balance makes him a tough customer. Double-A will be a key hurdle for Day, as it is for all pitchers lacking big-time fastballs. If Day can maintain his strikeout rate there, he'll be a strong candidate to join the low end of the Indians' rotation by late 2002.

10 - RHP Jamie Brown - Brown, 23, was a bit of a disappointment in 2000, failing to advance beyond the Double-A level for the second consecutive season. The 6'2", 205, 1996 21st round pick is a finesse hurler with a high 80s fastball, a curveball and changeup, none of which he can consistently get past higher level hitters. However, Brown can keep hitters off balance by variation of location and speed, and might eventually be a solid fit in a major league bullpen because of his ability to fool hitters the first time around the batting order. For Brown to remain a viable starting pitcher prospect, he'll need to develop a true out pitch for use against lefties. That's not likely going to happen. Look for Brown to be tried in a middle relief or setup role in 2001, and experience renewed success, possibly at the major league level.

OTHER PROSPECTS

LHP Mike Bascik - Bascik has very good control and he does a nice job of keeping the ball on the ground. His stuff isn't the greatest, but he knows what he's doing out there and that's a big part of the battle. He's not considered a top prospect, but if he performs this year like he did last year the Indians will have no choice but to give him a shot.

2B-3B Corey Erickson - Erickson has developed some power recently and that could be the thing that helps him advance. He plays a couple of positions, runs reasonably well and draws a fair number of walks, though he does tend to strikeout too much. Erickson probably won't be a star, but he can provide some pop and some versatility.

3B Nate Grindell - For a young hitter, Grindell has a lot of outstanding characteristics. He has tremendous power and has proven he can drive in runs consistently while not striking out very often at all. He could stand to walk more, but so long as the strikeouts are down that won't be a major issue. He's also shown some speed on the bases, which is an added bonus. He hit 18 home runs, had 36 doubles and drove in 98 runs at Low-A last year, but he also made 39 errors at third base.

OF Jon Hamilton - Hamilton doesn't have much home run power at this point of his career, but the ability to develop double-digit power is there. He runs reasonably well and draws a few walks, but really needs to cut down on the strikeouts to fulfill his potential.

RHP Miguel Jauregi - Jauregi has a big-time arm and he could be a fine relief pitcher in a very short time. His control is a problem and he falls behind in a lot of counts, allowing hitters to sit on his fastball, but his upside is nice. If he spots his fastball, there's no telling how fast he can rise.

OF Eric Johnson - Johnson can really run and he's got a very good idea of what it takes to be a good hitter. He's shown he can hit for average, he draws a lot of walks and steals a lot of bases, making him a candidate for top of the order duty down the line. He doesn't have much power, however, and he must continue to hit for average as he moves up the ranks in the minors.

RHP Willie Martinez - Martinez isn't a top of the line pitching prospect, but he's got a chance to be a decent major leaguer. He has a low 90s fastball and an above average curveball in his armory, though he's inconsistent. Martinez hasn't been prone to giving up a lot of hits, even at the Triple-A level, so if he can work ahead in the count on a regular basis he'll be just fine.

RHP David Riske - Riske is a good relief pitcher with the ability to help a major league team in the near future. He doesn't have a closer's stuff, but has picked up his fair share of saves in the minors because of his control and his ability to get ground ball outs. His fastball is about average and he's got a good breaking pitch to go with a tough mental approach on the mound.

2B Marcos Scutaro - Scutaro is a decent middle infielder with some offensive ability. He's not going to be a great hitter, but he does have a good eye at the plate and can run a little bit. He has demonstrated the ability to play both middle infield positions as well as third base, though second base is clearly his strongest position. There may be a major league utility role in his future.

RHP Roy Smith - Smith is a 6'7" righthanded reliever who came on strong with the Indians Double-A team last year. He spent the 1999 season playing for the St. Paul Saints, but he latched on with the Tribe and looked very good. His fastball isn't the greatest, but combined with his control and his secondary pitches he's very effective. His

1.96 ERA at Double-A last year most likely earned him a promotion to Triple-A for this year.

RHP Jose Vargas - Vargas has a live arm and pretty good control. He keeps the ball in the park and is adept at picking up strikeouts as well, which is a great combination. His future role is still uncertain as he can start and relieve, but his repertoire and his ability to keep the ball in the park would make him an ideal late-inning reliever.

RHP Jake Westrbook - Westbrook has good stuff, including a low 90s fastball and good breaking pitch, and he's pretty close to getting his shot at the majors. He's been inconsistent the past couple of seasons, but his overall ability leaves him with a better than average shot of sticking in the majors. The Indians might have a use for him soon, though he needs to be more consistent to regain his standing as a top prospect.

DETROIT TIGERS
ORGANIZATIONAL GRID

	AAA	AA	HI-A	LO-A
1B	Eric Gillespie - L - 25	Eric Munson - L - 22 Alejandro Freire - R - 25	Leo Daigle - R - 20	Jake Anthony - L - 23
2B	Chris Lemonis - L - 26 Marty Malloy - L - 27	Pedro Santana - R - 23	Terrance Freeman - B - 25 Reggie Nelson - R - 21	Carlos Jimenez - R - 20
SS	Jesus Azuaje - R - 27 Giomar Guevara - B - 27	Derek Mitchell - R - 25 Brian Rios - R - 25	Omar Infante - R - 18	Ramon Santiago - B - 18
3B	Rob Sasser - R - 25	Brant Ust - R - 21	Matt Boone - R - 20 Craig Da Luz - R - 25	Neil Jenkins - R - 19 Jason Drobiak - L - 21
OF	Billy McMillon - L - 28 Chris Wakeland - L - 26 Carlos Villalobos - R - 26 Pat Watkins - R - 27	Stoney Briggs - R - 28 Rod Lindsey - R - 24 Kurt Airoso - R - 25 Brian McClure - L - 26 Derek Besco - R - 24	Richard Gomez - R - 22 Juan Camilo - L - 22 Alex Steele - R - 24 Andres Torres - B - 22 Manuel Lutz - L - 24	Jerry Amador - R - 20 Corey Richardson - R - 23 Antonio McKinney - R - 22 Balmes Lara - R - 22 Cody Ross - R - 19
C	Brandon Inge - B - 23 Carlos Mendez - R - 26	David Lindstrom - R - 25 Mike Rivera - R - 23	Jorge Meran - R - 23	Maxim St. Pierre - R - 20 Inakel Vargas - R - 22
SP	Mike Oquist - R - 32 Steve Sparks - R - 35 Bart Evans - R - 29 Adam Bernero - R - 23 Mark Johnson - R - 25 Adam Pettyjohn - L - 23 Victor Santos - R - 23 Doug Walls - R - 26	Matt Miller - L - 26 Mike Maroth - L - 22 Tommy Phelps - L - 26 Shane Loux - R - 20 Randy Leek - L - 23 Nate Cornejo - R - 20	Craig Johnson - R - 24 Clint Smith - R - 23 Tim Kalita - L - 21 Rick Kirsten - R - 21 David Melendez - R - 24 Casey Rowe - R - 21	Calvin Chipperfield - R - 22 Jason Frasor - R - 22 Tommy Marx - L - 20 Andy Van Hekken - L - 20 Fernando Rodney - R - 19 Pablo Arias - R - 21 Jeff Leuenberger - R - 21
CLOSER	Brandon Reed - R - 25 Brandon Villafuerte - R - 24	Kris Keller - R - 22 Shane Heams - R - 24	Benny Lowe - L - 26 Stephen Bess - R - 23 Luis Pineda - R - 22	Greg Watson - R - 23

DETROIT TIGERS

In the last two seasons, the Tigers have radically over-hauled their minor league rosters, moving out the Mike Drumrights and Matt Drews who were long heralded, only to fall short in their quests for the majors. The Tigers still have plenty of rebuilding ahead, as their system has a glaring lack of star-quality players.

The Tigers drafted Eric Munson with the third overall pick in the 1999 draft with the firm belief that he would soon step in as a long-term solution in the middle of their order. Not so fast. Munson hasn't exactly overwhelmed minor league hurlers to date, and looked downright over-matched in a brief big league trial. Some of his power appears to have been lost in his transfer to the wooden bat, and his plate discipline is subpar. It's far from a sure thing that he'll ever be an adequate big league regular. One level behind Munson, Leo Daigle bears watching. His 6'3", 225, frame exudes power potential, but he hasn't yet found the key to it. Youth is firmly on his side, but he remains an outside sleeper prospect.

At second base, Pedro Santana offers an intriguing mix of speed, extra-base pop and sound defense. If Damian Easley continues to slip, Santana could be a candidate for major league time in 2001. He's a likely utilityman with an outside shot at a regular job. Carlos Jimenez can play both middle infield spots, and has low double-digit power/speed potential. He projects as a potential big league utilityman.

In Omar Infante and Ramon Santiago, the Tigers possess two high-upside shortstop prospects capable of eventually starting in the major leagues. Infante was one of the youngest High-A players in 2000, and he more than held his own at bat and in the field. He should develop extra base power as he matures, and already has excellent speed. He's raw, but has serious skills. Santiago is more polished than Infante, and has an arguably higher upside, especially in the field. He'll never be a masher, but could be a .280 hitter with 30 steals in the majors. The guess here is that Santiago will prevail in the battle for the 2003 shortstop job in Detroit.

Potentially viable alternatives to major league incumbent Dean Palmer abound throughout the system. Brant Ust leapt from rookie ball to Double-A in his first full pro season in 2000, and predictably struggled. He's a reliable defender and has some pop in his bat, but needs a lot of polish. He's no sure thing to be an eventual big league contributor. Matt Boone, brother of Aaron and Bret, son of Bob, grandson of Ray, major leaguers all; isn't nearly as assured of major league success as his relatives. He has some power potential and moves well at third base, but his development has been slower than anticipated. He's young, but needs to make a quantum leap in performance during the next year to remain a potential future big league starter. Neil Jenkins, a 1999 third rounder, looks like the best of the lot at this point. He has a serious power upside, and might fit in as a starter at either infield corner within three years. He certainly is a surer bet than Munson for future success.

Outfield help is limited. Speedsters Andres Torres and Richard Gomez are the only two with a significant chance to make a dent in the majors within the next couple of years. Torres is a switch-hitter with a bit of gaps power and decent plate discipline. He could be a fair fourth outfielder in the majors. Gomez is a slightly more well-rounded prospect who drives the ball with more authority. He's a sleeper to someday snag a starting job in the majors, possibly in 2003. 1999 fourth round pick Cody Ross has a polished game for his age. He hits the ball to all fields and makes consistent contact. He doesn't have a single eyecatching trait, a no-no for prospects hoping to be starting major league outfielders someday. He could become a solid 300 at bat big league contributor down the road.

Javier Cardona has made a few cameo appearances in the majors, to little effect. His power potential and defensive efficiency suggest a future as a long-term big league part-timer. The Tigers would love to see Brandon Inge eventually succeed Brad Ausmus as their everyday catcher. He's developing a power stroke, runs well for a catcher and is durable. He's still got some rough edges, and will never be a middle-of-the-order hitter, but is on target to arrive in the majors in some capacity by sometime in 2002. Maxim St. Pierre has some interesting complementary offensive skills (patience, speed) and a solid defensive game, and is a sleeper to eventually crack the majors in a supporting role.

There are no surefire pitching studs in the system, and only an average number of promising arms. Dave Borkowski has knocked around awhile, and is no closer to earning a big league rotation spot. His repertoire is limited and suggests a future as a major league middle reliever, at best. Lefty Mike Maroth suffered through a lost Double-A season in 2000, but has good control and could still be heard from if he develops a strikeout pitch. Even if he doesn't, Maroth could evolve into a viable relief specialist candidate because of his precision. Shane Loux likely has the highest upside among Tigers' pitching prospects. He combines command, power potential and youth, and has relatively few things to work on for a 20-year-old. He's no future ace, but could be a solid two or three starter down the road. Lefty Adam Pettyjohn was injured for the first half of 2000, but pitched well upon his return. He's the classic crafty lefty, but has proven able to keep the ball away from Double-A hitters' hot spots. He projects as a swingman or two-inning lefty arm out of the pen in the majors. Righty Nate Cornejo cracked the Double-A rotation at age 20 in 2000, a sign of future success. He's a strikeout pitch away from becoming a big minor league winner, and his odds are in favor of getting there. He's a potential major league mid-rotation starter. Tim Kalita, a southpaw with decent offspeed stuff, and Rick Kirsten, an extremely precise righty, don't have high-octane fastballs, but both have a shot to achieve in the high minors, if not in the majors. Calvin Chipperfield, 22, overwhelmed the much-younger Low-A hitters in 2000, but is no sure thing to do so at higher levels. His stuff and command are just average, and his 6'1", 170, frame is a finished product.

6'7" lefty Tommy Marx has a deceptive motion and a heavy fastball, and should ride those skills to at least a bullpen specialist role in the majors. If his command continues to improve quickly, he could be much more than that. Lefty Andy Van Hekken has shown precision and power in his pro career to date, and could break out to the upside as his 6'3", 175, frame matures. He's a sleeper to eventually claim a big league starting role. Remember the name, Fernando Rodney. He's only 19, can throw in the upper 90s, and though he has a lot of rough edges, could eventually star in the rotation or out of the pen. A major league closer job could be in his future.

TOP TEN PROSPECTS

1 - SS Ramon Santiago - Santiago, 18, more than held his own offensively and defensively as one of the younger players in a full-season league last year at Low-A West Michigan. The 5'11", 150, righthanded hitter has a surprisingly polished offensive game for his age and experience level. He consistently makes authoritative line drive contact, and could eventually become a 30 double, 10 homer producer given some physical development. He needs to learn to work the count a bit, but is way ahead of most recent 18-year-old shortstop prospects with the bat. He has game-breaking speed and fairly advanced baserunning instincts, and should continue to accumulate 40-50 steals per year as he advances. All that said, defense is Santiago's strongest suit. He has expansive range and a well above average throwing arm, but his most impressive trait might be his consistency on the routine play, a problem for many young shortstops. Midwest League managers recognized him as the circuit's best defensive shortstop last season. Santiago is the real deal, and could be the Tigers' shortstop by sometime in 2003. He won't be in the Jeter-A-Rod-Nomar-Tejada pantheon, but could eventually come close.

2 - SS Omar Infante - In Santiago and Infante, both 18, the Tigers possessed the youngest starting shortstops at both the High and Low-A levels. Though Santiago is considered the premier prospect, it was Infante who emerged as the High-A regular in 2000. Offensively, the 6'0", 150, righthander likely has a higher all-around upside than Santiago. The ball jumps off of Infante's bat, and he could evolve into a 20 homer guy with the expected physical development. His plate discipline is quite refined for his age, and he rarely strikes out. Though Infante's raw speed doesn't approach Santiago's, he is also a fine basestealer with advanced baserunning instincts. Defensively, Infante isn't quite as consistent as Santiago on the routine play, and is a bit behind in terms of range and arm strength as well. Still, Infante is certainly capable of evolving into a starting major league shortstop, and if the two both remain with the Tigers, could move to second or third base while Santiago stays at home. If he excels at Double-A in 2001 at age 19, then he's a freight train to the majors.

3 - RHP Shane Loux - Loux, 20, was the Tigers' second round draft pick in 1997. The 6'2", 205, righty has yet to dominate in his brief pro career, but has consistently shown flashes of excellence as one of the youngest competitors at each successive minor league level. Loux possesses a heavy low 90s fastball that he consistently keeps low in the strike zone, plus an improving curveball and a passable changeup. Loux's control is well above average, though he needs to work the corners of the plate a little more consistently. His lack of a true strikeout pitch, especially against lefthanders, and his tendency to leave the ball out over the plate has caused him to allow about a hit per inning thus far in his pro career. Loux also needs to watch his weight. Better conditioning might provide him with the additional movement on his pitches that he needs to make a bold step forward. Look for Loux to return to Double-A in 2001 and experience significant success for the first time in his pro career. He's two years away from the majors, and should evolve into a reliable mid-rotation starter once he gets there.

4 - 3B Neil Jenkins - Jenkins, 19, was the Tigers' third round draft pick in 1999. He's a one-tool power prospect at this stage of his development. He certainly has made a smooth transition to the wooden bat, however, driving some of his homers for extreme distance at Low-A West Michigan. The 6'5", 215, righthanded hitter has gap-to-gap power, but needs to develop plate discipline and learn to hit breaking pitches with some consistency before approaching his considerable potential. Defensively, there are issues. Jenkins is fairly slow to begin with, and lacks first step quickness. On top of that, however, his footwork was a bit messy last season, and his strong throwing arm was often untrue. The Tigers knew from the beginning that left field or first base might be Jenkins' eventual home, but hoped he'd be able to log some years at the hot corner first. It is Jenkins' bat that will get him to the majors, however. As long as his home run trend is positive and his strikeout and walk totals move in the right directions, Jenkins will remain on track for a 2003 or 2004 major league debut. He could be a 30-homer force in the majors down the road.

5 - RHP Nate Cornejo - Cornejo, 20, was the Tigers' 1998 supplemental first round draft pick. The 6'5", 200, righthander hurler advanced to Double-A by mid 2000, and was one of the youngest pitchers at that level. He raced through Class A ball largely on the strength of his 90 MPH fastball which he bores inside onto the hands of righthanded hitters. His relative lack of a breaking ball repertoire was not much of an issue in A-ball, but was after his promotion to Jacksonville in the Southern League. His curveball and changeup have the potential to be adequate major league offerings, but at this point he lacks a true out pitch for use against lefthanded hitters. The Tigers hope that Cornejo can add velocity and/or move-

ment by packing on 10-15 pounds of muscle onto his frame. However, he has a history of knee trouble, and there is question as to whether he could support the weight. Cornejo's still very young, with much development ahead. If he improves his breaking pitches and fine-tunes his already impressive command, Cornejo could eventually become a viable mid-rotation starter in the majors, with a 2003 arrival date.

6 - C Brandon Inge - Inge, 23, is a late-blooming catching prospect who functioned primarily as a shortstop and relief pitcher before turning pro. The 1998 second round pick now stands on the precipice of the major leagues, on the strength of an imposing arsenal of defensive skills and an intriguing offensive package for a catcher. The 5'11", 185, righthanded hitter is quite athletic. He straps on the gear every day without fail, has a quick release and above average arm strength, and communicates well with pitchers. Double-A Southern League managers recognized him as the circuit's best defensive receiver last season. Offensively, Inge has substantial pop to the gaps, and runs exceedingly well for his position. His plate discipline needs a lot of work, however, and was the prime reason for his struggles after a late-season promotion to Triple-A. Inge might be ready to back up Brad Ausmus in Detroit sometime in 2001. His progress with the bat will determine whether he evolves into the Tigers' eventual starter, or into a platooner or solid backup receiver.

7 - 1B Eric Munson - So what is this guy doing this far down on this list, you ask? Well, Munson, 22, has not developed into the offensive force the Tigers expected when they snared him with the third overall pick in the 1999 draft. The 6'3", 220, lefthanded hitter certainly can hit a mistake fastball a long way, but he has numerous holes in his swing and is all too eager to help pitchers out by expanding his strike zone. Munson has shown a maddening tendency to try to pull everything, and the resulting grounders to second make him a double play waiting to happen because of his lack of speed. Defensively, Munson moved to first base from catcher for good last year, and has never projected as better than average at either spot. He got a brief look in the major leagues last summer, and the amount of work he has ahead of him before he can succeed at that level was readily apparent. Unless Munson makes significant near-term strides, it's hard to see him evolving into a middle-of-the-order force in the majors. That's generally not considered a sufficient return on such a high draft pick.

8 - OF Andres Torres - Torres, 22, was the Tigers' 1998 fourth round draft pick. The 5'10", 175, switch-hitter is a speed merchant who is beginning to develop the other aspects of his all-around game. He has an excellent eye at the plate, and is learning to slap the ball on the ground and take advantage of his superior wheels. He'll never be a power hitter, so hitting .300-plus is a necessity for Torres to have a chance to be a force at higher levels. Defensively, he's a smooth center fielder who combines well above average range with an exceptional throwing arm. High-A Florida State League managers were impressed with his all-around skills, recognizing him as the fastest baserunner and for having the best outfield throwing arm in the circuit. He's a bit old for his level, and will have to make swift, significant impact at upper minor league levels to have a chance to start in the majors. The most likely scenario suggests Torres as a fourth outfielder and part-time leadoff man in the majors, with a late 2002 arrival date.

9 - LHP Tommy Marx - Here's a sleeper who could be on the verge of making a serious upward move. Marx, 20, is a 1998 third round draftee who had great difficulty finding the plate prior to the 2000 season. The 6'7", 200, southpaw had previously struggled with poor mechanics and a lack of confidence, but showed signs of putting it all together last season at Low-A West Michigan. He has solid peak velocity for a southpaw at around 90 MPH, and has learned to throw his curve for strikes consistently. He has a deceptive motion that is death to lefthanded hitters, and his changeup could evolve into a third plus pitch. Midwest League hitters batted well under .200 against Marx last season. He was sidelined by an elbow strain late last season, but could continue to make noise if he can maintain the mechanical consistency he displayed in 2000. If Marx can achieve at the Double-A level by the end of 2001, he'll jump much higher on this list, and will project as an eventual mid-rotation major leaguer.

10 - 2B Pedro Santana - Santana, 23, is a speed player who has been the Tigers' primary Double-A second baseman for two full seasons now. The 5'11", 160, righthanded hitter has surprising power to the gaps for his size, and combines well above average speed with solid basestealing technique. However, he made no strides in his major offensive problem area, plate discipline. Defensively, Santana covers quite a bit of ground, but isn't as surehanded as much younger, higher-ceiling prospects such as Santiago and Infante. Santana has not ventured from second base in his pro career, but it appears that he'll need to learn at least one more position to have a chance

for significant major league time with the Tigers. Santana will be the Tigers' Triple-A second baseman in 2001, but will need to show more patience at the plate, plus improved defensive consistency and versatility to have a chance to a near-term major league contributor.

OTHER PROSPECTS

3B Matt Boone - Boone has been slow to progress as a hitter despite coming from a great baseball family. His defense at third base was considered a strength up until 2000 when he made 43 errors at High-A Lakeland. Unless he becomes more patient at the plate, shows some more pop and becomes more consistent at the hot corner, he'll be known more for his family name than his own ability.

RHP Dave Borkowski - Borkowski has struggled at times because of his lack of anything consistent offspeed stuff, but he's still young enough to improve. His fastball is around 90 MPH and he does some different things with it, but at this point of his career he's too easy to hit against. If he improves his curve or change a little, there could be a future for him in the bullpen.

C Javier Cardona - Cardona is a solid defensive catcher with a good arm and a quick release. He's not a .300 hitter, but he has power and could improve himself in terms of batting average. As you would expect, Cardona doesn't run well and that doesn't matter. He could wind up nothing more than a part-time major league catcher, but has the ability to be a 15-20 home run guy if he lives up to his potential.

RHP Calvin Chipperfield - If he has another year in 2001 like he did last year, Chipperfield will begin to show up on some top prospects lists. He has outstanding stuff, very good control and is extremely difficult to hit against. Hitters in the Midwest League hit just .186 against him last year and he averaged more than a strikeout per inning as well. If he can simply do what he's done at Single-A against more experience hitters, he'll be in the majors pretty soon.

OF Richard Gomez - Gomez is a great runner with some offensive ability. His biggest flaw is that he strikes out too often, but he has some gap power right now and can absolutely change the flow of a game on the bases. As you would expect, Gomez can also cover a lot of ground in the outfield. If he can start to make a little more contact, you could see him hit closer to .300 with 10 home runs and 40-50 steals.

RHP Shane Heams - Heams has a big-time fastball and was good enough to pitch for the gold medal winning U.S. Olympic Baseball Team. Control is an issue with Heams, but because he's difficult to hit against he can often work around the occasional walk. He can be a strikeout machine when he's on and with some minor refinement, he could be a solid member of a major league bullpen.

LHP Tim Kalita - Kalita has the arm and the stuff to be a decent pitcher as he moves up the ranks, but he must improve his control. He's shown he can last deep into games and has good enough stuff to survive, but he's still raw and needs to work ahead in the count more often. Another positive trait is his ability to keep the ball down in the zone which results in a lot of ground balls.

RHP Rick Kirsten - Kirsten is a control pitcher who relies on changing speeds and locating his pitches. He averages six-plus innings per game, which is pretty solid. If he can keep older hitters off balance like he did the younger ones in Single-A, he will have a shot at making it to the majors.

LHP Adam Pettyjohn - Pettyjohn combines slightly above average stuff with excellent control. If he can work his fastball in and out, regularly hitting the corners, and keep hitters off balance with his breaking stuff, he'll be in the majors very soon. Pettyjohn doesn't project as a top of the rotation starter, but could be a nice fourth or fifth starter who knows what he's doing and works ahead in the count.

OF Corey Richardson - Richardson has the ability to be a good leadoff man down the line. He's not the greatest hitter right now and he has almost no power at all, but he's got tremendous patience and draws a ton of walks to go along with his outstanding speed. He walked 94 times at Single-A in 2000 and if he hits with a little more authority as he matures, he'll be on his way up.

LHP Andy Van Hekken - Van Hekken is a good looking lefthander with above average stuff and excellent control. He probably won't be a dominating strikeout-type pitcher when he advances to the upper levels of the minors, but he'll get a lot of ground ball outs and keep extra runners off base. He allowed just 37 walks while striking out 126 batters in 158 innings last year in the Midwest League and even more amazing was the fact that he allowed just three home runs all season.

OF Chris Wakeland - Wakeland is an older player who isn't a big-time prospect, but he's got power and runs a little bit, giving him a chance to be a bit of a sleeper. Strikeouts are a big problem for Wakeland, but if he can gain just a little more patience, he could be able to contribute at the major league level.

KANSAS CITY ROYALS
ORGANIZATIONAL GRID

	AAA	AA	HI-A	LO-A
1B	Kit Pellow - R - 26	Dave Willis - R - 25 Jose Amado - R - 25	Ken Harvey - R - 22 David Goodwin - R - 24 Ricardo Montas - R - 23	Emmanuel Santana - L - 19
2B	Emiliano Escandon - B - 25 Jeff Berblinger - R - 29	Rod Metzler - B - 25 J.P. Roberge - R - 27	Eric Nelson - B - 23 Corey Hart - B - 24	Thomas Lora - B - 21
SS	Ray Holbert - R - 29 Alejandro Prieto -R- 24	Nick Ortiz - R - 26	Mark Ellis - R - 23 Steve Medrano - B - 22	Willy Ruiz - R - 21
3B	Joe Dillon - R - 24	Larry Huff - R - 28	Henry Calderon - R - 22	Michael Clay - R - 23 Gregg Raymundo - R - 23 Donovan Ross - L - 22 Wilkins Mercado - R - 21
OF	Dee Brown - L - 22 Goefrey Tomlinson - L - 23 Les Norman - R - 31 Jeremy Carr - R - 29 Anthony Medrano -R- 25 Aaron Guiel - L - 27 Doug Jennings - L - 35	Mike Curry - L - 23 Jeremy Dodson - L - 23 Pat Hallmark - R - 26 Joe Caruso - R - 25	Alexis Gomez - L - 19 Jose Taveras - R - 23 Brandon Berger - R - 25 Brian Shackelford - L - 23	Byron Gettis - R - 20 Jacob Baker - R - 24 Norris Hopper - R - 21 Adam Neubart - R - 22
C	Izzy Molina - R - 29 Juan Brito - R - 20	Paul Phillips - R - 23 Dave Ullery - L - 25	Jeremy Hill - R - 22 Casey Dunn - R - 23	Brian Johnson - R - 23 James McAuley - R - 22 Mike Tonis - R - 21
SP	Brett Laxton - R - 26 Dan Murray - R - 26 Jamie Walker - L - 29 Jeff D'Amico - R - 25 Jeff Austin - R - 23 Chris George - L - 20 Chris Fussell - R - 24 Jason Rakers - R - 27	Kiko Calero - R - 25 Kris Wilson - R - 23 Junior Guerrero - R - 20 Jason Gooding - L - 25 Shawn Sedlacek - R - 24 Corey Thurman - R - 21	Jeremy Affeldt - L - 21 Matt Burch - R - 23 Mike MacDougal - R - 23 Brian Sanches - R - 21 Cary Ammons - L - 23 Ryan Baerlocher - R - 22	Ryan Douglass - R - 21 Jimmy Gobble - L - 18 Jesus Coa - R - 20 Tony Cogan - L - 23 Jason Kaanoi - R - 18 Wes Obermueller - R - 23
CLOSER	Paul Spoljaric - L - 29 Lance Carter - R - 25	Robbie Morrison - R - 23 Shawn Sonnier - R - 23	Justin Pederson - R - 25 Jim King - L - 22	Ryan Bukvich - R - 21 Jay Gehrke - R - 22 Carlos Pichardo - R - 22

KANSAS CITY ROYALS

As the Kansas City Royals have consistently pumped young talent onto their major league roster, the quality of their minor league system has quickly deteriorated. They haven't been able to restock the system adequately, particularly with regard to position player prospects.

At first base, Ken Harvey is a high average hitter, but his defensive shortcomings and lack of power output to date suggest that he has a future as a spare big league bat, at best. Teenager Chad Santos hung in there against Low-A pitching, and then showed power potential after a demotion to rookie ball. He's a sleeper to watch.

The cupboard is nearly bare at second base. Norris Hopper is a spray hitter with good speed who can also play the outfield, so could figure into the club's plans as an all-purpose backup.

Though 1999 ninth round pick Mark Ellis, at 23, was one of the older High-A regulars, his offensive exploits in the pitcher-friendly confines of his Wilmington home park mark him as a player to watch. He gets on base, can reach the gaps, runs well and is an exceptional defensive player. He could be a contributor in a part-time role in the majors down the road.

There's nothing going on at third base in the Royals' system.

Despite a poor start in 2000, outfielder Dee Brown remains the Royals' foremost position player prospect. He has a superior power/speed upside, and showed an improved attitude after an early-season wake-up call. Look for Brown to crack the major league roster in 2001, and eventually develop into an above average big league outfielder. Goefrey Tomlinson is a slap-hitting speedster who has been unable to stay healthy in the minor leagues. At best, he is a fourth or fifth outfielder in the majors, and could make a slight 2001 impact in Kansas City. 2000 Double-A lefthanded hitters Mike Curry and Jeremy Dodson could evolve into reserve big leaguers. Curry's patience and speed is mitigated by a lack of power, and Dodson's power potential, athleticism and plus throwing arm are offset by a poor offensive approach. Keep an eye on Alexis Gomez. He held his own as a High-A teenager in a pitchers' home park, and has the speed and gaps power to potentially evolve into a significant major league contributor.

Paul Phillips is a polished defensive catcher who rarely strikes out and has good speed for his position. He's a year plus away from contending for at least a share of the major league job, and could someday be a credible major league starter. Juan Brito's all-around skills are held in high regard, but he is far from polished in any aspect of his game. He needs to show consistency over a full season in a starting role before establishing himself as a viable major league prospect.

The Royals have focused on pitching talent in the upper rounds of recent drafts, with mixed results. 1998 first rounder Jeff Austin has quickly risen to Triple-A, but doesn't appear to have developed a true out pitch against top-flight hitters. It's hard to see the current incarnation of Austin excelling in the majors, but he's a dogged type who should eventually become big league timber. Lefty Chris George was also selected in the first round of the 1998 draft, and has made exceptional progress. His command could use a bit of work, but he's quite polished for age 20. He'll make the majors in 2002, and could someday be a number two starter. Junior Guerrero, 20, is a power pitcher who clearly was unnerved in his Double-A debut last season. Look for him to pull it together in his second shot there in 2001. His upside is arguably higher than George's, but his risks are higher was well. He's couple of years away from the bigs. 1999 first round pick Mike MacDougal didn't dominate High-A hitters at age 23 while pitching his home games in an extreme pitchers' park. That's not a good sign for his future, solid stuff notwithstanding. The guess here is that he'll be a fringe big leaguer at best. It took Corey Thurman a second High-A Wilmington season to break out. He's got borderline stuff but exceptional command, but will hard-pressed to repeat in the hitters' home parks that await him at higher levels. He's a big league sleeper prospect at best. 1999 second round pick Brian Sanches hurled a no-hitter for Wilmington last season, and is a fairly complete pitcher for a youngster. His lack of a Grade A heater or great size (he's 6'1", 175) make him no better than a big league mid-rotation candidate. Lefty Jimmy Gobble was yet another 1999 first round pick, and he held his own as an 18-year-old in Low-A ball in 2000. At 6'3", 175, a lot of physical development lies ahead, and his command is already big league quality. He too could someday be a major league mid-rotation starter.

TOP TEN PROSPECTS

1 - LHP Chris George - George, 20, was the Royals' supplemental first round draft pick in 1998. Though less heralded than fellow first round selection Jeff Austin, George's upward path through the system has been smoother. At the tender age of 20, the 6'2", 165, southpaw worked his way up to the Triple-A level by late last summer, and has tasted success all along the route. George's four-pitch repertoire features a low 90s fastball, a well above average changeup, plus a solid curveball and changeup. He varies speed and location well, and looks like a young Tom Glavine when he's hitting his spots. Despite pitching his home games in a hitters' park at Double-A Wichita last season, George impressed to the extent that he was recognized as the best pitching prospect in the Texas League by circuit managers. He did nibble around the edges of the strike zone too often, causing high pitch counts and relatively short stints. He'll need to nip that in the bud to similarly succeed at higher levels. He could help in Kansas City by late 2001, and looks like a future No. 2 major league starter.

2 - OF Dee Brown - Brown, 22, had dominated throughout his minor league career prior to last season, but only his positive reaction to his first serious bit of adversity salvaged what was shaping up as a poor 2000 season at Triple-A Omaha. The 6'0", 215, lefthanded hitter was cruising along with a low .200s average, a high strikeout total, and, most notably, a sullen attitude, when he was suddenly sent to the Florida Instructional League for a wakeup call. The 1996 first round pick promptly turned his season around upon his return to Omaha, again showcasing the power/speed package that makes him one of the more exciting offensive prospects in the minors. Brown can drive the ball to all fields with extreme power, and runs surprisingly well considering his rather stocky build. His lack of plate discipline was disappointing last

season, but he had shown a willingness to take pitches at lower levels. Defensively, Brown is limited to left field by his mediocre throwing arm, but he has worked hard to make himself a passable defender. Royals' Manager Tony Muser is a character guy, so Brown had better be on his best behavior to make the big club in the spring. Eventually, Brown should settle in as a .270 hitter with 25 homer power in the bigs, and maybe more.

3 - LHP Jimmy Gobble - Gobble, 18, was a supplemental first round draft pick in 1999. The Royals challenged him by immediately placing him on a full-season league team in his first full pro season, and after a slow start, the 6'3", 175, southpaw proved them right with a fine campaign at Low-A Charleston. Gobble features a low 90s fastball, an above average curveball and an improving changeup, and has uncanny command and solid mechanics for a youngster. Sometimes he catches a bit too much of the plate with his strikes, but hey, the kid is 18. His lean frame should easily accommodate another 15 pounds of muscle, and the resulting additional velocity and/or movement could make Gobble one scary prospect. Look for Gobble to bust into the mainstream consciousness in 2001 when he hurls his home games in the pitchers' paradise at High-A Wilmington. He's a lot like Chris George, and his career could follow a similarly steep upward trajectory. Gobble looks like a future No. 2 or 3 starter in the bigs, with a late 2003 arrival date.

4 - RHP Junior Guerrero - Guerrero, 20, would like to take a mulligan on his wasted 2000 Double-A season. The 6'2", 175, righthander was pushed to that level, where he was one of the youngest pitchers, after only nine High-A starts in 1999, and simply wasn't ready. Guerrero possesses an explosive, but fairly straight, mid 90s fastball, but his slider and changeup are not yet ready for prime time. The more polished Double-A hitters quickly became aware that Guerrero would eventually have to come in with his heater, and they sat on it. The hitter-friendly environment of his home park didn't help him either. Guerrero's control is fairly good for a young power pitcher, and once he begins to throw his breaking stuff for strikes, he could take off. Mentally, Guerrero held up well during his struggles last season, and the experience might do him good in the long run. Look for major improvement at the same level in 2001, putting him back on track for a near-term role on the Kansas City staff. If his breaking pitches don't come around, there will be room for him in short relief. Look for Guerrero to arrive in the major leagues as a situational bullpen righty in 2003.

5 - OF Alexis Gomez - Just a hunch here, but I have a feeling this guy will soon justify such a high rating. Gomez, 19, was challenged with a daunting jump all the way from the Gulf Coast League, the lowest rookie level, to High-A Wilmington, where he played his home games in an extreme pitchers' park. The 6'2", 160, lefthanded hitter responded with a solid all-around campaign, running the bases well and showing some line drive pop to all fields. Gomez was at times physically overmatched, and still has a way to go against quality breaking stuff, but performed just fine considering his age and experience level. He projects as a 15/30 power/speed threat and an above average defensive center or right fielder. Carlos Beltran's Wilmington numbers were comparable to Gomez', and Beltran was older when he passed through. Look for Gomez to explode onto the scene once he hits he enters the hitter-friendly environment at Double-A Wichita next season. Gomez has a solid chance to be a future No. 1 or 2 hitter in Kansas City, and could arrive by late 2002.

6 - RHP Jeff Austin - Austin, 23, was the Royals' first round pick, and the fourth overall selection in the 1998 draft. The 6'0", 185, righthander's career path has taken on a consistent pattern; he sputters through his first trial at each level, and improves markedly his second time around. For that reason and that reason only, his utter inability to get the ball past Triple-A hitters in 2000 should not construed as evidence that Austin will never cut it against upper level batsmen. Austin possesses a diverse repertoire including a low 90s fastball, a hard curve and a passable changeup, but his straightforward delivery is easy to read, and none of his offerings can be considered as true strikeout pitches, especially against lefthanded hitters. Austin's walk totals have always been low, but he has consistently allowed over a hit per inning because of poor location within the strike zone and a reluctance to pitch inside. Austin needs to take a major step forward at the Triple-A level, or else run the risk of becoming a wasted draft pick. The best guess is that he'll make some progress, and evolve into a low-end big league starter.

7 - RHP Brian Sanches - Sanches, 21, was the Royals' 1999 second round pick. He pitched in hard luck last season at High-A Wilmington, but showed flashes of brilliance, including an early-season no-hitter. The 6'1", 175, righthander has fairly ordinary stuff, including a 90 MPH fastball, an above average curve and a changeup which is in its formative stages. Sanches has some of the finer points of pitching down pat. He's a hard-nosed competitor who routinely keeps the ball low in the strike zone, and his ability to vary speed and location expertly gave him a solid strikeout rate last season despite a lack of raw gas. However, he did pitch his home games in pitcher-friendly Wilmington, a misleading prelude of what awaits him in the bandbox at Double-A Wichita in 2001. His Double-A performance will be a solid indicator of Sanches' eventual major league upside. Look for Sanches to emerge as mid-to-low-rotation starter in Kansas City, with an estimated arrival date of 2003.

8 - C Paul Phillips - Phillips, 23, was the Royals' 1998 ninth round draft pick. The 5'11", 175, righthanded hitter was slowed somewhat last season by a hip flexor, but when healthy, he showed fine defensive ability and a consistent line drive bat. Phillips is extremely difficult to strike out, but is almost as unlikely to take a walk. He has a little bit of pop to the gaps, but isn't much of a home run threat. He runs well for a catcher. He could settle in as a 10 steal per year guy, and can be used on the front end of hit-and-run plays with confidence. Defensively, Phillips is fundamentally sound, combining slightly above average arm strength with solid agility and fine game-calling skills. It doesn't appear that Phillips is going to develop an offensive game sufficient for him to start in the majors, but his glove will get him to the show as a backup capable of handling a 250 at bat workload. Phillips could get to Kansas City in September 2001.

9 - RHP Corey Thurman - Thurman, 21, was the Royals' fourth round draft pick in 1996. The 6'1", 215, righthander's stature within the organization had dropped after an awful 1999 season at High-A Wilmington, when he recorded a 4.88 ERA and allowed well over a hit per inning despite pitching his home games in an extreme pitchers' park. He got a second chance at Wilmington in 2000 and turned things around with a brilliant campaign that resulted in a late-season promotion to Double-A. Thurman's stuff doesn't match up to that of many other hurlers in the system. He has an upper 80s fastball and an average breaking ball arsenal. However, Thurman placed the ball on the edges of the strike zone consistently and threw strike one with regularity last season, and the results spoke for themselves. Though Thurman was hit hard in early Double-A starts, his ability to maintain a high strikeout rate is a good sign for his future. Thurman is a fringe starter prospect who could be a big league fit in the No. 5 spot or as a swingman or righthanded relief specialist. He'll contend for a big league role by early 2002.

10 - OF Goefrey Tomlinson - Tomlinson, 23, is a speed merchant whose lack of physical strength has made him a frequent injury victim and prevented him from developing the power game necessary for him to contend for starting major league outfield spot. The 6'1", 190, lefthanded hitter was set back by a deep bone bruise in his foot last season, but was a consistent on-base threat when healthy. Tomlinson waits out the count and hits line drives to all fields, but has only a touch of gaps power. Though he possesses well above average raw speed, his basestealing technique has progressed slowly, causing his success rate to be unacceptably low in the upper minors. Defensively, Tomlinson has excellent range, but his relatively weak throwing arm makes left field a better fit for him than center field. The 1997 fourth round draftee will have a difficult time crashing the deep Royals' major league outfield crew, even as a backup, but would be a fine reserve outfielder and bench bat given a change of scenery in 2001.

OTHER PROSPECTS

RHP Ryan Baerlacher - Baerlacher showed tremendous potential at Low-A last year and he could emerge as a top prospect sometime soon. He has a good arm, outstanding control and has a knack for polishing hitters off with the strikeout. Opponents hit just .209 against him during the 2000 season and he struck out 139 batters in 113-plus innings, which tells you what kind of stuff he has.

RHP Enrique Calero - "Kiko" Calero has a live arm, three good pitches and his control has improved quite a bit recently. He doesn't allow a lot of baserunners, or at least he didn't at Double-A last year, and he was once considered one of the Royals' better pitching prospects. He's a little old at 25 to have not seen Triple-A yet, but he could be a late bloomer.

OF Mike Curry - Curry is a burner who really knows how to get on base. He's not a great hitter, per se, but he draws a ton of walks and can really fly on the base paths. With a little more physical maturity, Curry could be a real weapon at the top of the order. Defensively, he can track down pretty much everything hit near him. He walked 94 times and had a .413 on-base percentage at Double-A last season.

OF Jeremy Dodson - Dodson has some power and speed, but isn't a polished hitter yet. He's beginning to draw more walks, but still strikes out quite a bit and makes too

many easy outs for a power man. He needs some fine tuning, but there is ability in him.

SS Mark Ellis - Ellis looks like he can be a very good all-around player. He hits for average, has outstanding patience at the plate, he runs well and has the ability to develop into a double-digit home run threat. He's still somewhat inconsistent at shortstop, but as long as he keeps hitting he'll be fine. Right now he looks like the ideal number two hitter, but he could develop enough punch to be more of an RBI man down the line.

1B-OF Pat Hallmark - Hallmark doesn't have a ton of power, but he can flat out hit. He's got the ability to hit well over .300 with double-digit power and very good speed. He's also not the kind of hitter who strikes out a lot and he draws a decent number of walks, which is a good combination. Hallmark is definitely someone to keep an eye on in the near future.

1B Ken Harvey - Harvey was one of the best college hitters available in the draft a couple of years ago and he's kept up that reputation nicely. Harvey is capable of hitting well over .300 and has the ability to develop into an excellent power hitter. He doesn't strike out very much and he walks enough to make himself effective at the plate. He just needs a little more time to learn how to hit the long ball.

RHP Mike MacDougal - MacDougal will soon be considered one of the Royals' best prospects. He has a mid 90s fastball with amazing life and he was considered three or four best pitchers in the Carolina League this past season. He still needs work on his secondary pitches and on control, but a power pitcher who gets movement on his fastball like a sinker ball pitcher would is a great commodity.

RHP Orber Moreno - Moreno is an overpowering pitcher with a chance to be a good closer in the near future. His upper 90s fastball is complemented by a decent slider and a solid changeup, making him a potentially dominant closer, even at the major league level. He missed all of last season because of arm problems, but is expected to regain his previous form and would still be considered a top prospect were he completely healthy.

1B Kit Pellow - Pellow has some power, but he's not a great hitter right now. He doesn't strike out too often, but at the same time he doesn't draw nearly enough walks. He was a below average third baseman, but has the ability to be pretty good at first base. He's not a top prospect, but his power could land him a major league bench job someday.

3B-OF Donovan Ross - Ross is a good hitter with some power potential and pretty good patience. He makes a lot of contact and has gap power right now, though his 13 home runs at Low-A last season leaves open the door for more production down the line. His defensive position is still uncertain, but he hasn't been terrible at either third or in the outfield.

RHP Shawn Sonnier - Sonnier is a closer prospect with a mid 90s fastball, power slider, and splitter. His control has improved and he is a bulldog of a pitcher on the mound. He was expected to be up in the majors sometime during the 2001 season and could be one of the surprises of the season. The Royals are very high on him.

MINNESOTA TWINS
ORGANIZATIONAL GRID

	AAA	AA	HI-A	LO-A
1B	Doug Mientkiewicz - L - 26	Tommy Peterman - L - 25 Todd Sears - L - 24 T.R. Marcinczyk - R - 26	Dan Leatherman - L - 23	Eric Sandberg - L - 20
2B	Luis Rivas - R - 20 Jeff Ferguson - R - 26	Steve Huls - B - 25	Ruben Salazar - R - 22 Ramon Borrego - B - 22	Luis Rodriguez - B - 20
SS	Mike Moriarty - R - 26	Cleatus Davidson - B - 23	Juan Lorenzo - B - 22	Tony Stevens - B - 21
3B	Casey Blake - R - 26	Michael Cuddyer - R - 21	Kevin Hodge - R - 23 Kyle Hawthorne - R - 22	Terry Tiffee - B - 20 Matt Scanlon - L - 22
OF	Chad Allen - R - 25 Brian Buchanan - R - 26 John Barnes - R - 24 Kevin Roberson - B - 32	Mike Ryan - L - 22 Bobby Kielty - B - 23 Papo Bolivar - R - 21 Rafael Alvarez - L - 23	Dustan Mohr - R - 24 Nestor Smith - B - 22 Michael Restovich - R - 21 Brian McMillin - R - 23 Nate Manning - R - 26	DeShawn Southward -R- 22 B.J. Garbe - R - 19 Kevin West - R - 20 Yustin Jordan - R - 21 John Edwards - R - 22 Craig Selander - L - 23
C	Javier Valentin - B - 24 Jeff Smith - L - 26 Marcus Jensen - B - 27 A.J. Pierzynski - L - 23	Matt LeCroy - R - 24 Allen Shrum - R - 24 Joe Sulentor - B - 23	Brandon Marsters - R - 25 Gabby Torres - R - 22	Kelley Gulledge - R - 21 Michael Wrenn - R - 22
SP	Dan Perkins - R - 25 Matt Kinney - R - 23 Alan Mahaffey - L - 26 Mike Romano - R - 28 Bryan Wolff - R - 28	Kyle Lohse - R - 21 Matt Carnes - R - 24 Ryan Mills - L - 22 Juan Rincon - R - 21 Brad Thomas - L - 22	Grant Balfour - R - 22 Joe Thomas - L - 25 Pete Fisher - R - 22 Adam Johnson - R - 20 Jon McDonald - L - 23 Ken Pumphrey - R - 23 Brent Schoening - R - 22	Joe Foote - R - 20 Brent Hoard - L - 23 Willie Eyre - R - 21 Jon Pridie - R - 20 Tim Sturdy - R - 21 Brian Wolfe - R - 19 Scott Blackwell - R - 21 Vincent Bonilla - R - 21
CLOSER	Brent Stentz - R - 24 Gus Gandarillas - R - 28 Jack Cressend - R - 25	Lee Marshall - R - 23 Danny Mota - R - 24	Mike Nakamura - R - 23	Ronnie Corona - R - 21 Tony Cento - L - 22

MINNESOTA TWINS

Considering the way that the Twins have crowded prospects onto their youthful major league roster, they have done well to maintain an adequate minor league talent base. Prospect quantity is a bit below average, but the quality of their top layer of prospects is solid.

Eric Sandberg established himself as a viable first base prospect with a powerful Low-A campaign in 2000. It remains to be seen whether he has the bat speed to duplicate his production against higher level pitching, Sandberg's mature approach at the plate labels him as at least a future major league part-timer, and potentially more.

Luis Rivas slid over from shortstop to second base at Double-A New Britain last season, in a move designed to speed his rise to the major leagues. Though he still needs to hit the ball on the ground more often to better take advantage of his speed, he is major league ready in many ways. His speed, surprising power potential and defensive brilliance mark him as a future major league starter, and a possible 2001 major league starter. Ruben Salazar drives the ball extremely well for his size (5'9", 162), and has played third in addition to second base. That versatility makes an attractive future utility option at the very least.

With Rivas now a second baseman, there are no shortstop prospects on the horizon. With youthful Cristian Guzman in place at the major league level, that's probably not such a big deal.

Michael Cuddyer is the Twins' third baseman of the not-so-distant future. He's a smooth defender and a natural hitter with a disciplined approach. Though he had disappointing Double-A power numbers last season, the 6'3", 202, righthanded hitter is destined to eventually develop his power stroke. He might need another year of seasoning, but Cuddyer will surely be the Twins' third sacker in 2002, and should be an above average major leaguer.

John Barnes had a spectacular Triple-A campaign last season, and is a candidate for a backup outfield job in the majors in 2001. He's a consistent line drive hitter who rarely whiffs, though his power and speed upsides are minimal. He'll be a decent complementary big leaguer. Mike Ryan is an intriguing prospect who can play second and third base in addition to the outfield. That versatility plus a live line drive bat could make a candidate for a deep reserve role in the majors. Switch-hitter Bobby Kielty made major strides in all facets of his game in 2000. This late bloomer has developed into an on-base and slugging threat, and could sneak onto the big league roster in 2001. He could become a viable starter in the majors, or at least a valuable backup. Papo Bolivar, 21, is a slap hitter who has always ranked among the younger players at each minor league level. However, he hasn't shown signs of developing noticeable power or speed, which will likely keep him in the upper minors for the foreseeable future. Strapping 6'4", 233, power prospect Michael Restovich had an uneven year at the plate last season, but remains an attractive middle-of-the-order option with surprisingly good speed. He needs to have a big Double-A season in 2001 to retain his star prospect status. He could be the Twins' left fielder by late 2002. 1999 first round pick B.J. Garbe, 19, had a disappointing initial full pro season. Though he is an exceptional all-around athlete, he just might turn out to be an aluminum bat wonder power-wise. Give him another season to show some pop before worrying too much.

With Matt LeCroy, Javier Valentin and Chad Moeller all spending significant time in the major leagues in 2000, the Twins are prospect central with regard to catchers. LeCroy and Valentin have substantial upsides, LeCroy has a serious power ceiling, and Valentin polished all-around skills. Moeller looks like a major league backup at best. A.J. Pierzynski has also logged major league time in the past. Despite his bulky 6'3", 220, frame, he's a slap contact hitter with just a bit of gaps power. As a lefthander, he could eventually form part of a productive big league platoon with either Valentin or LeCroy.

There isn't a lot of pitching depth within the organization. Jason Ryan has had a couple of chances at the major league level, and has proven eminently hittable. He's a fringe major league hurler who lacks an out pitch, especially against lefties. Former Red Sox' prospect Matt Kinney has blossomed into one of the Twins' foremost pitching prospects. His control has been an issue through much of his pro career, but his stuff hasn't. His high-octane fastball could make short relief his most suitable major league role. Righthander Kyle Lohse's development hit some snags in a miserable 2000 Double-A season. He has a well-rounded repertoire and good control, but his breaking pitches were flat and his location within the strike zone poor last season. He needs to make a quantum leap in performance at that level in 2001 to remain a near-term candidate for the big league rotation. Righthander Juan Rincon, 21, raced through Class A on the strength of his hard stuff, and found out the hard way in late 2000 that more is required to conquer higher-level hitters. He likely learned some lessons, and should fare much better in 2001. He projects as a future big league mid-rotation starter or middle reliever. 1998 first round pick Ryan Mills was still mired in Low-A ball at age 22 last season. The good news is, he endured much less of the mechanical difficulties that led to a miserable 1999 season. He needs to make a move soon to have even an outside chance of fulfilling his considerable potential, however. Righthander Joe Foote has middling stuff, but his solid command and ability to pitch in a variety of roles makes him a sleeper to watch, with an outside chance of landing on the fringes of the majors within a couple of seasons. 1999 sixth round pick Brian Wolfe, 19, is extremely raw, but could make a solid upward move once he adds movement to his pitches. His command and pitching savvy are solid. He could evolve into a late-rotation major league starter candidate.

Brent Stentz is a hard-throwing reliever who has been an effective minor league closer. He won't likely perform in that capacity in the majors, but could be an effective situational righty out of the pen.

TOP TEN PROSPECTS

1 - 2B Luis Rivas - Rivas, 20, is an excellent all-around prospect whose rise to the major leagues was accelerated by the departure of former golden boy Todd Walker from the organization last year. The 5'10", 175, righthanded hitter had been a shortstop prior to 2000, but the emergence of Cristian Guzman as a viable major leaguer at that

position made Rivas' move a logical one. He makes consistent, authoritative contact, possessing surprising power to the gaps for his size. If he can improve his plate discipline, he could evolve into a .300 hitter with 15-20 home run pop. He has exceptional raw speed, and is an aggressive baserunner who needs to study pitchers a bit more to maximize his basestealing potential. Defensively, his tools are quite sound. He has well above average range, and his plus arm might be wasted at second base. His tendency to boot the routine play has waned a bit, and with added repetitions, he could evolve into a Pokey Reese-like defensive second sacker thanks to his superior athleticism. Rivas' performance actually escalated after a late-season promotion to Triple-A, a great sign for his future. Rivas will likely be the Twins' second baseman in 2001. He might struggle in his rookie year, but should eventually become an impact player at the major league level.

2 - RHP Adam Johnson - Johnson, 20, was the shining light of the 2000 draft class, dominating immediately at High-A Fort Myers in the Florida State League while most of his contemporaries cut their teeth in rookie ball. The 6'2", 210, righty was selected second overall by the Twins most because of his signability, but then quickly proved to have the talent to justify his selection. He combines a low 90s heater with a slider that was simply too much for Florida State League hitters to handle. He allowed only 45 hits in 69 innings, fashioning a brilliant 92/20 strikeout/walk ratio. He has already made the transition from thrower to pitcher, no small feat for a first-year pro. He appears to be primed for 2001 Double-A success, and is the early line favorite to be the first member of his draft class to reach the majors. It could happen by September 2001; along with Brad Radke and Eric Milton, Johnson should nicely set up the top end of the Twins' rotation for many years to come.

3 - 3B Michael Cuddyer - Cuddyer, 21, was the Twins' first round draft pick in 1997. The 6'2", 190, righthanded hitter was moved from shortstop to third base prior to the 1999 season, and the shift has been a beneficial one. His quick reflexes, soft hands and strong throwing arm are of particular use at the hot corner, and his subpar speed isn't as much of a detriment as it was at shortstop. Offensively, the Twins have long expected him to develop into a prodigious home run hitter, but is hasn't quite worked out that way to this point. Cuddyer's compact, level stroke generated plenty of topspin line drives into the gaps at Double-A New Britain last season, but only a handful of homers. With his strength and body type, it remains quite possible that the relatively minor mechanical adjustments needed for him to add power production will occur. He is a patient hitter at the plate, and is an intense team leader type who does the little things necessary to win ballgames. If he develops a power stroke at the Triple-A level in 2001, he'll get to Minnesota quickly, and could become a star. Without power, though, he's basically Corey Koskie.

4 - OF Michael Restovich - Restovich, 21, was the Twins' second round draft pick in 1997. The 6'4", 233, righthanded hitter encountered the first patch of adversity in his brief pro career last season at High-A Fort Myers, getting off to a horrible start that it took him all season to overcome. He projects as a high-average, high-power hitter, but he needed to shorten his swing a bit in order to do the same damage to Florida State League hurlers as he had done at lower levels. Even with his midseason adjustments, most of Restovich's power was to the gaps; with refinement and added consistency, however, the Twins still believe he can evolve into a 30-homer threat. His plate discipline is fine, though he swings through his share of high fastballs. He runs quite well for his size, but he needs to pick his spots a little better on the bases, as over-aggressiveness has gotten him into trouble at times. Defensively, he projects as a left fielder because of pedestrian range and only an average throwing arm. Restovich needs to raise his offensive game significantly at the Double-A level in 2001. If he substantially increases his power numbers, he could evolve into an above average major league left fielder, with a targeted arrival date of late 2002.

5 - OF B.J. Garbe - Garbe, 19, was the Twins' first round draft pick, and the fifth selection overall in the 1999 draft. The 6'2", 195, righthanded hitter was a major disappointment with the bat at Low-A Quad City, where he hit for a low average with minimal extra base power. His transition to the wooden bat has been slow. The ball simply does not jump off of his bat at this stage in his development, and a retooling of his swing might be necessary. His approach at the plate is solid, and the deep counts he works ensure that he sees a lot of fastballs; he's just not doing anything with them. He runs quite well, but hasn't yet fully incorporated his speed into his offensive game. Defensively, Garbe is a natural center fielder with well above range and a very strong throwing arm. He has apparently overcome back problems that plagued him in 1999, as he was available for everyday play last season. Garbe will goes as far as his bat takes him. He was one of the youngest players in the Midwest League last season, so you can't

write him off due to one poor offensive year. If he doesn't perform significantly better in a Low-A encore in 2001, however, then it will be time to worry. At best, Garbe projects as a solid No. 1-2 hitter in a big league order, with an arrival date of 2004. He's got a lot of offensive work to do before then, however.

6 - OF Bobby Kielty - Kielty, 23, is quite an interesting story. He was not drafted out of high school, but opened a lot of eyes by tearing apart the wooden bat Cape Cod League in the summer of 1998. The Twins signed him as a free agent, and he proved his prospect status by enhancing his offensive production in 2000 after a daunting two-level jump to the Double-A Eastern League. At his age, he needed to do so to remain a viable prospect. The 6'1", 215, switch-hitter knows the strike zone, and can drive fastballs deep to the gaps and beyond fairly consistently. He is only an average baserunner, but his combination of on-base and slugging skills could make him a future second or third hitter option in the majors. Defensively, Kielty isn't a standout, possessing average range and a decent throwing arm. He's best suited for left field at upper levels. Kielty got a late start in pro ball, but has made up for nearly all of the time he lost. Kielty could surface in the major league lineup by the end of 2001, and projects as a solid, steady long-term big league performer.

7 - RHP Matt Kinney - Kinney, 23, is a former Red Sox' prospect who overcame a 1999 elbow injury to rise all the way to the major leagues last season. The 6'4", 200, righthander throws a lively low-to-mid 90s fastball and mixes it with a nasty slider. He has significantly enhanced his control over the years, and as a result averaged six innings per start for the first time in his pro career last season. He has apparently smoothed out mechanical difficulties that he endured in prior seasons, and also appears to be completely healthy. His fairly limited repertoire seemingly makes him a logical candidate for a shift to short relief, he could become a prototypical two-pitch power closer. For now, however, the Twins continue to envision him as a starter. Look for him to earn a spot on the Twins' roster sometime in 2001. He'll likely break in as a situational bullpen righty, but look for his role to escalate in importance over time.

8 - 1B Eric Sandberg - Sandberg, 20, has come out of nowhere to become a viable power prospect since being drafted on the 25th round in 1998. The 6'1", 215, lefthanded hitter has fairly advanced plate discipline for a youngster, legitimate longball power, and doesn't strike out very much for a masher. He is not particularly athletic; he's your basic station-to-station baserunner, and is a typically slow first sacker who will make the plays within his limited range. Sandberg will need to utilize his patience and power as the center of his offensive game. He'll draw walks wherever he plays, but needs to prove that he has enough bat speed to maintain his power numbers against more polished upper level hurlers. His first major test will come at the Double-A level, which he could reach by late 2002. At best, Sandberg could evolve into a Kent Hrbek-like run producer, with an estimated arrival date of 2004. He still has a way to go before his chances of reaching the high offensive standards set for major league first basemen can be ascertained.

9 - LHP Ryan Mills - Mills, 22, was the Twins' first round pick, and the sixth overall selection in the 1998 draft. The 6'5", 200, southpaw has battled ongoing mechanical and control problems throughout his pro career, and it has adversely affected his confidence. Though he did show some improvement from 1999, a totally lost year when he logged an 8.87 ERA and walked 87 batters in 95 Low-A innings his mechanics remain very inconsistent. Mills still has a tendency to alter his delivery from pitch-to-pitch, and the resulting high walk totals keep his outings quite short. His stuff remains solid; his fastball reaches the mid 90s, and his power curve serve as an out pitch against lefties. He also is fairly adept at working out of the jams he creates for himself. Despite all of the excitement, Mills did navigate three minor league levels last year, winding up at Double-A New Britain. Mills still has a chance to evolve into an achiever at the major league level, the bullpen could be his eventual destination, but needs to dominate somewhere in the upper in minors in 2001 to retain that chance. He'll reach the majors in 2002, at the earliest.

10 - RHP Kyle Lohse - Lohse, 21, was the Cubs' 29th round draftee in 1996, and came over to the Twins in the Rick Aguilera deal in 1999. The 6'2", 190, righthander dominated throughout most of his Class A tenure, but has hit the wall over the last season and a half since first being promoted to Double-A. His youth relative to his minor league level leads this observer to give him another chance, however. Lohse throws a 90 MPH fastball plus a slider and a changeup, and his walk rates have consistently ranked among the lowest in the minors. However, none of his pitches have enough zip to qualify as a true out pitch against upper level hitters, and his strikes tend to catch too much of the plate. Lohse has a good head on his shoulders. He endured his Double-A beating last season, refusing to cave in mentally. Still, he needs to tweak his

mechanics to squeeze out a tad more velocity and/or movement, and needs to paint the corners better to take the next step. He'll probably need to repeat at Double-A again, and needs to excel right away. If he does, he could project as a major leaguer by late 2002, and as an eventual mid-rotation starter.

OTHER PROSPECTS

OF John Barnes - Barnes is an outstanding hitter who only needs to add a little more home run power to be a force in the majors. He has walked more than he has struck out during each of the past two seasons and at 6'2" 205 pounds he has the strength necessary to be a home run threat. He hit .357 at Triple-A last year and had 37 doubles to with 13 home runs and 87 RBI. There's a chance he could be patrolling the outfield in the Metrodome by the end of the 2001 season.

1B Doug Mientkiewicz - Mientkiewicz has proven all he can in the minors and is should be ready for another shot at the Majors in 2001. He's got the ability to be a Mark Grace-type first baseman. He'll hit .300 with something like 15 home runs and he'll play outstanding defense at first base. He has developed more home run power over the past year, though he's not truly a threat to hit 20 at this point. He starred for the U.S. Olympic Baseball Team last Fall in Sydney, hitting two game-winning home runs, one a grand slam.

1B Justin Morneau - Rookie League players rarely make prospect lists unless they were recent first round picks, but it's hard to ignore Morneau's numbers from last season. He hit .402 with 21 doubles, 10 home runs and 58 RBI in 52 games. Even more impressively, he walked 30 times and struck out just 18 times. Any hitter this young with power and discipline needs to be watched closely.

RHP Danny Mota - Mota has quietly put together some decent numbers since being acquired from the Yankees in the Chuck Knoblauch deal. Mota has a very good fastball and outstanding control now that he's recovered from some arm problems he's had in recent years. At Double-A during the 2000 season Mota allowed just 19 hits and 8 walks over 28-plus innings while striking out 40. He had success in his few Triple-A appearances and could be ready for the majors by the end of 2001.

RHP Juan Padilla - Normally Low-A closers don't get much attention, but when you consider that the bullpen is one of the Twins' major areas of need, Padilla needs a mention. He dominated at Low-A during the 2000 season, using his excellent fastball to post a 16 saves and a 1.92 ERA over 32 appearances. He had 40 strikeouts and just nine walks in 33 innings, which could get him moved up the ladder quickly in years to come.

RHP Juan Rincon - Speaking of star Class A hurlers who hit the wall after reaching Double-A. Rincon, 21, is a 5'11", 175, righthander who carved up lower-level hitters in 1999 and early 2000 with a low 90s fastball plus an effective slider. However, both pitches are fairly similar in velocity, and Double-A hitters quickly discovered this after Rincon's mid-2000 promotion to Double-A New Britain in the Eastern League. Rincon then began to nibble around the edges of the plate, and his control, a prime asset at lower levels, began to waver. To avoid similar future upper level struggles, Rincon needs to develop his changeup into at least a passable third option. Then, he must regain the confidence and aggressive approach that he displayed in Class A ball. If Rincon can't put it together as an upper minor league starter in 2001, he could have a second life as a reliever. His ability to throws strikes and overmatch righties one time around the order could make him an effective situational righty. At best, Rincon would reach the majors to stay in late 2002.

RHP Jason Ryan - Ryan has decent stuff, but has been inconsistent in his major league opportunities. He's got an above average fastball, a curve and a slider, but none of them are "out" pitches. He relies on good control and working ahead in the count, which isn't necessarily bad, it just means he has less room for error. He had some success at Triple-A last year and could win a job at the bottom of a major league rotation sometime soon.

2B Ruben Salazar - Salazar is a good looking middle infield prospect with a solid bat. He's been able to hit .300 so far with pretty good pop for a second baseman. He makes contact and doesn't strike out too often, though he could stand to draw a few more walks. His defense is still a work in progress, but the ability is there.

NEW YORK YANKEES
ORGANIZATIONAL GRID

	AAA	AA	HI-A	LO-A
1B	Jon Zuber - L - 30 Nick Johnson - L - 21 Randall Simon - L - 25	Nick Leach - L - 22	Aaron Jones - L - 24 Ryan Soules - L - 24	Dion Washington - R - 23
2B	Carlos Garcia - R - 32 D'Angelo Jimenez - B - 22 Andy Stankiewicz - R - 35	Marc Mirizzi - B - 25 Nick Ortiz - R - 26	Seth Taylor - R - 22 Scott Kidd - R - 26	Torre Tyson - B - 24
SS	Alfonso Soriano- R - 22 Mike Coolbaugh - R - 28	Erick Almonte - R - 22	Teuris Olivares - R - 21	Victor Castillo - R - 19 Todd Mitchell - R - 21
3B	Kevin Orie - R - 27	Scott Seabol - R - 25	Andy Phillips - R - 23 Donny Leon - B - 24	Jeff Nettles - R - 21 Eric Olson - R - 21
OF	Kerry Robinson - L - 26 Felix Jose - B - 35 Ryan Thompson - R - 32 Mike Frank - L - 25 Jeremy Morris - R - 25 Alonzo Powell - R - 35	Marcus Thames - R - 23 Donzell McDonald - B - 25 Paul Ottavinia - L - 27 Richard Brown - L - 23 Luke Wilcox - L - 26 Tyrone Horne - L - 29	Billy Brown - R - 24 Alan Greene - B - 23 John Rodriguez - L - 22 Juan Rivera - R - 22	Andy Brown - L - 20 Pedro Santana - R - 21 Angel Valdez - R - 22 Dusty Rhodes - L - 24 Mike Vento - R - 22
C	Tom Wilson - R - 29 Julio Mosquera - R - 28 Brian Johnson - R - 32	Victor Valencia - R - 23 Rene Pinto - R - 22	Michel Hernandez - R - 21	Omar Fuentes - R - 20 Troy Norrell - R - 23 Brad Elwood - R - 24 Spencer Brazeal - R - 23
SP	Jake Westbrook - R - 22 Brandon Knight - R - 24 Ted Lilly - L - 24 Denny Lail - R - 25 Randy Flores - L - 24 Adrian Hernandez - R - 25 Mike Bertotti - L - 30 Randy Keisler - L - 24	Brian Rogers - R - 23 Jason Beverlin - R - 26 Christian Parker - R - 25 Brett Jodie - R - 23 Dave Walling - R - 21	Alex Graman - L - 22 Scott Wiggins - L - 24 Brandon Claussen - L - 21 Rosman Garcia - R - 21 Julio Rangel - R - 24 Todd Noel - R - 21	Ricardo Aramboles - R - 18 Mike Knowles - R - 20 Sam Marsonek - R - 21 David Martinez - L - 20 Scott Oliver - R - 23
CLOSER	Jay Tessmer - R - 27	Domingo Jean - R - 31	Jeremy Blevins - R - 22 Chris Wallace - R - 24	Jose Franco - R - 18 Brett Weber - R - 23

NEW YORK YANKEES

How strong is the Yankee organization? Well, despite giving up substantial talent to acquire veterans like David Justice and Denny Neagle for the stretch run, they still have one of the deepest minor league talent bases in the game. As usual, the bulk of this talent is acquired in the international free agent market, not from the draft.

Nick Johnson's injured wrist kept him out for the entire 2000 season. Pending his return to full strength, Johnson remains one of the premier prospects in the game. Johnson's lost season might buy Tino Martinez another year in the Bronx, but no more than that. Johnson remains a future force out of the number three hole. Former Dodger prospect Nick Leach hit for average at Double-A Norwich last season, but misplaced his power stroke. He likely won't meet the high offensive standards set for major league first sackers, but could eventually be a decent lefthanded bat off of a big league bench.

There are no viable second base prospects in the Yankee system.

Shortstop prospects abound, but with Derek Jeter in place, their futures are uncertain. Of course, one or more of the following players could be moved to second base or other positions, or used in next year's plethora of trading deadline deals. Alfonso Soriano, despite significant defensive struggles in a couple of brief major league trials last season, remains the real deal. His power/speed upside is superior for a middle infielder, and he possesses the raw athleticism to be a solid defender. Discipline is missing in all areas of his game, however. He'll remain a prime trading chip who should be someone's starting shortstop in 2001. A back injury suffered in a car accident cost D'Angelo Jimenez the 2000 season. He lacks Soriano's raw ability, but is more polished in all areas. The Yankees love Jimenez, and want him to be a big part of their 2001 squad as a multipurpose backup, or possibly as their starting second baseman. Erick Almonte began to develop a power stroke at Double-A Norwich last season. In this organization, Almonte will get lost in the shuffle, but elsewhere, he would be a near-term candidate for a big league utility role. Teuris Olivares had a somewhat disappointing High-A season in 2000, but the 6'0", 164, righty hitter also has a decent power/speed package for a shortstop. Like Almonte, however, he's going to have a hard time standing out in this company. Victor Castillo could break out to the upside in 2001. He was physically overmatched as a Low-A teenager in 2000, but has solid defensive skills and excellent speed to build upon. If he can develop even a passable offensive game, he could threaten for a supporting big league role down the road.

With Drew Henson off to Cincinnati as part of the Neagle deal, the Yanks are left without a standout third base prospect.

The Yankees also are surprisingly thin in the outfield, due in part to the inclusion of Jackson Melian in that same Neagle deal. Donzell McDonald can fly and has learned to take a pitch, but his complementary skills have not evolved to the point where he can be considered for a significant big league role. He's a 25th-man/pinch-running specialist at best. High-A outfielders John Rodriguez and Juan Rivera both have an outside chance to develop into big league role players. Rodriguez is a lefthanded line drive machine with a touch of gaps power, and Rivera has a substantial power upside, especially if his lean 6'2", 170, frame develops as expected. The Yanks have extremely high hopes for Wily Mo Pena, who can hit the ball a country mile. Unfortunately, he swings at virtually every pitch he sees. His first crack at a full-season league was a washout and the second needs to be better if he is to remain in the club's long-range plans. Like Pena, 6'6", 190, lefty Andy Brown can drive the ball, but has been held back by poor plate discipline. Brown could still develop into a major league contributor, but needs a big High-A season in 2001 to stay on track.

There isn't a lot of catching help on the horizon. Michael Hernandez is a durable defender who makes consistent contact at the plate, but doesn't likely have the offensive package to play every day in the upper minors, let alone the majors. Omar Fuentes is a defensive ace who added a bit of gaps power to an underwhelming offensive repertoire last season. He could eventually be a viable candidate for a backup major league job.

Despite dealing four pitching prospects to obtain David Justice and Denny Neagle last summer, the Yanks still have a relatively deep stable on hand. Former Expos' prospect Ted Lilly has battled nagging arm injuries, but remains a borderline prospect. The lefty's control remains good, but he has never developed a true out pitch for use against advanced hitters. He could be a midseason callup or a deep bullpen lefty in the majors in 2001. When the smoke cleared last July, lefty Randy Keisler surprisingly remained a Yankee. He has raced through the system, and now appears poised to join the major league club. He has the diverse repertoire and low 90s heat to start in the majors, but he might need to apprentice in the pen first. The Yanks groomed a number of promising arms on their two Class A clubs last season. Jeremy Blevins has started and relieved, but the Yanks envision him as a future closer. He might not have the gas to do it in the majors, but could evolve into a middle relief candidate there. Lefty Alex Graman is a finesse hurler who has happened to work his onto George Steinbrenner's good list - he was specifically declared off-limits to other clubs last July. Truth be told, Graman will be hard pressed to excel right away against higher level hitters, as his stuff doesn't yet square with his advanced mound savvy. He's no sure thing to make the majors. 1999 first round pick Dave Walling quickly worked his way to the Double-A level in his first full pro season, and was promptly strafed. No matter, Walling is an advanced craftsman who will learn from his struggles, and projects as a mid-rotation starter for the Yankees by 2003 at the latest. Righthander Todd Noel is a high-ceiling prospect whose development has been slowed by injuries. He's still a baby at 21, but must prove his health in 2001 to retain his prospect status. 6'2", 170, righty Ricardo Aramboles, 18, is one of the Yanks' high-profile international free agent signees. His stuff and command are exceptional for his age, but he needs to learn to set up hitters and keep his head during periods of adversity. Over time, he should develop into a premier starting pitcher prospect. 1998 34th rounder Brandon Claussen is on the verge of emerging as a legitimate prospect. The 6'2", 175, lefthander likely doesn't have a major league starting job in his future, but could evolve into a big league contributor.

Jose Franco, 18, is the Yankees' best relief pitcher prospect. He throws a hard, heavy fastball that should only get better with natural physical development. He could be a major league setup man.

TOP TEN PROSPECTS

1 - 1B Nick Johnson - It was a bizarre, wasted season for Johnson, 21, who had established himself as arguably the foremost position player prospect in the game over the previous two seasons. Initially sidelined with what was thought to be a minor muscle injury in his hand in spring training, Johnson never was well enough to practice, let alone play, during the 2000 season. Test after test was performed on his injured wrist throughout the season, but as of this writing, no definitive label had been placed on his mysterious soft tissue injury. When healthy, the 6'3", 195, lefthander had stamped himself as potentially the best offensive prospect to rise from the minors since the Andruw Jones/Vladimir Guerrero exacta. He had a ridiculous .525 on-base percentage at Double-A Norwich in 1999, combining a great eye with a compact, powerful stroke that drove the ball to both gaps with improving longball power. He's also an excellent defensive prospect, combining soft hands and fluid movements for a big man. It's a testament to Johnson's ability that he remains at the top of this list after his 2000 washout. If he totally recovers, he'll quickly get back on the road to the No. 3 spot in the big league batting order.

2 - SS Alfonso Soriano - Soriano, 22, remains a paradoxical prospect, possessing both amazing raw tools and baffling fundamental shortcomings. He somehow managed to avoid rising to the major league level for any meaningful period of time despite a spate of Yankee infield injuries, while simultaneously avoiding inclusion in one of the many second-half deals that put seemingly every available major league outfielder in pinstripes. The 6'1", 170, righthanded hitter possesses lightning bat speed and extreme power for his size. However, his utter ignorance of the strike zone has prevented him from dominating upper minor league pitching. He runs extremely well, but has yet to master the situational aspects of that phase of his game. All that said, Soriano's biggest shortcomings are in the field. He had brief, separate big league trials at both shortstop and third base, and inconsistent footwork, lack of aggressiveness and spotty accuracy with his arm all hindered him. Soriano will remain a highly sought commodity around baseball because of his immense talent, but it's hard to see where he fits as a Yankee. Look for him to be moved during the offseason, and be handed a starting shortstop job for a weaker ball club. He can and will become a major league star if he looks in the mirror and makes the obvious and necessary offensive and defensive adjustments.

3 - RHP Ricardo Aramboles - Aramboles, 18, has been through quite a bit in his brief pro career. Originally signed illegally as an underage player by the Marlins in 1996, the 6'2", 170, righthander underwent Tommy John reconstructive elbow surgery in 1998 and was written off as a prospect by many. He bounced back in 2000, staying healthy all season at Low-A Greensboro and showing improved velocity and extreme control. Aramboles' fastball reaches the low 90s, and he mixes in a curve and changeup. He should add a bit more juice as he naturally matures physically, and could be an extreme strikeout pitcher if he learns to paint the corners of the strike zone a bit better. There's still a bit of debate as to his true age, his birthdate is either 12/4/81 or 6/30/80, depending on whom you believe. Aramboles is a high-risk, high-reward prospect who still has a chance to develop into a number one or two major league starter. Double-A could provide a litmus test of his upside, he could get there in 2001, and reach the majors by early 2003.

4 - SS D'Angelo Jimenez - Talk about a rollercoaster ride. 2000 was supposed to be a breakthrough season for Jimenez, 22, who was expected to be a valuable all-purpose infield reserve at the major league level for the Yankees. A near-fatal offseason automobile accident changed all of that, however, as a broken bone in his neck promised to erase at least his 2000 season. A ferocious rehabilitation program got Jimenez back onto the field in the minors last August, however, and he was added to the major league roster in September. The 6'0", 160, switch-hitter's raw skills aren't as flashy as Soriano's, but they're pretty solid in their own right. Jimenez will work the count and take a walk, and possesses above average extra base power for a middle infielder. He has well above average speed, but needs to temper his aggressiveness on the basepaths a bit. Defensively, he is much smoother on the routine play than Soriano, and has soft hands and smooth throwing mechanics, though his arm strength isn't overwhelming. Jimenez can play second base, short-stop and third base, and can provide an added dimension to the Yanks' aging roster off of the bench. He'll be a valuable backup in New York in 2001, and could be their second or third baseman in 2002.

5 - LHP Randy Keisler - As with Soriano, it's kind of amazing that the Yankees' trade-filled Summer of 2000 ended with Keisler, 24, still a member of the organization. The 6'3", 180, lefthander was supposedly one of the players made available to the Indians as a player to be named later in the David Justice deal, in which fellow pitching prospects Jake Westbrook and Zach Day were

eventually delivered. The 1998 second round pick pitched brilliantly at times at Triple-A Columbus, combining a low 90s fastball, a decent curveball and an improving changeup. He threw strike one consistently, varied speed and location well, and lasted deep into ballgames thanks to relatively low pitch counts. Drafted as a 22-year-old, Keisler needed to race through the minors quickly to project as an eventual big league starter, and he has succeeded. Keisler is a solid bet to snare the fifth starter Look for Walling to fare better in a Double-A encore in role with the Yankees in 2001 spring training. Memo to Keisler, show up in Tampa in shape, or else run the risk of becoming the next version of Ed Yarnall. He could evolve into a poor man's Andy Pettitte, and last awhile in the Apple as a mid-rotation guy.

6 - OF Wily Mo Pena - Pena, 18, is one in a continuing series of high-profile international free agent signings by the Yankees. The 6'3", 190, righthanded hitter was signed to a $4.7 million major league contract back in April 1999. Pena's raw power is immense, but he has a lot to learn about hitting. At this stage in his development, Pena will swing at just about anything, and his propensity for burying himself in the count severely limits the number of fastballs he sees. He was overmatched by Low-A pitchers early in 2000, and continued to rack up poor strikeout/walk numbers in rookie ball before suffering a season-ending knee injury. Physically, he's an incredible speci-men for his age, and should pack on another 15 or 20 pounds of muscle as he matures. He has a 50 homer upside if he makes the necessary adjustments at the plate. His foot speed is average, but he projects as a solid defensive right fielder, combining good range and an excellent throwing arm. He'll get another Low-A shot in 2001, and needs to show significant improvement to remain a short-list top prospect. He still could become a star, but won't get to New York before 2004.

7 - RHP Dave Walling - Walling, 21, was the Yankees' first round draft pick in 1999. The 6'5", 210, righty was aggressively advanced to the Double-A level after a dominant High-A first half last season, and predictably struggled. The University of Arkansas product combines a low 90s fastball and a solid changeup, but needs to add a harder breaking pitch to fill out his arsenal. He's a finesse hurler who needs to keep the ball low in the strike zone to succeed, and inconsistency in that area keyed his Double-A struggles. Walling has an advanced feel for pitching considering his experience level, and is the type of pitcher who can keep his club in the game for six or seven innings even when he doesn't have his best stuff.

2001. He projects as a future major league mid-rotation starter, and could make his first foray into the Yankees' rotation sometime in 2002.

8 - LHP Alex Graman - Graman, 22, was the Yanks' third round draft pick in 1999. The 6'4", 195, lefthander outshone Walling in the eyes of many observers when the two pitched together in rookie ball that season, but Graman is a year older, and his upside a bit lower. Graman has a diverse four-pitch repertoire, featuring a 90 MPH fastball plus a nasty curve, a decent changeup and an entry-level slider. Graman is a control artist with a knack for setting up hitters, but might not have a true strikeout pitch against upper level hitters at this point. He has yet to establish himself as even a seven-inning pitcher, possessing below average stamina for a control hurler. At his age, it is imperative that Graman experiences immediate, significant Double-A success in 2001 to remain an A-list prospect. He pitched well in front of George Steinbrenner on more than occasion last season, supposedly gaining himself immunity from inclusion in any of the Yanks' in-season trades in 2000. Graman has a chance to slide into the low end of the Yanks' major league rotation by 2003, but has little margin for error.

9 - RHP Todd Noel - Noel, 21, was the Cubs' number one pick in 1996, and has since toiled in the White Sox', Marlins' and Yankees' organizations as well. The strapping 6'5", 230, righthander was limited to four High-A starts last season by recurring biceps tendinitis in his pitching arm. The loss of a full season at a key developmental stage in his career is quite significant, but Noel remains young and talented enough to make a run at a major league spot. His fastball routinely reaches the mid 90s, and Noel fills out a diverse repertoire with a curve, slider and changeup that all have major league potential. Noel's mechanics are still a work in progress, but he has shown solid control and could develop into a strikeout per inning threat with additional movement on his pitches. He has the body of a nine-inning hurler, but needs to unfurl a couple of 150 inning seasons to build towards such a stamina level. Noel needs to stay healthy in 2001 to get back on track towards the majors. His upside might be higher than that of any other pitcher on this list, but his flameout potential is higher as well. At best, he'll reach the majors in 2003.

10 - OF Andy Brown - Brown, 20, was the Yankees' first round draft pick in 1998. After a poor rookie ball campaign in 1999, the 6'6", 190, lefthanded hitter took some steps towards fulfillment of his immense power potential at Low-A Greensboro last season. Brown's swing remains a bit long, and his plate discipline quite poor, but the ball explodes off of his bat when he makes solid contact. He's comparable to the Indians' Russell Branyan at a similar stage in development, except that Brown appears to be capable of hitting for a higher average though he takes many fewer pitches. If Brown can significantly enhance his plate discipline, he could do major damage to the additional fastballs he would see. Defensively, Brown has adequate range and arm strength, but might be limited to left field at the big league level. If Brown's strikeout/walk ratio moves in the right direction in 2001, he'll be on track towards a possible late 2003 debut in the Bronx. He's a high-risk, high-reward type who could evolve into a major league middle-of-the-order force, or a Triple-A journeyman.

OTHER PROSPECTS

SS Erick Almonte - Almonte is an inconsistent defensive player and impatient hitter, but he's got the kind of pop and speed teams like out of their middle infielders. He needs to focus better in the field and avoid making errors on routine plays while becoming much more patient at the plate. He's shown a knack for driving in runs and could be a 20-20 guy someday, but he's got some work to do in the meantime.

RHP Jeremy Blevins - Blevins is a prospect who was used as both a starter and a closer last season. He has a very good arm and is getting better at throwing strikes early in the count, though he still has to prove himself against hitters above the Single-A level. He is a strikeout pitcher and he's worth watching over the next year or two.

RHP Ryan Bradley - Bradley has outstanding stuff, but control problems have hurt him recently. His fastball is in the low to mid 90s and he has a nasty slider, but if he's not working ahead in the count he gets hurt. He's been used both as a starter and as a reliever, though at this point he seems better served coming out of the bullpen.

LHP Brandon Claussen - Claussen has proven to be a strikeout pitcher early in his professional career and he has the stuff to maintain that standing as he moves up. His control isn't the greatest, though it's not terrible either, and he's very difficult to hit against. As he moves up the ladder, it will be important for him to work ahead in the count.

3B Elvis Corporan - Corporan is an erratic young third baseman with talent, but who is also still very raw. He strikes out an almost ridiculous amount at this point, but he has power potential and he runs reasonably well. His defense needs plenty of work still, but the ability to be a good defender is there.

RHP Zach Day - Day has an outstanding arm and can be absolutely overpowering at times. His control isn't pinpoint, but it's reasonably good. If he can improve his secondary pitches a bit and improve his control a touch, Day has a chance to be really good.

RHP Jose Franco - Usually, closers pitching at Low-A aren't worth writing about, but Franco is. He has a tremendous arm and is pretty much unhittable when he's on. Control is a bit of an issue, but because he doesn't give up many hits his walks haven't hurt him too much. He could advance pretty quickly over the next year or two if he keeps pitching like he did during the 2000 season.

C Michel Hernandez - Hernandez is a strong defensive catcher, but a work in progress at the plate. He has very little power and didn't hit for average last year either, but he has shown he can walk more often than he strikes out.

1B Nick Leach - Leach is a patient hitter who plays good defense, but he hasn't developed the power teams want from a first baseman. With Nick Johnson in his way, it's unlikely he'll advance very far with the Yankees, but he could turn into a solid lefthanded bat off the bench if he find the right opportunity. He's a Hal Morris/Mark Grace type of hitter, the type who teams are staying away from these days.

LHP Ted Lilly - Lilly has a low 90s fastball with good movement and a sharp curve, but he's yet to translate that into a legitimate shot at the majors. If he can develop his changeup further, he would increase his chances as a major league starter. He has the ability to strike hitters out, but often falls behind and has to give in to the hitter. He's not a top prospect right now, but he does have the potential to be a good major league pitcher.

OF Donzell McDonald - McDonald runs well and covers ground in the outfield, but hasn't developed as a hitter at all. He's 26 years-old this year and hasn't spent a full season above Double-A, which is definitely not a good sign. His patience is good and he's always a stolen base threat, but he must hit with more authority.

SS Teuris Olivares - Olivares has improved his consistency on defense over the past year, but still needs work at the plate. He has speed and a little bit of pop, but doesn't walk very often. With some work on his base stealing technique and some improved discipline at the plate, Olivares could be a good player.

RHP Jay Tessmer - He's not going to be a major league closer, but he could become a Scott Sullivan-like reliever who eats up some innings in middle relief and gives righthanded hitters problems because of his sidearm delivery. His fastball is nothing special, but he throws all of his pitches over the plate.

2B Torre Tyson - Tyson looks like he has a shot at being pretty good. He's got good wheels and a good eye at the plate, which leads one to believe he could be a factor at the top of the order as he moves up. He hasn't shown any power at all, but has been able to carry a decent batting average and play reasonably well at second base.

C Victor Valencia - Valencia has some power and draws some walks, though he's not exactly a finished product as a hitter. He strikes out a lot, makes feeble contact quite often and generally seems like he's pressing too much. Valencia is a capable defensive player, though he's probably looking at a career as a major league backup unless he smoothes things out at the plate.

OAKLAND ATHLETICS
ORGANIZATIONAL GRID

	AAA	AA	HI-A (Modesto)	HI-A (Visalia)
1B	Steve Decker - R - 34 Mario Valdez - L - 25	Jason Hart - R - 22 Todd Mensik - L - 25	Nick Sosa - R - 22 Mitch Gregg - L - 23 Jon Schaeffer - R - 24	Rafael Pujols - R - 22 Matt Howe - R - 23
2B	Jose Ortiz - R - 23	Jay Pecci - B - 23 Joe Espada - R - 24	Carlos Rosario - B - 20 Justin Hall - R - 23	Esteban German - R - 21 Monty Davis - R - 22
SS	Jorge Velandia - R - 25	Oscar Salazar - R - 22	Caonabo Cosme - R - 21	Angel Berroa - R - 20
3B	Mark Bellhorn - B - 25 Eric Martins - R - 27	Jacques Landry - R - 26	Gary Schneidmiller - R - 20 Christian Reyes - B - 22	Josh Hochgesang - R - 23
OF	Roberto Vaz - L - 25 Mario Encarnacion - R - 22 Bo Porter - R - 27 Eric Byrnes - R - 24	Justin Bowles - L - 26 Dionys Cesar - B - 23 Gary Thomas - R - 20 Mike Lockwood - L - 23 Greg Martinez - B - 28	Ryan Ludwick - R - 21 Jesus Basabe - R - 23 Rusty Keith - R - 22 Matt Forbes - R - 22	Hipolito Martinez - R - 23 Kirk Asche - R - 22 Omar Rosario - L - 22 Michael Wenner - R - 21
C	A.J. Hinch - R - 26	Cody McKay - L - 26 Brian Luderer - R - 21	Miguel Olivo - R - 21 Jose De la Cruz - R - 22 Aaron Nieckula - R - 23	Gerald Laird - R - 20 Javier Flores - R - 24
SP	Frank Lankford - R - 29 Ariel Prieto - R - 33 Jon Ratliff - R - 28 Justin Miller - R - 22 Scott Sanders - R - 31 Rich Sauveur - L - 36	Kevin Gregg - R - 22 Denny Wagner - R - 23 Tim Manwiller - R - 25 Marcus Jones - R - 25 Mario Ramos - L - 22 Eric Thompson - R - 22	Mark Seaver - R - 25 Juan Pena - L - 21 Justin Lehr - R - 22 Jon Adkins - R - 22 Matt O'Brien - L - 21	Jeff Schultz - R - 24 Wayne Nix - R - 23 Javier Calzada - R - 21 Scott Chiasson - R - 22 Keith Surkont - R - 23 Chris Enochs - R - 24
CLOSER	Scott Service - R - 33 Chad Harville - R - 23 Luis Vizcaino - R - 23	Bert Snow - R - 23 Leo Vasquez - L - 27	Jim Brink - R - 23 Brian Mazur - L - 22	Travis McCall - L - 22 Corey Miller - R - 23 Claudio Galva - L - 20

OAKLAND A's

Today's Oakland A's are living proof that the "old fashioned way" of building a ball club, from within via expert scouting and instruction, can still work in this day and age. Though their major league nucleus remains quite young, a great deal of talent remains on the farm. Some of those players will earn spots on the A's major league roster, and others will surely be dealt to acquire missing veteran pieces.

First baseman Mario Valdez was acquired from the Twins in a trading deadline deal last season. He has been a high minor league mauler for many years now, but has never found the right major league situation. He is a premium hitter who will make a major league impact somewhere; it might as well be Oakland. Don't be surprised if he's a major league contributor in 2001. 6'4", 240, behemoth Jason Hart has emerged as a legitimate power prospect. Bear in mind, however, that Hart has played in extreme hitters' parks in the last two seasons. Another big year at Triple-A in 2001 will prove he has a major league future, at least as a backup. Among others, Nick Sosa has some power potential and Rafael Pujols swings a lusty line drive bat, but they're darkhorses at best to get a sniff of the majors.

At second base, Esteban German slid backward a bit with a poor 2000 season. German has a great eye and is an expert basestealer, but hits too many lazy fly balls. He still could develop into a candidate to start in the majors, but needs to have a huge upper minor league season in 2001 to remain one. Switch-hitter Carlos Rosario has similar strengths and weaknesses as German, but has a much lower upside across the board. He's got an outside chance to emerge as a big league utility candidate.

Very quietly, Jose Ortiz has excelled in all facets of the game in recent seasons. He can play respectable defense at both middle infield positions, but his strength is hitting. Despite a diminutive 5'9", 160, frame, Ortiz can hit for both average and power right now in a part-time major league role. Oscar Salazar also has a chance to be a major league all-purpose reserve. He can play any infield or outfield spot, though he's nothing special with the glove anywhere, but is a reliable line-drive hitter with gaps power. Caonabo Cosme is showing signs of developing a solid power/speed package for a shortstop. However, he's been stuck in High-A ball for three years now, and has to make upper minor league noise now to have a chance at making an eventual big league impact. Angel Berroa, 20, is poised to bypass Cosme and Salazar, and could be a starting big league shortstop. His defense is excellent, and he hit the ball with surprising authority in his first full pro season in 2000. He's ready to break out.

Adam Piatt swings a lusty bat with legitimate big league extra base power, and will likely fit into near-future editions of the A's as a part-time designated hitter. He won't duplicate his gaudy minor league numbers in the majors. Onetime top prospect Mark Bellhorn has solid power potential and a good eye, but will have a hard time squeezing out a spot on the major league roster. A change of scenery might give him an opportunity for a big league reserve role elsewhere. Gary Schneidmiller, 20, has a great eye and plays a decent third base, but must develop some extra base power to have even an outside chance of reaching the majors. His youth is his greatest asset.

Outfield options are plentiful. Roberto Vaz is a relatively limited prospect with a bit of gaps power and decent speed, but will only get a big league cup of coffee at best. Mario Encarnacion, 22, considered to be the A's most talented position player prospect, hasn't shown the expected improvement at higher levels. He still has a chance to eventually start for the A's, but won't do so in 2001. His ability to play all three outfield positions makes him a viable fourth outfielder candidate. Eric Byrnes doesn't have Encarnacion's physical talent, but he simply hits wherever he goes. The righthanded hitter has a 15/15 power/speed upside, and is a sleeper to steal a major league backup job in 2001. He'll extract the most from his average raw tools. Gary Thomas, 20, stands just 5'6", 175, but he held his own as one of the youngest Double-A regulars. He's an above average defensive outfielder, but needs to hit the ball with more authority and use his speed more efficiently to keep moving up. He looks like a future big league fourth outfielder at this point. Ryan Ludwick likely bypassed Encarnacion as the chain's foremost power prospect last season. The 1999 second round pick still has a tendency to get himself out on bad pitches at times, but if he improves in that area he could eventually start, and possibly star, in the majors. Rusty Keith is a scrappy top-of-the-order type who evokes memories of another Rusty (Greer) at a similar stage in development. He gets on base and slashes the ball to the gaps regularly, and could draw attention to himself as a possible future major league supporting player with a big Double-A season in 2001. Among 1999 draftees, ninth rounder Kirk Asche, 11th rounder Michael Wenner and 23rd rounder Mike Lockwood all deserve mention, Asche for a 20/20 power/speed upside, Wenner for blazing raw speed, and Lockwood for power potential and a polished all-around game. All will have to raise their game significantly to stand out in such company and eventually earn consideration for major league roles.

Among catchers, A.J. Hinch is still hanging around at Triple-A Sacramento. His game has matured, and he would provide gaps power and solid defense as a big league backup or as a starter in the event of an injury to Ramon Hernandez. Miguel Olivo is the A's catching prospect most likely to eventually earn a starting role in the majors. His defensive skills are splendid, but his offensive game needs a bit of work. He needs to learn to take a pitch and add power via natural physical development. Brian Luderer, 21, has displayed a solid line drive bat in limited minor league roles. Before projecting a major league future, the A's need to see how Luderer performs over a full 400 at bat season.

Barry Zito joined the A's rotation late in 2000, and has a bright major league future. The southpaw has an advanced feel for pitching, a top-shelf curveball, and should be a fixture near the top of the A's rotation for a decade or more. Luis Vizcaino has a live fastball and a smooth delivery, but doesn't appear to have a sufficiently diverse repertoire to start in the majors. He could eventually become a serviceable major league setup man. Former Rockies' prospect Justin Miller is a finesse hurler who fared surprisingly well in the hitter-friendly environment at Double-A Midland. His ability to change speeds makes his average fastball seem harder. He could evolve into a viable big league swingman. Lefty Juan Pena, 21, blossomed into a legitimate starting pitcher prospect last season. He blew the ball by High-A California League hitters, and could get scarier as his 6'3", 195, frame

matures. He was held to five innings in most starts last year. If he maintains his strikeout rate over longer stretches at a higher level in 2001, watch out. Franklyn German has a prototypical 6'5", 210, pitcher's frame and decent stuff, but his pitches lack bite due to inconsistent mechanics. He's still a kid, but needs to make significant enhancements soon to assert himself as a prospect. 2000 eighth round draftee Justin Lehr showed excellent command at High-A Modesto, walking just over two batters per nine innings. Double-A will be a stern test for his average stuff, and could determine whether he has what it takes to eventually earn a supporting major league role. Righthander Eric Thompson, 22, surprisingly flourished at the Double-A level after a mid-2000 promotion, due to pinpoint precision within the strike zone. A repeat performance in 2001 could make him a sleeper to eventually garner a ninth or tenth man spot on a big league staff. 2001's breakout pitching prospects could include the likes of Javier Calzada and Claudio Galva, a pair of five-year minor league vets who made positive first full-season league impressions at High-A Visalia, combining slightly above average stuff with solid control.

TOP TEN PROSPECTS

1 - LHP Barry Zito - Along with Tigers' first base prospect Eric Munson, who didn't hang around long enough to get a hit, Zito, 22, was the only 1999 first round draft pick to advance to the major leagues in 2000 prior to the September 1 roster expansion. The 6'3", 200, southpaw made an immediate positive impression, showing a combination of stuff and savvy uncommon in such a youngster. Zito's repertoire includes a 90 MPH fastball, a nasty, drop-off-the-table curveball and a much improved changeup. Triple-A Pacific Coast League managers recognized his curve as the best breaking pitch in the circuit last season. He throws all of his pitches for quality strikes consistently, and his ability to change speeds and precisely locate the ball makes him a strikeout pitcher despite his lack of an overpowering heater. Zito needs to get hitters out earlier in the count more often, consequently keeping his pitch counts down and allowing him to last deeper into ballgames. Once he does so, he'll quickly entrench himself as the A's long-term staff ace.

2 - OF Ryan Ludwick - Ludwick, 21, was the A's second round draft pick in 1999. After an extremely slow start at High-A Modesto last season, the 6'3", 205, righthanded hitter went on a power binge that at one point included 19 homers over a 35 game stretch. Ludwick possesses extreme raw power to all fields; High-A California League skippers recognized him as the best power prospect in the circuit. Poor plate discipline was at the root of his early-season struggles. His numbers took off after he began to swing at fewer low, outside breaking pitches and high fastballs, and began to see more grooved fastballs as a result. He still has more work to do in this area, and could become a .300 hitter if he equalized his strikeout and walk totals. He also has a tendency to put undue pressure on himself. Though not speedy, he covers quite a bit of ground in center field because of the excellent jumps he gets. His above average throwing arm might make him a better fit in right field at higher levels. Ludwick should enter the majors sometime in 2003, and could be a long-term middle-of-the-order force if he continues to enhance his plate discipline.

3 - 2B Jose Ortiz - Ortiz, 23, has been flying under the radar of most talent prognosticators for years now because of his lack of size and raw tools. He just keeps performing, however, and has now established himself as a near-term major league factor. The 5'9", 160, righthanded hitter makes consistent contact and will take his share of walks, and possesses exceptional extra base power for his size. Though not a speed merchant, Ortiz has solid baserunning instincts, and picks his spots often enough to be a 20 steal resource over a full season. Defensively, Ortiz had enough range to be a solid minor league shortstop prior to 2000, but was shifted to second base to speed his rise to the majors. His defense was brilliant at his new home, as he combined expansive range and arm strength uncommon to second base. In fact, Triple-A Pacific Coast League managers rated him the best defensive second base prospect in the circuit. Randy Velarde is getting along in years, and Ortiz is ready to complement, if not totally replace him in 2001. Look for Ortiz to establish himself as a productive all-purpose major league infield backup, and a possible future long-term starter. His production on a per at bat basis should be well above major league average for his position.

4 - 1B Jason Hart - Hart, 22, was a fifth round draft pick in 1998. The strapping 6'4", 240, righthanded hitter appeared to be nothing more than all-or-nothing power prospect entering the 2000 season, but had a breakout season in all facets of the game at Double-A Midland in 2000. Hart smoothed out many of the rough edges of his offensive package last season, swinging at fewer bad pitches, and raising his walk total and batting average in the process. He's a deadly fastball hitter, possessing launching-pad power from gap to gap. Texas League managers recognized him as the best batting prospect in the circuit. That's not power prospect, but BATTING prospect. That word alone shows how far Hart has come. Defensively, Hart has worked hard to become a slightly better than average gloveman. He'll never be exceptionally quick at his size, but does have soft hands and acceptable range. The offensive standards for starting major league first basemen are extremely high, but Hart should be able to reach them. Of course, with Jason Giambi in town, there's no guarantee it will happen in Oakland. Hart will be major league ready in 2002, but might need a change of scenery to get a full-time big league job.

5 - C Miguel Olivo - Olivo, 21, is one of the foremost defensive catching prospects in the minor leagues. The 6'0", 180, righthanded hitter has a howitzer throwing arm and a flexible body, and moves well behind the plate. High-A California League managers recognized as him as the circuit's best defensive receiver. Olivo needs to add bulk as he physically matures to be able to handle the full-time grind of his demanding position, and also needs to improve his handling of pitchers. With the bat, Olivo has a quick, compact swing that generates some power to the gaps. Physical development should help that facet of his game as well, allowing some of his Class A doubles and triples to become upper minor league homers. His plate discipline is poor, and caused him to underachieve with the bat in his first crack at Double-A pitching in mid-2000. At this point, Olivo is an unpolished gem who could wind up either as the best defensive starting catcher in the AL not nicknamed Pudge, or as a Triple-A journeyman who gets himself out on a regular basis. The truth is likely somewhere in between - look for Olivo to join the A's for good by Opening Day 2003 at the latest, and evolve into a good-field, average-hit starting big leaguer.

6 - OF Mario Encarnacion - Encarnacion, 22, appeared to be on track for a near-term berth in the A's starting major league outfield, but his injury-plagued, subpar 2000 Triple-A season has at least temporarily put those plans on hold. The 6'2", 187, righthanded hitter has a lean, supple frame, and an extremely quick bat capable of generating above average home run power from gap to gap. However, an utter lack of plate discipline has transformed him into an upper-minor league strikeout machine. He has proven extremely vulnerable to outside breaking pitches and high fastballs, and has been slow to make the necessary adjustments. Encarnacion runs quite well, but not well enough to be the risk-taker that he is on the bases. Defensively, his range is adequate for center field, and potentially exceptional for right field, for which he has the requisite arm strength. Encarnacion is at a pivotal stage in his development. He still could mature into an eventual 30 homer/20 steal starting major league right fielder by 2002, or could stagnate near his current level and be overrun by the Ryan Ludwicks of this world.

7 - RHP Chad Harville - Harville, 23, was the A's second round draft pick in 1997. The 5'10", 180, closer prospect has been stuck in neutral for a couple of seasons now. He possesses an upper 90s fastball and a hard slider, but has not enhanced his command within the strike zone or added a viable third pitch that is significantly slower than the other two. Opposing hitters can confidently approach Harville by sitting on the fastball and adjusting to the slider. Still, not too many guys, especially among sub-six-footers, can crank the radar gun up to 98 MPH at will, so hope remains. The A's will continue to tinker with his motion to try to generate a little better movement on his fastball, and the search for the third pitch will continue. It could come together all at once for this high-ceiling prospect. Look for him to earn a righthanded setup role in Oakland in 2001, and to be ready to step into the closer role if he performs well and Jason Isringhausen falters.

8 - IF/OF Adam Piatt - Piatt, 24, was the A's eighth round draft pick in 1997. The 6'2", 195, righthanded hitter broke into the consciousness of talent evaluators with an incredible 1999 Double-A campaign in which he batted .345 with 48 doubles, 39 homers, 135 RBI and 93 walks at Midland in the Texas League. He bounced back and forth from Triple-A to the majors last season, proving to be a promising offensive prospect who lacks a true full-time defensive position. Piatt is a professional hitter, working the count well and pouncing on the most hittable pitch he sees in an at bat. He uses the whole field, and projects as more of a gaps-power hitter than a top-shelf home run threat at the major league level. Defensively, Piatt has adequate reactions and arm strength at third base, but has enhanced his value by also learning to play first base and left field. He fits in perfectly on the A's major league roster, both on the field and personality-wise. He'll have a hard time carving out a full-time role with this crew, but should be exceptionally productive on a per at bat basis in 350 or so plate appearances split between the aforementioned three positions and designated hitter in 2001.

9 - LHP Juan Pena - Pena, 21, came out of nowhere after a horrible High-A California League season (168 hits in 131 innings, 5.76 ERA) in 1999 to put up massive all-around numbers in a second season at that level. The 6'3", 195, southpaw is not truly overpowering, but improved mechanics allowed him to add movement to his 90 MPH fastball and his decent array of breaking pitches, drastically improving both his hits and strikeouts to innings pitched ratios to power-pitcher levels. Of course, the pivotal jump to the Double-A level awaits him, and that jump is even more fitful in the A's system, where the pitchers' nightmare that is Midland, Texas looms. Pena should be able to add another 10 to 15 pounds of muscle through natural physical development, allowing him to pitch deeper into ballgames. He averaged barely five innings per start in 2000 and become a viable major league starter prospect. At worst, Pena could become an interesting lefthanded situational relief prospect who could reach the majors in late 2002. If his 2001 Double-A experience goes well, Pena could become, much more.

10 - OF Gary Thomas - Thomas, 20, is an intriguing 1997 23rd round pick. He stands only 5'6", 175, but wended his way into substantial playing time at Double-A Midland last season, where he was one of the Texas League's youngest players. Offensively, the righthanded hitter projects as a top-of-the-order type, possessing well above average plate discipline and the ability to evolve into a consistent line drive hitter at upper levels. His offensive game was negatively impacted by nagging injuries last season, but he had shown some gaps power potential in High-A ball in 1999. His speed is a bit above average, and prior to 2000, he had proven himself a high percentage basestealer at lower levels. Defensively, Thomas is an exceptional outfielder with the range and throwing arm to play any of those three positions. Though he doesn't likely possess the offensive upside or the durability to be a major league starter, Thomas' array of skills would make him a useful 300 at bat part-timer or fourth outfielder in the big leagues. He needs to perform much better, however, in a second Double-A chance in 2001 to get back on track for a possible late 2002 major league debut.

OTHER PROSPECTS

OF Kirk Asche - Asche has good power potential and some speed, though he needs work on the finer points of hitting. He didn't hit for much of an average at Single-A Visalia last year and he struck out a ton. He's able to draw the occasional walk and if he can just cut back on the strikeouts a little without losing power he could advance quickly.

3B Mark Bellhorn - Bellhorn is a versatile infielder who has plenty of offensive potential. He strikes out a lot and isn't much of a hitter for average, but he has everything else. He has 20-plus home run power and 20-plus stolen base potential to go with the ability to draw plenty of walks.

RHP Scott Chiasson - Chiasson is a hard thrower with pretty good control. He's not overpowering, but his live fastball combined with his secondary pitches have been more than enough for him to be successful thus far. He's adept at finishing hitters off when he gets ahead and doesn't allow many hits or walks.

SS Caonabo Cosme - Cosme can really run and he's got some extra base power that could turn into double-digit home run power if he stops swinging like a madman. He strikes out a ridiculous number of times and even though he draw a decent number of walks, it's not enough to offset the whiffs. He's a good defensive shortstop.

SS Josue Espada - Espada is a good fielder with an idea of what it takes to be a decent hitter, though he has no power whatsoever. He draws a good number of walks when compared to the number of times he strikes out and he has above average speed, but his lack of punch at the plate might force him into a utility role down the line. He can play both shortstop and second base well.

2B Esteban German - German is a candidate for leadoff duty if he ever reaches the majors because of his outstanding speed. He stole 78 bases in 86 attempts at Single-A last season and that's a remarkable percentage. He needs work at the plate, where he has average patience and little power, but he's a good defender who can go a long way if he consistently gets on base and uses his speed.

C A.J. Hinch - Hinch is good receiver and decent hitter, but his lack of home run power and his struggles throwing out base stealers at the major league level are draw backs. He probably won't become a full-time starting catcher, but because he's got good leadership skills and works hard he should find his way into the majors as a backup.

3B Josh Hochgesang - Hochgesang, aside from having an unusual name, is a good prospect. His only flaw as a player at this point is his propensity for striking out. He's a good defender at third base, he has plenty of power and he runs well for a big man. He also draws a lot of walks, a sign he could cut back on the whiffs and hit more home runs as he advances.

RHP Justin Lehr - Lehr is a pretty advanced pitcher, considering he's able to keep his walks to a minimum while picking up a lot of strikeouts and keeping hitters from getting many hits against him. Lehr also does a fair job of keeping balls on the ground and in the ballpark, which will be useful as he moves up in the A's system.

OF Mike Lockwood - Lockwood jumped from Single-A all the way to Triple-A last year. Lockwood has outstanding patience at the plate and is a solid .300 hitter, though he could stand to hit a few more homers. Because he's not a speedster, Lockwood will need to improve his power numbers to be considered a top prospect, though he has already made significant strides in moving up as quickly as he did.

RHP Justin Miller - Miller has a good fastball and is more than able to punch hitters out when he gets ahead, but his control is lacking. If he can improve his repertoire just a bit and throw more first and second pitch strikes, Miller will be on his way. He's relatively difficult to hit against and hasn't been prone to giving up too many homers, but he's got to be ahead in the count to succeed against older hitters.

SS Oscar Salazar - Salazar is a pretty good hitter with some pop and he has the ability to play third base and outfield in addition to shortstop. He's not a home run hitter, but has shown he can reach double-digits while also hitting a bunch of doubles. Salazar isn't particularly skilled on the bases and his speed probably won't be much of a threat as he moves up, but as long as he hits he'll get chances to advance.

OF Roberto Vaz - Vaz is a line drive hitter with little pop and good speed. He's a little old to be considered a top prospect, but could be a good platoon player in the major leagues in the near future. Vaz doesn't strike out all that much, making him a candidate for pinch-hitting duty, and he draws a fair number of walks. He's not a particularly great fielder, but can hold his own in the outfield.

RHP Luis Vizcaino - Vizcaino appears to be on his way to a career in the bullpen. With A's multitude of young pitchers already in the starting rotation and the constant need for strong relief pitchers in the majors leagues, Vizcaino seems best served in that role. He has an above average fastball that gets good sinking motion and he's got reasonably good control, though it could stand to improve a little.

SEATTLE MARINERS
ORGANIZATIONAL GRID

	AAA	AA	HI-A	LO-A
1B	Brian Lesher - R - 29	Juan Thomas - R - 24 Greg Connors - R - 25	Craig Kuzmic - B - 23 Peanut Williams - R - 22	Shawn McCorkle - L - 22
2B	Carlos Hernandez -R- 24 Willie Bloomquist - R - 22	Jermaine Clark - L - 23	Robert Gandalfo - L - 22	Oscar Ramirez - R - 21 Ariel Durango - B - 21
SS	Jose Flores - R - 27 Chris Snopek - R - 29	Ramon Vazquez - L - 23	Antonio Perez - R - 18	Ruben Castillo - R - 19
3B	Chad Akers - R - 28	Luis Figueroa - R - 23 Ryan Medrano - R - 26	Bo Robinson - R - 24	Gorky Estrella - R - 23 Justin Leone - R - 23
OF	Anthony Sanders -R- 26 Chad Alexander - R - 26 Mike Murphy - R - 28 Mike Neill - L - 30 Charles Gipson - R - 27 Raul Ibanez - L - 28	Jake Weber - L - 24 Dwight Maness - R - 26 Alex Fernandez - L - 19 Adrian Myers - R - 25	Juan Silvestre - R - 22 P.J. Williams - R - 23 Harvey Hargrove - R - 24 Freddy May - L - 24 Terrmel Sledge - L - 23 Jaime Bubela - L - 21 Wilfredo Quintana - R - 22	Sean Parnell - R - 22 Chris Snelling - L - 18 Mike Abate - R - 21 Sheldon Fulse - B - 18 Orlando Hernandez - R - 21
C	Robert Machado - R - 27 Dusty Wathan - B - 26	Jim Horner - R - 26 Blake Barthol - R - 27 Juan Alcala - R - 22	Scott Maynard - R - 22 Travis McClendon - R - 27	Ryan Christiansen - R - 19 Kevin Robles - R - 22
SP	Ryan Anderson - L - 20 Pat Ahearne - R - 30 Ken Cloude - R - 25 Ryan Franklin - R - 27 Gil Meche - R - 21 Rod Henderson - R - 29 Kevin Hodges - R - 27 Joel Pineiro - R - 21 Frank Rodriguez - R - 27	Brian Fuentes - L - 24 Greg Wooten - R - 26 Allan Westfall - R - 25 Jason Turman - R - 24 Julio Ayala - L - 25 Jeff Farnsworth - R - 24 Josue Matos - R - 22 Brian Sweeney - R - 26	Chris Mears - R - 22 Enmanuel Ulloa - R - 21 Jeff Heaverlo - R - 22 Melqui Torres - R - 23 Caleb Balbuena - R - 23	Craig Anderson - L - 19 Cha Baek - R - 20 Rafael Soriano - R - 20 J.J. Putz - R - 23 Matt Thornton - L - 23
CLOSER	Todd Williams - R - 29	Aaron Scheffer - R - 24 Justin Kaye - R - 24	Brandon Parker - R - 24 Allan Simpson - R - 22	Aquilino Lopez - R - 20 Danny Delgado - R - 22 Julio Mateo - R - 20

SEATTLE MARINERS

In the last couple of seasons, the Seattle Mariners have done an amazing job of rebuilding what had been one of the weaker farm systems in the game. An influx of foreign-born, high-ceiling talent has supplemented some productive drafts, painting a bright future at the major league level. Starting pitching, also an area of depth at the major league level, is a specific strength.

First base is one area of weakness. Only High-A power threat Peanut Williams, who had a poor 2000 season, has a chance to someday play a significant big league role. Poor conditioning and plate discipline have held back the 6'3", 235, Williams.

In Jermaine Clark and Willie Bloomquist, the Mariners possess a pair of potential future major league starters. Clark, 23, is a seasoned offensive prospect, combining a consistent line drive bat with excellent plate discipline and above average speed. He's fairly ordinary defensively, and might need to learn another position to make himself a viable utility prospect. Clark, however, is likely to be passed by Bloomquist in 2001. He ravaged High-A California League pitching, smoking liners to all fields, making consistent contact and running the bases well. He's better with the glove than Clark, and is a natural team leader. Look for Bloomquist to land the Triple-A job in 2001, with Clark possibly becoming trade bait. Bloomquist is a future big league number one or two hitter. Switch-hitter Ariel Durango, 21, is a speed-burner with mediocre complementary skills who could become a utility prospect with significant development.

Shortstop Ramon Vazquez, 23, has been stuck at the Double-A level for two seasons now, and lacks a singular tool that would ensure him of a big league future. He's likely to kick around in the upper minors for quite awhile. Antonio Perez, 18, was the main consideration received in the Ken Griffey, Jr., deal. He has a tremendous power/speed upside for a shortstop, and excelled as the youngest player in the High-A California League last season. He's a future star, and though Alex Rodriguez stands in his way, the Mariners will find a place for Perez. Ruben

Castillo, 19, is another talented shortstop prospect. The 6'2", 155, righthanded hitter runs well, is an above average defender, and could add extra base pop as he physically matures. He's not in Perez' league, however.

Luis Figueroa, 23, a line drive hitter with solid plate discipline but no extra base power, is the best of a weak third base lot. One of the excess second base or shortstop prospects could wind up at the hot corner, especially if Alex Rodriguez signs a long-term deal.

Among upper minor league outfielders, only 19-year-old Double-A flycatcher Alex Fernandez has a significant chance of making a significant big league impact. He's far from complete at this stage in his development, but the 6'1", 205, lefthanded hitter has at least a 20/20 power/upside. He won't get anywhere near there until he learns to take a pitch, however. He needs another Double-A year. Without major improvement, a future major league job, let alone a starting role, will be in jeopardy. Juan Silvestre, 22, was one of the most productive hitters in the minors at High-A Lancaster last season, hitting for average and power. His tools are nothing special, however, and there's no guarantee that the 5'11", 200, righthanded hitter will ever play a significant major league role. He could be a decent future bench bat in Seattle. Lefthanded hitter Chris Snelling, 18, broke through in a big way at Low-A Wisconsin, establishing himself as one of the best all-around outfield prospects in the minors. The 5'10", 165, Australian has surprising power for his size, and his solid patience and defensive skills fill out the package. He'll start in the majors in center or right field at age 21 or 22. 1999 third round pick Sheldon Fulse, 18, is a speedburner who could break out in 2001. The former shortstop could evolve into a solid defensive outfielder and a gaps power bat. The Mariners need to see what he can do over 500 at bats.

At catcher, 6'2", 215, Scott Maynard is a durable receiver with a bit of power potential, but it's doubtful that he's major league timber. At best, he'll be a deep reserve. Ryan Christianson, 19, represents the Mariners' catching future. The 6'2", 202, righthanded hitter struggled through an uneven offensive campaign at Low-A Wisconsin, though he did display promising defensive skills. Look for things to come together for Christianson in 2001. He needs a year at each level, and should arrive in the majors in late 2003. He's a future major league starter.

Pitching depth is substantial. 6'10" lefty Ryan Anderson is the pick of the litter. The Mariners were able to resist recalling the 20-year-old Anderson before September 2000, allowing him to continue to refine the release point on his breaking pitch, the final piece in an All-Star package. He's better than Randy Johnson was at age 20, and it isn't close. He'll be in the rotation from Day One in 2001. Believe it or not, Anderson wasn't even the Triple-A ace in late 2000. That distinction went to righty Joel Pineiro, 21, a fine prospect in his own right. The 1997 12th round pick is a finesse hurler who needs to keep hitters off balance to succeed. He has a fine future as a major league mid-rotation starter, and could snag the fifth starter role in the spring. Righty Chris Mears, 22, slid backward in 2000 at High-A Lancaster after making the Futures Game in 1999. His stuff is just average, and his location within the strike zone must be exact for him to succeed. His future is uncertain, at best. 6'4", 190, righty Josue Matos has exceptional control and could make upper minor league noise if he adds velocity as he physically matures. For now, he projects as a big league swingman or middle reliever, but stay tuned. 6'2", 170, righty Enmanuel Ulloa has whiffed over a batter per inning at both Class A levels. He places his heavy fastball low in the strike zone, and will establish himself as a viable major league prospect if he maintains his strikeout rate at Double-A in 2001. 1999 first rounder Jeff Heaverlo, 22, was a mild disappointment at Lancaster, where the less heralded Ulloa was more consistent. Heaverlo has a diverse four-pitch repertoire, but leaves the ball out over the plate too often. Without significantly better command within the strike zone, he could be tattooed at higher levels. 2001 is a pivotal season for this potential future mid-rotation big league starter. Low-A Wisconsin's rotation featured multiple promising hurlers. Lefty Craig Anderson, 19, is a finesse hurler who consistently keeps the ball low in the strike zone. He needs to add some movement to his pitches to similarly excel at higher levels, but youth is clearly on his side. Cha Baek, 20, has a mid 90s heater, but inconsistent mechanics made it quite straight last season. Once he works out the kinks, he could hop onto the fast track. 6'1", 175, righty Rafael Soriano, 20, has a smooth delivery and a live fastball/slider combination. Addition of a third quality pitch would make him a top-shelf

prospect. Any one of the three aforementioned hurlers could slide into the middle of the Mariners' rotation within three years.

In the bullpen, righties Julio Mateo and Aquilino Lopez, both 20, have the highest upsides. Mateo is a finesse hurler who is a bit short on stuff, but he could evolve into a viable setup man. Lopez throws harder and could add more juice as his 6'3", 165, frame develops, he could close in the upper minors, and contribute in the bigs.

TOP TEN PROSPECTS

1 - LHP Ryan Anderson - Anderson, 20, was the Mariners' 1997 first round draft pick. The 6'11", 215, lefthander is often compared to former Mariner Randy Johnson for obvious reasons. Besides their stature, the two hurlers are both prototypical power pitchers who combine mid 90s fastballs with a sharp curve that serves as a second strikeout pitch. Anderson also throws a changeup that could be a viable third pitch at the major league level. Last season, he was recognized by circuit managers as the Triple-A Pacific Coast League's best pitching prospect, with its best fastball. Anderson has consistently ranked among the youngest competitors at each successive minor league level, but has posted ordinary won-lost records and ERA's at the upper levels. He tends to rely on his curve ball a bit too much, and occasionally gets a bit lazy with his mechanics, sacrificing both velocity and movement in the process. Still, Anderson has solid control for a power pitcher, and is clearly ahead of Johnson at a similar age. He projects as a surefire eventual big league ace. Expect him to be Rick Ankiel-like in the majors in 2001, occasionally dominating, but rarely lasting more than six innings in a start.

2 - SS Antonio Perez - Perez, 18, came over from the Reds in the Ken Griffey, Jr. trade. The 5'11", 175, switch-hitter was the youngest player in the High-A California League last year, where he impressed with his significant power/speed upside for a middle infielder, as well as his defensive potential. The ball jumps off of Perez' bat, with his extra-base power extending from gap-to-gap. He has a fairly advanced knowledge of the strike zone for his age, but could stand to shorten his swing a bit, sacrificing a bit of power for a higher average and more on-base potential. Perez has explosive raw speed, and is learning to pick his spots and read pitchers better, thereby getting bigger jumps. He could develop into a 25 homer, 40 steal guy. Defensively, he has well above average range and is quite consistent on the routine play for a youngster. His lack of superior arm strength might eventually cause him to slide back over to second base, his primary position in the Reds' system. That's especially true if Alex Rodriguez remains a Mariner. Perez has a chance to be a future major league All Star, and might be ready sometime in 2002.

3 - OF Chris Snelling - Snelling, 18, is a 1999 free agent signee out of Australia. The diminutive 5'10", 165, lefthanded hitter got off to an explosive start at Low-A Wisconsin last season before being sidelined by a broken hand and a damaged wrist ligament. Snelling is a complete offensive prospect who could be a fit in any of the top five spots in a batting order. He makes consistent contact, will draw a walk, and has surprising extra-base power potential for his size. His speed is just a bit above average, but he is an aggressive baserunner who could evolve into a 20 steal threat. Defensively, Snelling is a solid, fundamental center fielder whose range is enhanced by his knack for getting tremendous jumps on balls hit to the gaps. His arm strength is a bit above average, but not spectacular. His overall package caused Low-A Midwest League managers to recognize him as the circuit's most exciting player last season. To get back on the fast track, Snelling must prove his hands and wrists are healthy. Hitters tend to rely heavily on those appendages. Given that, he is a possible future .300 hitter and .400 on-base threat with 20/20 power/speed potential who could be ready for the majors sometime in 2003.

4 - C Ryan Christianson - Christianson, 19, was the Mariners' 1999 first round pick. The 6'2", 210, righthanded hitter handled the challenge of being the youngest everyday receiver in a full-season league last season, more than holding his own with the bat and glove at Low-A Wisconsin in the Midwest League. Christianson has made a smooth transition to the wooden bat. His longball power is real, and should intensify as he learns to drive the ball the other way. His plate discipline is fine for his age, though he still tends to chase the high fastball and strike out too often. He's a fly ball hitter with a compact uppercut stroke, and won't likely ever hit for a very high batting average. Defensively, Christianson is a durable horse who moves well for a big man behind the plate. His arm strength is a little above average at this point, but figures to improve as he continues to polish his throwing mechanics. Catcher has been a problem spot for the Mariners since the decline of Dan Wilson. Christianson should be a long-term solution at the position, and could arrive by late 2003. At worst, he projects as a .250-.260 hitter and 20 homer threat in the majors, and could be much more.

5 - 2B Willie Bloomquist - Bloomquist, 22, was the Mariners' third round draft pick in 1999. The 5'11", 180, righthanded hitter tore apart the High-A California League in the first half of 2000, leading the circuit in batting average and being recognized as its best defensive second base prospect by league managers. Though he scuffled terribly after a late-season promotion to Triple-A Tacoma, his status as a prospect was not significantly diminished. Bloomquist is a ballplayer; plain and simple. He makes consistent line drive contact with some pop to the gaps, will take a walk, and is an exceptional, instinctive baserunner despite a lack of overwhelming raw speed. Defensively, he has above average range and arm strength for a second baseman, as he was a top college shortstop at Arizona State. He's a baseball rat who can't get enough of the game, and his enthusiasm rubs off on his teammates. His offensive upside comes up short against, say, Antonio Perez, though Bloomquist could eventually be a .300 hitter with fair power and speed in the majors. He could work his way into the bottom end of the Mariners' lineup by late 2001. Long-term, he projects as a Tom Herr type, a solid, unspectacular player who seems to always be playing deep into October.

6 - RHP Joel Pineiro - Pineiro, 21, was the Mariners' 12th round draft pick in 1997. The 6'1", 180, righthander had a brilliant 2000 season at Double and Triple-A after struggling mightily in his introduction to the much older Double-A hitters in 1999. Pineiro is the antithesis of Ryan Anderson. He's a finesse hurler who only reaches the upper 80s with his fastball, though he maintains an acceptable strikeout rate because of his ability to mix in his above average curveball and decent changeup. Pineiro's mechanics and command within the strike zone were much more consistent in 2000 than in 1999, and even translated into flashes of brilliance in a brief major league trial. He gets ahead of hitters regularly, and his ability to retire them early in the count enables him to last deep into ballgames. Pineiro is a "feel" type of pitcher who needs to be clicking on all cylinders to consistently retire big league hitters. Guys like this can become Greg Maddux, or they can become the quite similar former Mariner prospect Bob Wolcott. Pineiro has a real shot to break north on the Mariners' roster in 2001, and projects as a long-term mid-rotation guy. Given the Mariners' starting pitching depth, he might have to serve an apprenticeship in the bullpen.

7 - OF Alex Fernandez - Fernandez, 19, was signed as a free agent out of the Dominican Republic in 1998. The 6'1", 205, lefthanded hitter was one of the youngest

Double-A regulars last season, and overcame a dismal start at New Haven in the Eastern League to put up reasonable offensive numbers. He's an extremely wild swinger, but has shown fairly consistent gaps power that could develop into 25-plus home run pop as he physically matures. Though he rarely walked last year, he did cut his strikeout rate markedly, a step in the right direction. Fernandez has above average raw speed, but isn't a particularly sound baserunner. He needs to develop a better feel for game situations, which should come with experience. Defensively, Fernandez has solid range and an above average throwing arm. Right field would seem to be the best fit for him down the road. This guy could be a major league star, or might never be a productive Triple-A player. He'll likely need to repeat at the Double-A level in 2001, and major improvement should be expected. Watch those walk totals, reaching even the modest total of 50 walks in a season could push him over the top in his quest to become a major league starter. That could happen in 2003.

8 - OF Sheldon Fulse - Fulse, 18, was considered a bit of a reach when the Mariners tabbed him with their third round draft pick in 1999. The 6'1", 170, switch-hitter has quickly proven himself a viable major league prospect, most recently at Low-A Wisconsin, where he was one of the Midwest League's youngest players last season. Speed is the centerpiece of Fulse's all-around game. He can flat out fly, and is far from afraid to use his chief weapon. In fact, he needs to learn to use his wheels more strategically on the basepaths. In any event, he's a future 50 steal threat if the rest of his game falls into line. He's a patient line drive hitter with little extra-base pop at this point, though some should develop as his lean frame naturally matures. Defensively, the high school shortstop has the speed and arm strength to play any of the three outfield positions, but needs to work on his route-running. Fulse is likely to return to the Low-A level to begin the 2001 season, but should quickly advance. He could be primed for a breakout year. If his power begins to develop, Fulse could quickly propel himself upward on this list and establish himself as a future (2004?) top-of-the-order threat in Seattle.

9 - RHP Enmanuel Ulloa - Ulloa, 21, was the Mariners' 21st round draft pick in 1997. The 6'2", 170, righthander nosed out his more highly touted 2000 High-A teammate Jeff Heaverlo, a 1999 number one pick who could reach the majors in 2001, for a spot on this highly competitive list. Ulloa is a driven player who has always possessed precise control, and has worked hard on his mechanics and his approach, consistently adding velocity and move-ment to his pitches in the process. Ulloa throws a lively low 90s fastball, and has developed his curve and changeup into solid complementary offerings. He gets ahead of hitters consistently, and has a chance to develop into a 200-inning major league horse given future physical maturation. He's an aggressive hurler who claims the inside part of the plate and doesn't nibble, which likely bodes well for the impending pivotal jump to Double-A. Ulloa could leap higher on this list with continued improvement in 2001, and should contend for a spot in the Mariners' rotation by late 2002. If he doesn't work out as a mid-rotation starter, he could be an excellent short reliever.

10 - LHP Craig Anderson - Anderson, 19, is a 1999 free agent signee out of Australia. The 6'4", 182, southpaw made an immediate full-season league mark as a precise, but somewhat hittable mound craftsman at Low-A Wisconsin. His fastball only reaches the mid to upper 80s, but he mixes it well with his above average curveball and changeup, maintaining an acceptable strikeout rate in the process. He walked barely two hitters per nine innings last season, but allowed about a hit per inning due to his tendency to leave the ball out over the middle of the plate. That could get him killed at higher levels, so Anderson will work on painting the corners better at High-A Lancaster in 2001. He'll never be a flamethrower, but if he can add 3-5 MPH via natural physical development, and he should, Anderson could develop into a very interesting prospect. It's too early to pronounce him a certain future major league starter, but he has the potential to evolve into a 200-inning mid-rotation horse.

OTHER PROSPECTS

2B Jermaine Clark - Clark is an exciting player who plays very consistent defense at second base and makes things happen on the bases. He's a very good contact hitter with a keen eye at the plate, in fact he got on base at a .421 clip at Double-A last year. If he keeps up that kind of offensive production, combined with his ability to steal 40 bases a year, he could be in the majors shortly.

RHP Ken Cloude - A couple of years ago Cloude looked like he could be a pretty good major league pitcher, but control problems and recurrent thrashings at the major League level have set him back. He's still relatively young and could come on because he has a live arm and pretty good stuff, but he's not likely to be an impact player.

2B Ariel Durango - Durango is a speedy second baseman who needs to be more disciplined at the plate. He doesn't have much power and probably never will, so striking out more than 100 times in a year is unacceptable. He has the ability to steal 50-plus bases if he learns how to draw a walk, but at this point he's got a lot of work to do.

3B Luis Figueroa - Figueroa is a good defender at the hot corner and he makes plenty of contact, but he has virtually no power and very little speed. He hit just one home run, only drove in 37 runs and didn't steal a single base. If he's going to move up and become a big leaguer someday, he needs to add some juice to his bat.

LHP Brian Fuentes - Fuentes is a 6'4" 220 pound lefthander with an above average fastball and a good changeup. His problem is control. He walked 70 batters, hit 13 and had 14 wild pitches in 139-plus innings during his second season at Double-A last year. He picks up a lot of strikeouts because he has a deceptive motion and because he changes speeds well, but he must improve his control quickly if he's going to have any impact in the majors. He's now 24 and should get his first shot at Triple-A this year.

RHP Jeff Heaverlo - Heaverlo is a good pitching prospect, but he needs to trust his fastball more. His best pitch is a slider, but he threw it too much last year. If he uses his 90 MPH fastball more effectively, he'll be tougher to hit against and he'd save wear and tear on his arm. He's got good mechanics and is the son of a former major leaguer, so expect him to make the necessary adjustments and move up the ladder pretty quickly over the next year or two.

IF Craig Kuzmic - Kuzmic is a 23 year-old switch-hitter with power who can play almost everywhere in the infield. He was a third baseman before the 2000 season, but he became more of utility defender last year. He slugged .496 drove in 104 runs and drew 71 walks at Single-A, but also struck out 124 times. He doesn't project as an everyday major leaguer, but his ability to play multiple positions, including catcher, plus his ability to hit well from both sides of the plate gives him a chance.

1B Shawn McCorckle - McCorckle is a good hitter with power potential. He strikes out quite a bit, as many young power hitters do, but he's also adept at drawing walks. With a little added strength, McCorckle could be a 30 home run guy down the line assuming he maintains his patience as the pitchers get tougher.

OF Juan Silvestre - Silvestre is a 22 year-old right-handed slugger with a big upside. He's got legitimate 30 home run power and 100 RBI potential, though he does strikeout too often. He doesn't run all that well and he doesn't draw many walks, but he's a decent defensive outfielder and he projects as a right fielder. If he can continue to maintain a high batting average to go along with his home runs as he moves up the ladder, the strikeouts won't be an issue.

RHP Rafael Soriano - Soriano is a good-looking young pitcher who hitters really struggle against. He's not over-powering as a general rule, but he's got reasonably good control for someone as young as he is and hitters only hit .225 against him at Low-A last year. He's got some work to do on his offspeed stuff and he needs to get stronger, but he's got time.

RHP Denny Stark - Stark has a live arm and is capable of dominating hitters when he's on. His control has improved over the past twelve months and he seems to have figured out how to pitch. Stark put up some nice numbers at Double-A last year, but it was his second year at that level and he's now 24 years old. He'll need to show something against Triple-A hitters before he becomes a real prospect.

RHP Greg Wooten - Wooten has phenomenal control but he lacks the raw stuff teams look for. He has had success against younger minor league hitters because he gets ahead in the count and changes speeds on them, but more experienced and aggressive hitters figure to give him problems. Still, his control gives him a shot at eventually advancing to the majors in come capacity.

TAMPA BAY DEVIL RAYS
ORGANIZATIONAL GRID

	AAA	AA	HI-A	LO-A
1B	Ryan Jackson - L - 28	Brian Becker - R - 25	Jose Velazquez - L - 24	Josh Pressley - L - 20 Dan Grummitt - R - 24
2B	Dustin Carr - R - 25 Brent Abernathy - R - 22	Rod Smith - B - 24	Jack Joffrion - R - 24 Derek Mann - L - 22	Frank Moore - L - 22
SS	Eddy De los Santos - R - 22	Nestor Perez - R - 23	Jorge Cantu - R - 18	Chris Schrock - R - 23 Ramon Soler - B - 18 Jace Brewer - R - 21
3B	Brooks Badeaux - B - 23	Jared Sandberg - R - 22 Paul Hoover - R - 24 Damian Rolls - R - 22	Andrew Beinbrink - R - 23	Yurendell DeCaster -R- 20
OF	Ozzie Timmons - R - 29 Alex Sanchez - L - 23 Jim Buccheri - R - 31 Randy Winn - B - 26	Kenny Kelly - R - 21 Scott Neuberger - R - 22 Joe Pomierski - L - 26 Garrett Butler - B - 24	Steven Goodson - L - 21 Brandon Backe - R - 22 Matt Diaz - R - 22 Kelvin Ryan - R - 21 Jeremy Murch - L - 21 Anthony Pigott - R - 24 Josh Hamilton - L - 19	Brian Martin - R - 20 Carl Crawford - L - 18 Jeremy Murch - L - 21
C	Pat Borders - R - 37 Toby Hall - R - 24	Jason Brown - R - 26 Neil Garcia - B - 27	Miguel Suriel - R - 23 Pete LaForest - L - 22 Ryan Ballard - R - 24	Chairon Isenia - R - 21 Castulo Valdez - R - 22 Danny Massiatte - R - 21
SP	Dan Wheeler - R - 22 Mickey Callaway - R - 25 Mike Duvall - L - 25 Cedrick Bowers - L - 22 Brad Cornett - R - 31 Dave Eiland - R - 33 Travis Phelps - R - 22 Matt White - R - 21	Travis Harper - R - 24 Bobby Seay - L - 22 Jesus Colome - R - 21 Delvin James - R - 22 Jason Standridge - R - 21 Jeff Sparks - R - 28	Adam Flohr - L - 23 Ed Kofler - R - 22 Alex Santos - R - 22 Cecilio Garibaldi - R - 22	Neal Frendling - R - 20 Joe Kennedy - L - 21 Jim Magrane - R - 21 Seth McClung - R - 19 Enger Veras - R - 19
CLOSER	Victor Zambrano - R - 25 Tony Fiore - R - 28 Lee Gardner - R - 25	Eddy Reyes - R - 24 Talley Haines - R - 23	Nathan Ruhl - R - 23	Jose Ortiz - R - 22 Jason Pruett - L - 21

TAMPA BAY DEVIL RAYS

The Devil Rays were the only minor league club with three teenage impact prospects in their everyday Low-A lineup throughout the 2000 season. They became even stronger at the trading deadline when three separate deals landed them second baseman Brent Abernathy, outfielder Jason Tyner and pitcher Jesus Colome, all certain future major league contributors. Things will shortly begin to get better for Rays' fans.

First base is not one of the deeper positions within the organization. Only Low-A prospect Josh Pressley, 20, a 1998 fourth round pick, has a chance to meet the high offensive standards of the position at higher levels. The 6'6", 220, lefthanded hitter hit a ton of doubles last season, and many should become homers as he matures. He also strikes out quite infrequently for a power hitter. He has a shot to start in the majors, and will at least be a decent part-timer.

The Rays obtained Brent Abernathy, 22, from the Jays for Steve Trachsel and Mark Guthrie at the trading deadline. He's a top-of-the-order sparkplug who rarely strikes out, slashes the ball to the gaps, and is an effective basestealer. He'll battle Miguel Cairo for the starting second base job in 2001, and should be an above average big league starter.

Eddy De los Santos, 22, is a fine defender, though he struggled with the bat the Triple-A level last season. He has low power and speed upsides, and little patience, so he projects as no better than a defensive replacement in the majors. Jorge Cantu, 18, was one of the breakthrough prospects of 2000. At his tender age, he rose to become the High-A shortstop by season's end. He moves smoothly in the field, with a quick release compensating for an average throwing arm. Offensively, the 6'1", 165, righthanded hitter makes consistent line drive contact, and could add power as he matures. He'll be a major league starter, and could be a star. Ramon Soler, also 18, has battled injuries for the last year and a half, but has raw tools comparable to Cantu's. In fact, he runs better and has a higher defense upside. Soler must prove his health before he can jump back onto the fast track.

Aubrey Huff, 23, parlayed an excellent Triple-A season into a trial at third base in the majors last year. Huff is a complete hitter, combining average, power and patience. His defense is steady, if unspectacular, and his ability to also play first base should help him stick in the majors. He could be the Rays' third baseman in 2001, and should eventually be above league average. Jared Sandberg, 22, is a raw power prospect who needs to learn to hit quality breaking pitches to the opposite field to reach his potential. He needs to make a major move soon to certify his top prospect status; don't bet on it happening. Juan Salas, 18, couldn't cut it in a full-season league in 2000, and had to return to rookie ball. The 6'2", 170, righthanded hitter can also play second base and has a decent power/speed upside, and is a name to watch for the future.

Jason Tyner, 23, is an utterly powerless prospect who came over from the Mets in the Rick White/Bubba Trammell deal. He's a speed merchant with solid defensive skills, and could be an asset at the major league level in a platoon role in 2001. Former Miami (Fla) quarterback Kenny Kelly, 21, is now a full-time baseball player, and has made great strides since making that decision. He had a fine Double-A season in 2000, combining a gaps-power bat and excellent baserunning ability into a productive package. With improved plate discipline, Kelly could be a solid major league leadoff man and center fielder. The real outfield action took place at Low-A Charleston in 2000. Josh Hamilton, 19, is one awesome all-around prospect. The 6'4", 200, lefthanded hitter's power upside is off the charts, and he also has 20-30 steal speed. Plate discipline is all he needs before becoming a minor league Triple Crown candidate and eventual major league All-Star. Hamilton's outfield mate, Carlos Crawford, 18, had a pretty nice season himself in 2000. He ranks among the fastest players in pro ball, and knows how to use his speed. His development with the bat has been dramatic. He's already a dangerous gaps-power hitter, and should eventually be an excellent number or two batter in a big league lineup. Like Hamilton, he's on the fast track.

Toby Hall, 24, is a late bloomer with solid defensive ability and a rapidly developing offensive game. He makes consistent contact and the long-expected power finally emerged from his 6'3", 205, frame last year. He could be ready to back up or platoon at the major league level sometime in 2001.

Dan Wheeler, 22, has spent some time with the Rays in each of the last two seasons, but his lack of a true out pitch has hurt him at upper levels. He rarely walks hitters, but doesn't paint the corners precisely enough to consistently retire quality hitters. 2001 is a key year, if he doesn't make the major league rotation, he may begin to be overrun by some talented younger hurlers. Lefthander Cedrick Bowers, 22, lacks an overpowering fastball, but his pitches move sharply, enabling him to maintain a respectable strikeout rate. Bowers must learn to retire hitters earlier in the count to start in the majors, he might be a better fit as a swingman or two-inning bullpen arm. Righty Travis Harper, 24, is a finesse hurler who needs to paint the corners to succeed against higher-level hitters. He has a feel for pitching and will likely squeeze the most from his natural skills and could earn one of the last spots on the Rays' 2001 staff. The Rays acquired flamethrower Jesus Colome from the A's at the trading deadline last season. He's a raw power prospect whose heater approaches 100 MPH, but his breaking pitches and his command have been slow to develop. If there isn't room in the rotation, he could become a big-time closer in the majors. Lefty Bobby Seay, 22, is a former number one pick who has made only halting progress in recent seasons. He has been injury-prone, and has never evolved into more than a five-inning pitcher. His makeup and attitude have also been concerns. It's tough to give up on a talented lefty, but the Rays' may be close to writing Seay out of their major league plans. Righty Matt White, 21, is another former number one pick who has developed more slowly than anticipated. His stuff can be downright nasty, but his command has been inconsistent and he lacks a true strikeout pitch. He's making some strides, and could be primed for a breakthrough 2001 season. The Rays still believe he'll be a long-term big league starter. It's time to deliver. Righty Travis Phelps, 22, showed surprising power at Double-A Orlando, and kept the ball on the outer edges of the strike zone consistently. He lacks the raw talent of many of the pitchers surrounding him, and will have to continue to perform similarly to be more than a bit player in the majors. 1997 first rounder Jason Standridge, 21, has generally needed a second look at each level to excel, but he has the mental toughness to learn from his struggles. Standridge has a diverse repertoire, and will

succeed at higher levels as long as he pitches in an aggressive manner. He's a prototypical mid-rotation starter who should have a long, productive career. Righthander Neal Frendling, 20, had a brilliant Low-A season, combining well above average power and command. He'll need to continue to place the ball well to maintain his strikeout rate at higher levels, as his low 90s fastball is solid, but not devastating. He could move onto the Rays' hot list with a repeat performance in 2001. Lefty Joe Kennedy and righty Jim Magrane are finesse hurlers who shone last season at Low-A Charleston. Kennedy lacks a strikeout pitch and could struggle at higher levels, but Magrane could break through in a big way in 2001. A successful two-level jump would certify Magrane as a likely future big league starter.

TOP TEN PROSPECTS

1 - OF Josh Hamilton - Hamilton, 19, has quickly justified his selection as the first overall pick in the 1999 draft. The 6'4", 200, lefthanded-hitting center fielder has won a string of honors in his brief pro career. He made the Low-A South Atlantic League All-Star team last season, and was rated the best batting prospect, power prospect, outfield arm and most exciting player by circuit managers in Baseball America's annual tools survey before his season was shortened by a torn right knee meniscus. He was the youngest player in last year's Futures Game, and went 3 for 4. He was also slated to be the youngest participant in the Arizona Fall League following the season. What's all the fuss about? Hamilton showed extreme power potential last season, a pretty amazing feat considering his fairly crude plate discipline. Once this guy learns to work the count and begins seeing more fastballs, watch out. He has above average speed and is a heady baserunner, but will likely physically outgrow the basestealing portion of his game by the time he reaches the majors. He has an absolute cannon for a throwing arm, and currently covers enough ground to play a solid center field. Again, physical growth will likely impact his defensive game as he advances, making him a natural right field prospect. Watch those walk totals, once they start to shoot up, Hamilton will get to the majors within a year. He actually could reach the majors by the end of 2001, and shapes up as a future major league No. 3 hitter and all-around stud.

2 - OF Carl Crawford - While 1999 first round pick Hamilton garnered most of the attention, Crawford, 18, their second round draftee that same year, has also certified himself as a possible future major league impact player. The 6'2", 195, lefthanded hitter focused on football when in high school, and was thought to be a long-term project baseball-wise. Not so; Crawford had a brilliant campaign as the youngest regular in the Low-A South Atlantic League, combining blazing speed with a consistent line drive bat and surprising gaps power. He has made a seamless transition to the wooden bat, and could develop into a 40 double, 15 triple, 20 homer threat given further physical development. Lack of plate discipline is a major shortcoming at this point, high fastballs and outside breaking pitches are his weaknesses, and he must lay off of them to become a top-flight leadoff prospect. He complements his excellent raw speed with sound baserunning instincts for a youngster. He could steal 50-plus bases in the majors someday. Crawford has exceptional range in the outfield, and projects as either a center or left fielder at higher levels. His arm strength is average at best. Crawford and Hamilton will soon present formidable obstacles at the top of the Rays' big league lineup and that day might not be far off. Crawford could reach Tampa Bay in 2003, and eventually be an All-Star.

3 - RHP Jesus Colome - In case you haven't noticed, the Rays' system is loaded at the top. Colome, 21, was acquired from the A's for reliever Jim Mecir at last season's trading deadline. The 6'4", 195, righthander is one of the hardest throwers in the minor leagues. His fastball routinely reaches the upper 90s, and was cited as the best heater in the Double-A Texas League by circuit managers last season. He combines it with a nasty slider, but has been slow to develop his changeup into a viable third offering. His strikeout rates haven't adequately reflected his power because of his lack of a true offspeed pitch. Though his command is spotty, that's to be expected for a youthful power hurler. His pitch counts have been high, and his stints short. Though his mechanics are unorthodox, they appear to work for him, and he has avoided arm trouble to this stage in his career. Colome's age suddenly increased by two years in 2000, diminishing his prospect status just a tad. With a solid offspeed pitch, Colome would project as a future ace starter. Without it, he could evolve into a lethal closer. Either way, he should earn a major league audition at some point in 2001 and begin a long career in a significant role in Tampa Bay the following season.

4 - 2B Brent Abernathy - Abernathy, 22, is a 1996 Blue Jays' second round draftee who was acquired at the trading deadline last season for pitchers Steve Trachsel and Mark Guthrie. The 6'1", 185, righthanded hitter is a natural leadoff prospect who makes consistent, authoritative contact to all fields and projects as a leadoff or number two hitter in the majors. Though he'll never be a true home run threat, he could be a 40 double Jody Reed clone at the plate in the bigs. He'll need to take more pitches than he did in the Triple-A International League last season to reach his potential, however. His raw speed is fairly ordinary, but Abernathy is an aggressive baserunner with sound instincts who could regularly steal 20 bases per season in the majors. Defensively, he's a dirty-uniform guy who gets the job done, though it's often not pretty. His skills, particularly his arm strength, aren't conducive to the other side of the infield, so a utility role isn't a good fit. Abernathy will be given every chance to win the Rays' second base job in 2001, and should succeed. He might not be a future All-Star, but should add grit to the upper portion of their batting order.

5 - 3B Aubrey Huff - Huff, 23, was the Devil Rays' fifth round pick in the 1998 draft. The 6'4", 220, Huff is a slightly watered-down, lefthanded version of college teammate Pat Burrell, a rookie stand out last season with the Phillies. Both players have big-time power potential, though Burrell's upside is noticeably higher. Both played third base at Miami (Fla) in college because of their superior arm strength. Burrell has already had to move to first base and then left field because of a lack of quickness at the hot corner, and Huff might eventually move across the diamond himself. It is Huff's bat that got him to the majors last season and will keep him there. His poor major league walk totals notwithstanding, Huff is a patient hitter who can drive the ball for distance from gap to gap, and he makes fairly consistent contact for a power threat. His ability to handle lefthanded pitching makes him a good bet to secure a full-time job in Tampa Bay in 2001. His overall offensive package led Triple-A International League managers to recognize him as the circuit's best batting prospect. Huff's no Burrell, but he should be a long-term fixture in the number five or six hole in the Rays' lineup, and likely has some 100 RBI seasons in him.

6 - RHP Matt White - White, 21, was a 1996 Giants' first round draftee who slipped through a draft loophole to a waiting $10 million free agent contract with the Devil Rays. The 6'5", 230, righthander's progress through the minors hasn't been as brisk as expected. Though White's fastball routinely reaches the mid 90s and his curve and changeup are viable secondary offerings, he has never established himself as a strikeout-per-inning hurler. His 2000 Double-A campaign did represent a breakthrough, however, White's mechanics were more consistent than ever before in his pro career, adding bite to all of his pitches and making him much less hittable. He needs to build off of this success and develop an attitude on the mound, while throwing quality first-pitch strikes on a more consistent basis. At his size, and with his repertoire, there's no excuse for White's inability to average more than six innings per start to this point in his career. His 2001 Triple-A season is a pivotal one. White could still emerge as the ace major league starter he was once expected to come, but his window of opportunity is closing. More likely, he'll become a reliable mid-rotation big league anchor, arriving sometime in 2001.

7 - SS Jorge Cantu - Cantu, 18, was signed as a free agent out of Mexico in 1998. The 6'1", 165, switch-hitter ranked as one of the youngest players to compete in a full-season league in 2000, and was promoted to High-A St. Petersburg after performing exceedingly well in the Low-A South Atlantic League during the first half. Cantu is a fairly wild swinger at this stage in his development, but makes fairly consistent contact and sprays the ball to all fields. He's likely to add 15 to 20 pounds of muscle as he naturally matures, and could develop 20 homer pop. His raw speed is only average, and he doesn't project as much of a stolen base threat. Defensively, his above average first-step quickness gives him solid lateral range, and an extremely quick release compensates for ordinary arm strength. Cantu has the all-around package to eventually be a major league starting shortstop, but development of adequate plate discipline is the key factor. The Rays will take their time with him, but if all goes well, he could be in the mix for a starting job by late 2003. He's no A-Rod, but could be a mid-level major league starter down the road.

8 - OF Kenny Kelly - Kelly, 21, was the Devil Rays' 1997 second round draft pick. The 6'3", 180, righthanded hitter is an exceptional athlete who was Miami (Fla)'s starting quarterback in the 1999-2000 season before deciding to focus on baseball on a full-time basis. His lack of baseball experience was as obvious as his talent at Double-A Orlando last season. Though he did exhibit a live line-drive bat with some gaps power to go along with well above average speed and defensive ability, many rough edges were apparent. Though Kelly's walk total climbed last season, his swing remains a bit long, and he's over-matched by quality breaking pitches. Though he should add some power potential as his frame naturally develops, his major league future lies at the top of the Rays' order, and his on-base skills need a lot of work. Kelly's a greyhound in the outfield, combining above average range and solid instincts with a strong throwing arm. With guys like Hamilton and Crawford around, Kelly has his work cut out for him to become a major league regular with the Rays. Look for him to at least become a valuable fourth outfielder, adding speed and defense to the club's bench attack. Substantial power development could carry him higher. He could arrive sometime in 2002.

9 - RHP Jason Standridge - Standridge, 21, was the Rays' first round draft pick in 1997. The 6'4", 205, righthander made his Double-A debut last season, struggling due to his inability to establish a true strikeout pitch. Standridge has quality stuff, combining a sinking low 90s heater with a curve and changeup that both project as adequate big league offerings. While he is able to consistently keep his pitches low in the zone, Standridge has a hard time making hitters miss. He also nibbled around the edges of the plate in his initial Double-A experience, leading to relatively high pitch totals and short stints. Don't be surprised if he makes the mechanical adjustments necessary to gain the added movement on his pitches necessary for Double-A success early in 200. He's a heady, determined sort who has always performed better in his second tour at a particular level. He's no future major league ace, but Standridge could evolve into a reliable mid-rotation anchor, and might arrive by late 2002.

10 - OF Jason Tyner - Tyner, 23, was the Mets' 1998 first round draft pick, and was acquired by the Rays at the 2000 trading deadline for reliever Rick White and outfielder Bubba Trammell. The 6'1", 170, lefthanded hitter certainly possesses some major league qualities, but his utter lack of home run pop makes one wonder whether his style of play has become extinct in today's power-oriented game. This guy hasn't homered since high school, honest. Though he has been a regular .300 hitter in the minor leagues, he was physically overmatched at times in last year's big league trials with the Mets and Rays. Tyner slaps the ball to all fields, makes consistent contact, and had shown an ability to work the count in the minors, though he hasn't done so in the majors. He can flat out fly on the bases, and was rated the best baserunning prospect in the Triple-A International League last season. However, the aggressiveness he routinely showed in the minors was also missing in action in the majors last season. Defensively, he has above average range and runs quality routes to fly balls, but will likely be limited to left field by his below average arm strength. Tyner will get a clear shot at a platoon job in Tampa Bay in 2001, at the absolute minimum. He had better show something, however, as the

Hamiltons and Crawfords are moving up fast. Tyner will likely carve a niche for himself at the major league level, providing on-base skills, speed and defense in a part-time role.

OTHER PROSPECTS

LHP Cedrick Bowers - Control is the only thing holding Bowers back at this point of his career. He has a solid low 90s fastball and a nasty curveball, but he's had trouble locating both. He had an outstanding season at Double-A last year, so big things could be coming for him. A shot at some major league time might not be out of the question come August or September.

RHP Neal Frendling - Frendling has a really good fastball and has been overpowering against young hitters so far. He also throws a good curve, a changeup and a sinker. Frendling didn't walk many batters at Low-A last year, but he had a fairly high number of wild pitches and hit batters which gives some indication that his command isn't perfect. If he can continue to develop his secondary pitches, Frendling has a chance to be very good.

C Toby Hall - Hall stepped up last year and put up some great offensive numbers at Double-A and Triple-A. He hit over .300 at both levels and showed a fair amount of power, though his patience could be a little better. Hall seems like a good defensive catcher and if he can overcome some of the problems young receivers run into.

RHP Travis Harper - Harper is a good pitcher with excellent control, though his stuff isn't all that great. He has a decent fastball, but not and overpowering one, and he's done well in the minors so far. He might be the kind of guy who takes a little time to settle in at the major league level and it's unlikely that he'll be a top of the rotation starter, but he could be a nice fourth or fifth starter, or maybe even a good reliever, because of his control and consistency.

3B Paul Hoover - Hoover had been a catcher until last season when he was used at all of the infield positions, in the outfield as well as behind the plate from time to time. Hoover has a good eye at the plate and he makes contact, but his lack of power at this point is a bit concerning considering he's a relatively large man. He's very athletic for someone originally considering a catcher and if things don't work out at a particular position for him, his versatility would come in handy on a major league bench.

RHP Travis Phelps - Phelps doesn't have great stuff, he's pretty much average across the board, but he's a gamer and he's aggressive. His control is good, but not great, and he's done a nice job of changing speeds so far, which gives him a chance to succeed later on. He was very good at Double-A in 2000 and could be a candidate for a shot at the majors before long.

1B Josh Pressley - Pressley is a good looking young hitter with tremendous hitting skills. He's yet to develop home run power, but his 44 doubles at Low-A last year are an indication that he could develop home run power as he matures. He doesn't draw all that many walks, but he also doesn't strike out much and that's a very good sign. His defense is very good and if he does happen to start hitting the long ball, he could advance quickly.

OF Alex Sanchez - Sanchez is can simply fly. He's got the speed to be a 50-plus stolen base man at the major league level and he's not a bad hitter either. He has no home run power at all and he doesn't draw many walks, but he puts the ball in play and with his speed that places a lot of pressure on opposing infielders to make plays cleanly. Even if he doesn't pan out as an everyday player, his speed should keep him in the bigs as a fourth outfielder.

3B Jared Sandberg - 2000 was a disappointing year for Sandberg and now there are questions about his offensive ability. After showing some power in 1999, he displayed almost none at Double-A last year and he struck out once every four at-bats. He's a good defensive player, though his range isn't all that hot, and he could still return to being a good player, but there are some questions about him at this point.

RHP Alex Santos - Santos was an accomplished and polished college pitcher out of the University of Miami when the Devil Rays drafted him and he should progress quickly over the next couple of years. He throws a 90 MPH fastball, a good curve and a decent change with decent control. He needs to work ahead in the count and avoid walks because he's not overpowering, but he knows what he's doing on the mound and has a good head on his shoulders.

LHP Bobby Seay - Coming out of high school, Seay was viewed as a potential front line starting pitcher. He hasn't quite lived up to that billing yet, but he still has a good 90-91 MPH fastball and above average curveball to work with. He needs to improve his control and change speeds more effectively, but the ability to succeed is definitely still there. He was finally healthy again in 2000 and that could be a good sign.

SS Ramon Soler - Soler is a burner who has leadoff skills and he's still just a teenager. If he can stay healthy, Soler could end up as another Rafael Furcal. He's a good defensive shortstop who could probably play second base if necessary and since the Devil Rays really don't have that many top middle infield prospects in front of him, he may not be too far from the majors, if he can stay healthy.

RHP Dan Wheeler - Wheeler has a low 90s fastball that moves a bit and a decent breaking pitch, but he's not fine enough with any of his pitches to get major league hitters out at this point. If he can refine his control, he has the stuff and the body to be a workhorse in the rotation, though he most likely won't be an impact pitcher.

TEXAS RANGERS
ORGANIZATIONAL GRID

	AAA	AA	HI-A	LO-A
1B	Jack Voigt - R - 34	Carlos Pena - L - 22	Travis Hafner - L - 23 Derek Baker - L - 24	Jason Jones - B - 23
2B	Jon Shave - R - 32 Chris Demetral -L - 30	Jason Romano - R - 21	Pedro Guerrero - R - 20 Jorge Diaz - R - 25	Inocencio Acevedo - R - 21 Steve Hine - L - 26
SS	Kelly Dransfeldt - R - 25	Danny Solano - R - 21 Mike Young - R - 23	Brandon Warriax - R - 21	Matt Halloran - R - 22 Ramon Martinez - B - 20
3B	Osmani Garcia - R - 26	Jason Grabowski - L - 24	David Meliah - L - 23	Hank Blalock - L - 19
OF	Mike Zywica - R - 25 Pedro Valdes - L - 27 Ruben Sierra - B - 34 Cliff Brumbaugh - R - 26 Rich Butler - L - 27 Jason McDonald - B - 28 Reed Secrist - L - 30	Juan Piniella - R - 22 Craig Monroe - R - 23 Tom Sergio - L - 25 Ryan Lane - R - 25 Harry Berrios - R - 28 Scott Podsednik - L - 24	Kevin Mench - R - 22 Corey Wright - L - 20 Douglas Garcia - L - 21 Amuarys Nina - R - 22 Steve Barningham - L - 24 Jason Bryan - R - 18 Chris Jaile - R - 19	Ricky Angell - R - 23 Brett Cadiente - L - 23 Cody Nowlin - L - 20 Adam Poe - R - 22 Monte Lee - R - 23
C	Randy Knorr - R - 31	Luis Taveras - R - 22 Jeremy Jones - R - 22 Josh McAffee - R - 22	Jimmie Romano - R - 23 Fred Torres - R - 20	Jason Torres - L - 21
SP	R.A. Dickey - R - 25 Corey Lee - L - 25 Brian Sikorski - R - 25 Jose Martinez - R - 25 Pete Munro - R - 25 Scott Randall - R - 24	Derrick Cook - R - 24 Trey Poland - L - 25 Joaquin Benoit - R - 20 Leiby Guzman - R - 23 David Elder - R - 24 Dave Lundberg - R - 23 Andy Pratt - L - 20	Travis Hughes - R - 22 Aaron Harang - R - 22 Colby Lewis - R - 20 Nick Regilio - R - 21 Alan Webb - L - 20 Matt Kosderka - R - 24	Frankie McGill - R - 20 Andy Cavazos - R - 19 Jovanny Cedeno - R - 20 Ryan Dittfurth - R - 20 Edwin Moreno - R - 19 Chris Russ - L - 21 Corey Spiers - L - 25
CLOSER	Jonathan Johnson - R - 25 Johan Lopez - R - 25	Chad Poeck - R - 27 Hank Woodman - R - 27	Doug Silva - R - 20 Emar Fleming - R - 23	Reynaldo Garcia - R - 22 Ryan Cullen - L - 20

TEXAS RANGERS

The Rangers have cultivated a number of solid prospects over recent seasons, but the best have either been traded (Fernando Tatis) or suffered serious injury (Ruben Mateo). Upper level pitching depth is thin, but a handful of high-ceiling position players will shortly be knocking on the major league door.

First baseman Shawn Gallagher's development has slowed over the last two seasons, and he now projects as no better than a major league role player. The 6'0", 187, righthanded hitter hasn't developed adequate plate discipline, and is just an adequate defender, leaving power as his sole plus tool. The Rangers' first baseman of the future is Carlos Pena. He has always possessed brilliant all-around tools, including a high power upside and solid defensive ability, but he blossomed over the past season after improving his plate discipline and learning to hit breaking pitches. He's at most a year away from starting for the Rangers, and should be a future All-Star in the majors.

Jason Romano, 21, will take his place alongside Pena in the major league infield before long. The 1997 first round pick is a top-of-the-order sparkplug who lines the ball with authority to the gaps, draws walks and steal bases. He has worked hard to make himself a bit above average defensively. He should be a 15 homer guy in the majors, and is a good bet to start in Texas in 2002. Pedro Guerrero, 20, is a solid defender with good speed, but has no offensive game at this stage. He needs another High-A season, and won't advance without significant development with the bat.

Kelly Dransfeldt is an above average defensive shortstop with excellent arm strength, but has never developed with the bat, largely due to poor plate discipline. He still could fit in as a major league utilityman if everything breaks his way. The Rangers have high hopes for Mike Young, acquired from the Blue Jays at the trading deadline. He has some pop to the gaps, runs very well, and plays more than adequate defensive at both middle infield positions. He's a better bet than Dransfeldt to garner a near-term utility berth in the majors. 5'9", 155, Danny Solano, 21, is a gritty type who works deep counts, makes the routine plays in the field, and does the little things well. His lack of raw tools and a proven secondary position works against him in pursuit of a major league backup role. Jose Morban, 20, has better defensive tools than all of the above prospects, but is quite weak with the bat. He was sent back to Rookie ball late in 2000, and struggled there as well. He's quite a ways away.

At 24, Jason Grabowski is a bit old to not have Triple-A experience, but his raw home run power keeps him in the major league hunt. The 6'3", 200, lefthanded hitter improved his plate discipline last season, and could emerge as a viable major league platooner or extra man by 2002 at the latest. Hank Blalock, 19, is a well-rounded prospect who could eventually be a major league standout. He has a natural lefthanded swing, and is capable of hitting for high average with power to the gaps. He has sneaky speed, and projects as an above average defender. He'll likely be ready for the majors by 2003, and could eventually approach the All-Star level.

Pedro Valdes has been an upper minor league masher for years now, and might finally seize a big league role with the Rangers. He can hit for average and power, has decent plate discipline, and at 27, is squarely at his peak. He could help the Rangers cope until Ruben Mateo recovers. Speedy Juan Piniella slid backward in his second Double-A season. A high-average hitter in the lower minors, Piniella lacks the power potential to compensate for his recent average drop off. His window of opportunity is closing. Craig Monroe, 23, is a late bloomer with a sizeable power/speed upside who has an outside chance to creep into the major league picture in 2001. The six-year minor league vet has improved greatly each of the last three seasons, and could continue to surprise. Kevin Mench, 22, led the NCAA in homers when he was in college, and has adjusted easily to the wooden bat in his brief pro career. The ball simply explodes off of his bat, and his solid plate discipline affords him a steady diet of fastballs to hit. He also runs quite well for his size (6'0", 215). Mench is a potential future big league starter who could make a two-level leap to Triple-A in 2001. Spray hitter Corey Wright, 20, has a chance to develop into a big league leadoff prospect. The 5'11", 165, lefthanded hitter is quite patient, and has greatly improved his basestealing technique. At the very least, he should be a viable major league backup outfielder by 2003 or so. Douglas Garcia, 21, is a slap hitter with few complementary skills who didn't fare well in his second High-A campaign. Mench and Wright will blow past him in 2001. 6'3", 190 lefthanded hitter Cody Nowlin, 20, showed signs of developing a power stroke last season. The 1998 second round pick could have a breakout season in 2001. Success at the High-A level by season's end would mark him as a possible future big league starter.

Luis Taveras, 22, is the Rangers' most advanced catching prospect. He is surprisingly durable, considering his slight 5'10", 165, frame, but lacks the standout offensive or defensive tools necessary to propel him much higher. He has an outside shot to back up in the majors. 1998 27th round pick Jeremy Jones, 22, surprised in 1999, eventually rising to Double-A on the strength of his consistent line drive bat. He too is a longshot for a significant eventual major league role, however. Watch Fred Torres, 20, a defensive ace who was one of the younger High-A regulars last season. If he develops power as his 6'0", 165, frame fills out, he could become a viable prospect.

The R.A. Dickeys, Jonathan Johnsons and Corey Lees have overstayed their welcome as prospects, and the Rangers have some talented youngsters ready to overtake them. Righty Joaquin Benoit, 20, was one of the younger Double-A starters last season. He can bring serious heat, but he currently has inconsistent mechanics and runs high pitch counts. A major improvement at the same level would keep him in the Rangers' rotations plans, otherwise, short relief could be in his future. Lefty Alan Webb, 20, was a key part of the package received from the Tigers in the Juan Gonzalez deal. Webb's mechanics were missing in action last season, and his strikeout rate plunged at the Double-A and High-A levels. Give him a mulligan for 2000, and give him one more chance to reclaim top prospect status in 2001. At best, he's a future mid-rotation major leaguer. At 5'11", 160, lefty Andy Pratt, 20, doesn't look like an impact pitching prospect, but he just might be one. His control is his prime asset, and he dominated Class A hitters by keeping them off balance. He predictably struggled in his Double-A debut, but still should make the bottom end of the Rangers' rotation by sometime in 2002. 6'4", 215, righty Colby Lewis is a four-pitch power hurler who could develop into a top-shelf prospect with im-

proved command within the strike zone. He'll be in the majors shortly after he evolves from thrower to pitcher. 1999 sixth rounder Aaron Harang is a 6'7", 240, behemoth with surprisingly sound mechanics for his size. His control is solid, and exceptional movement compensates for a lack of overpowering velocity. His Double-A performance in early 2001 will tell a lot about his eventual upside. Strong arms abounded at Low-A Savannah last season. Righty Jovanny Cedeno, 20, was likely the best of the group, evoking comparisons to (gasp) Pedro Martinez with his effortless motion and surprising velocity considering his 6'0", 160, frame. He should advance quickly, and has at least a mid-rotation big league upside. Fellow righties Andy Cavazos, Ryan Dittfurth and Edwin Moreno also showed flashes of excellence, and any one of the group could emerge as a solid prospect with the emergence of a strong secondary pitch.

Righty Doug Silva, 20, is the Rangers' best relief prospect. Though he lacks an overpowering heater today, more power should evolve from his 6'3", 190, frame. He keeps the ball low in the zone and has a chance to be an upper level closer and major league situational righty.

TOP TEN PROSPECTS

1 - 1B Carlos Pena - Pena, 22, was the Rangers' 1998 first round draft pick. The 6'2", 210, lefthanded hitter began to explore the limits of his offensive potential last season at Double-A Tulsa. Prior to 2000, Pena had been overaggressive at the plate, and was often overmatched by quality breaking stuff. He apparently has learned to lay off bad breaking pitches, causing his strikeout/walk ratio to significantly improve, and driving both his batting average and power production higher. Pena has a picturesque swing that generates serious power to all fields. Texas League managers recognized him as the circuit's best power prospect last season. He's quite athletic for his size, and is an instinctive baserunner and potentially excellent defensive first sacker. Pena is likely ready for the major leagues now, though he might be sent to Triple-A for the early portion of the 2001 season. He appears set to become a long-term major league fixture, and could evolve into an All-Star caliber first baseman.

2 - OF Kevin Mench - Mench, 22, was the Rangers' fourth round draft pick in 1999. The 6'0", 215, righthanded hitter was the NCAA home run king in 1998, but established himself as far more than an aluminum bat wonder with a massive High-A season last year in his first full pro campaign. He has extreme power potential to all fields, but projects as a high-average hitter because of solid plate discipline and his ability to make more consistent contact than most pounders. Mench also runs surprisingly well for a stocky guy, and is an instinctive baserunner with a knack for scoring runs. Defensively, Mench has just average range and a fairly ordinary throwing arm, and will likely be limited to left field or designated hitter as he advances. His offensive potential is real, however, and his lightning-quick bat speed and sophisticated approach at the plate should allow him to produce similarly at higher levels. Mench could move up quickly and contend for a starting job in Texas sometime in 2002. He could be a slightly souped-up, righthanded version of Matt Stairs.

3 - 3B Hank Blalock - Blalock, 19, was the Rangers' third round draft pick in 1999. The 6'1", 192, lefthanded hitter excelled as one of the youngest regulars in the Low-A South Atlantic League, stamping himself as one of the best hitting prospects in the low minors. Blalock has a natural stroke, combining the ability to make consistent line drive contact with a patient approach and burgeoning extra-base power potential. He's a doubles machine right now, and should develop 20-25 homer power as he matures physically. He has also emerged as a serious stolen base threat despite possessing only slightly above average raw speed. Blalock is an instinctive player with a feel for the game. He has solid range and plus arm strength at third base, and should evolve into at least an average major league defender. Blalock is a fast-tracker who should be in contention for the big league third base job by sometime in 2003. At the very least, he shapes up as his generation's Jeff Cirillo.

4 - RHP Jovanny Cedeno - Cedeno, 20, was signed as a free agent out of the Dominican Republic in 1997. The 6'0", 160, righthander has a chance to be a special pitcher. He unleashes exceptional power from his slight frame, mixing a low 90s fastball plus a nasty curve and a changeup. His pitches move sharply, and his mechanics are letter perfect, especially for his age. He has an innate feel for variation of location and speed, and often makes hitters look downright foolish. The one major drawback is his size. Right now, he's basically a six-inning pitcher, though he controls his pitch counts well enough to project as a nine-inning guy as his stamina evolves. The Rangers could roll the dice and see if Cedeno, who toiled at Low-A Savannah last season, can handle the much-older Double-A hitters in 2001. Don't bet against him succeeding. A little bit of Pedro Martinez' aura seems to be following Cedeno around. Double-A success in 2001

could stamp Cedeno as a potential major league ace, and move him to the top of this list.

5 - 2B Jason Romano - Romano, 21, was the Rangers' supplemental first round draftee in 1997. The 6'0", 185, righthanded hitter swings a lusty line drive bat, and has above average gaps power potential for a middle infielder. However, his best way to the majors is as a leadoff or number two hitter, and he needs to take more pitches and tinker with his stroke to produce fewer lazy fly balls to reach his potential as an on-base threat. He has well above average speed, but needs to study pitchers and learn to get better jumps. Defensively, he isn't the smoothest second base prospect around, but has above average range and a plus arm. Romano is a baseball rat who works hard on all facets of his game, so it's a solid bet that he'll squeeze the most from his ability. He likely needs a full Triple-A season, but enhanced on-base skills would put him squarely in the hunt for the major league second base job in 2002. He's a possible 20/20 power/speed threat who could be a long-term fixture in Texas.

6 - RHP Colby Lewis - Lewis, 20, was the Rangers' supplemental first round draft pick in 1999. The 6'4", 215, righthander has a prototypical power pitcher's frame, a diverse four-pitch repertoire, and fairly advanced command for a youngster. His fastball reaches the mid 90s, and Lewis mixes it with a curve, slider and changeup, all of which could evolve into above average major league offerings. Right now, however, his pitches lack exceptional movement, as evidenced by his allowance of over a hit per inning last season in the High-A Florida State League. He also has a tendency to catch too much of the plate with his strikes. Minor mechanical tweaking and additional experience should take care of the above concerns. Lewis might need a few more High-A starts to begin 2001, but should quickly move to the Double-A level, where he has the stuff to maintain or even improve his strikeout rate. Lewis has a chance to evolve into a number two or three major league starter, and should contend for such a role by 2003 at the latest.

7 - LHP Andy Pratt - Pratt, 20, was the Rangers' ninth round draft pick in 1998. The 5'11", 160, southpaw is an extreme finesse hurler who dominated Class A batters in two stints separated by late 1999 elbow surgery. Pratt's fastball only reaches the mid to upper 80s, and he relies heavily on his secondary offerings, an excellent changeup and a decent curveball. He routinely threw quality strikes on the edges of the strike zone, especially early in the count, to key his Class A success, and consistently kept hitters off balance by varying his pitch sequence. Like it does for many young finesse pitchers, however, it all blew up for Pratt when he was promoted to the Double-A level in mid 2000. His aggressiveness early in the count evaporated, as he nibbled and fell behind hitters, leading them to pounce on his ordinary fastball on hitter-friendly counts. Pratt remains a very promising prospect, however, because of his youth. Nothing more than failure can reasonably be expected from a 20-year-old extreme finesse pitcher at the Double-A level, unless you're dealing with a Greg Maddux. He'll do much better at the same level in 2001, and should contend for a berth in the Rangers' rotation by 2003. He projects as a future mid-rotation major league starter.

8 - SS Mike Young - Young, 23, was the Blue Jays' fifth round draft pick in 1997, and came to the Rangers in last year's trading deadline deal for Esteban Loaiza. It's a major break for the 6'1", 175, righthanded hitter, who appeared stuck behind the Felipe Lopezes and Cesar Izturises in the Jays' deep middle infield pipeline. A second baseman for most of his tenure in the Jays' system, Young will exclusively play shortstop for the Rangers. He's not a brilliant defender, his range is just a bit above average, but he's a heady player with a quick first step and above average throwing arm who possesses enough defensive skill to start in the majors. At bat, Young is a consistent line drive hitter with solid plate discipline and 40 double, 10 triple power, quite acceptable for a middle infielder. Young runs extremely well, and gets exceptional jumps, leading to high basestealing success rates. He could be a 20-plus steal source in the majors. Young has a chance to win the Rangers' starting shortstop job by 2002, and at the very least projects as a dangerous and valuable major league utilityman who could thrive in a 300 at bat role.

9 - OF Corey Wright - Wright, 20, was the Rangers' 12th round draft pick in 1997. The 5'11", 165, lefthanded hitter has steadily developed all facets of his game, and has very quietly been an effective top-of-the-order threat as one of the youngest competitors in his Low and High-A leagues during the past two seasons. He's a patient line drive hitter who slaps the ball to all fields, though he lacks significant extra-base pop at this stage in his development. His foot speed is only a bit above average, but Wright has greatly improved his ability to get a jump on pitchers, thereby improving his basestealing totals and success rate. To rate as a future big league starter, however, Wright will need to adjust his swing a bit to hit the ball on the ground more often, currently he hits too many lazy fly balls. Defen-

sively, Wright is solid, combining above average range with an ordinary throwing arm. He could be a fit in any of the three outfield slots as he advances, and projects as a viable future fourth outfield candidate in the majors, though he can't be totally ruled out as a leadoff guy. He'll get to the show in 2003 at the earliest.

10 - OF Craig Monroe - Monroe, 23, was the Rangers' eighth round draft pick in 1995. The 6'1", 195, righthanded hitter is a late bloomer who has been to the brink of being released on more than one occasion in his pro career. The Rangers continued to believe in his power/speed package, and Monroe began to repay them with an excellent Double-A season in 2001. Poor plate discipline held him back in his early years, but Monroe is now at least a 50 walk threat, and is laying waste to a substantial number of the additional fastballs he's been seeing since learning to work the count. His compact stroke produces power from gap to gap, and he now appears capable of hitting .270 or so in the majors, an unthinkable prospect prior to last season. Monroe can flat out fly on the bases, but has toned down his aggressiveness a bit. He projects as a high-percentage 20 steal threat. Defensively, Monroe has solid range, though his routes to fly balls often aren't the most direct. His above average arm strength makes him a natural fit for right field. Players who don't make it to Double-A before age 23 tend not to be productive big leaguers, but Monroe could be an exception. Don't be surprised if he functions as a productive fourth or fifth outfielder and bench bat for the Rangers, in 2002.

OTHER PROSPECTS

RHP Joaquin Benoit - Benoit is a very polished pitcher for someone so young. He's just 20 years old and has already experienced success at the Double-A level. He has an above average fastball that could improve as he matures and gets a little stronger, but what's most impressive is his control at this stage of his career. It's not perfect, but his control is better than you might expect for a kid. All he really needs is some polish on his offspeed pitches.

RHP Andy Cavazos - Cavazos has good stuff, including an above average fastball, but his control hurts him. He had 55 walks in just 82-plus innings at Low-A last year, but even worse than that he hurt himself by falling behind in counts and then giving up home runs. If he can be more fine with his fastball and improve his offspeed stuff, his performance will improve quite a bit.

RHP Ryan Dittfurth - Dittfurth throws hard and is definitely a strikeout pitcher, but he really needs to reign himself in. He's extremely wild and that leads to a lot of runs scored against him. Last year at Low-A he allowed just 127 hits and had 158 strikeouts in 158-plus innings, but he also walked 99 batters, hit another 17 and threw 16 wild pitches.

SS Kelly Dransfeldt - Not long ago Dransfeldt was considered the Rangers' shortstop of the future, but his offensive development has stalled a bit. He has the ability to hit for some power, but has problems with strikeouts. The problem is that his power numbers have dropped off at the Triple-A level and that's a concern. He's okay defensively, but not spectacular, and he runs a little bit. He needs to improve his strike zone judgment soon or he'll be stuck at Triple-A.

RHP David Elder - Elder is full of promise, but his wildness keeps him from fulfilling his potential. He's got a good arm and he gets good downward movement on his fastball, but his lack of control tends to overshadow his positive attributes. At Double-A last year he started 21 games and pitched 12 times out of the bullpen, picking up three saves. He has the ability to move up in either capacity if he throws strikes.

3B Jason Grabowski - Grabowski is an excellent hitter with good patience and above average power, but his defense has been just awful. He made 40 errors at Double-A last year and that's unacceptable no matter how much he hits. A position change could be in order sometime soon. Offensively, Grabowski has a chance to hit for power and average. He's very patient and even though he strikes out often, he walks nearly as many times.

1B Travis Hafner - Hafner is an outstanding hitter without a real position. He was used mostly as a designated hitter and first baseman at High-A last year, though he did play some third base as well. He's shown the ability to crush pitchers at the lower levels, hitting for average and power while driving in a lot of runs (.346, 22 HR, 109 RBI in 2000). The one thing to beware of with Hafner is his age. He was 23 playing at High-A and he'll need to prove himself against higher caliber pitchers in the future.

RHP Aaron Harang - Harang is not widely considered a prospect, but his excellent performance at High-A last year got him some attention. He's got a good arm and is very difficult to hit against, though he's not what you'd call overpowering. Florida State League hitters managed to hit just .220 against him and he walked just 50 batters while striking out 136 over 157 innings.

RHP Dan Kolb - Kolb has had some arm problems, but he has an excellent mid 90s fastball. He was moved to the bullpen for the 2000 season and he had considerable success, albeit in limited action. If he throws strikes, which he did last year, he can be an effective late-inning reliever in the majors sometime very soon.

LHP Corey Lee - Lee has all the raw stuff a pitcher needs to be successful, a low 90s fastball, a hard curve, a slider and a changeup. The problem is that he has no idea where any of them are going. He had an awful year at Triple-A last year, posting an 8.76 ERA and allowing 250 baserunners in 112 innings. If he ever "gets it," he could be a decent major leaguer.

OF Cody Nowlin - Nowlin has potential as a hitter, but he needs to be more patient. If he can draw more walks and make fewer weak outs on bad pitches, he could really come on. He doesn't run much but is a decent defensive outfielder. If he can boost his average some and knock a few more out of the park he'll be alright.

TORONTO BLUE JAYS
ORGANIZATIONAL GRID

	AAA	AA	HI-A	LO-A
1B	Kevin Witt - L - 24	Tim Giles - L - 24 Jay Gibbons - L - 23	Matt Logan - L - 20 Joe Dusan - L - 22	Kurt Keene - R - 21
2B	Chris Woodward - R - 24	Tony Schifano - R - 25	Glenn Williams - B - 22	Jaime Goudie - R - 21 Jimmy Alvarez - B - 20
SS	Cesar Izturis - B - 20	Felipe Lopez - B - 20	Jersen Perez - R - 24 Fausto Solano - R - 26	Doug Roper - B - 22 Brandon Jackson - R - 24
3B	Luis Lopez - R - 26 Rob Mummau - R - 28	Orlando Hudson - B - 22	Mike Rodriguez - R - 25 Mike Strange - R - 26 Chris Weekly - L - 23	Shawn Fagan - R - 21
OF	Vernon Wells - R - 21 Chad Mottola - R - 28 Ryan Freel - R - 24 Selwyn Langaigne - L - 24 Andy Thompson - R - 24	Scott Sollman - L - 25 Robert Perez - R - 31 Mike Peeples - R - 23 Ryan Fleming - L - 24 Dewayne Wise - L - 22	Garrick Haltiwanger - R - 25 Tony Peters - R - 25 Tyler Thompson - R - 24 Reed Johnson - R - 23	Shannon Carter - L - 21 Ryan Bundy - R - 22 Chivas Clark - L - 21 Alvin Morrow - R - 22
C	Charlie Greene - R - 29 Brian Loyd - R - 26	Mike Kremblas - R - 24 Joe Lawrence - R - 23	Josh Phelps - R - 22 Paul Chiaffredo - R - 24	Kevin Cash - R - 22 Juan Santos - B - 22 Jose Umbria - R - 22
SP	Gary Glover - R - 23 Kerry Taylor - R - 29 Clayton Andrews - L - 22 John Bale - L - 26 Leo Estrella - R - 25 Roy Halladay - R - 23 Joey Hamilton - R - 29	Matt McClellan - R - 23 Pasqual Coco - R - 22 Mike Kusiewicz - L - 23 Scott Cassidy - R - 24 Gustavo Chacin - L - 19 Mark Hendrickson - L - 26 Ryan Spille - L - 23	Joe Casey - R - 21 Charles Kegley - R - 20 Aaron Dean - L - 23 Yan LaChapelle - R - 24 Chris Baker - R - 22	Marcos Sandoval - R - 19 Matt Ford - L - 19 Cam Reimers - R - 21 Peter Bauer - R - 21 Ryan Houston - R - 20 Tyler Renwick - R - 21
CLOSER	Matt DeWitt - R - 22 Bob File - R - 23	Jarrod Kingrey - R - 23 Rendy Espina - L - 22	Orlando Woodards - R - 22 Scott Porter - R - 23 Robert Hamann - R - 23	Jerrod Payne - R - 21 Hugo Castellanos - R - 20

TORONTO BLUE JAYS

The perpetually productive Blue Jays' organization finally appears to be thinning out a bit at the lower levels. The Jays dealt from their primary area of strength, middle infield, at last year's trading deadline, sending Brent Abernathy to the Devil Rays and Mike Young to the Rangers to pick up some ammunition for their ill-fated wild card run.

First baseman Kevin Witt, 24, retains a substantial power upside, but has never developed the more salient areas of his game. The 1994 first round pick is likely running out of chances in Toronto, but could latch on as a bench bat somewhere in the majors next season. Matt Logan, 20, has been one of the younger players at his level each season, but has yet to show much of the power production expected from him. The 6'3", 200, lefty will likely repeat at High-A in 2001, and needs a 20 homer campaign to remain a potential future major league backup. 1999 second rounder Mike Snyder, 19, was sent back to rookie ball after a slow Low-A start, but remains a future power threat. The Jays hope he isn't a wooden bat wonder.

With Abernathy and Young no longer in the system, the Jays are low on second base prospects. Former Braves' prospect Glenn Williams, 22, showed decent extra base pop at High-A Dunedin, but at best is a future major league utility candidate. Former Dodgers' prospect Jaime Goudie, 21, runs well and has some pop to the gaps, but has been stuck at the Low-A level for awhile now. He'll be hard-pressed to advance much further.

The Jays possess two top-shelf shortstop prospects, one of whom will likely be moved to second base at the major league level. Cesar Izturis, 20, was one of the youngest Triple-A regulars last season. Izturis was unready with the bat, but did showcase superb defensive skills, including a howitzer arm. He'll need another Triple-A year to raise offensive game, but could then move in as the Jays' second sacker. Felipe Lopez, 20, who has an even higher all-around upside than Izturis, is the Jays' future shortstop. The switch-hitter struggled with the bat at Double-A Tennessee due to poor plate discipline, but has at least a 20/20 power/speed upside. He has better range than Izturis, and will be an above average major league defender. He needs another year of seasoning before stepping into the Jays' lineup for a decade or more.

Third baseman Orlando Hudson is a consistent line drive hitter with a good eye, and his ability to play multiple infield and outfield positions gives him a chance to eventually project as a major league utilityman. Robert Cosby, 19, a 1999 10th round pick, was dispatched to rookie ball after a subpar Low-A half season. The 6'2", 195, switch-hitter has decent speed but needs to develop a power stroke to make significant upward progress.

Despite a poor 2000 season, outfielder Vernon Wells, 21, remains one of the game's foremost prospects at his position. After a dreamlike 1999 season that saw him rise from Class A to the majors, Wells let down physically and mentally at Triple-A Syracuse. He has a 25/25 power/speed upside and is a greyhound in center field. Look for a big start at Triple-A in 2001 and a subsequent promotion into the Jays' lineup, where he will eventually become a star. Mike Peeples, 23, gets the most from his relatively ordinary skills. Though neither his strength nor speed is eye-catching, he's made a run at 20/20 in both of the last two seasons. His ability to also play second and third base gives him a chance to secure a reserve role in the majors by 2002. Speedy lefthanded hitter Shannon Carter, 21, made great strides at Low-A Hagerstown in his first year in a full-season league. Speed is the essence of his game, and he must continue to add extra base pop and plate discipline to work his way into the Jays' big league plans. The club's relative lack of lower level outfield prospects works in Carter's favor.

Josh Phelps, 22, is the club's most advanced catching prospect. He suffered through a poor Double-A season with the bat, but has at least a 15 homer power upside. Defensively, he is solid, combining a strong arm with sound game-calling skills. He needs a big comeback season to remain in the club's future plans. Former top infield prospect Joe Lawrence, 23, moved behind the dish at High-A Dunedin last season, and played quite well before a midseason injury. He could jump to Triple-A in 2001. His unique combination of gaps power, patience and speed for a receiver makes him a fit for a crack at a portion of the 2002 major league catching job, at least.

Pitching depth has thinned considerably in recent seasons. Righty Gary Glover, 23, endured a poor Triple-A season, as he has been slow to develop his secondary pitches. Glover could shift into a setup relief role next season, where his low 90s heater could serve him well once through the order. The Jays possess a trio of 2000 Double-A finesse hurlers who could contend for some major league starts in the near term. Righties Matt McClellan and Pasqual Coco and lefty Mike Kusiewicz all allowed about a hit per inning last season, but escaped major damage because of their ability to consistently throw strikes. All lack a true out pitch, and will require better precision within the strike zone to have a chance to thrive in the majors.

The Jays' paucity of low-level pitching talent caused them to rush lefty Gustavo Chacin, 19, and righty Charles Kegley, 20, to the High-A level a bit ahead of their time. The 5'11", 170, Chacin is the classical crafty lefty who needs to develop a strikeout pitch to succeed at higher levels. Youth is on his side, and he's likely to find that pitch in a second High-A season. Kegley is a 1999 11th round pick who needs to tweak his mechanics and significantly improve his command. He has a heavy fastball, and hitters struggle to make authoritative contact. He's a sleeper to break through in 2001. Low-A teenagers Matt Ford and Marcos Sandoval showed promise at Low-A Hagerstown. Ford, 19, is a 1999 third round pick who is likely the Jays' best pitching prospect. He has a solid feel for pitching for his age, and his ability to change speeds makes his slightly above average fastball seem harder. If he cuts the Double-A mustard sometime in 2001, he'll certify himself as a future mid-rotation major league starter. Sandoval is a finesse hurler with a rubber arm who has been used in a variety of roles in his brief pro career. The 6'1", 160, righty needs to add movement to his pitches via mechanical adjustment, and at this point, he's way too hittable to have a major league future.

TOP TEN PROSPECTS

1 - OF Vernon Wells - Wells, 21, was the Blue Jays' first round draft pick in 1997. The 6'1", 210, righthanded hitter took a step backward with a poor offensive Triple-A season in 2000 after a brilliant 1999 campaign which saw him explode from High-A to the major leagues in record time. Wells fell in love with the power stroke that he began to develop into his breakthrough season, and the slight loop in his swing padded his power totals a bit at the expense of a good chunk of his batting average. That's not a trade-off that the Jays were looking for from their number three hitter of the future. 2000 should serve as nothing more than a learning experience in the long run, however. Wells retains lightning-quick bat speed, and should eventually find the compromise point between batting average and power he could be a .300 hitter with 30 homer pop. He has well above average speed and solid baserunning instincts, and could be a 25 steal guy in the majors. He didn't slump defensively last season. He has expansive range and a plus throwing arm, and was recognized as the best defensive outfield prospect in the International League by circuit managers last season. Wells will be back with a vengeance in 2001 at the major league level, and could be a future All-Star.

2 - SS Felipe Lopez - Lopez, 20, was the Blue Jays' first round draft pick in 1998. The 6'0", 175, switch-hitter was challenged with a daunting two-level jump to the Double-A Southern League, where he was one of that league's youngest regulars. He struggled mightily with the bat against the older, more advanced pitchers, largely due to poor plate discipline. If he can improve in that area and get ahead in the count more often, his already impressive extra-base pop for a middle infielder could explode. He could evolve into a .300ish hitter with 25 homer power. His foot speed is well above average, but Lopez is quite raw with regard to baserunning technique. He needs to study pitchers' deliveries and learn to get better jumps, and that should happen with experience. Defensively, Lopez is state-of-the-art. He covers a lot of ground because of his speed and extraordinary first-step quickness, and he has well above average arm strength. Southern League managers recognized him as the best defensive shortstop prospect in the circuit. Even before the Jays began to deal from their minor league middle infield strength last season, there was no doubt that Lopez was the man they had in mind to be their next shortstop. He's a year away, and could rank in the upper half of the strong AL shortstop crop with the expected offensive development.

3 - SS Cesar Izturis - Izturis, 20, was signed as a free agent out of Venezuela in 1996. The 5'9", 155, switch-hitter was aggressively promoted two levels to Triple-A Syracuse last season, where he proved unready with the bat, but a superior defender with the glove. Izturis is a wild swinger with minimal extra-base power who makes fairly consistent contact. To eventually start in the majors, he'll need to become at least a 50 walk threat, and work the count to see enough fastballs to at least bat in the upper .200s. He can get it done; he was .308 High-A hitter in 1999. He runs extremely well, but needs to learn to pick his spots better and become a high-percentage basestealing threat. Defensively, Izturis shines and has exceptional range at either second base or shortstop, and more than enough arm to play any infield position. He was recognized for having the best infield arm in the International League by its managers last season. Izturis will likely defer to Lopez at shortstop and become the Jays' starting second baseman, most likely in 2002. His offensive development is the key to his future. Look for significant strides in his second Triple-A campaign in 2001.

4 - LHP Matt Ford - Ford, 19, was the Blue Jays' third round draft pick in 1998. The lean 6'2", 165, southpaw was one of the youngest Low-A South Atlantic League starters last season, and he surprised by striking out about a batter per inning despite ordinary peak velocity. His fastball only reaches the upper 80s, but he made significant strides with both his curveball and changeup last season, and showed solid ability to vary speed and location, especially for his age. Though Ford has solid control, he has a tendency to try to throw the perfect pitch too often, and racks up high pitch and low inning counts as a result. Ford should easily pack on another 15 or so pounds of muscle onto his lean frame, and the extra few MPH of velocity he could add might make him capable of maintaining such high strikeout totals at higher levels, including the majors. Watch those power/control numbers carefully, especially when he reaches Double-A. Success there could mark him as a future number two or three big league starter who could arrive by late 2003.

5 - C Joe Lawrence - Lawrence, 23, was the Blue Jays' first round draft pick in 1996. The 6'2", 190, righthanded hitter has played shortstop, third base and now catcher in his professional career. He has shown flashes of solid all-around potential during his pro career, but his last two seasons have both been shortened by ankle ligament tears. Offensively, Lawrence is an extremely patient hitter with above average gaps power for a receiver. He projects as a moderate-average hitter due more to his patience than his stroke, which is a bit long and has a slight uppercut. He

had pretty good speed before the ankle injuries, but can now be expected to run like a catcher. He's quite athletic for his position, and his plus arm strength and feel for the game give him a chance to develop into an above average defender despite the late start of his catching career. He backtracked a level to High-A for defensive transition purposes at the beginning of the 2000 season, but was the regular Double-A backstop by year-end. If he can stay healthy and have a productive Triple-A season in 2001, Lawrence could contend for at least a share of the big league job by the end of the year.

6 - LHP Gustavo Chacin - Chacin, 19, was a free agent signee out of Venezuela in 1998. The diminutive 5'11", 170, southpaw was a sleeper success story last season, rising all the way from rookie ball to the Double-A level by season's end. Chacin projects as the typical crafty lefty. His fastball only reaches the upper 80s, and he needs to mix it expertly with his curve and changeup to have a chance against upper level hitters. He is a battler with a knack for working out of jams, but predictably had some rough times in early Double-A outings because of a lack of both raw stuff and confidence against the much older hitters. Chacin needs to tweak his mechanics to squeeze out a bit more velocity and/or movement, and simply continue to accumulate experience against upper level batters. His High-A and Double-A time last season must be considered a bonus. He'll likely need to return to the High-A level to begin 2001, and should experience much more success this time around. He has a chance to evolve into a mid-range major league starter in 2004 after spending a year at each minor league level.

7 - RHP Pasqual Coco - Coco, 22, was signed as a free agent outfielder by the Blue Jays out of the Dominican Republic in 1994. The 6'1", 160, righthander actually made it to the majors for a midseason start in 2000, and established himself as a viable long-term starter prospect by maintaining his strikeout rate in his first Double-A season. Solid mechanics enable him to generate low 90s power from his slight frame, and he mixes his heater with an above average changeup and a developing slider. He has a quick motion to the plate, helping him control the running game. Coco has made major strides with his command, and should evolve into a reliable seven-inning hurler with more experience plus potential minor physical development. Coco's upper level success has to be considered at least a mild surprise after a mediocre second half of 1999 at the High-A level, but don't expect him to turn back now. Coco is a year away from making a strong challenge for a big league rotation spot. He could be a long-term fit in the No. 3 or 4 slot.

8 - C Josh Phelps - Phelps, 22, was the Blue Jays' 10th round draft pick in 1996. The 6'3", 195, righthanded hitter has unquestioned defensive skills, and has shown flashes of developing a longball power stroke that could transform him from a future major league backup candidate into a potential starter. Phelps has a long swing, which combined with an utter lack of plate discipline, caused him to struggle mightily in his first confrontation with more polished Double-A pitching last season. He has shown little aptitude for hitting quality breaking stuff to this point. He has carved up High-A Florida State League pitching in two separate opportunities, raising the dubious possibility that he has (gasp) High-A bat speed. Defensively, Phelps is legit. Though he has had elbow problems in the past, he possesses above average arm strength and is quite nimble behind the plate for his size. Phelps has at least a slight chance to develop into a .250-hitting starter with 20 homer pop in the majors, though it's a safer bet that he'll be a long-term big league backup, with an estimated arrival date of 2003.

9 - RHP Gary Glover - Glover, 23, was the Blue Jays' 15th round draft pick in 1994. The 6'5", 180, righthander signified that he possessed big league ability with an exceptional first half of 1999 at Double-A Knoxville, but has since struggled against Triple-A competition. Glover's best pitch is clearly his low to mid 90s fastball, but his inability to develop a second out pitch between his curve and changeup has held him back. His walk rates have been quite low, but his command within the strike zone has been poor. So let's see, he only has his fastball consistently working for him, and he tends to throw it down the middle of the plate. That's a bad combination. Glover clearly has a major league arm, but his window of opportunity to earn a spot in the Jays' rotation is beginning to close. The chance to narrow his repertoire and rely on hard stuff would give him hope of becoming an effective righthanded situational reliever. Watch how he's used in spring training in 2001. If it's as a reliever, he could sneak north with the big club and carve out a niche for himself.

10 - 1B Kevin Witt - Witt, 24, was the Blue Jays' first round draft pick in 1994. The 6'4", 200, lefthanded hitter was once envisioned as a potential middle-of-the-order force in Toronto, but has never developed the plate discipline necessary to stick at the major league level, though he had shown some positive signs in that area in 1999. He can drive a mistake fastball a long way, but Witt's swing remains long and he can still be overmatched by quality breaking stuff. He's quite slow afoot, making him a station-to-station baserunner and a fairly stiff defender. He's been tried at many positions throughout his tenure with the Jays, and he hasn't been particularly good at any of them. Witt has now played three full Triple-A seasons, not a good sign for someone hoping to make a living in the major leagues. A change of scenery would seem to be in his best interests. He still has the ability to fit in as a platoon first baseman or designated hitter in the majors, and could be quite productive on a per at bat basis. Given the right situation, he could be in the bigs in 2001.

OTHER PROSPECTS

RHP Scott Cassidy - Cassidy has the ability to dominate hitters at times. He's got a good arm, reasonably good control and a very aggressive approach. He's generally very tough to get a hit against and when he's on his game he rarely loses. If he can get off to a good start at Double-A this year, he could be moved up to Triple-A quickly.

RHP Leo Estrella - Estrella has a live arm and the ability to keep the ball in the ballpark. He's not overpowering by any stretch, but he's difficult to hit against and he is capable of picking up a fair number of strikeouts. He had good success at Double-A early last season and some form of success at Triple-A as well, so he may be ready for a shot at the majors before long.

RHP Charles Kegley - Kegley has a very live arm and is difficult to hit against, but he's got some serious control problems. His walks, wild pitches and hit batters combined almost added up to the number of innings he pitched last year, which is pretty scary. He needs to learn how to get the ball over the plate and he needs work on his other pitches as well.

LHP Mike Kusiewicz - Kusiewicz is a good looking lefthander who relies on control and changing speeds to get by. His fastball is about average and he has a good curveball, but control is his ticket to advancement. He had a strong year at Double-A in 2000 and that could be a springboard to future success for him.

RHP Matt McClellan - McClellan is a 6'7" righthander with an above average fastball, a good breaking ball and a deceptive motion. He still focuses too much on trying to strike hitters out and might be better served trying to get more ground ball outs because he's still unable to consistently last deep into games. He has held his own at every level so far, so there is hope for major league success.

OF Chad Mottola - He was a high draft pick coming out of college in the early 90's and has been slow to develop, but he dominated the Triple-A International League during the 2000 season (.309, 33 HR, 102 RBI, 30 SB) and he could still have a major league role someday. He has the ability to hit for average and power as well as good speed on the bases. The only flaw in his game is that he doesn't walk very often. Mottola is either a late bloomer or a Four-A hitter and the only way to find out which he is will be to see how he fares against major league pitching in the future.

IF-OF Mike Peeples - Peeples can play second base, third base and outfield and he's got offensive potential. He has better than average power and some speed, so if he can hit for a decent average and improve his ability to draw walks just a little bit he'll be on his way. Peeples isn't a top prospect, but because he can play several positions the opportunity to be a utility player exists if he doesn't pan out as an everyday player.

RHP Marcos Sandoval - Sandoval is extremely young (19 years-old) and somewhat advanced for his age, but he isn't physically mature just yet. He needs to get stronger and add a few miles per hour to his fastball before he becomes the prospect Toronto thinks he can be. He's still rough around the edges and needs refinement, but the raw tools are there.

RHP John Sneed - Sneed is a big righthander (6'6" 240) with an above average fastball and hard slider and a workable changeup. As long as he doesn't fall behind too often, Sneed will be fine. He has a commanding presence on the mound and the body one needs to be a workhorse, so all he really needs to do is prove that he can get more experienced hitters out.

2B Glenn Williams - Williams is a middle infielder with some pop in his bat. He's not a great hitter in terms of batting average at this point and he doesn't draw many walks, the two are distinctly connected, but he's got the ability to develop those skills. Williams doesn't run particularly well, but is solid in the field.

ARIZONA DIAMONDBACKS
5-YEAR DRAFT ANALYSIS

	1995	1996	1997	1998	1999
MAJOR LEAGUE STARS	N/A				
MAJOR LEAGUE STARTERS		#5 - P Brad Penny (Fla)			
MAJOR LEAGUERS		#1 - P Nick Bierbrodt #26 - OF Rob Ryan #32 - OF Jason Conti #42 - P Eric Sable			
SOLID PROSPECTS			#1 - OF Jack Cust		
POTENTIAL PROSPECTS		#13 - P Ben Norris #17 - 2B J. Rexrode (CWS)	#7 - OF Brian Gordon #36 - SS Alex Cintron	#5 - C J.D. Closser #12 - OF Victor Hall #15 - P Chris Cervantes #18 - P Bret Prinz	#2 - P Jeremy Ward #18 - 1B Lyle Overbay
ROUND 1-5 FLOPS					
GRADE		B	B	C	D

ATLANTA BRAVES
5-YEAR DRAFT ANALYSIS

	1995	1996	1997	1998	1999
MAJOR LEAGUE STARS					
MAJOR LEAGUE STARTERS	#3 - P Rob Bell (Cin)				
MAJOR LEAGUERS	#5 - P Kevin McGlinchy #39 - C Mike Mahoney (Cub)	#1 - P Jason Marquis #7 - SS Mark DeRosa			
SOLID PROSPECTS		#53 - 2B Marcus Giles	#2 - P Joey Nation (Cub) #5 - P Horacio Ramirez	#2 - P Matt Belisle	
POTENTIAL PROSPECTS	#4 - P Jimmy Osting (Phl)	#1 - 1B A.J. Zapp #3 - OF Junior Brignac #15 - 3B Mike Hessman	#1 - 3B Troy Cameron #4 - OF Cory Aldridge #8 - 1B Ryan Lehr	#3 - OF Ryan Langerhans #5 - OF Damien Jones #7 - P Scott Sobkowiak #17 - P Dan Curtis #29 - P Tim Spooneybarger	#2 - P Matt Butler #3 - 2B Pat Manning #5 - P Matt McClendon #12 - P Ben Kozlowski #49 - P Nathan Kent
ROUND 1-5 FLOPS					
GRADE	C	A	C	B	B

BALTIMORE ORIOLES
5-YEAR DRAFT ANALYSIS

	1995	1996	1997	1998	1999
MAJOR LEAGUE STARS					
MAJOR LEAGUE STARTERS		#10 - OF Luis Matos #14 - P Ryan Kohlmeier #25 - P John Parrish	#11 - 2B Jerry Hairston		
MAJOR LEAGUERS	#10 - OF D. Dellucci (Az) #35 - 1B Calvin Pickering	#2 - P Brian Falkenborg #13 - SS Augie Ojeda (Cub) #15 - P Josh Towers #33 - 3B Ryan Minor	#3 - P Matt Riley #8 - P Jay Spurgeon		
SOLID PROSPECTS			#1 - C Jayson Werth		#1 - P Richard Stahl
POTENTIAL PROSPECTS	#3 - OF Darrell Dent		#1 - OF Ntema Ndungidi #1 - OF Darnell McDonald #2 - P Sean Douglass	#1 - OF Mamon Tucker #3 - P Steve Bechler #6 - OF Tim Raines, Jr.	#1 - OF Larry Bigbie #1 - OF Keith Reed #1 - P Mike Paradis #1 - SS Brian Roberts #6 - P Erik Bedard #39 - SS Gary Cates
ROUND 1-5 FLOPS				#4 - P Chris Davidson #5 - P Josh Yarno	
GRADE	D	C	A	D	B

BOSTON RED SOX
5-YEAR DRAFT ANALYSIS

	1995	1996	1997	1998	1999
MAJOR LEAGUE STARS					
MAJOR LEAGUE STARTERS					
MAJOR LEAGUERS	#6 - P Matt Kinney (Min) #7 - 3B Cole Liniak (Cub) #9 - P Paxton Crawford #27 - P Juan Pena	#7 - P Rob Ramsay (Sea)	#3 - P Travis Harper (TB)		
SOLID PROSPECTS		#3 - 1B Dernell Stenson			#1 - P Brad Baker
POTENTIAL PROSPECTS	#5 - C Steve Lomasney #16 - OF Rontrez Johnson	#1 - P Chris Reitsma (Cin) #1 - P Josh Garrett #4 - OF John Barnes (Min) #8 - P Justin Duchsherer	#1 - P John Curtice (Cin) #2 - SS Aaron Capista #5 - P Greg Miller (Hou)	#1 - SS Adam Everett (Hou) #3 - P Mike Maroth (Det) #36 - OF Tonayne Brown	#1 - P Casey Fossum #10 - OF Brian Wiese
ROUND 1-5 FLOPS		#2 - 1B Gary LoCurto #5 - C Bobby Brito			
GRADE	B	C	D	D	C

ANAHEIM ANGELS
5-YEAR DRAFT ANALYSIS

	1995	1996	1997	1998	1999
MAJOR LEAGUE STARS	#1 - OF Darin Erstad		#1 - 3B Troy Glaus		
MAJOR LEAGUE STARTERS		#3 - P Scott Schoeneweis	#6 - P Matt Wise	#1 - P Seth Etherton	
MAJOR LEAGUERS	#2 - P Jarrod Washburn #4 - P Brian Cooper #5 - 2B Justin Baughman		#21 - OF Mike Colangelo		
SOLID PROSPECTS					#2 - P John Lackey #3 - P Phil Wilson #9 - SS Brian Specht
POTENTIAL PROSPECTS		#7 - OF Marcus Knight #26 - C Jason Dewey (Col)	#10 - P Steve Green	#5 - OF Darren Blakely	#13 - SS Alfredo Amezaga
ROUND 1-5 FLOPS		#4 - P Brandon Steele			
GRADE	A	C	A	C	A

CHICAGO WHITE SOX
5-YEAR DRAFT ANALYSIS

	1995	1996	1997	1998	1999
MAJOR LEAGUE STARS					
MAJOR LEAGUE STARTERS			#1 - P Jim Parque		
MAJOR LEAGUERS	#1 - 1B Jeff Liefer #2 - OF Brian Simmons	#2 - C Josh Paul #13 - P Chad Bradford	#1 - P Aaron Myette #5 - P Pat Daneker (Tor)	#1 - P Kip Wells #38 - P Mark Buehrle	
SOLID PROSPECTS		#5 - 3B Joe Crede			#1 - P Matt Ginter #3 - P Jon Rauch
POTENTIAL PROSPECTS	#7 - P Jason Lakman (Bal)	#1 - P Bobby Seay (TB) #4 - P Mark Roberts #16 - OF Jeff Inglin	#1 - SS Jason Dellaero #1 - OF Brett Caradonna	#1 - OF Aaron Rowand #2 - P Gary Majewski #3 - P Josh Fogg #7 - P Eric Fischer #34 - OF Terrell Merriman	#1 - P Jason Stumm #1 - P Brian West #1 - P Rob Purvis #2 - P Dan Wright #8 - P Dennis Ulacia #13 - 1B Casey Rogowski
ROUND 1-5 FLOPS	#4 - OF Ryan Topham				
GRADE	D	C	B	C	A

CHICAGO CUBS
5-YEAR DRAFT ANALYSIS

	1995	1996	1997	1998	1999
MAJOR LEAGUE STARS					
MAJOR LEAGUE STARTERS	#1 - P Kerry Wood		#1 - P Jon Garland (CWS) #3 - P Scott Downs (Mon)		
MAJOR LEAGUERS	#1 - P Brian McNichol #55 - P Justin Speier (Cle)	#5 - 2B Chad Meyers #10 - P Phillip Norton			
SOLID PROSPECTS				#1 - OF Corey Patterson	
POTENTIAL PROSPECTS		#1 - P Todd Noel (NYY) #4 - P Chris Gissell #29 - P Kyle Lohse (Min)	#5 - OF Jaisen Randolph #11 - P Mike Wuertz #26 - P Mike Meyers	#2 - 3B Dave Kelton #2 - C Jeff Goldbach #17 - 3B Eric Hinske	#1 - P Ben Christensen
ROUND 1-5 FLOPS		#3 - P Skip Ames			
GRADE	B	D	B	A	C

CINCINNATI REDS
5-YEAR DRAFT ANALYSIS

	1995	1996	1997	1998	1999
MAJOR LEAGUE STARS					
MAJOR LEAGUE STARTERS	#2 - P Brett Tomko (Sea)		#9 - P Scott Williamson		
MAJOR LEAGUERS	#5 - C Jason LaRue #8 - P Ray King (Milw)	#2 - P Buddy Carlyle (SD)	#2 - SS Travis Dawkins #5 - OF D. Wise (Tor) #7 - OF Mike Frank (NYY)	#17 - P B.J. Ryan (Bal)	
SOLID PROSPECTS				#1 - OF Austin Kearns #2 - OF Adam Dunn	
POTENTIAL PROSPECTS	#6 - OF Andy Burress	#20 - P Gene Altman (Mil)	#1 - 3B Brandon Larson #11 - P Clint Brewer #21 - P Rob Averette (Col) #25 - 1B Samone Peters		#1 - P Ty Howington #2 - OF Ben Broussard #21 - P Brad Salmon
ROUND 1-5 FLOPS	#3 - SS Andre Montgomery	#2 - P Randi Mallard #3 - P David Shepard			
GRADE	C	D	B	B	C

CLEVELAND INDIANS
5-YEAR DRAFT ANALYSIS

	1995	1996	1997	1998	1999
MAJOR LEAGUE STARS	#2 - 1B Sean Casey (Cin)				
MAJOR LEAGUE STARTERS					
MAJOR LEAGUERS	#14 - P S. Winchester (Cin) #25 - P Jason Rakers (KC)	#6 - P Paul Rigdon (Mil) #9 - P Sean DePaula #12 - SS John McDonald #56 - P David Riske	#1 - P Tim Drew		
SOLID PROSPECTS				#1 - P C.C. Sabathia	
POTENTIAL PROSPECTS	#3 - OF Chad Whitaker	#1 - 1B Danny Peoples #18 - P Mike Bacsik #21 - P Jamie Brown	#2 - C Edgar Cruz #3 - P Rob Pugmire #5 - OF Jon Hamilton	#2 - SS Zach Sorensen #6 - OF Tyler Minges	#6 - P Shane Wallace #19 - OF Travis Santini
ROUND 1-5 FLOPS	#4 - P Scott Harrison #5 - P Scott Schultz	#2 - P Ryan McDermott #5 - 1B Grant Sharpe			
GRADE	A	C	C	B	D

COLORADO ROCKIES
5-YEAR DRAFT ANALYSIS

	1995	1996	1997	1998	1999
MAJOR LEAGUE STARS	#1 - 1B Todd Helton				
MAJOR LEAGUE STARTERS	#2 - C Ben Petrick			#13 - OF Juan Pierre	
MAJOR LEAGUERS	#23 - P David Lee	#1 - P J. Westbrook (NYY)			#12 - P Craig House
SOLID PROSPECTS					#1 - P Jason Jennings
POTENTIAL PROSPECTS	#11 - P Scott Randall (Tex)	#3 - P Shawn Chacon #33 - P Josh Kalinowski	#1 - P Mark Mangum (Mon) #2 - P Aaron Cook #4 - 2B Chone Figgins #5 - P Justin Miller (Oak) #38 - P Ryan Price	#1 - C Jeff Winchester #1 - OF Choo Freeman #2 - OF Jody Gerut #2 - P Jermaine Van Buren #7 - 3B Matt Holliday #11 - P Ryan Cameron #3 - P Kevin Gordon	#2 - P Ryan Kibler
ROUND 1-5 FLOPS	#3 - P Chris Macca #4 - SS John Clark	#5 - P Jeff Sebring			
GRADE	A	C	C	B	B

DETROIT TIGERS
5-YEAR DRAFT ANALYSIS

	1995	1996	1997	1998	1999
MAJOR LEAGUE STARS					
MAJOR LEAGUE STARTERS	#57 -OF Gabe Kapler (Tex)			#1 - P Jeff Weaver	
MAJOR LEAGUERS	#2 - P Brian Powell (Hou) #11 - P David Borkowski	#1 - P Seth Greisinger #5 - C Robert Fick	#1 - P Matt Anderson		#1 - 1B Eric Munson
SOLID PROSPECTS					#3 - 3B Neil Jenkins
POTENTIAL PROSPECTS	#1 - P Mike Drumright (Fla)		#2 - P Shane Loux #3 - 3B Matt Boone #4 - P Alan Webb (Tex) #11 - 1B Leo Daigle	#1 - P Nate Cornejo #2 - P Adam Pettyjohn #2 - C Brandon Inge #3 - P Tommy Marx #4 - OF Andres Torres #14 - P Calvin Chipperfield	#4 - OF Cody Ross #6 - 3B Brant Ust #7 - P Tim Kalita
ROUND 1-5 FLOPS	#5 - P Rosario Ortiz		#5 - SS Heath Schesser	#5 - P Greg Peterson	
GRADE	B	D	C	B	B

FLORIDA MARLINS
5-YEAR DRAFT ANALYSIS

	1995	1996	1997	1998	1999
MAJOR LEAGUE STARS					
MAJOR LEAGUE STARTERS		#1 - OF Mark Kotsay			
MAJOR LEAGUERS	#2 - 1B Nate Rolison #3 - OF Randy Winn (TB) #19 - P Mike Duvall (TB)	#5 - P B. Billingsley (Mon)	#13 - OF Ross Gload (Cub)		
SOLID PROSPECTS			#14 - P Wes Anderson		#1 - P Josh Beckett
POTENTIAL PROSPECTS	#1 - OF Jaime Jones	#4 - P Blaine Neal	#2 - C Jeff Bailey #3 - OF Chris Aguila #10 -3B Kelley Washington	#1 - OF Chip Ambres #3 - 1B David Callahan #8 - P Marc Sauer	
ROUND 1-5 FLOPS	#5 - OF Rene Rascon				
GRADE	C	B	C	C	C

HOUSTON ASTROS
5-YEAR DRAFT ANALYSIS

	1995	1996	1997	1998	1999
MAJOR LEAGUE STARS					
MAJOR LEAGUE STARTERS		#20 - P Wade Miller			
MAJOR LEAGUERS	#1 - P Tony McKnight #4 - P Brian Sikorski (Tex)		#1 - OF Lance Berkman		
SOLID PROSPECTS				#1 - P Mike Nannini #7 - C John Buck	
POTENTIAL PROSPECTS	#2 - P Eric Ireland #5 - C Mike Rose (Az) #24 - P Jeriome Robertson #27 - 1B Aaron McNeal	#23 - P Roy Oswalt #29 - P Tom Shearn	#20 - P Tim Redding	#10 - 2B Keith Ginter	#1 - OF Michael Rosamond #9 - 3B Jon Helquist
ROUND 1-5 FLOPS		#2 - P John Huber #3 - 3B Brandon Byrd	#2 - C Cameron Hahn		
GRADE	D	B	B	B	D

KANSAS CITY ROYALS
5-YEAR DRAFT ANALYSIS

	1995	1996	1997	1998	1999
MAJOR LEAGUE STARS					
MAJOR LEAGUE STARTERS	#2 - OF Carlos Beltran		#1 - P Dan Reichert		
MAJOR LEAGUERS	#11 - OF Mark Quinn #25 - P Jeff Wallace (Pitt)	#1 - OF Dee Brown #3 - P Chad Durbin #6 - OF Jer. Giambi (Oak) #7 - P Scott Mullen	#9 - P Kris Wilson		
SOLID PROSPECTS				#1 - P Chris George	#1 - P Jimmy Gobble
POTENTIAL PROSPECTS	#5 - SS Steve Medrano	#4 - P Corey Thurman	#3 - P Jeremy Affeldt #4 - OF Goefrey Tomlinson	#1 - P Jeff Austin #2 - P Robbie Morrison #7 - OF Jeremy Dodson #8 - OF Norris Hopper #9 - C Paul Phillips	#2 - P Brian Sanches
ROUND 1-5 FLOPS					
GRADE	B	B	B	C	B

LOS ANGELES DODGERS
5-YEAR DRAFT ANALYSIS

	1995	1996	1997	1998	1999
MAJOR LEAGUE STARS					
MAJOR LEAGUE STARTERS		#4 - OF P. Bergeron (Mon)			
MAJOR LEAGUERS	#3 - P Onan Masaoka	#3 - SS Alex Cora #23 - P Ted Lilly (NYY) #38 - P Jeff Kubenka (Oak)			
SOLID PROSPECTS					#4 - 2B Joe Thurston
POTENTIAL PROSPECTS	#17 - OF Tony Mota	#1 - 3B Damian Rolls (TB) #5 - 1B Nick Leach (NYY)	#3 - 3B Ricky Bell #4 - C John Hernandez	#10 - P Lance Caraccioli	#8 - P T.J. Nall
ROUND 1-5 FLOPS	#1 - P David Yocum #4 - OF Judd Granzow #5 - P Sef Soto				
GRADE	D	B	D	D	C

MILWAUKEE BREWERS
5-YEAR DRAFT ANALYSIS

	1995	1996	1997	1998	1999
MAJOR LEAGUE STARS					
MAJOR LEAGUE STARTERS	#1 - OF Geoff Jenkins				
MAJOR LEAGUERS	#9 - UT M. Kinkade (Bal)	#3 - 1B Kevin Barker #13 - P Allen Levrault	#1 - P Kyle Peterson		
SOLID PROSPECTS				#2 - P Nick Neugebauer	#1 - P Ben Sheets
POTENTIAL PROSPECTS	#30 - OF Scott Kirby	#2 - P Jose Garcia #6 - P Paul Stewart #15 - P Al Hawkins	#3 - 3B Jeff Deardorff #5 - OF Frank Candela	#1 - P J.M. Gold #3 - OF Derry Hammond #6 - SS Bill Hall	#6 - SS Mark Ernster
ROUND 1-5 FLOPS				#5 - P Chris Pine	
GRADE	B	D	D	B	C

MINNESOTA TWINS
5-YEAR DRAFT ANALYSIS

	1995	1996	1997	1998	1999
MAJOR LEAGUE STARS					
MAJOR LEAGUE STARTERS	#1 - P Mark Redman	#1 - OF Travis Lee (Phl) #2 - OF Jacque Jones			
MAJOR LEAGUERS	#5 - 1B Doug Mientkiewicz	#4 - OF Chad Allen #7 - C Chad Moeller #13 - P Mike Lincoln	#1 - C Matt LeCroy		
SOLID PROSPECTS			#1 - 3B Michael Cuddyer #2 - OF Mike Restovich		
POTENTIAL PROSPECTS		#5 - OF Mike Ryan	#47 - P Joe Foote	#1 - P Ryan Mills #4 - P Pete Fisher #25 - 1B Eric Sandberg	#1 - OF B.J. Garbe #6 - P Brian Wolfe
ROUND 1-5 FLOPS			#5 - P Pete Blake	#5 - P Mickey Blount	
GRADE	C	C	B	D	D

MONTREAL EXPOS
5-YEAR DRAFT ANALYSIS

	1995	1996	1997	1998	1999
MAJOR LEAGUE STARS					
MAJOR LEAGUE STARTERS	#1 - C Michael Barrett	#2 - OF Milton Bradley			
MAJOR LEAGUERS	#4 - P J.D. Smart #5 - C Brian Schneider	#16 - 1B Andy Tracy	#1 - P - T.J. Tucker		
SOLID PROSPECTS			#1 - P Donnie Bridges		#2 - SS Brandon Phillips
POTENTIAL PROSPECTS	#2 - 2B Henry Mateo #3 - OF Kenny James	#1 - P John Patterson (Az)	#1 - 1B Thomas Pittman #1 - 3B Scott Hodges #1 - 2B Tootie Myers	#1 - OF Brad Wilkerson #1 - 3B Josh McKinley #20 - P Bran. Agamennone #44 - P Ron Chiavacci	#4 - OF Matt Cepicky #7 - 2B Bret Boyer #15 - OF Valentino Pascucci
ROUND 1-5 FLOPS			#1 - P Chris Stowe		
GRADE	C	B	B	C	C

NEW YORK YANKEES
5-YEAR DRAFT ANALYSIS

	1995	1996	1997	1998	1999
MAJOR LEAGUE STARS					
MAJOR LEAGUE STARTERS	#20 - 3B Mike Lowell (Fla)	#1 - P Eric Milton (Min)			
MAJOR LEAGUERS	#9 - P Mike Judd (LA) #19 - P Jay Tessmer		#1 - P Ryan Bradley #5 - P Randy Choate	#2 - P Randy Keisler	
SOLID PROSPECTS		#3 - 1B Nick Johnson		#3 - 3B Drew Henson (Cin)	
POTENTIAL PROSPECTS	#2 - OF Richard Brown	#5 - P Zach Day #6 - P Brian Reith (Cin) #30 - OF Marcus Thames		#1 - OF Andy Brown #5 - P Brian Rogers #34 - P Brandon Claussen	#1 - P David Walling #3 - P Alex Graman
ROUND 1-5 FLOPS	#4 - P Eric Boardman #5 - P Jason Wright	#2 - P Jason Coble #4 - C Vidal Candelaria	#2 - P Jason Henry		
GRADE	B	A	D	C	C

NEW YORK METS
5-YEAR DRAFT ANALYSIS

	1995	1996	1997	1998	1999
MAJOR LEAGUE STARS					
MAJOR LEAGUE STARTERS	#8 - P A.J. Burnett (Fla)				
MAJOR LEAGUERS	#10 - P Dan Murray (KC) #30 - P N. Figueroa (Phl)	#3 - P Ed Yarnall (Cin)	#13 - P Eric Cammack	#1 - OF Jason Tyner (TB)	
SOLID PROSPECTS	#11 - P Grant Roberts			#2 - P Pat Strange #18 - OF Brian Cole	
POTENTIAL PROSPECTS	#16 - P Lindsay Gulin (Cub)	#1 - OF Robert Stratton #5 - 1B Pat Burns #16 - P Dicky Gonzalez	#1 - P Geoff Goetz (Fla) #3 - 2B Cesar Crespo (Fla) #12 - P Nick Maness #24 - C Jason Phillips	#5 - 1B Craig Brazell #6 - OF Marvin Seale #14 - SS Gil Velazquez #17 - 2B Ty Wigginton	#10 - OF Prentice Redman
ROUND 1-5 FLOPS	#1 - SS Ryan Jaronczyk #3 - C Ryan Bowers #5 - SS Jeff Parsons				
GRADE	A	C	C	A	D

OAKLAND ATHLETICS
5-YEAR DRAFT ANALYSIS

	1995	1996	1997	1998	1999
MAJOR LEAGUE STARS			#6 - P Tim Hudson		
MAJOR LEAGUE STARTERS	#1 - P Ariel Prieto	#1 - 3B Eric Chavez		#1 - P Mark Mulder	#1 - P Barry Zito
MAJOR LEAGUERS	#2 - 3B Mark Bellhorn #10 - OF Ryan Christensen #17-2B David Newhan (Phl) #24 - P Steve Connelly	#3 - C A.J. Hinch #24 - P Brett Laxton (KC)	#2 - P Chad Harville #8 - 3B Adam Piatt	#8 - OF Eric Byrnes	
SOLID PROSPECTS					#2 - OF Ryan Ludwick
POTENTIAL PROSPECTS	#5 - C Danny Ardoin (Min)	#6 - 1B Nick Sosa #15 - P Kevin Gregg #21 - C Brian Luderer	#1 - OF Nat. Haynes (Ana) #23 - OF Gary Thomas	#2 - C Gerald Laird #5 - 1B Jason Hart #6 - 3B Gary Schneidmiller #15 - OF Rusty Keith	#8 - P Justin Lehr #9 - OF Kirk Asche #11 - OF Michael Wenner #23 - OF Mike Lockwood
ROUND 1-5 FLOPS				#3 - SS Kevin Miller	
GRADE	D	B	A	B	A

PHILADELPHIA PHILLIES
5-YEAR DRAFT ANALYSIS

	1995	1996	1997	1998	1999
MAJOR LEAGUE STARS					
MAJOR LEAGUE STARTERS	#2 - 2B Marlon Anderson	#1 - P Adam Eaton (SD)	#2 - P Randy Wolf	#1 - OF Pat Burrell	
MAJOR LEAGUERS	#1 - P Dave Coggin #23 - P A. Shumaker (Bal)		#5 - P Derrick Turnbow (Ana) #6 - P Tom Jacquez		
SOLID PROSPECTS		#2 - SS Jimmy Rollins		#2 - P Brad Baisley #9 - P Ryan Madson	#1 - P Brett Myers
POTENTIAL PROSPECTS	#1 - OF Reggie Taylor #12 - P Jason Kershner	#3 - P Kris Stevens #12 - OF Jason Johnson		#1 - OF Eric Valent #3 - OF Jorge Padilla #4 - OF Jason Michaels #15 - P Geoff Geary #18 - 1B Nate Espy #21 - SS Nick Punto	#9 - SS Julio Collazo #10 - OF Marlon Byrd #13 - P Frank Brooks
ROUND 1-5 FLOPS	#3 - P Randy Knoll	#5 - P Ira Tilton	#4 - OF Nick Marchant	#5 - C Kennon McArthur	
GRADE	C	A	B	A	C

PITTSBURGH PIRATES
5-YEAR DRAFT ANALYSIS

	1995	1996	1997	1998	1999
MAJOR LEAGUE STARS					
MAJOR LEAGUE STARTERS	#1 - OF Chad Hermansen #3 - P Bronson Arroyo	#1 - P Kris Benson			
MAJOR LEAGUERS	#11 - P Brian O'Connor	#5 - OF Tike Redman	#7 - OF Kory DeHaan (SD)		
SOLID PROSPECTS					#1 - P Bobby Bradley
POTENTIAL PROSPECTS	#2 - OF Garrett Long #4 - 1B Alex Hernandez	#3 - 3B Luis Lorenzana #4 - 1B Lee Evans #10 - 1B Carlos Rivera	#1 - OF J.J. Davis #3 - P John Grabow #10 - 2B Rico Washington	#2 - 1B Jeremy Cotton #17 - P David Williams #19 - P Jeff Bennett	#3 - OF Aron Weston #5 - C J.R. House #24 - 2B Josh Bonifay
ROUND 1-5 FLOPS					
GRADE	C	A	C	C	A

ST. LOUIS CARDINALS
5-YEAR DRAFT ANALYSIS

	1995	1996	1997	1998	1999
MAJOR LEAGUE STARS					
MAJOR LEAGUE STARTERS	#19 - 1B Chris Richard (Bal)		#1 - 2B A. Kennedy (Ana) #2 - P Rick Ankiel	#1 - OF J.D. Drew	
MAJOR LEAGUERS	#1 - P Matt Morris #10 - P Matt DeWitt (Tor) #17 - P Britt Reames #34 - OF K. Robinson(NYY) #54 - P Cliff Politte (Phl)	#1 - P Braden Looper (Fla)			
SOLID PROSPECTS		#3 - 2B Brent Butler (Col)		#4 - P Bud Smith	#4 - OF Ben Johnson (SD) #13 - 3B Albert Pujols
POTENTIAL PROSPECTS	#2 - SS Jason Woolf #2 - 3B Chris Haas			#2 - P Chad Hutchinson #2 - OF Tim Lemon #9 - SS Jack Wilson (Pit)	#1 - P Chance Caple #1 - P Nick Stocks #1 - 1B Chris Duncan #2 - P Josh Pearce
ROUND 1-5 FLOPS	#4 - P Rodney Barfield				
GRADE	B	C	A	A	B

SAN DIEGO PADRES
5-YEAR DRAFT ANALYSIS

	1995	1996	1997	1998	1999
MAJOR LEAGUE STARS					
MAJOR LEAGUE STARTERS					
MAJOR LEAGUERS	#1 - C Ben Davis #2 - 1B Gabe Alvarez		#1 - SS Kevin Nicholson		
SOLID PROSPECTS			#9 - P Junior Herndon	#1 - 3B Sean Burroughs	
POTENTIAL PROSPECTS	#19 - OF B. Pernell (Cub) #47 - C Wilbert Nieves		#2 - P Ben Howard	#5 - 1B Kevin Eberwein	#1 - OF Vince Faison #1 - P Gerik Baxter #1 - P Omar Ortiz #1 - P Mike Bynum #15 - P Jacob Peavy
ROUND 1-5 FLOPS	#5 - P Kenny Henderson	#4 - 3B Nate Dunn			
GRADE	C	D	C	A	B

SAN FRANCISCO GIANTS
5-YEAR DRAFT ANALYSIS

	1995	1996	1997	1998	1999
MAJOR LEAGUE STARS					
MAJOR LEAGUE STARTERS	#4 - P Russ Ortiz			#5 - P Ryan Vogelsong	
MAJOR LEAGUERS	#1 - P Joe Fontenot (Fla) #6 - P Joe Nathan #50 - 2B Edwards Guzman	#2 -SS Mike Caruso (CWS)	#1 - P Jason Grilli (Fla) #2 - P Scott Linebrink(Hou)		
SOLID PROSPECTS		#1 - P Matt White (TB)		#1 - 3B Tony Torcato	#1 - P Kurt Ainsworth #1 - P Jerome Williams
POTENTIAL PROSPECTS	#2 - P Jason Brester (Phi)	#8 - P Ryan Jensen #10 -OF Mike Glendenning	#5 - C Gius. Chiaramonte #15 - OF Mike Byas	#1 - P Nate Bump (Fla) #1 - P Chris Jones #1 - OF Arturo McDowell #2 - OF Chris Magruder	#4 - P Jeremy Cunningham #7 - 2B Joe Jester
ROUND 1-5 FLOPS	#5 - P Jim Woodrow	#3 - C Dave Kenna			
GRADE	B	B	D	C	B

SEATTLE MARINERS
5-YEAR DRAFT ANALYSIS

	1995	1996	1997	1998	1999
MAJOR LEAGUE STARS					
MAJOR LEAGUE STARTERS	#1 - OF Jose Cruz, Jr. (Tor)	#1 - P Gil Meche			
MAJOR LEAGUERS	#2 - OF S. Monahan (Col)		#12 - P Joel Pineiro		
SOLID PROSPECTS			#1 - P Ryan Anderson		#1 - C Ryan Christianson #3 - OF Sheldon Fulse
POTENTIAL PROSPECTS	#25 - P Brian Fuentes #27 - SS Ramon Vazquez	#5 - P Chris Mears #27 - P Josue Matos	#5 - 2B Jermaine Clark #8 - P Allan Simpson #21 - P Enmanuel Ulloa	#3- P Andy Van Hekken(Det)	#1 - P Jeff Heaverlo #3 - 2B Willie Bloomquist
ROUND 1-5 FLOPS	#4 - SS Duan Johnson	#3 - P Tony DeJesus #4 - P Denny Stark	#3 - P Pat Dunham #4 - P Scott Prouty		
GRADE	B	B	A	D	B

TAMPA BAY DEVIL RAYS
5-YEAR DRAFT ANALYSIS

	1995	1996	1997	1998	1999
MAJOR LEAGUE STARS	N/A				
MAJOR LEAGUE STARTERS				#5 - 3B Aubrey Huff #6 - P Ryan Rupe	
MAJOR LEAGUERS		#7 - P Mickey Callaway #34 - P Dan Wheeler	#2 - OF Kenny Kelly		
SOLID PROSPECTS			#1 - P Jason Standridge		#1 - OF Josh Hamilton #2 - OF Carl Crawford
POTENTIAL PROSPECTS		#4 - P Cedrick Bowers #5 - OF Alex Sanchez #16 - 3B Jared Sandberg #86 - OF Scott Neuberger	#9 - C Toby Hall	#4 - 1B Josh Pressley #16 - P Neal Frendling	
ROUND 1-5 FLOPS		#1 - OF Doug Johnson			
GRADE	C	C	C	B	A

TEXAS RANGERS
5-YEAR DRAFT ANALYSIS

	1995	1996	1997	1998	1999
MAJOR LEAGUE STARS					
MAJOR LEAGUE STARTERS	#3 - P Ryan Dempster (Fla)	#5 - 2B Warren Morris (Pit) #10 - P Doug Davis	#7 - 3B Mike Lamb		
MAJOR LEAGUERS	#1 - P Jonathan Johnson #4 - P Ryan Glynn #6 - P Dan Kolb #29 - P Mike Venafro	#1 - P Corey Lee #4 - SS Kelly Dransfeldt			
SOLID PROSPECTS			#1 - 2B Jason Romano	#1 - 1B Carlos Pena #9 - P Andy Pratt	#3 - 3B Hank Blalock
POTENTIAL PROSPECTS	#5 - 1B S. Gallagher (Mon) #8 - OF Craig Monroe	#1 - P Sam Marsonek (NYY) #7 - OF Juan Piniella	#2 - 3B Jason Grabowski #12 - OF Corey Wright	#2 - OF Cody Nowlin #5 - P Ryan Dittfurth	#1 - P Colby Lewis #2 - P Nick Regilio #4 - OF Kevin Mench #5 - P Andy Cavazos #6 - P Aaron Harang
ROUND 1-5 FLOPS					
GRADE	A	B	C	B	B

TORONTO BLUE JAYS
5-YEAR DRAFT ANALYSIS

	1995	1996	1997	1998	1999
MAJOR LEAGUE STARS					
MAJOR LEAGUE STARTERS		#1 - P Bill Koch			
MAJOR LEAGUERS		#3 - P Clayton Andrews #7 - 3B Casey Blake (Min)	#1 - OF Vernon Wells		
SOLID PROSPECTS		#2 - 2B Br. Abernathy (TB)		#1 - SS Felipe Lopez	
POTENTIAL PROSPECTS	#2 - C Craig Wilson (Pit) #10 - OF Ryan Freel	#1 - C Joe Lawrence #10 - C Josh Phelps	#5 - SS Mike Young (Tex) #8 - P Joe Casey #43 - 2B Orlando Hudson		#3 - P Matt Ford #11 - P Charles Kegley
ROUND 1-5 FLOPS	#4 - 1B Mike Whitlock #5 - P Jay Veniard				
GRADE	C	A	B	C	C

Predictive Scouting:
Beyond the Physical and Mental

Buck Showalter's highest compliment for a young player is, "His parents obviously did a good job." Derek Jeter won this praise immediately upon arriving to fill in for an injured Tony Fernandez in May 1995. Jeter had been correctly and tabbed as a cornerstone for the Yankees' emerging new dynasty.

What are the qualities which make up the "parents did a good job" ideal? How could a scout identify them and communicate them? To what extent can a scout see the content of player's character, beyond the visible on-field habits and observable aggressiveness?

Predictive scouting must go beyond the assessment of tools. Hitting ability, power, running speed, base running, arm strength, arm accuracy, fielding and range are merely physical. While mental character might be observable in on-field habits and aggressiveness, other qualities such as dedication and emotional maturity are difficult to assess from a distance. While a scout may make guesses using a trained eye, most scouts simply don't have the training to interview players for the purpose of predicting their future development.

The necessary interview skills do exist, and they are teachable. Using the same interview and listening skills that major corporations use to choose key professionals for top jobs, John Benson has a long and successful track record assessing the future outlook for promising young ballplayers. Interviews can accurately assess qualities such as:

- goal orientation,
- understanding of strengths and weaknesses,
- clarity of focus on what needs improvement,
- having a plan to grow and develop,
- cross-checking with coaches and managers for congruity of understanding,
- ability to visualize success short-term and long-term,
- dealing with adversity,
- staying within true capabilities, and
- not becoming too high or too low.

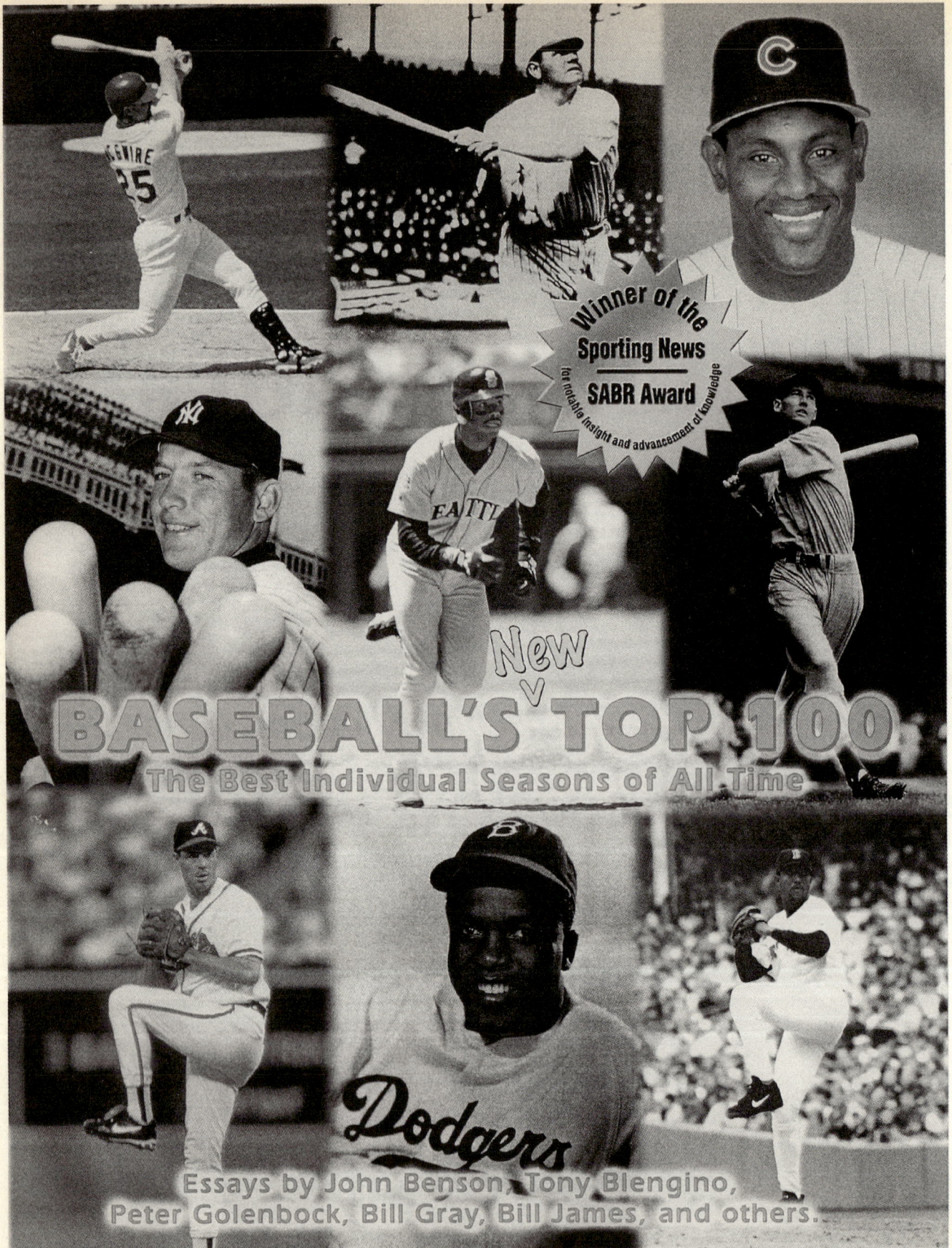

New

BASEBALL'S TOP 100
The Best Individual Seasons of All Time

Winner of the Sporting News SABR Award for notable insight and advancement of knowledge

Essays by John Benson, Tony Blengino, Peter Golenbock, Bill Gray, Bill James, and others...

ISBN # 1-880876-95-7
352 pages, hard cover, 8.5" x 11"
Retail Price: $24.95
Available: December 2000